MANAGING THE CHALLENGES OF WTO PARTICIPATION

This compilation of forty-five case studies do ...parate experiences among economies in addressing the challenges of participating in the WTO. It demonstrates that success or failure is strongly influenced by how governments and private-sector stakeholders organize themselves at home. The contributors, mainly from developing countries, give examples of participation with lessons for others. They show that when the system is accessed and employed effectively, it can serve the interests of poor and rich countries alike. However, a failure to communicate among interested parties at home often contributes to negative outcomes on the international front. Above all, these case studies demonstrate that the WTO creates a framework within which sovereign decision-making can unleash important opportunities or undermine the potential benefits flowing from a rules-based international environment that promotes open trade.

PETER GALLAGHER is Principal of Inquit Communications.

PATRICK LOW is Director of Economic Research and Statistics, WTO Secretariat, and a member of the Editorial Board of the *World Trade Review*.

ANDREW L. STOLER is Executive Director of the Institute for International Business, Economics and Law at the University of Adelaide.

MANAGING THE CHALLENGES OF WTO PARTICIPATION

45 Case Studies

Edited by

PETER GALLAGHER, PATRICK LOW AND
ANDREW L. STOLER

CAMBRIDGE
UNIVERSITY PRESS

CAMBRIDGE UNIVERSITY PRESS
Cambridge, New York, Melbourne, Madrid, Cape Town,
Singapore, São Paulo, Delhi, Tokyo, Mexico City

Cambridge University Press
The Edinburgh Building, Cambridge CB2 8RU, UK

Published in the United States of America by
Cambridge University Press, New York

www.cambridge.org
Information on this title: www.cambridge.org/9780521677547

First published 2005

A catalogue record for this publication is available from the British Library

Library of Congress Cataloguing in Publication data

ISBN 978-0-521-86014-7 Hardback
ISBN 978-0-521-67754-7 Paperback

CONTENTS

ACKNOWLEGEMENTS

We, the editors, should like to express our sincere thanks to the authors whose case studies appear here. Their insights make this book a unique record of how economies participate in the WTO. We are grateful for their interest in the project, their willingness to work within the constraints of a case study format and for bringing to us such a variety of stories and experiences of the management of trade policies. This project would not have been possible were it not for the early and enthusiastic support and funding it received from the WTO Secretariat and the Australian Government's aid agency, AusAID. On the WTO Secretariat side, particular thanks are due to the Deputy Director-General, Kiprkorir Aly Azad Rana, and the Director of the Institute for Training and Technical Co-Operation, Paul Rolian, who were sympathetic to and supportive of our objectives. Peter Versegi and Ian Anderson from AusAID saw the potential in the project from our first discussions on the fringes of the Cancún Ministerial Conference and offered valuable support. We also wish to thank Elizabeth Peak, Freya Beaumont, Lachlan Pontifex and Neil Young, who at various points in the project served as our AusAID day-to-day contact points. At the Institute for International Business, Economics and Law, James Redden and our WTO Visiting Fellow Peter Pedersen contributed to the editing of this volume. Jean-Guy Carrier of the WTO Secretariat also helped with editing and offered valuable advice and support on the production side. We should also like to express our appreciation to Finola O'Sullivan of Cambridge University Press for her encouragement and support. Finally, special thanks are due to IIBE&L's office manager, Marie Gutsche, as well as to Paulette Planchette and Souda Tandara of the WTO Secretariat, all of whom put in many long hours on this project.

Disclaimer

Opinions expressed in the case studies and any errors or omissions therein are the responsibility of their authors and not of the editors of this volume or of the institutions with which they are affiliated. The authors of the case studies wish to dissociate the institutions with which they are associated from opinions expressed in the case studies and from any errors or omission therein.

ABBREVIATIONS

ACP	African, Caribbean and Pacific Group of States
AD	anti-dumping
ADA	Anti-dumping Agreement
ASEAN	Association of South East Asian Nations
ATC	Agreement on Textiles and Clothing
AU	African Union
CARICOM	Caribbean Common Market
CB	capacity building
COMECON	informal name for Council for Mutual Economic Assistance (CMEA)
COMESA	Common Market for Eastern and Southern Africa
CSO	civil society organization
CVD	countervailing duties
DCs	Developing Countries
DDA	Doha Development Agenda
DRC	Democratic Republic of Congo
EAC	East African Community
EBA	Everything but Arms
EC	European Community
ECOWAS	Economic Community of West African States
EPA	Economic Partnership Agreement
ESA	East and Southern Africa
EU	European Union
FANR	Food, Agriculture and Natural Resources
FAO	Food and Agriculture Organization of the United Nations
FTAA	Free Trade Area of the Americas
GATS	General Agreement on Trade in Services
GATT	General Agreement on Tariffs and Trade
GDP	gross domestic product

I&S	infrastructure and services
IGAD	Inter-Governmental Authority on Development
IITC	Inter-institutional Trade Committee
IMF	International Monetary Fund
IOC	Indian Ocean Commission
ITC	International Trade Centre UNCTAD/WTO
JITAP	Joint Integrated Technical Assistance Programme
LDC	least developed country
LMG	Like-Minded Group
MERCOSUR	Southern Common Market
NAFTA	North American Free Trade Agreement
NFIDC	Net Food-Importing Developing Countries
NWGT	National Working Group on Trade
OECD	Organisation for Economic Co-operation and Development
PRSP	Poverty Reduction Strategy Papers
PTA	Preferential Trade Area
RECs	Regional economic communities
RIRN	Regional Integration Research Network Project
RTA	Regional Trade Agreement
S&D	special and differential treatment
SAARC	South Asian Association for Regional Co-operation
SACU	Southern Africa Customs Union
SADC	Southern Africa Development Community (successor to SADCC)
SADCC	Southern African Development Co-ordination Conference
SATRN	Southern Africa Trade Research Network
SCM	Agreement on Subsidies and Countervailing Measures
SHD&SP	Social and Human Development and Special Programmes
SIDS	small island developing states
SPS	sanitary and phytosanitary measures
SVE	small and vulnerable economies
TBT	technical barriers to trade
TIFI	Trade, Industry, Finance and Investment
TRIPS	Trade-Related Aspects of Intellectual Property Rights
TRQ	tariff rate quota

TRTA	Trade-Related Technical Assistance
UEMOA	Union economique et monétaire ouest-africaine
UNCTAD	United Nations Conference on Trade and Development
UNIDO	United Nations Industrial Development Organization
WTO	World Trade Organization

Introduction

PETER GALLAGHER, PATRICK LOW AND ANDREW STOLER

1 What is in this book

This book brings together forty-five case studies from economies around the world, each of which illustrates how governments, business and civil society manage their country's participation in the World Trade Organization.[1]

The case studies make a mosaic image of what it takes, at the start of the twenty-first century, to manage the integration of an economy into the global trading system and what the rewards, or penalties, of integration can be for economies of all sizes, including many of the world's poorest and most resource-poor economies.

They show, through 'real world' examples, that joining the WTO and taking advantage of WTO membership is not something to be left to government alone. It calls for the participation of many different 'stake-holders' in an economy, including goods and services producers, industry associations, consumer associations, civil society groups and academic analysts.

They also show that people representing those different national inter-ests and institutions take most of the significant decisions affecting an economy's participation in the global trading system. The WTO itself has only a secondary role; it helps to define the context of a trade policy decision but doesn't compel the choice of one policy over another.

The case studies include success stories, some stories of failure or frustration, one or two 'disasters' and some stories that are open-ended because the final outcome is not yet known.

---

[1] In this book we talk about participation of an economy, rather than a country, in the WTO. That is because we are not merely concerned with the way in which government actors have dealt with issues and opportunities. In each of the case studies, it is important to see how the government interacts with the local business community and other civil society elements in what might be called an economy-wide response.

Each of the case studies speaks for itself. The rest of this introduction provides some topical summaries of the case studies and identifies some of the ideas that emerge from them. But there are many more things in the cases themselves that we haven't covered here.

2 Playing the game

Do you remember watching a sporting event for the first time? A game whose rules you didn't understand?

Confusing, wasn't it? You could probably guess the objective of the game by watching the scoreboard, but without knowing the rules it can be very difficult to understand why the players are doing what they do and who's getting ahead in the game and who's falling behind.

Now, imagine that you are watching a game that has about 150 players on the field and no scoreboard. Imagine, too, that the rulebook for this game has twenty-eight thick chapters and thousands of pages of footnotes and clarifications, so that there is some doubt about whether even the players know all the rules. Watching each player in this game is a stadium filled with millions of followers – a mixture of supporters and critics – who are continually shouting encouragement or instructions to the players while betting furiously on the outcome of every play.

To make things even harder to follow, this game doesn't have a referee: the players have to manage the game for themselves. And without a referee to blame whenever the play seems to go against their team, some spectators have taken to abusing the staff at the stadium.

The multilateral trading system is not a game, of course; being a member of WTO isn't much like play. But the trading system managed in the WTO is a huge and frequently confusing enterprise in which a large and complex set of rules governs the way that governments – the main 'players' – interact.

As in some sports, the 'spectators' sitting just outside the field of play – billions of ordinary business people and citizens – are an important part of the 'game'. All the gains and losses end up in their hands and, ultimately, for reasons that we shall see in this book, the future of the game is also in their hands. But most members of the public don't understand the game very well and some of them suspect that the rules, which have been agreed among the players beforehand, are stacked against them.

This book is a sort of guide to the game, from a spectator's viewpoint or, to be more precise, from the viewpoint of more than forty spectators.

There continues to be a considerable amount of misunderstanding about the role of the World Trade Organization as an institution. One still hears complaints about giving up sovereignty to faceless bureaucrats on the shores of Lake Geneva. Most of this book demonstrates just how much sovereign discretion economies participating in the system wield. It really is true that the WTO is a member-driven organization.

We hope that the cases in this book will help dispel the mystery and encourage more people to take a more active role in the 'game' in future. When you read the cases, you will probably recognize many of the issues that they raise and the challenges faced by the people at the centre of the story. Many of the stories told here for the first time are repeated every day in economies around the world: you can probably find very similar stories in the business press in your own city.

The case studies

This book is the result of a project that has been jointly funded by the WTO and the Australian government's official aid agency, AusAID, to encourage better understanding of how the multilateral trading system works. Our sponsors agreed to allow us to seek case studies, predominantly written by observers and analysts in developing countries, that would detail some aspect of the way in which the stakeholders in a particular economy worked together to manage a problem or to make the most of an opportunity related to WTO membership.

We contacted authors in about fifty economies, many of them in academic institutions, and gave them a very short brief that left the choice of subject matter and approach entirely up to them. We did not ask for 'success stories' and we made it clear that the analysis of the issues, including their assessment of the value or role of the WTO, was a matter for their own judgement.

We have accepted for publication virtually all the cases that reached a final draft within the time constraints we placed on the authors. So, as much as possible, this is an 'un-retouched' snapshot of participation in the WTO seen – mostly – from around the developing world about ten years after the organization was founded.

3 The big picture

The cases in this book cover a wide range of commercial and government activities.

A **Bangladeshi** rock band finds that a 'Bollywood' movie producer has pirated one of its songs; band members use the provisions of the WTO to regain their rights.

The tiny Pacific island economy of **Vanuatu** decides to suspend its application for WTO membership when its inexperienced government administrators fail to find a sympathetic hearing from existing WTO members.

An 'inside' account of how **India** struggled to develop a national consensus on the liberalization of its protected agriculture sector.

The **Kenyan** government fights for the right, under the WTO Agreements, to import AIDS drugs manufactured elsewhere under 'compulsory licences' for use in Kenya. It finds that the issue of patent protection under its own legislation is not straightforward and that the patent law changes are not the biggest barrier to reducing the impact of the disease.

The tuna industry of **Thailand** fights to retain access to the European Union (EU) market on comparable terms to its competitors, but manages to avoid a costly formal dispute adjudication.

Chilean poultry exporters and government officials act urgently to handle an animal health emergency that could have killed exports to the vital European market, making effective use of international standards and notification procedures established by the WTO.

An exporter of traditional herbal medicines from **Nepal** runs into regulatory barriers he cannot understand or do much about until Nepal joins the WTO and the Nepalese government creates a regulatory framework that helps him to meet his customers' expectations of good manufacturing practice.

The **Mexican** government is backed into a corner, domestically, by the powerful Peasants' Union's revolt against imports from the United States under the North American Free Trade Agreement (NAFTA); the facts show, however, that the agreement has opened up new horizons for Mexican industry that could be extended by multilateral negotiation.

Nigerian industry is penalized by a system of import prohibitions that have strong political support but are economically costly – why Nigeria's WTO obligations don't offer a solution.

4 Some themes

Accession

The accession of developing economies to the WTO has proved to be a major challenge to their government administration as well as to the content of their trade policies. It's a gruelling procedure requiring the preparation of detailed memoranda on foreign trade policies and practices and a convincing commitment to implement the WTO Agreements – without access, in most cases, to the lengthy implementation delays that were available to members of the WTO when the agreements were first negotiated. They must also negotiate bilateral trade deals with their most important trading partners, intended to ensure that they 'pay' for the rights that they will acquire as WTO members. The process often involves years of detailed examination by a working party and lengthy rounds of negotiation.

During this time it is not at all unusual for domestic pressures on the government to mount, as business and civil society – lacking experience with the WTO and fearful of the consequences of market liberalization – demand more details about the benefits of membership and often question the impact of the WTO rules on the economy's sovereignty.

Several cases in this collection provide new perspectives from the inside on this difficult process.

Damedin Tsogtbaatar reveals how the objectives of the business community and even of the government were shaped by **Mongolia**'s historical experience before its accession bid. He shows how these false expectations led to ill-prepared negotiations, less advantageous accession terms than might have been achieved and subsequent disenchantment with the WTO that had a lingering effect on Mongolian trade policy.

Vanuatu, an island economy in the Melanesian group, was also ill-prepared for its attempts to accede to the WTO. It had few government and private-sector resources to support its accession efforts and lacked the administrative resources to inform its domestic stakeholders or adequately to prepare for the bilateral negotiations. The government of Vanuatu (population 200,000), like the government of China (population more than 1 billion), had chosen to make membership of the WTO an integral step in its objective of closer integration with the global economy. But economic reforms stalled along with the WTO bid, due in part to lack of adequate planning and national consensus on the objectives. The account by Daniel Gay reveals an unmistakeable bitterness in Vanuatu regarding the attitude of its major trading partners towards its WTO bid and even the role of the WTO secretariat.

In **China** the story of this historic change in economic direction is still unfolding, but the impression given by Gong Baihua of the Shanghai WTO Affairs Consultation Centre is that business and government are much more confident of their ability to control and to benefit from China's integration with the global economy.

Following the Vanuatu experience WTO members changed their approach to the accession of least-developed economies to reduce the administrative burdens on poor economies and to lower the bar to their entry. **Nepal** – whose accession had been slowed by political turmoil and security problems – was one of the first beneficiaries of this new approach, being invited to join WTO at the Cancún Ministerial meeting. P. R. Rajkarnikar tells the story of the leadership of a regional non-governmental organization (NGO), SAWTEE, in promoting consensus on membership during the final stages of the process and of the influence that SAWTEE's views had on specific issues relating to Nepal's accession such as plant breeders' rights.

Cambodia, too, was welcomed into the WTO at the Cancún meeting at a time when the constitutional machinery for ratifying the Agreement was not in place. Hach Sok and Samnang Chea examine the degree to which the accession was negotiated with the informed support of the business community and ask whether Cambodia, whose trade depends heavily on the export of garments, is well prepared for the future management of integration into global markets.

One of the most controversial aspects of recent accessions has been the demand by existing members that new members achieve still greater openness than is required by the current agreements. This was certainly one of the problems faced by **Vanuatu**.

The liberalization of markets that follows accession may also move the acceding economy to make consequential changes to its policies in order to take full advantage of accession. This is the case in **Vietnam** where, as Phan Van Sam and Vo Thanh Thu point out, liberalization of the banking sector – although not strictly required by the General Agreement on Trade in Services (GATS) – is essential to ensure that Vietnamese firms can make the best of their new opportunities for integration with global markets.

Disputes

How do developing countries fare under the WTO dispute settlement system? Does it work for or against their interests? Are they able to afford the legal advice that they need in order to bring a case? Are they able to achieve satisfactory resolution of their problems when they do not have the economic power to 'retaliate' if so authorized by the Dispute Settlement Body? Can they afford to fight one case after another if necessary to protect their interests in a global market?

Several case studies help to throw some light on the answers to these questions. One of the first cases after the creation of WTO involved a dramatic contrast in the economic size and resources of the disputants. John Breckenridge tells the story of **Costa Rica**'s successful assertion of its rights under the Agreement on Textiles and Clothing against US safeguard actions. The victory for Costa Rica in this case – due, says the author, to better preparation as well as the merits of its case – was a signal to other developing countries that the system would work to protect the interests of all members.

Pakistan, too, was successful in challenging US textile safeguards in the late 1990s, as Turab Hussain recounts. This case details some of the practical aspects of preparing a case and the potentially ambiguous 'victories' that formal dispute adjudication can bring. The government of Pakistan was party to a WTO dispute for the first time. According to the author it was not well equipped for the case and relied heavily on the specialist knowledge and funding resources of the textile industry association and its members. After persisting with the case before the Textile Monitoring Body and eventually before a disputes panel and an appeal, Pakistan's objections to the three-year US safeguard quota were upheld. But it had taken almost all of those same three years – and a lot of money – to win the case. Pakistan's victory was, in the view of the industry, mostly one of principle.

Nilaratna Xuto contributes a case study from **Thailand** in which close collaboration between government officials and industry leaders challenged proposed changes in EU tariff preferences. The Thai tuna case illustrates the operation of the conciliation procedures in WTO disputes, using the good offices of the Director General of the WTO. These provisions of the disputes mechanism do not capture headlines in the same way as a panel adjudication, but they offer many advantages as this case shows, including less contentious procedures, and significantly lower costs.

It is important to remember that no WTO dispute is supposed to be contentious. Of course, there can be a lot of heat generated between the disputants at the time. But the resolution of disputes serves a positive purpose for all WTO members by helping to smooth world trade and by clarifying how national trade regulations should operate to give effect to the principles of the WTO Agreements.

The WTO disputes system helps to do this even with regard to regional agreements, where disputes among the parties can be even more bitter than those among WTO members at large. An interesting instance of this is the story that Diana Tussie and Valentina Delich tell about the challenge that **Argentina** raised to Chilean variable levies imposed on imports of vegetable oils, after it had tried unsuccessfully to resolve the matter in the context of the Mercosur regional agreement.

Another surprising aspect of dispute settlement is the confidence-building effect that a successful case can have, affecting the attitude of government and stakeholders towards global economic integration. Junsok Yang's account of the case brought by **South Korea** against US anti-dumping measures on colour televisions confirms that preparation for a dispute that demands close collaboration between officials and business people has a positive impact on domestic trade policy-making. For South Korea the result was a more confident participation in the WTO and a more positive view of the benefits of 'globalization' of the economy.

The South Korean colour television dispute had its origins in anti-dumping actions taken in the 1980s. Today, anti-dumping actions continue to give rise to serious disputes, as we can see from B. Battarcharyya's very recent case study on the work that the **Indian** shrimp exporting industry and the government of India have undertaken to fight a dumping charge in the United States. Whether this and related cases also targeting shrimp exports will be subject to WTO challenge may be known by the time this book is published. Bhattarcharyya's account suggests, however, that in addition to the financial considerations a decision to pursue a WTO dispute should include an evaluation of the strategic interests of the industry in a lengthy legal tussle.

There is a valuable lesson on this same point in Jacqueline Krikorian's story of **Canada**'s unsuccessful defence of its discriminatory implementation of tariff benefits associated with its side of the US–Canada Auto Pact. She concludes that it was a case fought for the wrong reasons in an attempt to defend a policy whose original objectives had already been bypassed in the marketplace. Friction with trading partners, uncertainty for the automobile industry and a lot of expense might have been spared, in her view, if the Canadian authorities had elected not to defend their policies.

Standards and SPS

We asked all the case study authors to tell the story of a challenge or an opportunity faced by business in the world trading system. The stories that they tell range over many forms of trade barriers, but the most challenging seem to be those related to standards for health or safety, including food safety. Import regulations that fall under the provisions of the WTO's Agreement on Technical Barriers to Trade (TBT) or the Agreement on Sanitary and Phyto-Sanitary Measures (SPS) are multiplying around the world. They are typically complex regulations, frequently implementing standards that create a high hurdle for imports. Developing country exporters whose own governments may not implement similar standards sometimes find it difficult to understand what steps are required for compliance with these standards, even when the standards themselves have international sanction.

Bijendra Shakya's story about the Gorkha Ayurved company of **Nepal** illustrates all of these factors. The principal of the company, which exports herbal medicines, had to find out for himself about the meaning of the compliance requirements of his customers and to find ways of certifying compliance ahead of government moves to implement an appropriate regulatory structure.

Even legitimate SPS barriers can result in total import prohibitions, so that the stakes can be very high for developing country exporters with limited resources to manage compliance with stringent food health requirements. Rina Oktaviani's study of the EU barriers faced by the **Indonesian** shrimp industry shows how little room there is for manoeuvre in such cases and the critical importance of good information flows between government and industry in finding means, within the resources of the export industry, to meet the market requirements.

Excellent information flow and a high priority on transparency with authorities in export markets were keys to the successful management of the health emergency in **Chile**'s poultry industry, as told by Claudia Orozco. The Chilean industry and government officials on-site, as well as the Chilean representatives in Brussels and in the OIE (International Office of Epizootics) were immediately alert to the importance of informing all concerned about the nature of the outbreak of avian flu. They handled the emergency successfully because their openness maintained the confidence of the European authorities, allowing them to win agreement to the regionalization of the problem, reducing its commercial impact and making a solution easier to implement.

The Colombian authorities were not so forthcoming about a standards barrier that they imposed on the **Malaysian** latex condom industry, according to Norma Mansor, Noor Hasniah Kasim and Yong Sook Lu. This case suggests that it may be necessary to 'read between the lines' to understand the commercial impact of an apparently innocuous labelling requirement. It would have been possible for government officials on either side to make a mistake had it not been for the WTO standards

notification system that alerted the Malaysian firm to the potential problem with the Colombian labelling requirement and provided a mechanism
for an official Malaysian response. In this case, as in many potential trade
disputes that surface in the WTO, it appears that the proposal was quietly
withdrawn and the problem went away.

The non-discriminatory application of SPS barriers, such as those
affecting imports of farmed shrimp into the EU, means that they frequently affect a number of exporters at the same time. Several **Pacific
Island Forum** economies are potentially affected by the EU's health ban on
imports of traditional kava root products. These economies have already
banded together in their participation in the WTO, establishing a joint
representative office in Geneva to save on funds and to make the best use
of experienced personnel. Chakriya Bowman describes in her case study
how this initiative will help **Papua New Guinea**, **Samoa** and **Fiji** to work
closely together to respond to the unique threat to their multi-million
dollar exports of kava-based products.

Industries seeking protection press governments of both developed and
developing countries to implement standards or SPS barriers, because
they can offer much higher levels of protection than most tariffs. Isidro
Morales-Moreno's case study of **Mexican** agricultural policies following
the implementation of NAFTA describes instances of the use of SPS
barriers to reduce adjustment pressures on Mexican farmers.

Intellectual property

One of the most controversial aspects of the 1995 Agreement on Trade-
Related Aspects of Intellectual Property Rights (TRIPS) was the evidence
that rights-holders of trade-related intellectual property were mostly
in industrialized countries and that developing countries were mostly
importers of trade-related intellectual property. Critics said that the TRIPS
Agreement was more advantageous to the former than to the latter WTO
members who, nonetheless, faced heavy implementation obligations.

The cases set out in this book do not resolve the controversy, but it is
interesting that those we received that relate to TRIPS show developing
country export interest in intellectual property and some success stories,
as well as challenges on the import side.

S. C. Srivastava has provided a detailed account of the determined
legal defences mounted by the Tea Board of **India** to protect its registered
geographical indication (GI) of 'Darjeeling' in France, Japan and Russia.
Although the Tea Board's objections to the registration of marks that they

considered infringed their rights were not always successful – notably in France, where the Indian registration was not given reciprocal rights according to Srivastava – the case points to the heavy legal burden that the maintenance of a GI, like the maintenance of any trademark, can impose.

Amir Muhammed and Wajid H. Pirzada have compiled a case study related to recent negotiations between **Pakistan** and the EU on European access barriers to Basmati rice, in which the authoritative designation of rice as 'Basmati' may hold the key to maintaining Pakistan's access to the EU market. Unfortunately, as the authors point out, the government of Pakistan has not yet implemented its proposed legislation on the registration of such names.

Of course, copyright is unique among the major intellectual property categories in not requiring any registration process. One of the happiest outcomes for a developing country intellectual property rights-holder is to be found in Abul Kalam Azad's case on the triumphant defence of their copyright by the well-known **Bangladedshi** rock band, Miles. The band was able to obtain summary judgment in the Indian courts against the piracy of their music by a Bollywood producer, thanks to the rights established by the TRIPS Agreement.

Darker and more complex problems figure in Ben Sihanya's case study on the parallel importing and compulsory licensing of patented AIDS drugs in **Kenya**. The case provides an insider's report on efforts to ensure a supply of effective, low-cost drugs for the fight against AIDS in Africa, and examines the controversy over the TRIPS Agreement's restrictions on trade in compulsorily licensed drugs. The Kenyan objective, according to Sihanya, was to ensure that the patents served the interests of both rights-holders and consumers. This balance was expressed in Kenyan law as well as in the TRIPS Agreement. Part of the challenge in 'reinterpreting' the provisions of the TRIPS Agreement was to maintain this balance of interests when the compulsorily licensed drugs were made available for export. But, in Sihanya's view, the change to the TRIPS provisions did not necessarily address the most significant barriers to effective public health delivery to AIDS victims.

Services

Although services form a rapidly growing part of developing country trade and already provide a significant contribution to a higher balance in their trade account, the level of developing member commitments under GATS remains low. A developing country with significantly higher service commitments than many others is **Argentina**. As Roberto Bouzas and Hernán Soltz argue, this is most likely to be the result of a coincidence in time between multilateral liberalization efforts and domestic policy reform. In this case the multilateral negotiations were seized upon as an opportunity to push domestic reform.

Soledad Salvador and Paola Azar study the efforts made in **Uruguay** to develop a new 'institutional channel' for public/private-sector co-ordination on GATS issues. The authors believe that the dialogue suffered from a lack of commitment on both sides, and from some institutional resistance and poor information flows that fed existing suspicions – on the part of unions and civil society organizations, for example – about the objectives and consequences of services liberalization. They point to the need to evaluate objectively the domestic impacts and opportunities of services market access. Without such evaluation, the authors argue, the personal views of negotiators and officials may assume more importance than agreed national objectives in determining the GATS commitments eventually subscribed.

J. P. Singh presents a case that contrasts the superficially similar approaches to GATS negotiations of two small Central American economies, **Belize** and **Costa Rica**. Noting the low level of commitments offered by developing countries in the GATS negotiations, he asks why economies with vibrant service sub-sectors and in serious need of foreign investment or with sizable service export surpluses make such low commitments.

> The evidence that follows for the two countries confirms the essentially bottom-up nature of GATS: both countries choose particular sectors for commitment – at levels acceptable to domestic actors. Interestingly, they also exhibit significant policy differences: Costa Rica was positioning itself to take advantage of being a service-based export-led economy; Belize remains ambivalent about the role of services in general and GATS commitments in particular.

Linda Schmid has a services success story to tell about the experience of telecommunications liberalization in the small Caribbean island economy of **Barbados**, whose flavour can be represented by this cameo from her account:

> An itinerant gardener who makes his way to work and carries his tools with him on his bicycle passed me while I was in a traffic jam. I needed help with my garden, flagged him down, and asked if he might be available. I reached for a pen and paper. He pulled out his cell phone, entered my data,

and that evening I had a phone message to schedule a garden site visit. He was using his cell phone as a client database. Individuals with minimal economic means are employing this lower cost technology to enhance the way they work and communicate with others.

She notes, however, that creating regulatory institutions to oversee a competitive market in telecommunications or other newly liberalized services sectors such as banking, insurance or securities is a challenge to WTO members with limited financial and human resources.

Malathy Knight-John and Chethana Ellepola would, presumably, agree about the regulatory challenges. Their account of the implementation of the provisions of the GATS Telecommunications Reference Paper points to gains for **Sri Lanka** from the liberalization of the telecoms market that followed GATS. But they also identify wide gaps between the global expectations reflected in the Reference Paper and Sri Lanka's performance in the crucial area of interconnection. The authors describe a complex political economy created by a large number of small players and a small number of large public switched telecommunication network operators who, in the absence of an effective post-liberalization regulatory regime, have been able to cartelize aspects of the market.

Advocacy and 'democratic accountability'

Where do WTO decisions come from? From the member governments: there is no other source of decisions in the WTO. Not even the recommendations of the disputes panels or the Appellate Body become decisions of the WTO until the member governments say so.[2]

So, how do individual member governments decide what to say on any particular issue? That question lies at the heart of what might be called the 'democratic accountability' issue for any intergovernmental organization like the WTO. Do the decisions of the WTO have 'democratic' credentials in the sense that the member governments' policies and regulations are based on a democratic mandate and on the processes that we expect in any democracy such as public information, consultation with stakeholders and accountability to citizens for the decisions taken?

The case studies in this book show that the answer is, in general, 'yes'. We see evidence in almost all cases that governments are ready to *inform* and *consult* with private-sector stakeholders when they are preparing for

---

[2] Although it would be very unusual, not to say difficult, for the member governments to reject a recommendation of a panel (possibly as modified by the Appellate Body).

a WTO decision or negotiation. Most governments seem to appreciate, too, that such consultations are essential to ensure that government is well informed about the consequences of its actions in the WTO.

There are, however, two different aspects to this co-ordination with stakeholders: *advocacy* – which can be 'lobbying' for private benefit or something more public-spirited – and *accountability*, which means, at a minimum, government responsiveness to the demands of stakeholders and citizens.

In most of the cases in this book there is an element of advocacy by producers that prompts governments to inform and consult. Producers whose interests are at stake in a trade policy measure are likely to lobby for government consideration and support particularly where a foreign trade remedy measure is involved (Pakistan – cotton, India – shrimp, Costa Rica – garments) or some other external event threatens changes in market access terms (Thailand – tuna, Malaysia – condoms, Chile – poultry). In most of these cases we see the formation or expansion of producer coalitions designed to address a specific, WTO-related trade challenge to trade in a particular product. In several of these case studies the authors also suggest that the experience gained by the coalition, and the links it develops with the government in the course of the events recounted in the case, will continue to provide a base for co-ordination in the future.

Jean-Marie Paugam, for example, tells the story of the co-ordination of **French** negotiating positions, particularly on agriculture, in the lead-up to the Cancún ministerial meeting. Although France exercises its influence on the WTO agenda through the European Community's position, Paugam provides an analysis of a very well-informed, experienced, sophisticated stakeholder community whose inputs into both the French and Community's negotiating position is persistent, co-ordinated and effective. 'Overall', Paugam notes, 'in keeping with theoretical predictions, protected producers are more likely to organize themselves efficiently when their interests are concentrated and their consumers dispersed. In a context of declining agricultural support, concentrated potential "losers" proved very active.'

Two other case studies also use the agricultural sector to analyze the challenges of including non-governmental actors in the decision-making process. The study on **Venezuela** by Rita Giacalone and Eduardo Porcarelli shows that the issue is not simply whether both government and the private sector are serious about engaging in dialogue. They refer to the need for 'avoidance of politicization' in consultative processes and argue that 'private-sector associations should carefully tread the waters of domestic politics in order to have the right to participate ... ' Shishir Priyadarshi's study of decision-making on agriculture in **India** traces an open and generally successful consultative process. But he also notes that this inclusiveness and transparency may have pre-conditioned the government's stance and favoured a defensive posture.

Niel Joubert's study of the development of the anti-dumping regime in **South Africa** reveals that even where consultative mechanisms are well established, they may simply serve to bless decisions that have already been taken or positions that have been defined in anticipation of negotiations with other countries. Joubert notes that governments may well have to choose trade-offs that disregard non-governmental stakeholder inputs, but this does not necessarily mean that these were disregarded from the outset.

There seems to be a qualitative difference between the lobbying of producers in the context of WTO negotiations – where the potential responses of the government are constrained by the need to reach reciprocal agreements with trading partners – and lobbying where the government is not so constrained.

From **Nigeria**, for example, Ademola Oyejide, Olawale Ogunkola and Abiodun Bankole bring us a case of an import prohibition policy that seems to escape the constraints of the General Agreement on Tariffs and Trade (GATT) rules because it falls under a WTO exception. The authors argue that the policy has failed despite a degree of popular support. Although its nominal purpose is to secure the economy's balance of payments, the latter is determined primarily by developments in the world oil market; the import prohibitions have relatively little impact. The real force behind the use of this policy instrument, according to the authors, is the protection of domestic producers, but there is little evidence that protection has produced the desired result of a greater degree of import replacement or higher export earnings.

Sometimes producers join in sector-wide or even cross-sector advocacy that may include non-producer interests (Philippines – co-ordination, Brazil – G20, India – agriculture, Kenya – co-ordination, France – co-ordination). Here the need to accommodate divergent interests is likely to defeat attempts at 'lobbying' on behalf of product or sector objectives and to result in more strategic 'advocacy' by the private sector, taking account of economy-wide goals.

Pedro da Motta Veiga brings us an example of this broadly based policy advocacy in his insider's account of **Brazil**'s role in the formation of the G20 group of developing countries and the interaction of Brazilian ministries and industry in those events. He writes:

> Brazil's negotiations strategy was driven not only by the internal dynamics of the agricultural negotiations in the WTO, but also by a broader shift in the country's foreign economic policies – especially in its trade negotiations strategy – towards a view where the North–South axis acquired a growing relevance. Brazil's leadership in the setting of the G20 is perhaps the best example, at the multilateral level, of the country's new 'southern' stance in trade negotiations.

In several cases, too, we see evidence of *accountability*: that is, the willingness of governments to take responsibility for their decisions or to share with stakeholder representatives responsibility for decisions (India – agriculture, Chile – poultry, Thailand – tuna, Brazil – G20, Barbados – telecommunications, Philippines – agriculture, China – consultation).

Donah Sharon Baracol gives us an insight into the **Philippines** formal consultation process on agriculture negotiations: the Task Force on WTO Agriculture (Re)Negotiations (TF-WAR). The Task Force was formed as a result of grass-roots demand for a review of the Philippines negotiating approaches before the Seattle Ministerial meeting, and it remains, according to Philippines officials, a principal source of information for agricultural industry stakeholders as well as of guidance for the government in formulating its position. The strength of the consultation process and its broad base provides, according to the author, a form of security for Philippines negotiators against the pressures of third parties in the negotiations.

But consultation and co-ordination are expensive: they use resources that are scarce in any economy – especially small and developing economies – such as the time and attention of government officials and private-sector representatives. We also find several cases where the challenges described by the author are due to consultation and accountability mechanisms that are under-resourced and unco-ordinated (Uruguay – services, Kenya – co-ordination, Botswana – co-ordination) or slow to start (Pakistan – textiles, Uganda – co-ordination, Malawi – co-ordination).

Several African case studies contain examples of co-ordination problems and failures due in part to the cost of building appropriate institutions.

Walter Odhiambo, Paul Kamau and Dorothy McCormick are critical of the consultative process in **Kenya** that is managed through the

National Committee for the WTO (NCWTO). The membership of the national consultative body – responsible for recommendations on all aspects of Kenya's participation in WTO – was based in part on its 'enquiry point'/notification obligations under the Uruguay Round agreements. The committee is large and hierarchically structured, and has a heavy agenda of meetings. But without political commitment, funding, legal status, decision-making powers or consistent participation from the private sector it has provided limited inputs into government decisions. For all its shortcomings, however, the authors believe that it has had an impact on the dissemination of information and on an increased private-sector awareness of the WTO in Kenya.

Tonia Kandiero argues that stakeholders in **Malawi** have reason to be disappointed with the organization of their representation in the WTO, and suggests that changes are needed in the co-ordination of technical assistance to Malawi to ensure that its need for a better understanding of the WTO and more effective representation can be met.

Nichodemus Rudaheranwa and Vernetta Barungi Atingi-Ego from **Uganda** list six areas of investment needed to support full participation in the WTO, and argue that developing countries need to consider investments in trade negotiating capacity and the resourcing of their stakeholder consultation mechanisms as a development project, creating the institutions needed for trade-led growth.

The case studies related to accession to the WTO (see above) show that the process frequently leads to the creation of organized coalitions.

An 'agent of restraint'

The authors of the Nigerian case study draw a lesson that may have wider application:

> Nigeria's membership of the WTO provides it, in principle, with a strong external trade policy surveillance mechanism. But the role of the WTO as an 'agent of restraint' in favour of good trade policy is feasible only to the extent that two important conditions are met. First, the government whose behaviour is to be 'restrained' must be committed to good trade policy and thus be willing to tie its own hand and use an external treaty obligation to strengthen its hand against local vested interests.

Governments are usually aware that to change a trade measure such as a tariff, a quota or a subsidy means hurting someone – possibly someone now relying on low-cost imports – who will never forget the hurt.

It also means helping someone else who will never remember that the government did them a favour by raising a trade barrier.

Thus many governments learn to be grateful that the rules of the WTO limit what they could otherwise easily do: lift rates of protection or give new subsidies. As a matter of fact, it is rare that the WTO rules absolutely prohibit a government from taking whatever action the latter deems necessary. But the role of the WTO as an 'agent of restraint' in favour of good trade policy proves valuable to governments around the world every day, because every day governments are under pressure to raise a barrier – or simply to maintain a barrier – to help some industry or other.

Take the case of the **Philippines** customs valuation measures brought to us by Ramon L. Clarete. The case provides a history of efforts by the Philippines government and Congress to develop a transparent, effective means of valuing imports to ensure that neither importers nor, potentially, customs officials could defraud the government of its revenue from duties and that protection levels would be maintained while the government met its obligation to base collections on transaction values. Working within the restraints imposed by the WTO Agreement on Customs Valuation enabled the Philippines authorities to bypass pressure from interested lobbies and adopt a more transparent system, with post-entry audits, that has lowered barriers to trade and has increased customs revenue.

Two special regions

We have taken special care in this book to include cases from the smallest and most disadvantaged economies, particularly the island economies of the Pacific such as Vanuatu, Papua New Guinea and Fiji, and land-locked economies such as Botswana, Laos, Mongolia, Nepal and Zambia.

We expected to find that these economies faced specific problems and we hoped to find some useful ideas or perspectives that would emerge from their common experience and help them – and others – to find specific solutions in the future.

What we found was that these economies face many of the same problems and opportunities as other economies, but have fewer resources to manage them and face greater penalties if things go wrong.

In **Botswana**, a land-locked economy of southern Africa, the narrowness of the economy's productive base and its dependence on a very small number of export destinations has resulted in informal and ad hoc trade policy-making, according to Kennedy K. Mbekeani. He reports, however, that a lack of information resources in the responsible agency – experienced personnel, analytical capacity and relevant inputs from stakeholders – is the single biggest challenge to the management of Botswana's trade policy.

Botswana's land-locked neighbour, **Malawi**, has similar resource problems and similar failures of stakeholder consultation according to Tonia Kandiero, who describes the complex of supply-side constraints and policy shortcomings that have prevented Malawi from taking full advantage of its WTO membership.

Small, resource-limited economies often face difficulties in finding adequate resources to participate in negotiations. Sanoussi Bilal and Stefan Szepesi ask whether **Zambia** and **Mauritius** have been able to 'economise' on these resources by using possible synergies between different negotiating fora and multilateral negotiations. The issue was whether these two countries were able to use their participation in regional negotiations under the Southern African Development Community (SADC) and the Common Market for Eastern and Southern Africa (COMESA) to facilitate participation in the WTO. The answer was that little exists by way of direct impact, but that there could be indirect synergies such as raising awareness, training, making information available and capacity building. But the ability to make use of these opportunities depends crucially on pre-existing capacity, and this was clear from comparisons between Zambia and Mauritius.

Buavanh Vilavong and his colleagues detail the difficulties faced by the **Laotian** garment industry after the garment quotas were eliminated in some of the largest export markets in January 2005. They show how, in a small, land-locked economy that is still on the road to WTO membership, the challenges of increasing productivity while maintaining access to tariff preferences are linked, creating some crucial hurdles for the industry.

Andrew Stoler paints a picture of the tough choices facing **Fiji** with the erosion of sugar preferences in the European market. Preference erosion is a widespread problem for developing economies; Fiji has moderated it by securing the extension of some regional preferences. But it appears that Fijians may be failing to make the best of their options for growth due to failures of consensus and co-ordination at a policy level.

Fiji's approach to dealing with its many problems compares poorly to what is happening in another small island state, **Mauritius**, which, as Andrew Stoler explains, is wrestling with many of the same kinds of issues. In Fiji, political tensions stand in the way of successful co-operation between government and business. In Mauritius, government and business have a long tradition of working together for mutual benefit.

The government of **Papua New Guinea** (PNG), like the governments of the other islands of the Pacific, faces a major challenge sustaining its membership of the WTO. Despite having the largest economy in this group, the burdens of membership weigh heavily on PNG according to Chakriya Bowman. But, with the help of donors including Australia and the EU and with the support of the WTO Secretariat, the island economies of the Pacific Islands Forum have found a unique response to this challenge to their administrative resources: a Joint Representative Office in Geneva. Chakriya Bowman describes a specific instance in which this joint representation has helped the Pacific Islands Forum manage a standards-based threat to their exports of kava to Europe.

5 Who's in charge?

What do these case studies tell us about the role of the WTO in an economy's trade policy?

There are probably as many answers to that question in this book as there are cases: the role that the WTO plays is subtly different in each account, depending on the history of the economy or its economic or constitutional circumstances. But it is clear in every case that WTO rules and WTO activities comprise only one factor among many economic, administrative, social and even constitutional factors that affect the way in which trade and related policies are decided.

In several cases governments are struggling to develop or to prosecute successful trade policies or to participate in the WTO because they lack human, administrative or financial resources. The challenge is particularly evident in the poorest economies such as Malawi, Botswana and the island economy of Vanuatu. But the case studies of Nigeria and Venezuela suggest that greater wealth does not necessarily bring with it more successful trade policy administration. Something else is needed.

Nor is the size of the economy necessarily an indicator of whether it will enjoy success in the protection of its rights or prosecution of its objectives in the WTO. We have case studies from some of the largest economies (France, Brazil and India) that show a sophisticated process of policy development based on contributions from well-informed private-sector organizations and experienced trade policy administrators. But we also have case studies – such as those from Costa Rica, Pakistan and Thailand – that show how middle-sized and even small economies with less experience in multilateral affairs can achieve significant 'wins' in the WTO.

Cases from southern Africa and the Pacific confirm that there is a 'threshold' level of the human and administrative capacity and resources that are needed to implement WTO agreements and to maintain an effective presence 'at the table' of WTO negotiations. The Papua New Guinea case indicates that there may be innovative ways to overcome some of these constraints, but this possible 'exception' only proves the rule.

Beyond that threshold, however, the case studies in this book show over and over again that the key to the successful management of participation in the WTO and the global trading system is co-ordination: among government agencies (as we see in case studies from India, Brazil and France), and between the government and private sectors (as we see in case studies from the Philippines, India (shrimp), Thailand, Mauritius, Costa Rica, Chile, Nepal (accession), Pakistan (textiles) and Argentina (services)).

Cases revealing a high level of interaction, information exchange and collaboration between business or civil society institutions and government are all 'success stories'. Cases where, for a variety of reasons, this collaboration and information exchange breaks down (Venezuela, and to a lesser extent Uruguay) or where it does not get going (Kenya (co-ordination), Vanuatu) or where there is a misalignment of priorities between government and the private sector (Fiji, Canada (automobiles), Mongolia) tell a less happy story.

This common thread through the stories of success on the one hand and failure or frustration on the other leads, we think, to a conclusion about the role of the WTO that deserves specific emphasis. Beyond the 'threshold' mentioned earlier, the crucial factors in the success of an economy's trade policy are home grown. The WTO itself is not the prime determinant of whether an economy achieves its objectives in the world trading system. The Agreements constrain government actions in the regulation of trade, but none of those constraints appears in any of these case studies as a hurdle for governments or for businesses. On the contrary, where WTO members in the stories told here directly invoke the rules (Pakistan (rice), Costa Rica (textiles), South Korea (television)) or make use of the framework of rules and obligations (Bangladesh (copyright), Chile (SPS)) the outcome is positive for developing country business. Where the rules act to constrain or direct government choices (Nigeria, Vietnam, Canada) the constraints seem likely to lead to more opportunities for trade and growth.

Decisions by the WTO determine the outcome in a small number of the case studies we have collected; for example, in some of the disputes case studies (Pakistan (textiles), Costa Rica (textiles etc.)). But in most case studies, including some disputes that were resolved without WTO adjudication (Thailand (tuna), Pakistan (rice)), there is no direct intervention by the organization in the events or trends described. The case studies tell us that the decisions that matter to members most of the time are not made in Geneva. They are decisions made by governments in direct contact with other members within the framework of the WTO system, or they are decisions made autonomously by governments about the allocation of resources within their own economies.

Perhaps the question we should ask is not 'who's in charge' but 'where does the responsibility lie' for trade policy and for achieving success in the global economy. The answer is not – in either case – the WTO. The answer is the 'stakeholders' – in each member economy of the WTO, public and private sectors together.

1

Dispute settlement between developing countries: Argentina and Chilean price bands

DIANA TUSSIE AND VALENTINA DELICH*

The WTO is playing a novel role in regional trade relations. Access to a multilateral dispute settlement system is helping to scrutinize and anchor the more lax regional disciplines. Although accessible only to highly profitable sectors because participation is too costly and time consuming, the WTO provides the intangible benefit of exposure. Pressure through exposure can help countries unable or unwilling to retaliate to obtain more favourable results than in bilateral or regional instances. In fact, WTO rulings act as a magnifying glass of countries' (WTO-incompatible) trade policies. In this picture, reputation, a high-value asset to attract business and negotiate trade agreements, is thus at stake. A dispute between Argentina and Chile over variable levies for edible vegetable oils is a case in point.

1 The problem in context

After a tariff reclassification in 1999, the Chilean price band system (PBS) resulted in higher customs duties for edible vegetable oils. In normal circumstances Argentina might have been able to absorb the drop that this implied in market share, but the restriction came in a very threatening international context for the sector. This is a flagship sector in Argentina: it weighs heavily in trade and production and thus its interests cannot be dismissed lightly. As a result, this issue became the first legally handled dispute with a regional partner to be submitted to the WTO. Due to the number of coterminous issues that peppered the relationship between the two countries, shelving for political reasons was always a risk.

Argentina is one of the top vegetable oil producers in the world. Total production, which includes soy, sunflower, peanut, olive, cotton, linseed,

* FLACSO, Argentina.

corn, turnip, edible mixes and *tung* oils, amounted to about 5,283 thousand tons in 2001 (CIARA 2004). Nearly all domestic production is exported, with foreign sales varying between 80% and 90% of total production. Low domestic consumption, together with high productivity turns Argentina into the leading world exporter of sunflower and soy oil, followed by Brazil and the United States. Currently, exports of vegetable oil and fats represent about 28% of the value of total food exports and around 10% of the value of total exports.

Export performance has been erratic over the last seven years, due mainly to international market circumstances. Changes in both global demand and supply of grains led to a price drop in 1997–2001. On the demand side, south-east Asia and Russia, two of the most important buyers, were undergoing deep economic crises and thus making decreased purchases. On the supply side, the implementation of the deficiency loan system for soy in the United States, the production of Round-up-Ready (genetically modified) soy and a record harvest of sunflower and soy in two of the main world producers, namely Argentina and Brazil, contributed to increased global production of seeds. In particular, during the period 1999–2001 prices were 10% lower than those registered at the beginning of the decade and almost 40% below the 1997 peak (Schvarzer and Heyn 2002: 7). Locally, the collapse of prices meant that seven factories closed. Even the biggest companies were struck: Molinos closed one of its plants and dismissed 270 employees.

The price drop affected the operation of the Chilean PBS: it resulted in the collection of *ad valorem* customs duties of up to 64.41% for oils and 60.25% for wheat flour in 2000, thus violating the ceiling set at 31.5% in the Uruguay Round. At that time the Chilean market was purchasing about half of Argentina's total exports of mixed oils (US$26 million). Sales of oil mixes to Chile soared while total exports to this market began to contract due to a fall in soy and sunflower that had been the object of safeguard measures. The Chilean market, despite its small size (US$80 million), was strategic in the sense that geographical proximity translated into accessibility for small and big exporters alike.

The determination of business to litigate was stoked when Chile reimbursed to Bolivia, but not to Argentina, duties collected on a (subsequently lifted) safeguard.[1] Moreover, collective action was relatively easy

---

[1] This is a prime example of the *legal spaghetti bowl*. While the safeguard duties affected both Bolivian and Argentine products, Bolivia had recourse to a bilateral agreement with Chile with a binding dispute settlement system. As the ruling confirmed that the safeguard was

to articulate, given that production is highly concentrated. Pressure to take Chile's measures to the multilateral dispute settlement system mounted and finally the government decided to do so. The fact that the Andean Community also has a PBS in place attracted the interest of business in turning the result of the conflict into an exemplary action of broader regional consequence.

The multilateral legal incident

It was not until diplomacy and regional jurisdictional representation proved ineffective that the conflict escalated to the multilateral level. Argentina first submitted the dispute to the Administration Commission of the Mercosur–Chile Agreement (Economic Complementary Agreement 35 (ECA35)). Chile had made a commitment in ECA35 neither to include more products nor to modify in any other way its PBS. After obtaining a favourable (though not binding) recommendation from the regional Group of Experts, Argentina decided to raise the issue at the WTO when Chile's reluctance to comply became obvious.

At the WTO, the dispute revolved principally around two issues:

(1) whether the PBS was a violation of GATT Article II (bound tariffs); and

(2) whether the PBS was the kind of measure that should have been 'tariffied' according to Article 4.2 of the Agreement on Agriculture (AA).[2]

The PBS applies to agricultural products. When a product subject to the PBS arrives in Chile, the customs official will impose the *ad valorem* duty (8%) only when the reference price (RP) falls between the lower and upper thresholds of the PBS. The RP is not the price of that particular transaction but a price that the Chilean authorities determine each Friday using the lowest free on board (FOB) price in so-called markets of interest.[3] The applicable RP for a particular shipment is determined with reference to the date of the bill of lading. Once the reference price for the shipment has been determined, the customs official proceeds to compare it with PBS thresholds. The PBS, in turn, is determined annually on the basis of FOB prices observed on particular international markets over the course of the

---

not compatible with the Bolivia–Chile Agreement, and therefore duties had been illegally collected, Chile had to reimburse the duties.

[2] According to Art. 4.2, WTO members shall not maintain, resort to or revert to any measures of the kind which have been required to be converted into ordinary customs duties (there is a footnote listing measures except as otherwise provided for in Art. 5 and Annex 5).

[3] Markets of interest include Argentina, Australia and Canada.

preceding 60 months. Unlike the prices used for the composition of the PBS, the reference prices are not subject to adjustment for 'usual import costs'. If the RP is below the 'floor', the customs officer will impose specific duties to reach the floor. If the RP is above the floor, then the officer must reduce the duties down to the floor price.

Argentina argued that the PBS violated Article II(b) of GATT 1994 on the grounds that by virtue of its structure, design and mode of application it potentially led to the application of specific duties in violation of the Chilean bound tariff. Argentina alleged that in practice the PBS resulted in the collection of *ad valorem* customs duties exceeding the bound ceiling tariff of 31.5%. In addition, Argentina considered the PBS to be a variable levy or a minimum import price inconsistent with the AA, since Article 4.2 required that such measures be converted into ordinary customs duties.

Chile argued, in contrast, that the PBS duties are ordinary customs duties and therefore not subject to tariffication, and that there are two separate conditions to be met for a measure to be prohibited: it must be listed in Article 4.2 note 1[4] and it must be requested by a member country. The PBS was not listed and no member had ever requested tariffication. In addition, Chile argued that ECA35 was signed after the Uruguay Round; since it explicitly allows the PBS,[5] Argentina cannot claim that the PBS is prohibited.

The panel found that the PBS was a measure of the kind which should have been converted into ordinary customs duties and that by maintaining it, Chile had acted inconsistently with the AA. The panel also found that PBS duties could be considered as 'other duties or charges of any kind' imposed on or in connection with importation, under the second sentence of Article II(1)(b). Since Chile did not record its PBS in the 'other duties and charges' column of its Schedule, the panel found that the duties were also inconsistent with Article II(b) of GATT 1994.

The panel recommended that Chile bring the questioned measures into conformity with its multilateral obligations (April 2002).[6] The route to

---

[4] The measures listed therein are quantitative import restrictions, variable import levies, minimum import prices, discretionary import licensing, non-tariff measures maintained through state-trading enterprises, voluntary export restraints or similar border measures other than customs duties.

[5] Art. 24: 'When using the Price Band System provided for in its domestic legislation concerning the importation of goods, the Republic of Chile commits, within the framework of this Agreement, neither to include new products nor to modify the mechanisms or apply them in such a way which would result in a deterioration of the market access conditions for MERCOSUR.'

[6] Currently, Argentina is questioning Chile's implementation of the report.

this pronouncement was marked by an interactive, time-consuming and costly process of building legal arguments and finding economic data. The Argentine government juggled constantly to avoid issue-linkage and political tension with Chile while at the same time upholding the claim of business. In the section that follows, we present the main attributes and idiosyncratic characteristics of the actors involved and the way in which they interacted in this case.

2 The players

The main Argentine players at the multilateral level were the government, in particular the Directorate for Multilateral Dispute Settlement (DISCO) at the Foreign Affairs Ministry, and the oil sector, in particular the Association of Argentine Edible Oil Industries (known by its Spanish acronym, CIARA). Other players included public officials in the Economy Ministry, the law firm contracted to work on the Argentine side and the freshly inaugurated business think tank, the Institute for International Agricultural Negotiations (Spanish acronym INAI). We first introduce the institutional/organizational features of the public sector, then profile the private sector and finally the way in which they interacted to build the case through the different fora and contexts.

The public sector

The process for requesting the government to pursue a trade dispute using the WTO Dispute Settlement Understanding has not been subject to regulation. There are no standing operating procedures to deal with a claim stemming from business or any guidelines on how different government offices should co-operate on bringng a case. There are no established proceedings for matters such as the window to which business must direct this kind of claim; what evidence must support it; how the government must handle the claim in terms of administrative proceedings; or under which circumstances the government should advance the private sector's claims or not. In practice, the Ministry of Foreign Affairs puts together the cases and then upholds them internationally. While the decision to open a consultation (or to settle a dispute) always involves a political decision, the responsibility for its development, the co-ordination with business, the daily management of the dispute as well as the leading technical role pertains to DISCO. Since its creation in 1999, DISCO has managed thirty-nine conflicts, including consultations, mutually agreed solutions and panels. Considering Argentina's negligible share of world trade, the number of cases is relatively high.

In contrast to the procedural void for WTO claims, the steps for business petitions are clearly stipulated within Mercosur's dispute settlement system. The first step in a Mercosur controversy is usually a consultation through the Trade Commission (headed by the Economy Ministry). If the conflict leads to the establishment of a Mercosur tribunal, the Economy Ministry retains a leading role throughout the case.[7]

Interestingly enough, in the Mercosur–Chile Agreement, private-sector petitions for dispute settlement are not contemplated. However, the legal officer who handles Mercosur disputes in the Economy Ministry was also in charge of Mercosur–Chile, interacting with the private sector in the same manner as if it were a Mercosur case.

> I am a member of the Administration Commission of ECA35 and therefore I was fully acquainted with all the details. I am in charge of Mercosur cases. Given that the Foreign Affairs Ministry desk that oversees Mercosur–Chile relations does not have dispute settlement experience, the Economy Ministry took the lead in this case: my interaction with private sector was not impaired by the lack of a formal procedure for petition.[8]

A flagship sector

The industry is a flagship business. First, foreign sales represent about 10% of total exports, in a context in which foreign currency is badly needed for complying with external payments. Production and commercialization generate about 8.5% of total employment (Bertello 2004). Second, the concentration of plants (and its upstream and downstream activities) in powerful provinces allows the industry to carry additional clout. Finally, the fact that there are relatively few actors makes collective action relatively easy to articulate.

Locally owned companies account for most of the production. Co-operatives have lost market share while foreign-owned plants have stepped up production capacity since 1994 and have notably increased their leverage within the sector (Ferrugia and Guerrero 2000: 122–5). The main exporters are Cargill and Vicentin. In 2001 Aceitera General, Deheza,

---

[7] Usually, the experts of the Ministry of Economy who have prepared the case in previous instances are designated as Argentine representatives before the Mercosur Tribunal.

[8] Dr Marina García del Rio, Legal Senior Adviser at the Ministry of Economy, interview, 25 June 2004.

Dreyfus and Bunge Argentina started to compete with Vicentin for second place; these five companies have gained market share rapidly, reaching more than 70% of the market today.

The logic of collective action is essentially co-operative. As a business source noted, 'Generally, we consult and take steps to act together as Argentine companies in international conflict situations.'[9]

Companies articulate their demands through CIARA, which acts as broker and spokesperson and has a fluid and long-standing relationship with the government. CIARA was set up in 1980 with the objective of protecting and promoting the interest of the oilseed processing industry, and it now groups most of the vegetable oil and protein meal producers. When facing barriers in foreign markets, collective action is the first move. But once preliminary studies estimated the cost to be as high as US$1 million to initiate a case on soy, some companies opted out. At times a company decides to invest in the protection-seeking country rather than litigate, as was the case with anti-dumping duties in Peru.

In addition, INAI, the business think tank, provided technical assistance. INAI has a small but highly qualified staff – a manager, two lawyers and an economist. It was originally created in 1999 by the three Grains Exchange Markets (Rosario, Bahia Blanca and Buenos Aires) with the aim of strengthening capabilities for dealing with agricultural negotiations. Subsequently other organizations joined, CIARA being one of them.

Altogether, cohesiveness, 'political muscle' and expertise were the three pillars on which business proceeded following the initiation of demands.

3 The process and the outcome

The conflict was first brought to a regional forum: the ECA35 Administration Commission. The legal officer at the Economy Ministry in charge of Mercosur dispute settlement was responsible for oral presentations and submissions, working closely with CIARA to obtain data and articulate legal arguments. She emphasized that

> In this instance costs are very low because there is no need for an external law firm. It is also a very flexible process, taking into account that the problem started in March 1999 and by April 2000 there was a recommendation from the Group of Experts.[10] Beyond the validity of our arguments, key

---

[9] Interview, 2 June 2004.
[10] The Group of Experts is formed by one expert from Chile, another from Mercosur and the other – acting as president – from a non-member country.

to our winning strategy was to appoint Mr Sortheix as an expert. He is internationally recognized as a high-level expert on customs classification. Although he did not chair the Group, his knowledge and experience made him a natural leader.[11]

The regional dispute system was out of the public eye and at the same time it was both fast and low-cost. Chile did not, meanwhile, modify its reclassification. On the contrary, safeguards were applied in order to strengthen the legal basis of the increased protection. As observed by the Legal Senior Adviser,

> We first believed that the reason had to do with the fact that the Mercosur–Chile dispute settlement system was not binding. We subsequently worked hard to negotiate and pass a binding dispute settlement system. But after Chile's refusal to comply with the WTO's ruling I have come to believe that the political economy underpinnings of a conflict are as determining of compliance as the features of the institutional mechanism.[12]

The expectation that Chile would comply with the ECA35 Group of Experts recommendation was widely shared. CIARA was convinced, because 'Chile has such a good reputation in international trade circles'.[13]

In two meetings held at the Ministry of Foreign Affairs, Chilean self-righteousness came as a surprise to everyone. Banking on their own spotless reputation (and Argentina's tarnished record in this respect), the visiting team defiantly bragged that exporters would eventually come to accept the restriction and would not consider taking up the question in the multilateral arena.

To continue the story, after Chile's refusal to change the PBS, business urged the Argentine government by means of a public letter to find a bilateral solution. Although CIARA was already in contact with the Ministry of Foreign Affairs, a formal letter was sent out, triggered by two other market shifts. Firstly and most importantly, India (Argentina's most important market) nearly doubled import tariffs on raw sunflower and soy oil. This threatened sales to a market that purchased 20% of exports. Second, China (Argentina's third buyer) attempted to introduce non-trade barriers that practically implied the closing of the market. The letter, addressed to the Minister of Foreign Relations by the Director of CIARA, asked for 'a rapid

---

[11] Dr Marina Garcia del Rio, interview, 25 June 2004.
[12] Dr Marina Garcia del Rio, interview, 25 June 2004.
[13] Raquel Caminoa from CIARA, interview, 9 June 2004.

and energetic claim with the adoption of bilateral instruments necessary to neutralize the negative effects of these measures'.[14]

Meanwhile, the government was concerned with other priorities in terms of its agenda with Chile: it was waiting for the Chilean Senate to ratify a bilateral mining agreement. This treaty was of strategic economic importance because it was expected to lead to a US$10,000 million investment along the Andean frontier and to double the mining exports of the two countries. CIARA thus feared that mining interests would overshadow their case, and pressure on the government for the case to be taken to the WTO was stepped up. CIARA also pulled strings across the Andes, requesting a meeting with the Chilean Minister of Foreign Affairs. But it was not until five weeks after the signing of the mining agreement on 29 August 2000 that the government went into action and on 5 October requested consultations with Chile at the WTO. Argentina requested the formal establishment of a panel in mid-January 2001.

The decision to go to the WTO received a political push. According to a Ministry of Foreign Affairs official,

> There were two moments when political drive was decisive. First, to request the establishment of a panel; second, during the panel process when some actors wanted to drop the case in favour of a mutually agreed solution. After a detailed technical explanation, the authorities decided to continue the case.[15]

DISCO was responsible for dissecting and drafting the legal and economic arguments of the case. The workload to present the first brief on time was quite hefty for all the actors involved, but mainly for DISCO staff – four full-time and two part-time officials.[16] CIARA and INAI experts collaborated in reading drafts, but DISCO officers were the ones working up to thirteen hours a day to get things done on time. In addition, a public officer from the Secretariat of Agriculture was asked to join some meetings because of 'his experience in dealing with Chileans'.[17] This

---

[14] *La Nación*, 15 June 2000. [15] Interview, 14 July 2004.

[16] According to the public officials involved, the workload was gigantic and the Ministry of Foreign Affairs offered them no encouragement. The resolution of these disputes remains out of the range of those who decide promotions within the ministry and salary is far below market rates.

[17] Dr Facundo Vila, Foreign Affairs Ministry and former lawyer at DISCO, telephone interview, 7 June 2004. Accordingly, Lic. Jorge Iturriza said that 'I think I was important because I was acquainted with the Chileans after the negotiation of the Mercosur–Chile Agreement.'

recruitment was seen to be necessary because a mutually agreed solution is still highly possible during the first stage of a dispute.

The interaction between DISCO and the private sector was intense and constructive throughout the dispute. CIARA paid for running costs and for the fees of the law firm. The contribution of the law firm, providing a first draft for the demand and being available for specific consultations, was less useful than expected. Both public and private actors agreed that its contribution could have been more useful had the firm been hired to fine-tune all the submissions rather than being responsible for the first brief. During the initial stages of the procedure some of the arguments directly related to facts, and the pool of local expertise could have done the job.

> Only about 10% of their original ideas remained in the final paper. They were used as a general guide. As we proceeded it became obvious that the firm did not have much expertise on agricultural issues. I guess that the budget constraint was an obstacle at the time of selection.[18]

One public official has noted that

> when interacting with a law firm one has to keep in mind that their interests do not coincide with the government. The law firms are tied to results while governments in addition have a systemic interest. When the government raises a case it also considers questions such as the impact on the AA, or the spill-over of the case onto general trading relations.[19]

The cost of the law firm amounted to about US$200,000, of which an important part pertained to the claim on the AA. CIARA provided data and information related to the sector and INAI contributed to the building of arguments. In particular, INAI performed the economic analysis of the working of the Chilean PBS and reviewed the legal arguments of the case, especially Article 4.2 of the AA.

> The contribution of the private sector in terms of people, provision of information and economic resources was impeccable. It cannot be replicated again except in one instance. I can think of only one other Argentine sector with the same global interests and with the skills to follow, to facilitate

---

[18] Vila, interview, 7 June 2004.   [19] Interview, 14 July 2004.

all logistical aspects and to provide and manage a data base [referring to another flagship sector, the producer of seamless pipes[20]].[21]

The working dynamic for building the case included meetings between the officials of DISCO, representatives of CIARA and INAI's experts, when the drafts of the law firm were reformulated. Occasionally, there were other participants (such as the Secretariat of Agriculture or representatives from leading firms such as Molinos and Nidera). At the WTO, sessions could technically be held in any official language; but, after the initial presentations in Spanish led to a member of the panel yawning and dozing off, a decision was taken to switch to English. In this context, an interviewee remarked that

> It is tiring and time consuming to wait for the translation in hearings. But more relevantly, translation of documents may take ten days, so that panellists turn up without time to read them. This is a disadvantage vis-à-vis documents submitted promptly in English by the defendant. Panellists know where their arguments are headed while they have no clue about ours, and this is a great handicap.[22]

The Argentine delegation did not have external lawyers outside the room where sessions took place. By the second session the delegation started to feel that they were winning the case: most of the questions were directed to Chile and the questions denoted that the concerns of the panel tended to be in line with the Argentine position. The general tone also seemed 'pushy' when confronting the Chileans' arguments.[23]

But not all the issues raised during the dispute were technical. Political calculations kept cropping up from all corners. First, business had to deal with those favouring diplomacy over litigation. Moreover, business feared that the President might withdraw the demand if Chile eliminated sanitary restrictions on beef. In order to avoid backsliding, the Grains Exchange and CIARA wrote a formal letter to the President backing the specialists and emphasizing that if the government dropped the dispute,

---

[20] In this sense, other regional developing countries, such as Brazil and Venezuela, are following the same pattern in litigation in only taking up flagship sectors. Brazil has litigated against Canada in defence of Embraer, a world leader in small aircraft manufacture, and has recently taken on the United States and the EU on sugar, poultry and cotton. Venezuela's case on environmental standards with the United States was in defence of the PDVSA, accounting for 80% of Venezuelan exports.

[21] Vila, interview, 7 June 2004.   [22] Interview, 14 July 2004.

[23] Vila, interview, 7 June 2004.

it would seriously damage trade prospects. They argued that the WTO decision would pave the way for tackling similar conflicts with the European Union and the Andean Community.[24] Eventually, the fact that the case was becoming a 'winning case' helped to overcome other political calculations.

The struggle at home was mirrored at the WTO. The adoption of the panel recommendation (and the Appellate Body report) did not mean that the issue was closed. Chile has not complied so far, and still has its PBS in place. In this sense, several actors coincided in the view that the major flaw of the WTO is the reliance on unilateral retaliation. While some actors interviewed suggested financial compensation as an alternative, others emphasized trade compensation. However, some influential public officials have remarked that one must keep in mind the original objectives in assessing overall results. When the case started, oils were subject to a 70% tariff. Since the dispute the maximum is 31.5%, with a double assurance: a WTO ruling and a Chilean Congress law. In addition, vegetable oil was excluded from the PBS, and there is now an interpretation of how a variable levy minimum price works with considerable value as precedent.

True, for Argentina the tangible gain was the cap on Chilean tariffs as a result of the initiation of the WTO case.[25] There were also intangible gains in terms of reputation. In this sense, perhaps the biggest loss for Chile might also be an intangible in terms of its reputation for compliance. The WTO acted as a magnifying glass for a country's reputation.

4 Challenges confronted in the process

The government's principal challenges were twofold: to construct a (winning) case at the WTO with no financial resources and scarce human skills, while at the same time avoiding issue linkage so as not to poison relations with a strategic regional partner. Business, in turn, had to articulate and sustain collective action, raise funds to cover the costs involved in litigation and absorb economic losses during the protracted proceedings. Both government and business had to accept a new partnership if success was to be achieved.

---

[24] *La Nación*, 18 March 2002.
[25] In effect, a short time after the process began, Chile announced that the PBS would not result in a tariff higher than the one binding at 31.5%.

The government strategy was to isolate this conflict from other bilateral issues and manage each in its own time. Such de-linking happened at least twice. First, at the time of signing the mining agreement in 2000 and, second, in 2003 to isolate the case from the sanitary restrictions applied to Argentine beef. In addition, by relying on CIARA and INAI experts and, to a lesser extent, on the external law firm, DISCO was able to overcome its limited financial and technical resources. Still, DISCO officials stressed the colossal personal effort undertaken to comply with deadlines under the WTO dispute settlement system and also the feeling that being a developing country always implies, if not negative, at least sceptical expectations regarding performance: 'When asked, the international community doubts our capacity to defend ourselves and when acting as claimant our capacity to handle and lead the case.'[26]

Litigation costs and collective action are usually two barriers for business. The fact that the vegetable oil sector is structurally concentrated in only a few hands allowed the litigation strategy to be followed with relatively low transaction costs. Ultimately, the fact that the sector is a global player was an important source of leverage over the domestic policy process.

At the time of influencing policy, business had to wade through a maelstrom of informal channels, since there is no regulation or window for dealing with petitions for multilateral trade dispute settlement. This institutional vacuum posed a dual risk: on the one hand it could have allowed the government arbitrarily to dismiss the business claim and, on the other hand, it could have triggered an internal dispute among government agencies, ultimately impeding effective co-ordination of the case.

Last but not least, the protracted WTO process might have jeopardized Argentina's market share in Chile: 'When you are out of a market for about two years, it is extremely difficult to win back positions.'[27]

Faced with no prospect for compensation and with an accumulated loss of US$50 million, both business and government agents considered the question of retaliating against Chilean products. But retaliation was a completely inadequate solution. From the business angle, retaliation could not offset the losses. From the government perspective, retaliation was likely to poison overall relations with Chile.

---

[26] Interview with a Ministry of Foreign Affairs official, 14 July 2004.
[27] Interview with a business informant (confidential), 2 June 2004.

5 Lessons for others

Recourse to the WTO dispute settlement procedures is not for everyone, nor is it a routine action that can be undertaken lightly. It is costly and time-consuming and thus discriminates in favour of big business and countries. At the same time it has political repercussions, especially if used against a close partner. However, the Argentine experience indicates that the WTO does contribute to limit discretionary trade practices; it acts as an international magnifying glass held to countries' trade practices. Moreover, it was perceived as a neutral third party on a regionally divisive issue.

In particular, the main lessons left by this case are as follows.

In terms of the domestic institutional setting, the lack of clear and pre-established mechanisms to handle disputes is detrimental to all actors. While the private sector risks arbitrary neglect or dismissal of its case, public agencies bear uncertainty about their competencies and decisions. The considerable cost and expertise required is a problem for developing countries. One feasible cost-effective solution would be to reallocate public officials to create a permanent and multi-disciplinary corps of experts to handle trade disputes. In this way, experience and learning could be accumulated by the same agency and legal outsourcing would be limited to fine-tuning and/or data collection when needed.

In terms of business participation, a key element of their successful involvement was the sense of shared responsibility with the public sector for the final outcome. It would have been impossible to do the groundwork for the case without the provision by business of factual information, statistical data and financial collaboration.

In terms of capacity building, the case was a shared learning experience among all actors. While business was able to assess with much more precision the costs and benefits of potential cases post-Chile, the confidence of public agents was built up and they subsequently felt encouraged to take up litigation in the case of other products.

In terms of bargaining strategy, the government's temporal de-linking of issues and taking them one at a time was crucial for the avoidance of cross-sectoral pressures at home and issue linkage in bilateral relations with Chile. In terms of the sector in question the key was calculating beforehand the maximum and minimum losses the sector was able to forego.

In terms of the WTO process, beyond practical matters (such as the cost of the process, the need to present the case in English or the importance of having business representatives 'next door') an already well-known problem became evident: the pointlessness of recourse to retaliation. In effect, if the offending measure is not rescinded and the demanding country does not want to shoot itself in the foot to retaliate, it ends up empty-handed. Non-compliance and the low pay-off of retaliation restrict the impact of the action.

Bibliography

Ferrugia, Olga and Guerrero, Irene (2000) 'El complejo oleaginoso en la Argentina y en la provincia de Santa Fe', in Mario Lattuada, Olga Ferrugia and Irene Guerrero, eds., *El complejo oleaginoso*, Ediciones del Arca: Ituzaingo & Rosario, pp. 98–136.

Franco, Daniel (2004) 'Aceite de soja. Análisis de cadena alimentaria', Secretariat of Agriculture, available at http://www.alimentosargentinos.gov.ar/0–3/olea/Aceite_Soja-r19/A_soja.htm (accessed 24 May 2004).

Franco, Daniel (2004b) 'Aceite de girasol. Análisis de cadena alimentaria', Secretariat of Agriculture, available at http://www.alimentosargentinos.gov.ar/0–3/olea/a_girasol_3/Aceite_girasol.htm (last accessed 24 May 2004).

Schvarzer, Jorge and Heyn, Iván (2002) 'El comportamiento de las exportaciones argentinas en la década del noventa. Un balance de la convertibilidad', CESPA, technical paper, November.

www.ciara.com.ar

www.copal.com.ar

www.indec.gov.ar

2

Argentina and GATS: a study of the domestic determinants of GATS commitments

ROBERTO BOUZAS AND HERNÁN SOLTZ*

The commitments undertaken by Argentina in the General Agreement on Trade in Services (GATS) appear generous when compared with those of other Latin American countries. Based on this finding this case study tries to identify the main factors that shaped Argentina's services offer under GATS. Although the complexity, extension and coverage of GATS lists makes it very unlikely that one single factor can account for the content of a national offer, our research suggests that the government's desire to 'lock in' domestic policy reforms at a time of profound economic change was a major factor shaping the offer's content. We found the case study interesting because it underlines the domestic roots of international trade policy-making and illustrates the way in which the international trade regime can be used instrumentally by national authorities willing to consolidate their policy preferences.

The case study is based on a comparative examination of Argentina's GATS schedules and open interviews with many of those who participated in the policy-making process.[1] The report is organized into four sections. Section 1 briefly summarizes the factors that can shape trade policy formation. Section 2 makes a comparative assessment of the coverage and depth of the Argentine list of offers. Section 3 reports our main qualitative findings about the major factors that shaped its content. Section 4 draws some conclusions from the case study.

---

* Roberto Bouzas is Associate Professor, Universidad de San Andrés. Hernán Soltz is at FLACSO, Argentina. We are very grateful to those who agreed to share their time and experience with us. Although this summary risks misrepresenting individual opinions, we hope that it will provide an accurate account of trends and events.
[1] We interviewed – either orally or in a written form – more than a dozen public-sector officials directly engaged in the negotiations. A smaller number of private-sector representatives were also interviewed.

1 Determinants of trade policy formation

In their study of the determinants of financial services commitments, Harms, Mattoo and Schuknecht (2003) refer to the vast body of theoretical and empirical work arguing that 'trade policy formation is determined by self-interested politicians granting protection or liberalization to special interests'. According to this view, one key factor behind trade policy formation would be the relative influence of alternative interest groups. This hypothesis may be useful to understand trade policy-making in normal times, but it may shed less light during periods of stress and deep policy reform.

Apart from the role of domestic interest groups, multilateral trade negotiations can also be regarded as a strategic game in which governments look for reciprocal concessions. Thus, the level of concessions made by one country at one point in time may be upheld with the expectation of obtaining larger gains in future bargains. In line with this view, Harms, Mattoo and Schuknecht (2003) maintain that 'the incentive to trade off current gains from unilateral liberalization against even larger gains from reciprocal opening in the future would seem to be most important for countries that faced high protection in their areas of export interest *and* possessed, alone or as a group, sufficient negotiating leverage to extract liberalization commitments from their trading partners' (emphasis in original). Argentina fits in this category, since it was both an exporter of temperate agricultural products and an active member of the Cairns group.[2]

At first sight, the Argentine case does not seem to fit well with any of these explanations. The political economy behind services liberalization is unclear, since trade unions in the reformed sectors were probably more powerful than the consumers potentially benefiting from higher quality and – presumably – lower priced services. Similarly, there may have existed strong bargaining considerations for upholding concessions in order to extract more reciprocal benefits in the future. Where does Argentina fit? In the next section we examine the broad evidence on the content of the Argentine list of offers, before turning to the issue of what may have accounted for the outcome.

---

[2] In their study of the determinants of financial services commitments, Harms, Mattoo and Schuknecht (2003) argue that, at least in the area of financial services, 'a government's decision to liberalize may be affected by the economic environment, particularly the degree of macroeconomic stability and the quality of prudential regulation', although they underline that the relationship is 'not obvious'.

2 Argentina's GATS schedules

This section reviews Argentina's GATS schedules and compares them with those of its neighbours. Berlinski and Romero (2001) were the first to point out that Argentina's GATS commitments had a relatively high sectoral coverage and level of openness, higher even than Chile (generally taken as the Latin American paradigm for an open and deregulated economy).[3] Table 2.1 shows that Argentina made binding market access commitments for 232 items (out of a total of 620[4]), 144 of them bound with no restriction ('none').[5] This means that Argentina undertook market access commitments for 37.4% of total negotiable items, nearly a third of which had no restrictions. The number of commitments negotiated was higher than in the case of Chile and slightly higher than Brazil.[6] The contrast between the Argentine offer and those of its neighbours deepens when the comparison is made using the ratio of no-restriction commitments to the total number of negotiated items. In effect, while Argentina bound 62.1% of its commitments under the 'none' category, the Brazilian and Chilean ratios were only 22.3% and 31.0%, respectively. Cross-country differences in national treatment are slightly less marked than in market access, but they maintain the same pattern (see Table 2.2).[7]

---

[3] The standard methodology used by Berlinski and Romero (2001) is subject to well-known limitations, of which they are well aware. First, the absence of commitments should not be taken as equivalent to the existence of restrictions, since a low level of commitments can reflect strategic behaviour. Second, the summary ratios used in Tables 2 and 3 (see below) provide little information about the nature or economic significance of existing restrictions and/or concessions. Third, for the same reasons the ratios developed by Hoeckman (1995) provide a fragile basis for cross-country or cross-sector comparisons. However, a qualitative examination of the offers seems to confirm the more 'liberal' bias of Argentina's offer.

[4] Six hundred and twenty is the product of 155 sub-sectors and four modes of supply (cross-border trade, consumption abroad, commercial presence and movement of natural persons).

[5] Commitments made in the original list (GATS94) and in four additional protocols (Financial Services – July 1995, Movement of Natural Persons – July 1995, Basic Telecommunications – April 1997, and Financial Services – November 1997). Argentina made commitments in addition to the GATS94 list only in the Basic Telecommunications protocol.

[6] Considering exclusively the GATS94 list, the sector coverage undertaken by Argentina and the degree of openness it offered were considerably higher than the Latin American average. Brazil and Chile were also above the Latin American average in terms of sectoral coverage, but well below in terms of depth of commitments.

[7] In the GATS94 list, Argentina's share of no-restriction commitments was even higher than the OECD average (but the sector coverage was lower). Brazil has yet to ratify the commitments undertaken in the Financial Services and Telecommunications protocols. If these still not ratified protocols are not considered, Brazil's sector coverage ratio falls from 36.1% to 25.2% and the non-restriction to total commitments ratio from 22.3% to 12.2%.

Table 2.1. *GATS: commitments on market access*

	Argentina		Brazil		Chile		Latin America average		OECD average	
	GATS94	Plus protocol	GATS94	Plus protocol	GATS94	Plus protocol	GATS94	Plus protocol	GATS94	Plus protocol
Number of negotiated commitments	208	232	156	224	140	168	119	na	330.4	na
Number of no-restriction commitments	136	144	19	50	36	52	49.1	na	188.9	na
Number of negotiated commitments as percentage of total GATS list[1]	33.5	37.4	25.2	36.1	22.6	27.1	19.2	na	53.3	na
Number of no-restriction commitments as percentage of number of negotiated commitments	65.4	62.1	12.2	22.3	25.7	31.0	41.3	na	57.2	na

[1] Total GATS list = 620.
Source: Based on Berlinski and Romero (2001).

Table 2.2. *GATS: commitments on national treatment*

	Argentina		Brazil		Chile		Latin America average		OECD average	
	GATS94	Plus protocol	GATS94	Plus protocol	GATS94	Plus protocol	GATS94	Plus protocol	GATS94	Plus protocol
Number of negotiated commitments	208	232	156	224	140	168	nd	nd	nd	nd
Number of no-restriction commitments	136	154	27	77	48	73	nd	nd	nd	nd
Number of negotiated commitments as percentage of total GATS list[1]	33.5	37.4	25.2	36.1	22.6	27.1	nd	nd	nd	nd
Number of no-restriction commitments as percentage of number of negotiated commitments	65.4	66.4	17.3	34.4	34.3	43.5	nd	nd	nd	nd

[1] Total GATS list = 620.

Source: Based on Berlinski and Romero (2001).

The cross-country comparison of market access commitments across service sectors displays differences and similarities (see Table 2.3). First, Argentina, Brazil and Chile show uneven coverage ratio across sectors. None of the countries made commitments in the fields of education, environmental services, social and healthcare services, recreational, cultural and sporting services, and other services. In addition, Chile undertook no commitments in construction and construction-related engineering and distribution services. Consequently, in the case of Chile market access commitments were concentrated in only five sectors (business services, communications, financial services, tourism and transportation).

Second, in four out of five sectors in which Chile undertook market access commitments (business services, communications, financial services and tourism), the coverage ratio was lower than that of Argentina. Only in the case of transportation (where Argentina made no offer) do the commitments made by Chile show a higher – but still very low – coverage ratio. Interestingly enough, Chile's coverage ratio is lower than that of Brazil in communications, financial services and transportation.

Third, when the sectors in which the three countries made commitments are compared, financial services shows the highest coverage ratio, followed by communications and business services.

As far as the depth of commitments was concerned, in most cases where Argentina undertook market access commitments it did so under the no-restrictions modality ('none'). The exceptions were communications, financial services and the horizontal restrictions applicable to Mode 4 (see below). In addition, in most sectors where Argentina made market access offers the degree of openness committed was higher than the OECD average (see Table 2.4).

3 The making of Argentina's GATS offer

Stage 1: learning what services negotiations were about

Argentine trade officials had traditionally focused on trade in goods (particularly temperate agriculture products) and were thus not prepared for undertaking international negotiations in services. This confronted them with the imperative to understand the nature of the issues under negotiation and the implications of alternative modalities and commitments.[8]

---

[8] This, of course, was not unique to Argentine trade officials. The first academic works dealing with trade in services were published in the second half of the 1980s.

Table 2.3. *GATS: commitments on market access by sector (sub-sectors with commitments/total number of sub-sectors)*

	Argentina	Brazil	Chile	Latin America average	OECD average
Business services	34.8	23.9	23.9	21.1	68.1
Communication services (1)	37.5/62.5	4.2/66.7	25.0/50.0	16.9/na	36.6/na
Construction and construction-related engineering services	80	100	0	26.3	82.2
Distribution services	60	60	0	10	65.6
Educational services	0	0	0	3.8	44.4
Environmental services	0	0	0	1.6	70.8
Financial services (2)	94.1/94.1/94.1	76.5/82.4/88.2	76.5/82.4/82.4	44.5/na/na	88.9/na/na
Social and healthcare services (not included in (1))	0	0	0	7.8	15.3
Tourist services	100	25	75	67.2	72.2
Recreational, cultural and sports services (excluding audiovisual services)	0	0	0	8.8	37.8
Transport	0	14.3	5.7	8.4	27
Other services	0	0	0	0	0.1
Maximum	100	100	82.4	67.2	88.9
Minimum	0	0	0	0	0.1

(1) GATS 1994/GATS Fourth Protocol.
(2) GATS 1994/GATS Second Protocol/GATS Fifth protocol.
Source: Based on Berlinski and Romero (2001).

Table 2.4. *GATS: commitments on market access: average openness level on a scale of 0–4 (with 4 being complete liberalization), by sector*[1]

	Argentina[2]	Brazil	Chile	Latin America average	OECD average
Business services	3.5	1.2	1.4	2.3	3.2
Communication services	3.5	2.5	2	2.4	3.2
Construction and construction-related engineering services	3.5	1.5	0	2.5	3.2
Distribution services	3.5	1.8	0	2.3	3.1
Educational services	0	0	0	1.3	2.8
Environmental services	0	0	0	0.5	3.2
Financial services	2.3	0.7	1.5	1.6	2.3
Social and healthcare services (not included in 1)	0	0	0	2.7	2.6
Tourist services	3.5	1.5	3.5	2.6	3.2
Recreational, cultural and sports services (excluding audiovisual services)	0	0	0	3.1	3.3
Transport	0	1.3	2	2.8	3.1
Other services	0	0	0	0	3.3
Average	3.3	1.5	2.1	2.2	3.0
Standard deviation	0.5	0.6	0.9	0.7	0.3
Maximum	3.5	2.5	3.5	3.1	3.3
Minimum	2.3	0.7	1.4	0.5	2.3

[1] Figures only include commitments undertaken in GATS94.

[2] All commitments made by Argentina in Mode of Supply 4 include horizontal restrictions, thus leading to a maximum average openness level of 3.5.

Source: Based on Berlinski and Romero (2001).

Apart from that novelty, services negotiations were characterized by inherent complexities. On the one hand, the service sector includes a broad range of activities, most of them heavily regulated by different layers of government. Since border barriers are an exception (and when they exist they are seldom the most relevant restriction on services trade), national officials had to review a large number of dispersed domestic regulations and understand their relevance for the issues under negotiation (such

as market access and national treatment). On the other hand, statistical information on services trade was scarce, unreliable and generally
unsuited for providing a basis for negotiation (Marchetti 1999). These
challenges were compounded by the fact that GATS adopted a broad definition of 'services trade', which included *domestic* sales of services made
by foreign-owned companies established in the *domestic* market (strictly
speaking, 'investment in the provision of services').

Immediately after the launching of the Uruguay Round (UR) in 1986,
the Argentine government allocated the functional responsibility for the
technical work on services trade to the Economy Ministry, at that time
still responsible for the conduct of international trade negotiations. In
1988 that agency produced one of the earliest proposals on services negotiations submitted to the GATT by a developing contracting party.[9] When
responsibility for international trade negotiations was transferred to the
Ministry of Foreign Relations and International Trade in 1989, a small
task force was organized in the newly created Secretariat of International
Economic Relations (the Economy Ministry staff hitherto responsible for
the negotiations were transferred to the new agency). One of the first activities of the task force was to make a survey of those domestic regulations
with implications for international trade in services. This demanded regular consultations with other public-sector agencies, such as the Central
Bank, the Insurance Superintendent, the Secretaries of Communications, Transportation and Tourism, the National Immigration Service and
other agencies with normative and regulatory responsibilities for public
utilities.

Many public officials interviewed underlined that one of the major
obstacles faced was not so much that of gathering the required normative
information, but interpreting it in the light of what was necessary to build
a national list of commitments. Moreover, in areas where there was not
a single responsible agency (such as business services), the task force had
to engage directly in identifying existing regulations and drawing direct
inputs from the private sector (such as professional associations). During
this stage the task force consulted regularly with the private sector (first
informally and later through formal channels) to identify sensibilities, barriers to access to third markets, and domestic regulations relevant to the
preparation of the list of commitments.[10] Commercial representations

---

[9] This contrasted with the more 'defensive' stance adopted by other developing countries,
such as India and Brazil.

[10] All the interviews indicated that the response given by the private sector was very passive.

abroad also researched market access and regulatory restrictions that affected Argentine service suppliers. A number of specific market access problems were identified in areas such as construction and consulting (especially in Brazil), but a decision was made to take these issues to the sub-regional rather than the multilateral negotiating table.

Stage 2: accounting for Argentina's GATS offer

Argentina submitted an initial offer at the beginning of 1991, more than two years before the presentation of the final list in 1993. We were unable to reconstruct the changes made to the initial offer, but some public officials interviewed mentioned that the final list was 'technically superior' to the initial offer (due to an ongoing 'learning process') and responsive to some requests made by other contracting parties (particularly the United States). However, there seems to be a consensus that the major factor that shaped the content of Argentina's final offer was the environment of deep regulatory change that prevailed between 1990 and 1997, when the last protocol was negotiated. In effect, during these years Argentina entered into an ambitious process of reform in which economic institutions were overhauled. The GATS offers largely reflect this phenomenon.

The list of Argentina's horizontal commitments (exceptions) is very short. In line with what most countries did, in Mode 4 it includes binding commitments only for senior business employees (executives, managers and specialists).[11] The Argentine list also includes a horizontal restriction to the acquisition of real estate in border areas (150 sq km inland and 50 sq km in coastal regions) in Mode 3, which remains unbound.[12]

Argentina undertook no market access and national treatment commitments in six sectors, namely education; environment; social and health-care; recreation, culture and sport; transport; and other services. These exclusions were not unique to the Argentine offer, but very much in line with those of other developing countries, which have typically undertaken very few commitments in these areas.[13] In sectors such as social and

---

[11] Argentina also did not participate in the negotiations through which a small number of countries adopted additional commitments for movement of physical persons. This was the third protocol, adopted in July 1995 and in force since January 1996.

[12] Current legislation demands prior authorization from the Border Superintendent. Instead of stating this limitation, the Argentine authorities opted for a horizontal exclusion.

[13] The Latin American average for the ratio of negotiated commitments as a share of total negotiable items in these sectors is less than 10%. The ratio is also comparatively low in OECD countries (except for environmental services), but still higher than the Latin American average.

healthcare services and education, one major reason for omission was the extensive presence of the public sector. In others, such as environmental and other services, technical uncertainties and poor information may have also played a role. In transport, the limited extent of commitments was a result of the combination of the Argentine authorities' preference for a 'clean list', the uncertainty as to the evolution of some regulatory frameworks (such as in the railways), and the lack of interest of OECD countries in agreeing in certain areas.[14] In the business services sector, where the Argentine offer shows a comparatively low coverage ratio, domestic interest groups, technical complexities and limited information also played a role, taking into consideration in particular the limited availability of qualified human resources. The preference for a 'clean list' shows itself in the fact that in those areas in which Argentina made commitments, these were taken under the 'no restrictions' modality.[15] *Ex post facto*, some testimonies also pointed to strategic considerations ('we should keep some bargaining leverage').

In the five remaining service sectors (of which finance and communications stand out in terms of economic significance), the extent of the commitments was comparatively generous in terms of both coverage and depth. Argentina undertook all its commitments in financial services during the UR, meaning that it did not take part in the negotiations of the second and fifth protocols. This suggests that strategic or reciprocity considerations, the last of which was at the centre of financial services negotiations, did not play a relevant role. Instead, the evidence seems to suggest that the financial services offer was used as a 'lock-in' device for autonomously taken policy reforms. The only sub-sectors unbound were services auxiliary to insurance (including broking and agency services), other financial services and new financial services (except national treatment for commercial presence, bound without restrictions). Most restrictions on financial services applied to cross-border trade. Insurance and insurance-related services were either unlisted or listed with restrictions (except maritime and air transportation insurance). Insurance services were unbound for Modes 1 and 2 (market access and national treatment).

---

[14] In some activities (such as air and maritime transportation) there was limited interest on the part of OECD countries in undertaking commitments. In effect, after the conclusion of the UR the Argentine government made commitments in the context of the negotiations for a protocol on maritime transportation, but these negotiations broke down. The US administration did not push for negotiations in coastal maritime services and air transportation either.

[15] Except the horizontal restrictions that affect Mode 4.

Mode of supply 3 was restrained by the suspension of new authorizations for establishment (removed in 1998).[16] Reinsurance services were listed with no restrictions except for commercial presence, subject to the same constraint as general insurance services.[17] Banking services were listed with no restrictions, except for cross-border trade (unbound). Argentina's offer in banking services is quite open when compared with other countries in the region, and the depth of commitments is similar to the OECD average.

In the case of communications Argentina undertook commitments for approximately two-thirds of the total number of negotiable items.[18] Telecommunication services were bound in the context of the negotiations of the basic telecommunications protocol agreed after the conclusion of the UR.[19] Local telephone services, domestic and international long-distance, international data transmission and international telex services were bound without restrictions after 11 August 2000 for Modes 1 and 3. Mobile telephone services and PCS were bound without restrictions, but in the case of PCS the authorities retained the capacity to determine the maximum number of operators per area. Domestic data and telex transmission, electronic mail, voice mail and electronic data interchange were bound with no restrictions. The Argentine offer did not include the provision of satellite facilities of geo-stationary satellites operating fixed satellite services, which, in addition, was excluded under the GATS Article II exception.[20]

---

[16] Strictly speaking, until 1998 the access of foreign firms was possible through the acquisition of existing insurance firms (Berlinski 2002). Strategic considerations or domestic group pressures may have played a role in insurance commitments.

[17] The United States and the EU pressed the Argentine government to deepen its commitments in insurance. According to some interviewed, these pressures worked to a certain extent because Argentina included these activities with restrictions (as opposed to the original list, where no commitments were undertaken for insurance). Cross-border trade (except for freight insurance) is unbounded and the authorization of new entities is suspended (however, the deregulation implemented in 1998 ended the suspension in the establishment of new insurance firms).

[18] No commitments were made for postal, audiovisual and other services. Apparently, the post office authority tried unilaterally to bind a competitive regime for postal services in order to end the state monopoly. Audiovisual services were left unbound in line with the stance adopted by many other countries (again, the preference for a 'clean list' or human resource constraints may have been stronger than the desire to bind existing regulations).

[19] Argentina also adopted a voluntary reference paper that established additional commitments concerning interconnection charges and the independence of regulatory agencies.

[20] The exclusion was a result of the existing contract with a private firm in charge of exploiting the two orbit positions allocated to Argentina, which required strict reciprocity. Later, Argentina negotiated bilateral reciprocal agreements with the United States, Canada,

In the sector of construction and construction-related engineering services all sub-sectors were bound with no restrictions except for general construction works for civil engineering, which was excluded. The reason for excluding this sector is related to domestic interest groups and, according to some of the negotiators, strategic considerations such as keeping leverage for future negotiations, including regional preferences under GATS Article V (Stancanelli 1997).

In distribution services, Argentina bound with no restrictions retailing and wholesale trade services and franchising. No commitments were undertaken for commission agents' and other services. Tourism and travel services, at last, were bound with no restrictions.

Based on this examination and our interviews, it is a plausible hypothesis that Argentina's GATS offer was seen as a mechanism to send a strong signal of commitment to economic reform and to 'increase the costs' of future policy reversals. This liberalization drive was led by the Economy Ministry, headed by the architect of the economic reforms and a former Minister of Foreign Relations (1989–90). According to testimonies, in a context of deep regulatory reform the outstanding policy guideline behind Argentina's commitments in GATS was to strengthen the reform process, either by 'locking-in' reforms already undertaken or by submitting a 'clean list' that would show limited government interventions. In the words of a senior negotiator, the GATS was regarded as 'an opportunity to bind internationally some of the reforms undertaken' (Stancanelli 1997). Another senior trade official wrote that the predominant thrust of Argentina's services offer was to provide 'an anchor to domestic reform' (Niscovolos 1991) and to 'prevent a return to protectionist policies' (Niscovolos 2003).

In a few sectors (such as business, insurance, construction and construction-related engineering services) the pressure of domestic interest groups may have also played a role. However, in general the participation of the private sector in the preparation of Argentina's list of offers was very limited. Most negotiators interviewed referred to the limited engagement of the private sector and the lack of technical preparation and understanding of the GATS. According to various testimonies, meetings

---

Mexico, Brazil, Netherlands and Spain. Satellite services was one of the toughest issues in negotiations with third parties, particularly the United States. Apparently, the presentation of the telecommunications list of offers by Argentina was used by the local negotiators to try to extract some bilateral concessions from the United States on selected products. This may have been a reaction to the demands of the US government concerning the level of commitments to be undertaken in this sector.

organized to gather information to build the Argentine offer frequently ended in a list of demands over domestic policies (such as tax policy) rather than international negotiations. The GATS was regarded as something distant and unrelated to business concerns, probably increasing the discretion of national authorities.[21]

4 Conclusion

The elaboration of the GATS list of commitments faced many technical and information obstacles. In contrast to the GATT agreement, negotiating the GATS required close co-operation between different governmental agencies and an adequate understanding of a regime still in the making. In addition, the extended regulations which typically characterize the service sector demanded a significant effort to understand their meaning and significance from the standpoint of market access and national treatment. Doing this work ideally required multi-agency teams of highly trained personnel, which were frequently scarce.

Argentina's list of commitments in the GATS was characterized as 'exemplary'. Indeed, the available evidence suggests that Argentina undertook broader and deeper commitments than its neighbours, including an outward-oriented country such as Chile. Moreover, in sectors such as telecommunications and financial services Argentina's commitments were close in coverage to the OECD average. In those sectors in which Argentina undertook commitments, they were even deeper than the OECD average.

The major driving force behind the construction of the Argentine list of commitments seems to have been to 'lock in' economic reform initiatives, especially in communications and financial services (two of the service sectors with the largest economic impact). Other participants demanded concessions from Argentina (especially in telecommunications), but the extent of commitments seems to have been basically driven by domestic considerations, rather than external pressures or strategic considerations. This approach may reduce leverage in future multilateral as well as preferential negotiations, as shown by intra-Mercosur negotiations and other inter-regional preferential negotiations, such as that between Mercosur and the European Union.

---

[21] In 1987, shortly after the launching of the Uruguay Round, the private sector created the Unión de Entidades de Servicios (UDES), which reunited several service business federations. However, UDES had very limited success in mobilizing the private sector or making substantive contributions to the policy-making process.

Placing bargaining or strategic considerations in a secondary place as opposed to unilateral reforms may be justified on efficiency grounds. The objective of this case study was not to criticize a particular policy choice, but to underline the domestic roots of trade policy-making and, in this particular case, the driving force of policy-makers willing to 'lock in' a policy regime and send strong signals to the market. If the anticipated efficiency gains do not materialize in the future, responsibility should not be assigned to the rules that govern the multilateral trading regime but to the peculiarities of the domestic policy-making process.

Bibliography

Berlinski, J. (2002), *Dimensiones del Comercio de Servicios en la Argentina*, Buenos Aires: ITDT/Siglo XXI Editores.

Berlinski, J. and Romero, C. A. (2001), 'Las concesiones de Argentina, Brasil and Chile en el GATS y la competitividad internacional de Argentina', processed.

General Agreement on Trade in Services.

Harms, P., A. Mattoo and L. Schuknecht (2003), 'Explaining liberalization commitments in financial services trade', World Bank Policy Research Paper 2999, March.

Hoekman, B. (1995), 'Assessing the General Agreement on Trade in Services', in W. Martin and A. Winters, eds., *The Uruguay Round and Developing Countries*, Washington, DC: World Bank.

Marchetti, J. (1999), 'El comercio de servicios en la Argentina: evidencia, intereses comerciales y estrategias de negociación', *Boletín Informativo Techint* 300, Oct.–Dec. (Buenos Aires).

Niscovolos, L. P. (1999), 'Comercio internacional de servicios: Argentina en el ALCA, la OMC y el MERCOSUR. Algunos aportes para enfocar la negociación hemisférica', in *Panorama del MERCOSUR* 3, Centro de Economía Internacional – Secretaría de Relaciones Económicas Internacionales – Ministerio de Relaciones Exteriores, Comercio Internacional and Culto, Buenos Aires, July.

Niscovolos, L. P. (2003), 'Comercio internacional de servicios. Liberalización y derecho a regular, marco conceptual and aportes para las negociaciones', *Boletín Informativo Techint* 311, Jan.–April (Buenos Aires).

Stancanelli, N. E. (1997), 'El comercio de servicios. Cuestiones principales desde una perspectiva latinoamericana', CEI, Centro de Economía Internacional – Secretaría de Relaciones Económicas Internacionales – Ministerio de Relaciones Exteriores, Comercio Internacional and Culto, Buenos Aires.

3

Rock 'n' roll in Bangladesh: protecting intellectual property rights in music

ABUL KALAM AZAD[1]

1 The problem in context

'"It's daylight robbery in *Murder*," screamed a cult Bangladeshi rock band, and its plea has been heard', writes the *Telegraph* of Calcutta in its front-page story on 'tune-lift' in the Hindi movie *Murder* (*Telegraph*, 20 May 2004). Miles, a very popular Bangladeshi music band (see box) has accused music director Anu Malik, a music-mogul of the Mumbai movie world, of committing pure piracy of one of its original compositions.

On receiving messages from fans in the United States, the United Kingdom, Australia and India that their song 'Phiriye Dao Amar Prem' (Give me back my love) had been copied in the soundtrack of *Murder*, Manam, Hamin and other members of Miles collected a copy of the movie and sat down to watch it themselves. When the song 'Jana Jane Jana' was being played, the band members could hardly believe their ears. Only the language was different – Hindi. Otherwise, 'the lyrics are a shadow of ours, the tune is the same. Even the beat break-ups, the use of guitar and filler notes are the same. How could Anu do such thing?' wondered Hamin, one of the guitarists and vocalists of Miles. 'Even when a musician is inspired by a song, he can only copy eight measures. But this is a complete copy of Phiriye Dao,' added Hamin (*Bombay Times*, 18 July 2004).

The Bengali song 'Phiriye Dao' was composed by Miles for its music album 'Prathasa' (Hope) in 1993. It was released in Bangladesh and Pakistan. In 1997 this same song was included in a music album named 'Best of Miles, Vol. 1' released by the Asha Audio Co. of Calcutta, and it became very popular in both Bangladesh and West Bengal, India.

---

[1] Professor, Department of Economics, University of Chittagong.

Now the song has been used in the soundtrack of the Hindi block-buster movie *Murder* without, of course, the permission of its original composers.

The Mumbai (previously Bombay) movie world known as 'Bollywood', in imitation of the United States' Hollywood, earns millions of dollars by producing and exporting its films, typically including music and dance, romance and comedy, all over the world, including Bangladesh. Compared with India's, Bangladesh's movie/music production is just a dwarf. Bangladesh runs a huge trade deficit with India, and the import of movies/music from India contributes significantly to it.

Under such circumstances, copying and reproducing a Bangladeshi song without any payment of royalties is not only unethical but also a blatant violation of the intellectual property rights recognized by the World Trade Organization. It hurts, in this particular case, the business interests of the Bangladeshi rock band Miles.

'Just as Santana cannot leave a concert without performing "Black Magic Woman", we cannot conclude a concert without performing "Phiriye Dao". Our songs have a huge potential for the non-Bengali audience. We had planned to release their Hindi versions. Our plans to go Hindi are in jeopardy. We are open to singing for Hindi films too. The offer should have come to us', said Hamin in a description of how the copying of their song had hampered Miles' prospects, including, of course, business prospects (*Bombay Times*, 18 July 2004). And it goes without saying that since Bangladesh is the 'home' of Miles, so when its business interests are hurt, Bangladesh's business interests also are hurt.

2 The players involved

The decision to seek redress and preparations

The members of Miles discussed among themselves the possibility of seeking and getting compensation for the injury caused to their business prospects. It was decided that they should contact lawyers, people well versed in matters relating to the WTO, and the Ministry of Commerce.

The relevant people in the Ministry of Commerce showed keen interest in the case. They contacted their counterparts in the Ministry of Commerce in India, who suggested that Miles should seek redress to the problem by taking the violators of copyright to court. The Bangladesh Ministry of Commerce advised the members of Miles accordingly, and asked the Commercial Counsellor and others in the Calcutta office of the Bangladesh deputy high commission to extend all possible co-operation to the band members in this regard.

By approaching some individuals well-versed in WTO matters, the band members learned that they can claim protection for their work under the copyright and related rights provisions of the Agreement on Trade-Related Aspects of Intellectual Property Rights (TRIPS). The main provisions on copyright and related rights in the TRIPS Agreement are contained in the Berne and Rome Conventions. In addition, the TRIPS Agreement contains provisions related to

(a) computer programs and databases;
(b) rental rights to computer programs, sound recordings and films;
(c) rights of performers and producers of phonograms; and
(d) rights of broadcasting organizations.

In the case of Miles, Article 11 and Article 14 of the TRIPS Agreement are the most relevant ones. According to Article 11, member countries are required to provide authors of computer programs, sound recordings and cinematographic films the right to authorize or to prohibit the commercial rental of their copyright works. In addition, Article 14 provides that the performers shall have, 'in respect of a fixation of their performance on a phonogram', the right to prevent the reproduction of such fixation.

On being advised by the Ministry of Commerce and bolstered by the knowledge of the rules of WTO, members of Miles finally decided to go to the court of law. 'By going to court, we are registering our protest against such an unethical deed', said Hamin to the *Bombay Times* (18 July 2004).

Preparations for a legal suit

Sinha and Company, a Calcutta law firm, was contacted on behalf of Miles for filing suit against the violators of copyright. Accordingly, lawyers of the firm served notices on the offenders, prepared relevant documents including 'notations' of the original and copied songs, collected audio-cassettes of the two songs and so on. Finally, after the expiry of the notice period, a writ petition was filed on behalf of Miles in the Calcutta High Court on 17 May 2004 against the producer Mahesh Bhat and the music director Anu Malik of the film *Murder*, the singer of the song, Amir Jamal, the recording firm Saregama (India) Ltd and the audio company RPG Global Music (London).

In the writ petition it was claimed that the defendants had collaborated on copying core elements from the petitioners' song 'Phiriye Dao Amar Prem' in the soundtrack 'Jana Jane Jana' of the movie *Murder*. It was further claimed that the themes of the two songs had been similar and their melodies identical. Even the use of chords was the same in both the songs. 'This is gross infringement of the International (Intellectual) Property Rights as well as the Copyright Act', stated Pratap Chatterjee, the lawyer for the petitioners (*Telegraph*, Calcutta, 20 May 2004).

As compensation for the 'injury' caused to the business interests of the petitioners, 50 million rupees were demanded from Anu Malik, Mahesh Bhat, Saregama India Ltd and RPG Global Music; in addition, 'total reimbursement' for the expenditure incurred in filing the case also was demanded. A court order was also sought for appointing a receiver or special officer to seize the entire lot of soundtrack software from Saregama's Dum Dum studio. Besides this, the band's lawyers demanded that the respondents 'should be directed to disclose upon oath details of cassettes and CDs distributed by them to various vendors and retails'.

3 The outcome and challenges

The verdict

On hearing the petition, the Hon. Justice S. K. Mukherjee took *prima facie* cognizance of the matter and passed an interim order on 19 May 2004. In his learned judgment, the justice ordered the respondents to remove the song from the soundtrack of the movie *Murder*. The court order further barred the respondents from manufacturing, selling, distributing or marketing any music cassette or disc containing the song.

Triumph of the rule-based international trade regime

The verdict of the Calcutta High Court in the Miles case was a triumph of the rule-based international trade regime. Previously, intellectual property right (IPR) laws were applicable mainly within national boundaries, and only the nationals of a country could benefit from such laws; India was no exception to such practice. The Indian Copyright Act empowered the government to extend the benefits of the Act to the nationals of other countries (i) if India had entered a bilateral treaty with that country; (ii) if India and the country concerned had been parties to a common international convention guaranteeing protection to intellectual property rights; or (iii) if the Indian government was satisfied that the country concerned had adopted measures to reciprocate similar protection to the works of Indian nationals.

But Bangladesh and India had neither signed any bilateral agreement nor been parties to any common international convention related to the protection of property rights in literary and artistic works before 1995. So, according to the provisions of the Indian Copyright Act, Bangladesh would not have the right to claim IPR protection for its citizens' works in India before 1995.

However, both Bangladesh and India became members of the WTO on its formation in 1995, and the Indian Copyright Act was amended accordingly to make it compatible with the TRIPS Agreement. The amendment to Chapter IX of the Act, entitled 'International Copyright: power to extend copyright to foreign works', inserted a new section after s. 40 which reads as follows:

> 40A (1) If the Central Government is satisfied that a foreign country (other than a country with which India has entered into a treaty or which is a party to a convention relating to rights of broadcasting organizations and performers to which India is also a party) has made or has undertaken to make such provisions, if any, as required for the protection in that foreign country, of rights of broadcasting organizations and performers as is available under this Act, it may, by order published in the Official Gazette, direct that the provisions of Chapter VIII shall apply –
>
> . . .
>
> (c) to performances that are incorporated in a sound recording published in a country to which the order relates as if it was published in India.

In addition to making necessary amendments to the Copyright Act of 1957, the Indian government also issued the International Copyright Order 1999, extending the benefits of the provisions of the Indian Copyright Act to nationals of all WTO member countries. This automatically granted Bangladesh, as a member of the WTO, the status of receiving copyright protection in India for its citizens' works.

In the present case, both India and Bangladesh as members of the WTO are bound by its rules. When some nationals or business firms of India infringed the copyright (included in the IPR) of the Bangladesh nationals – members of the band Miles – it was possible for the latter to seek legal redress for the injury caused by such infringement of copyright. And this was particularly provided for in the WTO rules (National Treatment Principle of TRIPS).

Thus although the TRIPS Agreement was not the first of its kind to enable copyright owners to defend their rights in foreign countries, because of the variations in standards of protection and eligibility criteria, it was previously possible for someone to violate the intellectual property rights of nationals of other countries and exploit it for commercial purposes both within and outside the country, that is for both domestic supply and export. The TRIPS Agreement, by ensuring a minimum standard of protection and eligibility criteria, was intended to put an end to such violations of intellectual property rights beyond national boundaries. The case described here serves as a concrete proof of such an intention.

The present case is a further proof of the fact that Bangladesh was a special beneficiary of the provisions of the TRIPS Agreement. Prior to amendment to make it TRIPS-compatible, the Indian Copyright Act provided for the extension of copyright protection to the works of nationals of other countries provided that that country also granted reciprocal treatment to the works of Indian nationals. But in this case, the Bangladesh band Miles obtained 'National Treatment' although Bangladesh still has until 2006 (an allowance of grace period for Bangladesh as a least developed country (LDC)) to accord similar treatment to the nationals of India (or any other country, for that matter).

But availing themselves of the benefits of the provisions laid down in the WTO rules involved costs and challenges for the copyright owners of Bangladesh. These were in terms of money, time, lack of information and uncertainty about the outcome, compensation and the amount thereof. In this particular case, the band has won only the first round of the battle. It is yet to secure a verdict on the nature and amount of monetary compensation commensurate with the damage caused to the band's business prospects.

4 Lessons for others

Reactions to the court order

Nevertheless, the members of Miles were very happy with the decision of the court. In particular they were pleased because not only did they get their copyright recognized, the recognition came promptly too. 'We were impressed by the promptness with which the first hearing in the Calcutta High Court was completed and the injunction order was passed. Normally, it does not happen so quickly. We proceeded systematically, organizing everything very carefully. Particularly, we submitted the technical nota-tions of our song and that of the "copied" song', said the members of the Miles (*Prothom Alo*, 26 May 2004).

Mahesh Bhat, the producer of *Murder*, responded to the injunction order by removing the song from the soundtrack of the movie. However, in his defence he said that the song had been bought from the Jeddah-based Pakistani singer Amir Jamal. 'We had bought the song from Amir Jamal ... and it was only recreated by Anu', Mahesh Bhat told a *Telegraph* reporter when contacted on his cell phone (*Telegraph*, Calcutta, 20 May 2004).

But the most interesting and vindicating confession came from Anu Malik, the music director of *Murder*. Recording his reactions for the first time since the controversy over the song 'Jana Jane Jana' surfaced, Malik confirmed that 'This song, as well as "Kaho Na Kaho" (another song from *Murder*) were taken from a Pakistani singer by the producers and the music company. I have not even recorded that song, leave alone composed it' (*Telegraph*, Calcutta, 26 May 2004). Malik said that he had been shocked to be dragged into this controversy: 'The people who bought the song from the Pakistani singer must also clarify that I had nothing to do with it.'

Manam Ahmed, the Miles keyboard player, was asked in an interview about the statements made by both Mahesh Bhat and Anu Malik that the controversial song was purchased from the Pakistani singer Amir Jamal. In reply, Manam Ahmed mentioned that this song had been composed in 1993 for their album 'Prothasa', which had even become popular in Pakistan. It was released in India again in 1997 by the Asha audio company of Calcutta. 'If Amir Jamal was the original composer of the song, why did not he come up with a complaint during the last ten year period?' asked Manam (*Prothom Alo*, 10 June 2004).

Manam Ahmed's contention was confirmed by the audio company Asha of Calcutta. S. D. Lahiri, the proprietor of Asha, said, 'The song appears in our 1997 release "Best of Miles Vol. 1". The *Murder* track has reproduced ditto the entire musical arrangement of the Miles number, including the specific guitar parts' (*Telegraph*, Calcutta, 20 May 2004). On the other hand, shrugging off their responsibility in the whole episode, S. F. Karim, business manager for Saregama India Ltd, said, 'We have little role in this, except reproducing and printing what the producer and music director have given us. Had it been non-film music, we would have had a more proactive part in the composition' (*Telegraph*, Calcutta, 20 May 2004).

In short, the members of Miles are very happy with the outcome. They are happy to see that their rights have been established. On the other hand, the violators of copyright have also learned that they cannot get away scot-free after perpetrating such infringement of others' copyright. They can be expected to be more cautious in future. But above all, this case upholds the fact that intellectual property rights, like other property rights, are inviolable. This will simultaneously serve as a warning to would-be violators of intellectual property rights and as an encouragement to creative people all over the world by reassuring them that their creative works will not be pirated. And all of these follow from the TRIPS Agreement – one of the three major instruments that constitute the legal rights and obligations of the WTO.

History of Miles at a glance
1982
First public appearance on Bangladesh Television as **Miles**.
First solo public concert at Shilpakala Academy Auditorium, Dhaka. Capacity attendance of 2,000.
First album released in English, entitled 'Miles': three original songs, seven covers.

1983–1990
Played at the Sonargaon Pan Pacific Hotel's discotheque and coffee shop in Dhaka six nights a week. Many solo and joint concerts.

1986
Second album released in English, entitled 'A Step Further': seven original songs and three covers.

1991
First Bangla album, 'Protisruti', released: twelve original Bangla songs, bringing the band unprecedented popularity with a number of hit songs.

1991–1992
A number of television appearances performing the Bangla songs.

1992
First concert outside Bangladesh, in Bangalore, India: UK rock music performed in three-hour solo concert. Attendance 7,000.
Second Bangla album, 'Prottasha', was released with twelve original Bangla songs: record-breaking sales. To date the highest-selling album of Miles' music in Bangladesh.

1993

Numerous television appearances, and many concerts with audiences of 12,000 plus.

Signed with Pepsi Cola for a sponsorship agreement of one year, which included exclusive concerts organized by Pepsi.

1994

First CD released as the 'Best of Miles', from Hollywood, United States, the first ever CD of a Bangladeshi band. Sold very well in United States, United Kingdom, Japan, United Arab Emirates and Bangladesh.

Solo three-hour concert in Chandigarh, India, of UK rock music. Attendance 5,000.

Two concerts in the Gulf states of Abu Dhabi and Dubai. Audiences 1000–1500.

Numerous concerts in Bangladesh.

Asia's largest cable TV network Star TV's music channel 'V' and 'MTV' Asia covered Miles' concert and tour news.

1995

Many concerts in Bangladesh colleges and universities, as well as private dinner-dance performances.

1996

Solo two-and-a-half-hour concert in Calcutta of mostly Bangla songs. Audience 7,000.

Released third Bangla album (the band's fifth), 'Prottoy', containing eleven original songs, a high-selling album in Bangladesh and abroad, giving the band its third consecutive hit album.

Successful major tour of United States and Canada over two months, performing in New York, Dallas, Oklahoma, Chicago, Florida and Montreal to audiences of 500 to 2,500 people, ticket prices ranging from $20 to $100.

1997

Increasing air-play of Miles' Bangla and English songs on India's FM Radio, and increasing press and record company interest there. Release of the band's first singles cassette, 'Prayash', two original Bangla songs performed as extended dance songs. Supported by earlier TV performances, they were very well received.

BBC conducted and aired a number of interviews with Miles in various programmes along with some of their most popular Bangla songs.

Interview with Miles published in London's oldest Bangla newspaper, *Janomot*.

Band's seventh disc recorded, partly in India and partly in Bangladesh.

1998

Performed in many charity concerts to audiences of 1,000 to 20,000 people.

Performed another successful concert in Calcutta to an audience of about 6,000 people.

Made a number of music videos through the year for satellite TV channels including MTV.

First compilation album released in India as 'Best of Miles' (Vol. I), a 'perennial seller' in record company language, with huge radio play.

Second compilation album 'Best of Miles' (Vol. II) released six months later, also topping the charts. The two albums received great reviews in the local press, making Miles very well known in West Bengal, India.

1999

Performed in concert in Chittagong stadium, with an audience of over 30,000.

Second guitar player taken on by the band.

Performed at Shibpur Engineering College, Calcutta, in front of an audience of 5,000 – Miles' fifth performance in India, the highest number of concerts by any band from Bangladesh.

4

4

Barbados: telecommunications liberalization

LINDA SCHMID*

1 The problem in context

Telecommunications liberalization is a deliberate process in Barbados that offers insight into how economies participate in the World Trade Organization (WTO) and handle the global market. This case study will examine telecommunications liberalization in Barbados as a reflection of its participation in the multilateral trading system and as a response to consumer and market demand. The study will demonstrate how Barbados chose to use WTO instruments domestically and through the establishment of an independent regulator. The case will describe the catalysts for telecommunications regulatory reform, the roles of primary stakeholders, and their key decisions. The challenges and results of liberalization will be highlighted, and stakeholders will recommend improvements to the process.

Barbados is a small island state in the Caribbean heavily dependent on international trade in services. Tourism and financial services represent the majority of services exports and the main source of foreign exchange.[1] Barbados is a hub for firms operating in the Caribbean due to the island's airlift capability and comparatively well developed transportation and communication links. Sugar, rum and crude petroleum are significant export products. Their dependence on government support and diminishing preferential trading arrangements has shifted production 'towards niche markets of higher-priced "luxury items" ... cut flowers, speciality sugar, as well as research and development of special varieties and specialised rums', according to economist Sherryl Burke Marshall.[2] International trade in services is the mainstay of the economy, providing

---

* Trade in Services Officer, International Trade Centre, Geneva. Previously Trade Director for Caribbean Trade and Competitiveness Program, USAID.
[1] Barbados National Strategy for Trade Capacity Building, Ministry of Foreign Affairs and Foreign Trade, October 2003.
[2] Sherryl Burke Marshall, Economist, Prime Minister's Office, interview, 15 April 2004.

consistent, annual export revenues. Barbados undertook telecommunications reform in recognition of the fundamental importance of telecommunications infrastructure to international trade in services.

Barbados is at the forefront of policy development for small island states
to ameliorate their narrow range of resources, limited scale economies,
and disproportionately high transportation and communication costs. As
an example, in 1997 Barbados adopted the value added tax (VAT) to reduce
dependence on tariffs and better position itself for trade negotiations. This
is an iconic adjustment for a small island economy interested in the benefits of reduced tariff levels. As another demonstration of its leadership,
Barbados supports implementation of the Caribbean Single Market and
Economy for 'the development of the region . . . as it seeks to integrate into
the new global economy'.[3] Telecommunications liberalization also exemplifies policy leadership for a small island economy interested in greater
integration into the global market of international trade in services.

The island is a founding member of the WTO, dedicated to engagement in the multilateral trading system. Economist Sherryl Burke
Marshall observed, 'Barbados participates in the WTO to benefit small
countries and small island states'. A primary interest is special and differential treatment and special status for small island developing states.[4]
Barbados participated in early negotiations of the General Agreement on
Trade in Services (GATS), made additional commitments in telecommunications services, and is a signatory to the Telecommunications Reference
Paper.[5] As an economy deeply reliant on tourism and financial and international business services, Barbados has undertaken liberalization of its
telecommunications market to enhance its competitive position and economic growth. In 2002 Senator Tyrone Barker noted, 'the government
of Barbados is committed to liberalization of telecommunications, since
this process will permit Barbados to meet its commitments as a member
of the WTO and signatory to the GATS'.[6]

In consultation with stakeholders and telecommunications experts,
the government developed a pragmatic approach to telecommunications

---

[3] Barbados National Strategy for Trade Capacity Building, Ministry of Foreign Affairs and
Foreign Trade, October 2003.
[4] Sherryl Burke Marshall, Economist, Prime Minister's Office, interview, 15 April 2004.
[5] Barbados Draft Consolidated Schedule of Specific Commitments [GATS], WTO Document
S/DCS/W/BRB, 24 Jan. 2003.
[6] Senator Tyrone Barker, Parliamentary Secretary, Ministry of Economic Development,
speech to the Workshop on Costing Interconnect and Access Services in the Caribbean,
October 2002, http://www.commerce.gov.bb/fyi/news00p.asp?artid=82.

liberalization. It renegotiated its contract with the incumbent network, then enacted a package of legislation to transform the regulatory environment and prescribe market reform in stages. The legislative package reflects the tenets of the Telecommunications Reference Paper. Barbados chose to create provisions in its legislation on the disciplines of interconnection, independent regulator, universal service, allocation of scarce resources and competitive safeguards. These principles are of primary importance to liberalization due to the nature of the telecommunications industry. New entrants to the market must have the ability to interconnect to the incumbent network at a reasonable cost in order to provide services. An independent regulator is necessary to provide objective market oversight. Competitive safeguards are necessary to prevent anti-competitive practices by market participants. Implementation of these provisions has played a leading role in transforming the telecommunications market in Barbados.

After the passage of new legislation and the consequent establishment of an independent regulator, Barbados undertook market reform in stages. The approach is designed to provide a smooth market transition from a monopoly to a competitive environment. The Internet Service Provider (ISP) market for Internet access and domestic mobile phone services were opened to competition first. This involved the issuance of licences to competitive providers and their interconnection with the incumbent network. The process was protracted due to delays by the incumbent and required active oversight by the independent regulator. The final phase opens international long-distance and fixed line services to competition. The independent regulator will rebalance rates to ensure that the price of the service accurately reflects its cost.[7] The transformation of the telecommunications market has faced universal challenges and is a direct result of pressure from the Barbadian public and private sectors.

2 The local and external players and their roles

Barbados has a vibrant trade community with numerous vocal interests. According to a trade association representative, 'Barbados has a culture of participatory engagement ... people work together and share information ... The government is very deliberate in including different actors

---

[7] Rate rebalancing is the adjustment of rates charged for domestic and international telephone services. The result of the adjustment should be a rate that reflects the actual cost of providing the service, http://www.ftc.gov.bb/.

in the decision-making process.' National stakeholders help to manage Barbados' engagement in trade negotiations and implementation of trade commitments. They come together formally as the 'Social Partnership' to voice their concerns and advise on trade priorities and unilateral reform. Representatives from the private sector, labour and non-governmental organizations (NGOs) exercise a well-established consultative mechanism with the government on trade policy.[8] The Chamber of Commerce, the Private Sector Trade Team, the National Union of the Fisherfolk Organization, and the primary union and employer organizations exemplify participants. Those in the Social Partnership, new telecommunications providers, telecommunications users, public officials and the press played important roles in moving Barbados to telecommunications liberalization.

Knowledge of the external market and disappointment with services domestically energized consumers to call for reform. Omar Holder, a recent graduate of Barbados Community College, recalled, 'Liberalization was due to public complaints about cost ... [and] comparison with services available in other markets'.[9] New technology at a low cost propelled consumers to support telecommunications liberalization. A student at the University of West Indies Cave Hill Campus, Sian Cumberbatch, explained, 'the state of the telecommunications system before liberalization forced many to go around the system by using call-back services and other technological means to bypass the licensed service provider'.[10] Consumers were vocal about the need for lower telecommunications prices. The *Nation* newspaper reported, 'Barbadians have become more cognizant of their rights as consumers and now are willing to speak out on business decisions that affect them.'[11] Consumer activism helped to press the transition to liberalization forward.

High fees were having a detrimental effect on business. Firms found that companies were avoiding establishment of subsidiaries on the island due to the high cost of telecommunications. Barbados needed an economically priced, dynamic communications infrastructure to compete internationally, according to a prominent Barbadian businessman. Barbados recognized the uniqueness of the telecommunications service sector and 'its dual role as a distinct sector of economic activity and as the

[8] Barbados National Strategy for Trade Capacity Building, Ministry of Foreign Affairs and Foreign Trade, October 2003.
[9] Omar Holder, graduate, Barbados Community College, interview, 7 May 2004.
[10] Sian Cumberbatch, student, University of West Indies at Cave Hill, interview, 7 May 2004.
[11] 'Telecommunications Giant in for a Fight', *The Nation*, 1 Sept. 2003.

underlying transport means for other economic activities', as described in the first clause of the GATS Telecommunications Annex.[12] The high cost of the underlying transport network was creating a drag on the economy. Telecommunications users helped to create momentum for structural change in the market.

Service firms were keen on liberalization of telecommunications services. Hotels, tour operators and travel services recognized the need for a state-of-the-art network infrastructure for local and international clients. Banks, insurance firms and retailers are heavy data users that require economically priced telecommunications services to be competitive. 'The "customer card" used [to collect purchasing data at checkout lines] in grocery stores relies on heavy-duty [data] transfers and low-cost telecommunications… without affordable data transfers the product would not be a viable business service or venture', explained a prominent businessman. Service companies are already at a disadvantage in the lending market due to regional loan practices that fail to recognize intellectual property and soft assets as a basis for working capital. Barbadian service firms advocated telecommunications reform to lower the cost of communications.

The advent of the Internet and public awareness of this new phenomenon created a demand for Internet access, mobile phones and greater bandwidth. According to Anthony Gunn, managing director of Carriaccess Communications, 'New technologies changed the nature of communications services and how they are delivered to consumers'.[13] This created market space for new communication businesses. Barbadian computer professionals were eager to grab this business opportunity. Entrepreneurs responded to consumer demand for new services, and a nascent information communication technology (ICT) sector developed to build websites, create online marketing strategies for firms and provide new ICT services. Barbadian consumers and businesses wanted to use, access and offer competitively new communication technologies at home. Entrepreneurs clamoured for change in the market.

Public officials recognized how a modern information communication technology infrastructure would facilitate economic and social development. They analyzed how the global technology boom could add value

---

[12] General Agreement on Trade in Services, Telecommunications Annex, http://www.wto.org.

[13] Anthony A. R. Gunn, managing director, Carriaccess Communications, interview, 7 April 2004.

to people's lives by providing access to information and knowledge. 'The technology environment was changing, evolving, electronic government was coming into existence and cheaper communication infrastructure was a priority', commented economist Sherryl Burke Marshall.[14] Barbados is interested in developing a knowledge-based economy; telecommunications liberalization and the Barbados educational technology program 'Edu-tech' are designed for that purpose. Teachers and health professionals were aware of the opportunities for online education and online health services. The public sector viewed telecommunications liberalization as a means to better serve constituents. The government decided to develop a strategy for transition to an open market.

Another driver towards telecommunications liberalization was the press. Newspaper editorials lambasted monopoly pricing and journalists began asking questions about the telecommunications market and the absence of services that existed in foreign markets. Radio talk shows addressed the issues of telecommunications liberalization. The print and broadcast media investigated the state of the market and aired the views of consumers, firms and public officials. Journalists wrote articles about the industry and covered the public debate. The press served an important role in making industry information available and publicizing the varied aspects of the liberalization debate. 'The press made the voters aware of the telecommunications issues', said Grady Clarke.[15] The media's decision to focus on telecommunications and provide coverage helped restructuring efforts.

The vibrant trade community of Barbados helped to set the stage for market reform. Exposure to information technology advances in the external market energized consumers to call for reform. Demand grew for Internet access, mobile phones and greater bandwidth. Businesses were suffering from the high cost of communications services from the monopoly. Services firms that are by their very nature heavily dependent on telecommunications infrastructure were proponents for change. Public officials were interested in the economic and social benefits of a modern information communication infrastructure, and they were ready to make the difficult decisions to change the structure of the market in Barbados. The press fanned enthusiasm for change. 'As a signatory to the WTO General Agreement on Trade in Services, Barbados had joined the global movement towards liberalization and committed itself to liberalizing

---

[14] Sherryl Burke Marshall, Economist, Prime Minister's Office, interview, 15 April 2004.
[15] Grady Clarke, managing director, Caribbean Credit Bureau Ltd, interview, 6 June 2004.

telecommunications and encouraging competition within the sector', noted Senator Tyrone Barker.[16]

3 Challenges faced and the outcome

Barbados faced the challenge of liberalizing its telecommunications market from a powerful incumbent with a firm hold on the telecommunications network. Public sentiment in favour of the transformation was evident, and the government used various means to address the challenge. One of the first obstacles to telecommunications liberalization was opposition from employees of the incumbent. Introducing competition to the monopoly was a risk to those employed by the incumbent, although over the long term telecommunications liberalization will cause the market to grow and increase employment in telecommunications services. In the short term, the incumbent inevitably has to lay off employees. Of a population of approximately 260,000 people in Barbados, 2,887 were employees of the incumbent provider.[17] Thus there was vocal opposition from labour to reform that would allow competition with the incumbent. The government decided that the anticipated benefits of a liberalized market in telecommunications outweighed the cost of initial dislocation and job loss. The government changed the legal structure of the market.

The central tenet of liberalization was the introduction of competition. The government negotiated a Memorandum of Understanding with the incumbent in October 2001 to bring an early end to its monopoly licence.[18] The monopoly arrangement had provided investment in infrastructure by the provider with a guaranteed return on investment over a twenty-year period. The fees on international telephone calls were to subsidize low-cost local and universal service. This arrangement worked to some degree in a static telecommunications environment; however, with new technology and demand for state-of-the-art services, the 'monopoly bargain' was inadequate. Incumbent services did not keep pace with new services and lower costs in other markets. As a monopoly, the incumbent had no

[16] Senator Tyrone Barker, Parliamentary Secretary, Ministry of Economic Development, speech to the Workshop on Costing Interconnect and Access Services in the Caribbean, October 2002, http://www.commerce.gov.bb/fyi/news00p.asp?artid=82.

[17] Barbados Chamber of Commerce and Industry Business Directory, http://www.bdscham.com.

[18] Cable and Wireless News Release: Cable and Wireless and the Barbados Government Sign Memorandum of Understanding, 16 Oct. 2001, http://www.candw.ky/aboutus/pressreleases/PRpages/2001arch.html.

economic incentive to match developments abroad. The Memorandum envisioned a transition period of twenty-one months ending in August 2003. The transition process continues with the opening of international long-distance service delayed to the beginning of 2005.

To transform the legal structure of the market, Barbados considered multilateral instruments. Barbados is party to the three components of the GATS that govern telecommunications services. The GATS Telecommunications Annex ensures service providers' access to and use of public telecommunication transport networks and services, transparency in the access and use of those services, and a commitment to technical co-operation. The Basic Telecommunications Services Agreement provides for scheduled commitments in, for example, voice telephony, data transmission and private leased circuits. The Telecommunications Reference Paper has a heavy focus on the telecommunications network's interconnection with technical, procedural and commercial disciplines, and the provision of an independent regulator. The Paper contains regulatory principles on competitive safeguards, universal service and publicly available licensing criteria. Barbados chose to use the Reference Paper as a basis to help design a regulatory environment that supports competition.

Barbados integrated the principles of the Telecommunications Reference Paper into a package of legislation and worked to apply those provisions to ensure a competitive telecommunications market. The 2001 Telecommunications Act[19] requires compliance with 'international obligations with respect to telecommunications'. Provisions of the Act reflect the principles of the Reference Paper. Part VI of the Act, on network interconnections, states that a carrier shall provide interconnection services to its public telecommunications network on terms that are transparent and non-discriminatory; in a timely fashion, at charges that are cost oriented and 'at points, in addition to network termination points offered to end-users, subject to the payment of charges that reflect the cost of construction of any additional facilities necessary for interconnection'. These and other provisions echo the language of the Reference Paper on its five subsidiary principles on interconnection. Access to the incumbent network is pivotal to opening the market.

The passage of this legislation demonstrates how Barbados decided to use WTO instruments domestically. Part IV of the 2001 Telecommunications Act sets out licensing requirements in conformity with the public availability of licensing criteria discipline in the Reference Paper. Part VII

---

[19] 2001-36, http://www.ftc.gov.bb/.

has universal service obligations under conditions that are 'transparent, non-discriminatory, non-preferential, and competitively neutral', consistent with the Reference Paper. Parts IX and X govern use of scarce resources 'on a non-discriminatory basis' consistent with the Reference Paper. Part VI refers disputes on interconnection to an independent body consistent with the Reference Paper. Barbados established the Fair Trading Commission (FTC) via legislation to monitor and investigate service providers and promote and maintain effective competition in the economy.[20] In 2002, the chairman of the Fair Trading Commission acknowledged the government's new telecommunications policy as a means to meet its obligations as a signatory to the GATS.[21]

Barbados has created the legal environment and an independent regulator to help liberalize the telecommunications market and dislodge the incumbent's hold on the market. The Telecommunications Act authorizes 'the ownership and operation of telecommunications networks; the provision of telecommunications services on a competitive basis; and the prevention of unfair competitive practices by carriers and service providers'. Yet the incumbent is moving very slowly and has made interconnection with its backbone very difficult. For ISPs the incumbent's execution of this process was slow. In the cellular market, licences were granted to four competitive providers but interconnection to the backbone was fraught with problems. 'In 1998 the government said it would deregulate. The process has taken six years and is still going on. From November to January we had newspaper wars on the issue. They focused on the incumbent's refusal to co-operate', said Anthony Gunn.[22] To provide services competitors are reliant on interconnection to the fibre-optic network owned and operated by the incumbent. Although there is a legal requirement to provide access, the incumbent has no economic incentive. Gunn added that 'the incumbent frustrated the process by inaction, over-quoting and red tape'.

The Barbados Fair Trading Commission is wrestling with a problem that regulators in the most sophisticated telecommunications markets tackle – how to loosen the grip of an obstructive incumbent loath to give up its profit centre. Regulators in developed and developing economies use different means to oversee and discipline reluctant incumbents including

[20] Mr Justice Frank King, Chairman, Fair Trading Commission, Barbados, Canto Conference, 18 June 2002, http://www.ftc.gov.bb.

[21] Ibid.

[22] Anthony A. R. Gunn, managing director, Carriaccess Communications, interview, 7 April 2004.

due process, incentives and punitive measures. Adherence to due process helps to develop public confidence in the independence of the regulator and the fairness of its decisions. As an incentive to the incumbent, a regulator may offer new licences to provide new services with the potential for new earnings. Regulators also use punitive measures in the form of fines or sanctions if more stringent means are necessary to influence the incumbent. The Reference Paper does not reach this level of detail but advises, 'regulators shall be impartial with respect to all market participants'. The problem of dislodging a monopoly is a universal challenge in developed and developing economies.

Barbados continues to use a pragmatic approach to the incumbent. The Fair Trading Commission is exercising its authority to monitor and investigate the conduct of all providers and to promote and maintain effective competition in the economy[23] through regulatory hearings and adjudicative deliberations. FTC proceedings allow providers and interested parties to present their positions on regulatory issues in a transparent manner for consideration. The FTC has handed down rate adjustment and interconnection decisions affecting the operation of the incumbent and competitive providers. In a January 2005 decision, for example, the FTC reiterated its earlier findings that the incumbent had not provided sufficient or complete information to justify domestic rate changes.[24] At the same time, the incumbent will receive a new licence along with other new market players to provide long-distance services. The FTC is using incentives rather than punitive measures to continue the transition. Adhering to due process open to the public and the press has helped to validate the decisions of the FTC and continue telecommunications reform.

Creating a procompetitive telecommunications environment is also a universal challenge. The pace of the transition is slow in Barbados but consistent with liberalization in developed markets. As a WTO member, it has benefited from the proactive use of multilateral instruments in its market. The considered process of liberalization has introduced new providers and services at a lower cost. The Minister of Energy and Public Utilities said before the House of Assembly that, within six months of cellular service competition, 'we have seen the rates charged plummeting'.[25] An observer noted that 'the incumbent only lowered its prices for particular services

---

[23] Mr Justice Frank King, chairman, Fair Trading Commission, Barbados, Canto Conference, 18 June 2002, http://www.ftc.gov.bb.

[24] FTC Decision and Order in the Matter of the Application for a Review of the Decision of the Fair Trading Commission Dated 20th July 2004, No. 4 of 2004, 17 Jan. 2005.

[25] '50% Hooked', The Nation, 27 Oct. 2004.

when the new entrants offered new services. Unless new entrants were in the market, the incumbent would not have lowered its prices.' Despite the difficulties with the incumbent, Barbados has experienced positive outcomes from telecommunication liberalization. At the end of 2004, in response to competition the incumbent reduced its high-speed Internet access rates by 22%.[26] In early February 2005, the three major players in the mobile market lowered their long-distance rates by almost 50%.[27] These changes can be attributed to new legislation and a regulatory environment that supports competition. The continuing transformation of Barbados' telecommunications market will depend on the independent regulator's ability to oversee the incumbent.

The benefits that have accrued to the market from liberalization in ISP and mobile services are also incentives for continuing the transition. Shantal Munro-Knight noted, 'Liberalization has drastically reduced [telecommunications] costs... calls have become cheaper for the consumer... incoming calls on cell phones are now free.'[28] Competitive mobile services in Barbados have provided cost savings to consumers and businesses. Telecommunications rates have fallen drastically, according to a local telecommunications expert. Mobile communications are functioning as a conduit for traditional and new services and minimizing the need for fixed line infrastructure. For example, a Barbadian firm plans to offer credit checks for display on cellular phones as a service to small retailers. Mobile phones are being used in some markets to pay bills, take photographs and provide short messaging services. As an affordable piece of technology that offers new services to many individuals, the mobile phone is an important benefit that continues to fuel the transition.

Greater telecommunications penetration and lower cost will also sustain the transition. Cellular mobile penetration rates have risen to over 50% of inhabitants and the number of Internet users has increased from 15,000 in 2001 to 100,000 in 2003.[29] 'Deregulation of the cellular/mobile market brought prices down and connected gardeners, fishermen – everyone', according to Anthony Gunn.[30] He added that the 'most significant

---

[26] Cable and Wireless Press Release, 3 Dec. 2004, http://www.candw.com.bb.

[27] 'Cingular Cuts Charges', *The Nation*, 4 Feb. 2005.

[28] Shantal Munro-Knight, Programme Officer, Caribbean Policy Development Centre, interview, 6 April 2004.

[29] International Telecommunications Union Statistics, http://www.itu.int/itu-d/ict/statistics/.

[30] Anthony A. R. Gunn, managing director, Carriaccess Communications, interview, 7 April 2004.

impact of deregulation is growth in the telecommunications market In 2002, annual telecommunication investment grew by 64%.[31] Consumption has increased and individuals who could not afford telecommunications services previously were able to become consumers at lower prices.' The introduction of affordable pricing methods has expanded penetration. The ability to prepay for mobile services has made mobile phones accessible to those who could not afford subscriber service.

In Barbados, mobile telephones are providing technology services such as text messaging, Internet access and databases to individuals with limited resources for personal computers. A local resident gave this personal account.

> An itinerant gardener who makes his way to work and carries his tools with him on his bicycle passed me while I was in a traffic jam. I needed help with my garden, flagged him down, and asked if he might be available. I reached for a pen and paper. He pulled out his cell phone, entered my data, and that evening I had a phone message to schedule a garden site visit. He was using his cell phone as a client database. Individuals with minimal economic means are employing this lower cost technology to enhance the way they work and communicate with others.

Telecommunications liberalization has had a multiplier effect on the economy, created additional business and added to government revenues. Omar Holder, the recent University of West Indies graduate, said, 'telecommunications liberalization creates business for other companies... [for] example advertising ... [and] prepaid phone cards'. He observed, 'there are taxes on cell phone calls, thus money goes to the government [providing] direct increase in government revenue'. Liberalization has increased employment in the telecommunications sector. Central Bank governor Marion Williams 'projected that during 2004, the ongoing liberalization of the telecommunications market will gain momentum... the level of employment should increase in ... telecommunications industries, with the projected expansion and economic activity and the coming on stream of the new cellular phone providers'.[32] Increases in employment and access to new technology at a competitive price are the incentives that will continue to drive the liberalization process forward in Barbados.

---

[31] International Telecommunications Union Statistics, http://www.itu.int/itu-d/ict/statistics/.
[32] 'Economic Growth Expected in 2004', Web Posted SIDSnet, 6 February 2004, http://sidnet.org/latestarc/other-newswire/msg00077.html.

4 Lessons for others (the players' views)

Stakeholders offered different views on the transition, encompassing the renegotiation of the Memorandum of Understanding with the incumbent, the creation of new legislation, the establishment of an independent regulator and the actual move to market reform. From witnessing this process, an observer asked the question, 'Can countries that liberalise afford a watchdog?' Extricating a monopoly provider from a potentially booming industry requires a swift, expert, independent agency that knows the industry and the issues at hand. Barbados experienced postponements in spectrum licensing and delays in the liberalization phase of international and fixed line services.[33] According to Anthony Gunn, 'the private sector was not sufficiently involved in the legislative or regulatory adjustments that were made'.[34] Greater government consultation with the new value-added telecommunications providers in the market could have helped to provide a check on the interests of those defending the status quo.

Creating regulatory institutions that are technically and procedurally adept at overseeing a pro-competitive market in telecommunications or other newly liberalized services such as banking, insurance or securities is a challenge to WTO members with limited financial and human resources. It is not only a question of cost but is also a question of technical and management know-how and the ability to assess the respective markets. These structures can also be highly politicized. There is a human dimension to bringing an independent regulatory institution into existence. The regulator must be staffed with skilled experts in the sector and individuals with expertise in a competitive market and procedural knowledge. There are also potential regulatory gaps with a new regulator and a steep learning curve for procedure. 'Commission hearings are an expensive process . . . ultimately borne by the consumer . . . perhaps there could have been a way to streamline the process', noted an observer of the transition.

In hindsight, a local entrepreneur observed that the government 'should have talked to other telecommunications providers in earlier stages'. There should have been a more aggressive interpretation of telecommunications law. He advised that the regulator 'should have taken a more hard-nosed approach toward the incumbent . . . for example, by having them open their books'. The Fair Trading Commission 'should have

---

[33] Ian Worrell, vice-president, Corporate Communications, Sunbeach Barbados, Case Study: Barbados, CARIBCAM Mobile Conference, November 2003.
[34] Anthony A. R. Gunn, managing director, Carriaccess Communications, interview, 7 April 2004.

been more aggressive in combating delaying tactics'. Advanced information technology services in Barbados would have been out of the starting
blocks earlier in that case. Due to the slow pace of change this entrepreneur
moved his firm's data processing and Internet back-office services to
another market; he noted that 'the press had done a fair job of reporting
on the telecommunications issues'. The coverage would have been better
if they had employed a specialist in telecommunications.

Public attention to the process has helped. The press reported diligently on Fair Trading Commission hearings on interconnection charges.
The Barbados Association of Nongovernmental Organizations (BANGO),
The Barbados Consumer Research Organization Inc. (BARCO) and other
stakeholders participated as interveners to express their concerns. They
are monitoring rebalancing and rate adjustment and working to ensure
that the incumbent is not given preferential treatment.[35] Shantal Munro-
Knight of the Caribbean Policy Development Centre (CPDC) noted that
the process of telecommunications liberalization is important to the constituents of CPDC. She said that the Centre is 'examining the conditions
under which the telecommunications incumbent is de-monopolizing –
CPDC is looking at rates, interconnection and other issues'.[36] The Centre
is interested in maintaining universal service and concerned with what
will happen when the market levels off. As a signatory to the Telecommunications Reference Paper, Barbados 'has the right to define the kind of
universal service obligation it wishes to maintain'.[37] NGOs' attention to
regulatory proceedings complements due process and acts as an additional
check on the actions of the incumbent.

Barbados uses different WTO instruments to enhance its domestic
policy environment. In addition to the Reference Paper, the 'Trade Policy
Review Mechanism helps the government to best tinker with the structures in place to better integrate itself into the world economy... As an
actor in the global market, Barbados works to make interfacing with the
international community more transparent and easy', observed economist
Sherryl Burke Marshall.[38] The mechanism is a vehicle for the government

---

[35] Fair Trading Commission Hearing Report in the Matter of the Utilities Regulation Act
2000-30 and in the Matter of the Application by Cable and Wireless (Barbados) Limited to
the Fair Trading Commission for Rate Adjustments pursuant to Section 16 of the Utilities
Regulation Act 2000-30, February 2004, http://www.ftc.gov.bb/.

[36] Shantal Munro-Knight, Programme Officer, Caribbean Policy Development Centre, interview, 6 April 2004.

[37] WTO Telecommunications Reference Paper, http://www.wto.org.

[38] Sherryl Burke Marshall, Economist, Prime Minister's Office, interview, 15 April 2004.

to see what they are doing and make sure it makes sense, she added. Review results are intentionally made public to enhance transparency in the marketplace. According to a member of a Barbados trade association, 'As a country integrated into the world economy, it was natural for Barbados to be part of a body that governs trade and investment, the World Trade Organization.'

Barbados also works with WTO members in different WTO Councils to consult on trade issues. In February 2004, the island formally presented to WTO members its implementing legislation for the TRIPS Agreement. As a 'conscious policy of modernising its system of intellectual property rights', Barbados undertook legislative reform and shared those results with WTO members in the Council for Trade-Related Aspects of Intellectual Property.[39] As part of that process, Barbados responded to questions from Australia, Japan and other WTO members about its new legislation. Affirmative engagement in the Trade Policy Review Mechanism in 2002 and engagement with WTO members in the TRIPS Council demonstrates how a small island state makes use of its WTO membership.

The experience of Barbados with telecommunications liberalization exemplifies how WTO members use the organization to their benefit. The Barbadian desire for a dynamic information communications market for the island propelled the transition to a liberalized environment. As an economy dependent on trade in services, Barbados adjusted domestic policy using WTO instruments as a reference to improve telecommunications services as a unique activity and as the foundation for other service activities. The phased approach to telecommunications liberalization in Barbados made the Internet accessible, expanded mobile communications, and brought in new technology services despite interconnection delays. The oversight of an active, independent regulator, public scrutiny and access to new services will continue to fuel the transition. Barbados works with other members in the WTO to benefit small island economies through astute use of WTO instruments, active engagement and articulate leadership to mitigate the challenges of liberalization and make real the benefits.

---

[39] Council for Trade-Related Aspects of Intellectual Property Rights Review of Legislation, Barbados, IP/Q/BRB/1, 9 Feb. 2004.

5

Services commitments: case studies from Belize and Costa Rica

J. P. SINGH*

1 The problem in context

Belize and Costa Rica made modest commitments in the General Agreement on Trade in Services (GATS) at the Uruguay Round and the Fourth (Telecommunications) and Fifth (Finance) protocols negotiated thereafter in 1997. Costa Rica's commitments reflect status quo bindings of market liberalization, Belize's commitments reflect less than that. This is not surprising: most developing countries used the provisions of GATS to commit a few sectors at levels which were already open and to the extent allowed by their domestic policy contexts.[1]

Belize and Costa Rica also present an interesting puzzle: why did these economies with vibrant service sub-sectors, in serious need of foreign investment in others, and with sizable service export surpluses, make low commitments? Borrowing a Costa Rican trade official's words, why did they make 'timid commitments' in services?

The evidence that follows for the two countries confirms the essentially bottom-up nature of GATS: both countries choose particular sectors for commitment – at levels acceptable to domestic actors. Interestingly, they also exhibit significant policy differences: Costa Rica was positioning itself to take advantage of being a service-based export-led economy; Belize remains ambivalent about the role of services in general and GATS commitments in particular.

This chapter shows that GATS commitments as such present a static picture; the decision-making processes leading up to them reveal the dynamics behind thinking about the role of services in economies. After

* Communication, Culture and Technology Program, Georgetown University, Washington, DC.

[1] Rudolf Adlung et al. (2002), 'The GATS: Key Features and Actors', in Bernard Hoekman et al., eds., *Development, Trade, and the WTO*, Washington, DC: World Bank, p. 262.

Table 5.1. *Demographic and economic profiles*

	Belize	Costa Rica
Total population (2003)	266,440	3.96 million
Land area (km^2)	22,965	51,000
Average annual per capita income	$3,237 (2002)	$4,193 (2003)
Literacy	76%	96%
Share of services in GDP	59% (2003)	58.1% (1999)
Percentage of workforce in services	60% (2003)	63.7% (1999)

Sources: World Trade Organization, *Trade Policy Report: Belize*, 14 June 2004; World Trade Organization, *Trade Policy Report: Costa Rica*, 9 April 2001; US Department of State, *Background Notes*, available at http://www.state.gov/r/pa/ei/bgn, accessed 22 October 2004.

profiling the countries and their GATS commitments, this case study outlines the major players, the challenges they faced and the lessons to be learned from them.

2 The political economic context

Belize and Costa Rica exhibit significant similarities and contrasts. Both are small economies with similar service-sector characteristics (Tables 5.1 and 5.2). The percentage shares of workforce in services and of services in GDP, and the growth of services trade are particularly important. Much of the service-sector growth is due to the growth of tourism in each country. Both economies are in transition from being primarily agriculture-export driven to seeking diversification. In both countries, officials regularly cite the proximity to the United States and the ability to speak English as important competitive advantages. Of course, there are marked contrasts: Belize has a much smaller population with lower rates of higher education. Belize's offshore financial and business registry services probably account for the second-largest export item; Costa Rica is concentrating on information technology for diversification.

In terms of politics, both are democratic countries with predominantly a two-party system. Both avoided the patterns of authoritarianism that plagued Latin America. Costa Rica's more than fifty years of democratic decision-making confers considerable legitimacy on state instruments

Table 5.2. *Services and merchandise trade*

	Year	Belize	Costa Rica
Balance of commercial services	1992	37	108
trade (US$ million)	1995	29	62
	1998	28	230
	2001	56	763
Balance of merchandise trade	1992	−159	−599
(US$ million)	1995	−115	−583
	1998	−139	−2777
	2001	−273	−1554
Ratio of commercial service to	1992	1:1.06	1:2.27
merchandise exports	2001	1:0.98	1:2.47

Source: International Trade Statistics 2003, WTO, and author's calculations.

and their ability to define gradual change.[2] Belize gained independence from the United Kingdom in 1981, and the state's role is neither clearly defined nor institutionalized; it exhibits the 'highly personalistic' leadership defining the Caribbean.[3]

The history of structural adjustment in Costa Rica during the 1980s may account for the differences in liberalization in the two economies. Officials note that the international choices made in the 1990s reflected the liberalization process that started with the economic crisis in 1982. By 1989, when Costa Rica joined GATT (General Agreement on Tariffs and Trade), these policies were in place and perceived to benefit the country. Accession to GATT went smoothly and Costa Rica was asked to make few concessions. Officials speak freely of the help received from the United States, especially under President Ronald Reagan, in exchange for their support in the fight against the Contras in Nicaragua. On GATT, Francisco Chacon, Vice-Minister of Foreign Trade (1994–8), says: 'We were gaining a lot and paying very little'.

[2] 'Costa Rica largely fits the democratic stereotype. One of the hallmarks of the Costa Rican political system is its emphasis on consultation and persuasion; impatient external agencies tended to feel this approach hamstrung reform' (1990), 'The Politics of Adjustment in Small Democracies: Costa Rica, the Dominican Republic, and Jamaica', in Joan M. Nelson, ed., *Economic Crisis and Policy Choice: The Politics of Adjustment in the Third World*, Princeton, NJ: Princeton University Press, p. 208.

[3] Jacqueline Anne Braveboy-Wagner (1993), 'English-speaking Caribbean', in Joel Kreiger, ed., *The Oxford Companion to World Politics*, New York: Oxford University Press.

3 GATS commitments

At the Uruguay Round, Belize committed itself only to liberalizing a few medical services, including neurosurgery.[4] They are unbound for Mode of supply 4 (movement of natural persons) 'except for senior managerial personnel and technical experts not available in the local labour market'.[5] 'What drove us into GATS was a feeling that we were expected to become members and buy into the whole packet as it was a single undertaking. With no experience and national sensitivities about interaction at multilateral level we tried to identify sectors that were least problematic', says Richard Reid, Senior Economist at the Trade Policy Unit in Belize's Ministry of Foreign Trade.

Belize later made commitments in telecommunications negotiations that ended in 1997. Given that Belize Telecommunications Ltd (BTL) had a fifteen-year monopoly until 2002, the commitments are for limited liberalization in online information and database retrieval, electronic data interchange and online information or data processing. No commitments were made in sectors such as tourism and financial services, already liberalized enough to allow for commitments.

Costa Rica made status quo bindings but presented a more detailed schedule of specific commitments in four out of the twelve possible services and, later, for financial services – banking – in the Fifth Protocol.[6] The Uruguay Round commitments are limited to Mode 2 or consumption abroad in the following sectors: computer and related services (falling under business services in CPC), education services, social and health services, and tourism and travel-related services. A horizontal commitment is taken for commercial presence (Mode 3) under market access applying only to sectors listed in the schedule of specific commitments – in this case higher education and travel agencies and tour operators, and later to the commitments undertaken for banking under the Fifth Protocol. The banking bindings are for Mode 3 in market access and national treatment allowing affiliated companies or subsidiaries to provide customer deposits, transfer financial information and leasing services. Most-favoured-nation (MFN) exemptions are taken in professional, advertising and land transportation services allowing foreign professionals

---

[4] GATS follows the United Nations Central Product Classification (CPC) system that lists eleven service sectors and a twelfth miscellaneous category. Neurosurgery falls under the sub-category of business services listed under professional services.

[5] WTO document S/DCS/W/BLZ. 24 Jan. 2003.

[6] WTO document GATS/SC/22/Suppl.1. 26 Feb. 1998.

to practise in Costa Rica only if reciprocity agreements exist with their home countries, excluding countries in the Central American Common Market (El Salvador, Guatemala, Honduras and Nicaragua). Overall, the limited commitments reflect the degree to which the Costa Rican market was already open.

4 Local and external players and their roles

Government

Costa Rica's is a presidential system of government. The constitution vests enormous power in the president, checked by informal consensus-building politics. The formal limits on presidential power on trade include working through the Ministry of Foreign Trade (COMEX) and ratifying trade treaties in the fifty-seven-member Legislative Assembly.[7] However, the Assembly can only approve or reject a trade treaty – 'a permanent "fast track" in favour of the executive branch'.[8] The role of successive presidents in steering the Costa Rican economy is thus extremely important. State instruments overall reflect enormous legitimacy; 'the state is a ship where the crew know where it is going' – the economic crisis merely began to change this role 'from participant to regulator', says Roberto Echandi, special adjunct ambassador for US Trade Affairs at COMEX.

COMEX was formally created in October 1996 to reflect the increased importance of trade since economic reforms began in 1982.[9] It consolidated trade-related functions allocated earlier to various government departments, including the Ministry of Foreign Relations. However, COMEX undertakes extensive consultations with other ministries and government bodies involved in international trade policy, including agriculture, the central bank, tourism and transport. During the Uruguay Round there were thirty COMEX staff members, including ten

---

[7] For an excellent review see Roberto Echandi (1997), 'The Uruguay Round Agreements: Constitutional and Legal Aspects of their Implementation in Costa Rica', in John H. Jackson and Alan O. Sykes, eds., *Implementing the Uruguay Round*, Oxford: Clarendon Press.

[8] Ibid., p. 411. Another important feature is that laws afford equal protection to foreign firms and citizens making national treatment a permanent feature. Service liberalizations are thus about market access and not national treatment. Based on an interview with Echandi.

[9] The economic crisis followed the breakdown of the import substitution industrialization strategy, falls in coffee prices and hikes in oil prices. In 1981, the colón was drastically devalued, wages dropped, and inflation rose above 18%. A string of loans was obtained from the International Monetary Fund (IMF), the International Bank for Reconstruction and Development (IBRD) and the United States.

negotiators. Key positions were occupied by well-respected technocrats, a legacy of the reform efforts begun earlier, notes Eduardo Lizano, former president of the Central Bank of Belize and a well-known intellectual.

The constitutionally guaranteed monopolies in several service sectors, including wireless, insurance, energy, coal and oil, are of enormous significance. Thus Costa Rica did not sign the Fourth Protocol on telecommunications, although it held observer status. For finance, it liberalized banking but not insurance. The monopolies responsible for insurance and telecommunications are the National Insurance Institute (INS) and the Costa Rican Electricity and Telecom Institute (ICE).[10]

In sum, services trade in a multilateral context was important to Costa Rica by the 1990s in spite of the domestic obstacles. In the 1990s 'there was consensus at some level that services is an area where Costa Rica can benefit... That's translated into politicians who understand these types of activities. They incorporate this into their discourse', says Anabel Gonzáles, Special Ambassador for US Trade Affairs in Costa Rica. Roberto Echandi adds, 'Small is beautiful... We want to be perceived as a small country with a positive agenda. We understand the importance of rules to generate services and foreign direct investment.'

Belize is a parliamentary democracy with a bicameral legislature, the National Assembly, consisting of twenty-nine directly elected members of the House of Representatives and twelve appointed members of the Senate. While the economic crisis in Costa Rica served to institute economic reforms, Belize inherited a system of imperial preferences in commodity exports that did not face serious challenges until the late 1990s. It joined GATT in 1983. However, finding its feet securely on the ground after independence in 1981, combined with the lack of any economic crisis, meant that Belize was not an active participant in the Uruguay Round. 'In 1994, we were sleeping. At that time, our minister didn't tell us what was going on. Trade was divided into two–three ministries... agriculture and trade were at cross-purposes', says Fred Hunter Sr, a former cabinet minister.

Belize created a Ministry of Foreign Trade in the mid-1990s, but it lacked technical expertise and resources. The Trade Policy Unit (TPU) carries out negotiations. During the Uruguay Round, there was only one staff member assigned for negotiations (there are now five). Richard Reid,

---

[10] They were kept informed by COMEX during the telecommunication and banking negotiations. Based on interviews with Jaime Coghi, a counsellor at the Costa Rican permanent mission to the WTO.

who has been with the TPU since its inception, remembers that tariff bindings were the most important issue: 'Everything else was going for what you can. We were still fighting to create a real ministry of foreign trade.'

Primary commodity producers – in sugar, citrus and bananas – hold tremendous political clout, with politicians responding to these preferences. Thus, Belize did not prioritize its services sector in the 1990s. Others note that this may still be the case. 'Belize has yet to define what it wants to be', says David Gomez, managing partner of Launchpad Consulting in Belize, who was deputy permanent representative at Belize's Mission to the UN–WTO in Geneva in 2001–2. Furthermore, investment laws in Belize are not specific enough, giving politicians tremendous leeway and making the system clientelistic. Officials and industry representatives cite several instances of ministers making commitments internationally without technical input or consultations.

Industry

In Costa Rica, the Uruguay Round and subsequent sectoral negotiations featured the rising prominence of COMEX, inter-ministerial co-ordination, entrenchment of an economic reform programme and consultations with parastatal bodies such as ICE and INS. However, direct consultations with industry on services matters were limited. Nevertheless, there were other important influences. The formation of the private Costa Rican Investment Board (CINDE) in 1982 is important. CINDE identifies the revealed comparative advantages, works closely with COMEX, and aggressively seeks to attract foreign direct investment (FDI). Its crowning achievement came in November 1996 when Intel announced that it was going to build a $300 million semiconductor plant in Costa Rica.[11] CINDE's early identification and prioritization of electronics and service-related sectors contributed to success, says Edna Camacho, the director general of CINDE. According to Ronald Jiménez, the vice-president of CAMTIC (Costa Rican Chamber of Information and Communication Technologies), the software sector had begun to grow in

---

[11] 'In the late 1980s, CINDE had explicitly decided to follow a strategy of attraction, marketing itself to a specific group of potential investors, rather than spreading its fairly limited resources across a hodgepodge of ambiguous leads.' Debora Spar (1998), *Attracting High-Technology Investment: Intel's Costa Rican Plant*, Foreign Investment Advisory Service Occasional Paper 11, Washington, DC: World Bank, p. 8.

Costa Rica in the late 1980s. At that time there were around twenty-five firms; now there are more than two hundred.

Meanwhile, the banking sector had also begun to grow incrementally since the early 1980s. COMEX officials met with the Costa Rican Banking Association (ABC) during the Fifth Protocol negotiations and see bankers as their foremost partners in arguing for services liberalization; for its part, the ABC views economic reform as slow.[12]

In Belize, no industry consultations were undertaken during the Uruguay Round. The telecommunications negotiations were different: the government was interested in eventually liberalizing but recognized BTL's monopoly until 2002. Even a status quo binding with marginal liberalization in a few sub-sectors was then a good precedent. The Trade Ministry sent over the schedule of specific commitment to BTL officials to fill out. 'The WTO commitments were a no-no to us. At that time, it didn't occur to us that we wouldn't get another fifteen-year licence', says Robert Young, director of telecommunications, Public Utilities Commission, Belize, who formerly worked at BTL. However, it is unclear whether the limited liberalization bindings made in sub-categories reflected input from BTL, trade ministry officials or external agencies, according to Gilbert Canton (chairman) and Robert Young of the Public Utilities Commission, Belize.

There is also no evidence that the tourism industry, the biggest service export sector in both Costa Rica and Belize, was consulted during the Uruguay Round negotiations. As explained later, this reflected the state of organization of the tourism industry in each country and the inability of various tourist service providers (hotels, restaurants, tour guides, transport operators, etc.) to view themselves as service exporters.[13] Even when they do so they may not seek foreign markets and may be protectionist towards their own. Both countries, however, have industry associations and government bodies that are involved in prioritizing tourism.

Civil society

Civil society groups were not directly involved in GATS, but their indirect influence in democratic politics is important. In Costa Rica the state had

---

[12] Based on interviews with COMEX officials and Jorge Monge, the president of ABC. Monge identified infrastructure – roads, telecommunications, airports – and education as sectors where change over the last twenty years has been slow.

[13] Based on interviews with William Rodriguez, president, Costa Rican National Chamber of Tourism (CANTUR), and Andrew Godoy, executive director, Belize Tourist Industry Association. CANTUR and BTIA are industry associations.

to build a constituency for its economic reforms in the 1980s. While many of the structural adjustment reforms were top-down and dictated by external agencies, they were eventually accepted by society because of state efforts. GATT was prioritized in terms of the country's international trade strategy, and officials shied away from using GATT to push reforms that were unpopular, except for tariff bindings in agriculture. This built early legitimacy for GATT instruments. Nonetheless, there is a twist to the story. Part of the welfare state had worked for Costa Rican society. This applies to ICE and INS, making liberalization in these areas impossible. The case of INS is interesting because it provides for a variety of public services beyond insurance. 'INS is everyday life. It pays for firemen and other services', says Eduardo Lizano. As for ICE, consumers viewed it as providing reasonably good services at low costs. 'Costa Ricans reflect themselves in ICE', says Johnny Rivera, a former ICE official who is now telecommunications manager for the Western Union call centre in Costa Rica.

The main bases of political support in Belize are the primary sectors; bananas alone employ nearly 10,000 people. It may have hampered the ability of policy-makers in Belize to prioritize services early on. 'Services may have been a new animal to some of them and at the end of the day they need to cater to local needs', says Joseph Waight, a Ministry of Education advisor who was with the Ministry of Finance during the Uruguay Round. The legacy is that WTO is viewed in terms of agriculture and not services.

External agencies

For services negotiations neither country received much external assistance. Nor were there any particular external pressures on them, at least during the Uruguay Round, to liberalize services.

5 Challenges faced

Services were new to the GATT agenda, and both countries made limited commitments, but there are differences in the ways in which the two countries responded.

Knowledge of services agreement

Both countries viewed the Uruguay Round in terms of commodities rather than services. Both countries also knew that the idea of positive lists meant that maintaining the status quo or making token commitments was enough to sign on to GATS.

Without an in-depth knowledge of the domestic services market or the evolving services agreement, Belize opted for the least costly option, making limited commitments in medical services. Trade in preferential commodities was profitable and Belize's efforts went into preserving these preferences. By the time of the telecommunications and financial services agreements, officials had better knowledge of GATS. Belize used the status quo binding in telecommunications to begin the process of reform in that sector. However, the knowledge of services sectors was not uniform; Belize did not make status quo bindings in already liberalized financial services.[14] Each of the following reasons was given by a different official interviewed:

> It was too early. We were just building regulatory capacity.
>
> There was a lack of supervisory capacity.
>
> When we think of financial services, we do not think of WTO at all.
>
> The Ministry of Foreign Trade didn't even ask us.
>
> The Ministry of Foreign Trade asked us but it would have meant undoing our fixed exchange rate system and opening the capital market account.
>
> There were concerns about money laundering and the United States was trying to prevent us from offering any kind of offshore financial services at all.
>
> Vested interests in banking didn't want the opening.

The real reason, according to Yvette Alvarez, former deputy governor of the Central Bank of Belize, was that most of the efforts of the bank were devoted to passing appropriate legislation for offshore banking and anti-money laundering. There was no political capital or time left to spend on crafting a WTO commitment.

As for Costa Rica, it made a thorough investigation of its services sector but also played it politically safe by committing to the status quo. However, as seen above, service exports were beginning to get politically prioritized.

The commitments in banking followed more than a decade of banking liberalization. The most significant move was the 1995 law that allowed banks to accept current-account deposits, now part of Costa Rica's WTO

---

[14] Belize provides a variety of offshore services: trusts, mutual funds, international insurance, international business corporations registry, international banking, offshore investment schemes. The offshore services began to develop in 1990. By the end of the decade, concerns were being raised about money laundering and tax evasion and, more recently, terrorism financing. In 2000, the OECD blacklisted Belize for its financial services sector.

commitment.[15] Eduardo Lizano comments that the pressures for this reform came from domestic banks and from USAID for helping the country to pay its national debt.

Co-ordination and technical capacity

International trade policy involves co-ordinating several ministries and expertise to advance one's interests effectively. GATS, in particular, demands inter-ministerial co-ordination and also the task of making myriad domestic producers realize that they are exporting services. National treatment and market access commitments across the four modes of supply make GATS even more a highly technical exercise.

During the Uruguay Round Belize started creating the Ministry of Foreign Trade and its Trade Policy Unit. The task of educating various service sectors that they are service exporters may have stood in the way of making commitments. For example, tourism officials admit that educating operators on GATS is difficult. It may be too daunting for small ministries to perform. TPU officials in Belize note that keeping up with all the international trade agreements with the European Union, the United States and CARICOM (Caribbean Community and Common Market) and with other countries keeps them busy, 'they do not have time to do the type of "information and sensitization" needed to keep service providers attuned to GATS', says Tracey Hutchinson, a trade economist at the TPU.

Calculating the impact and implications of commitments is hard, too. Officials note that these competencies did not exist at the CARICOM level either, which may have been 'asked to commit to sectors where we don't know what we're committing away or committing to', says Carla Barnett, chief executive officer of the Ministry of National Development and former Deputy Secretary General of CARICOM. Take the instance of tourism. Most of the data on the tourist industry earnings come from the 7% hotel tax levied by the Belize Tourism Board. These data are supplemented by a few surveys, but Belize does not systematically collect tourism data. The tourism industry accounts for about 18% of foreign direct investment and about 25% of employment, but these figures reflect

---

[15] The controversial new banking law was ushered in by President Figueres. His father, José Figueres Ferrer – also known as Don Pepe – had ushered in state monopolies and import substitution industrialization after the Revolution of 1948. The son was alternatively considered a traitor or as best positioned to carry out this reform.

the hotel sector data. Officials note that systematic data collection may even show that more than two-thirds of Belize's GDP comes from tourism-related activities.[16]

Costa Rica named and empowered COMEX as its lead agency for trade matters towards the end of the Uruguay Round. 'Our position was that we were new players and didn't have knowledge or expertise and therefore we prioritized. In services, the ideas of positive lists allowed us to make commitments that were in our interest,' says Francisco Chacon. While Costa Rica was careful, its schedule of commitments, as mentioned earlier, was far more detailed than was the case for Belize.

In Costa Rica the tourism sector is relatively open and growing, making it more difficult for industry operators to see the wisdom of committing to GATS (this holds for Belize, too). William Rodriguez, president of the Costa Rican Chamber of Tourism, admits: 'First time I heard we have to be committed, my response was, "we've always been open".' Costa Rica, did, however, make limited commitments in tourism during the Uruguay Round.

Balancing interests and sequencing liberalization

There were two challenges to balancing domestic interests and sequencing services liberalization: moving beyond agriculture to prioritize services, and finding ways for liberalizing sectors that were historically private or state monopolies.

Belize's strategy in telecommunications employed the GATS schedule in binding status quo but also allowed liberalization in three sub-sectors. By the mid 1990s the government of Belize was interested in liberalization but hamstrung by the BTL monopoly. Until 1987, BTL was a Cable and Wireless monopoly (as in other parts of the Caribbean). When making the commitments, the Director of Telecommunications, serving as the de facto regulator in the Ministry of Telecommunications, announced that telecommunications would be liberalized in 2002.[17] The commitments were followed by the Public Utilities Act of 1999, which allowed for a new regulator in anticipation of liberalization in 2002.[18]

---

[16] Tourism data drawn from interviews with Tracy Traeger, Director, and Evan Tillett, Deputy Director for Finance and Tourism, Belize Tourism Board.

[17] Neville D. Samuels (2000), 'Low Teledensity and Limited Access to Telecommunications in Belize: A Problem of Diffusion', Master's thesis, Communication, Culture and Technology Program, Georgetown University.

[18] The telecommunications market opened in 2002 when Intelco started providing network services to government and mobile services everywhere. An August 2004 exposé showed

Costa Rica's commitments seemed to follow, rather than precede, domestic liberalization. At a macro level, structural adjustment was a top-down process and thus the case of these sectors might be unique.[19] In banking, the commitments reflected the domestic market. In telecommunications, even Costa Rica's observer status at the WTO negotiations had to be justified to ICE. By the late 1990s, liberalization pressures for telecommunications continued to build. Multinationals, in particular, needed a suitable infrastructure, which included telecommunications. As telecommunications services became sophisticated, societal needs could not be met either. Nevertheless, legislation introduced by the government to liberalize telecommunications in 2000 had to be withdrawn because of opposition from ICE and sections of Costa Rican society. 'Welfare state for Costa Rica worked even if import substitution industrialization didn't. Everybody had a telephone and at low prices. ICE was identified with the welfare state. This wasn't a failure of the state', says Roberto Echandi.

6 Lessons for others

Costa Rica has both a positive view of the WTO and a proactive services strategy. Belize is beginning to identify its service priorities but has limited resources and perceives the WTO negatively. What can be learned from contrasting the two experiences?

Prioritizing services

Costa Rica is widely perceived as a success story in terms of using international trade to its advantage. 'Our country is convinced that active participation in the multilateral system of trade generates very important benefits for all its members, not only through trade liberalization, but also in establishing a system of rights and obligations based not on political or

---

that the government used social security to fund the development of Intelco, a firm in which the Prime Minister had a share.

[19] COMEX officials insist that domestic liberalization needs to precede and has preceded international commitments. Others disagree. Commenting on insurance and telecommunication commitments made in the recently concluded Central American Free Trade Agreement (CAFTA), Eduardo Lizano says: 'I am grateful that the Americans pushed us on insurance and telecommunications. We were worried that insurance and telecommunications would be excluded until Zoellick [US Trade Representative Robert Zoellick] came to Costa Rica.' The context for COMEX officials' comments might be the concentrated opposition to CAFTA among trade unions and students.

economic power, but in clear and fair rules, that are supported by an effective system of problem resolution', noted Tomas Dueñas, the Costa Rican Foreign Trade Minister,[20] on the occasion of the visit of WTO Director General Mike Moore to Costa Rica on 28 August 2001.

Several pillars of Costa Rican strategy are identifiable; while embedded in successful workings of constitutionalism and democratic politics, they offer insights for countries looking to diversify their economic portfolios. First, Costa Rican officials speak of globalization as hubs and spokes in which the United States is a hub and countries such as Costa Rica the spokes. Roberto Echandi notes that Mexico first worked this out with regard to NAFTA (North American Free Trade Agreement). Second, COMEX and CINDE identified key sectors for prioritization by tracking revealed comparative advantage rather than an extensive scientific study. Currently, the foyer of CINDE's main office near San José displays pictures emphasizing three sectors: electronics, medical devices and services. Third, Costa Rica made limited commitments, but the early prioritization of services allowed for identification of both the strengths and inefficiencies in sub-sectors. Fourth, while there is no consensus whether Costa Rica uses international commitments to usher domestic reform or vice versa, it is undeniable that the Costa Rican elite thinks hard about ways to embed the reform process in society and takes international obligations seriously. Costa Rica submitted its initial offer for services at the Doha Round in April 2004.[21]

It is unfair to contrast Belize with Costa Rica when it lags far behind in resources and educational advantages. Its TPU, for example, has only five staff members. But Belize seems to be moving in the same direction as Costa Rica, albeit in timid and often ambiguous ways. Yvonne L. Hyde, the Belize ambassador in Brussels, says: 'We have a saying in the Caribbean: "one step forward and two steps backwards".' There is talk of services prioritization, but it lacks teeth. 'People in Belize are afraid of change. It is not lack of education. Costa Rica would embrace it much more than we do', says Ambassador Hyde. Eamon Courtney, Minister of Foreign Trade and Investment, noted at the country's Trade Policy Review in Geneva on 12 July 2004, 'Tourism, information technology, non-traditional agriculture and financial services are but just a few of the options we are exercising to harness the intelligence and industry of the Belizean people. We are therefore alarmed by the continuous machinations of some to shift the

---

[20] Mr Dueñas' comments were translated by Laura Stein of Georgetown University.
[21] WTO document TN/S/O/CRI of 21 April 2004.

rules to maintain their advantages.' A step forward, but not without expressing caution about the system of preferences.

The political machinery remains beholden to agricultural interests; economic diversification is difficult. 'Services are important to our economy. What's lacking from the highest offices of our government is an understanding that services are tradable', says Tracey Hutchinson of the TPU.

Belize, like Costa Rica, created institutions (such as the investment promotion agency Beltraide) to promote investment and diversification, but services are yet to receive political and economic priority in terms of resources. Belize does not have an initial offer in services at the Doha Round and is waiting for CARICOM to frame a common position.

Technical capacity

In Costa Rica, COMEX's Gonzales notes that the most effective way for the WTO to utilize its resources for capacity building and to help small economies use the multilateral system effectively might be to send twenty to thirty graduates each year to the United States or other places with well-known higher education institutions to study international trade law and how the multilateral system works. They attribute their success to such education and to the subsequent appointment of technocrats to trade policy and diplomacy positions. They note that WTO technical capacity-building often falls victim to letting countries admit that they lack capacities rather than taking a serious inventory of how best to utilize their resources.

While officials in Belize admit to the need for capacity building, they are not convinced that the one-week or three-month courses that the WTO offers are particularly helpful. They have participated in sixty-three WTO capacity-building programmes since 1998. While appreciating WTO efforts, Courtney noted in Geneva that 'attachments of experienced experts to national governments would be very effective in providing direct capacity building'. Clearly, both Belize and Costa Rica are arguing for long-term solutions to capacity building.

National co-ordination

Belize emerged from the 1990s convinced of the need for domestic consultations. The National Trade Negotiation Commission (NTNC) was set up in 2002 to bring together the private sector, civil society and government representatives. A Trade Technical Team (TTT), composed of representatives from various ministries, advises the NTNC.[22] The discussions in the NTNC, however, are reactive rather than proactive in framing negotiation and development strategies; government officials and industry representatives note that services have not come up in NTNC discussions, which focus mostly on the threats to the system of agricultural preferences.

Costa Rica continues to deepen its processes of domestic consultations; the vaunted system of state persuasion in Costa Rica can be interpreted as the state's ability to set the broad outlines of economic strategies, themselves a result of formal and informal consultations. The recently concluded Central American Free Trade Agreement (CAFTA) negotiations featured industry and society representatives sitting in rooms, the so-called *cuarto junto*, next to Costa Rica's negotiators for up-to-date consultations.

7 Perceptions about the WTO

Belize has not seen tangible benefits from participation in the WTO. While officials admit that isolation is not an option and would send the wrong signal to the international community, they point to losses that they attribute to the WTO. Referring to the threats to the system of preferences at the WTO, Orla K. Coleman, a junior economist at the TPU, says, 'sugar will leave a bad taste'.

Costa Rican perceptions are the opposite. Its growth and diversification through trade (it currently exports more than 3,500 products) are attributed to the multilateral system in which the WTO is a key actor. Costa Rica has used the dispute settlement procedure effectively, resulting in rulings in its favour. Most Costa Ricans, therefore, have no difficulty in favouring the international trading system and its system of rules. As a proxy, the following numbers from a recent poll on CAFTA are instructive.[23]

---

[22] WTO, *Trade Policy Review: Belize*, report by the Secretariat. WT/TPR/S/134, 14 June 2004, p. 17.

[23] Costa Rica, Public Opinion #97: CID-Gallup. Made available to the author at COMEX. Conducted 17–22 April 2004.

Nearly half of Costa Rican adults (43%) consider themselves as knowing 'a lot' or 'something' about the commercial free trade agreement that Central America negotiated with the United States.

Two-thirds of those interviewed (66%) assume that CAFTA will bring benefits to the country.

Former minister Chacon says that the debates on trade in Costa Rica are pragmatic and not academic, in spite of the opposition to trade in some sections.[24] Costa Rica uses such pragmatism to its advantage: 'If you're small, think hard to be constructive to be taken seriously. If you're destructive, who cares?' says COMEX's Echandi.

---

[24] Graffiti on the walls of San José, especially around the University of Costa Rica, reads 'No TLC' meaning 'no tratado de libre comercio' (no free trade treaty), referring to CAFTA.

6

Inter-agency policy co-ordination in Botswana

KENNEDY K. MBEKEANI*

1 The problem in context

Participation in the WTO

Botswana is a founding member of the WTO; it joined the General Agreement on Tariffs and Trade (GATT) in 1987 and opened its mission in Geneva in 2001. The mission also serves other Geneva-based UN and specialized agencies. The Ministry of Trade and Industry is responsible for foreign trade policy formulation and implementation, negotiations on bilateral agreements, licensing and regulation of domestic trade and regulation, and monitoring of domestic consumer issues. Within the Ministry, the Department of International Trade is responsible for foreign trade policy, including co-ordination of WTO negotiations.

Botswana's new foreign trade policy is aimed at achieving free and dependable access for its exports and lowering the cost of importing goods by reducing tariffs and trade barriers. Reduction of tariffs on imported inputs is aimed at promoting manufacturing for export and domestic consumption.

Botswana's foreign trade policy has been influenced by the concentration of the direction of its exports (to Europe and South Africa). Diamonds, the main export commodity, are exported to the United Kingdom under a special arrangement with De Beers, while beef enters the European Union (EU) market under preferential access under the Cotonou Agreement (formerly the Lomé Agreement). The little that Botswana manufactures is exported mainly to South Africa duty free under the Southern African Customs Union (SACU) Agreement. The bulk of Botswana's imports (almost 80%) come from South Africa.

---

* Senior Research Fellow, Botswana Institute for Development Policy Analysis (BIDPA).

The advisor in the Ministry of Trade indicated that

> For a long time, because the market for the main export commodity [dia-
> monds] trades as a monopoly through De Beers and the other significant
> export product [beef] receives preferential market access, Botswana did not
> see the need to actively participate in WTO negotiations. South Africa was
> setting external tariffs for all of the SACU member states and to a large
> extent negotiating in the WTO on their behalf. For a long time, because of
> the SACU set-up, the Ministry of Trade and Industry was not considered
> important. SACU issues were handled by the Ministry of Finance.

Botswana's own domestic market has been under threat since South
Africa emerged from the apartheid era and has gradually opened up its
market to foreign competition. The first real test was when South Africa
negotiated a free trade agreement with the EU; this agreement was a
de facto free trade agreement with all the SACU member states. The
second eye-opener was the challenge faced by the EU in the WTO on its
discriminatory preferential market access (under the Lomé Agreement) to
a select number of African, Caribbean and Pacific (ACP) countries. This
meant that preferences enjoyed by Botswana (mainly for its beef exports)
were coming to an end.

Jay Salkin, a leading Botswana economist based at the Botswana Institute for Development Policy Analysis (BIDPA), believes that Botswana's
renewed interest in the WTO is due to the low level of employment in the
diamond sector and the erosion of preferences to the European market:

> While the diamond sector is by far the leading sector of the Botswana
> economy in terms of its contribution to gross domestic product and foreign
> exchange earnings, its contribution to employment is extremely low (under
> 3.6%) due to the high capital intensity of diamond mining and the fact that
> most of the diamond is exported in rough form. As a result of the low
> contribution to employment and fear of losing the market for beef in the
> EU, the authorities have adopted an industrial strategy aimed at promoting
> non-diamond industries both for export and local consumption.

He also feels that 'The strategy could only be achieved through active
participation in the WTO to gain access to new markets and at the same
time opening up its own (SACU) market.'

Others feel that the current Minister of Trade (Jacob Nkate) and his
predecessor (Tebelelo Seretse) provided renewed interest in WTO issues
and exposed capacity constraints within the Department of International
Trade. Seretse played a key role during the Doha Ministerial Conference
(she was one of the vice-chairs), while Nkate was the spokesperson for
the ACP group in Cancún.

Interagency co-ordination

The Department of International Trade is responsible for overall co-ordination of WTO negotiations. This co-ordination is carried out via ad hoc contacts between officials appointed by the relevant ministries and ad hoc meetings with relevant representatives from the public and private sectors. The department selects which other ministries participate in the consultative process. Consultations are based on briefings by the department as well as background papers, draft national positions prepared by the Ministry of Trade and negotiating proposals from other WTO members.

Although the core functions of the Department of International Trade deal with foreign trade, especially the WTO, the conclusion from the interviews is that it is not capable of performing its functions as would be desired. All the stakeholders interviewed were dissatisfied with the adequacy of its services, efficiency of delivery and overall effectiveness. Most people interviewed had complaints regarding its operations.

The advisor for the Ministry of Trade feels that the capacity constraints within the department limit its ability to co-ordinate WTO issues:

> The Department of International Trade is not considered very effective because it has a limited number of staff to deal with, among others, WTO matters, the EU, the Cotonou Agreement, SADC, SACU [Southern African Customs Union] and bilateral agreement matters. The majority of the staff do not have a good understanding of trade issues, especially the WTO. Their academic training was not in economics or law. This has, therefore, made it difficult for the Department to perform its task effectively.

The stakeholders cite several examples of lack of consultation between the lead ministry and other stakeholders. The Director of Planning in the Ministry of Agriculture indicated that the Department of International Trade does not include their input in the country's position:

> There are many instances where the Ministry of Trade officials have attended important WTO General Council meetings without consulting the Ministry of Agriculture, even when the issues under consideration are related to agriculture. The mechanisms for intra-government co-ordination and consultation with domestic stakeholders are weak. The country's positions in the WTO are formulated through ad hoc consultative processes, which include a select number of government departments and the business society. A senior trade official in the Ministry of Trade drafts a position paper which is then shared between government departments and the permanent representative to the WTO. The paper is then passed on to Cabinet for approval without input from the stakeholders.

Others interviewed indicate that the lack of interest in WTO issues is explained by the absence of political leadership. Ministers of Trade do not hold their portfolios long enough to appreciate WTO issues and in turn fail to provide the necessary political leadership. The executive director of the Exporters Association of Botswana (EAOB) feels that the high turnover of trade ministers allowed officials of the ministry, who did not consult with other stakeholders, to become passive participants in WTO processes:

> Between the Singapore Ministerial and Cancún Ministerial, we have had six ministers of trade. Our ministers are always having to catch up and are therefore unable to provide the political leadership that is required to ensure that we effectively participate in the WTO processes.

The lack of inter-agency co-ordination in Botswana is evident in the fact that the country has not made any commitments in the services negotiations despite liberalizing the telecommunications and banking sectors.

Economic background

Botswana's growth performance has been very impressive. During the 1980s the country experienced real GDP growth averaging 10% a year, before slowing down in the 1990s to 5.4% per year due to slower growth in mineral sector activity. The rapid growth of real GDP has lifted Botswana from being a low-income to a middle-income country. GDP per capita has increased from US$1,150 in 1980 to US$3,066 in 2003.

Exports have played a very important role in the economic development of Botswana, growing at an impressive annual average of 21% since 1980 (Figure 6.1). Exceptionally high growth rates in exports (25% per year) were recorded between 1983 and 1987.

The value of exports increased from P348 million in 1982 to P8.3 billion in 1996; and to P14.6 billion in 2001. A slowdown in world demand for diamonds between 1990 and 1993 affected overall growth in exports.

Botswana's exports are concentrated around seven major products: diamonds, vehicles, copper-nickel, meat and meat products, soda ash, hides and skins and live animals, and textiles.

Diamonds dominate Botswana's exports. From the mid-1980s to the late 1990s, the average annual share of diamonds in total exports was 75% (Table 6.1). In recent years, the share has increased to 84%. Other

Table 6.1. *Botswana's exports, as percentage of total*

Product	1996	1998	2000	2001
Diamonds	70.97	70.26	82.73	84.84
Vehicles	13.78	10.78	1.91	2.02
Copper-nickel	5.37	4.89	5.84	4.08
Textiles	2.34	3.39	1.71	1.31
Soda ash	0.84	1.10	0.69	0.88
Cereals	0.05	0.14	0.13	0.11
Fruits and vegetables	0.02	0.01	0.01	0.00
Milk and milk products	0.00	0.00	0.00	0.00
Live animals, meat and related products	2.85	3.76	2.17	2.96
Other products	3.78	5.66	4.81	3.79

Source: Central Selling Organization.

Figure 6.1. *Annual export growth 1982–2001*

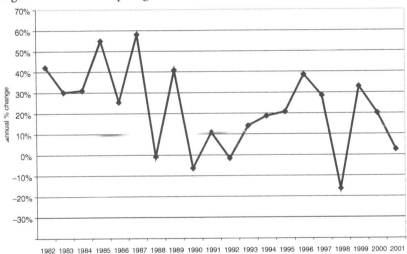

traditional exports, such as meat and copper-nickel, have either levelled off or decreased in importance. The share of textiles has also been declining.

Botswana's direction of exports has remained highly concentrated. Until 2000, the United Kingdom, Switzerland and South Africa took up over 90% (see Table 6.2). The only major change in the direction

Table 6.2. *Direction of Botswana's exports (as a percentage of total exports)*

	1995	1998	2000	2001
South Africa	21.13	16.54	6.50	6.42
Switzerland	30.75	16.33	13.33	0.01
United Kingdom	37.26	55.59	69.92	85.83
Rest of the world	10.86	11.54	10.24	7.75

Source: Central Selling Organization.

of Botswana exports was a shift in the destination of diamonds from Switzerland to the United Kingdom.[1]

The share of exports to South Africa has been steadily declining in recent years; in the period from 1995 to 2001, they fell from 21% to just over 6.4%. This has been mainly due to the decline in motor vehicle exports.

Despite several efforts by the government to promote non-traditional exports, Botswana's export basket remains highly concentrated. The high proportion of diamonds in total exports remains a major concern to both policy-makers and the business community.

2 Local and external players and their roles

Government

The Ministry of Trade and Industry

The Department of International Trade in the Ministry of Trade and Industry is the institution responsible for the overall co-ordination of WTO negotiations. Co-ordination of WTO negotiations is carried out through ad hoc contacts between officials appointed by the relevant ministries and ad hoc meetings with relevant representatives from the public and private sectors (i.e. industry associations selected by the Ministry of Trade). Consultations occur on a needs basis and circumstances determine who is consulted. Consultations are based on briefings by the Ministry of Trade as well as on background papers, draft national positions prepared

---

[1] The shift results from an internal arrangement at De Beers, which exclusively markets Botswana's diamonds, and does not reflect a change in demand. In the past all Botswana's diamond exports went to Switzerland, but eventually ended up in London at De Beers' Central Selling Organization, now the Diamond Trading Company.

by the Ministry of Trade, and negotiating proposals from other WTO members.

According to the Advisor in the Ministry of Trade, inter-agency co-ordination is poor due to weaknesses in the Department of International Trade. Other stakeholders share the same view.

> The Ministry of Trade and Industry is crucial to Botswana's effective participation in the WTO. However, its internal weaknesses, as well as its poor linkages with stakeholders, make it a liability in the process. (Executive director, Exporters Association of Botswana)

> The Ministry of Trade is unable to provide guidance to the Geneva mission on issues of interest to the country. This may be attributed to shortage of qualified staff. As a consequence, Botswana's participation in the WTO is severely constrained. (Permanent Secretary, Ministry of Foreign Affairs)

The Exporters Association of Botswana also complained about the slow response of the Trade Ministry's staff, the lack of transparency and the inaccessibility of senior ministry officials.

There is a general feeling that the Department of International Trade does not have the necessary capacity and competence to co-ordinate WTO issues. The department has only four people working on international trade issues, including the WTO.

Ministers of trade

The high turnover of ministers of trade is also seen as one of the main reason for weak inter-agency co-ordination on WTO issues. Botswana had six different ministers of Trade in the period between the Singapore Ministerial conference and the Cancún Ministerial conference. The Executive Director of the Exporters Association of Botswana has cited this as a reason for the lack of consultation by the Department of Trade (see above). The high turnover does not provide the necessary political leadership to deal with WTO issues and consult widely.

> South Africa has maintained the same Minister of Trade since the Geneva Ministerial (Conference) and you could see that with time his knowledge of WTO issues grew and so was the knowledge of his officers. With us, it is one Minister per WTO Ministerial conference. They always have to catch up but with a weak support structure in the Ministry, we always end up observers. (Director of Planning, Ministry of Agriculture)

Jacob Nkate and Tebelelo Seretse have shown an interest in WTO issues. This has led to the setting up of new structures for consultations on

WTO issues. The Cabinet recently approved the establishment of a high-level trade negotiating committee composed of heads of ministries, state organizations and industry leaders.

However, others are sceptical of the new arrangement. They feel that without improving the competence of the officials in the lead ministry – the Ministry of Trade and Industry – the committee will fail to provide the necessary guidance to negotiators and the mission in Geneva.

Non-government bodies

Consultations with non-government bodies occur on a needs basis, and circumstances determine who is consulted. Participants are industry and business associations, and research institutions (e.g. the Botswana Institute for Development Policy Analysis (BIDPA) and the University of Botswana) selected by the Ministry of Trade.

The Ministry of Trade and Industry indicated that they find it difficult to attract sufficient industry interest and attendance at WTO consultations; these consultations normally occur before ministerial conferences and attendance is normally very low. The ministry feels that industry does not see the relevance of WTO negotiations.

However, the industry and other non-governmental institutions feel that the ad hoc nature of the meetings does not warrant the allocation of scarce resources. They also feel that their institutions have little, if any, impact on the preparatory process for negotiations.

Two institutions are key to providing analytical support on WTO issues: the University of Botswana and BIDPA. The University of Botswana indicated that it is not consulted by the Ministry of Trade. The head of the Economics Department stated that

> We have never made any formal input into Botswana's position at the WTO, nor have we been notified of planned changes to current activities and practices. Excessive government control accounts for its inefficiency and ineffectiveness. The department would, ideally, have a role to play, especially in terms of research and analysis. The dearth of analysts to tackle issues related to trade and exports requires that we should seek to venture into this important area (WTO issues).

BIDPA indicates that it is only consulted just before WTO ministerial conferences. Its executive director comments that 'We would like to collaborate more with the Ministry of Trade on WTO issues and avoid the current ad hoc arrangement.'

Foreign external players

A number of external players are involved in formulating Botswana's position at the WTO.

SACU

Even though the Ministry of Trade and Industry is responsible for foreign trade and SACU member states are individually represented in the WTO, Botswana's foreign trade policy has traditionally been determined by South Africa. Under the SACU Agreement, other member states of SACU – Botswana, Lesotho, Namibia and Swaziland – applied import duties set by South Africa and were provided with compensation for surrendering their tariff-setting powers to South Africa. South Africa's Department of Trade and Industry (DTI) has traditionally formulated and co-ordinated SACU's trade policy. The Industrial Development Corporation (IDC) – the business arm of the DTI – and the South African Parliamentary Committees assist the DTI in carrying out periodic reviews and assessments of trade polices.

However, the SACU Agreement allows smaller members to make submissions in sectors where they need protection (including protection from South African exports).

> Even though South Africa was setting external tariffs for all of us [SACU member states] we were able to protect certain areas of interest to us such as beef. The situation was not as it is portrayed. We could make submissions to South Africa and the submissions were almost always taken on board. In addition, we did not have the necessary expertise and capacity compared to South Africa's Board of Tariff and Trade to effectively participate in tariff setting. (Secretary for Financial Affairs in the Ministry of Finance, Botswana)

Recently the SACU Agreement has been renegotiated to allow active participation of the smaller member states in the formulation of trade policy. SACU member states are now required to negotiate jointly with third countries and participate in setting common external tariffs. However, there is a feeling that South Africa will take the lead because Botswana and other SACU states have the capacity neither to negotiate a series of trade agreements nor to provide analytical backup.

SADC Council of Ministers and African Trade Ministers' meeting

The SADC Council of Trade Ministers usually meets before key meetings of the WTO to prepare a regional position, formulated on the basis of country positions. Botswana has traditionally not been very active in promoting positions at the regional level, as it usually followed South Africa's position.

Once a SADC position has been agreed upon it is taken to the annual meeting of African Trade Ministers which then formulates an African position.

ACP coalition

African, Caribbean and Pacific countries meet before key WTO ministerial conferences to formulate a joint position. Such a coalition ensured the renewal of the Cotonou waiver which was of interest to Botswana. But it also blocked the launching of negotiations on the new issues, of which trade facilitation was of benefit to Botswana. At the Cancún Ministerial Conference, the Botswana Minister of Trade was the spokesperson for the ACP.

3 Challenges faced and the outcome

Negotiating capacity

Considerable capacity is needed for effective participation in the design, enforcement and use of the rules and institutional mechanisms that shape the global economy. As a latecomer to full participation in the trading system and negotiating rounds, Botswana has experienced great difficulty in participating effectively in the WTO processes. The Doha Round presents complex challenges to Botswana: the broadening of the new issues will require additional human and institutional capacity and bring a number of challenges in its wake.

A shortage of staff explains the deficiencies in trade-related expertise and negotiating skills. The country lacks the capacity for effective participation in the negotiation process, and has had a limited impact on the design of the new rules. Knowledge of multilateral and regional trade policies, institutions and agreements is limited. As the WTO process becomes even more complex and technical, it is essential that Botswana develop the capacity to articulate its interests and defend its rights within the WTO framework.

The consensus emerging among the stakeholders who were interviewed is that the Ministry of Trade and Industry, as the co-ordinating ministry on WTO issues, needs to develop an internal capacity by training people to align their skills with the complexity of WTO negotiations. These must come from the non-governmental bodies, government and the private sector.

Trade ministers also tend to be poorly informed on the WTO and regional agreements and rules, and other government officials and private-sector actors tend to be even less knowledgeable. One reason is the high turnover of trade ministers.

Analytical capacity

SADC countries face an enormous task in their efforts to manage the activities arising from the Doha Work Programme. Botswana needs to carry out careful analytical work that identifies what the policy issues are and what Botswana's interests are in the many areas covered by the Doha Declaration. Such analytical issues must be complemented by a solid empirical foundation that accurately reflects local polices and practices.

There is a need to build greater analytical capacity in the research and policy communities, and ensure that this is designed to increase the number of researchers and analysts in the region who are familiar with modern analyses of trade and trade policy and the operation of the global trading system. Improving the quality of policy analysis will lead to better prepared negotiating briefs, through the preparation of high-quality analytical studies designed to illuminate key trade issues. Improved organization and availability of quantitative and qualitative data on trade-related issues and 'demand-driven policy analysis' will assist Botswana in preparing thorough and professional negotiating briefs.

> Data limits our ability to do more analytical work on trade issues. For example, the latest trade data we have is for 2001. How do you expect us to advise on the flow of trade? How can you initiate any anti-dumping investigations with a lag of three years? (Johnson Maiketso, BIDPA researcher)

Involvement of other stakeholders

There is widespread recognition of the need to involve a wide range of other ministries in the consultations in order to benefit from their expertise, sectoral knowledge and contacts. The effectiveness of trade policy-making is constrained by limited government and private-sector access to information on international trade developments, issues and agreements. The dissemination of policy-relevant trade information is often inconsistent.

4 Lessons for others

It is evident that the Ministry of Trade and Industry is key to Botswana's effective participation in the WTO. Weaknesses within it seem to be the root cause of the absence of formal and effective domestic inter-agency co-ordination. Key stakeholders that would otherwise provide valuable input into Botswana's participation in the WTO are not consulted. It is therefore important that structures are instituted that will address the problem. These will include:

improving capacity within the Ministry of Trade and Industry;
improving inter-government consultation; and
improving consultation with other stakeholders.

Capacity of the Ministry of Trade and Industry

Lack of capacity in the lead ministry on WTO issues translates into an inability to have effective inter-agency co-ordination. The Department of International Trade should be responsible for the country's representative office in Geneva. It should be entrusted with the task of inter-ministerial co-ordination of all WTO-related issues, relying on Botswana's permanent representative at the WTO to establish and maintain relationships with other WTO members and the WTO Secretariat.

The Botswana mission in Geneva requires clear instructions from the capital on the positions that should be taken in WTO meetings; and must be able to channel information and briefings to the Department, which in turn should transfer this to the government bodies affected and other stakeholders.

The mission in Geneva should be large enough to allow participation in all major WTO committees and meetings. The current arrangement, with one junior trade officer, is inadequate. The office should provide the Department with regular information and reports on the positions taken by other WTO members; furthermore, the Department should respond in a timely manner after consulting with all the key stakeholders.

The absence of an information centre in the Ministry of Trade and Industry is one of the reasons for poor dissemination of information to stakeholders. An information centre can be given the task of streamlining information flows within the government and to other non-government institutions on WTO-related issues.

Intra-governmental co-ordination

Co-ordination of government positions for negotiations should be conducted through an inter-ministerial group, which should co-ordinate the different points of view of the ministries with an interest in the negotiating process and elaborate Botswana's position for WTO negotiations. The group should also follow up on the implementation of agreements reached at the WTO and hold regular meetings and facilitate regular technical exchanges between relevant ministries.

Seminars on WTO issues and processes for ministry officials not directly involved in the negotiations should be organized; this will stimulate the interest of other government departments as they will begin to see their roles in WTO negotiations.

There is need to develop a strong co-ordination process between Geneva and the capital that will include reports, feedback and relevant minutes of meetings sent from Geneva to the capital and the sending of representatives. The inter-ministerial group should invite officials from Geneva, on an ad hoc basis, to brief meetings held in the capital.

Consultation with other stakeholders

There is a great potential for private-sector organizations to contribute to Botswana's participation in the WTO. For example, the Exporters Association of Botswana is an indigenous business organization with a wealth of knowledge on small to medium-sized business operations; BIDPA has established a reputation for rigorous, thorough and balanced policy research and analysis that informs major public policy initiatives.

Botswana should advocate an open and transparent approach to trade negotiations and use a broad range of consultation mechanisms to seek the views of stakeholders. The Ministry of Trade and Industry should meet frequently with all the stakeholders, including the country's negotiating team for economic partnership agreements (EPAs) and other regional and multilateral trade agreements, to keep them informed of progress in the negotiations and to answer specific questions they may have. Through the Joint Integrated Technical Assistance Programme (JITAP), Botswana has set up a high-level national trade policy negotiating committee. The committee, expected to meet regularly for an update on all trade negotiations and to plan future trade negotiations, encompasses all relevant ministries

and government departments, public institutions, private-sector organizations, NGOs and academic and research institutions. However, the
Ministry of Trade and Industry has not provided this committee with
the leadership it requires to ensure regular meetings and the exchange of
information.

7

Brazil and the G20 group of developing countries

PEDRO DA MOTTA VEIGA*

1 Introduction

It is widely known that Brazil, as a major exporter of agricultural and
agro-industrial goods, has adopted an offensive stance in negotiations
on the liberalization of trade in agriculture taking place in the WTO, as
well as in other negotiating processes. In line with this Brazil has participated actively in the Cairns Group – a coalition of developed and
developing countries exporting agricultural products – both during and
after the Uruguay Round. As the launching of a new multilateral round
of trade negotiations was being discussed, Brazil pushed for including in
the agenda ambitious goals related to market access and the reduction
or elimination of export and domestic support schemes. Moreover, in
the Free Trade Area of the Americas (FTAA) and EU–Mercosur negotiations, Brazil has presented proposals consistent with those developed in
the multilateral arena.

However, in the months preceding the WTO Ministerial Conference
in Cancún in September 2003, an interesting process of strategy-shifting
took place, involving Brazil's stance in negotiations on agriculture.

Without breaking with the Cairns Group and giving up its pro-trade
liberalization stance in agricultural negotiations, Brazil led the setting of
an issue-based developing countries' coalition aimed at bargaining jointly
during the Ministerial Conference and beyond. This new coalition, the
G20, brought together developing countries which traditionally adopted
differing – even opposed – positions in the agricultural negotiations in
the WTO; the simultaneous presence of Argentina and India in the group
is the best example of this novelty.

It is worth noting that the shift in Brazil's negotiations strategy was
driven not only by the internal dynamics of the agricultural negotiations

in the WTO, but also by a broader shift in the country's foreign economic policies – especially in its trade negotiations strategy – towards a view where the North–South axis acquired a growing relevance. Brazil's leadership in the setting of the G20 is perhaps the best example, at the multilateral level, of the country's new 'southern' stance in trade negotiations.

2 The local and external players: roles and interaction

One of the more interesting features of the decision-making process leading to the establishment of the G20 was that it involved intensive interaction between public and private domestic actors and between these actors and external players. Even more interestingly, the domestic and external dynamics became more and more interconnected as the G20 was set up and became a relevant player in agricultural negotiations at the WTO.

The 'domestic' interplay involved continuous co-ordination between public agencies and between public- and private-sector representatives, leading to the setting up of new structures and institutions, including a non-governmental organization (NGO) focused on technical research related to agricultural negotiations which is financed by the main private associations of the Brazilian agribusiness.

On the domestic front, the adoption by Brazil of increasingly assertive and autonomous positions in agricultural trade negotiations has been backed, in structural terms, by the impressive modernization Brazilian agribusiness underwent during the 1990s.

By the late 1980s, agricultural exports concentrated on primary goods – coffee, cocoa and cotton, among others – and were strongly regulated by state-owned sectoral bodies. As a consequence of this and until the beginning of the 1990s, the private sector did not show a great deal of interest in trade negotiations, and the participation of agribusiness representatives in the Uruguay Round was very timid. During the negotiations to launch the sub-regional integration process, the private sector adopted an essentially defensive stance, focused on the alleged risks of competition in the domestic market arising from the elimination of tariffs among Mercosur member countries.

From 1995 onwards, driven by large investments, a strong expansion of agribusiness productivity took place in Brazil. This process speeded up at the end of the decade, and sector representatives began to push the government to adopt more aggressive negotiating positions in agriculture, in the FTAA and EU–Mercosur trade talks. In the WTO, the new position taken by the private sector was crucial for the government's decision to ask for the setting up of agricultural-products-related dispute settlement panels in their actions against the United States and the European Union (EU).

In early 2003, summing up these evolutions in attitudes, the Brazilian Minister of Agriculture called for the adoption of an 'autonomous position' in the agricultural negotiations, a position which also reflected – as shown below – some disappointment towards the recent performance of the Cairns Group. At that time, the main sectoral Brazilian agribusiness associations created a research institute geared to providing technical support to the ongoing agricultural negotiations at the WTO as well as at the preferential fora.

As the so-called 'Harbinson paper' was made public in the WTO talks, during the first half of 2003 a working group, created as a joint initiative by the ministries of Agriculture and Foreign Affairs, undertook a cautious and detailed analysis of the paper, criticizing it and formulating technically sound proposals on each of the points it raised. Later on, the working group expanded to integrate other ministries, governmental agencies and private representatives related to the agriculture and agribusiness sectors.

A similar position was adopted once the joint EU–US document on agriculture was made public, in the weeks preceding the Cancún Ministerial Conference: 'the day after the document was issued, the working technical group began to work on this new proposal, analyzing and assessing each paragraph, deconstructing it', according to a participant of the group from the private sector.

On the external front, the political origin of this coalition can be traced back to the Brasilia Declaration signed between Brazil, India and South Africa in June 2003. According to the Brazilian Minister of Foreign Affairs, the G20 'was not born in Cancún or in Geneva, during the weeks preceding the WTO Ministerial Conference. It emerged from the political trust built up between Brazil, India and South Africa some months earlier.'

The creation of the new coalition also seems to be related to a growing feeling of disappointment with the Cairns Group and its positions on agricultural negotiations before Cancún.

In the view of a private-sector representative, the WTO informal mini-ministerial, held in Egypt in July 2003, made it explicit that Australia was exerting the strongest leadership within the Cairns Group; however, it did not wish to adopt a more aggressive stance in the negotiations, favouring instead the EU–US bilateral understanding as a first step towards untying the agricultural knot in the multilateral negotiations. According to this private sector representative, 'the G20 began to emerge in Egypt, when it became clear that Australia and the Cairns Group would not seek to counterbalance the EU and US common interests'.

The timid reaction of the Cairns Group to the EU–US joint document on agriculture – issued some weeks before Cancún – strengthened the incentives, on the Brazilian side, to look for political alternatives to what was being perceived as a new Blair House Agreement, excluding the interests of developing countries. As a Brazilian diplomat put it, 'Cairns was paralyzed and Brazil seized the opportunity created by this "leadership vacuum" to gather support to its paper in Geneva'.

However, the document prepared by the public–private working group in Brasilia turned out to be very aggressive as far as market access demands were concerned. In the view of high-level officials, this stance could isolate Brazil in the negotiations, jeopardize efforts to build a coalition around the Brazilian paper, and compromise the objective – most valued by the Brasilia authorities – of attracting some of the most important developing countries to this new coalition.

One of the consequences of this, according to a Brazilian diplomat, was that

> Brazil had to reduce its ambition in market access issues in order to gather the support of India and China for its demands against developed countries' domestic and export subsidies. It had also to emphasize the idea of proportionality of concessions to be made during the negotiations: developing countries were supposed to pay less than the developed ones in the agricultural negotiations.[1]

The historical evolution of G20 also includes a period of intense activity in Geneva prior to Cancún. As a Brazilian diplomat puts it,

> the group met frequently at the level of heads of delegation in Geneva prior to Cancún. The group also met (and continues to meet) at the technical level to discuss specific proposals in the context of the WTO agriculture negotiations, and to prepare technical papers in support of the group's adopted common platform. The frequent contacts and meetings at the ministerial level in Cancún further consolidated the group and made it possible for the G20 to resist the strong pressure to break its common position.

---

[1] It is worth noting that, within the Brazilian Government, divergent positions did exist as far as the agricultural negotiations were concerned: the ministry in charge of the agrarian reform and issues relating to the small-scale agriculture supported defensive positions in these negotiations, while the Ministry of Agriculture had a strongly pro-liberal stance, supported by the modern agribusiness sectors. Hence, the G20 platform, less ambitious in the market access issue and more attentive to developing countries' concerns related to food security and small-scale agriculture, helped to generate a broad domestic consensus around the official position.

In the words of a leading negotiator,

> Since its inception the G20 had established close relationships with other groups in the WTO with a special interest in the agricultural negotiations. The G20 is not a closed group. On the contrary, it is open to the participation of other interested countries that share its objectives and positions. It is thus only natural for the group to have close contacts with other groups. A majority of G20 countries are members of the Cairns Group and there is a large degree of coincidence between the positions of both groups which naturally support each other and try to co-operate for their common purpose: the faithful implementation of the Doha mandate.

The frequent contacts with other groups and coalitions did not jeopardize the identity of the newly born G20. Making reference to the relationship between the G20 and the Cairns Group, a Brazilian diplomat stressed that

> each has its own personality. The G20 tries to strike a balance between the interests of trade liberalization and the development objectives of its members. Cairns is more focused on trade liberalization. Their respective agendas and interests coincide as regards the need to end trade-distorting policies in agriculture and for the opening of developed countries' markets. The difference lies in the definition of special and differential treatment for developing countries, especially in the area of market access. The G20 clearly accepts the need for a dual approach to market access that fully takes into account the needs of rural development and the situation of countries with a large rural population. The Cairns Group acknowledges in its platform the need for special and differential treatment for developing countries, but defends – as is only natural due to its composition, where major exporters of agricultural products play a central role and where developed and developing countries are present – a policy more committed to open markets in agriculture, in both developed and developing countries.

As the G20 is composed only of developing countries and as it tries to combine the broader interests of economic and social development, especially in rural areas, with trade liberalization, it has established strong ties to other developing country groups: 'the African Group recognized the existence of common ground with the G20 in the Cairo Communiqué and some African countries have joined the group since Cancún. Others have indicated their interest in the group's work and may join in the future', according to a high ranking diplomat.

These ties and contacts produced some non-negligible impacts on the dynamics of the agricultural negotiations at the Cancún Ministerial

Conference: 'At Cancún, the G20 maintained frequent dialogues with the Cairns Group and the African Group and the G20's reaction to the Derbez text incorporates elements of the position of both groups. In the case of the African Group the issue of cotton was taken up by the G20 as part of its platform.'

3 Challenges and the outcome

The first challenge: the establishment and the composition of the G20

The G20 was created in response to the EU–US text on agriculture. Why the focus on agriculture? The common position reached by the United States and the EU created the risk of reducing the scale of ambition set in Doha with consequences, in the light of the central role of agriculture in the Doha Development Agenda (DDA), for the whole of the Round. And why an alliance of developing countries? The US–EU common paper revived the North–South polarization in a crucial area of negotiation and generated concrete risks of marginalization for the interests of the developing countries in this central issue. The understanding between the two major trading partners had the potential to affect the ambitious targets set at Doha, especially as far as developing countries' interests and development issues were concerned: 'developing countries from both sets of interests came together when they realized that the EU and the United States had joined forces and come up with a text that was highly unsatisfactory'.[2]

Hence the first challenge faced by Brazil's strategy was the setting up of an issue-based coalition composed exclusively of developing countries. On the one hand, southern coalitions – bloc-type coalitions – in trade negotiations were broad in scope but their effectiveness has proved very limited. On the other side, the most successful experience in the setting up of a North–South issue-based coalition – the Cairns Group – had, in the view of Brazilian diplomacy, run out of steam. As stressed by two analysts, 'the coalitions of today, including the G20, having learnt from the failings of their predecessors, utilize some elements of both the bloc-type coalitions and issue-based alliances'.[3]

As emphasized by one of the leading official Brazilian negotiators, 'the establishment of the group and its composition involved a political decision and sent a message to all participants in the Round, especially the

[2] Narlikar and Tussie (2003).
[3] Idem.

developed countries, that there was a new factor to be taken into account in the negotiations. The creation of the group was a political statement.'

According to a representative of the Brazilian private sector, the setting up of G20 'challenged not only the agricultural policies of the developed countries, but the legitimacy of the model adopted by those countries to negotiate in multilateral fora, presenting their agreed position as a fait accompli to developing countries'.

From the Brazilian point of view, the decision to form a coalition of developing countries with heterogeneous interests in the agricultural negotiations represented a significant shift in the country's negotiation position on this issue; it was now driven by the offensive interests of a large exporter but also by the objective of breaking the North–South protectionist front in agricultural negotiations through the setting up of a new 'southern agenda' on agriculture, albeit less ambitious than the Cairns Group's agenda.

The second challenge: building consensus and retaining cohesion in the G20

The second challenge faced by Brazil in the emerging coalition involved the ability to build a consensus among developing countries with heterogeneous interests in the multilateral negotiations on agriculture. Cohesion of the coalition has been a major concern of Brazilian diplomacy, and consensus-building within the G20 required that much attention be directed to the design of negotiating technically consistent proposals in order to avoid the G20 being labelled as a coalition that merely sought to block progress and was uncommitted to a positive outcome for the WTO Ministerial Conference. As a Brazilian diplomat recalled, 'At Cancún, the group not only presented its views and influenced the elaboration of the proposed final text of the conference, but, also, after the presentation of this text, it met for several hours and prepared a number of concrete amendments to the text for the final round of negotiations which unfortunately never took place.'

The co-ordination between technical experts from the Brazilian government and the private sector, and the experience accumulated in Brasília during the months preceding Cancún played here a central role, allowing Brazil – and then the G20 – to develop a sound, substantive position dealing with the complex issues involved in the agricultural negotiations.

The battle to maintain the cohesion of the G20 was described by one of the main Brazilian negotiators at Cancún as follows:

Even before the Ministerial Conference, some developed countries tried to dismiss the group, by refusing to take its proposals seriously and by accusing the group of trying to introduce an ideological dimension in the negotiation, by importing into the WTO positions and tactics that had their origin in the North–South dialogue. This reflected a sort of annoyance with an attempt by a group of developing countries to try to interfere with the agreement between the EU and the United States which should represent the basis for the results on agriculture at Cancún. The attempts by many countries from the G20 and other groups to change the bilateral deal to better reflect their interests were met with a negative reply.

Once the G20 was set up, another battle began at Cancún, as some developed countries attempted to divide the Group and to create difficulties in its relations with other groups in the WTO, especially the Cairns Group and the African Group. In spite of strong pressures put on members of the group, the G20 remained united during the whole of the conference, with the withdrawal of only one delegation from the group. Another delegation, Nigeria, joined the group in the final stages of the meeting. After Cancún a small number of countries also left the group, but others became members, for example Tanzania and Zimbabwe.

The outcome: a high level of legitimacy and Brazil becomes a major player in agricultural negotiations

In spite of criticisms from developed countries and the fact that no agreement on agriculture was reached at the end of the day in Cancún, the G20 was perceived by public opinion, in both the North and the South, as a legitimate and constructive effort by developing countries to advance their interests in the WTO negotiations and to defend the idea, officially agreed in Doha, of a development round.

Since Cancún, the G20 has been widely recognized as a major new player in agricultural negotiations, and one whose interests should be taken into account if some agreement on this issue is to be reached in the WTO. In December 2003 the EU's chief negotiator, Pascal Lamy, participated in the G20 ministerial meeting, held in Brasília, implicitly confirming this understanding. Another G20 ministerial meeting was held in São Paulo in June 2004, and during the first half of 2005 the group embarked on technical and political consultations with a view to injecting momentum in ongoing agricultural negotiations.[4]

The G20 is clearly today an important partner in the agricultural negotiations in the WTO and the five main partners remain in the group.

---

[4] A G20 website was recently created and a link to this website can be found on the homepage of Brazil's Ministry of Foreign Affairs.

The failure of the Cancún Ministerial Conference and the consolidation of the G20 help to explain the Non-Group-5 (NG-5), created in March 2004, which put together three major developed players in the agricultural negotiations (United States, EU and Australia – the leader of the Cairns Group) with Brazil and India, respectively the most liberal and the most protectionist member of the G20.

In the view of Brazilian diplomats and representatives from civil society organizations, once the period of 'blame-shifting' that followed Cancún was left behind, the initiative of setting up the NG-5 reflected the recognition that the process of decision-making in agricultural negotiations had to change to integrate the G20.

Beyond that, the setting up of the NG-5 is considered to be a very important initiative, as the technical and political work of its members paved the way for concrete proposals which proved essential to consensus-building in Geneva on the negotiations framework. As one NGO representative put it, 'After the meeting of the NG-5 in São Paulo in June 2004, consensus was reached among members as far as the export and domestic subsidies were concerned, and the market access issues remained as the only area of dissent. A very important step was made in this meeting, making the work carried out in Geneva in July 2004 easier.'

According to Brazil's Minister of Foreign Affairs, 'The G20 has produced a change in the dynamics of agricultural negotiations, which migrated from the Blair House model to the NG-5 model as far as decision-making is concerned . . . It is not by chance if the text on framework presented for discussion in July 2004 represents a progression from the G20 point of view as compared with the text presented at the beginning of the WTO Ministerial in Cancún.'

The official view in Brazil on the 1 August 'package' is quite positive, although it is widely recognized that a lot of work remains to be done. The adopted framework is perceived as a text which respects the Doha mandate and its level of ambition, and represents a substantial improvement as compared with the text submitted in Cancún as far as agricultural negotiations are concerned.

4 Learning from the experience

The assessment of the strategy of setting up the G20 is widely positive in Brazil, despite the setback of the WTO Ministerial Conference where the coalition made its début. Brazil continues to participate in the Cairns Group, and has made significant efforts to keep the G20 coalition alive and has involved itself – with India – in the NG-5, which put together the major players in the multilateral negotiations on agriculture.

Many lessons can be learnt from the Brazilian experience of setting up the G20, but two will be emphasized here. The first relates to the importance of the domestic dimension in the formulation of the national position on a negotiation issue central to Brazil. The domestic dimension is about political negotiations involving groups with different views and interests as far as trade negotiations are concerned: in the case of Brazil, these negotiations played an important role in shaping the option of building a coalition with other developing countries and in balancing liberalization goals and development objectives.

The technical and institutional component of the domestic dimension in setting up the G20 are worth highlighting. Technical preparation and permanent co-ordination among public agencies and with the private sector helped to build domestic consensus supporting the official position in the negotiations. These mechanisms have been kept active before, during and after the Cancún Ministerial, and it seems correct to assert that they have become more and more dense and complex. Capacity-building initiatives in the private and public sector made their contribution in this way: the Ministry of Agriculture has created a specific institutional structure to deal with trade negotiations in a systematic manner; agribusiness sectoral associations have supported a research institution charged with presenting technical proposals for agricultural negotiations, and they have participated in the Brazilian Business Coalition – a forum representing industrial, agribusiness and services sectors in trade negotiations.

The second lesson refers to the convenience (or not) of replicating the coalition-setting initiative in the area of non-agricultural market access. The assessment of one leading negotiator is clear-cut on this point:

> After Cancún, and in the light of the role the G20 played at the conference, there have been some suggestions that the group could perhaps play a larger role encompassing other areas of the WTO agenda or even the broader agenda of co-operation for development. Perhaps this is only natural and reflects the need that is felt in many quarters for a new coalition to revitalize the debate on development issues in international fora. This is even more true in the light of growing fatigue with orthodox adjustments, self-regulating market forces as an answer to development problems and the negative aspects of globalization. Nevertheless, the G20 is perhaps not the answer and to try to expand the mandate of the group would possibly jeopardize its unity. One of the strengths of the G20 is its ability to combine a political stance with a focused approach to agricultural negotiations.

Bibliography

Brazilian Mission in Geneva (2003 and 2004), *Carta de Genebra*, various issues.

Hugueney Filho, C. (2004), 'The G20: Passing Phenomenon or Here To Stay?', processed.

Jank, M. S. and M. Q. Monteiro Jales (2004), 'On Product, Box and Blame-Shifting: Negotiating Frameworks for Agriculture in the WTO Doha Round', ICONE, 14 May.

Narkilar, A. and D. Tussie (2003). 'Bargaining Together in Cancún: Developing Countries and their Evolving Coalitions', mimeo.

8

Cambodia's accession to the WTO: 'fast track' accession by a least developed country

SAMNANG CHEA AND HACH SOK[*]

1 The problem in context

In 1994, Cambodia applied for membership of the WTO. Following the Doha Declaration of November 2001 that eased membership conditions for least developed counties, Cambodia's membership was finally approved in September 2003 at the Cancun Ministerial Conference. However, membership did not become effective until a year later because an internal political deadlock in Cambodia after the July 2003 elections delayed ratification.

Some Cambodian policy players were surprised by approval of Cambodia's membership of the WTO, as negotiations had been conducted without the active participation of stakeholders. There was neither comprehensive research nor public debate on the costs and benefits of joining. According to a survey done by the Economic Institute of Cambodia just days after this approval, more than half of Cambodians living in Phnom Penh, the capital, had never heard of the WTO.[1] None of the country's parliamentarians knew about the substance of the negotiations. The government was expected to reveal detailed agreements with the WTO at the ratification debate in the National Assembly. Critics say that Cambodia has just thrown itself in at the deep end by becoming a member of the WTO.

With an estimated average per capita income of US$300, Cambodia is the poorest and least developed country in the east Asian region, and one of the poorest in the world.[2] Since its emergence from war and upheaval,

---

[*] Samnang Chea is a researcher at the Economic Institute of Cambodia, specializing in the WTO and globalization. Hach Sok is Director of the Economic Institute of Cambodia.
[1] EIC, 'An EIC Survey – WTO and Social Justice', *EIC Annual Report* 1, October 2004.
[2] EIC, 'Cambodia's Economic Developments and Reform Progress in 2003–2004', *EIC Economic Watch*, 1, October 2004.

Cambodia has been very keen for economic recovery, to integrate itself into the world community by means of internal reforms. Though initial reforms have produced some positive results, the country is still plagued with major socio-economic problems. Its engine of growth for the past few years – the garment industry – is facing uncertainty and is looking towards the WTO for solutions.

The government and some business people have high expectations of WTO membership. They expect it to help protect and expand markets for Cambodian garment exports and other products after the removal of US quotas from 2005, even though Cambodian industries have not been well known for their cost-effectiveness and competitiveness. Civil society members are more sceptical, as apparently membership comes with many conditions with which the country as a whole may not be able to comply, even with a five-year grace period. There seem to be reasonable doubts that the benefits will really exceed the costs associated with membership.

To some, however, the conditions imposed for WTO accession may just be what the country needs for genuine institutional and policy reforms. Cambodia will indeed have a steep learning curve. It is, in effect, a litmus test according to which accession will make or break the country after its ratification by the National Assembly.

The objective of this case study is to tell the story of Cambodia's accession process, and the ways in which policy-makers, the private sector and civil society perceive and deal with the issues of WTO membership.

2 The roles of stakeholders in the accession process

The membership application

Given the important role of international trade in alleviating poverty and promoting economic growth, Cambodia initiated ambitious preliminaries to becoming a member of the Association of South East Asian Nations (ASEAN) and the WTO. The Cambodia government filed an official WTO application on 8 December 1994, and a working party was established two weeks later to consider it. According to Lu Laysreng, then Under-Secretary of State for Commerce, the Council of Ministers agreed to push for Cambodian entry into the WTO: 'It is very important for Cambodia to join the WTO, because it provides facilities for us to move into a world association of business people.' Cambodia then started to work on a number of issues that had to be resolved to enable

Cambodia to join the WTO, including lower tariff rates, the adoption of an accounting system based on the Anglo-Saxon model, and the adoption of a hybrid legal system integrating Anglo-Saxon and French standards.[3]

After attending the four-day ministerial conference in Singapore in December 1996 as a new official observer, Cambodia understood that it was not easy to be a WTO member, but the Minister of Commerce, Cham Prasidh, remained determined: 'Cambodia will enter the WTO after the country joins ASEAN ... by the end of 1997,' he said. 'If we are late joining the WTO, we are alone in trade', he warned.[4]

Membership was delayed due to political turmoil and state institutions that were not ready. Street fighting in July 1997 between the two ruling coalition parties delayed the plan to join ASEAN, which effectively slowed down the WTO accession process. There were many other issues, including the judicial system, administrative reform and trade policy, that needed to be considered to comply with WTO standards. It was not until April 1999 that Cambodia was permitted to join ASEAN, a milestone for the country's economic integration.

In June 1999 a memorandum on Cambodia's foreign trade regime was submitted to the WTO, consisting of more than 100 pages answering 179 questions asked by the organization. In January 2001, questions and answers relating to the memorandum and conditions for accession were circulated.[5] Cambodia organized five sets of multilateral negotiations through a working party from June 2001 to July 2003, and nine bilateral agreements from August 2001 to August 2003.

The speed of the accession process seemed to accelerate after the Doha Round held in November 2001, just two months after the terrorist attack on the World Trade Center in the United States. One of the great achievements of the Doha Round was the Doha Declaration, which would help least developed countries to join the world trading system more easily. During his visit to Cambodia just after the Doha Round, WTO Director-General Mike Moore declared that he would be very disappointed if Cambodia did not become a member within the next year, before he left his post on 1 September 2002. However, he played down his ambitious view, stating, 'It is always difficult work, and there is much to be

---

[3] Ek Madra, 'Cambodia to Press for WTO Membership', *Cambodia Daily*, 4 March 1996, p. 11.

[4] Ek Madra, 'Commerce Minister Sees WTO by End of 1997', *Cambodia Daily*, 16 Dec. 1996, p. 12.

[5] WTO, 'Accession of Cambodia: Questions and Replies', January 2001.

done ... It is especially difficult when there is a vacuum [here] of public administration and public laws.'[6]

In August 2001 a team of experts from six world organizations came to Cambodia to assess the country's ability to join the WTO. Funded by a trust fund provided by donors, managed by the World Bank, the team spent three weeks researching and assessing Cambodia's strengths and weaknesses in preparation for its possible entry into the WTO. Cambodia was selected as one of three pilot countries to receive integrated framework attention. 'This is a pro-poor trade strategy', according to Sandy Cuthbertson of the Centre for International Economics.[7] The first public forum on Cambodia's effort to join, gathering together experts, government officials and civil society, was held in August 2002.[8]

The negotiation process

The working party met for the first time on 16 April 2003 to consider the memorandum, and on 22 July it indicated that Cambodia would become a member of the WTO in September 2003. At Cancún in Mexico, on 11 September 2003, WTO ministers approved Cambodia's membership agreements, and invited the country to become the 147th member. It would have been the first least developed country to join the WTO through a full working party negotiation process. However, Cambodia's parliament had yet to ratify the agreed terms, and because of the delay Nepal instead became the first least developed country to enter the WTO. Cambodia had to wait until early September 2004, when the Cambodian parliament unanimously ratified accession to the WTO after the resolution of the political impasse.

Not many had known about the membership, however. Just after the Cambodian protocol of accession was approved by the WTO in September 2003, the Economic Institute of Cambodia (EIC), a newly established think tank institute, conducted a survey in Phnom Penh among workers, business people and leaders of civil society, on Cambodia's accession to the WTO. Only 40% of workers and 50% of small and medium-sized business had heard of the WTO. During a forum organized by EIC on

---

[6] Matt Reed, 'Director of WTO Says Quick Entry a Matter of Gov't Will', *Cambodia Daily*, 28 Nov. 2001, p. 14.

[7] Brian Calvert, 'Panel: Cambodia's Fitness To Join WTO under Review', *Cambodia Daily*, 9 Aug. 2001, p. 14.

[8] Richard Sine, 'Public Forum Debates Virtues, Vices of WTO', *Cambodia Daily*, 22 Aug. 2002, p. 14.

29 October 2003, about a month and a half after Cambodia was invited to join the WTO, many civil society members expressed their concerns about the possible negative impacts of WTO accession on the poor, but they still felt confident that Cambodia could overcome these challenges. 'We cannot reverse our decision on WTO membership. Our motto is that we must take risks, otherwise there is no change,' said Keat Sokun of the Cambodia Centre for Human Rights.[9]

According to some in civil society, Cambodia had been inspired since 1994 to join this global trading club, but the information was not widespread, especially in the private sector. Only the Ministry of Commerce and few line ministries were actively involved and participated in the accession process.

Cambodia may not, nevertheless, have done enough homework before joining the world trade body. Raoul M. Jennar of Oxfam Belgium maintained a critical view: 'Negotiations were conducted in the highest secrecy. There was no debate at the National Assembly, or in the press, or among NGOs... Government, parliamentarians, journalists and associations all share the responsibility for this silence... Government negotiators rejected any assistance offered by international NGOs and only listened to WTO propagandists... One can regret that Cambodians did not wonder during the negotiations and that they did not consult the 29 least developed countries who are members of the WTO.'[10] Oxfam-GB's country director Michael Bird also felt that 'very little work has been done to assess the kinds of impacts of WTO policies'.[11]

However, the government rejected these assessments. Sok Siphana, Secretary of State for Commerce, refuted the statement: 'we have to have WTO accession because the fate of 220,000 workers is at stake, if we don't enter'.[12]

The ratification of WTO membership

After eleven months of political deadlock, Cambodia finally had a government and the National Assembly began the ratification process. During the debate in the National Assembly on 31 August 2004, Assembly

[9] 'Quotable Quotes', *EIC Economic Review*, 2, November 2003, p. 16.

[10] 'National Assembly Ratifies Entry to WTO', *Business Press Review*, 6–12 Sept. 2004, p. 8.

[11] Michael Coren, 'WTO Reforms: Commercial Court Seen as Key Problem', *Phnom Penh Post*, 23 May–5 June 2003.

[12] Bill Bainbridge, 'Mexican Wave: WTO Set to Welcome Cambodia', *Phnom Penh Post*, 29 Aug. 2003.

President Prince Norodom Ranariddh said, 'the vote approving Cambodia's WTO accession gave the country a space in history among other poor nations inside the global trade group'.[13] And the opposition party had no objection to the WTO accession, but articulated many anxieties. 'I think entering into the WTO is necessary; it is a global force. There is no country, especially small and poor country like Cambodia, that cannot be marginalized by this global trend, so we must encourage and push to be a full member of the WTO,' said opposition leader Sam Rainsy.[14] The accession to the WTO was unanimously ratified by the Cambodian parliamentarians, and Cambodia would officially become a member of the WTO in mid-October 2004.

The journey Cambodia embarked upon to join the WTO was like running a marathon, according to Suos Someth, Cambodia's first permanent representative at the WTO and ambassador to the UN agencies: 'You may not be the winner, but you will run the 42 kilometres like the others instead of staying outside the competition and watching the others run.' Cambodia's progress should be viewed optimistically. 'It takes a long time to build a nation. Economic growth indicators may paint a bleak picture ... they are only indicators to say where we are going.'[15]

Cambodia is hoping that WTO membership will facilitate its trade negotiation with other economies. As a small country it may not have the bargaining power to negotiate bilaterally with developed countries, but 'If we don't have the WTO, it would be a much longer wait because you have to knock on one door at a time',[16] says Secretary of State for Commerce Sok Siphana. Cambodia can use the WTO as an international force to negotiate.

WTO membership will offer Cambodia access to the world market that is expected to attract both local and foreign direct investment to help overcome its current weak production capacity. As Cambodia intends to change anyway, it can incorporate the changes imposed by the WTO that are indeed challenges that the country wants to turn into opportunities and benefits. But this can be achieved only if the government has the political will to remove the trade constraints that have stifled the private sector. Accession is expected to force reform in both legal and economic

[13] 'National Assembly Ratifies Entry to WTO', *Business Press*, 6–12 Sept. 2004, p. 1.

[14] Sam Rainsy, debate in the National Assembly, 31 Aug. 2004.

[15] Michelle Vachon, 'New WTO Representative Optimistic for Economy's Future', *Cambodia Daily*, 31 Oct. 2001, p. 10.

[16] Bill Bainbridge, 'Mexican Wave: WTO Set to Welcome Cambodia', *Phnom Penh Post*, 29 Aug. 2003.

policy. The country can benefit fully from globalization if, and only if, all economic players participate in optimizing their benefit. The role of the government is vital in involving the private sector, farmers and civil society in trade, requiring genuine reform and strong political will.

3 The challenges ahead

The primary objective of Cambodia in becoming a member of the WTO is to protect its fledgling garment industry after the removal of export quotas at the end of 2004 under the Multi-Fibre Agreement (MFA) arrangements, which will be applicable to all members of the WTO. The industry has become a significant part of the Cambodian economy and needs to be sustained. It is estimated it employs more than 200,000 workers, and indirectly contributes to the livelihood of more than 1 million in rural areas. By 2002, garment exports had grown to form up to 96% of the country's total exports of goods, from about nil six years previously. About 70% of garment exports have gone to the United States, and were Cambodia not a member of the WTO, the United States might have imposed a high import tariff which would almost certainly have ensured a quick collapse of the non-competitive Cambodian garment industry, rife as it is with high bureaucratic costs.

The market niche

The garment industry itself seems to aim for a market niche that gives its products some competitive advantage – the offer of products that are produced by workers whose labour rights are upheld. Sok Siphana of the Ministry of Commerce says, 'Companies will always go to China for their profit, yet profit alone is not always the basis for business; image-conscious multinationals will continue using Cambodia because of our high labour standards.'[17]

The Garment Manufacture Association of Cambodia (GMAC) – it was most active in pushing Cambodia towards WTO membership – continues to welcome the International Labour Organization (ILO) inspection of working conditions at garment factories to ensure the support of the human-rights-conscious buyers in the marketplace. According to Ray Chew of GMAC, 'We need to promote a national brand name based

---

[17] Daniel Ten Kate, 'Can Cambodia's Garment Industry Survive?' *Cambodia Daily*, 6–7 Sept. 2003, p. 4.

on compliant labour standards. Today, buyers are talking about social accountability.'[18]

On the government side, efforts to reduce negative social impacts are also expressed: 'We have to educate workers about the influence of globalization, and push employers to respect labour laws in their factories,' states Ing Kunthaphavi, then secretary of state for Women's Affairs and Veterans.

It remains to be seen, however, just how much business will be retained simply by Cambodia's reputation for good labour standards.[19] 'How much we can link the ILO and labour law to increase sale remains to be seen,' said Tan Keat Chong, general manager of PCCS Garments Ltd. 'If that can be achieved, there is a fighting chance this industry can survive.'[20]

Nevertheless, experts think that this kind of niche market can succeed only in the short term. In the long run, it may not be possible to sustain an industry growth that is largely driven by competition in costs and product quality. The cost of labour compliance will help to make total production costs uncompetitive. According to a GMAC study on the survival of the garment industry after the bilateral textile agreement expires, buyers still insist on lower prices regardless of Cambodia's high labour standards.

Government officials, however, are optimistic that the country will retain jobs created by the volatile garment industry. Minister of Commerce Cham Prasidh maintains, 'After joining the WTO, the garment industry will not move anywhere, but will stay in Cambodia. While some garment factories want to move to China, there are twenty-six new companies applying to open new factories. So the existing will stay and the newcomers will move in because there will be quota free conditions after 2004. Cambodia introduces a strategy to link international trade to labour conditions.'[21]

Legislation and reform implementation

The challenges facing Cambodia in this area are twofold: enacting all necessary reform legislation for membership in time and carrying it out. As part of its accession to the WTO, Cambodia has made a large number of commitments in legal and judicial system reforms, including the

---

[18] 'Quotable Quotes', *EIC Economic Review*, November 2003, p. 16.   [19] Ibid.
[20] Daniel Ten Kate, 'Can Cambodia's Garment Industry Survive?' *Cambodia Daily*, 6–7 Sept. 2003, p. 4.
[21] Cham Prasidh, debate in the National Assembly, 31 Aug. 2004.

enforcement of the rule of law and the establishment of a specialized commercial court. According to a government source, forty-seven laws and
regulations are needed to fulfil WTO membership requirements. Fourteen
laws and regulations have already been adopted, while the other thirty-
three are to be passed within the next two years. However, the political
deadlock after the elections of July 2003 has already delayed this ambitious scheduling. Effectively, the schedule imposes the passing of more
than two laws and sets of regulations per legislative working month. On
past experience, however, the Cambodian parliament is not likely to meet
the deadline; it has, on average, taken three months to adopt a piece of
legislation.

If carried out properly, these commitments would stimulate other
related economic reforms that will be conducive to improving investor
confidence. Cambodia has committed itself to drastic institutional
reforms that will supposedly take place during a transitional period of
five years, under the Doha Agreement on a least developed country
accession. Given the current weak administration and institutions, it is
highly unlikely that those reforms will be achieved unless there is a genuinely strong political will. Cham Prasidh, Minister of Commerce, warns,
'Whether Cambodia will fully benefit from the WTO depends on what it
will achieve in the future. WTO gives Cambodia a lot of opportunities,
but it is not sure that the opportunities will become a full comparative
advantage if we do not do some necessary reforms, such as administration
and legal reform.'[22]

Increasing supply capacity for exports

On the business front, improving the competitiveness of the private sector
will be a prime challenge for Cambodia. WTO membership will open foreign markets to Cambodian exports as well as opening the local market to
imports. To survive, and perhaps prosper, in either one or both of the markets, the Cambodian private sector will need to be competitive to take on
the world. The current indication is that the local production sector may
have difficulties in competing with foreign producers. Business people
consistently cite increasing corruption and lack of available credit as the
two most important constraints that have prevented the sector from being
more competitive and attracting appropriate long-term investments. The
opposition leader agrees that WTO membership will open up the market

[22] Ibid.

for domestic producers, but questions whether Cambodia can take advantage of the larger market:

> WTO will give possibilities and a global market to the farmers, artisans, craftsman and producers. If we don't have that market, we cannot go to mass production and cheap products ... Joining the WTO is a necessary component but not sufficient. There are many other necessary jobs to do to achieve the objectives ... You have the right to sell to the global market, but ask yourself what can you really sell to those markets? You have the right to sell, but you have nothing to sell, so what for?[23]

The first concern of trade liberalization is the issue of reciprocity of benefit, and the government needs to ensure that the country will have sufficient production capacity to benefit from the larger market. Cambodia is classified as an import country with limited production capacity, and seems unlikely to have a larger production capacity soon. The government also expresses the same concerns. According to Under-Secretary of State Chhim Narith at the Ministry of Commerce, Cambodia will not get any benefit from the WTO, if it does not have its own products or factories.

The decision to join the WTO was made without any real analysis of its advantages, says Jean Claude Levasseur, Representative of the UN Food and Agriculture Organization. 'If we do not help people build their own capacities, the WTO will not help them ... Cambodian rice is not popular yet, meaning that farmers need to make major changes before rice becomes a viable export.'[24] The main problem, according to the executive director of CEDAC,[25] Yang Saing Koma, is that Cambodia is not well prepared. He says that farmers now produce mainly for themselves; it will take a long time before they can produce enough and become sufficiently organized to enter the market. He believes that export-oriented agriculture will favour large agribusiness interest rather that the majority of Cambodia's poor.

Thus the benefit of the WTO may be limited because of Cambodia's weak production capacity, and disadvantages could increase. Cambodia has experienced a current-account deficit of more than 10%. Opening the door to foreign goods may increase the deficit, thereby increasing the difficulty for the government financing either through reserves or by borrowing, or both. Moreover, liberalizing trade in services will open the market for foreign competition that may suffocate local suppliers, including

---

[23] Sam Rainsy, debate in the National Assembly, 31 Aug. 2004.
[24] Alex Halperin, 'Can Cambodian Rice Ever Make It in the World?', *Cambodia Daily*, 6–7 Sept. 2003, p. 6.
[25] Cambodian Centre for Agricultural Studies and Development.

small and medium-sized enterprises. There will always be industries in which foreign competitors are more efficient than domestic producers. When import barriers are lowered, the foreign producers will be able to attract the domestic consumers with lower prices and high quality. Domestic firms competing in those markets will face downward pressure on sale and profit, which in turn can lead to lower wages, job losses and perhaps even company closure.

'Cambodia has nothing to export to the potential global market and on the other hand, foreigners send their products to Cambodian market, taking the market share from Khmer farmers. Cambodian products cannot compete with the neighbouring countries; how would we compete in the global market if we cannot even compete in our own market,'[26] asks Sam Rainsy. The government maintains that since the local market has been virtually free up to now, it has already been so flooded with export products that formal trade liberalization will make little difference. 'Demand from about 13 million people has already been fulfilled; therefore when we join the WTO, I do not expect that it will have a new impact or an inflow of products that have not already reached Cambodia.'[27]

Agriculture issues

Cambodia has basically forgone its rights under WTO membership to use high tariffs and farm subsidies in agriculture, while others are still holding on to them. According to Oxfam, some of the requirements imposed on Cambodia go far beyond what the United States and the European Union are willing to commit themselves to in the present round of negotiations. Tariff ceilings are a case in point. The Cambodian government has committed to limiting its tariff to an average rate of about 30% for agriculture produce and 20% for industrial products.

Cambodia has also agreed not to subsidize its agricultural exports, although under the Agreement on Agriculture, other least developed countries are not required to undertake such a commitment. Critics say that this provision will effectively seal off Cambodia's right under the Agreement on Agriculture to introduce export subsidies on any agricultural product in the future when necessary to protect the livelihood of poor farmers, or to effect development priorities. However, the government argues that the agreement will not affect agricultural development,

[26] Sam Rainsy, debate in the National Assembly, 31 Aug. 2004.
[27] Sok Siphana, debate in the Senate, 6 Sept. 2004.

as Cambodia has never had any export subsidies on agriculture, and the government can always increase its import tariffs on agricultural products to protect local producers. Besides, according to Minister Cham Prasidh, the government is committed to a really free trade environment: 'We are a pragmatic country; Cambodia cannot afford farm subsidies which are not good thing for long-term competitiveness... The government does not believe that the subsidy is a good strategy for sustainable development of the agriculture sector, while the international trend calls for the elimination of the subsidy.'[28]

Given WTO membership, Cambodia needs to live, and perhaps prosper, under a low- or nil-tariff regime. Globalization calls for reduction in tariffs, which are still the main source of government revenue, accounting for 73% of tax revenue. Cambodian tariff rates, at an average of 29%, are already low compared with other least developed countries and Cambodia cannot afford to go lower.[29] Under a succession of International Monetary Fund (IMF) programmes Cambodia has embarked upon a rapid trade liberalization exercise. Average tariff rates have been halved since 1996. A further reform was introduced in 2001, including a sharp reduction in maximum tariff levels. In addition to the shock caused by such rapid reform, the reduction in applied tariff rates demanded by the IMF and the World Bank weakened Cambodia's bargaining position of during the WTO accession process.

Competitiveness

Perhaps one of the most challenging tasks facing Cambodia is to make local industries competitive. Cambodian products are not ready for competition in the global market, since their production costs are not competitive for such reasons as poor infrastructure, high energy prices and corruption. According to a World Bank report[30] the most corrupt government agencies are the customs office and CamControl.[31] 'If these two institutions are not well managed and controlled, it will destroy the Cambodian economy, increase unemployment and make the Cambodian people poorer and poorer', observes Sam Rainsy.

---

[28] Cham Prasidh, debate in the National Assembly, 31 Aug. 2004.
[29] Uy Sambath, official of the Ministry of Economy and Finance.
[30] World Bank, 'Cambodia – Seizing the Global Opportunities: Investment Climate Assessment and Reform Strategy', August 2004.
[31] CamControl is a state institution belong to the Cambodia Import–Export Inspection and Fraud Repression Department at the Ministry of Commerce.

Cambodian agriculture products are not competitive when compared with those of its neighbouring countries, not because of production costs, but because of high trade costs that involve some unregulated practices in the exporting process. But Minister Cham Prasidh explains that in the agriculture sector, the high price of Cambodian products stems from a small economy of scale. Therefore the government will help farmers to form an association from which they will benefit. In addition some corrupt practices in customs valuation will automatically disappear when the government introduces a computerized system.[32]

Protection of intellectual property rights

The implementation of copyright law will affect education and other fields relating to human resource development. In a poor country such as Cambodia, books, CDs and VCDs with copyright simply cannot be afforded because they would be too expensive for the average citizen. Pirated CDs, VCDs, and DVDs as well as copied books, unlicensed films and even imitations of circus performances and pantomimes may soon cease to exist in Cambodia. With the majority of the population earning less than one dollar per day, the enforcement of copyright law would take away the livelihood of thousands, and cut off many from educational and entertainment materials.

4 Concluding remarks

Even though it may not have been well thought through, WTO membership may just be a panacea Cambodia needs in order to improve its own governance and credibility. Cambodia has made a large number of commitments relating to the institutional reforms as part of its terms of accession to the WTO, especially to speed up its legal and judicial system reforms in order to transform Cambodia to a country governed by the rule of law. These commitments, if carried out, would stimulate other related economic reforms to improve investor confidence.

There are many crucial challenges ahead to test the government's resolve to make WTO membership work for the country.

Much more legislation needs to be in place and, perhaps more significantly, to be implemented. The production base needs to expand so that the country can draw benefits from exports to the world market. Industries

---

[32] Cham Prasidh, debate in the National Assembly, 31 Aug. 2004.

and agriculture will have a new regime: growing with low or nil tariffs and no subsidy. Industries are to be competitive. And the protection of intellectual property rights will compel the Cambodian government somehow to make copyright materials available to the country's poor majority.

A market niche is to be built on upholding workers' rights in the expectation that it will help to sustain growth. Indeed, Cambodia has so far enjoyed the quota system granted by the United States, the main reason for the dramatic expansion of its garment industry. It is thus quite clear that the current success of the garment industry depends exclusively on the artificial comparative advantage known as special treatment that will be phased out at the end of 2004. Hence the niche market, such as linkage between labour standards and the market, will be undoubtedly helpful in the short term, while long-term growth will be more dependent on high quality and low-cost labour.

9

Canada and the WTO: multilevel governance, public policy-making and the WTO *Auto Pact Case*

JACQUELINE D. KRIKORIAN*

In 1994 the Canadian Parliament adopted legislation to implement the Uruguay Round with virtually no opposition. The measure was easily passed by the House of Commons with a vote of 185–7.[1] There was general acceptance that the World Trade Organization (WTO) was a necessity for Canada both to participate and to compete in the new international order. Not only did legislators believe that the WTO Agreement would enhance and facilitate Canadian exports, but there also was an expectation among parliamentarians that the new rules-based dispute settlement mechanism would act as a counter-force to US unilateralism in the international arena. Roy MacLaren, the Minister for International Trade, explained that the arrangements would particularly benefit 'small and medium-size trade players like Canada, which are inherently vulnerable to the threat of unilateralism by the economic giants'.[2]

The debates in the House of Commons on the Uruguay Round focused, however, on more than just the merits and advantages of the trade regime. Concerns were expressed about its impact on a number of key Canadian

* Postdoctoral Fellow, York University, Ontario. The author gratefully acknowledges the many individuals who met her to discuss the case and its implications. She also would like to thank David R. Cameron, Dennis DesRosiers, Ran Hirschl, John H. Jackson, Maura Jeffords, Bruno Julien, C. Christopher Parlin, David Schneiderman, Debra Steger, Michael Trebilcock, Robert C. Vipond, and the Fellows at the Institute of International Economic Law at Georgetown University Law Centre, 2001–3, who provided input and assistance with this project in varying capacities.
[1] World Trade Organization Agreement Implementation Act (Bill C–57), c. 47, S.C. 1994. For a more detailed review of the parliamentary measure see Debra P. Steger, 'Canadian Implementation of the Agreement Establishing the World Trade Organization', in John H. Jackson and Alan Sykes, eds., *Implementing the Uruguay Round* (Oxford: Clarendon Press, 1997), 242–83.
[2] Roy MacLaren, Minister for International Trade, *House of Commons Debates* (27 Oct. 1994), 7319.

industries. One such debate pertained to auto manufacturing. Thousands of Canadians in central Canada depended on this sector for employment, and questions were raised about the WTO Agreement's effect on the industry.

The Minister of Trade assured parliamentarians, however, that the new trade regime would not have any negative impact on Canadian automobile sales and production:

> Nothing in the Uruguay Round adversely affects, or indeed affects, the Canadian automobile industry, other than the reduction in tariffs on manufactured goods. It provides greater opportunity for the export of Canadian-made vehicles to third countries beyond the United States. There's certainly nothing adverse in the agreement for the Canadian automobile industry.[3]

In fact, MacLaren advised members of the House of Commons Standing Committee on Foreign Affairs that he actually expected the Japanese to expand their Canadian auto production in the immediate future as both the North American Free Trade Agreement and the Uruguay Round arrangements enhanced 'the opportunity for investment by other automobile companies from overseas'.[4]

Contrary to MacLaren's assurances, however, both Japan and the European Communities filed complaints against Canada[5] targeting the country's auto industry only three years after the adoption of the new trade agreement. Officials from Tokyo and Brussels contended that a bilateral treaty signed by Canada and the United States in 1965 – the Agreement Concerning Automotive Products[6] (Auto Pact) – was both in substance and in implementation inconsistent with the WTO Agreement.

---

[3] Roy MacLaren, Minister for Trade, appearing before the House of Commons Standing Committee on Foreign Affairs and International Trade, *Minutes of Proceedings and Evidence of the Standing Committee on Foreign Affairs and International Trade*, no. 9 (3 Nov. 1994), 22.

[4] Ibid.

[5] *Canada – Certain Measures Affecting the Automotive Industry* – Complaints by Japan (139) and the European Communities (142), report of the Panel, WT/DS139/R and WT/DS142/R, 11 Feb. 2000, report of the Appellate Body, WT/DS139/AB/R and WT/DS142/AB/R, AB–2000–2, 31 May 2000, and Arbitration under Art. 21.3(c) of the *Dispute Settlement Understanding* (DSU), WT/DS139/12 and WT/DS142/12, 4 Oct. 2000, hereinafter referred to as the *Auto Pact Case*. As the European Communities and the Japanese complaints were similar in nature, they were consolidated and heard by a single panel pursuant to Art. 9.1 of the DSU.

[6] Agreement Concerning Automotive Products, Canada and the United States, 16 Jan. 1965, Can. T.S. 1966 No. 14., 17 U.S.T. 1372 (entered into force 16 Jan. 1966) [Auto Pact].

The Auto Pact effectively constituted a sectoral free trade agreement for cars and car parts. As Buddy Drury, Minister of Industry, explained to the House of Commons in 1966, Canada entered into the arrangement with the United States to overcome the problems associated with developing a strong auto-manufacturing base in a small domestic market. Limited production volumes and duties on imported parts effectively prohibited Canadian auto manufacturers from competing in the sector. 'No matter how carefully the Canadian vehicle and parts producers managed their businesses, no matter how diligently they took advantage of the latest technologies, they faced higher costs' than their non-Canadian competitors who operated in larger markets.[7] The Auto Pact remedied this problem by effectively mandating US car companies to increase their production in Canada in order to sell their vehicles duty-free in its domestic market.

From the Canadian perspective, the Auto Pact had proved to be an enormous success over the years. Auto- and auto parts manufacturing in Canada developed and thrived under the policy and the Auto Pact 'evolved into a powerful symbol of prosperity and patriotic pride'.[8] In 1984 alone, for example, Canada produced approximately 1.5 million automobiles that accounted 'for almost a third of the country's $719 million trade surplus'.[9] For a nation of only 25 million, this was no small feat.

Consequently the WTO challenge resulted in significant media attention across the country. Canadians were angry about the matter, as not only had the government in Ottawa assured the public that the country's automobile industry was compatible with the WTO Agreement, but the Auto Pact held a kind of sacred status among Canadians since it had guaranteed employment for thousands of workers over the years. The challenge was viewed as an attack upon the country's policy-making autonomy, and many believed that there would be dire economic consequences if the arrangements were abandoned. Such concerns were further fuelled by North American auto manufacturers who would be adversely affected by any changes to the Auto Pact. Ford Canada President, Bobbie Gaunt, for example, explained that 'scrapping the auto pact would result, within five years, in the loss of 116,000 jobs and a reduction in real GDP of some $10 billion'.[10] Similarly, former trade negotiator Gordon Ritchie,

---

[7] C. M. Drury, Minister of Industry, *House of Commons Debates* (5 May 1966), 4746.

[8] Mary Janigan, 'An Industry on the Line', *Maclean's* (9 Aug. 1999), 40.

[9] Douglas Martin, 'Canada's Lucky Car Industry', *New York Times* (17 Oct. 1984), D1.

[10] Bobbie Gaunt, president, Ford Canada, in a speech to the Saskatoon Chamber of Commerce, quoted in Peter Morton, 'Big Three Want No Changes to Auto Pact', *Financial Post*

retained by the 'Big Three' North American auto manufacturers (General
Motors (GM), DaimlerChrysler and Ford) as a consultant,[11] contended
that any alteration to the status quo 'would unquestionably permit the
Japanese and the European producers to capture a bigger share of the
market over time with production from overseas'.[12]

The United States was not subject to the WTO challenge because it had
obtained a waiver on the major issue of the dispute under the General
Agreement on Tariffs and Trade (GATT). This waiver enabled it to participate in the Auto Pact without adhering to the trade agreement's
most-favoured-nation (MFN) clause. This provision requires contracting
parties to treat like products from other member states similarly despite
their country of origin. Canada never sought a waiver because it originally
implemented the Auto Pact in such a way that allowed any car manufacturer to participate in the programme, thereby avoiding a conflict with
MFN requirements. It was only in 1989 with the passage of the Canada–
US Free Trade Agreement that Canada became susceptible to a challenge,
as it terminated the right of any new auto manufacturers to participate
in the programme. The key issue in this dispute, therefore, pertained to
the manner in which Canada had implemented the Auto Pact since the
1980s.

The WTO challenge posed a significant problem for the government
of Canada in two respects. On the one hand, the Auto Pact had become a
national symbol for Canadians. The WTO complaint created a public relations problem for officials in Ottawa, who had emphasized the value of the
WTO for the country without expressly acknowledging any of its potential implications. Second, the government was subject to intense pressure
by domestic stakeholders who benefited from the agreement. The way
in which the Auto Pact was put into effect provided a competitive edge
to some of the country's most important employers. The Big Three had
a real economic stake in the maintenance of the status quo because it
provided them with a significant advantage over their Japanese and European competitors. The Canadian Auto Workers union (CAW) actively
supported the North American auto manufacturers who employed its
workers.

(13 Sept. 1997), 5. See also similar comments made by Buzz Hargrove, president, Canadian Auto Workers (CAW), 'It's the End of the Line, Canada is Terminating a Model Trade
Agreement', *Globe and Mail* (19 Feb. 2001), A11.
[11] Greg Keenan, 'Big Three Hire Lobbyist Gordon Ritchie to Advise Companies as Ottawa
Reviews Auto Policy', *Globe and Mail* (10 Dec. 1996), B16.
[12] Gordon Ritchie, quoted in Janigan, 'An Industry on the Line'.

1 *The Auto Pact Case*

In 1965 the Auto Pact and the measures Canada adopted to implement it – the Motor Vehicles Tariff Order (MVTO) and the Special Remission Orders (SROs) – allowed a company that made automobiles in Canada to import cars and car parts duty-free if two main conditions were met. First, it had to maintain a minimum production-to-sales ratio based on its 1964 model year. Effectively, this meant that for every car sold in Canada, one car had to be made in Canada. Second, a car manufacturer had to achieve a minimum level of Canadian value added (CVA) in its local production that was at least equivalent to that which existed in its 1968 model year. In addition to the CVA requirements set out in the Canadian implementation measures, those car makers participating in the Auto Pact in 1965 – Ford, General Motors, DaimlerChrysler (then Chrysler) and American Motors – provided officials in Ottawa with letters that not only explained how they intended to implement the Auto Pact, but also additional CVA undertakings.

Under the terms of the Auto Pact, only cars and car parts imported from the United States that met the production-to-sales ratio and CVA requirements were entitled to the duty-free programme. In its implementation of the treaty however, Canada extended the same duty-free treatment to all GATT members. Consequently, auto manufacturers from other countries, such as Volvo from Sweden, were entitled to the same duty-free terms on meeting the CVA and production-to-sales ratio requirements. Moreover, the way in which Canada implemented the agreement also made it possible for auto manufacturers such as Ford to bring, for example, Brazilian-made engines into Canada free of duty – giving the Brazilians and others a stake in the operation of the system as well.

The extended eligibility for non-US auto manufacturers for the duty-free treatment ended, however, in 1989 with the Canada–US Free Trade Agreement. At the insistence of the US trade negotiators, this treaty closed the right of other companies to participate in the Auto Pact.[13] No longer would car manufacturers from other countries be entitled to duty-free imports even if they met the CVA and production-to-sales ratio requirements. This was particularly problematic for a number of Japanese companies that had been in the process of ramping up their Canadian production to meet Auto Pact conditions. In other words, and rather

---

[13] As one source explained, the United States was so anxious to prevent companies like Toyota from becoming a member of the Auto Pact that a footnote was included in c. 10 of the FTA to prohibit them from gaining access by buying a small company to get in.

ironically, the Canadian policy designed to encourage foreign investment was amended in such a way as to remove any incentive for non-Auto Pact members either to implement or to expand auto production in Canada, and, in the process, effectively entrench the competitive edge of existing Auto Pact participants over their foreign rivals.

In 1996, despite opposition from Ford, GM, DaimlerChrysler and the CAW, the federal government formally amended the Auto Pact benefits. It removed the approximately 9% duty on the importation of all auto parts. Any car manufacturer, whether or not it met the terms of the Auto Pact, could bring auto parts into Canada duty-free after 1996. Although this was always the practice because of duty remission and drawback programmes, the government effectively entrenched the duty-free parts programme into law and ensured that auto manufacturers were treated equally in this respect.[14] The federal government maintained, however, the 6.7% import duty, later dropped to 6.1%, on new cars. In other words, Auto Pact members who continued to meet the CVA and production-to-sales ratio requirements retained the right to import new cars without paying duties, unlike their non-Auto Pact competitors. And it was this issue that underpinned the WTO challenge.

The catalyst for the dispute, however, came in June 1998, with the release of the federal government's report on the auto industry.[15] Contrary to expectations among a number of foreign auto manufacturers such as Toyota, the report did not repeal the 6.1% duty on new cars. Consequently, within two months, officials from Japan and the European Communities brought a challenge against Canada at the WTO.

At the heart of the European and Japanese WTO complaints, therefore, was the belief that there needed to be a 'level playing field' in the Canadian market.[16] Tsuneyoshi Tatsuoka, counsellor for economic affairs at the Japanese embassy in Ottawa, explained that 'some Japanese companies are being discriminated against' and 'we find the outcome [of the report] very disappointing'.[17] The patchwork set of duties on new car imports appeared to be without purpose or meaning:

---

[14] For a review of the debate surrounding this measure, see the Senate of Canada, *Proceedings of the Standing Committee on Banking, Trade and Commerce*, issue no. 6 (2 Dec. 1997).

[15] Industry Canada, *The Automotive Competitiveness Review, A Report on the Canadian Automotive Industry* (June 1998).

[16] Delegation of the European Commission in Canada, Press Release, 'WTO Appellate Body Confirms that Canada Auto Pact is Contrary to WTO rules', 31 May 2000, obtained on 19 Jan. 2002, at www.eudelcan.org/english/5B2–24.cfm.

[17] Tsuneyoshi Tatsuoka, counsellor for economic affairs, embassy of Japan, quoted in Heather Scoffield, 'Japan Considers Challenging Canada's Auto Tariff', *Globe and Mail* (12 June

General Motors can bring in Saabs from Sweden duty-free, Ford Canada can do the same with Jaguars from Britain and DaimlerChrysler with Mercedes-Benz vehicles from Germany. Cami, a joint venture between Suzuki and GM, and Volvo Canada, now owned by Ford, also have duty-free import privileges. Yet other foreign-owned auto manufacturers with Canadian subsidiaries must pay the 6.1% duty on vehicles they import from overseas because they aren't in the club. These include Toyota, Honda, Nissan, Mazda, BMW, Volkswagen and Hyundai.[18]

David Worts, executive director of the Japanese Automobile Manufacturers Association of Canada, explained, 'Differential treatment under the current two-tiered auto policy clearly favours one group of automakers over another.'[19] And Toyota Canada president Yoshio Nakatani was even more blunt, noting that 'it is not only unfair' but also 'discriminatory'.[20]

The specific complaints brought by the European Communities and Japan before the Panel and the Appellate Body were complex, as they alleged that the Canadian measures were inconsistent with a number of provisions in several WTO agreements including the GATT 1994, the Agreement on Subsidies and Countervailing Measures (SCM), the Agreement on Trade-Related Investment Measures (TRIMS),[21] and the General Agreement on Trade in Services (GATS).[22]

The most significant issue raised by the challenge pertained to the MFN clause. The tribunal members at both the Panel and the Appellate Body recognized that although on the face of it the Canadian measures were not discriminating against products based on their country of origin, that was their effect:[23]

1998), B6. See also Simon Avery, 'Japanese Car Makers May Take Case to WTO', *Financial Post* (11 June 1998), 1, and Heather Scoffield, 'Japan To Take Canada to WTO over 6.7% Imported Car Tariff', *Globe and Mail* (1 July 1998), B1.

[18] Neville Nankivell, 'Let Consumers Drive Auto Policy, Not the Big Three', *National Post* (7 June 2000), C19.

[19] Japanese Automobile Manufacturers Association, 'JAMA Canada Disappointed by the "Status Quo" Results of the Federal Auto Review on Tariffs and Trade Policy', *Canada NewsWire* (10 June 1998).

[20] Yoshio Nakatani, president, Toyota Canada, quoted in Tony van Alphen, 'Toyota Attacks Trade Policy, Demands Same Duty-Free Status Big Three Enjoy', *Toronto Star* (13 Feb. 1997), E8. See also Greg Keenan and Heather Scoffield, 'Toyota Assails Tariff Decision', *Globe and Mail* (11 June 1998), B1.

[21] Agreement on Trade-Related Investment Measures (TRIMS) in the Multilateral Agreements on Trade in Goods, Annex 1A of the WTO Agreement.

[22] General Agreement on Trade in Services (GATS), Annex 1B of the WTO Agreement.

[23] *Auto Pact Case*, report of the Panel, paras. 10.38–10.50, and report of the Appellate Body, paras. 78–86.

The measure maintained by Canada accords the import duty exemption to certain motor vehicles entering Canada from certain countries. These privileged motor vehicles are imported by a limited number of designated manufacturers who are required to meet certain performance conditions [in Canada] ... The advantage of the import duty exemption is accorded to some motor vehicles originating in certain countries without being accorded to like motor vehicles from *all* other members.[24]

Consequently, it was held that Canada's measures were inconsistent with the MFN provisions set out in Article I:1 of the GATT 1994.

The Panel also found that the CVA requirements were inconsistent with the national treatment clause in GATT 1994. The national treatment principle requires that imported goods be given the same treatment as like domestic goods in respect of all laws and requirements affecting their sale, purchase, transportation, distribution or use. The Panel held that the CVA requirements in the MVTOs and SROs 'confer an advantage upon the use of domestic products but not upon the use of imported products' because 'they adversely affect the equality of competitive opportunities of imported products in relation to like domestic products'.[25] Canada did not challenge this finding before the Appellate Body.

Japan and the European Communities also contended that the Canadian measures implementing the Auto Pact were inconsistent with provisions of the subsidies agreement. This agreement does not prohibit subsidies per se, but does prohibit subsidies contingent on export performance. The analysis of the subsidies complaint was extensive, but at the same time only one specific finding was made against Canada. The Appellate Body, confirming the Panel's decision, held that the production-to-sales ratio was not only a subsidy, but also was contingent on export performance contrary to Article 3.1(a) of the SCM Agreement. It recognized that the effect of production-to-sales ratio requirements, which in some cases was 100:100, necessitated a manufacturer to export motor vehicles.[26]

The last set of challenges brought by officials from Japan and the European Communities pertained to the services agreement. The Panel held that the Canadian measures implementing the duty import exemption were inconsistent with both the MFN and the national treatment provisions[27] of the GATS. Canada appealed against the finding pertaining to the MFN clause, but did not appeal against the conclusions reached

---

[24] Ibid., report of the Appellate Body, para. 85 (emphasis in original).
[25] Ibid., report of the Panel, para. 10.85.
[26] Ibid., report of the Appellate Body, para. 104.   [27] GATS, Articles II:1 and XVII.

regarding national treatment. Although it would not have affected the outcome of the dispute, this perhaps was a mistake, as the Appellate Body reversed the Panel's MFN findings and was sharply critical of the Panel's interpretative approach to the GATS. This appeal tribunal noted that the Panel not only failed to substantiate its analysis and findings pertaining to the MFN clause, but also did not even properly determine whether the measure at issue was within the scope of the services agreement.[28]

In the light of these findings, both the Panel and the Appellate Body held that the Canadian measures pertaining to the import duty exemption were inconsistent with a number of provisions in the WTO Agreement, and therefore requested Canada to bring its measures into conformity. An arbitrator awarded Canada eight months in which to make the necessary changes.[29]

2 The policy-making process in Canada in response to the WTO challenge

Canada defended the Auto Pact despite a recognition there was little chance of success. The government always knew that it had a problem with the Auto Pact and the MFN provisions of the GATT and later the WTO Agreement. As Michael Hart, a former Canadian trade negotiator, explained, there was little doubt that the Auto Pact was in clear violation of Canada's WTO commitments. He noted that it was 'an "open-and-shut case" of discriminatory trade practices'.[30] In fact, officials were so certain that Canada had little prospect of winning the case that there was a discussion whether or not even to appeal the matter after the loss at the Panel level. As one official in the Department of Foreign Affairs and International Trade (DFAIT) publicly explained, 'We don't want to raise expectations,' because 'The Auto Pact can't be saved.'[31]

Yet despite facing almost certain defeat, Canada vigorously defended and then appealed on the matter at the WTO. This can be attributed to three main factors. First, there was considerable public pressure on federal officials to take a strong stand not only in favour of the cherished Auto

---

[28] *Auto Pact Case*, report of the Appellate Body, paras. 167, 174, 181, 182.

[29] Ibid., report of Arbitration under Art. 21.3(c), DSU, para. 56.

[30] Michael Hart, quoted in James Baxter, 'Officials See Silver Lining in Cloud of Lost Trade Disputes', *Ottawa Citizen* (13 July 1999), C1, C2.

[31] Source in the Department of Foreign Affairs and International Trade (DFAIT), quoted in Ian Jack, 'Ottawa To Appeal WTO on Auto Pact', *National Post* (17 Dec. 1999), C1.

Pact but also against 'interference' by an international body on a matter of domestic public policy. Once the WTO claim was made public, the significant media attention and the corresponding 'court of public opinion' limited the government's ability to enter into a negotiated settlement. At that point, the government had virtually no choice but to defend the Auto Pact vigorously even in the face of certain defeat. It did not want to be seen to be allowing an international body to 'dictate' its auto policy.

Second, government and labour leaders alike hoped that if Canada defended the 6.1% duty on new car imports, the car manufacturers would make an effort to stave off any future plant closures.[32] There was a widespread belief that auto manufacturers would take the government's defence of the Auto Pact as a sign of good faith and maintain facilities such the one in Sainte-Thérèse, Quebec, that were facing likely closure. In fact, in the aftermath of the case, Industry Minister John Manley publicly reminded auto manufacturers of the government's expectations in this regard, stating that 'Having taken the action we did on [maintaining the new car] tariff, that ought to be taken into account when the future of [the car plant in] Sainte-Thérèse comes up.'[33]

Third, and arguably most importantly, Canada defended this challenge at the WTO because of extensive lobbying by Ford, GM and Daimler-Chrysler. Domestic stakeholders influenced both the government's decision to defend the case at the WTO and the nature and manner in which the case proceeded. In other words, the auto manufacturers were key players in Canada's response to the WTO challenge and were not simply advised in the aftermath of its decisions. The federal government consulted with the representatives of the Big Three car manufacturers, the CAW and, to a lesser extent, the provincial governments, at every stage of the WTO process. The auto industry itself was, in fact, so influential in shaping Canada's response to the WTO challenge that André LeMay, DFAIT spokesman, actually stated that the stakeholders and not the government would determine whether there would be an appeal after the loss at the Panel level: 'You have to realize it's not our decision ... Basically we're dealing with the unions and with the industry to see whether or not they want to appeal this.'[34]

---

[32] Buzz Hargrove, president, CAW, quoted in Simon Avery, 'Japanese Car Makers May Take Case to WTO', *Financial Post* (11 June 1998), 1.

[33] John Manley, Minister of Industry, quoted in Ian Jack, 'GM Told To Weigh Tariff in Ste-Thérèse decision', *Financial Post* (7 Oct. 1998), 17.

[34] André LeMay, quoted in 'Tweaking the WTO', *Globe and Mail* (16 Feb. 2000), A16.

The government of Canada in conjunction with its stakeholders, and not the WTO, determined how the trade regime's decision would be implemented. After considerable consultation, officials in Ottawa made a number of changes to its regulatory framework that were advocated by the Big Three. First, in September 2000, it removed all references to the production-to-sales requirements in relevant provisions that were found to be inconsistent with the subsidies agreement.[35] Second, in February 2001 the government amended the schedule to the Customs Tariff, and repealed the Motor Vehicles Tariff Order, 1998, and three other remission orders made pursuant to the Financial Administration Act.[36]

In addition, officials in Ottawa raised the 6.1% tariff for all imported vehicles from sources other than the United States. In other words, instead of eliminating the tariff altogether, officials imposed it on all companies operating under the Auto Pact including the North American companies when they imported from countries outside the United States. Though perhaps not undertaken in the spirit of free trade, it technically ensured that Canada adhered to the WTO decision while at the same time minimizing any potential effect on the competitive position of the North American auto manufacturers vis-à-vis their foreign rivals.

Ironically, considerable pressure was exerted by the representatives of Ford, GM and DaimlerChrysler in both the public and private arenas for the tariff on new cars to be applied to all auto manufacturers. Maureen Kempston Darkes, president of GM, for example, publicly demanded that the federal government impose the tariff on all auto manufacturers in order to fulfil the WTO requirements. She explained that 'Under no circumstances, should they remove the tariff ... We want no unilateral reduction of tariffs, so that means it would go on everybody.'[37]

---

[35] Order Amending the Motor Vehicles Tariff Order, 1998, SOR/2000-342.

[36] Order Repealing the Motor Vehicle Tariff Order, 1998 and Amending the Schedule to the Customs Tariff, SOR/01-81, Order Repealing Certain Remission Orders Made under the Financial Administration Act (2000–1), SOR/01-82, Order Repealing Certain Remission Orders Made under the Financial Administration Act (2000–2), SI/01-30, and an Order Repealing Certain Remission Orders Made under the Financial Administration Act (2000–3), SI/01-31.

[37] Tony Van Alphen, 'Tax Us Too, Big Three Auto Firms Say', Toronto Star (19 Feb. 2000). For similar comments see Mark Nantais, president of the Motor Vehicle Manufacturers Association, quoted in Keenan, 'Big Three Hire Lobbyist'; Michael Sheridan, Director of Government Relations, Ford, quoted in Heather Scoffield, 'Luxury Vehicles May Be Hit by Tough WTO Auto Pact Ruling', Globe and Mail (31 May 2000), B1; and Michael Walker, director of government relations, DaimlerChrysler, quoted in Greg Keenan, 'Auto Tariff Kills Big Three's Edge, Ottawa To Slap 6.1% Duty on Vehicles Imported from outside North America', Globe and Mail (25 Jan. 2001), B1.

As an editorial in the *Globe and Mail* explained, the North American auto manufacturers received significant benefits with such an approach:

> The 6.1-per-cent tariff gives the [Big Three] a leg up on competition in the luxury car segment and allows for higher pricing of their own luxury vehicles, where the Big Three harvest all the tariff-made fruit as profit. The tariff also increases the cost differential between luxury cars and medium-priced cars. This provides room for higher pricing in the mid-market segment, because there is less risk of purchasers bleeding over into lower-end luxury car models.[38]

Moreover, the effect of maintaining the tariff had a disproportionately greater impact on Toyota and Honda. For example, between January and August 1999, DaimlerChrysler, Ford, GM and Suzuki imported approximately one new vehicle for every twelve new vehicles imported by non-Auto Pact members – largely from Japan – who paid the 6.1% duty.[39]

The immediate economic impact of the changes was twofold. First, the prices of some imported cars increased. As Dennis DesRosiers of DesRosiers Automotive Consultants explained, an additional 30,000 vehicles, approximately 2% of annual auto sales in Canada, were subjected to the 6.1% tariff. Most of these vehicles were luxury cars such as Mercedes and Jaguar imports. Second, government revenues increased from the extension of the tariff. DesRosiers estimated that the increase in import duties would amount to $250 million per year.[40]

At first blush, it might appear that the medium- to long-term impact of the WTO decision in the *Auto Pact Case* will be significant, as there has been a staggering drop in Canadian automotive production:[41]

> In 1999, Canada assembled 3.1 million new vehicles, ranking us fourth in the world in automotive output. By 2001, our output shrank by 20%, dropping us to seventh place, and we will fall to ninth by 2005 (passed by

---

[38] Editorial, 'Reject the Auto Manufacturers' Appeal for Higher Taxes', *Globe and Mail* (1 June 2000), A16.

[39] Information derived from vehicle import statistics provided by DesRosiers Automotive Consultants and company reports, reproduced in Greg Keenan and Heather Scoffield, 'Higher Tariffs Loom Following WTO Auto Ruling', *Globe and Mail* (14 Oct. 1999), B1.

[40] Dennis DesRosiers, DesRosiers Automotive Consultants, quoted in Tony Van Alphen, 'Auto Tariff Extension Seen of Little Impact', *Toronto Star* (26 Jan. 2001).

[41] For an alternative perspective see Stephen S. Poloz, vice-president and chief economist, EDC, www.globeandmail.com (22 May 2002), who contends that 'Canada's auto sector is performing well relative to the rest of the economy. Vehicle assembly is maintaining its share, and vehicle parts are a leading growth sector. These characteristics are symptomatic of an industrial sector in transformation, not long-term decline.'

booming Mexico and China). With the announced or anticipated closure of three or more assembly plants, and a likely downturn in North America vehicle demand (once zero-per-cent sales incentives are lifted), things can only get worse.[42]

However, a closer examination of the Canadian automotive sector indicates that these changes to the auto sector are a reflection of a cyclical downturn in the economy. Explained Jim Stanford, an economist for the CAW, 'The demise of the Auto Pact did not cause the current decline in the Canadian auto industry, almost all of which would have occurred even if the Auto Pact had remained in force.'[43]

The reality is that, despite the public outcry, the loss of the Auto Pact will have little effect on Canada. The thresholds set out in the production-to-sales ratios and the CVA requirements were based on production levels in the mid-1960s and had been exceeded for over a decade. John Manley, Minister of Industry, recognized that the production-to-sales ratios were outdated, noting that 'The Auto Pact was based on the fundamental premise that we should produce one vehicle for every one that's sold in Canada, and we're now producing two for every one that's sold.'[44] Nor did the CVA requirements retain any significant meaning. As one observer noted, 'they were so low, they were met by the labour costs alone'.

More importantly, as automotive experts unanimously agree, the 1965 treaty did not play a role in investment or production decisions during the previous ten years.[45] Auto manufacturers did not base their decisions to build auto plants, invest in existing auto plants, or close auto plants, on their desire to retain the right to bring in new automobiles duty-free – and that was the only remaining benefit of the Auto Pact. As

---

[42] Buzz Hargrove, president, CAW, 'Our Future's on the Line', *Globe and Mail* (21 May 2002), A17.

[43] Jim Stanford, economist, CAW, 'An "Auto Pact" That's Perfectly Legal, A System of Taxes and Grants to Promote Auto Investment and Production in Canada', unpublished ms. presented to the Meetings of the Canadian Economics Association in Calgary, Alberta (May 2002), 1, quoted with permission.

[44] John Manley, Minister of Industry, quoted in Mark MacKinnon and Greg Keenan, 'Historic Auto Pact To Die in Feb., US Big Three Tariff Exemption Will End', *Globe and Mail* (5 Oct. 2000), B1.

[45] Dennis DesRosiers, quoted in 'Auto Pact's End Creates Uncertainty', *Toronto Star* (14 July 1999), 'Auto Pact Has No Effect on Investment, Ottawa Says', *Financial Post* (2 June 1999), C2, Michael Robinet, Detroit-based automotive analyst, quoted in Ian Jack, 'Canada Loses Face in Row with Europe over Beef', *National Post* (13 July 1999), C3, and Melvyn Fuss, Department of Economics, University of Toronto, quoted in Philip Demont and Natalie Armstrong, 'WTO ruling Will Have Little Impact, Experts Say', *Ottawa Citizen* (14 Oct. 1999), C3.

Othmar Stein, vice-president of public and government affairs for DaimlerChrysler Canada, noted, 'Auto manufacturers have invested heavily in
Canada because it makes good business sense,' observing that the 'Canadian industry is extremely competitive'.[46] A low dollar, cheaper labour
costs, government-sponsored healthcare and an educated workforce were
the factors that shaped investment decisions regarding auto manufacturing in Canada. Automotive expert DesRosiers effectively agreed, explaining that the end of the Auto Pact was considered to be 'employment
neutral',[47] and equated the event to 'the couple that has been separated
for twelve years without having their divorce finalized'. He noted that 'The
auto sector, for all intents and purposes, was separated from the Auto Pact
by the FTA and then NAFTA. It was already 98% redundant'.[48]

Perhaps, therefore, the biggest effect of the WTO decision in the *Auto
Pact Case* is not in terms of the economy, but in the political arena. It
created a serious public relations problem for the Canadian government.
Officials lost a legal dispute they knew they were going to lose and, in the
process, generated considerable negative media attention. As evidenced by
the plant closure in Sainte-Thérèse, auto manufacturers did not change
their plans because of the government's support in the WTO process.
As one observer explained, 'Canada defended this case because the 1965
treaty was important symbolically. And in hindsight, maybe it was unfortunate that the government pursued the case the way it did. The GM plant
in Sainte-Thérèse closed because it was in trouble for a long time, and
Ottawa took a lot of heat for it because of the WTO decision. Looking
back, maybe it was unfortunate the government did prosecute the case.
The Auto Pact was dead anyway, the fundamentals of the industry were
good, and Canada had commitments from the Japanese. In hindsight,
maybe Canada shouldn't have brought the case forward as the loss of the
Auto Pact was very symbolic and hurt the government significantly.'

3 Some tentative observations

In the aftermath of the WTO decision in the *Auto Pact Case*, Canada had
two options for bringing itself into consistency with its obligations. It
could, for example, have chosen a trade liberalizing route and eliminated

[46] Tony Van Alphen, 'WTO Aftermath Ruling Not Seen as a Job Threat', *Toronto Star* (15 Oct.
1999).
[47] Dennis DesRosiers, DesRosiers Automotive Consultants, quoted, ibid.
[48] DesRosiers quoted in James Baxter, 'WTO Sets Date for End of Auto Pact', *Ottawa Citizen*
(5 Oct. 2000), D5.

the tariff on imported vehicles from non-US sources on all auto imports, or it could eliminate the discrimination by levying the tariff on everyone – which it did. Being consistent with one set of trade obligations, therefore, does not always mean that you need to liberalize trade. In this case, Canada actually increased trade barriers in order to protect its domestic stakeholders' competitive position over their Japanese and European rivals.

In other words, this review of the Auto Pact Case demonstrates that decisions emanating from the WTO are implemented from within state borders. Competing domestic interests, not the international trade regime, set the parameters of public policy. In the process, governments are able, at best, to limit or, at worst, to circumvent, any potential impact of a WTO decision by implementing the decision in a manner that best suits its country's interests. In this respect, the state retains control over policy-making at the national level.

The government of Canada defended this challenge at the WTO for two reasons. First, there was considerable public pressure on Canadian officials to protect the Auto Pact as it had become a potent symbol of economic prosperity. Extensive media coverage surrounding the matter ensured that the government was under pressure to take a strong public stance against the WTO challenge, even if privately officials knew that there was little hope that the country could win its case.

Second, there were intensive lobbying efforts by the Big Three to keep the provisions of the Auto Pact for as long as possible in order to maintain their competitive advantage over foreign car manufacturers. Government officials took these concerns seriously and adhered to the wishes of auto manufacturers both in defending the action at the WTO and in implementing the decision.

The problem, however, with the Canadian government's strategy was that it resolved only its immediate problem and did not deal with any long-term implications. If the public outcry was significant when the case was filed, it was even worse on Canada's defeat at the WTO. Defending the case did not simply delay the inevitable but fuelled the controversy and intensified public anger at the outcome. Had the government simply conceded that changes were necessary at the early stages of the conflict, possibly even prior to the complaint being filed, it could have controlled the outcome rather than simply appear to be reacting to a legal decision being made elsewhere. This was, in other words, a case that arguably should never have gone to the WTO. Canada should have dealt with the problem in 1998 in a manner that best protected the national interest rather than focusing solely on the interests of its stakeholders. Would it really have been an error to provide Japanese car manufacturers such as Toyota and Honda with an incentive to increase their auto production in Canada just like that received by the North American auto manufacturers? After all, wasn't that the very purpose of the Auto Pact – to encourage investment in Canada?

10

The SPS Agreement and crisis management: the Chile–EU avian influenza experience

CLAUDIA OROZCO*

1 The problem

In May 2002, Chilean sanitary authorities were notified of a possible outbreak of avian influenza[1] (AI – also known as bird flu). Until then, highly pathogenic avian influenza (HPAI) had never occurred in Chile[2] or in any other country in South America.[3]

Chilean authorities and the poultry industry were suddenly confronted with huge challenges: (i) the control of a highly contagious viral disease that can produce very high levels of mortality; (ii) the eradication of the disease in order to regain the status it had as a disease-free country; and (iii) the need to maintain the confidence of its major trading partner to ensure that the safeguard sanitary measure adopted by the European Commission would not be transformed into a permanent measure.

* Independent consultant, specialist in WTO law and negotiations, Brussels.
[1] Influenza infections can affect all avian species, in particular chickens, turkeys and ducks. At the time of the Chilean outbreak, influenza infections were divided into two groups: highly pathogenic avian influenza (HPAI) classified under List A of the World Organization for Animal Health (formerly the International Office of Epizootics – OIE), and low pathogenic avian influenza, which causes a mild disease and was not listed by the OIE as a notifiable disease.

List A includes 'transmissible diseases that have the potential for very serious and rapid spread, irrespective of national borders, that are of serious socio-economic or public health consequence and that are of major importance in the international trade of animals and animal products'. List B includes 'diseases that are of serious socio-economic or public health consequence and that are of major importance in the international trade of animals and animal products'. This classification of diseases will change as of 2005. OIE website, http://www.oie.int.
[2] Chile País Libre de Influenza Aviar, Government of Chile, Servicio Agrícola y Ganadero, Dec. 2002.
[3] Avian Influenza in Chile, Report of the Mission carried out in Chile from 17 to 25 July, Drs Ilaria Capua and Stefano Marangon, OIE Experts.

The first outbreak occurred in a broiler breeder farm that hosted 617,800 breeders and a hatchery and was located near a broiler operation containing nearly 1.5 million broilers.[4] It was followed by a second outbreak in a turkey breeder farm that held four dark houses for young birds containing a total of 26,000 birds, four breeding houses with 24,000 birds and a hatchery.[5]

At the time of the outbreak, the poultry industry[6] in Chile was concentrated in seven companies producing over 400,000 tons a year of fresh poultry meat[7] with an average annual growth of 11.4%.[8] Exports amounted to US$69 million in 2001, $44 million in 2002 and $72 million in 2003,[9] with Mexico and the European Union (EU) accounting for over 80% of total exports.[10] The industry was concentrated in three regions[11] quite apart from two others where poultry is reared for domestic consumption.[12]

Following the outbreak Chile's avian influenza-free status was affected and access to export markets was closed.

The Chilean authorities adopted an extensive and rigorous sanitary programme aimed at controlling the spread of the disease and eradicating it in as little time as possible. This approach reflected Chile's strict sanitary policy towards exotic diseases on List A of the World Organization for Animal Health (OIE) and aimed at regaining market access as soon as possible. The Chilean authorities sought to obtain from the EU regionalization of their territory, once and if the disease was controlled and until it could regain disease-free status. This two-stage approach represented the quickest way in which to restore access to export markets.

The authorities succeeded, from a sanitary point of view, in controlling the spread of the disease immediately and eradicating it soon after. They succeeded in proving Chile's sanitary status to the EU, so that the EU

---

[4] Ibid.   [5] Ibid.
[6] Poultry meat, poultry meat products and preparations, live poultry (ratites) and hatching eggs.
[7] Asociación de Productores Avícolas de Chile, website http://www.apa.cl.
[8] Average annual growth between 1990 and 2003. Asociación de Productores Avícolas de Chile, website http://www.apa.cl.
[9] Asociación de Productores Avícolas de Chile, website http://www.apa.cl.
[10] By 2003 the EU became the main destination of, and accounts for over 50% of, total exports. Ibid.
[11] Regions V (Valparaiso), VI (O'Higgins) and RM (Region Metropolitana).
[12] Regions VII and IX.

granted regionalization three months after imposing a ban on imports and within six months had lifted the safeguard measure.

The handling of the crisis, both by Chile as exporting country and the EU as importing member is a success story for both WTO members and the world trading system. It demonstrates that a developing country with well-organized institutions can manage difficult sanitary problems in a manner that allows a complex decision-making WTO member to respond positively to market access demands.

2 Local and external players

Chile

Four players were important in Chile's management of the crisis:

1. The Ministry of Agriculture and Livestock had overall political responsibility for the management of the situation.

2. The Agriculture and Livestock Service (SAG) is an independent organization that reports to the Ministry of Agriculture and has technical, administrative, financial and legal autonomy. SAG's main objectives are to avoid the introduction of exotic diseases into the national territory, to prevent any spread within the country and improve health status through control and/or eradication of diseases considered to be important. It has a National Directorate,[13] thirteen regional offices[14] and sixty-three local offices.[15]

In the management of the AI crisis SAG was responsible for the technical decisions adopted, primarily the decision to depopulate infected farms, to avoid vaccination, to carry out a census of the entire country and to adopt a strict sanitation programme for the infected and adjacent areas. These decisions were guided by the primary goal of controlling and eradicating the disease through a 'stamping-out' strategy, in order to regain disease-free status.

A second set of decisions adopted by SAG involved the suspension of export certificates and the immediate notification of the situation to trading partners and international organizations. Finally, SAG seems to have been responsible for the policy of transparency that permeated the management of the entire crisis.

---

[13] Responsible for legislation, policy, co-ordination, supervision and control.
[14] Responsible for the co-ordination and supervision of technical operations.
[15] In charge of implementation of activities and on-the-spot operations.

3. The Ministry of Foreign Affairs, Market Access Department at the Economic Directorate, and the Chilean missions to the EU and the WTO.

The ministry was responsible for relations with the EU and the WTO. From the Market Access Department, Macarena Vidal[16] co-ordinated and led presentations to the WTO Sanitary and Phytosanitary (SPS) Committee and co-ordinated with Francisco Bahamonde[17] at the Chilean mission to the EU all contacts and presentations to the Directorate General for Health and Consumer Protection (SANCO) at the European Commission.

4. The private sector, which included poultry producers, the Association of Avian Producers (APA) that represents over 95% of poultry producers, the Association of Egg Producers (ASOHUEVO) and the Association of Medical Veterinarians Specializing in Aviculture (AMEVEA).

These key players worked within several committees formed by the government to discuss and co-ordinate decisions and strategies.

At the political level a committee was formed by the Minister of Agriculture, the Under-Secretary of Agriculture, the national director of SAG, the chief of the Livestock Protection Department of the Ministry of Agriculture and advisers from the Ministry of Agriculture. This committee met regularly with representatives of the industry and its Associations.

At the technical level a committee was formed by the permanent veterinary staff of SAG, the technical staff of the poultry industry, the administrative staff of SAG and representatives of medical veterinarians specializing in poultry farming and academia.

At the operational level a structure was formed comprising professional and technical staff from SAG and specially hired officials to implement the operative actions.

More than seventy professionals and technicians were dedicated exclusively to the eradication campaign, with direct costs to the public sector of US$683,000.

In addition, producers' veterinarians, under the supervision of official veterinarians, undertook several sanitation programme activities.

The European Union

The European Commission was responsible on behalf of the EU. Within the Commission, the Directorate General for Health and Consumer

---

[16] Advisor on Sanitary and Phytosanitary Issues, Market Access Department, Economic Directorate, Ministry of Foreign Affairs.
[17] Agriculture attaché, exclusively responsible for agriculture and SPS issues.

Protection (DG SANCO) took the lead, through Directorate E[18] responsible for Food Safety and Directorate F in charge of the Food and Veterinary Office.[19]

DG SANCO, on the basis of scientific advice and support from the European Food Safety Authority, is responsible for the EU's policy and legislation on food safety, animal health, animal welfare and plant health within the EU. Its tasks include responsibility for control systems in third countries in order to ensure compliance with EC measures for exports to the EU.

Concerning Chilean exports of poultry, Directorate E was involved at two stages, first when authorizing Chile as a third country for exports. For several years Chile has been listed as a third country from which the member states authorize imports of fresh meat,[20] live poultry and hatching eggs,[21] meat products,[22] and minced meat and meat preparations.[23] These decisions required complete knowledge of the sanitary situation of the country as well as of its legal and institutional framework and the organization of the industry. The authorizations included granting SAG the authority to issue export certificates, which ensure that the product complies with EC legislation. The Directorate relied on the findings of missions performed by the Veterinary Office.

Second, Directorate E prepared decisions concerning the safeguard measure.[24] As chair of the Standing Committee on Food Chain and Animal Health DG SANCO–Directorate E was responsible for circulating all information received from Chile, incorporating the item in the agenda of the committee and preparing the draft for the proposed measure to be voted on by the committee. In addition it was responsible for the required inter-service consultations (with DG Trade, DG Agriculture, DG External Relations, the Secretariat General and the legal service) and drafted the final proposals for decisions to be formally adopted by the College. Directorate E made proposals concerning two decisions. The first one requested member states to ban imports from Chile.[25] The second

---

[18] Food Safety: Plant Health, Animal Health and Welfare, and International Questions.
[19] Food and Veterinary Office.
[20] Commission Decision 94/85/EC, OJ No. L 44, 17/2/1994, p. 31.
[21] Commission Decision 95/233/EC, OJ No. L 156, 7/7/1995, p. 76.
[22] Commission Decision 97/222/EC, OJ No. L 89, 4/4/1997, p. 39.
[23] Commission Decision 2000/572/EC, OJ No. L 240, 23/9/2000, p. 19.
[24] Regulation 2002/178/EC of the European Parliament and of the Council, OJ No. L 031, 1/2/2002, p. 1.
[25] Commission Decision 2002/607/EC. OJ No. L 195, 24/07/2002, p. 86.

accepted temporary regionalization of Chile's territory, thereby reducing the impact of the ban on Chilean products.[26]

Directorate F completed a routine mission on 3–11 December 2001 to 'assess compliance with relevant EC requirements for imports into the EU of poultry meat, poultry meat products, live poultry and hatching eggs'.[27] The report was an important input for the decisions taken by DG SANCO and the Standing Committee, as it was a recent comprehensive study of the legal and institutional organization and capabilities of the Chilean sanitary system, including its attributions, the system of laboratory services, animal health controls, veterinary supervision and food safety controls.

Knowledge of the Chilean system allowed DG SANCO to understand fully and assess the information submitted by the Chilean authorities concerning the evolution of the crisis.

World Organization for Animal Health

A third player that indirectly influenced the outcome of this case was the OIE, which aims at ensuring transparency in the global animal disease and zoonosis situation. It collects, analyzes and disseminates scientific veterinary information; provides expertise and encourages international solidarity in the control of animal diseases; safeguards world trade[28] by publishing health standards for international trade in animals and animal products; and promotes veterinary services.

The participation of the OIE was defined by its aim of ensuring transparency in animal health. In this regard the OIE manages the World Animal Health Information System, based on the commitment of member countries to declare through the OIE their main animal diseases, including zoonoses. It includes the rapid alert system for notification to members of an outbreak of a notifiable disease and a database for the notification of the animal health status of its members.

On 30 May, SAG notified the OIE of its first suspicion of AI, and on 5 June it confirmed the presence of HPAI.[29] Thereafter SAG submitted six

---

[26] Commission Decision 2002/796/EC, OJ No. L 277, 15/10/2002, p. 21.

[27] Final Report of a Mission carried out in Chile from 03/12/01 to 11/12/01 in order to assess compliance with relevant EC requirements for imports into the EU for poultry meat, poultry meat products, live poultry and hatching eggs. European Commission, Health and Consumer Protection Directorate-General. DG (SANCO)/3430/2001.

[28] Within its mandate and under the WTO SPS Agreement, OIE Mission, OIE website http://www.oie.int.

[29] Influenza Aviar en Chile, Sospecha. Hernan Rojas Olavarria, Chief Veterinary Officer (CVO), Department of Livestock Protection, Agriculture and Livestock Service (SAG), Ministry of Agriculture, *Informaciones Sanitarias*, Vol. 15, No. 22, 31/5/2002, p. 85.

follow-up reports informing the OIE of the evolution of the disease and the sanitation programme.[30] On 19 December SAG notified the OIE that it declared the entire Chilean territory free of HPAI.

In addition, and responding to a request from SAG, the OIE was instrumental in identifying AI experts who could audit and advise on the sanitation programme. OIE recommended two Italian experts, Dr Ilaria Capua (virologist) and Dr Stefano Marangon (epidemiologist)[31] who carried out a mission in Chile on 17–25 July. The mission was organized and financed by SAG.

The experts' mission took place when most of the emergency work had been completed and thousands of tests and samples had been collected. Its main task was to audit the sanitation programme and help SAG to gather and interpret information on laboratory tests and epidemiological data.[32]

3 Facts[33]

Following a legal requirement to notify the SAG regional office of any suspicion of AI or Newcastle disease, on 23 May 2002 a broiler breeder farm (Mitil) notified an unusually high mortality rate, which, after an

---

[30] Influenza Aviar en Chile, Informe de Seguimiento No. 1 Hernán Rojas Olavarria, Chief Veterinary Officer (CVO), Department of Livestock Protection, Agriculture and Livestock Service (SAG), Ministry of Agriculture, *Informaciones Sanitarias*, Vol. 15, No. 24, 14/6/2002, p. 95. Influenza Aviar en Chile, Informe de Seguimiento No. 2 Hernán Rojas Olavarria, Chief Veterinary Officer (CVO), Department of Livestock Protection, Agriculture and Livestock Service (SAG), Ministry of Agriculture, *Informaciones Sanitarias*, Vol. 15, No. 25, 21/6/2002, p. 103. Influenza Aviar en Chile, Informe de Seguimiento Nos. 3 y 4 Hernán Rojas Olavarria, Chief Veterinary Officer (CVO), Department of Livestock Protection, Agriculture and Livestock Service (SAG), Ministry of Agriculture, *Informaciones Sanitarias*, Vol. 15, No. 27, 5/7/2002, pp. 114–15. Influenza Aviar en Chile, Informe de Seguimiento No. 5 Hernán Rojas Olavarria, Chief Veterinary Officer (CVO), Department of Livestock Protection, Agriculture and Livestock Service (SAG), Ministry of Agriculture, *Informaciones Sanitarias*, Vol. 15, No. 32, 9/8/2002, p. 149. Influenza Aviar en Chile, Informe de Seguimiento No. 6 (Informe Final), Hernán Rojas Olavarria, Chief Veterinary Officer (CVO), Department of Livestock Protection, Agriculture and Livestock Service (SAG), Ministry of Agriculture, Informaciones Sanitarias, Vol. 15, No. 39, 27/9/2002, p. 186.

[31] Both from the Istituto Zooprofilattico Sperimentale delle Venezie, Virology Department, OIE and National Reference Laboratory for Avian Influenza and Newcastle Disease.

[32] Dr Ilaria Capua.

[33] Based on the description contained in Notificación de Influenza Aviar, Government of Chile, Servicio Agrícola y Ganadero, Octubre 2002; Chile País Libre de Influenza Aviar, Government of Chile, Servicio Agrícola y Ganadero, December 2002; and Avian Influenza in Chile, Report of the Mission carried out in Chile from 17 to 25 July, Drs Ilaria Capua and Stefano Marangon, OIE experts.

official inspection carried out the next day by SAG veterinarians, led to HPAI being suspected. This first notification activated the National Emergency System for Animal Health.

Days later, surveillance actions caused a second outbreak of AI in a turkey breeder farm 4 km away (Tremolen) to be detected.[34] Laboratory tests confirmed the presence of HPAI in two sectors of the farm.

These two breeding farms, designated as the infected area, were put under official quarantine and after serological testing SAG ordered the destruction of the flock. In Mitil, SAG's decision covered 100% of the bird population (460,000 birds) and the destruction of over 100,000 hatching eggs. In Tremolen it covered two breeding sectors (18,000 birds). The procedure was completed within a few days and carcasses were buried on the spot. Animals in two other sectors at Tremolen that did not appear to be infected were put under permanent surveillance and stringent biosecurity measures to ensure that the virus would not circulate. The quarantine declared in the infected area also meant the control and restriction of all movements of products into and out of the area, disinfecting of vehicles and new biosecurity measures. It covered the period up to 15 December 2002 and was lifted on that date when the sanitation process was completed and the absence of viral activity was verified.

A peripheral zone 10 km in diameter surrounding the infected area was established for surveillance and increased sanitary controls: intense testing[35] for sixteen commercial farms and increased testing[36] for 258 farms that hosted birds were put into effect.

Throughout the rest of the country a monitoring programme was carried out for all poultry farms in order to diagnose the scope of the outbreak.[37]

Private veterinarians supervised by officials from SAG implemented these initial measures.

By 21 June, when preliminary laboratory tests indicated the possibility of HPAI, as a preventive measure SAG stopped certifying exports of live poultry and hatching eggs, live ratites and hatching eggs, fresh meat from poultry, ratites, wild and farmed feathered game and poultry meat preparations, and poultry meat products. By the end of June both outbreaks were typified as the HPAI virus by the OIE reference laboratories (Ames

---

[34] On 9 and 10 June two more notifications were received but laboratory examinations rejected the presence of AI.
[35] Every seven days.   [36] Every fifteen days.
[37] Between 1 June and 15 July over 79,000 serum samples were tested for AI.

in the United States and Weybridge in the United Kingdom). Apparently it had started as a low pathogenic AI and mutated into a highly pathogenic one.

These findings were notified by SAG to Chile's trading partners and the OIE.[38]

By then, one EU member state had already adopted a safeguard measure and banned all relevant imports from Chile, including consignments certified before 21 June that were already on their way.

To regulate and harmonize the situation within the EU member states and with Chile's decision to stop certification of exports, DG SANCO included the item on the agenda of the July meeting of the Standing Committee on Food Chain and Animal Health. It prepared the draft for a safeguard measure and completed the required inter-service consultations. The European Commission adopted Decision 2002/607/EC of 23 July, requiring member states to prohibit the importation of products from Chile and requiring them to authorize the importation of certified exports for meat obtained from animals slaughtered before 21 June. This decision was applicable until 1 January 2003, the six months foreseen by OIE guidelines. It was to be reviewed, in the light of the evolution of the disease, before 20 September 2002.

Between mid-June and the end of September the first four steps of a six-step sanitation programme were implemented in the infected zone:[39] (i) the fermentation of waste and beds; (ii) appropriate burial; (iii) the washing and cleaning of all places and equipment related to the production chain; (iv) the disinfecting of houses, equipment and materials used both indoors and outdoors. All that remained were steps (v), a period of silence of four weeks, and (vi), concerning verification of the absence of viral activity by populating the sheds with new susceptible birds demonstrably negative to AI.[40] New biosecurity measures in all breeding farms had also been implemented and surveillance and testing in the unaffected sectors in Tremolen were maintained.

Throughout this period in the adjacent peripheral area of surveillance, authorities completed a census of all breeding farms, implemented controls on the movements of animals, adopted biosecurity measures similar to those adopted for the infected area and continued surveillance and

---

[38] Notifications by Hernán Rojas Olavarria, Chief Veterinary Officer (CVO), Department of Livestock Protection, Agriculture and Livestock Service (SAG), Ministry of Agriculture.
[39] In Tremolen, these four steps were implemented between mid-Aug. and the end of Oct.
[40] These two last steps were completed by the second week of Dec.

testing.[41] At first brigades were organized with technicians and specialist professionals looking at the places of residence of the workers at Mitil and Tremolen and testing all the owners of birds living nearby in order to see whether the virus had spread beyond the workplace. In addition, all farms hosting birds in the entire area were identified and at least two tests per owner were performed.[42]

In the disease-free zone, a national monitoring programme was carried out on all poultry farms. Two censuses were completed and farms voluntarily adopted new biosecurity measures suggested by SAG.

By the end of September, three months after the last of the livestock had been eliminated and when revision of Decision 2002/607/EC was due, the Chilean authorities were well on their way to completing the sanitation programme adopted for the infected area, the adjacent area and the disease-free part of the country.

At that time the Chilean authorities requested DG SANCO to consider the regionalization of their territory. In accordance with Article 6 of the SPS Agreement, Chile submitted all relevant information to show that the identified area was free of avian influenza and that this condition was unlikely to change.

The request was preceded by the regular submission of information at the end of each sanitation action[43] and a meeting in Brussels at which Chilean veterinary authorities presented evidence of the definitive extent of the outbreak (two sources), the sanitation programme in place and evidence of the disease-free situation of the rest of the country.

On the basis of the information presented by Chile, DG SANCO proposed a new measure, which was approved by the Standing Committee. Inter-service consultations were completed and by 14 October Decision 2002/796/EC was adopted, providing for the temporary regionalization of Chile and authorizing exports from the areas that had not been affected by the disease.[44] The EC based its decision on the fact that since early June, when the two outbreaks had been confirmed, no further outbreaks had occurred; that SAG could guarantee that the disease problem was confined to regions V and VI, with well-controlled borders as regards the

---

[41] Every twenty-one days in commercial farms and every forty-five days for small farms hosting birds.

[42] Workers on poultry farms are forbidden by sanitary measures to have birds at their place of residence.

[43] The regular submission of information was positively highlighted by Maria Pittman and Eva Maria Zamora from Directorate E, SANCO.

[44] Commission Decision 2002/796/EC, OJ No. L 277, 15/10/2002, p. 21.

movement of animals, personnel and vehicles; and that extensive screening had been performed which gave positive results, indicating that the disease had been successfully eradicated.

4 Challenges faced and the outcome

The Chilean authorities and the poultry industry had been faced with huge challenges: the control and eradication of the first ever occurrence of HPAI in South America and the need to maintain the confidence of its major trading partner to ensure that the sanitary measure would be promptly lifted in order to re-establish its exports.

SAG, the Ministry of Foreign Affairs and the Chilean mission to the EU successfully and ably represented Chile's domestic producers to regain market access in as short a time as possible.

Clearly the costs borne by the state[45] and the private sector[46] would have been wasted without appropriate guidance and actions by the Chilean authorities. It was SAG which led the rapid implementation of a national structure that allowed thorough monitoring, testing and the implementation of a sanitary programme in the infected and adjacent areas. SAG and the Ministry of Foreign Affairs ably maintained contact with the EU authorities. They regularly submitted information to DG SANCO and were able to present scientific evidence of the status of the disease and the sanitation programme. This contact at technical level allowed each party to work in various languages in order to keep up with the speed of events.

At the request of the Chilean authorities, the parties met twice in Brussels: in July to make a presentation of the situation including the results of the testing programme, guarantees of the sanitary status of products certified for export and guarantees of the suspension of certification of exports. A second meeting was held in September, when the Chilean authorities presented a report on the definitive extent of the outbreak, the evolution of the sanitation programme and evidence that a large part of the country was disease-free.

---

[45] These costs, including hiring additional veterinary staff, performing nationwide testing, depopulation and quarantine programme, amounted to US$683,000. Chile País Libre de Influenza Aviar, Government of Chile, Servicio Agrícola y Ganadero, December 2002.

[46] Including additional professional staff, loss of animals and costs of testing, these costs amounted to US$5,675,000. No state compensation was available to cover these costs. Ibid.

SAG used OIE experts to audit and, as the relevant international organization, to validate its sanitation programme. The mission served its purpose, and SAG was able to corroborate the appropriateness of the measures and the strategy adopted, and was useful in rectifying aspects of the sanitation programme by including components recommended by the mission and which until then had not been considered.[47]

The Chilean producers were faced with the very onerous consequences of the decisions adopted by SAG.[48] Nevertheless, even in the light of these decisions, the producers and the APA collaborated with SAG at all times and contributed to the rapid implementation of the emergency measures. Private veterinarians supervised by official veterinarians carried out some of the most important tasks such as the emptying of farms and sampling. They shared the objective set by the veterinary authorities, of solving the sanitary problem and regaining market access to and the confidence of trading partners.

For Chile's private sector the experts' mission was valuable in four ways: first, academically, due to the considerable experience and research brought by the experts on dealing with AI; second, concerning epidemiology data and suitability of biosecurity measures; third, in their validation of the procedures used by officials in laboratories; and fourth, due to their recommendations concerning measures to adopt in the period following the eradication of the disease.

The European Commission was faced with the challenge of closing the market during the period when trade in poultry meat, meat products, meat preparations and live animals represented a threat to animal health in the EU. It was also faced with the challenge of reopening market access immediately after the threat was removed. This required an assessment of the validity of the scientific evidence presented by Chile and the commitment to remove the sanitary measure once the sanitary conditions were shown to be sound.

Faced with these challenges, the parties had recourse to the WTO Agreement on the Application of Sanitary and Phitosanitary Measures. On the one hand, paragraph 1 of Article 6 includes the obligation of importing members to ensure that their SPS measures are adapted to the sanitary characteristics of the area – whether it is the entire country, part of it or

---

[47] Chile País Libre de Influenza Aviar, Government of Chile, Servicio Agrícola y Ganadero, December 2002.

[48] Suspension of exports certificates, depopulation of infected animals, complete sanitation programme, additional biosecurity measures.

parts of several countries. It also indicates the criteria that members must take into account when adapting a measure to regional conditions.[49] On the other hand, paragraph 3 of Article 6 of the Agreement establishes an obligation on the exporting country claiming that an area within its territory is disease-free to provide the necessary evidence in order to demonstrate objectively that the area is currently and likely to remain disease-free. For this purpose, it requires the exporting member to grant access to the importing member for inspection, testing and other relevant procedures.

In addition, paragraphs 5 and 6 of the Preamble of the SPS Agreement recognize the importance of international standards, guidelines and recommendations vis-à-vis sanitary measures that ensure the desired protection and minimize negative effects on trade. In this context it recognizes the relevance of the OIE.

The relevant provisions of the SPS Agreement demonstrated its full value thanks to actions taken by these two administrations. Within three months the authorities of both parties – Chile and the EU – were able to satisfy themselves that, faced with a very serious sanitary problem, trade could be partly restored without in any way compromising sanitary standards.

The European Commission adopted a sanitary measure requesting its member states to ban imports from Chile.[50] This measure was notified to the WTO.[51] Three months later, when evidence showed that the disease had not spread, it granted temporary regionalization[52] and notified the WTO of this step.[53] Important from the trade perspective is the fact that the safeguard measure was adopted from the outset as a measure with an expiry date – 1 January 2003. Its lifespan of nearly six months reflected the recommendations of the OIE with no need for additional procedures to restore full market access for Chilean products.

On 19 December 2002 Chile notified the OIE that on the basis of scientific evidence it declared itself free of avian influenza.

In this way, the EC succeeded in guaranteeing that products introduced to the European market complied with EU sanitary and health standards.

---

[49] 'In assessing the sanitary or phytosanitary characteristics of a region, Members shall take into account, *inter alia,* the level of prevalence of specific diseases or pests, the existence of eradication or control programmes, and appropriate criteria or guidelines, which may be developed by the relevant international organizations.' Agreement on the Application of Sanitary and Phytosanitary Measures, Art. 6, para. 1.

[50] Commission Decision 2002/607/EC. Official Journal L 195, 24/07/2002, p. 86.

[51] G/SPS/N/EEC/172, 25 July 2002.

[52] Commission Decision 2002/796/EC, Official Journal L 277, 15/10/2002, p. 21.

[53] G/SPS/ N/EEC/174, 1 Oct. 2002.

The rapid response by the EC was influenced by several factors such as (i) its knowledge of the institutional and legal framework that existed in Chile for export of poultry, through the mission of the Veterinary Office and the recently negotiated Association Agreement[54] and their knowledge of the structure of the industry;[55] (ii) Chile's transparency; and (iii) the report from the OIE experts' mission, which was an important element in establishing credibility, and assuring the appropriateness of the measures taken and the significance of the laboratory results. All three factors contributed to creating the necessary confidence of the Standing Committee in accepting the information submitted by Chile and its request to be regionalized.

5 Lessons to be learned: the players' views

Chile

Government officials from SAG confirming and explaining the policies outlined in official documents,[56] Macarena Vidal[57] from the Ministry of Foreign Affairs, and Felipe de la Carrera and Pedro Guerrero from the APA all highlight three elements as key to the success of the management of this crisis:

1. Transparency: SAG was transparent in providing all the information possible on the situation from the moment it had any suspicion of the presence of AI. Even before HPAI was confirmed, and on the basis of preliminary laboratory results, SAG suspended the issuing of export certificates and informed its trading partners, the relevant international organizations and the private sector. Thereafter, the details of the sanitation programme and all measures adopted were regularly supplied to the European Commission and the OIE.

2. Teamwork between all levels of actors connected with the poultry industry (entrepreneurs, producers' associations, private veterinarians

---

[54] Council Decision 2002/979 Agreement Establishing an association between the European Community and its member states, of the one part, and the Republic of Chile, of the other part.

[55] The industry is at the same time located in large spaces but concentrated within three regions in Chile. According to Ms Pittman these factors contributed to the control of the disease and the avoidance of its spreading to other farms.

[56] Notificación de Influenza Aviar, Government of Chile, Servicio Agrícola y Ganadero, October 2002; Chile País Libre de Influenza Aviar, Government of Chile, Servicio Agrícola y Ganadero, December 2002.

[57] Advisor on Sanitary and Phytosanitary issues, Market Access Department, Economic Directorate, Ministry of Foreign Affairs.

and universities). This teamwork was key to the successful control of the disease. It allowed the immediate implementation of an emergency plan that avoided the spread of the disease and the implementation of new non-binding biosecurity measures in the disease-free area to reinforce prevention of the disease. Government officials, OIE experts and the private sector stressed this element. They all agreed to label it as 'of vital importance'.

3. The active participation of Chile in international organizations such the WTO and OIE, informing them about the problem and the sanitation programme, coupled with the visit from OIE experts, resulted in a fair understanding of the situation in Chile.

The Chilean authorities indicated that if a similar situation were to arise again, only one element would be handled differently: the participation of entrepreneurs. It should be recognized that producers in the same production chain might have different interests depending on their individual output. The example mentioned was the discussion and analysis of vaccination as an alternative control measure.

At the same time, they raise their concern that although Article 6 of the SPS Agreement mandates regionalization, not all WTO members show the political will to implement it in a reasonable way. Lack of active implementation of this provision would greatly and unduly penalize a transparent, thorough and costly exercise such as the one performed by Chile. Consequently, and in the light of positive experiences such as this case, Article 6 of the SPS Agreement should be further developed.

The APA indicated that two other lessons learnt are the importance of taking extreme biosecurity measures in producing farms and the importance of producer associations able to lead the crisis on behalf of producers and able to relate rapidly with the public sector on an ongoing basis. They mention that one element requiring improvement is the ability of their laboratories to complete diagnoses in a rapid and efficient manner.

DG SANCO

Henri Belveze,[58] Maria Pittman[59] and Eva Maria Zamora,[60] offering their views in a personal capacity, highlight the same elements as key to the rapid reopening of the market for Chilean poultry exports.

---

[58] Deputy head of unit.   [59] Veterinary administrator.   [60] Veterinary administrator.

1. The transparency with which the Chilean authorities acted, at the outset of the outbreak of the disease and throughout the process.

2. The quality of the information regularly provided by Chilean authorities, which at all times was complete, coherent and consistent, including when questions were raised or follow-up information was requested. Equally important was the quality of the delegations present at the bilateral meetings held in Brussels. The delegations included veterinary and scientific experts able to address technical questions allowing for a rich exchange of information.

3. The quality of the veterinary services in Chile, which had been documented as recently as December 2001 by the European Veterinary Office. Of particular importance was the responsibility allocated by Chilean law to SAG to adopt necessary measures to guarantee the sanitary status of the country. In the absence of a recent mission by the Veterinary Office an urgent mission could have been necessary before the regionalization proposed by Chile was accepted.

4. The quality of the relationship between technical officials.

5. Chile's reliance on advice from experts recognized by the OIE.

In addition to these elements, it is the view of these DG SANCO officials that Chile's management of the crisis and the rapid response by the EU is an example to be followed by other WTO members. It is their view that other WTO members, faced with equally complete and scientifically valid information on the disease-free status of an exporting member, would not follow expedited procedures for accepting regionalization or, worst, would not accept the disease-free status of a member. According to these officials, some WTO members request a full risk assessment financed by the exporting country regardless of existing information concerning the last outbreak of the disease. Consequently, they consider that it would be useful to develop Article 6 of the SPS Agreement further, to establish guidelines that would lead to a similar positive response by all WTO members and avoid unduly penalizing trade after a sanitary situation is resolved.

OIE experts

Dr Ilaria Capua explains that from a sanitary point of view, the success of this case is primarily due to the rapid response offered by the Chilean veterinary authorities. In a short time a system of field veterinarians reporting, testing and handling information was organized. It all meant that a highly contagious disease 'did not get out of control'. In addition, the structure of the industry (an element also highlighted by DG SANCO[61]) posed an advantage for the control of this disease. The industry was concentrated in three regions, and breeding farms were physically separated from slaughterhouses and cutting plants.

Dr Capua considers that it is not possible to derive general lessons, as a sanitary response varies depending on the type of disease, the type of industry, the set-up of the industry and the set-up of the government.

Nevertheless Dr Capua emphasizes that this case shows that a developing country is able to manage a sanitary crisis successfully when its institutional organization allows for a fast response and when the authorities co-ordinate their efforts with industry.

Dr Capua mentions that success requires co-ordination with the private sector. In this particular case it was key to completing in such a short time the extensive testing of the industry and the stamping-out measures taken in the infected farms. This was key to avoiding the spread of the disease.

6 Conclusion

The circumstances surrounding the case thus indicate that this success story was no accident.

It seemed to be the natural consequence of thorough work by the Chilean veterinary authorities for years before the sanitary emergency appeared, coupled with commitment, institutional organization and collaboration with the private sector, trading partners and international organizations throughout the management of the crisis. The institutional organization of the veterinary services, particularly their independence and legal responsibilities, allowed them to take costly but necessary decisions expeditiously within an intergovernmental system of exchange of information and consultation. The case demonstrates that it is possible for a developing country to handle complex SPS emergencies which, if not controlled within days, can have potentially drastic consequences. It also demonstrates that by being transparent with importers the necessary confidence that the case has been resolved can be developed.

Both trading partners benefited from the legal and institutional framework set up by the WTO SPS Agreement. Based on their experience both argued for further developments of Article 6 of the SPS Agreement.

---

[61] Maria Pittman.

11

Shanghai's WTO Affairs Consultation Center: working together to take advantage of WTO membership

GONG BAIHUA*

1 The problem in context

China's accession to the World Trade Organization in 2001, following fifteen years of difficult negotiations, was a watershed event both for the WTO and its members and for China. Chinese government officials and those who followed the progress of the negotiations over the years knew that accession would bring with it the necessity of a large number of reforms in domestic economic policies, many of which would require adapting the outlook of Chinese business establishments. Those who understood the WTO also knew that it would be difficult to implement certain of the accession-related changes in ways that met the expectations of China's trading partners.

WTO membership also brought with it the opportunity to take advantage of new market access opportunities and new protections now available to China under the rules-based system of the WTO. As a non-member of the WTO, China found that its exports were often the subject of discriminatory treatment in overseas markets. In addition, as a country that was making the transition from a centrally planned economy to one where market forces would set prices and determine resource allocation, China often saw its exporting enterprises subjected to anti-dumping actions that treated Chinese exporters unfairly – often because of China's designation as a 'non-market economy'.

Shanghai has been at the forefront of China's economic reforms and opening-up to the outside world, and has played the leading role in China's adaptation to world trade rules. It was experts from the Shanghai Institute of Foreign Trade who, in early 1985, first proposed to the Chinese central government that China's GATT membership be resumed. This was

* Chief Officer for Information Services, Shanghai WTO Affairs Consultation Centre.

followed by the establishment of a Shanghai Research Centre on GATT, which drew upon the expertise of researchers from Shanghai and other Chinese universities.

The Shanghai WTO Affairs Consultation Centre (the Centre), sponsored by the Shanghai People's Municipal Government, is a professional, non-government consulting institution set up to provide legal and policy advice on WTO affairs, as well as WTO-related training services. Since its establishment, the Centre has contributed greatly to the fulfilment of China's WTO accession commitments, especially through support given to the central and regional governments in their adaptation to the WTO regime.

This case study examines the underlying rationale for the establishment of the Centre, the people in Shanghai and elsewhere who have contributed to the work of the Centre and the challenges faced by the Centre since its establishment. It is overall a story about how local government (supported by the central government) has been able to work with universities and trading enterprises successfully to establish and maintain an institution that is a model within China for how to organize to take full advantage of WTO membership. It is a model that should also be adaptable to other countries' situations.

2 The local and external players and their roles

A combination of external developments and local visionaries contributed to the eventual establishment of the Centre. Even then, it was not a project that could be realized overnight. In retrospect, Shanghai was probably the only city in China where progressive local government officials, academics and the business community could have achieved the critical mass necessary to set the Centre's establishment in motion in the pre-WTO period.

When China and the European Union (EU) reached bilateral agreement on the terms of China's WTO accession and signed an accord to this effect in May 2000, it became clear that China's WTO accession process was being accelerated. At the important annual Chinese central government Economy Work Meeting, the then President Jiang Zemin and Premier Zhu Rongji declared that preparation for WTO accession should be actively carried forward. To step up preparation for WTO accession, the Development Research Centre of the Shanghai People's Municipal Government, the Shanghai Planning Commission, the Shanghai Economy Commission and the Shanghai Foreign Relations and Trade Commission led the development of a 'Shanghai Action Plan Regarding China's Accession to WTO', which contained eighteen guidelines on WTO accession preparation. The publication of this action plan by the municipal government in August 2000 symbolized an important shift in Shanghai's WTO preparation work from a research phase to a more active implementation phase.

One of the major initiatives of the Action Plan was to set up a professional WTO consulting institute in Shanghai. In October 2000 this initiative culminated in the founding of the Shanghai WTO Affairs Consultation Centre. Those core individuals who planned the organization and activities of the Centre in these early days decided that the broad scope of the Centre's planned activities called for a management team that would be interdisciplinary in nature. In line with this thinking, the chief officers of the key divisions of the Centre come primarily from Fudan University, the East China Institute of Politics and Law and the Shanghai Institute of Foreign Trade. All of these individuals work for the Centre on a contract basis. Overall, there are six divisions in the Centre: the Consulting Services Division, the Information Services Division, the Training Services Division, the Monitoring and Early-Warning of Trade Remedy Measures Division, the Research Services Division and the Post-doctoral Programme Division. The Centre also has a high-level advisory committee with members from home and abroad, including the former director general and deputy directors general of the WTO, and some renowned WTO experts and scholars from China.

The peak decision-making body of the Centre is the Board of Trustees, which comprises representatives from Shanghai's various WTO-related government departments and industry associations. Under the leadership of the Board of Trustees, the president of the Centre takes care of daily business matters. The current president is Dr Xinkui Wang, who is also the president of the Shanghai Institute of Foreign Trade.

3 Challenges faced and the outcomes

During the period in which China's GATT status and the Uruguay Round were negotiated, the Development Research Centre of the Shanghai Municipal People's Government arranged for foreign trade and international law specialists to conduct a number of policy-focused research projects on the implications for Shanghai of resuming China's GATT membership and the Uruguay Agreements. Following the creation of the WTO in 1995, these specialists extended their work to cover issues related to the General Agreement on Trade in Services (GATS) and the Agreement on Trade-Related Aspects of Intellectual Property Rights (TRIPS).

Research experts in Shanghai continued their work after the WTO's establishment and began to focus on the eventual implications for China and their region of the country's planned accession to the WTO. Through the research and monitoring of the negotiations, it became clear that joining the WTO and adequately implementing the commitments that China would be asked to undertake would not be an easy task. In the late 1990s it was also becoming clear that China's growing industrial export base and highly competitive position in world markets would increasingly subject Chinese exporters to trade harassment in other markets – in particular to anti-dumping actions where China was often discriminatorily treated as a non-market economy.

In response to this research, the Shanghai Municipal People's Government recognized that Shanghai's preparation for China's WTO accession needed to be made as early as possible, and that further and more detailed work was needed on the challenges and opportunities that would follow accession. This work was initiated by the Development Research Centre of the Shanghai Municipal People's Government, the Shanghai Planning Commission, the Shanghai Economy Commission and the Shanghai Foreign Relations and Trade Commission, and was undertaken by a number of departments and WTO specialists. A research report on the impact on Shanghai of China's WTO accession was completed by the time the Sino-US WTO accession agreement was signed in November 1999.

When the decision was finally made on 26 October 2000 to establish the Shanghai WTO Affairs Consultation Centre, it was done purposefully, with the Centre being backed both by a written constitution and also by a clear statement of its mandate. In the documentation issued at that time by the original executives of the Centre, it was described as being the new 'driving force behind Shanghai's endeavour to turn itself into "One dragon head and three centres" and provide the city greater room for growth in the world'. The objective of the Centre was clearly described as taking active measures to cope with the opportunities and challenges that Shanghai would face after accession to the WTO. It was decided at the start that, constitutionally, the Centre's main functions would be to provide training, information, study, information and legal aid services which are related to WTO affairs; to assist governments, enterprises and public institutions to familiarize themselves with and to adopt practices that are in accordance with the relevant WTO rules; and to expand trade and economic co-operation with other countries around the world.

From the outset, the presence of the Centre appears to have been beneficial for Shanghai, in view of the clear need to strengthen and promote both Shanghai's and China's very important WTO accession-related work. In this respect, the Shanghai Municipal People's Government has made a point of consulting the Centre before promulgating its WTO-related regulations and policies. The Centre has also received strong praise for its work from abroad. The embassies of WTO members – including those of the United States, the European Union, Japan and Australia – have all communicated actively with the Centre. Indeed, the Centre has become a significant channel for communicating information related to WTO affairs.

In terms of its operations, the Centre provides the following major services to governments, enterprises and the public:

1. Consultancy services. Since its foundation, the Centre has provided consultancy services in relation to the central government's participation in WTO multilateral trade negotiations; supported the central government in efforts to modify laws and regulations to conform with China's accession commitments; supported local enterprises in defending their rights under WTO rules through remedies such as anti-dumping and other safeguard measures; formulated development blueprints for domestic enterprises to cope with various trade barriers; and provided early warning in relation to anti-dumping or other safeguard measures. The 'WTO Consultation Online Hotline' set up by the Centre has also become a major resource for its stakeholders.

2. Information services. The Centre has been collecting and disseminating WTO-related information through various channels since its establishment, and has become an important information source for the central and regional governments, enterprises and scholars alike. The Centre's website[1] reports WTO-related news from both home and abroad. Its 'WTO Reference Centre in Shanghai', set up by the WTO Secretariat, has become the major collection of WTO-related materials in Shanghai. The *WTO Newsletter* edited by the Centre is issued every two weeks, and covers a wide range of both domestic and foreign WTO-related news. The Centre also translates and publishes the WTO Appellate Body's reports and other monographs concerning WTO issues on an annual basis, to provide its readership with a timely and in-depth understanding of WTO affairs.

3. Training services. The Centre provides training programmes on WTO affairs for various WTO specialists and participants, such as government officials and lawyers. Since 2001, the Centre has delivered the

[1] www.sccwto.net.

'50/100 Senior Expertise Training Project on WTO Affairs' to more than 1,000 trainees. More than one hundred of these trainees have undergone further professional training in other major WTO member countries. Some of these have returned to take up key WTO-related posts in government and business enterprises.

4. Research work. The Centre benefits from a far-reaching research network made up of doctorate advisers, professors, and well-known experts and scholars in China and overseas who collaborate in their research into WTO-related issues.

5. Forum on WTO affairs. A major success of the Centre over the years has been the establishment of its annual WTO affairs forum as a globally recognized forum on China and WTO issues. An initiative of the municipal government, the WTO affairs forum takes place annually in November during the Shanghai International Industrial Fair. Advisors to the Centre and WTO experts from China and overseas are invited to the Centre for the forum, which provides a unique opportunity to review the problems and opportunities associated with China's progress in realizing the benefits of WTO membership.

In providing its information and consultancy services the Centre relies heavily on a network of WTO liaison officers in government, business enterprises, intermediary organizations, industry associations and related departments across Shanghai. This provides the Centre with both a feedback mechanism on the state of compliance with WTO accession requirements and, potentially, a vehicle for addressing particular issues that arise in this context. To the extent that such problems are then addressed, this has the potential to result in far-reaching improvements to Shanghai's business environment.

The practical orientation and value of the Centre are illustrated by two case studies on issues on which it has focused in recent years. Both the case studies addressed here demonstrate not only the expertise developed by the Centre on WTO issues over the years but also the direct and practical ways in which enterprises can benefit from the Centre's expertise.

Case study 1: automobiles – auctioning licence plates
and national treatment

In Shanghai, individuals seeking to purchase and register an automobile for their own use must obtain a licence plate for the proposed vehicle through a monthly auction conducted by the municipal government authorities. The system is designed both to reduce the total number of automobiles released onto the streets of the city at any one time and also to act as an important revenue source for the municipality. The reasons for the auction are domestic, and nothing in the system is supposed to be designed in a way that would affect international trade.

On 7 August 2002, US consulate staff informed the Centre that, to their knowledge, Shanghai's monthly licence plate auction for individual and private-company buyers was relying on one method of auctioning and allocating licence plates for domestically produced cars and that another method was being employed in the case of licence plate auctions for imported cars. The US authorities alleged that the imported cars were being subjected to discriminatory treatment that adversely affected market access for imports.

After being informed of the allegations, the Centre's specialists immediately began an investigation, and notified the Shanghai Municipal Development Planning Commission. An examination of the July auction rule used by the Shanghai International Commodity Auction Co. Ltd, as outlined on its website, showed that plans called for 3,000 licence plates for domestically produced cars to be auctioned, compared with just thirty licence plates for imported cars. On further investigation it also became apparent that the Commodity Auction Co. had set a floor price at auction for imported cars (26,000 yuan), but that no similar floor price existed in the case of domestically made cars. The practical effect was that domestically made cars were available at considerably lower prices (the average winning sealed bid at auction was 20,904 yuan).

In terms of the relevant laws and regulations, the Centre's specialists acknowledged that the Chinese government's accession commitments required imported cars and auto parts to be given 'national treatment'. The Centre's specialists also recognized that there was an indispensable relationship between a car and its licence plate, such that any restriction applied to a licence plate also applied to the car. Accordingly, given the WTO national treatment principle[2] and the general elimination of quantitative restrictions,[3] the different systems put in place by

---

[2] GATT Art. III (national treatment) states: 'The contracting parties recognize that internal taxes and other internal charges, and laws, regulations and requirements affecting the internal sale, offering for sale, purchase, transportation, distribution or use of products, and internal quantitative regulations requiring the mixture, processing or use of products in specified amounts or proportions, should not be applied to imported or domestic products so as to afford protection to domestic production.'

[3] GATT Art. XI (General Elimination of Quantitative Restrictions) states: 'No prohibitions or restrictions other than duties, taxes or other charges, whether made effective through

the regional government for the acquisition of domestically made and imported cars resulted in different treatment and were therefore inconsistent with China's WTO commitments. Under WTO rules, this had a direct effect on the extent to which the Chinese government was meeting its WTO obligations, as it is responsible for abolishing 'regional regulations, rules and other regional measures that contradict WTO obligations and duties'.[4]

To avert a potential trade dispute and protect Shanghai's reputation as a place to do business, the Centre was committed to addressing this particular example of non-compliance. It entered into negotiations with the Shanghai Municipal Development Planning Commission and suggested that any different treatment by the licence plate auctioning systems be discontinued. As a result, since October 2002 there has been no floor price for imported cars and no difference between domestically produced and imported cars in terms of limits placed on the number of cars auctioned.

In this case, the Centre's approach was to build up a contact network, and seek a number of opinions on whether the relevant laws and regulations were in line with WTO rules. This included the opinions of representatives of foreign enterprises. At the same time, the Centre carried out its own investigations and analysis, and was able to work with the relevant government departments on a quick and practical solution. In this respect, the Centre was an important link between government departments and the business sector.

Case study 2: an early-warning system for anti-dumping disputes in China

China's enterprises have exploded onto the international trade scene in recent years and have rapidly established major footholds in most major export markets. By the end of 2003, China's total trade volume reached US$850 billion. At the same time, Chinese exporters became the number one target of trade remedy measures taken by other governments around the world. Based on official statistics, counting from the first anti-dumping action taken against Chinese exporters in 1979 up to July 2004, Chinese exporters have been subjected to a total of 643 investigations

quotas, import or export licences or other measures, shall be instituted or maintained by any contracting party on the importation of any product of the territory of any other contracting party or on the exportation or sale for export of any product destined for the territory of any other contracting party.'
[4] Report of the Working Party on the Accession of China, para. 70.

covering regular and specific trade remedy measures initiated by thirty-four countries and regional groupings. More than 4,000 individual export products have been involved in these investigations.

While there has been this steep rise in trade remedy cases against China, many Chinese exporters lack the knowledge of the trade rules or the financial resources required to defend their interests. The Shanghai municipal government and the Centre recognized trade remedy actions early on as an area where the Centre could provide practical assistance to Chinese manufacturers and exporters. Working with the Ministry of Commerce in Beijing (MOFCOM) and with the Shanghai municipal government, the Centre started a project in mid-2002 aimed at developing a monitoring and early warning system on trade remedy measures with the objective of providing professional services to governments, exporters, manufacturers, chambers of commerce and trade associations.

Under the leadership of Dr Wang Xinkui, president of the Centre, Dr Yao Weiqun, associate president, and his professional team at the Centre were charged with developing a unique online monitoring and early warning system on trade remedy measures against China based on the use of information technologies. Prior to implementing the system in practice, the design team proceeded in phases. In the first phase of the design stage (Version 1.0, setting the United States as its subject), the monitoring and early warning system (V1.0) covers bilateral trade conflicts between China and the United States involving anti-dumping, and all the past and ongoing cases in this field are analyzed online to provide basic information for an early warning of future possible conflicts. At the same time a subsystem of this Version 1.0 was developed for transitional textiles safeguard measures taken by the United States against Chinese textile exports.

Over a two-year development period, the team gained a rich experience working with companies, chambers of commerce, trade associations and other professional services as it sought to hone its information technology interface with aspects of economic and trade patterns in combination with WTO rules. Over time, a system has gradually evolved that integrates computer science with the operation of trade and economic variables. In July 2003 the Centre launched the two prototype early warning systems in trial form. The first sign of success came with the issuance by the Centre's experts of an early warning report based on a petition by six US textile manufacturers' associations to the US Department of Commerce, aimed at initiating a procedure for transitional textile safeguard measures.

In June 2004 the Centre announced the establishment of V1.0 for anti-dumping disputes between China and the United States, in response to the increasing number of anti-dumping disputes with developed countries following China's WTO accession (WTO statistics show that of 2,416 anti-dumping cases being investigated at the end of 2003, about one-seventh involve China).

In its first stage, the V1.0 system covers 189 varieties of export goods in eighteen categories (mainly textiles, home appliances, steel and furniture) which are contained in the items accounting for some 60 per cent of China's annual total exports to the United States. Registered companies receive information on the quantity, future prices and dumping margins of Chinese products exported to the United States. Companies can also obtain monitoring reports on US trade remedy measures, and receive training services to help them respond to anti-dumping investigations or charges. They can register as members and access the information by logging on to two websites.[5]

One measure of the Shanghai Centre's success with the system is news that the Chinese Ministry of Commerce is now considering plans to develop early-warning systems on trade disputes in other major harbour cities, as a precursor to a nationwide world trade services system.

4 The Shanghai WTO Affairs Consultation Centre: lessons for others

The Shanghai WTO Affairs Consultation Centre is practically unique in the world in terms of its organization, focus and role. It is an important example of how government, business, academia and outside experts can think ahead to both the problems and opportunities likely to arise in connection with participation in the WTO system and then take action to organize themselves to deal with these problems and opportunities.

Although China is a developing country, Shanghai is undoubtedly a relatively rich region, both within China and in comparison with many other areas around the world. Clearly, there may not be many others (inside or outside China) with the resources to develop the high technology trade remedy measures early-warning system that the Centre has put into place. But there are surely less resource-intensive alternatives that could still provide value for money as government, business and outside experts work together to provide practical assistance to those seeking to draw maximum benefit from the rights and obligations of the WTO system.

---

[5] www.sccwto.net and www.shcei.gov.cn.

Within China, the Shanghai Centre has been recognized both by the central government in Beijing and by other neighbouring authorities as a valuable model for co-operation. The Centre's influence, therefore, is not limited to Shanghai but extends throughout China and beyond. Its experience vindicates the decision by the Shanghai Municipal People's Government to establish the Centre. Its example is one that could be followed by other countries striving for WTO membership, as well as those already in the WTO seeking to draw greater benefit from the opportunities provided by the multilateral trading system.

12

Costa Rica's challenge to US restrictions on the import of underwear

JOHN BRECKENRIDGE*

1 The problem

Setting the scene

In March 1995 the United States claimed that its domestic underwear industry was being seriously damaged or threatened with actual damage by imported cotton and man-made-fibre underwear[1] from Costa Rica and six other countries.[2] The United States initiated consultations with the countries alleged to be damaging or threatening its industry with the intention of invoking the transitional safeguard provisions of the Agreement on Textiles and Clothing (ATC).[3] During the course of these consultations, three of the seven countries agreed to quantitative restrictions on the imported underwear that would be allowed into the United States. However, after failing to reach agreements with Costa Rica, Honduras, Thailand and Turkey, the United States in June 1995[4] introduced restrictions on the importation of cotton and man-made-fibre underwear backdated to take effect starting in March 1995.

With the unilateral introduction of restrictions, the case was referred to the Textile Monitoring Body (TMB) for review and recommendations regarding the matter as required by the ATC. The TMB found that the United States had not demonstrated that its industry had suffered serious damage. However, it could not reach consensus on whether the existence of an actual threat of serious damage had been demonstrated, and thus recommended further consultations among the parties.

---

* Independent consultant based in Geneva, Switzerland.   [1] US textile category 352/652.
[2] The other countries were Colombia, Dominican Republic, El Salvador, Honduras, Thailand and Turkey.
[3] ATC, Art. 6.
[4] Thirty days after the 60-day consultation period as required by Art. 6.10 of the ATC.

The United States eventually reached agreements with Honduras, Thailand and Turkey after further consultations. However, the United States and Costa Rica were unable to reach a mutual understanding after consultations in August 1995 and November 1995. On 22 December 1995 Costa Rica began the dispute settlement process under Article XXIII of the General Agreement on Tariffs and Trade (GATT 1994) and the corresponding provisions of the ATC.

Why did Costa Rica decide to pursue the dispute settlement process? This key decision had significance beyond the immediate details of the specific dispute. The case was the first formal dispute settlement case to address issues arising from the intended liberalization of trade in textiles as embodied by the ATC and the first case in which a small developing country initiated a dispute against the United States.[5]

WTO context

In 1995 the newly created WTO and the recently concluded Uruguay Round of negotiations that culminated in the 1994 GATT offered its members improved access to the world trading system. All members had negotiated and agreed to these mechanisms, which, in the best judgment of the members, represented fundamental principles of free or liberalized trade that would serve the best interests of the members and the world trading system. However, in 1995 many of these mechanisms (chief among these being the Understanding on Rules and Procedures Governing the Settlement of Disputes (DSU)[6] and the ATC) remained largely untested. Given the immense discrepancies in relative political and economic influence among the members, would the system withstand the intense, but inevitable, political and economic forces that would be brought to bear on specific dispute cases?

At the time of this dispute, members could not predict how the new DSU process would function. Developing countries, in particular, were concerned about the new system's fairness.[7] In recent years, developing

---

[5] Costa Rica's case was only the fourth dispute brought against the United States. The countries bringing dispute cases prior to Costa Rica were Venezuela, Brazil and Japan.

[6] GATT 1994, Art. XXIII.

[7] Although this may have been the concern of developing countries and some observers at the time, there are those who now believe that the system favours developing countries. That is, it has become politically difficult for a large country like the United States to bring a dispute case against a small developing country because no one likes a bully, but it is easy for a small developing country to bring a case against a large developed country because

countries have initiated more than half of all new dispute cases.[8] However, at the time when Costa Rica initiated its case, no small developing country had brought a case against a large developed country. Many observers viewed confronting the United States as a risky strategy – not only for Costa Rica, but also for the DSU process in general. How would the United States respond to a ruling against it? Unwillingness by the United States to abide by such a ruling could undermine the credibility of the entire process.

Textiles in the world trading system

The Short-Term Cotton Arrangement (STA) of 1961 for the first time formally acknowledged special treatment of the textile sector in the world trading system. This special arrangement for cotton, which began as a one-year agreement, led to a sequence of arrangements on textiles spanning more than forty years. The Long-Term Arrangement (LTA) lasting from 1962 to 1973 and the Arrangement Regarding International Trade in Textiles (better known as the Multifibre Arrangement or MFA) lasting from 1974 to 1994, for all practical purposes exempted the textiles sector from GATT rules and discipline.[9] The ATC, which succeeded the MFA in 1994, explicitly acknowledged the need to integrate the textile sector into GATT and set a definitive end date (31 December 2004) for the special treatment of the sector. However, at the time of the Costa Rica–US dispute the liberalizing impact of the ATC remained unclear. And the history of textile treatment in the world trading system justified a certain level of scepticism.

Costa Rica's perspective on the problem

Costa Rica had just approved the Uruguay Round. The administration gained domestic political support for the agreement by promising that if the country was willing to undertake trade liberalizing reforms, Costa Rica would benefit from increased rights and opportunities within the

everyone loves an underdog. However, developing countries point out that they need the protection of a formal dispute process. They say that the large developed countries do not need a formal process to put pressure on their trading partners.
[8] 'WTO Dispute Settlement 1995-2003: A Statistical Analysis', *Journal of International Economic Law*, 2004.
[9] M. Raffaelli and T. Jenkins, *The Drafting History of the Agreement on Textiles and Clothing*, Geneva: International Textiles and Clothing Bureau, 1995.

world trading system. Now, almost before the ink on the new agreement had dried, the promise of new rights and opportunities seemed in jeopardy. From Costa Rica's perspective, the United States' efforts to impose restrictions were inconsistent both with the spirit of the ATC's goal of integrating textiles into the GATT and with the ATC provisions for transitional safeguard measures. Costa Rica believed that the United States, as part of a systematic strategy, was attempting to maintain control of a vertically integrated industry by requiring countries to use US fabric in garments intended for the US market. The restrictions effectively only applied to underwear garments made with fabric not of US origin. In essence, the United States was attempting to protect its fabric industries rather than the domestic underwear industry. This strategy would allow the United States to control the entire production chain while utilizing cheaper labour from Costa Rica (and other developing countries) for assembly. Costa Rica argued that the transitional safeguard measures available under the ATC did not provide for restrictions to be applied to the products of one industry (underwear garments) in order to protect the interests of another industry (fabric).

Of course, focusing only on the legal issues and the facts of the case ignores the political complexities of Costa Rica's decision to pursue a dispute settlement case through the WTO. Many diverse political and economic stakeholders with potentially conflicting priorities and interests influence a decision to pursue a formal dispute settlement process. Several other countries were in a similar situation to that of Costa Rica, yet only Costa Rica chose to proceed with a dispute settlement case. What were the internal dynamics in Costa Rica that led to the decision to pursue the case?

2 The local and external players

Government players

Within Costa Rica, three governmental entities actively influenced the course of events. The Ministry of Trade handled technical trade-related matters and relations – particularly in the context of WTO issues. The Ministry of Foreign Affairs was responsible for matters of international relations. Costa Rica's embassy in Washington, typically headed by a politician with significant clout in the Costa Rican government, handled matters of specific interest to the United States–Costa Rica relationship. These groups did not always see eye to eye on policy matters. The Ministry of

Trade had only gained the status of a formal agency in the late 1980s and was, therefore, a relatively new governmental entity. The gradual evolution of a group handling trade issues into a formal agency meant that the Trade Ministry's jurisdiction was not clearly established in law, which sometimes led to conflicts with the Ministry of Foreign Affairs. The Ministry of Foreign Affairs tended to believe that trade issues were a subset of foreign relations and should be managed within the context of its broad perspective on Costa Rica's international relations. The prospect of bringing a dispute settlement case against the United States strained the relationships between these agencies, since the Ministry of Foreign Affairs and the Washington embassy did not initially support the action.

When Costa Rica became aware of the US plan to impose quantitative restrictions on the underwear industry, the Minister of Trade, José Rossi, gave responsibility for the case to a team of young lawyers.[10] Irene Arguedas, Francisco Chacón, Roberto Echandi and Anabel González had all received law degrees from top US universities and had developed a reputation as serious and competent technocrats. They provided Costa Rica with the necessary technical and legal capacity to handle a dispute settlement case.

Private-sector players

In the period leading up to the dispute, clothing manufacturing had been one of the fastest growing export sectors in the Costa Rican economy, largely because the country had begun to process imported textiles into garments for export. This activity had benefited greatly from the US value added tariff provisions[11] and preferential access to the US market under the Caribbean Basin Initiative. Industry growth also coincided with a Costa Rican economic reform programme designed to raise domestic value added to products of export interest. The textiles and clothing industry achieved significant gains in the value added/output ratio.[12]

Consequently, the textile and clothing industry was an important industry at the time of the dispute, and although the restrictions only

---

[10] Everyone on the team was under 35 years of age and two of the team were under 30. Even the minister was still in his thirties.

[11] This is sometimes referred to as '807 Trade' in reference to the chapter in the former US tariff schedules by which it was covered. At the time of the dispute this trade was covered by item 9802.00.80 of the Harmonized Tariff Schedule of the United States (HTSUS).

[12] Trade Policy Review of Costa Rica, 1995 (document WT/TPR/S/1).

affected a segment of the overall industry, the potential economic consequences to the textile and clothing sector as a whole were significant.
Costa Rica was a relatively high-cost, although globally competitive, producer of textiles and clothing. However, committing to the use of relatively
high-cost US fabric would almost certainly undermine Costa Rica's long-
term competitiveness in the global textile and clothing market. In order
to remain competitive Costa Rica would need the flexibility to source its
fabric from the lowest-cost suppliers.

Generally, the Costa Rican textile sector was very supportive of pursuing the dispute. However, US multinational corporations had substantial
investments in the textile sector and lobbied actively and publicly against
pursuing the dispute case.

3 Challenges faced and the outcome

Costa Rica needed to gain the domestic support of key Costa Rican stakeholders to pursue the case at all. The Ministry of Foreign Affairs and the
Costa Rican embassy in Washington held similar views concerning the
decision to pursue the DSU process – given the narrow economic stakes
in this particular case, the potential pay-offs of the underwear dispute
did not justify risking the broader relationship with the United States.
However, it was not just inter-bureaucratic quarrelling, but fundamentally different points of view that led to the divergent attitudes among the
agencies towards this trade dispute. From the perspective of the Ministry
of Trade these differing points of view represented a generation gap. They
perceived the prevailing view among their colleagues in the Ministry of
Foreign Affairs, who tended to be much older, as derived from an earlier
era when the economy had been geared toward the Central American
market and focused on import substitution. The Trade team believed that
the Ministry of Foreign Affairs underestimated the importance of the
WTO rules-based trading system to Costa Rica's economic development
strategy, and hence viewed the potential dispute as primarily a textile
issue. The Trade team viewed trade, and Costa Rica's full participation in
a rule-oriented international trading system, as essential to the country's
economic future.

While the team from the Ministry of Trade did not believe that the case
should be pursued at all costs, they were motivated by strategic considerations in addition to the economic stakes. Roberto Echandi, a member
of the legal team, stated the strategic point as follows:

[In] the Uruguay Round, a balance had been reached regarding the incorpo-
ration of textiles to the normal rules of trade (away from the unilateralism
and discrimination of the Multifibre Arrangement). After such a balance
was reached, here came the United States and unilaterally attempted to
ignore the deal. That was extremely dangerous to an economy as dependent on trade and on the US market as was Costa Rica's.

The Ministry of Foreign Affairs and the Washington embassy characterized the Ministry of Trade's position as unduly influenced by the
'romantic' and 'theoretical' ideas of a group of naïve technocrats. In their
opinions, realpolitik should prevail.

The domestic textile industry did not automatically support pursuing
the case either. As Irene Arguedas, a member of the team from the Ministry
of Trade, recalls, two different types of companies worked behind the
scenes to influence the decision to pursue the dispute settlement process.
The first were those who were vertically integrated with the US industry
and sourced their cut fabric from US suppliers. These companies could
export their product back to the United States under the Guaranteed
Access Level (GAL) programme[13] and were in favour of an amicable or
negotiated solution. The other group of companies consisted of those
who sourced their fabric from places other than the United States. They
were not eligible to export their product to the United States under the
GAL programme. The access of these companies to the US market would
be directly affected by the specific limit (SL) quota restrictions and they
were correspondingly more interested in pursuing the dispute.[14]

In the face of the strong reservations of key political players within
Costa Rica and the aggressive lobbying by the US trade officials and US
multinationals with investments in the textile industry,[15] the Ministry of
Trade had to make strong and persuasive arguments to go ahead with the

[13] Guaranteed access levels, or GALs, are the specific negotiated quota levels for particular
products being given more favourable treatment because the products are made from
fabric formed and cut in the United States. Generally the GALs being proposed by the
United States as part of its overall restraints considerably exceeded the levels of current
trade and would, therefore, have no real impact on trade in such products.

[14] It should be noted that a similarly challenging political dynamic was mirrored in the
structure of the US industry. Companies using a totally domestic process to manufacture underwear would likely be threatened by increased imports of underwear. However,
companies using 807 programmes to assemble their product abroad could benefit from
increased imports. Therefore consensus among industry on the trade dispute in the United
States was likewise unlikely.

[15] Members of Costa Rica's trade team say that lobbying efforts on the part of the United
States in this case were among the most aggressive they have witnessed.

case. However, even within the Ministry of Trade, team members were reluctant to pursue the case, especially alone.

Members of the Ministry of Trade team recall that 'in order to avoid bearing the burden of testing the system alone' they attempted to forge alliances with other countries. First, they sought the support of other Central American countries facing similar issues to Costa Rica. However, those countries feared the potential double consequences of losing a dispute settlement case and/or losing access to the US market. Next, Costa Rica attempted to gain support from Turkey, Pakistan and India. Costa Rican trade officials travelled to Geneva to meet with the ambassadors to the WTO. Although these countries acknowledged that they faced similar issues, they did not believe that they could forge the domestic coalitions necessary to bring a dispute case to the WTO. India said that it would support Costa Rica at the WTO with a third-party submission, but would not join as a complainant in the case.[16] Costa Rica would have to make the decision to pursue the case alone to test 'whether the concepts and principles of GATT would in fact apply to the textiles sector'.

Ultimately, José María Figueres, the president of Costa Rica, decided to initiate the dispute settlement process. He was a former Minister of Trade himself, and had recently studied strategy and competition while pursuing a degree at Harvard University. Consequently he appreciated the strategic argument that the case transcended the economic considerations of the underwear industry. Failing to take a stand on what Costa Rica perceived as a threat to its rights under the GATT could eventually lead to a larger, and economically substantive, risk – the erosion of Costa Rica's ability to participate in and benefit from the world trading system.

Once the decision was made to pursue the case, the administration still had to decide how to handle its prosecution. Although the Ministry of Trade legal team was well educated and had a reputation for good work, they were also perceived in some quarters as too young to lead Costa Rica's challenge in such an important case. Therefore, several attempts were made to secure outside counsel to assist with the case. However, given the amount of research the in-house team had already conducted on the specific issues, they found that they already knew more than the 'experts' they interviewed. In addition, the costs of retaining outside legal counsel were very high. Eventually, concerns about the limited value to be added by an external counsel relative to the costs and the fact that the

---

[16] India clearly had an interest in the case, as it subsequently brought two textile-related cases against the United States (DS 32 and DS 33) just months after the Costa Rican case.

case seemed legally straightforward, led the key stakeholders to allow the existing trade team to handle the case.

Despite the concerns about pursuing the case and managing its prosecution, Costa Rica prevailed in both the dispute settlement process and the subsequent legal appeal. Not only did Costa Rica receive favourable rulings, but the United States also accepted and conformed to the decisions.

From Costa Rica's perspective there were several positive outcomes in addition to the legal outcome of the case. First, the case helped to build the perception domestically (and internationally) that small countries could benefit from membership of the WTO. Second, without substantively damaging the relationship, Costa Rica gained an increased level of respect from the United States and more generally among WTO members. Finally, the country gained significant experience and expanded its capacity with regard to international trade and legal issues, while the legal team within the Ministry of Trade further enhanced its reputation for credibility within the Costa Rican government.

4 Lessons for others (the players' views)

Costa Rica, despite its concerns about 'testing the system' alone, used the mechanisms available to it as a WTO member to ensure that important principles of the multilateral trading system (as agreed upon by the members' economies) were appropriately applied. The 'system' worked as intended in this case. Almost ten years after the dispute, both developed and developing countries regularly use the DSU process. This case, as an early test of the system, clearly pointed to some lessons.

Anabel Gonzales of the Costa Rican legal team identified one general lesson related to managing trade disagreements: 'Never underestimate a trade conflict. Pay attention to it from the beginning and throughout the process.' The United States probably underestimated both Costa Rica's resolve and its capacity to prosecute the case. While the other countries identified by the United States as posing a threat to its underwear industry quickly agreed to settle with the United States, Costa Rica did not. When the case went before the dispute settlement panel, many discrepancies in the information provided by the United States substantively undermined the credibility of the claim that its industry was being damaged.[17] The Costa Rican trade team handling the case believed that if the

---

[17] See WT/DS24/R.

United States had seriously thought that a dispute settlement panel would eventually scrutinize the case, they would have assembled the data supporting their case more carefully.

While there were not many things that the team from the Ministry of Trade would perhaps have done differently if given the chance, Costa Rica's experience in navigating the DSU process suggests several additional lessons. Despite Costa Rica's success in this case, Irene Arguedas emphasizes that countries should use the DSU as a genuinely last resort: 'First, it is key to exhaust every possibility there may be to try to avoid the dispute and settle with your partner.' Pursuing a dispute case is intellectually demanding, time-consuming, resource-intensive and politically stressful. Only when the alternatives have been exhausted and the potential risks of not pursing the case are substantial should countries initiate a case.

It is important for complainants to be well prepared. They must have a detailed understanding of the case issues and believe that there are substantive legal grounds for bringing the case. As Anabel Gonzales puts it, 'Before taking your case to the [dispute settlement process], make sure you know it and [are confident] it is a winner.' Having the capacity to handle the case is part of being well prepared. Technical and legal expertise is essential to being prepared for what is often described as an intense process. Irene Arguedas makes the point this way.

> Once the process is launched, it moves according to the time periods provided by the [DSU], which are short (though adequate). It means that there is no time to learn! Therefore, in order to be able to face adequately this kind of challenge, it is key to have good in-house technical and legal expertise. Capacity building is normally a challenge and resources are usually lacking, but, in the absence of that, chances of success are minimal.

The members of the Costa Rican legal team believe that it has become even more difficult to handle a dispute settlement case as the process has evolved and parties have become more sophisticated than they were in the early days of the system. While capacity building is often difficult, it can nevertheless not be overlooked.

Even if a country thinks that the DSU process is its last resort, and that it has a well-prepared case, it should make sure it has the solid support of key players in government, industry and other stakeholders before proceeding with the case. Irene Arguedas says, 'It is absolutely crucial to have solid support from the government and from at least an important part of the industry. In our case, the support of the President ... was key.'

In addition to government and industry stakeholders, Anabel Gonzales suggests developing strong relationships with the domestic and international press. The Costa Rican team held regular informational meetings for the press to educate them on the issues and keep them informed about developments. While building relations with the press will not win a case, having the public media supporting a case is generally an advantage in maintaining domestic support. Ultimately, forging a solid and reliable domestic coalition is at least as important as preparing a quality case.

Finally, even when a country has exhausted other options, fostered capacity, prepared a solid case, and forged domestic support, building relationships with allies can enhance the case. In this case, India's third-party submission supporting Costa Rica's case was symbolically important. In addition, discussions with India during the case and India's contributions to the oral hearings were very helpful to the Costa Rican team.

In reflecting on the case nearly ten years later, members of the Costa Rican team all expressed enthusiasm for the opportunity to have played an active role in the dispute settlement process. Although the underwear case is nearly a decade old, liberalization of textiles within the world trading system continues to present challenges for member economies. As the ATC's 31 December 2004 deadline for the full integration of textiles into the GATT approached, the battle over textile quotas continued. Textile trade groups from countries that benefited from quotas continued to lobby aggressively for delays in their scheduled elimination.

13

Fiji: preparing for the end of preferences?

ANDREW L. STOLER*

1 The problem in context

This case study of Fiji explores the way in which its government and people are preparing to deal with the expected end of preferential trading relationships, and is based largely on interviews conducted in Fiji over several days in August 2004. In March 1997 the WTO Secretariat published its report of Fiji's first review under the Trade Policy Review Mechanism (TPRM).[1] Paragraph 37 of the report's summary observations provides a good starting point for the current study. It reads, in part:

> Fiji's economy depends heavily on sugar, tourism and clothing. The need to lessen the dependence on the sugar industry may become more urgent as Fiji's preferential status in its sugar export markets is eroded in the long term. Similarly, the clothing sector, also facing an erosion of preferential access, could require efficiency gains to remain competitive. Diversification of the economy will, however, require attention to the problem of shortages of professional and technical personnel that have resulted from the high rates of emigration over the past decade.[2]

What has happened in Fiji since 1997 to facilitate diversification of the economy away from reliance on preference-dependent sectors and what policies and strategies are being pursued to this end? Can this small island nation adapt its workforce and economy to cope with the challenges of the early twenty-first century? Fiji's successful adaptation to change would be important to both the country and the region, while failure would probably have grave consequences.

---

* Executive Director, Institute for International Business, Economics and Law, University of Adelaide.
[1] WTO Secretariat, *Trade Policy Review – Fiji*, Document WT/TPR/S/24, 13 March 1997, Geneva: World Trade Organization.
[2] Ibid., p. xiii.

2 The local and external players and their roles

Fiji's political and economic relations with the countries affording it preferences for its exported goods – mainly Australia, New Zealand and the
European Union (EU) – have long been key to the islands' prospects for
success. As a sign that Fiji's relations with the EU are more significant
than its need to participate in the WTO, Fiji maintains an embassy in
Brussels that – as a part-time responsibility – looks after developments in
Geneva. Decisions made in Canberra, Brussels and Wellington are criti-
cally important to policy-makers in Suva. This is a tough position to be
in, and one would expect that it would encourage Fijians to co-operate
with each other as a way of promoting a common cause.

The government and the state-owned sugar company have traditionally
played a central role in Fiji's economic development. The government's
Native Land Trust Board and the Fijians it represents is another central
actor. Foreign investors are also important, particularly in the garment
sector, where they dominate the ownership of the industry. The government and private-sector outside investors should be working together.

However, even a few days on the islands are sufficient to give an outside
observer the impression that politics have deeply divided key local players.
The role played in Fiji's affairs by these local actors will hopefully be
apparent in the section that follows. In many cases the local players seem
to have permitted their disagreements with fellow Fijians to guide their
actions in ways that are unlikely to advance what some would imagine
should be commonly shared goals.

3 Challenges faced and the outcomes

Fiji's trade and economic prospects are heavily dependent on developments in a few key economic sectors. The challenges faced in these sectors,
current policies and likely prospects are explored below.

Sugar

The sugar sector of the global economy is undoubtedly one of the most
distorted, given the plethora of production and export subsidies and
extremely restrictive access barriers complicating sales to the world's
major sugar-consuming markets. Tragically, sugar is also a commodity
that many developing countries have come to depend upon as a mainstay
of their local economy and as a principal source of export earnings.

At present, the sugar sector in Fiji is central to the overall wellbeing of the national economy. The industry contributes 7%[3] of the country's GDP, and generates between $250 million and $300 million in revenue each year.[4] The sugar industry directly employs some 35,000 people, while around 220,000 people – including farmers, cane cutters, truck drivers and mill workers – depend directly or indirectly on the sugar sector for their livelihoods. In international trade terms, sugar is the country's second most important export, after garments.

The sugar industry has benefited significantly over the years from access to the EU's preferential trade regime for sugar. Under the arrangement, the EU pays prices substantially above world market price levels for imports of sugar from specified ACP[5] countries – up to three times the world price – with about half of the preferential import quota allocated to Mauritius and the rest divided among sixteen other ACP suppliers. Although the programme is quite complicated in its operation, its bottom line effects are easy to understand. At the time of writing, the world market price for raw sugar stood at around 35 cents a kilogramme; the cost of sugar production in Fiji amounts to about 42 cents a kilogramme. Roughly 48% of Fiji's annual sugar production is exported to the EU at a price nearly three times the world price level, about 25% of production is consumed locally and the rest is exported mainly to the world market at a price that reflects a significant loss relative to the cost of production. Already, these statistics reveal a fragile situation – but additional internal and external dynamics are combining to make the picture even more dire.

Within the EU, changes are being debated to sugar policy that, if implemented, would drastically cut the price paid for preferential sugar imports from ACP countries. The scheme, as it has existed up to now, is collapsing in part under the weight of dramatically increased imports of sugar into the EU from least developed countries under the 'Everything But Arms' (EBA) preference arrangement. None could have anticipated nor imagined how quickly EBA sugar suppliers could ramp up their production. Reportedly, sales of EBA sugar into the EU from countries such as Sudan, Bangladesh, Mozambique and Zambia have reached a level of around 1.8 million tons in just over two years. On top of this, the WTO case brought against the EU sugar regime by Brazil, Australia and Thailand

---

[3] Theodore Levantis, Frank Jotzo and Vivek Tupule, 'Ending of EU Sugar Trade Preferences, Potential Consequences for Fiji', *ABARE Current Issues* 03.2, 2002, p. 2.
[4] Arthur McCutchan, *Fiji Business*, August 2004, p. 3.
[5] African, Caribbean and Pacific.

could require the EU to cut the intervention price for sugar by up to 40%. A final external factor to take into account is competition from Brazil. Officials in both Fiji and Mauritius have told the author that Brazilian sugar suppliers are probably unique in being able to sell on the world market at world prices and still make a profit – although there are allegations of heavy subsidies to the industry in that country. Moreover, Brazil's sugar-producing capacity is reportedly growing rapidly, further exacerbating competitive pressure on suppliers such as Fiji.

Against this rather bleak global picture, how is Fiji preparing for the likely end of preferences for its sugar exports? By all accounts, the situation of the industry is bad and getting worse. Rather than working hard to make the industry more competitive in an effort to remain in the sugar business, the government, farmers and the sugar industry all appear to be working at cross-purposes. Ross McDonald, the chairman of the board of the Fiji Sugar Corporation, has been quoted as saying, 'My observations are that generally all the stakeholders are pulling in their own direction.'[6]

Looking at the current situation in Fiji's sugar industry, an outside observer could be tempted to reach the conclusion that an unconscious decision has been made to abandon the industry even before the end of the EU's preference scheme. A critical problem is that of land tenure. Some 87% of the land in Fiji is owned by ethnic Fijian extended families and managed by the Native Land Trust Board (NLTB), and most of the farmland devoted to sugar cultivation was leased, mainly to Indo-Fijians, for thirty-year periods under the provisions of the Agriculture Landlord and Tenants Act of 1976. Those leases, the bulk of which have evidently expired over the past three to four years, are not being renewed. The Indo-Fijians are leaving farms and the ethnic Fijians are evidently not taking up sugar farming in their place. Consequently, sugar production has fallen dramatically as land is taken out of production.

A further problem, not unrelated to the land tenure issue, is the fact that farmers have allowed many fields to degrade to the point where some landholdings have supplied as many as twenty ratoon crops.[7] Part of the

---

[6] McCutchan, *Fiji Business*, p. 4.

[7] In the first year of a sugar cane crop, stalks of cane are planted in freshly ploughed ground, and when the crop matures the cane is cut and the stump left in the soil. New cane will grow from these stumps, although its quality in terms of sugar content will generally decline with each passing year. Cane grown from stumps of the previous harvest is known as a 'ratoon' crop, and experts say that after a maximum of three ratoon crops the stumps should be removed, the ground re-ploughed and new stalks planted. A twentieth-generation ratoon crop would likely produce considerably lower sugar yield.

reason for this can be ascribed to the reluctance of farmers to invest in new plantings when they expect to leave the land. Another fact that cannot be ignored is that the Fiji Sugar Corporation pays farmers for the weight of cane delivered to the mills, with no regard to the cane's sugar content. Sugar mills in Fiji are antiquated and have benefited from very little investment over the years. Bagasse, the by-product of sugar-cane processing, which in Mauritius is used to power electricity production in specially configured plants, goes to waste in Fiji because the electricity company and the sugar company cannot agree on the price to be paid for the bagasse. Finally, despite the millions of tons of sugar it has exported to the EU at intervention price levels over the years, the Fiji Sugar Corporation is reportedly insolvent and remains in business only through government grants and guaranteed loans. In these circumstances, it has clearly not been in a position to undertake the kind of product development research and marketing activities that have characterized the Mauritian sugar industry.

Is there a coherent sugar strategy for the future? If so, it is not apparent according to the views of people who should know. The government is watching very closely the debates in Brussels and hoping to hang on to whatever benefits it can for as long as possible. Even if sugar production in Fiji has declined dramatically in recent years, it will be years before there can be a wholesale changeover to alternative agricultural production.

Luke Ratuvuki, the chief executive of the Ministry of Agriculture, Sugar and Land Resettlement, observed that there are many other crops that can be successfully cultivated in place of sugar, but the transition will take some time. Fruits, maize, rice and vegetables are all possible, but the government is interested in ensuring that there is value added through local processing and this will require substantial amounts of (mainly foreign) investment. Cut flowers might be another option, but transportation apparently poses problems. Exporting cut flowers to rich overseas markets requires reliable and reasonably priced air transport. According to Ratuvuki,[8] Air Pacific – which is practically the monopoly international air service to Fiji – typically has its cargo space booked out long ahead of time and charges rates which would make cut flower shipments non-competitive.

If the NLTB's policy of systematically terminating leases of agricultural land to non-ethnic Fijians was designed to have produced economic and social benefits for the indigenous community as part of a government 'blueprint' launched four years ago, that policy seems to have failed

---

[8] Interview with the author, 18 Aug. 2004.

spectacularly. According to an article in the *Fiji Times*,[9] a recently issued Asian Development Bank report found that the Fijian population in squatter settlements had increased dramatically, with 5,295 Fijian squatter households in the Central Division compared with 3,377 Indian squatter households. In what some dismissed as a highly partisan reaction to the report, the Labour Party's leader in the Fijian parliament, Mahendra Chaudry, was quoted in the newspaper article as saying that 'the notion of landless Fijians is preposterously ironic, given the fact that about 90% of land in Fiji is owned by Fijians'.

The garment sector

The garment-producing sector is the most important industrial sector in Fiji today and can generally trace its origins to a combination of domestic incentives, the existence of the global scheme of allocated trade for textiles and apparel under the GATT's Multifibre Arrangement and the WTO successor arrangement, and special preferential trading arrangements put in place by Australia and New Zealand under the South Pacific Regional Trade and Economic Co-operation Agreement (SPARTECA). Most of Fiji's garment factories are foreign-owned and many depend upon preferential access for their continued profitability. In the 1990s the production and export of garments grew rapidly, but in recent years the industry has been hit by three factors that could well threaten its long-term viability.

A first major problem concerns the impending end of quota arrangements under the WTO's Agreement on Textiles and Clothing (ATC). Faced with the potential closure of many foreign-owned plants that were established in the country solely to take advantage of Fiji's quota in developed country markets, the government in Suva has had to consider its position in the WTO. According to Isikeli Mataitoga,[10] chief executive officer of the Ministry of Foreign Affairs and External Trade, the government is attempting to address this problem by joining with other textile and apparel exporting countries in the so-called 'Istanbul Consensus Group' to seek a three-year extension of the restrictive trading arrangements under the WTO.

Such an extension is likely to be problematic. In any event, far more important to the future of the garment industry in Fiji is the SPARTECA

[9] Imran Ali, 'Blueprint Failed', *Fiji Times*, 20 August 2004, p. 3.
[10] Interview with the author, 18 Aug. 2004.

arrangement and preferential access to the Australian market. As the orig-inal SPARTECA scheme drew to a close in 1999, Fiji lobbied Australia for a new scheme that would include relaxed rules of origin for certain cate-gories of products. A new SPARTECA-wide scheme was agreed and ready for implementation when the 2000 coup in Fiji put everything on hold, leaving the industry in limbo for some time and hitting many producers very hard. The arrest of the coup leader and the installation of an interim government allowed the new preferential arrangements to go into effect, but with a termination date of end-2004.

In July 2004, just months before the termination date, Australian Prime Minister John Howard agreed (on the fringes of a South Pacific Forum meeting in Apia, Samoa) to an extension of the treatment. According to Mark Halabe,[11] managing director of Mark One Apparel, the Howard government's agreement to extend preferential treatment to imports of garments from Fiji is a success story of government working with industry in Fiji. He also gives credit to lobbying assistance from the Australian textiles, clothing and footwear (TCF) industry and his Australian buyers who helped to convince the government in Canberra that the preference scheme should be extended.

Halabe is an Australian national whose garment factory, located in a tax-free factory zone fifteen minutes' drive from Suva, employs about 600 people – mostly indigenous Fijians. On the day of the author's visit to the plant, the production line was focused on work shirts and vests, most of which incorporated reflective safety materials. State-of-the-art comput-erized fabric mapping and cutting machines ensure rapid and accurate cutting of shirt parts and an efficient use of fabric. Other high-tech equip-ment sews pockets and flaps onto the shirts in seconds, supplementing the work of employees at industrial sewing machines.

Halabe is of the view that while extension of the WTO ATC quotas may or may not benefit some segments of the Fijian garment sector, the seven-year extension of preferential treatment in the Australian market will set up a situation where some segments of the industry will be well positioned to survive over the longer term in a non-preferential environment. Part of the reason for this optimism is that the new seven-year preference arrangement for Fiji is thought likely to be related in its operation to the Australian government's Strategic Industry Plan that incorporates important incentives for the use of productivity enhancing equipment. In addition, Halabe hopes that several million dollars might be made

---

[11] Interview with the author, 19 Aug. 2004.

available to the garment industry in Fiji to fund training and assist in recapitalization of production facilities.

Today, Fiji's garment sector employs some 14,000 people, with garment exports exceeding the value of sugar exports (although the statistics collected by the government in Suva evidently mask the importance of the sector by subsuming textiles and clothing statistics within a broader category of 'manufacturing'). After China, Fiji is the second most important supplier of garments to the Australian market, with a market share of about 6%. Where will the industry be in seven years' time, when the preferential regime expires?

In Halabe's view, the industry has a long-term future even without a preference in the Australian market. Although he readily admits that the Fijian industry will never be able to compete with Chinese suppliers on price, he considers that there are other factors that will keep Fiji in the Australian market. Chief among these is the fact that Fijian manufacturers will be more responsive to the needs of their customers in the relatively small Australian market than is likely to be the case with Chinese producers who concentrate on realizing economies of scale through massive production runs aimed at far larger markets in the United States, Japan and Europe. The Fijian industry on the other hand has a long history of relationships with Australian buyers and will be able to supply quality garments, on time and at a stable price. In seven years' time it is likely that continued differential labour costs will see the migration to Fiji of most garment manufacturing now taking place in Australia.

Alternative opportunities for the future

Naturally enough, Fiji's economic and trade prospects for the future are not limited to sugar and garment production; a number of other alternatives present themselves. In recent years, mining – mainly for gold – has accounted for as much as 3% of GDP, but a combination of technical difficulties in production and wide swings in the world price for gold have undermined the sector's viability. Fiji is the location of the world's largest mature mahogany plantation and the country is poised to benefit from the harvesting of this renewable resource. Exploitation of the mahogany plantation has reportedly been delayed by political infighting over how the revenue from the timber should be shared. The author was told by more than one interviewee that tensions over this question contributed to the impetus for the 2000 coup.

According to Luke Ratuvuki, the commercial fishing sector has grown rapidly in recent years and holds great promise for the future. The industry specializes in fresh and chilled tuna, as well as canned tuna. The canned product is exported mainly to the United States and EU countries, while substantial quantities of sashimi-grade tuna are exported to Japan. Fiji has acted to retain a certain amount of the exploitation of this sector for locals by limiting foreign fishing fleets to set quantities.

Tom Vuetilovoni, Fiji's Minister for Commerce, Business Development and Investment, is quick to point out that Fiji has some important success stories. Fiji Water, a locally bottled mineral water, has benefited from effective marketing to become the second-ranked mineral water in the lucrative US market. He notes that the fact that the Southern Cross cable passes through Fiji on its way from Australia and New Zealand to the United States creates important opportunities for Fiji as a regional centre of information communications technology (ICT) activities. ANZ Bank, for example, has located a significant call centre in Fiji.

Vuetilovoni admitted that a complicating factor limiting growth in the ICT/Internet sector is the very high price currently charged by Fiji's monopoly telecommunications company for Internet service provider (ISP) access. This situation is likely to change as the monopoly seeks government approval to realign its cost and pricing structure, which up to now has used high Internet and international connection charges to cross-subsidize cheap local calls. The company is seeking the right to offer different packages, some of which will dramatically lower Internet access charges.

Other services sectors present a mixed picture for Fiji. Not surprisingly, tourism features importantly in the government's plans for the future. There have also been promising discussions with foreign-based film-makers, many of whom have evidently found Fiji to be a cost-effective location.

Brian Singh, chief executive officer for the Ministry of Labour, Industrial Relations and Productivity, admits that one problem Fiji faces in the services sector harks back to the WTO Trade Policy Review's comment on the shortage of professional and technical personnel. According to Singh, Fiji has no long-term plans for future skills training. The problem of a lack of skilled personnel has become critical in some sectors. In the construction industry, for example, a lack of trained local labour has led to the importation of substantial numbers of construction workers from the Philippines. The construction sector is not the only segment of the economy with a labour shortage. Evidently the growth in the supply of trained local hotel staff has not kept pace with the anticipated expansion of the tourism sector, contributing to concerns that expatriates might need to be hired for catering and catering administration jobs in Fijian hotels and resorts.

Traditionally, Fiji draws most of its overseas tourists from Australia, New Zealand, Japan and the United States, and the sector is very important in terms of its contribution, directly and indirectly, to employment, foreign exchange earnings and the viability of the national carrier, Air Pacific (a major stake in which is held by the Australian airline Qantas). Although exclusive five star and 'five star plus' accommodation is available in Fiji, most of the industry's development to date has been centred on the middle-class Australian and New Zealand tourist markets, which tend to be price-sensitive. In this context, it seems clear that a more competitive and efficient aviation transport sector in the Pacific, able to provide good quality service at reasonable prices will be a key factor in the development of the tourism industry in Fiji and neighbouring islands.

The future of the sector was the focus of discussion at the July 2004 Fiji Tourism Forum. At that meeting, the chief executive of Air Pacific, John Campbell, was reported to have issued a number of warnings about the future prospects for tourism in Fiji.[12] As a strategy for countering competition from 'no frills' airlines that were beginning service to Fiji, Air Pacific had cut ticket prices from Australia and New Zealand by up to 30% only to find that its ability to fill its flights was being compromised by a number of negatives in the Fiji hotel and resort sector. According to Campbell, a major problem is that many Fijian hotels are raising their prices for rooms, food and drink, and telephone calls to levels that are threatening to price them out of business. He commented that a lack of quality hotel rooms is also a problem in the market, compounded by the fact that electricity and water supplies are not matching demand, with the consequence of potential 'brown-outs' compromising the industry's ability to provide services of a quality expected by tourists. Campbell also cited infrastructure problems and deficiencies at Nadia and Nausori airports, resulting in long immigration lines and slow baggage delivery as issues that required priority attention if the sector is to grow.

Another issue that has arisen recently to complicate the tourism sector relates to the way in which tourist resorts are financed. As is now commonplace in many tourist locations, developers in Fiji have supplemented their

[12] Robert Keith-Reid, 'Air Pacific Chief Warns Tourism Industry', *Fiji Islands Business*, August 2004, p. 13.

sources of financing by selling units in resort hotels to private investors who are normally expected to turn the unit over to the hotel management in exchange for a share of the income. These private investors, naturally enough, enjoyed benefits and tax breaks similar to the resort developer – benefits the Fijian government proffered in the belief that additional hotel rooms would enhance the prospects for tourist arrivals and spending on the Fijian economy. Things went awry at one major development when it became known that many of the private-sector investors in hotel units were opting to pocket the tax benefits from their investment and then live in the units they had purchased instead of making them available for use by tourists. The government reportedly reacted to this development by suspending the benefits it had previously made available to the private sector investors, effectively ending this form of tourist development financing.

4 Lessons for others: Fiji's approach to loss of preferences

Many people would argue that in the world of 2004 the sugar industry is not the industry to pursue as a means of making money. Many of them would also argue that the best course of action for a country in Fiji's circumstances would be to get out of the industry. Such comments ignore the fact that sugar continues to be a mainstay of the Fijian economy and the country's most important employer. That said, there can be little doubt that an unhappy combination of political infighting, misdirected policies and a lack of investment in new technologies and infrastructure has put the Fijian sugar industry on a long downhill slide. In the absence of a major turnaround effort, Fiji anyway appears to be on its way out of this industry. As Ross McDonald put it recently, 'We now have this one window of opportunity and it's an opportunity we have to take. We have to stop pointing fingers at everybody else and work together to get the industry moving again. The alternative is a disaster, and that's something we cannot contemplate.'[13] If the Fijian sugar sector is to prepare for the end of preferences, it must face a long and tough internal reform before it can hope to be competitive in world markets.

The outlook is far more optimistic for the garment sector. While it is true that both the government and industry's first reaction to the end of preferences has been to seek a further extension of special trading arrangements (both in Australia through SPARTECA and in the WTO through

---

[13] McCutchan, *Fiji Business*, p. 7.

association with the Istanbul Consensus group), there are nevertheless reasons to think that Mark Halabe's vision of Fiji as a cost-competitive niche supplier of quality garments to the Australian market is a real possibility. But that industry needs to remain focused and to take advantage of the time remaining for preferential trade to undertake needed training programmes and investment in technologies contributing to efficiency gains. The Fijian government will likely need to co-operate as well. From the interviews conducted by the author, it seems that many of the garment producers now in Fiji would probably leave if the government implemented its rumoured plans to end the tax-free factory scheme.

Fiji's failure to deal effectively with skilled labour shortages that were already apparent in 1996 when the WTO Secretariat conducted its trade policy review must be viewed as a serious concern. With the sugar industry in long-term decline and limited opportunities to create employment for Fijians in sectors such as the construction industry and tourism, it makes no sense at all for the country to be importing workers from the Philippines and elsewhere when it could be training its own nationals in these areas.

Political instability has hit Fiji hard in recent years. Many comments were made to the author about the number of companies which saw their businesses undermined or ruined by the events of 2000. Although the country seems to be settling down under the rule of law – something that has been demonstrated this year by the government's acceptance of the jailing of the Vice Prime Minister – one cannot escape the impression that many serious economic issues are still treated as political footballs in Fiji. Too many stakeholders are still pulling in their own directions instead of co-operating for the common good; this is not preparing Fiji particularly well for the day when its preferential trade arrangements disappear.

14

The road to Cancún: the French decision-making process and WTO negotiations

JEAN-MARIE PAUGAM*

1 The problem in context: how does France participate in multilateral trade negotiations?

France is a major trading power and has steadily followed a long-term path of trade liberalization since the launch of the European Common Market. 'France's exports rank fourth for goods and third for services, with a structural surplus representing approximately 2 per cent of GDP. Five millions jobs are based on exports. Foreign companies are responsible for one-third of our industrial production.'[1] While not directly engaged in negotiations in the WTO, France participates in the European common trade policy and is deemed a 'pivotal' state, particularly on agriculture. Yet little research attention has been devoted to the political economy of trade reform in France.

This study surveys French decision-making relating to trade, from summer 2002 to the Cancún WTO Ministerial. It focuses on market access issues, which by no means embrace France's trade negotiating priorities. Following Rodrik, we assume that 'all the political economy models provide a particular story about how organized groups or individual voters can take political action to reinforce or alleviate the income-distributional consequences of trade flows . . . The conclusion in common is: trade is not

---

* Senior Research Fellow, IFRI (Institut Français des Relations Internationales). This study relies on the views of decision-makers, and only public sources – speeches, press communiqués, articles, statements, and reports from government, administration and civil society stakeholders – are used to report the opinions and decisions of political authorities. Speeches available on government websites are only referenced by dates. The study is further based on selected interviews of public and private decision-makers and on inside analysis provided by 'players'.
[1] H. Testard, 'Notes Bleues de Bercy', N-269, April 2004.

free because politically influential groups can be made better off by policy interventions on trade.'[2]

One of the suggestions presented in this paper is that standard assumptions about the influence of organized groups on trade reforms are globally verified: France's political economy entails no cultural exception. Another suggestion is that institutional settings, both at national and at European Union (EU) level, substantially affect the outcome of French decision-making.

2 The players and their role: setting the French political economy variables

Conventional models root the demand side of trade policy in individuals' preferences, channelled through organized groups, and the supply side in policy-makers' preferences expressed through the institutional structure. While acknowledging that 'values, identities, and attachments, play an important role in explaining the variations in preferences over trade',[3] this paper concentrates on decision-making, thus dropping the analysis of French public opinion preferences. One reason is that opinion polls do not reveal, *prima facie*, striking differences between French and other European opinions on trade, the WTO, or even the Common Agricultural Policy (CAP).[4]

Policy-makers' preferences

Trade and agriculture. Players acknowledge that a consensus exists among policy-makers: agricultural goods are not considered common goods, because what is at stake outweighs trade interests. President Chirac of France often stated this vision:

> It is essential to remember that agriculture does not reduce to the trading framework in which international negotiations too often pretend to lock it . . . Before involving international trade, debates over agriculture, on the global scale, are really debates over food sovereignty, which relies above all on agricultural development. The goal that we must pursue in agricultural matters is to achieve food security for all. Trade negotiations must not lose sight of it.[5]

---

[2] Rodrik (1994), 'What Does the Political Economy Literature on Trade Policy (Not) Tell Us that We Ought To Know?', NBER, 1994.

[3] Mayda and Rodrik (2002), 'Why Are Some People (and Countries) More Protectionist than Others?', Department of Economics and JFK School of Government, Harvard.

[4] 'Eurobarometer', October 2003; 'Views of a Changing World', Pew Global Attitudes Project, June 2003.

[5] 13 June 2003.

Diplomatic advisers to the Trade and Agriculture Ministers explain, 'The WTO negotiations always cloud political issues with coded language. Behind technical negotiations, what is always at stake is the very legitimacy of agricultural policies. France systematically reformulates what the negotiation really is about, politically.'

Trade and diplomacy. The French elite may grant second-rate status to trade policy. 'Trade policy is not a French notion; trade is considered a by-product of diplomacy', suggests Hubert Testard, Deputy Chief Trade Negotiator. Players admit that French trade policy integrates broader foreign policy options. Some mention the stakes of transatlantic relations and development policies in that regard.

Trade and partisan politics. Players do not support the claim of a right/left partisan divide on trade.[6] 'The right may seem slightly more flexible on public services and the left on agriculture. Such nuances are infinitesimal. There is no French political divide on trade policy', asserts Philippe Gros, permanent delegate to the WTO.

Institutional design

For Damania and Frederiksson,[7] 'to influence trade policy, special interest groups must influence all such (collective or individual) actors with veto rights over policy changes. The empirical literature ... has ignored the fact that trade policy is determined by more than one veto player.'

Three features are particularly relevant for trade policy within the French democratic framework. The French Constitution grants pre-eminence to the president, over the government, on foreign policy (*domaine réservé*). The Trade Minister[8] runs a specialized administration (DREE)[9] within a strongly institutionalized interministerial decision-making process: a secretariat (SGCI)[10] headed by the Prime Minister's office exclusively clears French positions on EU policies. Parliament's involvement is slight.

As an EU member state, France promotes its positions through the EU Council of Ministers (Foreign Affairs); trade policy decisions are prepared

---

[6] H. Milner and B. Judkins, 'Partisanship and Trade Policy: is there a left–right divide on trade policy?', Columbia University (2001).

[7] R. Damania (2004), 'Trade policy: what's welfare got to do with it?', University of Adelaide and P. G. Fredriksson, Southern Methodist University.

[8] Delegated to the Minister of Economy, Finances and Industry.

[9] Direction des Relations Economiques Extérieures.

[10] Secrétariat Général du Comité Interministériel pour les questions de coopération économique européenne.

by the Article 133 Committee, where the EU Commission consults with member states, other Council formations are also relevant, particularly those relating to agriculture, environment and development. To that end, building coalitions with other EU member states is needed. A good bilateral dialogue with the EU Commission, at all levels, is also considered a decisive channel.

Players adapt their strategy to this multi-dimensional institutional design.

Lobbying strategies. 'We simultaneously promote our positions at all levels', says Francis Delemotte, Head of International Trade of UIC.[11] Marc Maindrault, his counterpart at MEDEF,[12] adds: 'Many businesses privilege trade lobbying through European Industrial Branches Federations. These are the heart of power: they hold the information that the Commission needs to elaborate its proposals. Other important business organizations can influence the Commission, for instance the European Round Table.' Hence the lobbying efforts may prove asymmetrical: 'Offensive sectors tend to go to Brussels, while defensive one speak both in Brussels and Paris. So the government hears much more from the latter', analyzes Laurence Dubois Destrizais, Assistant Secretary for Multilateral Affairs, Trade Ministry.

Bureaucratic influences. The confrontation of administrations' views can modify the influence of vested interests: some administrations represent selected political constituencies, others global interests. 'The interministerial process allows us to blend purely conceptual approaches of trade liberalization with grounded facts and sector-specific stakes. It makes our positions more accurate,' thinks Fabrice Gourdellier, Head of the Trade Policy Unit of SGCI. Most players support this claim.

Political strategy. Positions taken by the government must be interpreted against the background of EU competences. Sylvain Lambert, diplomatic adviser to the Agriculture Minister, stresses that 'France does not talk as a first-rank negotiator. Its role is not to substitute for the EU negotiator but to nuance his arguments, remind him of priorities and signal red lines.' Hubert Testard remarks that 'We are not overall defensive on the WTO. But since 80% of the negotiating time is spent on agriculture, the political level is forced to intervene more on it, which gives a defensive tone to our positions.' Otherwise, the government's positions on trade must be understood within a global dialogue with the Commission: trade negotiations are but one dimension within EU policies (CAP, competition, economic co-ordination, fiscal discipline and so on).

---

[11] Union of Chemical Industries.   [12] A French major employers' union.

Bilateral relations. Member state coalitions are decisive. Within the wider Franco-German dialogue, the Trade Minister regularly consults with German counterparts. 'Germany is the only country with which we have such an institutional dialogue', observes Philippe Gros. Players suggest that the Franco-German agreements on CAP reform were decisive in the making of EU positions for Cancún. But they also stress a difficult Franco-German co-ordination on trade, due to opposing defensive priorities. Thus, case-by-case coalitions are also built with other countries, depending on issues.

Vested interests and organized groups

Vocal agricultural lobbying

'We make sure that our voice is heard at the national and European levels',[13] claims Patrick Ferrere, Director General of FNSEA.[14] Players see the French agricultural lobbying on WTO negotiations as better organized and more efficient than other sectors. Agricultural organizations maintain a constant public pressure on the government at each step of the trade negotiations. What is at stake? Ferrere explains:

> 'France is *the* agricultural country in Europe. Our agriculture represents roughly 25 per cent of Europe's total agriculture, and accounts for 400,000 equivalent full-time jobs involving 1.2 million people through seasonal activities. The agro-food industry employs 600,000 people. Both factors make it the first French employer. These incomes have multiplying effects on all our rural life. Therefore, recognizing agriculture was, and remains, the condition for French participation in European integration. Due to higher labour, environmental, sanitary and quality standards, our agriculture bears higher costs than anywhere else. This is why, since its inception, Europe has twinned its trade and agriculture policies: controlling market access is a prerequisite to organizing agriculture.

In 2000, agriculture and the agro-food industry accounted for 2.3% and 3% of French GDP, respectively. France received 22% of the €44.5 billion spent by the EU-15 in 2002 on the Common Agricultural Policy (CAP). Benefits from subsidies are highly concentrated. Main public supports for market regulation break down as: arable crops (57%), bovine meat (22%) and the dairy sector (6%). With a decreasing number of farms since 1990, the average farm payments 'almost doubled in real terms, to

---

[13] Through participation in the Comité des Organisations Professionnelles Agricoles de l'Union Européenne/Comité Général de la Coopération Agricole de l'Union Européenne (COPA-GOCECA).

[14] The main French farmers' union.

reach €18,679 in 2003, 81% of which came from the EU'.[15] The highest farm payment averages were geographically very concentrated.[16]

'Public support for our agriculture has been very substantially reduced since 1992', observes François de la Gueronnière, Deputy Director for International Affairs at the Agricultural Ministry. 'First, because price support as a CAP tool has been much reduced since 1992; second, because subsidies and production have been essentially decoupled, which eliminates most of the trade distorting effects.' This analysis is consistent with OECD findings.[17]

Hence virtual high stake 'losers' as a result of liberalization are increasingly concentrated. Conversely, players hardly identify a 'winning side' from agricultural negotiations.

First, the EU is not seen as a prospective international market player. 'We really target the EU-25 market: 450 million consumers', says Patrick Ferrere. Gueronnière adds, 'Since the Uruguay Round the assertion of our agricultural export vocation faded. The agricultural surplus was then viewed as a major asset to balance our current account and strengthen the exchange rate. It is no longer the case. We now maintain a non-agricultural trade surplus and the euro took over from the franc, which eliminated the exchange rate problem. So our focus in trade negotiations shifted to the defensive side.' Moreover, major French agro-food exports, such as wine and spirits,[18] do not rely on CAP supports.

Second, throughout CAP reforms, structural contradictions with the WTO Agricultural Agreement remained. Hubert Testard observes: 'There was a structural incompatibility between the Agreement on Agriculture and historical CAP instruments. This essentially ended with the 2003 CAP reform.' As Ferrere stresses,

> First, the WTO undermines the CAP concepts of price and production support. Second, it does not acknowledge the supply side management limiting EU production since 1984, yet this allowed the Cairns Group and the United States to take over former European exports in third markets. Third, market access negotiations focus on tariffs and ignore the European demands for labelling of food origin, geographical indications and sanitary requirements.

---

[15] 'Les concours publics de l'UE dans les quinze Etats membres' and 'Les concours publics à l'agriculture en 2003', MAAPAR, 2004.

[16] 'Les concours publics à l'agriculture française: bilan des aides 1990 à 1997', Economie et statistique N°329-330, 1999, INSEE.

[17] Tangerman, 'Overcoming Discrimination against Agricultural Exporters', Paris: Cordell Hull Institute, July 2004.

[18] 40% of agro-food exports in 2001.

Third, the US instruments are considered under-disciplined. 'With deficiency payments, marketing loans, food aid, export credit, the US farmers get the full set of possible supports', adds Ferrere. For all players, no domestic political support for agricultural reform can be built without strictly balancing the EU and US concessions.

Weak corporate lobbying

Players remark: 'Businesses are silent'; 'MEDEF's negotiating positions are much too general'; 'Businessmen almost never take up multilateral issues with ministers'; and 'The president of MEDEF never speaks on the WTO.'

Jacques Desponts, chairman of MEDEF's and UNICE's[19] WTO committees, considers that

> French business lobbying remains domestically centred. It is extremely hard to have businesses express priorities on trade negotiations. The first MEDEF position was constructed for Seattle and we achieved a similar position with UNICE. Yet French companies do not invest enough time in UNICE compared with northern Europeans. As a result, they are cashing the horserace bets in reverse order: we get 'agriculture, industry and services' instead of 'services, industry and agriculture'.

Other business players concur. Dominique Jacomet, Vice-Chairman of UIT,[20] notes:

> Internationalization in our sector is rooted in the multilateral system. We have strong interests, offensive and defensive, in WTO rules: TRIPS enforcement, tariff peak elimination, anti-dumping ... So we are very active internationally, at all levels. However, the priority given to agriculture hardly allows France to promote our interests.

Why are industrial and services sectors not better at trade lobbying?

First, WTO market access may have lost relevance. Hubert Testard notes that 'a major change since the Uruguay Round comes from the trillion dollars of accumulated foreign direct investment, mainly involving multinational companies. They reduced pressure on market access. The big benefits of tariff reductions would now fall on small and medium-sized enterprises (SMEs), less influential than multinational groups within MEDEF.' Others observe that France trades mostly within the EU, with preferential trading zones and OECD countries maintaining average low tariffs.

---

[19] Union of Industrial and Employers' Confederations of Europe.
[20] Union of Textile Industries.

Second, evaluating the gains does not prove to be easy. 'It is hard to measure robustly national gains from trade liberalization. Some statistics cannot be isolated from the EU's. It is almost impossible to reach a simple measure of gains in the services sector. Thus policy-makers must balance certain and measurable losses in agriculture against vague and uncertain gains in other sectors', says Mathilde Lemoine, economic adviser to the Trade Minister.

Third, the lobbying strategies of businesses vary. Marc Maindrault analyzes:

> MEDEF permanently updates its negotiating priorities with information from members' organizations. But the information is uneven because sectoral interests are diverse. Some branches efficiently monitor their WTO interests, others less so. Some have domestic and European objectives, without a stake in the WTO. Some federations represent one, or two, major groups: these have their own international strategies, without relying much on collective action. Major leaders directly discuss their important issues with the Trade Commissioner.

Politically efficient NGOs

Non-governmental organizations (NGOs) in France are considered influential on policy-making. Mathilde Lemoine explains: 'They have a political approach to the negotiations. They usually focus on a single issue, for instance access to medicine. They bring in experience on the ground, especially on the development dimension. They have reactive international networks: policy-makers understand that NGOs may promote their political priorities more swiftly than heavy diplomatic channels.'

French authorities thus hold regular meetings with 'civil society', associating NGOs, businesses, trade unions and members of Parliament in trade negotiations. Business lobbies deplore the fact that an indiscriminate process grants disproportionate influence to NGOs. 'Businesses make trade, not NGOs', says Jacques Desponts.

3 Challenges and the outcome: the forming of French positions in the Cancún market access negotiations

This section analyzes the way in which the decision-making process translated French political objectives into the Cancún market access negotiations (agriculture, industry, services). For each major negotiating step,

France took part in the consensus provided by the EU member states to the Commission.

French political priorities

Re-elected in 2002, President Chirac expressed his priorities for the Doha Development Agenda, particularly during France's presidency of G8 in 2003. (i) He gave his overall vision of the trading system: trade is good for the economy if 'openness to trade, defined in the WTO framework, comes with precise rules of the game'.[21] (ii) He drew the French 'red lines': 'France favours free trade but not under any conditions. It trustfully takes up the Doha Round and will be vigilant on three sectors: cultural goods, which can never be considered common trading goods; agriculture, in order that the Doha Decision be compatible with the CAP; services, so that openness does not undermine great public services as education and health.'[22] (iii) He asserted his vision of development, focusing on the needs of the poorest countries, especially African countries. In a major address, the president made three proposals for Africa's trade: 'A moratorium decided by all developed countries on destabilizing export subsidies directed towards Africa, during the WTO negotiations'; 'a special and privileged trade treatment for Africa' through 'a common and unique' preferential scheme amongst developed countries; a new endeavour against commodities prices volatility, 'in particular cotton'.[23]

The government promoted the presidential options. Trade Minister François Loos stated: 'we want trade liberalization to come with the laying of a regulation'.[24] He subsequently insisted on his priority on access to medicines as a major regulatory issue for the WTO. The Agriculture Minister defended the compatibility between development and the CAP.[25] The government rejected the Cairns Group's arguments: 'No, the CAP does not strangle the poor countries!'[26]

Agriculture: 'the chicken and egg story'

'The chicken is the CAP, the egg is the WTO', the EU Trade Commissioner Pascal Lamy often said,[27] pointing out systemic links between the internal

---

[21] 21 May 2003.   [22] 30 April 2003.   [23] 21 Feb. 2003.   [24] 9 July 2002.
[25] 'The Case for the Defence', *Economist*, 9 Jan. 2003.
[26] H. Gaymard, F. Loos et P. A. Wiltzer, *Le Figaro*, 21 Dec. 2002.
[27] 'Cancún: agriculture et libéralisme', *Le Figaro*, 9 Sept. 2003.

and external dimensions of agricultural reform. The French priority was really the chicken. 'The WTO was not really on the political agenda. What politically mattered was the CAP reform proposed by the Commission. WTO negotiations were but one of the many variables of CAP reform', assesses Fabrice Gourdellier. However, the EU Commission saw Cancún as a deadline motivating the reform. The Agriculture Minister explained to the French Parliament that 'nothing that has happened in Brussels over the past few months can be understood unless it is linked with the discussions before the WTO'.[28]

Chicken

The Franco-German dialogue was decisive for CAP reform. Step one occurred in October 2002, when the German Chancellor and the French President agreed to cap the CAP budget for 2006–13. Sylvain Lambert explains: 'At stake was the future of the *acquis communautaire* in the EU-25. Germany accepted the phasing in of farmer's direct payments for new members. France agreed to keep the CAP budget under control with a stabilized global envelope and budget correctors if the ceilings are reached.'

Step two resulted from the Luxembourg CAP reform of June 2003. France had vigorously opposed a deep reform, initially not planned to take place before 2006 (Agenda 2000). Minister Gaymard made it clear: 'About the evolutions of the CAP, I wish to restate our complete opposition to the decoupling proposed by the Commission.'[29] Nevertheless, the Franco-German dialogue reached an agreement endorsing the idea of 'partial decoupling', which paved the way for the Luxembourg agreement. The general 'decoupling' of subsidies was decided, with room for manoeuvre left to governments willing to keep minimal links between subsidies and production levels. Patrick Ferrere stresses that 'farmers resented Luxembourg as a major fracture: the EU was no longer willing to regulate agricultural markets and shifted supports from production to farm incomes. This raises a fundamental question of the legitimacy of subsidies: farmers want to work, not to sit and wait.' Nevertheless, 'the reform came about without dramatization or major conflict', observes Sylvain Lambert.

Egg

France systematically engaged the WTO negotiations in defending the CAP status quo, while never departing from the EU consensus.

[28] 11 March 2003.   [29] Berlin, 17 Jan. 2003.

First, the EU negotiating offer included: a Uruguay Round tariff reduction formula – a 55% reduction in domestic subsidies and a 45% reduction in export subsidies. Farmers criticized an offer 'which exhausted the full room for manoeuvre of the European Union before the real start of the negotiations'.[30] The French government nevertheless endorsed it.[31]

Second, Stuart Harbinson, chair of the WTO Agriculture Negotiating Group, presented two draft 'modalities' for negotiations: France, the EU, and a majority of WTO members rejected both as unbalanced.

Third, at the G8 Evian summit the EU had endorsed the French proposals for Africa, including a moratorium on all destabilizing export subsidies. 'The Africa initiative signalled our readiness to move, provided all others would. It is still on the table', analyzes Anne Cazala, diplomatic adviser to Trade Minister Loos. But the G8 stonewalled and watered down the proposals and the moratorium was not agreed.

Fourth, the CAP reform changed the EU negotiator's mandate. For Sylvain Lambert,

> the EU had fully delivered for Cancún. Looking at the facts instead of ideology, European agriculture is the only sector that has been reformed three times since the Uruguay Round. Meanwhile the United States raised support 70% and partially re-coupled their subsidies with the Farm Bill. This refutes arguments about our alleged defensiveness on agriculture. But reforming the CAP cannot be the only game in town. So we refused to pay once in Brussels, twice in Geneva.

The fifth crucial step resulted from the transatlantic agriculture agreement of August 2003. It departed from previous EU positions, especially with the concept of a 'blended tariffs formula'. France was surprised by the Commission's proposal but did not reject the move. The Agriculture and Trade Minister jointly 'took note of the agreement between the EU Commission and the American negotiator on some of the topics of agricultural negotiations in the WTO' and stated that 'the government will exert the highest vigilance in respect of the mandate given by the Council to the Commission, who negotiates on behalf on the European Union, and in particular in respect of commitments made in the Luxembourg agreement of 26 June, reforming the CAP'.[32] Laurence Dubois Destrizais explains: 'The Commission presented the EU–US agreement as a fait accompli. But

---

[30] Agrisalon.com, 17 Dec. 2002.
[31] Agrisalon.com, 12 Feb. 2003.   [32] 13 Aug. 2003.

while it was a clear change of strategy, the Commission had not crossed the red lines.'

Eventually, Cancún failed before agriculture was negotiated. 'The agreement between the transatlantic negotiators had shown that the USA were not ready to put figures on a "modality paper,"' thinks Sylvain Lambert. 'This is why agriculture was not discussed in Cancún.'

So the egg did not challenge the chicken.

Non-agricultural market access: the lonely long-distance runner

'Ministers Mer and Loos launched an evaluation process to assess our offensive and defensive commercial interests. It helped progress towards a more offensive French attitude in spite of our agricultural sensitivity. The tariff negotiation was the main focus of businesses, yet they could hardly reach an aggregated vision of their offensive interests', relates Christophe Lecourtier, international counsellor to the Economy and Finance Minister. 'Under low pressure from businesses, the process was essentially fed by efforts from a few industrial sectors and economists to measure France's interests', reminds Laurence Dubois Destrizais.

The evaluation was positive.

> The net job surplus derived from trade and investment is estimated between 500,000 and 600,000 net job creations over the last ten years. It is a very clear positive result, which leads the Ministry of Economy and Finance to pro-mote, both in the domestic inter-ministerial debate and the negotiations, a globally offensive attitude, even though we have an agricultural sensitiv-ity. We also assessed our defensive industrial interests, which involve some labour-intensive sectors, and they represent less than 10% of the tariff lines.

'We are resolutely offensive and we argue for the elimination of all duties over 15%', declared Minister Loos.[33] Hence, while most of its political cap-ital was invested in agriculture, France fed the EU demands for ambitious industrial results. It supported the first Commission proposal of a tariff 'compression mechanism' (a complex harmonizing formula within tar-iffs bands) and sectoral negotiations for textile, clothing and footwear. In April 2003, France demanded improvements in the negotiating modali-ties proposed by Ambassador Girard, chair of the non-agricultural market access (NAMA) negotiating group.[34] In August 2003, France supported a

---

[33] 8 April 2003.
[34] For the EU, 'Girard's formula' favoured protectionist countries, since its results depend upon each country's initial bound tariffs levels.

transatlantic agreement endorsing the previous US call for a 'Swiss formula'. In Cancún, France and the EU asked for improvements in Chairman Derbez's draft 'modalities' for NAMA. Cancún's failure left the business unfinished.

Services: hot political agenda, cold bureaucratic work

French political interest in services goes back to the Uruguay Round 'cultural exception' debate. Priorities were crystal clear for Cancún: two out of three presidential 'red lines' (culture and public services) fell on the services negotiations. They were shared by policy-makers and unchallenged by businesses.[35] Cultural diversity objectives were enshrined in the EU negotiating directives and Commissioner Lamy broadly shared the French position on public services.[36] France also promoted offensive demands. Minister Loos stressed: 'France is the world's third service exporter. The sector now provides 72% of jobs against 57% in 1980. We have an excellent negotiating position since the EU has already reached a high level of liberalization. Our objective is reciprocity from other countries, taking into account their level of development.'[37]

Nevertheless, France experienced strong NGO pressure during the preparation of the European services offer. Major campaigns were initiated against the General Agreement on Trade in Services (GATS) at national and EU levels.[38] NGOs asked for transparency of the EU offer and argued in defence of public services, national regulatory rights and access to basic services in developing countries. The campaigns had political effects. When the EU released its offer to the WTO (April 2003), the 'AGCS [GATS]-free campaign' could claim fifty French local government areas (four regions, twenty *départements*, twenty-six municipalities) as self-declared 'GATS-free zones'. Members of parliament put questions to the government. The political debate then – temporarily – faded after the release of the Commission proposals on an NGO website.

The political debate stimulated a heavy inter-ministerial process, but problems were not found where the NGOs had indicated. Fabrice Gourdellier relates,

---

[35] J. M. Messier, former chair of Vivendi Universal, was unanimously criticized for declaring the 'death of the French Cultural Exception' in 2001.
[36] European Parliament, 10 March 2003.
[37] 25 Feb. 2003.   [38] See www.agcs.free.fr.

We started in November 2002 organizing sectoral meetings to identify the limits of our 1994 commitments, check the corresponding legislations, and assess our negotiating margins. In the end, we narrowed down to six sensitive issues needing discussion with the Commission. For the decisive 133 Committee meeting, only one technical problem was left, on Mode 4. We were not alone amongst member states. So the issue went to the Council of Ministers which eventually adopted the offer, with an interpretative statement. Mode 4 was especially difficult in the inter-ministerial debate because of conflicting bureaucratic cultures: DREE was unfamiliar with migration policies while the Department of Populations and Migrations had barely confronted the European process, much less the WTO.

Eventually, the services negotiations became peripheral to Cancún core political issues.

4 Lessons for others

On its road to Cancún, France stuck to the European consensus and its long-term commitment towards progressive trade liberalization and multilateral negotiations. In so doing, French decision-making on trade revealed the following features.

1. Overall, in keeping with theoretical predictions, protected producers are more likely to organize themselves efficiently when their interests are concentrated and their consumers dispersed. In a context of declining agricultural support, concentrated potential 'losers' proved very active. 'There is a clear vision from the political level that our interests in the negotiations mainly involve agriculture, thus are fundamentally defensive', confirms Anne Cazala.

2. The national bureaucratic process influences decision-making in mitigating vested interests' influence: economic analysis and the inter-ministerial co-ordination importantly contributed to the identification of France's interests.

3. The EU negotiating competences substantially impact the strategy of organized groups and the shaping of their interactions with domestic policy-makers and administrations.

4. Consistency with Rodrik's claim (1994) that 'there is a natural status quo bias to policy-making whenever some of the gainers (or losers) from reform cannot be identified *ex ante*'. Most players' perceptions support the claim. 'Eventually our effort objectively to measure gains and losses was partly undermined by the macro-economic context of recession and the political interference of the CAP reform', notes Christophe Lecourtier.

The textile industry echoes: 'Until Cancún we intensely promoted ambitious tariffs negotiations. There we felt overwhelmed by non-industrial
stakes. Since then, the worsening economy, China's soaring exports, and
the approaching deadline for quota elimination changed the mood. Our
companies are turning to more defensive demands.' For Philippe Gros,
'Our decision-making often leads us to favour defensive interests in the
negotiations. A key problem is that the political level lacks a real "control
board" to balance economic interests objectively.'

5. France may lack more institutionalized government-to-business consultations on trade policy. Emmanuelle Butaud, director for international
affairs at UIT, remarks: 'Consultations take place on a case-by-case basis,
usually under short notice linked with the 133 Committee's agenda, and
with little feedback afterwards.' All business and agriculture representatives deplore the fact that they are denied access to official membership
status in the French delegations to the WTO ministerial conferences. Business representatives therefore suggest that institutionalized consultations
would significantly help in streamlining decision-making at national level
and with interaction with the EU.

15

Decision-making processes in India: the case of the agriculture negotiations

SHISHIR PRIYADARSHI*

1 The problem in context

India submitted a very detailed and comprehensive proposal[1] as part of the ongoing negotiations on agriculture in the WTO in January 2001. It covered all aspects of the negotiations and remains one of the longest proposals ever submitted by any member. This study examines the manner in which this negotiating proposal was finalized, the consultations that were undertaken and the actual decision-making process that led to the submission of the proposal. It attempts to identify the main protagonists and the key stakeholders, the role that each one played in the process and the extent to which, in their view, they succeeded in getting their concerns reflected in the proposal. Finally, the study also tries to ascertain from the stakeholders their perception of the WTO as an organization, including in the context of the WTO's perceived influence on the process and final outcome.

Agriculture has been, and perhaps will remain for some time, a key issue in the WTO, with the power to influence negotiations, packages and the outcomes of Ministerial Conferences. It is equally sensitive, if not even more so, in the Indian context. To understand these sensitivities fully, including India's emphasis on self-sufficiency, it is important to keep in mind the extreme shortage of food grain that the country faced in the 1950s and 1960s. It was only the success of the 'Green Revolution' that helped India overcome its dependence on food aid. The criticality and

* Counsellor, Development Division, World Trade Organization. The views expressed in this case study do not reflect those of the WTO or its members and are purely an expression of the author's assessment of decision-making processes in India in the context of the agriculture negotiations. The study is based on a number of interviews that he carried out in July–Aug. 2004. The author wishes to thank all those people who agreed to be interviewed, without whose valuable inputs and insight this case study would not have been possible.
[1] G/AG/NG/W/102, 15 Jan. 2001

sensitivity of the Indian agriculture sector can be further gauged by the following factors:

the share of agriculture in the national GDP is a huge 24%;

a little over 700 million people, that is about 69% of the population, are dependent on the rural economy for their livelihood;

a very large majority of this rural population survives on an annual per capita income of US$175 as compared with the current national per capita income of US$480;

nearly 70% of cultivable land, that is about 100 million hectares out of 142 million hectares, continues to be vulnerable to the vagaries of the monsoon; and

even though India is the second-largest agricultural producer in the world, its yields are still very low when compared with some of the other producers.

This would show why agriculture is such a key issue for India in the WTO, and the constraints that were probably factored in while finalizing the Indian proposal. Additionally, the rural population in India, which is largely agro-based, has a political mind of its own, and has the power (and often the inclination) to prove the political 'pundits' wrong. This was amply demonstrated in the recently held elections in which the ruling, and favoured, National Democratic Alliance was voted out of power, largely because the rural population felt neglected, and in fact somewhat bypassed, by the much touted process of economic liberalization. This power which the rural population wields makes the decision-making process in agriculture even more sensitive and consequently subject to even greater political scrutiny.

2 The local and external players and their roles

The federal government

The main protagonists in the context of the agriculture negotiations at the federal level in India are the Ministry of Commerce and Industry (MOCI), the Ministry of Agriculture (MOA) and the Ministry of External Affairs (MEA).

The MOCI is mandated with the primary responsibility for all WTO-related issues. The government of India orders regarding the allocation of business state that it is the MOCI which handles all issues related to 'International trade and commercial policy, including tariff and non-tariff barriers'.[2] Within the MOCI, the Trade Policy Division (TPD) is responsible for the work relating to the WTO. It is headed by a Special Secretary, who is assisted by two senior joint secretaries and a team of nearly twenty middle-management-level officers. The Permanent Secretary of the MOCI is kept in the loop but for most issues the final decision and the negotiating positions are largely formulated in the TPD itself.

On the other hand, the MOA is the nodal ministry for all issues relating to agriculture, including the work relating to the Food and Agriculture Organization of the United Nations (FAO). However, the situation is somewhat ambiguous when it comes to agriculture issues within the WTO. International trade negotiations no doubt come within the ambit of the MOCI, but the MOA feels that when it comes to trade negotiations in agriculture then it should be the lead protagonist. In fact, as a former official of the Agriculture Ministry pointed out, 'the first step taken by the government, which set the ball rolling on the agriculture negotiations, was taken by the MOA and not by the MOCI, in the form of a seminar organized in conjunction with the FAO in June 1999'. This ambiguity is compounded because the consultative process between the two ministries is not institutionalized and, in the past, largely depended on personal relationships between the officials heading these divisions. Nonetheless, it is clear from the feedback provided by various officials that on issues related to agriculture the MOCI has been careful to avoid finalizing positions before obtaining the explicit approval of the MOA.

The role of the MEA as a stakeholder, especially in the context of the agriculture negotiations, is less clear. Its expertise in the negotiating process is not in doubt, since it has negotiated most international agreements; what the MOCI does doubt, however, is the MEA's expertise in the substance of the negotiation – and especially so in the case of agriculture. This perhaps explains why the MEA does not appear to have been involved in the consultative process to any significant extent.[3]

The state governments

The state governments were not regarded as significant stakeholders during the Uruguay Round (UR) and their involvement was minimal during

---

[2] Government of India's allocation of business orders of June 2004.
[3] Unlike most foreign missions, that invariably lobby for their government's position, there is very little evidence of Indian embassies abroad performing similar lobbying in the context of the agriculture negotiations. This could perhaps be explained by the minimal involvement of the MEA in the drafting of the agriculture proposal.

the pre-UR consultations. This is surprising, not only because are some of the Indian states larger than many WTO members, but also because agriculture is a state subject.[4] In fact, some state governments had, soon after the conclusion of the UR, filed a case in India's Supreme Court on the grounds that the government of India had no authority to accept obligations arising out of the Agreement on Agriculture (AOA) because of agriculture's status as a state subject. The government of West Bengal reiterated these concerns in May 2001, saying that 'agriculture is a state subject, therefore all agreements, legislations etc., are within the exclusive domain of the state governments', and that it was unacceptable that 'the government of India had signed the AOA... without first arriving at a consensus among the state governments'.[5] It is clear that a number of state governments have significant sensitivities regarding agriculture; these appear to have been taken into account during the consultative process. At the same time, it is also true that awareness of WTO-related issues is very superficial in the states, including amongst the state bureaucracy, and the positions taken by them are largely political rather than being based on the likely implications of the proposals. T. S. R. Subramanian said that 'in most states, the WTO and its rules are regarded as a distant entity without any immediate consequences for the state government, and perceived as a largely esoteric subject'.[6]

Industry

There are two main industry associations in India. The first, the Confederation of Indian Industry (CII) was established as a non-government, industry-led and industry-managed organization. It has been playing an increasingly active role in putting forth the views and concerns of industry to the government. Its membership extends to over 4,800 companies from the private as well as public sectors. According to N. Srinivasan, Director-General of the CII, it 'provides a platform for

---

[4] The government of India has designated certain subjects, including agriculture, as state subjects, which are areas where the basic and residual authority to legislate has been delegated to the state governments. Areas such as external affairs, defence and finance have been placed in the corresponding list of areas falling within the competence of the central government. Interestingly, there is also a concurrent list on which both the central and state governments can legislate.

[5] Views expressed in a meeting of Chief Ministers convened in May 2001.

[6] Interview with T. S. R. Subramanian, former Cabinet Secretary, who normally, though not necessarily, is the most senior civil servant in the country.

sectoral consensus-building and networking'.[7] He categorized the CII as fulfilling two functions, namely 'creating an awareness amongst its members on key WTO issues and providing inputs to government, based on the feedback received from industry'. The second industry association, the Federation of Indian Chambers of Commerce and Industry (FICCI), was established in 1927, and according to Manab Majumdar, the association's Project Leader (WTO), FICCI has been at the forefront of 'analyzing the impact of events through a multi-disciplinary approach involving representatives of business, academia, policy-makers and foreign experts, and evolving problem-solving responses'.[8]

These organizations do not seem to have been consulted during the Uruguay Round. Srinivasan put it very aptly when he said that 'for a long time the relationship between the government and industry was based on a "we–they" syndrome; the UR reflected the tenuousness of the relationship, with the government taking most decisions on its own'. Today, the situation has changed dramatically and these associations are not only consulted regularly, but also provide critical inputs to government on trade issues. Srinivasan felt that 'the turning point of this relationship was the Seattle Ministerial Conference when, for the first time, representatives from industry were formally a part of the Indian delegation'.

Academic institutions and think tanks

During the UR, academic institutions and think tanks did not feature in the consultative process at all. Since the UR they have become much more involved, even though this participation is still somewhat marginal because most of them do not have the resources needed to conduct a meaningful analysis. At times, they also lack the sectoral expertise that the modern multilateral process requires, something which is not uncommon amongst academic institutions around the world. However, a number of institutions and think tanks were consulted during the drafting of the agriculture proposal. These included the National Council for Applied Economic Research (NCAER), the Indian Institute of Foreign Trade (IIFT), the Indian Council for Research on International Economic Relations (ICRIER) and the Research and Information System for the Non-Aligned and other Developing Countries (RIS). Dr Anil Sharma, a senior economist in NCAER, said that 'our inputs were sought so that

---

[7] Interview with N. Srinivasan, Director-General, CII.
[8] Interview with Manab Majumdar, Project Leader WTO Issues, FICCI.

MOCI could take informed positions on various issues and use the analytical data that we provided to convince domestic lobbies about the appropriateness of these positions'.[9] Biswajit Dhar of the IIFT said that 'even though the terms of reference of the prescribed work were very broad, the actual inputs sought by the ministry were invariably needs-based'.[10] A former official of the MOA stated that these institutions 'provided valuable inputs, especially in analyzing the micro-level impact of liberalization in agriculture, both that had already been undertaken and that which was being proposed'.

Civil society

Civil society in India, in the same way, perhaps, as in any other country, is extremely heterogeneous. It is not difficult to find groups actively defending or opposing any point of view in relation to a particular issue. This is not to belittle their contribution to the overall debate, a fact which seems to be well accepted. There is an increasing recognition in most government circles that consultations with civil society are very important. However, there is still a big question mark as to which non-governmental organization (NGO) to invite to the consultative process, as there are a very large number of active NGOs to choose from. As Amrita Narlikar said, 'the process of involving NGOs seems to be a self-affirming process with the more critical ones being often excluded from the inter-ministerial consultations; the checks and balances, so necessary in such a process of consultation, seem to be missing'. Officials appeared to have somewhat preconceived notions of the views of civil society. A former official of the MOA said that 'the views expressed by the civil society representatives are always protectionist in nature. According to them, Indian agriculture is simply not trade-driven; their only objective is, therefore, to ensure that the livelihood of the subsistence farmers is protected.'

3 Challenges faced and the outcome

Perhaps the most significant challenge that was faced in arriving at an outcome (that is the final negotiating proposal) was to put in place a process that would take into account the very diverse views and positions of the various stakeholders, while ensuring that a cohesive proposal could be

---

[9] Interview with Dr Anil Sharma, Senior Economist, NCAER.
[10] Interview with Biswajit Dhar, head of the WTO Unit, IIFT.

prepared. The process went through a number of different phases: the initial identification of the key issues; consultations with the non-governmental stakeholders, including industry associations; the initial drafting of the proposal; holding regional and inter-ministerial consultations; and the final approval by the Cabinet.

Identification of key issues

As a first step towards identifying the main issues that would need to be addressed in the agriculture negotiations, the MOCI and MOA asked the NCAER and IIFT to analyze the experience of implementing the AOA and to make appropriate recommendations on the critical issues facing Indian agriculture. Interestingly, the basic approach to Indian agriculture does not seem to be the same as far as these institutions are concerned. For example, Dr Anil Sharma of the NCAER feels that 'Indian agriculture is quite competitive and India should adopt a more aggressive stand in the negotiations'. On the other hand, IIFT had a more conservative approach and was more closely aligned to the MOA's position on the need to protect the agriculture sector. A former official of the TPD said that 'though their inputs were very useful, they did not often factor in the political sensitivities of the issues that they were analyzing'. Giving one such example, the official said that according to the econometric analysis carried out by NCAER a somewhat lower bound rate was proposed as being sufficient to take care of probable import surges for a particular food security-sensitive commodity, but since such a low bound rate was not politically acceptable, it was modified while finalizing the proposal.

The ministries also contacted a number of well-known agricultural scientists. Some very useful suggestions appear to have come out of these interactions. For instance, M. S. Swaminathan, one of the most renowned agricultural economist in India, came up with the suggestion that India should press for a livelihood box, in which all the country's concerns on rural development and poverty alleviation could be aired.[11] This concept seems to have been taken on board even though India's final proposal talks of a 'food security box' rather than a 'livelihood box'. At the same time, the policy framers also had to factor in views such as those expressed

---

[11] As quoted in the 3–16 Feb. 2001 issue of *Frontline Magazine*, in which Dr Swaminathan is reported to have made this suggestion in a convocation address given by him at the Kerala Agriculture University on 29 Dec. 2000.

by Devinder Sharma, a trade and food policy analyst who, at that time, wrote that

> five years after the World Trade Organization came into existence, the antici- pated gains for India from the trade liberalization process in agriculture are practically zero. And yet, undaunted by the negative fallout from the implementation of the WTO's Agreement on Agriculture, the Ministry of Agriculture is aggressively pushing for the second phase of reforms. The entire effort of the free trade initiative is to destroy the foundations of food self-sufficiency so assiduously built over the years.[12]

Consultations with industry

Indian industry representatives appear to have been involved in the entire consultative process. Srinivasan stated that 'in addition to providing feed- back to MOCI, CII also lobbied and presented the industry's view on key issues to people like Mr Lamy and Mr Zoelick, whom we met on sev- eral occasions'.[13] Manab Majumdar said that 'FICCI had constituted an agriculture task force, whose primary mandate was to provide inputs to the government on agriculture issues'.[14] He, in fact, felt that it was not the government but the industry associations which needed to do more, including by apportioning more resources into their analysis of WTO issues. However, one criticism levied at industry associations by some of the stakeholders was that they tended to adopt positions on policy issues that looked suspiciously similar to those of the government and that they were rarely critical of government. However, both the representatives of CII and FICCI disagree: Srinivasan said that 'we did not hesitate to criticize the government, although such views are often expressed in private con- sultations, rather than in public statements of disagreement'. Majumdar was of the view that 'we do have differences with the government but we tend not to wash our dirty linen in public'.

Inter-ministerial consultations

Even though the two key ministries, the MOCI and the MOA, appear to have initiated the process somewhat independently, they do seem to have kept each other involved and informed on developments. Subsequently, the interaction between the two ministries increased even more and

[12] Devinder Sharma, 'WTO and Indian Agriculture: The End Result Is Zero'.
[13] Interview with Srinivasan.   [14] Interview with Majumdar.

culminated in what was practically a joint negotiating proposal. But the path to the final common position was not all that smooth. Officials from both ministries admitted that there were – at times serious – differences on the position the two ministries wanted to adopt on key issues. R. C. A. Jain, in trying to explain the reasons for these differences, said that 'MOCI, understandably, has a broader perspective and sees agriculture as one of the sectors being negotiated, whereas for MOA it was difficult to accept such an approach as agriculture is a very sensitive sector in which compromises cannot be made'.[15] He also felt that differences arose because 'MOCI's mandate was to increase India's share of global trade, while MOA wanted to ensure that domestic production and the livelihood of small farmers was in no way threatened.' A former expert who was closely associated with the drafting process said that 'the two ministries were like the two sides of a convex lens; the inevitability of their relationship being signified by the two joined ends of the lens, while the differences amongst them on the approach to key issues is illustrated by the bulging middle part of the lens'.

State-level consultations

The central government organized very wide-ranging consultations on WTO agriculture issues. In the June–July 2000 issue of MOCI's monthly newsletter mention is made that 'in the process of preparing India's negotiating position on agriculture, the government initiated regional consultations at various places, besides national level consultations, with a view to generating greater awareness of the issues and to receive views and suggestions which would facilitate a consensus regarding India's position'. However, some people still feel that these consultations were more of a formality rather than a process that led to significant changes. T. S. R. Subramanian said that 'the discussions in these state-level consultative meetings often remained superficial because of a lack of in-depth knowledge of WTO issues at the state level'.[16] An official of the Ministry of Agriculture said that 'rather than contributing to the substantive aspects of the negotiating elements, these discussions tended to largely reflect a fear "psychosis" of the WTO, and views simply did not emanate in these consultations that the agriculture negotiations should be seen as an

---

[15] Interview with R. C. A. Jain, former Secretary, Ministry of Agriculture.
[16] Interview with Subramanian, who earlier had also worked as Joint Secretary in the Trade Policy Division (TPD) of the MOCI.

opportunity; instead, there was an overwhelming feeling that this was a threat which had to be countered'. A former official of the MOA said that 'an attempt was made to explain that the agriculture negotiations did not represent the kind of threat people made it out to be, but it was very difficult in view of the unidirectional nature of views that were being expressed. The best we could do in these circumstances was to build the negotiating proposal around the objective of maintaining the status quo.'[17]

Finalization of the proposal by the Cabinet

All these meetings and consultations played an important role in giving final shape to the Indian proposal. The Commerce Ministry's website specifically mentions that

> the Indian proposal jointly formulated by the Department of Agriculture and Co-operation and Department of Commerce, reflects the broad consensus which was achieved through a series of regional-level meetings, meetings with the state governments, interaction with political parties, representatives of farmers' organizations, various autonomous institutions, agricultural universities and eminent agricultural economists.

As for the involvement of India's WTO mission in Geneva, an official said that the mission was always kept in the picture and provided useful feedback, especially about the likely reactions of possible/potential alliance partners to the different elements of the proposal. The final draft was submitted to the cabinet early in January 2001. While it was not possible to consult the file on the cabinet note (all such notes are secret), officials involved with the exercise indicated that since most ministries had been consulted beforehand practically no changes took place during the examination by the cabinet. Once approved by the cabinet, the proposal was transmitted to Geneva.

It was the culmination of this intense consultative process that led to India's negotiating proposal being submitted to the Special Session on Agriculture in January 2001. As a very detailed proposal, it broadly reflects the concerns and attempts to address the issues that were raised during the consultative process. While all three pillars of the negotiations are covered, it starts with a detailed proposal on food security in which it proposes the setting up of a food security box which encompasses all the special and differential treatment flexibilities. In the other sections, there is an evident

---

[17] Interview with R. Agarwal, former Director of the MOA.

thrust on seeking adequate reduction of tariffs, including tariff peaks, in developed countries, while seeking flexibility not to reduce tariffs on its food security crops. There is also a clear reference to the linkage between an a priori reduction in trade distorting domestic support in developed countries, and reductions in tariffs in developing countries. It seeks the complete elimination of all export subsidies. At the same time, it proposes that all measures taken by developing countries for poverty alleviation, rural development, rural employment and diversification of agriculture should be exempted from any reduction commitments.

The perception of the WTO's role in the process

The documented records and the oral interviews that were conducted clearly show that the Indian proposal on agriculture was finalized mainly through a bureaucratic process based on consultations with stakehold-ers. Julius Sen has pointed out, in relation to the proposals on WTO issues, that 'India's negotiating positions are almost without exception recommended by Commerce Ministry officials, examined by the Com-mittee of Secretaries, and then approved by the concerned Cabinet sub-committee'.[18] Clearly the process was bureaucratically driven and subject to fairly wide-ranging domestic consultations. And yet, to many, the WTO seems to have a significant influence, on both the process and outcome. The general perception is that the WTO is pushing the agenda for global economic reform and that the agriculture negotiations are a part of this WTO-led reform agenda. Feelings against the WTO are expressed even more strongly in the context of reductions in tariffs, especially on agri-culture products, which many of the stakeholders felt would open up domestic markets with negative implications for rural employment and agriculture production. The fact that the WTO does not have an organi-zational mandate of the kind that the World Bank and the IMF have, and that it is a completely member-driven organization, where the agenda is set and executed by the members on the basis of explicit consensus, does not seem to be a well known, or an accepted fact. Instead, as Amrita Narlikar said, 'the general public seems to have a very opinionated view of the WTO, and even certain civil society organizations and other insti-tutions who would be expected to have a better understanding of the WTO, more often than not seem to have a negative perception of the

---

[18] Interview with Julius Sen, a former Indian administrative service officer, now an Associate Director and Senior Programme Adviser at Enterprise LSE, London School of Economics.

organization'.[19] Biswajit Dhar, who writes for a number of newspapers, also said that because of such a perception 'it is not always very easy to take a pro-WTO line in public writings'.

A number of reasons were put forward to explain this perception. The Indian ambassador to the WTO felt that this was because 'the general public still regards the WTO as a developed country club, pushing the agenda at the behest of the major players and global MNCs'.[20] Another, perhaps more historical, explanation was given by a former official of the Commerce Ministry, who said that 'when India signed up to the Uruguay Round Agreements the long-term implications of many of the obligations it was undertaking were far from clear. Later, when quantitative restrictions had to be lifted and patent protections tightened, there was a public outcry. At that stage it was convenient to attribute the responsibility for these decisions to the WTO.' The former Indian ambassador to the WTO supported such an explanation, when he said that 'the public at large has a very negative perception of the TRIPS Agreement and there is a feeling that developing countries, including India, were literally coerced into accepting the agreement; a feeling that is still very deeply entrenched in the Indian psyche and colours the general perception of the WTO even today'. These feelings become even more pronounced in the context of agriculture. A former official of the MOA said that 'self-sufficiency in agriculture is still seen as the single most important achievement after independence, and there is a feeling that the WTO is out to undo this very achievement by its insistence on liberalization, without acknowledging the importance of self-sustainable domestic production'.

Not that balanced views were not forthcoming. Srinivasan of the CII said that their members understood that 'the WTO only provides a platform for negotiations and it was up to member countries to negotiate outcomes of interest to them'. Others too acknowledged that many positive things had come about because of the WTO. For instance, Biswajit Dhar said that 'the consumer in India today has a much wider choice, mainly because of the removal of quantitative restrictions'. Subramanian said that 'there has been a vast improvement in the efficiency and in the customer service of the banking sector after foreign banks were allowed to open up branches in the country'. But these positive outcomes are rarely acknowledged. Subramanian, in fact, equated the WTO to the British Raj

---

[19] Interview with Amrita Narlikar, Lecturer in International Relations at the Centre of International Studies, University of Cambridge.
[20] Interview with K. M. Chandrasekhar, Indian ambassador to the WTO.

in India, which, according to him, 'got blamed for things, but never got credit for the positive changes it introduced'.

4 Lessons for others (the players' views)

It is not very easy to generalize, or to draw lessons from a process which had so many protagonists, especially as their contributions were spread out both geographically and temporally. Some of the decision-making processes have definitely been institutionalized and it would not be wrong to assume that they would be followed whenever decisions are being taken on other WTO-related issues. It is also clear that the consultative process in India had come a long way, especially as compared with the situation before the Uruguay Round, and the debate on the various tenets of trade policy had been thrown open to a much wider audience. As the present analysis shows, very wide-ranging consultations, spread out over more than two years, were held while finalizing negotiating the proposal on agriculture. As obtained from the records of the Commerce Ministry, in addition to a very large number of informal consultations, a total of fourteen formal consultative meetings were held with stakeholders between 1999 and 2001.

The inclusiveness of the consultative process is also borne out by the reactions of some of the key stakeholders. The associations representing Indian industry appear to be largely satisfied with the consultative process. The Director-General of CII said that 'we were involved at all stages of the process', and that the 'final proposal adequately reflects the concerns that we brought to the government's attention'. Similarly, Manab Majumdar of FICCI said that 'the process of consultations followed during the course of finalizing the agriculture proposal reflects the exponential increase in interaction between government and the industry associations'. However, the position is less clear as far as the involvement of the actual agricultural producers is concerned. Where rural agricultural worker unions exist, their political priorities seem to limit their capacity to organize themselves at the grass-roots level; they also appear reluctant to go beyond their own immediate spheres of interest. Clearly, therefore, the ability of agricultural workers' groups to influence the government still remains very limited. To some extent their views were reflected in the stance taken by the MOA, whose officials were generally satisfied with the final proposal. Jain felt that this was because 'of a clear understanding at the political level that on issues of substance the views of MOA would prevail'.[21] There is also

---

[21] Interview with Jain.

no denying that the process was kept very transparent. Flyers were put out on the official website at every stage, and comments appear to have been regularly solicited from the various stakeholders. However, it also appears that the political bosses preferred to play safe and were more comfortable with a defensive strategy rather than pushing aggressively for market reforms. As a former Cabinet Secretary said, 'the politicians do not want to lose their domestic support for events taking place in far away Geneva and therefore tend to adopt an intransigent stand, especially on an issue like agriculture, where that domestic constituency is as large as 700 million people'.[22]

It would, therefore, not be wrong to conclude that the Indian position and policy approach to the agriculture negotiations in the WTO were arrived at on the basis of some very intensive cross-sectoral and inter-ministerial consultations, and then adopted at the highest possible level in the government. Apart from the officials in the ministries of Commerce and Agriculture, representatives of various autonomous institutions, agricultural universities and eminent agricultural economists were also involved in the process. In addition, inputs were sought from the state governments, representatives of different political parties and civil society. Clearly, therefore, this was a decision taken by the government on the basis of expressed domestic concerns.

Such a decision-making process would seem to fit in with the mandate and role of the WTO as a facilitator of an inter-governmental dialogue that leads, among other things, to binding decisions on the governments involved. The WTO, as is well known, though perhaps not well enough propagated, is not an independent or self-contained entity with the constitutional legitimacy to take decisions in the name of its members. Rather, it is a vehicle for decision-making among national governments vested with sovereign authority. The present analysis strengthens this view, since clearly in the formulation of India's agriculture negotiating proposal there is very little, if anything at all, that can be attributed to extraneous factors, including the WTO. And yet the spectre of the WTO, not as an institution mandated merely to facilitate the negotiating process, but as an institution attempting to influence domestic decision-making process, does not seem to have completely disappeared. The WTO is still perceived somewhat negatively. The general view seems to be that it is an institution seeking to undermine domestic policy space. There is clearly a lack of understanding about the WTO's mandate and the member-driven nature of the organization. The dichotomy between a decision-making process

---

[22] Interview with Subramanian.

which was no doubt completely domestic and clearly very democratic, and the perception of the WTO as an organization attempting to influence domestic decision-making processes, is perhaps best summed up by excerpts from two different interviews that the Union Agriculture Minister gave recently. While speaking to the *Financial Express*, he said 'let me make it amply clear that India will not succumb to any pressure . . . we will take a pragmatic view on various issues . . . we will not compromise on safeguarding the interests of the small and marginal farmers'[23] – a statement that clearly emphasizes the domestic imperatives of India's position in the agriculture negotiations. However, in another interview[24] given very soon afterwards, he still referred to the 'threat from the WTO', a threat whose only basis is perhaps a continuing, though hopefully diminishing, legacy from the Uruguay Round, when the responsibility of certain politically uncomfortable decisions had been apportioned to the WTO.

[23] Interview with Sharad Pawar, Minister of Agriculture, *Financial Express*, 7 June 2004.
[24] Interview with Pawar, *India Today*, 5 July 2004.

16

Protecting the geographical indication
for Darjeeling tea

S. C. SRIVASTAVA*

This case study relates to the geographical indication (GI) protection of Darjeeling tea. It tells the story of the unauthorized use and registration of 'Darjeeling and Darjeeling logo' by Japanese companies already registered in Japan by the Tea Board of India. The study also refers to the unauthorized use and attempted registration of the words 'Darjeeling and Darjeeling logo' by some other developed countries.

1 The problem in context

India is the world's largest producer of tea, with a total production of 846 million kg in the year 2002, supplying about 31 per cent of the world's favourite hot drink. Among the teas grown in India, Darjeeling tea offers distinctive characteristics of quality and flavour, and also a global reputation for more than a century. Broadly speaking there are two factors which have contributed to such an exceptional and distinctive taste, namely geographical origin and processing. Thus Darjeeling tea has been cultivated, grown and produced in tea gardens in a well-known geographical area – the Darjeeling district in the Indian state of West Bengal – for over one and a half centuries. The tea gardens are located at elevations of over 2000 metres above sea level.

Even though the tea industry in India lies in the private sector, it has been statutorily regulated and controlled by the Ministry of Commerce since 1933 under various enactments culminating in the Tea Act, 1953. The Tea Board was set up under this Act. A major portion of the annual

* Research Professor, Indian Law Institute, New Delhi. Formerly Professor, Chairman and Dean, Faculty of Law, Kurukshetra University (India), and University of Calabar (Nigeria). The author acknowledges with thanks the help received from the Tea Board of India for providing requisite information.

production of Darjeeling tea is exported, the key buyers being Japan, Russia, the United States, and the United Kingdom and other European Union (EU) countries such as France, Germany and the Netherlands.

Efforts made by the Tea Board to ensure the supply of genuine Darjeeling tea

In order to ensure the supply of genuine Darjeeling tea, a compulsory system of certifying the authenticity of exported Darjeeling tea was incorporated into the 1953 Tea Act in February 2000. The system makes it compulsory for all the dealers in Darjeeling tea to enter into a licence agreement with the Tea Board of India on payment of an annual licence fee. The terms and conditions of the agreement provide, *inter alia*, that the licensees must furnish information relating to the production and manufacture of Darjeeling tea and its sale, through auction or otherwise. The Tea Board is thus able to compute and compile the total volume of Darjeeling tea produced and sold in the given period. No blending with teas of other origin is permitted. Certificates of origin are then issued for export consignments under the Tea (Marketing and Distribution Control) Order, 2000, read with the Tea Act, 1953. Data is entered from the garden invoices (the first point of movement outside the factory) into a database, and the issue of the certificate of origin authenticates the export of each consignment of Darjeeling tea by cross-checking the details. The customs authorities in India have instructed, by circular, all customs checkpoints to check for the certificates of origin accompanying the Darjeeling tea consignments and not to allow the export of any tea as 'Darjeeling' without this certificate. This ensures the sale-chain integrity of Darjeeling tea until consignments leave the country.

Legal protection at domestic level

CTM Registration

In order to provide legal protection in India the Tea Board of India registered the 'Darjeeling logo' and also the word 'Darjeeling' as certification trade marks (CTMs) under the (Indian) Trade and Merchandise Marks Act, 1958 (now the Trade Marks Act, 1999).

GI registration

The Tea Board of India has also applied for the registration of the words 'Darjeeling' and 'Darjeeling logo' under the Geographical Indications of

Goods (Registration and Protection) Act, 1999 (the Act) which came into force with effect from 15 September 2003, in addition to the CTMs mentioned above.

Under the Act:

(a) No person shall be entitled to institute any proceeding to prevent or recover damages for the infringement of unregistered geographical indications.

(b) A registration of geographical indications shall give to the registered proprietor and all authorized users whose names have been entered in the register the right to obtain relief in respect of infringement of the geographical indications. However, authorized users alone shall have the exclusive right to the use of the geographical indications in relation to the goods in respect of which the geographical indications are registered.

(c) A registered geographical indication is infringed by a person who, not being an authorized user thereof,

(i) uses such geographical indications by any means in the designation or presentation of goods that indicates or suggests that such goods originate in some other geographical area other than the true place of origin of the goods in a manner which misleads the public; or

(ii) uses any geographical indications in such a manner which constitutes an act of unfair competition including passing off in respect of registered geographical indications; or

(iii) uses another geographical indication to the goods which, although literally true as to the territory, region or locality in which the goods originate, falsely represents to the public that the goods originate in the region, territory or locality in respect of which such registered geographical indications relate.

(d) The purpose of the GI Act is to create a public register, and

(e) The GI Act confers public rights.

Status of registration of GI

The registration of the marks applied for by the Tea Board of India has not yet been granted. The Registrar has, however, after examining the application for registration filed by the Tea Board of India advertised for any expression of opposition. It is only after considering opposition, if any, that the Registrar may decide to register the GI of the Tea Board.

Advantages of GI protection at domestic level and export markets

The reasons for the need for additional protection for GI over and above the CTM has been set out by the chair of the Tea Board of India as follows.

- When CTM registration is not accepted in a jurisdiction where protection is sought, for example, France for Darjeeling;
- because GI registration is necessary to obtain reciprocal protection of a mark mandate under EU Regulation 2081/92; and
- registration gives clear status to a GI, indicating a direct link with geographical origin.[1]

Quite apart from the aforesaid reasons the GI Act in India has also been enacted in order to comply with its obligation under the Agreement on Trade-Related Aspects of Intellectual Property Rights (TRIPS), which requires WTO members to enact appropriate implementation legislation for GI.

Steps taken at international level

Registration of Darjeeling tea and logo

In order to protect 'Darjeeling' and 'Darjeeling logo' as GI, the Tea Board of India registered the marks in various countries, including the United States, Canada, Japan, Egypt, and the United Kingdom and some other European countries, as a trade mark/CTM. In this context it is relevant to note that on 3 August 2001 the UK Trade Registry granted registration of the word 'Darjeeling' as of 30 March 1998 under the UK Trade Marks Act 1994. The United States has also accepted the application of the Tea Board for the registration of 'Darjeeling' as a CTM in October 2002.

The appointment of the International Watch Agency

In order to prevent the misuse of 'Darjeeling' and the logo, the Tea Board has since 1998 hired the services of Compumark, a World Wide Watch agency. Compumark is required to monitor and report to the Tea Board all cases of unauthorized use and attempted registration. Pursuant to Compumark's appointment, several cases of attempted registrations

---

[1] Tea Board of India, 'The Experience of Indian Tea Producers: Protection of Darjeeling Tea', paper presented at the World Wide Symposium on Geographical Indications, San Francisco, 9–11 July 2003 [WIPO/GEO/SFO/03/8].

and unauthorized use of 'Darjeeling' and Darjeeling Logo have been reported.

The assistance of overseas buyers

In order to ensure the supply of genuine Darjeeling tea, the Tea Board has sought the help of all overseas buyers, sellers and Tea Council and Associations in so far as they should insist on certificates of origin to accompany all export consignments of Darjeeling tea.

2 Local and external players and their roles

The Tea Board of India, the sole representative of tea producers in India, is responsible for the implementation of the government's regulations and policies. It is vested with the authority to administer all stages of tea cultivation, processing and sale (including the Darjeeling segment) through various orders issued by the government. It works in close co-operation with the Darjeeling Planter's Association, which is the sole producers' forum for Darjeeling tea. Both the Tea Board and the Darjeeling Planter's Association (DPA) have been involved at various levels in protecting and defending the 'Darjeeling tea' and 'Darjeeling logo'. The primary objects are (i) to prevent misuse of the word 'Darjeeling' for tea sold worldwide; (ii) to deliver the correct product to the consumer; (iii) to enable the commercial benefit of the equity of the brand to reach the Indian tea industry and ultimately the plantation worker; (iv) to achieve international status similar to champagne or Scotch whisky in terms of both brand and equity and governance/administration.

The Tea Board of India assumed the role of complainant in making and filing opposition or other legal measures whenever cases of unauthorized use or attempted or actual registration of Darjeeling and Darjeeling logo were brought to its notice. Such legal measures are generally taken where negotiation failed. For instance, in February 2000 in Japan the Tea Board of India filed an opposition against Yutaka Sang yo Kabushiki Kaisa of Japan for registration of the trade mark 'Darjeeling Tea' with the map of India, the International Tea KK of Japan for registration of Darjeeling Women device in Japan under class 30/42 (tea, coffee and cocoa) and against Mitsui Norin KK for the use in advertising of the 'Divine Darjeeling' logo. These opposing parties defended the invalidation action filed against them.

Some disputes relating to Darjeeling tea have been settled through negotiation undertaken by the Tea Board of India with the foreign companies concerned with the help of their respective governments. Thus, the Tea Board with the help of the Indian government continues to negotiate with France at various levels over the activities of the French trademark authorities. Moreover BULGARI, Switzerland agreed to withdraw the legend 'Darjeeling Tea fragrance for men' pursuant to legal notice and negotiations.[2]

In one of the cases in France, the Tea Board of India put the applicant Comptoir des Parfums (which advertised in March 1999) on notice, and drew its attention to the prior rights and goodwill in the name of Darjeeling as the GI for tea, requiring it to withdraw its application voluntarily. Based on the correspondence the applicant consented to the amendment of all specifications of goods by the addition of 'all those goods being made of Darjeeling tea or recalling the scent of Darjeeling tea'. The amendment proposed by the applicant was found by the examiner to be descriptive of the goods in question.

'The Tea Board of India feels that a partnership with the buyers in the major consuming countries such as Germany, Japan and the United Kingdom would be the only long term solution to the problem of possible passing off.' However, it strongly opposes any attempt at individual registration in the case of private labels or its misuse in specific overseas jurisdictions.[3]

3 Challenges faced and the outcome

The Tea Board of India has faced a series of hurdles, challenges and difficulties in the protection and enforcement of the word 'Darjeeling' and of the Darjeeling logo. Some of the major challenges faced by the Tea Board's effort to protect 'Darjeeling' and the Darjeeling logo in Japan, France, Russia, the United States and other countries are given below.

Unauthorized use and registration of Darjeeling Tea and logo in Japan

In the first case the Tea Board filed an invalidation action against International Tea KK, a Japanese Company, over the registration of the Darjeeling logo mark, namely, Darjeeling women 'serving tea/coffee/coca/soft drinks/fruit juice' in the Japanese Patent Office (JPO) on 29 November

---

[2] Source: N. K. Das, 'Geographical Indications: Protection of Darjeeling Tea', WIPO Symposium on Geographical Indications, San Francisco, 11 july 2003.
[3] See Tea Board of India, 'Experience of Indian Tea Producers'.

1996 with the trademark registration number 3221237. The impugned registration was made notwithstanding the registration in Japan of the identical Darjeeling logo mark by the Tea Board of India, with the trademark registration number 2153713, dated 31 July 1987. The Tea Board also filed a non-use cancellation action. On 28 August 2002 the JPO Board of Appeal held that the pirate registration was invalid because it was contrary to public order and morality. With regard to the Tea Board's non-use cancellation action, the JPO decided that International Tea KK had not furnished sufficient evidence to substantiate its use of registration and thereby allowed the appeal of the Tea Board.

In the second case, the Tea Board of India opposed the application for 'Divine Darjeeling' in class 30 (Darjeeling tea, coffee and cocoa produced in Darjeeling, India) filed by Mitsui Norin KK of Japan advertised on 29 February 2000. The opposition was mainly on three grounds, namely (i) 'divine' is a laudatory term and accordingly the mark for which protection is sought is merely 'Darjeeling', which is clearly non-distinctive; (ii) 'Divine Darjeeling' is misleading in so far as 'coffee and cocoa produced in Darjeeling' are concerned, all the more so because the district of Darjeeling does not produce coffee or cocoa; (iii) Darjeeling tea qualifies as a geographical indication under international conventions including TRIPS and ought to be protected as such in Japan, a member of TRIPS.

The JPO Opposition Board dismissed the invalidation action filed by the Tea Board of India primarily on the ground that the mark 'Divine Darjeeling' as a whole was not misleading or descriptive of the quality of goods. However, the non-use cancellation action succeeded, because the registered proprietor was not able to place on record adequate evidence to prove the use of the mark in Japan.

In yet another case the Tea Board of India brought an invalidation action against Japanese trade mark registration of 'Darjeeling tea' with a map of India in class 30 by Yutaka Sangyo Kabushiki Kaisa, on the ground that the registration was contrary to public order and morality. This action was rejected on the ground that 'the written English characters "Darjeeling tea" and the map of India for the goods of Darjeeling tea are used as an indication of the origin and quality of Darjeeling tea and will not harm the feelings of the Indian people'. However, the non-use cancellation action filed by the Tea Board succeeded, because the registered proprietor was not able to place on record sufficient evidence to prove the use of the mark in Japan.

A perusal of these decisions reveals that the JPO did not decide the contention of the Tea Board of India relating to the TRIPS Agreement, which requires WTO members to provide the legal means to prevent the use of a GI for goods originating in a geographical area other than the true place of origin in a manner which misleads the public to constitute an act of unfair competition. Indeed, non-disposal of the argument that the procedural guidelines of WTO be followed dilutes the effect of the TRIPS Agreement.

Other instances of defending GI against developed countries

France. While the Indian system protects French GIs, France on the other hand does not extend similar or reciprocal protection to Indian GIs. Thus French law does not permit any opposition to an application for a trademark similar or identical to a GI if the goods covered are different from those represented by the GI. The owner of the GI can take appropriate judicial proceedings only after the impugned application has proceeded to registration. The net effect of such a provision has been that despite India's protests, Darjeeling has been misappropriated as a trade mark in respect of several goods in class 25, namely, clothing, shoes and headgear. The French Examiner – even though he found evidence in favour of the Tea Board of India (i) on sufficient proof of use of 'Darjeeling' tea in France, and (ii) that the applicant had slavishly copied the name Darjeeling in its application – held that the respective goods 'clothing, shoes, headgear' and 'tea' are not of the same nature, function and intended use, produced in different places and sold through different networks. The Examiner also held that even if the applicant has slavishly copied the Tea Board's Darjeeling logo (being the prior mark), the difference in the nature of the respective goods is sufficient to hold that the applicant's mark may be adopted without prejudicing the Tea Board's rights in the name 'Darjeeling'.

In another case the Tea Board opposed the application against the advertised marks for Darjeeling in classes 5, 12 and 28 by Dor François Marie in France. The French Examiner rejected the Tea Board's opposition and held that the respective goods did not (i) have the same nature, function and intended use; and (ii) share the same distribution circuits. However, he held that although the applicant's mark constituted a partial reproduction of the Tea Board's prior figurative registration for the Darjeeling logo, the designated goods lacked similarity to that of the Tea Board's prior marks and the logo, therefore, may be used as a trade mark without prejudicing the prior rights of the Tea Board.

Russia. The Tea Board filed an application for unauthorized use by a company of the word 'Darjeeling'. This application was objected to on the ground of conflict with an earlier registration of the identical word by a company named 'Akorus'. The Russian Patent Office overruled the objection and accepted the application of Tea Board of India for the word 'Darjeeling'.

United States. The Tea Board is opposing an application filed by its licensee in United States to register 'Darjeeling nouveau' ('nouveau' is the French for 'new') relating to diverse goods and service such as clothing, lingerie, Internet services, coffee, cocoa and so on in respect of first flush Darjeeling tea. The registration application is under consideration even though 'Darjeeling' is already registered under US CTM law.

Other countries. Quite apart from the above, in several cases the Tea Board of India opposed attempted registration and unauthorized use of the word 'Darjeeling' in Germany, Israel, Norway and Sri Lanka before the Patent Office of the country concerned.

Costs of protection and enforcement for the industry and the government

Another major challenge faced by the Tea Board of India relates to legal and registration expenses, costs of hiring an international watch agency and fighting infringements in overseas jurisdictions. Thus during the last four years the Tea Board of India has spent approximately US$200,000 for these purposes. This amount does not include administrative expenses including the relevant personnel working for the Tea Board, the cost of setting up monitoring mechanisms, software development costs and so forth. It is not possible for every geographical indication right holder to incur such expenses for protection. Further, like overseeing, monitoring and implementing GI protection, the high cost of taking legal action can prevent a country from engaging a lawyer to contest the case, however genuine and strong the case may be. Moreover, a lack of expertise in the proper handling of highly complex legal language is another challenge to be met.

4 Lessons for others

The Tea Board of India appears to be not satisfied with the policy as well as the approach of the patent authority in Japan and France. In order to deal with the situations described above, India, along with several other member countries of the WTO, wants to extend the proposed register for

GI to include products or goods, other than wines and spirits, which may be distinguished by the quality, reputation or other characteristics essentially attributable to their geographical origin. The main advantage would be to develop a multilateral system of notification and registration of all geographical indications. In this connection, a joint paper has recently been submitted to the Two's TRIPS Council. The Doha Ministerial Declaration under paragraphs 12 and 18 also provides a mandate for the issue of providing a higher level of protection to GIs to products other than 'wines and spirits' to be addressed by the TRIPS Council. According to the Tea Board, (i) extension of protection under Article 23 for products other than wines and spirits is required where no legal platform exists to register a GI or a CTM which is a TRIPS obligation, for example Japan; (ii) once the scope of protection is extended it would not be necessary to establish the credentials/reputation of a GI before fighting the infringement of similar 'types', 'styles', or 'look-alikes'; and (iii) additional protection would rectify the imbalance created by the special protection of wines and spirits.[4]

The experience in defending GI in France, the United States and Japan further strengthens the Tea Board's perspective on the subject. Despite a registration of 'Darjeeling' as a GI in France, the Tea Board was unsuccessful in defending it because French law does not permit any opposition to an application for a trade mark, similar or identical to a GI. Likewise, India's efforts to protect 'Darjeeling' in Japan did not succeed because the prefix 'Divine' has not gained currency in the Japanese language.[5] From the experiences described above it is felt that it is high time to evolve a rule that no application for registration of a GI of the same or similar goods or products or even similar type, style or look-alike already registered in that country be ordinarily entertained by the competent authority of the country concerned. Further, the GI status and apprehended or actual violation of GI should be published at both domestic and international levels. Moreover, adequate steps should be taken to evolve rules and procedures for GI or CTM registration in all the member countries of the WTO. This would prevent conflict to a great extent. Finally, a vigilance cell should be established to check the violation and misuse of the GI of any product.

[4] Ibid.   [5] Ibid.

17

The Indian shrimp industry organizes to fight the threat of anti-dumping action

B. BHATTARCHARYYA*

This case study deals with the way in which the Indian shrimp industry responded when faced with an anti-dumping action in the United States. It also indicates the potential impact of the anti-dumping action on the fragmented, small-producers-dominated industry.

1 The case history

On 31 December 2003, the Ad Hoc Shrimp Trade Action Committee (ASTAC), an association of shrimp farmers in eight southern states of the United States, filed an anti-dumping petition against six countries – Brazil, China, Ecuador, India, Thailand and Vietnam. The petition alleged that these countries had dumped their shrimps in the US market. Though the actual petition was made by the Ad Hoc Shrimp Trade Action Committee, whose members are located in Alabama, Florida, Georgia, Louisiana, Mississippi, North Carolina, South Carolina and Texas, the Southern Shrimp Alliance (SSA) had been organizing the process of seeking redress.

The petition meeting statutory requirements, on 21 January 2004 the US Department of Commerce (DOC) announced the initiation of anti-dumping investigations against the six countries. Products covered include warm water shrimp, whether frozen or canned, wild caught (ocean harvested) or farm-raised (produced by aqua-culture), head-on or head-off, shell-on or peeled, tail-on or tail-off, deveined or not deveined, cooked or raw, or otherwise processed in frozen or canned form.

The Department notified the International Trade Commission (ITC) of its decision on initiation. On 17 February 2004 the International Trade Commission announced its decision that there was a reasonable

* Distinguished Professor in International Business, IILM, New Delhi, and Hon. Dean, Institute For International Trade and Law, New Delhi.

indication that the US shrimp industry is materially injured or threatened with material injury by imports, allegedly at less than fair value, from the six identified countries. As a result, the Department of Commerce continued with its investigations and gave its preliminary determination on 28 July 2004. The ratio of preliminary duty varies between 3.56% and 27.49% for three mandatory respondents selected by the DOC. The weighted arranged rate for India is 14.2%, and the average rate for China is 49.09%, for Brazil 36.91%, for Vietnam 16.01%, for Ecuador 7.3% and for Thailand 6.39%.

2 The national and international context

The trouble had started much earlier than December 2003. On 26 February 2002, Reggie Dupre, a Louisiana state senator, alleged that tainted farm-raised Asian shrimp was being diverted from Europe and dumped on the US market. Dupre was calling for a congressional investigation into food safety and unfair pricing, as local fishermen voiced concern that imports had depressed the prices they got for the locally harvested shrimp. By September 2002, shrimp industry representatives from eight southern states had got together to fight the case against imported shrimp from certain countries. 'We stand a better chance of success when all shrimp-producing states come on board', as George Barisich, president of the United Commercial Fisherman's Association, observed.

On 22 October 2002, representatives of the shrimp industry from the eight southern states voted to form the Southern Shrimp Alliance to fight unfair competition from imported farm-raised shrimp from certain countries. There was, however, a basic problem. It was estimated that it might cost more than US$3 million in terms of legal expenses to go for an anti-dumping petition.

There were also problems associated with divergent trade interests. Shrimp importers and distributors were afraid that a long-drawn-out battle would affect the supply of imported shrimp and adversely affect their business. Wally Stevens, president of the American Seafood Distributors Association, described how the salmon industry in Maine had filed an anti-dumping petition against Norway in 1990, hoping to stabilize prices. Twelve years after winning and spending up to $10 million, salmon was selling at half the price prevailing at the time of the beginning of the dispute. 'This is definitely not the right way to go. It consumes an immense amount of money and is not a long-term solution in terms of maintaining viability.' In a statement in January 2003, Stevens said that his organization, in support of 'free and fair trade', would oppose any anti-dumping action by the SSA.

In the meantime, countries threatened with the prospective action started reacting. Vietnam, one of the countries identified almost at the beginning of the SSA exercises and also highly dependent on the US market for shrimp exports, was the first to protest. Foreign Ministry spokeperson Phan Thuy Thanh said in a statement on 12 September 2002 that 'I can say with certainty that Vietnam has never dumped its shrimp, and its shrimp have been sold at market prices.' Thailand was another country to lodge a protest. Kenneth Pierce, of Willkie Farr & Gallagher, representing the Thai Frozen Foods Association, condemned the move to consider anti-dumping action against Thai shrimp exports. 'Thailand's shrimps have never been dumped in the United States, nor have they caused material damage to US shrimp', he said in a statement on 25 November 2002. As evidence mounted of the SSA's determination to go ahead with the petition on anti-dumping, other threatened countries also started taking preventive actions. Rokhmin Dahiri, the Indonesian Maritime and Fisheries Minister, denied allegations that the Indonesian government subsidized its shrimp farmers. He said in a statement on 25 August 2003 that the price of shrimp on the domestic market was much lower than the export price. The dumping charge was baseless and, therefore, the United States should exclude Indonesia from the proposed anti-dumping investigations. The government of Bangladesh took similar action, and Vietnam also started working out alliances. Nguyen Thi Hong Minh, Vietnamese Deputy Fisheries Minister, said in a statement on 4 August 2003 that the Vietnamese shrimp businesses and their counterparts in south-east Asia, India and China as well as US shrimp importers were considering measures including lobbying to prevent a lawsuit.

The Indian government and the Indian shrimp industry were aware of the threat. Arun Jaitley, the then Minister for Commerce, made a statement in June 2003 after his official visit to the United States: 'We are anticipating an action against our shrimp exports because our share in the US market is on the rise.' During the whole of 2003, the SSA went through the process of raising the required resources and trimming the number of countries against which dumping action was to be brought, as the cost of the legal battle increased with the number of countries. After a compromise with the Mexican shrimp industry, the number of countries was ultimately brought down to six.

The main contentions of the petitioners were as follows.

The six named countries accounted for 74% of shrimp imports in the US market.

Imports from the six countries increased from 466 million lb. in 2000 to 650 million lb in 2002.

Import prices of the targeted countries had dropped by 28% in the previous three years. The average unit value of the targeted countries in 2000 was $3.54; this had fallen to $2.55 in 2002, on a headless, shell-on equivalent basis.

The average dockside price for one count size of gulf shrimp dropped from $6.08 to $3.30 per pound from 2000 to 2002.

The United States was the most open market in the world. High tariff rates in other large importing countries provided a powerful incentive for exporters to increase shrimp shipments to the United States. Likewise, the US market also served as the market of last resort when shrimp shipments were denied entry to other markets such as the European Union due to the discovery of unacceptable levels of contaminants.

3 The Indian shrimp industry and its response

The first concrete signal that India might be included in the US industry's anti-dumping petition was received by the Indian government in June 2003. That anti-dumping investigations against Indian shrimp imports might be initiated was hinted at during bilateral talks when the then Commerce and Industry Minister Arun Jaitley had met his counterpart in Washington at that time. The reason given was that India's shrimp exports to the United States had been rising rapidly during the previous three years, from $255.93 million during 2000–1 to $299.05 million during 2002–3.

India's marine products industry has been one of the major export success stories. From an export base of just Rs. 450 million in 1971–2, it increased to Rs. 68,810 million in 2002–3. Shrimp is the mainstay of India's marine product exports.

Japan has traditionally been the biggest export market for India's marine products, followed by the United States, China and several EU countries. There was an over-dependence on the Japanese market, as shrimp is the major export item which Japan imports in huge volume. However, in the recent past, there has been a gradual decline in the intake from Japan with an increasing absorption in the United States, as well as some other countries. The United States, traditionally a buyer of small-sized shrimp from India, has now started buying many other varieties, including black tiger shrimp, resulting in its occupying the top slot in India's export markets of marine products, replacing Japan in 2002–3.

Success in India's shrimp export is directly attributable to the development of shrimp culture. Assisted by the Marine Products Export Development Authority (MPEDA), shrimp culture has developed as a major industry in several coastal states. It is mostly an enterprise of small and medium farmers, and has led to the utilization of otherwise unproductive areas in the coastal region, contributing to improvements in the socio-economic conditions of the rural poor in the shrimp farming areas. It has created direct employment of about 300,000 people and indirect employment to over 700,000.

The Indian government has played an important role in the promotion of marine product exports, including the development of shrimp farming. The MPEDA is a government-sponsored body whose mandate covers the development of the industry as a whole, including export promotion. It is under the administrative control of the Department of Commerce and is headed by a senior officer of the Indian Administrative Service. Its governing council comprises senior officials of the central and state governments as well as representatives of the marine products industry.

The Seafoods Exporters Association of India (SEAI) is the nodal body of the exporters community and is represented on the MPEDA governing council. There is, therefore, close co-ordination between these two bodies which are primarily responsible for organizing the shrimp industry's as well as the government's response to the US anti-dumping investigations.

After the statement of the Commerce Minister on the possible threat to Indian shrimp exports to the United States, these two bodies went into action. To explore the possibilities of avoiding the anti-dumping action and, if necessary, to take legal action, a delegation comprising senior members of the SEAI went to Washington in September 2003, and after discussions in various quarters, decided to sign an agreement with the law firm, Garvey Schubert and Barer, to be the counsel in the United States for the anti-dumping investigations. After returning to India, the SEAI informed its members through a circular letter that 'Ms Lisbeth Levinson, a partner in the firm, will personally and exclusively handle our case.'

Regarding the extremely damaging potential of the proposed anti-dumping action, the SEAI pointed out to its members that in July 2003 the United States had imposed anti-dumping duty ranging from 44% to 63% on catfish fillet imports from Vietnam which would remain in force for five years. There will be annual reviews to decide whether the duties need any adjustments upwards or downwards. The Association warned its members that any such move against India's shrimp exports would ring the death knell of the industry.

The Association also realized the importance of other related regulatory provisions for Indian shrimp exports to the United States. The SEAI informed its members that within twenty days of filing the case, the United States could start imposing anti-dumping duties which would be returned only if the Indian exporters won the case. Since this anti-dumping duty would have to be paid by the US importers, the SEAI cautioned that they might stay away from India, and therefore the business would start to become affected long before the case came to its final conclusion.

The game plan worked out by the MPEDA and the SEAI was comprehensive. It involved approaching the central government, developing contacts with counterpart bodies in other countries which might be named in the petition, and putting their house in order, to raise resources.

By October 2003, the plan had started taking shape. In a statement on 8 October 2003, K. Jose Cyriac, the chairman of the MPEDA, said, 'We are discussing the issues with other countries which are likely to be labelled with dumping charges.'

The SEAI president, Abraham Tharakan, after describing the petition as extremely unfair, said that in addition to calling for government support it would seek to co-operate with major exporting associations in Vietnam, Thailand and China and to forge an alliance among the Asian exporters. Some twenty-five Indian companies export to the United States, and the industry anticipated that the case might be filed against six or seven big players. However, the SEAI decided to fight the case from the platform of the organization as a mark of solidarity.

'We will back each indicted company', said Ranjit Bhattacharye, secretary-general of the SEAI, whose management committee decided that it would defend the industry's position, meet the cost of the legal process and not leave the cost to be borne by those Indian firms that might be selected for investigations.

The SEAI has estimated a total budgetary requirement of Rs. 70 million to fight the case. Of this, SEAI would mobilize Rs. 40 million internally and the remaining Rs 30 million would be collected from its members, depending on the volume and value of their individual exports to the US market.

When the initiation decision came on 21 January 2004, both the organizations were unhappy, but they were expecting it and were therefore ready to act. According to the SEAI, 'with over 75% of the US producers having signed the petition, proceeding with the hearing was a fait accompli'.

Both Jose Cyriac and Abraham Tharakan left for the United States to take further action to protect the interests of the Indian shrimp exporters.

The SEAI had worked out plans to contest the dumping allegations on various grounds. It put forward two major differences between the Indian and the US sea-caught shrimp and offered reasons why Indian shrimp is cheaper.

First, there are specific variations between the shrimp caught off the south-west coast of the United States and in Indian waters, so that prices are bound to be different. 'The threat for the domestic shrimp farmer in the United States comes from China, Thailand, Indonesia and Ecuador. India's shrimp exports are predominantly of black tiger and scampi varieties which are not cultivated in the United States', according to the president of SEAI.

Second, while fishing in the United States is a capital-intensive activity calling for major investment, in India shrimp capture is carried out with a very low level of capital and requiring hardly any investment. This makes the cost of production considerably lower in India compared with that for shrimp sea-caught off the US coast.

Jose Cyriac observed, after the decision to initiate investigations, that the cost of cultured and captured shrimp in India was far lower than that of shrimp caught and bought in the US market, enabling Indian exporters to compete with US shrimp in price. Further, the petition filed before the US Department of Commerce had mixed up count and weight (shrimp is sold by size and the number of shrimp constituting 1 kg), providing another avenue to contest the case.

When the ITC decision on the preliminary affirmative decision came on 17 February 2004, the Indian shrimp industry termed it 'discriminatory and unjust'. Tharakan of the SEAI said, 'We are deeply disappointed and upset by the verdict.' Asserting that the Indian shrimp industry has not been resorting to dumping, he was confident of ultimate victory: 'We have a strong case against US shrimpers. We are certain that we will win the case despite the setback.' Tharakan said that there was no possibility of the United States succeeding in imposing an anti-dumping duty on Indian shrimp as it was not sold below the cost price. On the contrary, it was sold to US importers at a price higher than that for Japan and for other countries.

On receipt of the preliminary decision, Indian exporters who were mobilizing funds said that they would fight the case till the end. Jose Cyriac commented: 'The government is unhappy with the US verdict.

But it is only a preliminary finding. We will help the Indian exporters fight the case in the United States.'

The government itself came out with a statement on 18 February 2004, when S. N. Menon, special secretary in the Department of Commerce, said, 'We will fight it out. We are all geared up to fight the case and the industry has already hired lawyers for this.' Menon observed that India had a strong case as India was exporting mainly 'tiger shrimps which are not found there and that too, in unprocessed form'. Noting that 80% of shrimp consumption in the United States is met through imports, Menon said that unprocessed Indian shrimps generated about 1 million jobs in the US food processing industry, therefore, any action against Indian shrimp would adversely affect the US food processing sector. The SEAI and its members were getting ready for the next set of actions. After the preliminary positive determination by the ITC, the next step was for the Department of Commerce (ITA) to prove whether there had been dumping and at what level. As part of that exercise, a few leading firms would be selected from each country and detailed questionnaires would be sent to them.

According to Sandu Joseph, the secretary of the SEAI, a team of US DOC officials would visit Kerala, a major shrimp producing state, in June or early July. 'They will visit our shrimp farming factories and verify our accounting practices. Our factories and accounts are open. We want to prove that we are not producing and exporting cheap shrimp to the United States.'

Joseph also referred to the support the Association could mobilize in the United States. The SEAI had been receiving 'favourable support' from a group of US congressmen to fight the anti-dumping investigations. Joseph said that more than a dozen members of the Congress had written to US Commerce Secretary Donald Evans, asking him to use fair and reasonable procedures in the investigative process.

While the industry and the SEAI, as well as the Indian government, are fairly confident of the strength of their case, the biggest problem being faced by the shrimp exporters is the uncertainty caused by the anti-dumping investigations.

After the announcement of the preliminary ITC determination, Sandu Joseph commented that 'We have been badly affected. There is no shrimp export happening to the US now.' He said that Indian shrimp exporters had not received any export order from the United States since 17 February 2004.

By April 2004 there was widespread concern among the exporters, growers and other stakeholders. Shrimp exports to the United States had come almost to a standstill due to the uncertainty regarding the contingent applicability and incidence of the anti-dumping duty.

According to Joseph Zavier, general secretary of the Kerala Boat Owners Association, with almost insignificant exports to the United States since February the shrimp catch had been reduced by 40–45%. The price per kilogramme of white shrimps, Rs. 280 a few months previously, had crashed to Rs. 100 in April, while the price per kilogramme of another variety of prawn had fallen from Rs. 80 to Rs. 40.

In Tamil Nadu and Andhra Pradesh, two large southern states, shrimp farming is done in large barren areas converted into farms. Mohammad Nayeem, once a prosperous shrimp farmer in Andhra Pradesh, is now a broken man. He owns 100 acres of shrimp farm and used to sell the products at a price of Rs. 450–600 per kilogramme, but after the ITC decision the price had crashed to Rs. 220, while the cost of production was Rs. 250.

In Kerala, shrimp farming is mostly done in paddy fields, converted into shrimp farms, on the fringes of backwaters. According to Rajan P. Mambaly who is one of those who has given his land under lease for shrimp farming, the duty, if imposed, will hit him and the farmers hard, as the net price to the growers would come down to the extent of the anti-dumping duty.

The preliminary determination came on 28 July 2004. In a media briefing on 29 July 2004 the chairman of the MPEDA observed, 'We are not happy with the preliminary determination of the duty rates. The final determination would be on 16 December 2004 and we will fight the case further and try to bring it down to zero level.'

The investigation has now moved into the final determination stage. As part of the procedure, DOC officials visited India in August–September 2004 for onsite verification of the information and data submitted by the mandatory respondents during the preliminary phase of the investigations.

WTO-related issues

India's shrimp export to the United States came under difficulties before, when the United States banned the import of captured shrimp from certain countries, including India, in 1976. It was on the ground that trawling for shrimp by mechanized means had been adversely affecting certain varieties of sea turtles. The dispute on the US ban on the import of shrimp caught without using turtle extruder devices during harvesting was taken to the WTO Dispute Settlement system by the affected countries, including India. The WTO ruled against the United States and asked it to make the regime WTO-compatible. However, since that had not yet happened, India's exports to the United States of aqua-culture shrimp and shrimp caught by non-mechanized means were being made on the basis of certification by the MPEDA, as required under the law.

The trade lobbyists in the United States, such as the Consuming Industries Trade Action Coalition (CITAC), the Seafood Distributors Association and others which were against the imposition of anti-dumping duties on imported shrimp, have raised the issue of the Continued Dumping or Subsidy Offset Act 2000, popularly known as the Byrd Amendment. They want the Act to be repealed or modified to make it WTO-compatible.

Under the Amendment, the US government distributes the anti-dumping and anti-subsidy duties to the US firms that brought forward the cases.

The Act was perceived to violate WTO rules by several countries. Eleven members of the WTO (Australia, Brazil, Canada, Chile, India, Indonesia, Japan, South Korea, Mexico, Thailand and the EU) requested the establishment of a Panel, while six others (Argentina, Costa Rica, Hong Kong, China, Israel and Norway) joined as third parties, supporting the complainants.

On 16 September 2002, the Panel Report recommended the repeal of the Byrd Amendment, as it was held to be a WTO-incompatible response to dumping and subsidization. Offset payments constitute a remedy, in addition to the imposition of an anti-dumping or anti-subsidy duty and this is not envisioned under the WTO rules. Following a US appeal in October 2002, the Appellate Body in its report in January 2003 confirmed the Panel's central finding that the Byrd Amendment is WTO-inconsistent.

The deadline for the US to bring the Byrd Amendment into WTO conformity expired on 27 December 2003. As a consequence, the EU has requested the WTO to authorize retaliatory measures in January 2004. The issue is currently before the WTO and the United States has, as yet, taken no action towards ensuring WTO compliance. However, at the meeting of the WTO Negotiating Group on Rules (26–28 April 2004), the United States said that it was 'beyond question that countries have the sovereign right to distribute government revenues as they deem appropriate', but added that the United States intended to implement the Byrd Amendment ruling.

4 Lessons learnt

The crisis caused by the anti-dumping petition of the Ad Hoc Group has been so far handled competently. The two nodal agencies, one a government body (the MPEDA) and the other a private trade body (the SEAI) have co-ordinated their approaches. One reason for this of course is that the SEAI is represented in the management of the MPEDA. Several visits by the representatives of those two bodies to Washington at critical points also helped to bring an understanding of the nature of the problem and how to face it. This resulted in the selection and appointment of the legal counsel, as early as September 2003. The importance of co-ordinated action by the threatened partners, even those outside India, was appreciated and was worked on by the trade representatives with their counterparts in several Asian countries included in the petition.

Another achievement has been the speedy resolution of the issue of financing. The fact that the Association decided to bear more than 50% of the total costs from its internal resources and the rest from the contribution of members according to the value of their respective exports was critical. Equally critical has been the government's steadfast support for the shrimp industry.

But what remains unaddressed is the issue which is in fact generic and therefore affects all cases, including the shrimp case. Anti-dumping cases take a long time to be finally decided. During this period, trade is affected because importers are risk avoiders and will, therefore, be likely to shift to new sources of supply until the uncertainty is resolved. Industry people pointed out that an anti-dumping case was initiated against Indian leather goods in South Africa two years ago. Although the case was ultimately settled in India's favour, the market was lost to India, because of the uncertainty caused by the transitional decisions.

There is, therefore, a huge human element in such cases where the products originate in small and medium-sized enterprise sectors, and a large number of poor and marginal farmers, artisans or unskilled or semi-skilled labour are engaged in the production of such goods. As of now, there is no institutional mechanism, in the form of a safety net, to take care of this problem. The Indian shrimp industry is one where the problem is acute because of the way in which it is organized. As observed earlier, the industry is fragmented and dominated by small fishermen and farmers.

Uncertainty for any reason create risks which they are not equipped to bear. This case has highlighted the need for the government to look at this issue. Since the Indian government has already indicated its decision to fight an adverse judgment, the need is more acute.

The shrimp industry in India had always focused on one or two major markets for growth. Previously it was Japan and during the last few years, it has been the United States. It has now learnt the importance of diversification. A. J. Tharakan, the SEAI president, has said that they are exploring alternative markets to make up for the loss of the lucrative US market. 'But it will be a long drawn-out process. It is not easy to establish your presence.'

This is why it is important to start early – a lesson the industry appears to have learned from this experience.

18

Indonesia's shrimp exports: meeting the challenge of quality standards

RINA OKTAVIANI AND ERWIDODO*

1 Background

Among Indonesia's fishery products, shrimps contribute the largest foreign exchange earnings. The total value of shrimp exports in 2002, for example, was US$840 million, accounting for about 50% of the total value of fishery exports. However, shrimp exports have been declining during 2000–3. In 2000, Indonesia exported 144,035 tons (US$1,003 million) of shrimp, but this declined to 127,334 tons in 2001 and 122,050 tons in 2002, or around US$940 million and US$840 million, respectively (Central Bureau of Statistics 2003). As an archipelagic country, Indonesia has 17,508 islands and 81,000 km of coastline which provide an excellent resource for brackish-water shrimp farming to support the growth of shrimp exports.

Japan is the largest export market for Indonesian shrimp, followed by the European Union (EU) and the United States. From the total export amount (122,050 tons) in 2002, 60% was shipped to Japan, 16.5% to the United States and 11.5% to the EU. Indonesia's shrimp exports to Japan were, on average, 53,000 tons per year, or about 30% of Japan's total shrimp imports. Meanwhile, Indonesia's share of (frozen) shrimp exports to the United States is only 5–6%, which is much lower than that of Thailand (31%), Ecuador (20%) and Mexico (13%). Other export competing countries are Bangladesh, China, India, the Philippines, Taiwan and some Latin American countries.

The shrimp business in Indonesia is now under serious challenge, both internally and externally. Internally, the shrimp business faces many

* Rina Oktaviani is a Lecturer in the Department of Socio-economic Studies, Faculty of Agriculture, Bogor Agricultural University; Erwidodo is a Senior Researcher at the Centre of Agro-socio-economic Research (CASER), Ministry of Agriculture, Indonesia.

problems, especially in the production (farming) phase, such as disease infestation, shortage of shrimp fry, shrimp feed and medicine, regional planning and infrastructure, and farmer empowerment. Externally, the current flooding of relatively 'cheap' imported shrimp into Indonesia has had a detrimental effect on the profitability of businesses. Some of them went bankrupt and a large number have been in financial difficulties. Depressed world prices had begun in 2002, when the US government enacted an anti-dumping measure against China, Thailand, Vietnam, Brazil and Ecuador. This low price will potentially reduce incentives for doing business, reduce the quality of Indonesian shrimp and eventually reduce Indonesia's competitiveness in the world market.

The other external challenge is associated with quality standards used by major importers, namely Japan, the United States and the EU. Indonesia's shrimps have been found to be infected by viruses and highly contaminated by antibiotics such as oxytetracyline, chlortetracyline, and chloramphenicol (*Kompas*, 3 January 2004). The EU has since September 2001 required virus-free as well as antibiotic-free shrimp imports, the relevant regulation[1] strictly obliges all imported shrimp to be free from chloramphenicol,[2] which is commonly used as for controlling disease by shrimp growers to fight against a number of viruses, and thus to increase shrimp productivity. The Indonesian government has long banned the use of chloramphenicol for animal health protection and as a supplement ingredient in animal feed.[3] The government, along with the Indonesian Fishery Business Association (GAPPINDO), has actively encouraged farmers to abandon the use of chloramphenicol, particularly during the harvest stage of cultivation.

Considering the Indonesian production system, efforts to meet this quality standard would likely be the major constraint and challenge for Indonesia's shrimp production in the near future. It was reported that brackish-water shrimp ponds in Indonesia amounted to 380,000 hectares, 80% of which is cultivated traditionally. Shrimp production using this system is vulnerable to virus infestation, and the use of antibiotics such as chloramphenicol is common.

---

[1] EU-No. 001/705/EC.

[2] A chloramphenicol content of less than 0.5 ppb used to be allowed to enter the EU market. Some analysts and traders raised their objection to this regulation by claiming that chloramphenicol is naturally produced by Streptomyces venezuela in the soil and plankton which is eventually eaten by shrimps.

[3] Surat Edaran Dirjen Peternakan 1143/IV-a tanggal, 19 Nov. 1982.

2 The problem in context

This study is aimed at identifying policy and actions in response to the above two challenges, namely coping with 'cheap' imported shrimps and meeting importers' quality standard. The following are research questions regarding the first challenge: what are appropriate government policies in response to such a challenge? Should Indonesia temporarily ban shrimp imports, as is now being urged by GAPPINDO? Is there any alternative to border measures (protection)?

With regard to quality, the following questions need to be answered. What must the government do to help the shrimp business (particularly traditional shrimp growers) to comply with the quality standard set by the importing countries? What role can the government adopt to help growers increase productivity as well as the quality of shrimp products? What must shrimp growers do to solve their problems and at the same time capture maximum gains stemming from trade liberalization? What can Japan, the EU and the United States do, in a mutually collaborative spirit, to help Indonesia's shrimp producers to comply with the required quality standard without necessarily increasing their production costs? How can the so-called 'trade facilitation' under the Doha Agenda soon be realized to help developing countries to gain from trade liberalization? More specifically, how can Indonesia (or its delegations) put this on the agenda of the next WTO round or in bilateral negotiations?

The Japanese market

Indonesia's shrimp exports to Japan have been declining during the period 2001–3. Total exports in 2001 were 55,617 tons (70.3 billion yen), declining to 53,607 tons (65.6 billion yen) in 2002 and 52,367 tons in 2003. The exports to Japan are mainly frozen, whose volume grew at a rate of less than 1%, while its value dropped by 8% during the same period. Meanwhile, fresh and canned shrimp exports declined significantly, by 8% and 36% respectively.

The declining export trend will probably continue. Japanese importers have recently refused to import shrimps from Indonesia since they are contaminated by chloramphenicol (*Bisnis Indonesia*, 20 January 2004).[4]

---

[4] It was reported that Chinese shrimps have been rejected by Japanese importers because they have been found to be contaminated with chloramphenicol.

According to Mohammad Ramli, PT Bosowa Dataran's manager, Indonesian exporters are now obliged to attach a letter of declaration indicating
that they are exporting chloramphenicol-free shrimps. Fortunately, there
Japanese importers have shown understanding and co-operation towards
Indonesia's exporters in undertaking pre-shipment inspection to avoid
any possibility of rejection.

The European Union market

The September 2001 EU regulation obliging all imported shrimp to be free
from chloramphenicol was discussed intensively during the second meeting of the ASEAN Fishery Federation (AFA) in Bangkok (4–6 November
2003). AFA member countries revealed their concern about the potential
adverse effects of such a regulation. To mitigate the immediate adverse
effects, AFA has proposed to the EU the gradual implementation of a zero
chloramphenicol content over five years, namely 3 parts per billion (ppb)
for the first three years, 1.5 ppb for the remaining two years and finally
zero ppb. Some analysts and traders raised their objection to this regulation, pointing out that chloramphenicol is naturally produced by Streptomyces venezuela in the soil and in plankton which is eventually fed to the
shrimps. A zero content of chloramphenicol in shrimp may therefore be
impossible.

The US market

The US Shrimp Trade Action Committee, an ad hoc committee of the
Southern Shrimps Association (SSA), sent an anti-dumping petition to
the Department of Commerce and the International Trade Commission
dated 31 December 2003 (*Bisnis Indonesia*, 2 January 2004). It sought anti-
dumping action against six shrimp exporting countries, namely Brazil,
China, Ecuador, India, Thailand and Vietnam, claiming that these six
countries practised unfair trading which harmed the US shrimp grower.
Indonesia was, fortunately, not included in this anti-dumping action.

There are two implications of the US action that need to be considered.
First, although Indonesia was not included in the anti-dumping action,
this measure should be considered as a sign of a future threat to the Indonesian shrimp business and exporters. The US government may decide to
take action against Indonesia in future, particularly if Indonesia is found
to be re-exporting imported shrimps from China, Thailand and Vietnam.
There are signs that some 'rent seeking' traders may be undertaking

'transshipment' of imported shrimps from these three countries to the main export destination, including the United States. Indonesia's shrimp imports from China, Thailand and Vietnam have been increasing recently, as a result of the US anti-dumping action against these countries (*Kompas*, 10 July 2004).

Second, this anti-dumping measure will obviously open a window of opportunity for Indonesia to increase its shrimp exports (and its share) to the United States. High tariffs on Chinese and Vietnamese shrimp imports will make Indonesian shrimps more competitive in the US market. The question, however, is whether Indonesia is able to take advantage of this opportunity. Since the United States imposed anti-dumping duties on Thailand, China and other main exporters, Indonesian exports of shrimp to the United States have increased significantly, from 15,253.5 tonnes in January–August 2003 to 26,679.3 tonnes in January–August 2004, or by about 75% (Putro 2004). The increase has been mainly associated with cultivated shrimps.

3 The players and their roles

Responses to chloramphenicol contamination

There are two choices for shrimp growers in response to the chloram-phenicol problem: the first is using synthetic chloramphenicol that would increase shrimp production and result in shrimp that were 'free' from salmonella, but contaminated with chloramphenicol. Second, by aban-doning the use of chloramphenicol, growers could produce chloram-phenicol (mostly) free shrimp, but would probably reduce their shrimp production due to salmonella infestation. The second option, if chosen, would not free shrimp growers from the quality problem, as the EU also requires salmonella-free (non-contaminated) shrimps. Needless to say, shrimp growers in Indonesia are thus facing a dilemma. For develop-ing countries such as Indonesia, producing salmonella-free as well as chloramphenicol-free shrimps appears to be a difficult, if not impossi-ble, goal to attain at the moment. A more sensible and fairer solution would be for the EU governments to help developing country exporters to comply with such standards. Facilitation through trade, such as tech-nical and financial assistance, can be set up bilaterally or, though WTO fora, multilaterally.

Natural chloramphenicol can easily be distinguished from its synthetic counterpart by a special instrument introduced by the EU. The question is whether this device can be cheaply accessed by typical small-scale Indonesia shrimp growers. The EU should also be willing to bear part, if not all, of the pre- and post-inspection costs regarding quality standard inspection procedures. It is a challenge not only to the Indonesian government but to all world leaders to promote freer and fairer trade in line with the Doha Agenda of the WTO.

Responses and Action to Cheap Imported Shrimp

The world market price of white shrimp is expected to drop due to a peak harvest in many shrimp-producing countries. China, for example, will likely produce more than 350,000 tons of white shrimps in 2005, while Vietnam and Thailand will each produce around 250,000 tons. If shrimp imports from these countries are not controlled, the domestic price of shrimp in Indonesia will certainly be depressed, and shrimp growers will suffer large losses.

The price of white shrimps declined continuously throughout 2004. It dropped from US$7.2 per kg in April to US$6.2 in October, and around US$5.8 in December. The instability in world prices has been transmitted to the domestic market. The domestic price of white shrimp in May 2003 was Rp 36,000 per kg, dropping to Rp 18,000 per kg in December; it increased to around Rp 30,000 in January 2004, then fluctuated somewhat in the course of the year, settling in the range of Rp 25,000–Rp 26,000 per kg in the last two months.

Indonesia's shrimp imports from China, Thailand and Vietnam increased in the period June–August 2004, as a result of the US anti-dumping policy towards these countries. The imported shrimps eventually depressed Indonesia's domestic prices, since some of them are marketed domestically. At the same time unit production costs have been reported as increasing (to more than Rp 20,000 per kg) in line with an increase in the prices of feed and shrimp fry (*Kompas*, 10 July 2004).

The issue of low-priced imports is a very controversial one for the Indonesian shrimp industry. GAPPINDO urged the government to impose either a high tariff or non-tariff barriers including an import ban, arguing that cheap imported shrimp will destroy domestic production and hurt shrimp growers. However, the Association of Cold Storage Firms strongly disagreed, on the grounds that they would be possibly facing a shortage of shrimps for their needs. After a series of meetings with the relevant stakeholders, the government, through a joint decree issued by the Ministry of Marine Affairs and Fisheries and the Ministry of Trade, decided on a six-month ban on the import of shrimps from Brazil, China, Ecuador, India, Thailand and Vietnam from 28 December 2004.

In addition to protecting domestic shrimp growers, the import ban was also aimed at responding to the US government's concern over the possibility of transshipment through Indonesia. The US Department of Commerce reminded the Indonesian government to be alert to the transshipment activities of countries that are the targets of the US anti-dumping duties (*Bisnis Indonesia*, 20 November 2004). This reminder was sent in relation to Indonesia's increasing shrimp imports from China and Thailand during the period of 2003–4, particularly during the last few months.

The Indonesian government, through the Ministry of Marine Affairs and Fishery, announced the formation of the Indonesian Shrimp Commission on 8 October 2004, consisting of government policy-makers, academicians and business representatives (GAPPINDO). Its mission is (i) to prepare a draft of the shrimp industry's development policy, including production, processing and international marketing development policy; (ii) to harmonize the downstream and upstream shrimp industries; and (iii) to empower the shrimp entrepreneurs, especially in terms of technology, management and financial capacity (Pasaribu 2004).

The shrimp market needs to become more diversified in terms of both product and market in order to counter cheap shrimp imports. This calls for a high level of technical assistance from both the government and international organizations (such as the FAO) in order to increase the value added of the product, such as quick-frozen, peeled, butterfly-cut shrimp, and cooked products. Industry development through technical assistance can be implemented by offering simple, low-cost technologies for value adding and by matching buyers and sellers to facilitate market diversification. Indonesia can also promote a locally specific or national quality brand (seal) the better to compete in the international market.

In order to foster the development of the national shrimp industry, the government should focus on promoting the conducive regulation of the business environment, such as consistent regulations, a regional master plan and land zoning, improving public infrastructure, promoting research and development, in particular into productivity and quality enhancing, as well as into disease-resistant technologies. These are all public domain undertakings which because of their high cost could not be tackled by private enterprises and shrimp growers. This view was put forward by the chairman of the Nusantara Fishery Community, Masyarakat Perikanan Nusantara-MPI, who stated that government had so far been too busy to tackle such technical matters as cultivation practices.

It is worth noting the performance of the Shrimp Club, established in Lampung by GAPPINDO, with a total memberships of thirty-eight firms comprising farmers, hatcheries, and feed producers and suppliers. The club mostly produces Venname shrimp, accounting for about half the total Venname shrimp production in Lampung. According to the head of the Shrimp Club, the club's activities include giving technical assistance to members, establishing partnerships with the provincial government, undertaking productivity-enhancing studies, running experimental trials for new shrimp varieties such as Udang Biru (Litopenaeus stylirostris), and establishing long-term contracts with exporters and other market outlets including hypermarkets.

The successful experience of Nurdin Abdullah, president of PT Hakata Marine Indonesia (HMI), offers new hope of changing the sad story of Indonesian shrimp into a success story. He invited Japanese investors to establish a joint-venture firm specializing in the production of high-quality shrimp fry and food products. At present, not only does the firm supply high-quality shrimp fry, but it has been able to produce and supply 'ShrimpGuard', a disease-preventing antibody which can be added to shrimp food, which was developed jointly with Kyushu Medical in Japan. The main intention is to rebuild the shrimp industry in south Sulawesi so that it becomes the leading province producing giant tiger prawn (*udang windu*), which has been reported as being Indonesia's second-largest export earner. Nurdin Abdullah is committed to improving the province's production potential (*Kompas*, 29 November 2004).

In order to comply with international safety and quality standards, Indonesia needs technical assistance from its trading partners, which are mainly developed countries, including technology transfers, equipment, expertise and training, and trade facilitation. Other initiatives need to be promoted. More joint ventures with investors from major export destinations need to be established in the near future. Through such initiatives, transfers of technology and market-based knowledge can be expected to take place, and developing country exporters will gradually be able to meet the quality standard set by developed countries.

4 Lessons for others

Indonesia's shrimp business has been facing serious constraints and challenges, only some of which have been partially tackled. The most critical
challenges are related to quality standards, including freedom from anti-
biotic contamination, imposed by developed country importers, with
which the Indonesian shrimp growers lack the capacity to comply. Other
problems are the low productivity and high cost of production of domestic
shrimps. This last problem creates difficulties in managing trade policy
against cheap imported shrimps from major shrimp exporters such as
China, Thailand and Vietnam.

In response to the EU quality standards, the Indonesian government has
issued a number of regulations including that of banning cloramphenicol use. In 2001 the government reiterated a chloramphenicol banning
regulation that had been enacted in 1982, and established a special task
force, at both the regional and national levels, to enforce the ban. Regular monitoring is carried out in all major shrimp producing regions.
This action has been a success, as shown by the fact that only 8.6% out
of a total sample of 10,115 from seven provinces was found to contain
cloramphenicol.

The Indonesian government has recently tightened the conditions of
issuance of import quality and health certificates in order to avoid the
possibility of shrimp transshipment to the United States via Singapore.
This initiative is a response to the increasing trend of transshipment using
Indonesia's export certificates, and has been found to be very effective in
controlling transshipments and in avoiding Indonesia being involved in
possible circumventions through transshipments. In addition to imposing a temporary import ban, Indonesia has also prepared an instrument
for the management of the importation of shrimps. In order to stabilize domestic prices and to support domestic shrimp growers, shrimp
importers are obliged to absorb domestically produced shrimps according to an import-absorption ratio. This instrument is expected to be
effective in guaranteeing that farmers receive reasonable farm-gate prices
for their shrimps during the peak harvest period.

Any barrier to trade means an increasing cost for trading. For a developing country exporter like Indonesia, the quality standard imposed
strictly by importing countries is difficult and costly to meet. Producing salmonella-free as well as chloramphenicol-free shrimps appears to
be difficult, if not impossible, to attain at present. A more sensible and
fairer way is for developed countries (such as Japan, the United States

and EU countries) to help developing country exporters to comply with such quality standards. Trade facilitations, such as technical and financial assistance, can be set either bilaterally or multilaterally though WTO fora.

Last but not least, the government must provide a better environment for doing business as well as promoting new investment in the shrimp business. Among others things are improving relevant public infrastructures, promoting consistent regulations and laws and their enforcement, and political stability. In the case of the shrimp business, the government must increase its research and development budget to promote disease-resistant varieties and productivity-enhancing technologies. All these are considered as non trade-distorting domestic supports that is, 'green box' supports as defined by the WTO Agreement on Agriculture.

Bibliography

Central Bureau of Statistics (2003), *Statistical Yearbook of Indonesia 2002*, Jakarta: Central Bureau of Statistics.

Central Bureau of Statistics (2004), *Statistical Yearbook of Indonesia 2003*, Jakarta: Central Bureau of Statistics.

Bisnis Indonesia (2 Jan. 2004), 'Udang RI Lolos Tuduhan Dumping' (Indonesian Shrimp Released from Anti-Dumping Act) www.bisnisindonesia.com.

Bisnis Indonesia (20 Jan. 2004), 'Jepang Tolak Udang Gunakan Antibiotik' (Japan Refuses Antibiotic-contaminated Shrimp) www.bisnisindonesia.com.

Dursin, R. (2001), 'Indonesia: Shrimp Farming Destroying Mangroves', Inter Press Service.

Kompas (26 April 2000), 'Industri Tambak Udang Ancam Ekosistem Pesisir' (Shrimp Pond Industry Destroys Coastal Ecosystem), www.kompas.com.

Kompas (3 Jan. 2004), 'Segera Benahi Udang untuk Meningkatkan Pangsa Pasar' (Reorganize Shrimp Business Immediately to Increase the Market Share). www.kompas.com.

Kompas (10 July 2004), 'Dipertimbangkan Larangan Sementara Impor Udang' (Temporary Shrimp Import Ban To Be Considered), www.kompas.com.

Kompas (15 Oct. 2004), 'Harga Udang Dunia Tertekan Panen Raya' (Shrimp World Price Decrease Due to Harvest Period), www.kompas.com.

Kompas (27 Oct. 2004), 'Di Sumatera Utara: Ribuan Hektar Tambak Udang Ditelantarkan' (North Sumatera: Thousands of Hectares of Brackish-Water Shrimp Ponds are Abandoned), www.kompas.com.

Kompas (26 Nov. 2004), 'Impor Udang Melonjak 75 Persen' (Shrimp Imports Rise 75%), www.kompas.com.

Kompas (29 Nov. 2004), 'Nurdin Mengembalikan Kejayaan Udang SulSel' (Nurdin Restores Shrimp Development in North Sulawesi), www.kompas.com.

Kompas (28 January 2005), 'SKB Larangan Impor Udang Segera Dicabut' (Joint Letter on Shrimp Import Ban To Be Released Immediately), www. kompas.com.

Kuljis, A. M and Brown, C. L. (2004), *A Market Study of Specific Pathogen-Free Shrimp*, Centre for Tropical and Subtropical Aquaculture Publication 112, aquanic.org/publicat/usda_rac/tr/ctsa/spfmkta.htm.

Pasaribu, A. P. H. (2004), 'Press Conference on the Indonesian Shrimp Commission by the Head of the Centre of Information', Jakarta: Ministry of Marine Affairs and Fisheries.

Putro, S. (2004), 'Perkembangan Pasar Utama' (Development of Main Market), paper presented at National Shrimp Workshop, Jakarta, 2 Dec. 2004.

Seitz, W. D., Nelson, G. C. and Halcrow, H. G. (1994). *Economics of Resources, Agriculture, and Food*, New York: McGraw-Hill.

Siregar, P. R. (2001), *Indonesia: Mounting Tensions over Industrial Shrimp Farming*, WRM Bulletin No. 51, October 2001.

Subardjo, S. (2004), 'APCI dan Kesepakatan Makasar' (APCI and Makasar Commitment), paper presented at National Shrimp Workshop, Jakarta, 2 Dec. 2004.

Sukadi, F. (2004), 'Kebijakan Produksi Udang Budidaya' (Shrimp Culture Production Policy), paper presented at National Shrimp Workshop, Jakarta, 2 Dec. 2004.

Suryadarma, J. (2004), 'Lompatan Besar dimulai dari Langkah Kecil' (A Big Jump Is Started from a Small Step), paper presented at National Shrimp Workshop, Jakarta, 2 Dec. 2004.

19

Patents, parallel importation and compulsory licensing of HIV/AIDS drugs: the experience of Kenya

BEN SIHANYA*

1 The problem in context: patent issues in access to AIDS drugs in Kenya

Patents, the WTO Agreement on Trade-Related Aspects of Intellectual Property Rights (TRIPS) and Kenya's Industrial Property Act, 2001 have been singled out as the main scapegoats in the problem of accessing AIDS drugs in Kenya. This has prevented the pursuit of a more realistic national health policy and strategy to address the problem. Remarkably, AIDS-related deaths are also associated with limited care and support. AIDS is generally undermining Kenya's survival, development, productivity and competitiveness.

The daily number of deaths in Kenya from AIDS has reached about 300, and Dr Patrick A. Orege, the Director of the National AIDS Control Council (NACC), reports that there are 1.5 million people living with HIV/AIDS (PLWHA) in Kenya.[1] Another report, by Noel Wandera, puts the PLWHA figure at 1.2 million.[2] The reporting and computation of AIDS-related deaths is controversial; there are indications that as compared with other African countries, and even in absolute terms, infection rates in Kenya may actually be declining.[3]

---

* Lecturer in Intellectual Property, Constitutionalism and Communications Law, University of Nairobi Law School. The author holds a Ph.D. in intellectual property from Stanford University. I am grateful to Dr Patrick Low and an anonymous WTO reviewer for insights, and to Daisy Ajima, a graduating student at the University of Nairobi Law School, for the excellent research assistance she provided.

[1] See Patrick Orege, 'The Need for Antiretrovirals', *Sunday Standard* (Nairobi), 29 Aug. 2004, p. 20.

[2] See Noel Wandera, 'New Health Plan to Benefit Aids Patients', *East African Standard* (Nairobi), national news section, 27 Aug. 2004, p. 4.

[3] See *Daily Nation* article, 27 Aug. 2004.

Remarkably, a publication issued in August 2004 by the African Civil Society Governance and AIDS Initiative (GAIN), 'HIV/AIDS, Democracy and Governance in Africa', states that recent statistics published by UNAIDS on HIV prevalence show that 'previous estimates appear to have been too high'.[4]

The document goes on,

> There have recently been suggestions that even the lower figure for HIV numbers in Africa is too high, and that the real figure may be as much as 25% lower. Downward revisions in estimated prevalence rates arise chiefly because of the revision of assumptions about the representativeness of data sources used for estimating national prevalence rates. For example, HIV rates in small towns are typically higher than in villages, but data from antenatal clinics in small towns have often been used as the basis for assessing rates in rural areas, which leads to overestimation. As population-based methods for measuring HIV prevalence are becoming more common, prevalence estimates are usually reduced. However, there are serious methodological difficulties with population surveys, in particular because of the relatively large number of individuals who refuse to provide a sample. Until assessment methodologies are improved, there will remain a high level of uncertainty about prevalence estimates.[5]

GAIN concludes that 'it is important to listen carefully to the statisticians, who always insist that it is impossible to know the exact number of people living with HIV and AIDS, and that the best use for surveillance statistics is to identify trends over time rather than "correct" prevalence levels'.[6]

AIDS drugs are expensive: this is partly because of royalties that must be paid to patent holders under the TRIPS Agreement and Kenya's Industrial Property Act, 2001,[7] but also because of limited research and development

---

[4] See generally Kenya AIDS Watch Initiative (KAWI) website at http://www.kenyaaidinstitute. org (last visited 22 Oct. 2004).

[5] Ibid.   [6] Ibid.

[7] Aspects of the TRIPS and patent problem in access to AIDS drugs in Kenya have been captured in three of my studies: Ben Sihanya, 'Constructing Copyright and Creativity in Kenya: Cultural Politics and the Political Economy of Transnational Intellectual Property', JSD (doctoral) dissertation, Stanford Law School, 2003 (forthcoming book, 2005); Ben Sihanya, 'TRIPS and Access to Drugs, Food and the Relevant Technologies in Kenya: Reforming Intellectual Property and Trade Laws for Sustainable Development', research report for EcoNews Africa (Nairobi), on addressing the impact on Kenya of the intellectual property regime under the TRIPS Agreement – preparations for the Cancún WTO meeting, 2003; Ben Sihanya, 'Patent Wars Raging over Aids Cure', *Daily Nation*, Opinion: Pandemic, 17 Dec. 2003, at p. 9. Cf. Arthur Okwemba, 'Kenya Now Producing Aids Drugs:

(R and D) on diseases affecting Kenyans. Non-governmental organizations (NGOs) such as Médecins Sans Frontières (MSF), Action Aid and
other health campaigners have argued that more than 50% of Kenyans live
on US$1 a day and cannot afford the expensive antiretroviral (ARV) drugs
or to maintain optimal nutrition levels associated with effective drug use.
Following calls by experts throughout the 1990s, the Industrial Property
Act has finally been amended to allow for the parallel importation of
generics from India, Brazil and other countries.[8]

There have also been controversies regarding compulsory licensing.
First, many stakeholders argue that Kenyan firms do not have the capacity
to manufacture or distribute such drugs. Second, NGO activists and others argue that the pharmaceutical industry in Kenya is largely oligopolis-
tic and firms have not been keen to process drugs under a compulsory
licence. Third, accessing AIDS drugs has revealed more serious health
policy problems: even non-patented drugs have not been easily accessible, or they have expired in the central storage facilities, or they have been
pilfered through rent-seeking Ministry of Health bureaucrats.

2 The local and external players and their roles

The Kenyan government's position on patents has been that intellectual
property rights should be exercised for the mutual benefit of rights holders and consumers. According to Mboi E. Misati, a senior patent examiner
at the Kenya Industrial Property Institute (KIPI), 'the TRIPS Agreement
should ensure a balance of the rights and the duties of the rights holders vis-à-vis the poor'.[9] Kenya has also argued that the TRIPS Agreement should reflect the socio-economic development of Kenya and other
developing countries; that the TRIPS Council should work closely with

---

But Subtle Pressure Is Already Being Put On Government to Stop Licensing', *Daily Nation,*
Horizon, Science/Technology/The World of Ideas, 1 April, 2004, pp. 23–4; Correspondent,
'Move by Pharmaceuticals Could Limit US Funding', ibid., p. 23.

[8] It is significant, if ironic, that the Act had been promulgated in 1989 partly to protect
Kenyan scientists and the Kenya Medical Research Institute (KEMRI) over the claim that
they had invented a drug for AIDS, Kemron.

[9] See Arts. 28, 30, 31, 32 of the TRIPs Agreement and Part VII (ss. 53–59) of Kenya's IPA 2001
(on the rights of the patent holder). See Mboi Misati, Senior Patent Examiner, Kenya Industrial Property Institute (KIPI), 'The TRIPS Agreement and Access to Essential Medicines in
Kenya', paper presented at a seminar on 'The Role of Intellectual Property Rights in Health
Research and Development', organized by the Kenya Medical Research Institute (KEMRI),
24–25 Feb. 2004.

all stakeholders in order to ensure that the TRIPS Agreement is not in conflict with the public interest, including public health. Kenya's main areas of concern include access to medicines to address public health and nutrition, and its position has been to encourage patent protection but to relax the law to facilitate research and development.[10] The relaxation should be exercised so that it does not infringe the rights of the patent holder.[11]

The key negotiators have also played a key role in advancing these concerns. Kenya, South Africa, Malawi and Lesotho started a campaign within the WTO to relax patent protection on drugs. Activists and other players observe that this campaign was successful because they worked closely with other governments. NGOs claim credit for helping developing countries frame policies on the initiatives while also lobbying policy-makers in the European Union (EU) and the United States, where major pharmaceutical companies were based. For instance, activists advised the South African government on its Medicines Act. In February 1999, US campaign members proposed adding provisions to African trade legislation to cut off funding to agencies that pressed African countries to adopt intellectual property laws exceeding the requirement of the TRIPS Agreement.[12]

Developing country negotiators were also reportedly well briefed and qualified. NGOs worked closely with the southern African states as they advocated a new essential medicine strategy as a means to counter US and EU trade pressure on patent issues. Dr Olive Shisana, the key negotiator for the African countries, was reportedly tough and well informed.[13] Generic manufacturers also made a difference; pharmaceutical companies in developing countries have also played a critical role in the process. For instance, India's Cipla offered generic substitutes for HIV drugs which would cost US$350 a year for the treatment. This is a small fraction of the price charged by Western firms holding patents on the drugs.

Pressure from developing countries placed the issue of public health on the agenda of the Doha Ministerial Conference. Article 1 of the Doha

---

[10] Relaxation of the patent regime would involve repealing some of the rules on using a patent without the owner's consent. This includes declining to produce the article in reasonable quantities, which implicates Art. 31(f) of the TRIPs Agreement. And Kenya championed the amendment of this article. See Misati, 'TRIPS Agreement'.

[11] Ibid.

[12] See Angene Wilson, 'Good News about AIDS-Case Countries: Lesotho, Kenya, Malawi and South Africa', available at www.rpcr.org (accessed on 24 Aug. 2004).

[13] Ibid.

Declaration recognizes the gravity of health problems afflicting developing countries, including AIDS, malaria and tuberculosis. Article 6 empowered the Council to find an expeditious solution by the end of 2002.[14]

There were many formal and informal sessions to execute this mandate.[15] Various problems were recognized in the TRIPS Agreement as identified by the African Group of which Kenya has been a leader.

1. The first impediment was that Article 31(f) of the TRIPS Agreement restricts the use of compulsory licensing to authorising 'predominantly for the supply of the domestic market of the member authorising such use'. This means that a country making use of a compulsory licence must manufacture the product locally for the domestic market. Thus, the country must have sufficient local manufacturing capacity. This is not the case in most of the developing countries. There are three main problems: (i) Kenya and many other developing countries argue that they are too poor to set up factories and they lack sufficient local manufacturing capacity; (ii) the domestic market is too small to attract sufficient investment in the pharmaceutical sector; and (iii) if the domestic market cannot be expanded, economies of scale cannot be achieved.

The series of meetings to execute the mandate of the Declaration comprised representatives of developing and developed countries. Kenya, together with forty-one members of the African Group that it chaired, demanded a broader approach in designing the solution and an interpretation of the effective use of compulsory licensing so as to facilitate strategies to supply the current needs of members.

Kenya argued for Article 31(f) of the TRIPS Agreement to be either deleted or amended; it also argued for subsequent interpretations to ensure sufficiency in manufacturing capacity for Kenya to make use of compulsory licensing. The EU supported the amendment conditionally to ensure non-diversion and transparency. No decision had been reached as the deadline under the Declaration of the end of 2002 drew near. The first decision was made on 24 November 2002, but the African Group argued that it was unsatisfactory and unworkable. It considered this was 'a step back from Doha because it created further restrictions on the current flexibilities in the TRIPS Agreement'.[16]

---

[14] For the search for a solution, see below.
[15] The discussions encompassed product coverage, beneficially importing member, eligible supplying member, transfer of technology, meaning of domestic market, legal mechanisms, transition period, exclusive marketing rights and non violation complaints.
[16] Nelson Ndirangu, Kenya's trade attaché in Geneva, on behalf of the African Group.

The decisions on the implementation of paragraph 6 of the Doha Declaration[17] of 30 October 2003 clarified some of the issues. Article 2 of the Decision would waive the obligations of an exporting country under Article 31(f) of the Agreement with respect to the granting of a compulsory licence.

According to some, this waiver should be revised to be an actual amendment rather than an interim measure which can be repudiated at any time. There should be a permanent change to the provision to provide for certainty, since pharmaceutical companies need some certainty before they can invest in the industry.[18]

2. Some members have proposed that Article 30 of the TRIPS Agreement be interpreted broadly to give WTO members the right to allow production without the consent of the patent holder to address public health needs in another country.[19]

The first comprehensive decision was given in the Perez Motta text.[20] It was unsatisfactory to Kenya and other developing countries as it did not tackle most of the problems. In the course of rejecting it, the chairman of the African Group[21] expressed disappointment and frustration, saying that the Decision was neither a practical solution nor was it workable. He described it as a step back from Doha.

In a speech read by the African representative,[22] the African Group stated:

> The African Group is disappointed and frustrated by the progress made so far. The group feels if the discussions continue on the same line as they have been conducted to date, then it is unlikely that the desired solution will be forthcoming, and particularly one meant to address the public health problems afflicting Africa. Members may wish to seriously reflect on the reasons why the African group raised the issue in the TRIPS Council prior to the Doha conference and their subsequent expectations after the issue

---

[17] The Decision was adopted by the General Council in the light of a statement read out by the chairman of the African Group; it can be found in Job (03)/177 of the WTO. This statement was reproduced in the minutes of the General Council to be issued as WT/GL/M/82. See the footnotes to the Decision.

[18] Interview with Evans Mboi Misati, chief patent examiner at KIPI, Nairobi, 17 Aug. 2004.

[19] Art. 30 of TRIPS provides for 'limited exceptions to the exclusive rights conferred by the patent provided that such exceptions do not unreasonably conflict with the normal exploitation of the patent and do not unreasonably prejudice the legitimate interests of the patent owner, taking into account the legitimate interests of the third parties'.

[20] The text was named after the then chairman of the Council, Eduardo Perez Motta.

[21] Nelson Ndirangu, Kenya's trade attaché in Geneva.

[22] Ndirangu, on behalf of the African Group.

in the Doha [Declaration] as stated in the various communications of the TRIPS Council. This probably gives them a better understanding of the nature of the solution Africa expects.

Lobbying efforts finally began to yield some advances. By the conclusion of the Cancún Ministerial Conference in September 2003, members had agreed to relax the provisions of the TRIPS Agreement. For instance, they agreed that a patented technology required for the production of medicines and allied kits should be accessible to deserving WTO members on favourable terms. The final text of an acceptable decision was adopted on 31 August 2003.

Additionally, the Kenyan government, including the Ministry of Health and the Ministry of Trade and Industry, as well as the Kenya Industrial Property Office (KIPO), played a major role in the discussions on public health and patents. KIPO prioritized and advised on the reform of patent law and policy, and sought and secured the enactment of the Industrial Property Act's provisions on compulsory licensing, parallel importation and government use, as well as the transformation of KIPO into the Kenya Industrial Property Institute (KIPI).

Businesses which played a part in the process included pharmaceutical companies, pharmacies, importers and exporters.[23] The most visible player in the campaign was Cosmos Industries, which lobbied the government to allow compulsory licensing.

Many local and international civil society associations and research outfits also participated. These included the Consumer Information Network (CIN),[24] MSF,[25] Health Action International (HAI), Kenya Aids Watch

---

[23] Pharmaceutical companies such as Cosmos and Cipla lobbied the government extensively to allow for parallel importation and compulsory licensing.

[24] EcoNews Africa participated in lobbying through research, media campaigns, and general lobbying and raising public awareness, including through articles. It commissioned a study by the author: 'TRIPS and Access to Drugs, Food and the Relevant Technologies in Kenya: Reforming Intellectual Property and Trade Laws for Sustainable Development', research report for EcoNews Africa Nairobi, on addressing the impact on Kenya and the intellectual property regime under the TRIPS Agreement, March 2003. This report drew from earlier work with MSF and KIPI, among others, leading to IPA 2001. Oduor Ong'wen and Karin Gregow of EcoNews were key players in the research, advocacy and lobbying process. See also Oduor Ong'wen, 'Intellectual Property Rights Promote Piracy', *East African Standard*, 14 July 2004.

[25] MSF and HAI participated by organizing a conference on 15–16 June 2000 in Nairobi on 'Improving Access to Essential Medicines in East Africa: Patents and Prices in the Global Economy'. For conference documents see www.accessmedicine. msf.org. The conference was also supported by the Rockfeller Foundation. See http://www.harweb.org/mtgs/nairobi (last accessed 16 March 2003). Innovative Lawyering played a role in addressing the legal issues, especially intellectual property.

Institute (KAWI), Christian Children's Fund (CCF),[26] Oxfam, EcoNews Africa and Innovative Lawyering.[27]

A statement posted by MSF on their website captures the developments and the perspectives of the players. We cite it *in extenso*:

> Kenya Coalition on Access to Essential Medicines today warned that the Kenyan government needs to carefully examine the extent of the reductions and the impact that this could have on more long-term access to life-saving medicines. The government should be guided by the fact that a generic manufacturer (CIPLA of India) has offered to provide US quality approved antiretrovirals at US$800–1000 per person per year. If the big pharmaceutical companies give an 85% reduction on the current global price of US$15,000 per patient per year, as announced publicly in May, then the price would be US$2,250. This means that twice as many patients would be able to be treated in Kenya by using medicines supplied by the Indian manufacturer than with the big pharmaceutical company offer which is being negotiated.
>
> In order to have the right to import these affordable medicines, Kenya would need to issue compulsory licences to override patents, which is their right within international trade law (TRIPS within WTO). According to the law, inexpensive generic drugs can be legally manufactured locally or imported (cf. stipulations on 'governmental use' and 'compulsory licensing' provided by the Kenyan Industrial Property Act, 1989). Negotiations on price cuts should never substitute these rights or hamper the implementation of these provisions. The Kenyan Coalition points out that the price cuts coincide with upcoming discussions about a new Industrial Property Bill, 2000. This Bill should create opportunities to improve access to cheaper drugs by softening the conditions for compulsory licensing and by introducing parallel imports, all of which are legal under international WTO TRIPS law. Price negotiations should not compromise any proposed amendments to the Bill, 2000, which are in favour of access to drugs.
>
> . . .

---

[26] The Christian Children's Fund (CCF) has been responding to this global call to action with innovative programmes based on a seven-point strategy focusing on home-based care; psychosocial support for orphans and other vulnerable children; HIV/AIDS prevention; nutrition and child health; educational assistance and vocational training; promotion of positive living for people with HIV/AIDS; and sustainable livelihoods through income-generating activities. See generally www.christianchildrenfund.org (last accessed 24 Aug. 2004).

[27] Innovative Lawyering participated through the author, its chief strategist; I worked with MSF and other agencies in advocating progressive reforms to IPA, 1989, and by working with EcoNews Africa in producing the research report cited in n. 7 above.

Therefore, the Kenya Coalition on Access to Essential Medicines encourages the Kenyan government and UNAIDS to recognize that although there could be short-term benefits from the deal, these could be outweighed by negative consequences in the long run, unless serious efforts are made to stimulate generic production of antiretroviral drugs by local manufacturers and/or to import inexpensive drugs. The introduction of generic drugs will increase competition and will lead, according to general market rules, to considerable price reductions.[28]

3 Challenges faced and the outcome

Many players focused on legal provisions: patents. They lobbied the government and the National Assembly to facilitate legislative reform. They also convened fora to condemn the WTO, TRIPS, and pharmaceutical transnational corporations (TNCs). The process of coming up with a comprehensive Industrial Property Act on the issues was also characterized by intense lobbying. In a press conference in 2001 the Coalition for Access to Essential Medicines warned the government of the possibility of powerful pharmaceutical companies using 'not too transparent' ways to woo MPs to vote against a Bill aimed at facilitating access to cheaper medicines.[29]

Dr Chris Ouma, Action Aid's national co-ordinator, HIV/AIDS Programme Kenya, argued that

> MPs should think about the plight of their people. They now have the power to alleviate their suffering ... But we know [the MPs] are also under pressure from pharmaceutical companies ready to use subtle but not-very transparent ways of pushing their case ... We cannot be sure the MPs we have talked to will vote for the Bill. Things have been happening that leave us worried.[30]

As indicated, domesticating the TRIPS Agreement was a major first step in complying with the WTO Agreement. President Daniel arap Moi on 27 July 2001 assented to the Industrial Property Act replacing the

---

[28] Available at www.msf.org (last accessed 24 Aug. 2004). There is an explicit and implicit assumption that normal market conditions and principles (or the market mechanism of demand and supply) operate efficiently in Kenya, especially as far as HIV/AIDS drugs are concerned.

[29] See Ken Opala, 'Don't Quit Anti-Aids Drugs War, MPs told', *Daily Nation*, (Nairobi), 11 May 2001.

[30] Ibid.

Industrial Property Act, 1989.[31] Thus Kenya revised the Industrial Property Act, partly to be WTO/TRIPS-compliant, and also took the opportunity to address one of the most critical issues in the post-TRIPS dispensation: access to HIV/AIDS drugs. S. 58(2) of the 2001 Act limits a patentee's rights:

> The rights under the patent shall not extend to acts in respect of articles which have been put on the market in Kenya or in any other country or imported into Kenya *by the owner of the patent or with his express consent.*

The words in italics were added through an amendment a month after the Act was passed.[32] There was extensive lobbying against this provision by NGOs that believed that it did not sufficiently limit the rights of a patent holder. According to the Kenya Coalition on Access to Essential Medicines, a lobby group bringing together several local and international NGOs in Nairobi,[33] the contentious amendment is especially troubling because it was introduced just a month after the 2001 Industrial Property Act was enacted.[34]

> We are shocked that the amendment to an Act, which we were involved in, was drafted and passed without the consultation of any of the stakeholders in the civil society ... it seems some of the important gains that the IPA [brought about] have now been taken away.[35]

In December 2001 Kenya's Assistant Minister for Trade and Industry, Albert Ekirapa, explained to an enraged National Assembly that his ministry had not given a commencement date because the Attorney General's office had not drafted subsidiary regulation to govern its implementation

---

[31] Act No. 3 of 2001, *Kenya Gazette Supplement*, 60 (2001).The Act came into effect via a notice issued on 28 March 2002 which indicated that the commencement date would be announced by notice. The commencement date was 1 May 2002.

[32] *Kenya Gazette*, 49 (2002).

[33] The members are Action Aid, the Association of People Living with AIDS in Kenya (TAPWAK); Health Action International (HAI Africa); Network for People Living with HIV/AIDS (NEPHAK); Women Fighting AIDS in Kenya (WOFAK); Society for Women and AIDS in Kenya (SWAK); Nyumbani; Federation of Women Lawyers of Kenya (FIDA); CARE International; Médecins Sans Frontières (MSF); DACASA; Pharmaciens Sans Frontières (PSF); Kenya Medical Association (KMA); Consumer Information Network (CIN); and Campaigners for AIDS-Free Society.

[34] The main issue in this contention was the speed with which the amendment was drafted. See Dagi Kimani, 'New Law Blocks Import of AIDS Generics in Kenya', *East African*, 1 July 2002.

[35] Lisa Kimbo, the Co-ordinator of the Kenya Coalition on Access to Essential Medicines, on 1 July 2003.

six months after it had been passed. The same office, however, took less than a month to draft the amendment. Partly because of this controversy, the amendment was withdrawn[36] and the Act was reinstated to its original condition. The Industrial Property Act also provides for government use under s. 80.

The first applicant for a licence was Cosmos Industries. It sought to be allowed to produce a drug, the product of Glaxo SmithKline and Boehringer Ingelheim of Germany. On realizing that the government was about to issue a licence, Boehringer offered a voluntary licence, slowing down the negotiations on the licence. According to Dr William Mwatu, the company's East Africa Medical and Regulatory Director,

> Cosmos would be able to manufacture zidovudine and larnivudine, as well as a combination of the two, for sale in Burundi, Kenya, Rwanda, Tanzania and Uganda... this action we believe will go a long way to help increase access to [the life-prolonging drugs], and also have another health-care company play a significant role in addressing the HIV/AIDS crisis in Kenya.[37]

While signing the agreement in Nairobi, the chairman and managing director, Prakash Patel, said, 'The door of access to essential medicines for the people of Kenya and East Africa will now be open.'[38] Cosmos will be Africa's second manufacturer of generic ARV drugs, after the South African company Aspen Pharmacare, which announced a similar move in early 2004. Cosmos Industries received its licence from Glaxo SmithKline in 2004.

The Minister of Trade and Industry, Dr Mukhisa Kituyi, made a quotable speech at the presentation ceremony:

> Nevertheless it is a road to success. When I was informed that there was a company that had filed an application for government's use of antiretroviral patents as provided under the Industrial Property Act, 2001, I was really delighted. Kenya is a signatory to major international treaties on intellectual property like the convention establishing the World Intellectual Property Organization [WIPO] and the [TRIPS] Agreement. We therefore have an obligation to protect and respect the rights of all patent holders.[39]

---

[36] *Kenya Gazette*, 23 Aug. 2003.

[37] See Konchora Gurancha and Mutahi Rukanga, 'Aids Drug Prices To Drop', *East African Standard*, 23 Sept. 2004, p. 40; see also Jeff Otieno, 'Patients Set To Benefit from Cheap Aids Drugs', *Daily Nation*, 23 Sept. 2004, p. 4; UN Office for the Co-ordination of Humanitarian Affairs, 'Kenya To Produce ARVs in Weeks', at www.irinnews.org.

[38] Ibid.

[39] This speech is reported in full on the Ministry of Trade and Industry's website (http://www.tradeandindustry.go.ke/speech). It is analysed briefly by Jeff Otieno on the website.

The Minister also cited the constitutional protection of property in the context of access to HIV/AIDS drugs:

> Our Constitution also provides for the sanctity of property and the government indeed respects the Constitution, being the supreme law of the land. Similarly, the government has a duty to provide for easy access to antiretroviral drugs to its citizens who are living with HIV/AIDS, more so when the AIDS pandemic was declared a national disaster.[40]

Dr Kituyi then addressed the immediate stakeholders in the licence transaction:

> I am therefore very grateful to the two parties, Glaxo SmithKline and Cosmos, who negotiated and agreed on acceptable terms for a voluntary licence. It is my hope that many other pharmaceutical companies in Kenya will follow this noble example to enable the people living with HIV/AIDS to easily access antiretroviral drugs. Once again, Kenya has taken the lead in this region and I am glad to note that the territory referred to in the voluntary licence includes Kenya, Uganda, Tanzania, Burundi and Rwanda.[41]

The Minister was optimistic about the impact of the licensing arrangement, and about KIPI's role in the administration of intellectual property:

> It is my hope that this function will mark the beginning of a truly healthy competition in the manufacture of not only antiretroviral drugs but all other health drugs in the country for the benefit of all. This will certainly have the ripple effect of creating the much needed wealth in Kenya. Finally let me also take this opportunity to thank KIPI for the role it has played in the negotiations between the two parties here and the eventual registration of the voluntary licence as one of the Institute's mandate under the Industrial Property Act, 2001. My ministry is keen to see all its departments carry out their mandates as provided for under the respective legislations.[42]

Another problem identified in Kenya is that the influx of generics may lead to an influx of counterfeit drugs. KIPI has devised some rules for identifying a counterfeit, which it defines as a pharmaceutical product availed to the market or presented to it and intentionally tailored to derive and ride on the reputation or goodwill of another good through labelling or marking. 'The counterfeits are not necessarily substandard goods. But they infringe the patent. Goods are counterfeits when a person

---

[40] Ibid.   [41] Ibid.   [42] Ibid.

other than the owner of the patent makes them without the patentee's licence.'[43]

Significantly, there is widespread ignorance in Kenya on the importance of intellectual property rights. Local manufacturing companies are generally afraid to invest in compulsory licensing or parallel importation for fear generally of taking on the pharmaceutical giants.[44] They do not actually realize that they have the legal backing to do so. Even trained lawyers do not actually commit enough time on the complex and wide area of intellectual property.

Beyond the patent debate

The debate on patents has not resolved the problem of access to AIDS drugs. Critics observe that most of the government's resources on AIDS are spent on emoluments, workshops and spurious awareness campaigns.[45] They cite, for example, the KSh 13 million spent on the International Conference on AIDS and Sexually Transmitted Infections in Africa (ICASA),[46] when the 2003 conference was held at Nairobi's Kenyatta International Conference Centre (KICC), on 21–26 September 2003.

> Numbering just about a hundred, activists under the aegis of the Pan-African AIDS Treatment Access Movement (PATAM) spoke, kicked, railed and acted up against many 'enemies' of access to treatment for HIV/AIDS in Africa: Big Pharma, the unfeeling, profit-focused multinational corporations, and African leaders who have refused to provide treatment for their

[43] KIPI, 'Detailed Analysis in Response to Shako and Co. Advocates – Differentiating Between Counterfeits and legally Imported Pharmaceutical Products' (2004).

[44] As per Misati, 'TRIPS Agreement'.

[45] For instance, Dr Margaret Gachara, the former director of the government's AIDS body, the National AIDS Control Council (NACC), was on 30 Aug. 2004 convicted and sentenced to one year in jail for fraudulently earning about KSh 27 million (or KSh 2 million per month) in emoluments and for abuse of office, when NACC spent much less on some crucial programmes. See *Daily Nation*, 26 Aug. 2004; Jillo Kadida and Mark Agutu, 'Gachara Is Jailed for One Year: Former Aids Control Boss Is Found Guilty of Fraud and Abuse of Office', *Daily Nation*, Tuesday, 31 Aug. 2004, p. 48. Critics also observe that in 2004 the Ministry of Health organized a two-day women's conference at Kasarani in Nairobi on AIDS, at which about KSh 30 million were spent. This was opened by President Mwai Kibaki and allegedly organised by an NGO fronted by the Health Minister's daughter. See *East African Standard* and *Daily Nation*, 23 Feb. 2004 and after, including nation reporter and KNA, 'Abrupt End to Aids meeting', *Daily Nation*, 23 Feb. 2004.

[46] The ICASA Conference is a forum held under the auspices of UNAIDS where every two years African scientists, social leaders, political leaders and communities come together to share experiences and updates on the responses to the HIV/AIDS pandemic.

peoples. 'You talk, we die,' yelled the activists, as they mounted a blockage of the VIP and heads of governments lounge at the Kenyatta International Conference Centre, venue of the 13th International Conference on AIDS and STIs in Africa (ICASA).[47]

At the conference one speech after another was read by participants expressing their disappointment in the way the WTO and the government were working toward achieving access to drugs. One person living with AIDS, Nomfundo Dubula,[48] on behalf of people living with HIV, said during the closing ceremony of the ICASA conference:

I want to say that as communities and people living with HIV we are angry. Our people are dying unnecessarily. African leaders, the ball is in your hands. You have to decide whether you want to lead a continent without people. So, stop playing hide and seek whilst people are dying. The World Health Organization has declared antiretroviral therapy a state of global emergency and our leaders are still in a state of denial. The Doha and the UNGASS declarations have opened the way to decide about the future of Africa, so, when is your action? The Doha declaration on health is hope, and it must be implemented. Two years ago, the Abuja declaration promised 15% of the budget on health but up to now that has not happened. How many people must die? Please, move from talks to real action. I also want to address the WHO. WHO has promised to give technical assistance in the procurement of drugs. Now we need your assistance in our countries to ensure that cheaper generic drugs reach every country, with or without manufacturing capacity.

You also have a key role in ensuring resources for poor countries. The 3 by 5 initiative should also ensure that all treatment programmes include treatment literacy efforts. On our side, we commit ourselves in educating our people and ensuring adherence. We need real leadership in the implementation of effective strategies to reach the 3 by 5 target. We will assist you in this effort if you show commitment and independence in prioritizing people's health over any other interest. I want to refer to the drug companies, whose bags are full with profits. Stop squeezing poor Africans which only represent 1.3% of your global market. Don't delay access by giving exclusive licenses that are only transferring the monopoly to local companies blocking competition. Your diagnostics are still too

---

[47] See http://www.equinetafrica.org/newsletter/newsletter.php?id=1542 (accessed 24 Aug. 2004). See generally the speeches at the conference at www.listkabisa.org equinet-newsletter: [Equinet-news], equinet newsletter October 2003: 'Stop Playing Hide and Seek Whilst People Are Dying'.

[48] He is from the Treatment Action Campaign in South Africa and represents the Pan African Treatment Access Movement.

expensive and inaccessible. Provide low prices and allow our governments to bring us life-saving essential drugs and the essential monitoring
systems.[19]

Government procurement of drugs, which is not constrained by the
WTO, the TRIPS Agreement or the Industrial Property Act, 2001, is largely
inefficient. It further illustrates the policy defects highlighted in the fore-
going appeal.

There is limited support for research and development, a matter that has
arisen with regard to about five announcements of alleged breakthroughs
in AIDS drug development. These 'patent races' or 'wars' include Kemron,
Dr 'Stone's' 'Ozone therapy', collaboration between the Universities of
Nairobi and Oxford, and the work of Professor Arthur Obel.

Obel developed Pearl Omega, which was challenged by the medical pro-
fession and the Kenya AIDS Society (KAS) for, inter alia, not conforming
to standards under Kenya's health law and policy regarding clinical testing,
efficacy, approval and registration of new drugs.[50]

KAS went to court[51] and claimed that its members (patients) would be
harmed, and that Obel's representation that he had found a cure could be
counter-productive, as there might be recklessness based on false hope.
Justice Gideon Mbito upheld Obel's right to process and distribute the
drug, thus making important pronouncements on the policy of AIDS
research: Obel had taken great personal risks in researching a dangerous
disease. Such researchers need incentives. The Court of Appeal[52] upheld
the decision (also on a technicality), partly because patients' suffering was
alleged but not proved.

Issues regarding incentives and intellectual property have invariably
arisen in the five major AIDS drugs announcements. In Kemron there were
two major contests of ownership and control. The first pitted the Kenya
Medical Research Institute (KEMRI) (or scientific researchers) against
traditional healers and herbalists, who claimed a share because they had

---

[49] See equinet newsletter, 'Stop Playing'. The '3 by 5' is the global target of providing
3 million people living with HIV/AIDS in developing and middle-income countries with
life-prolonging antiretroviral treatment (ART) by the end of 2005 (source: WHO website,
accessed in April 2005).

[50] Kenyan medical practitioners also expressed concern, because Obel did not disclose the
ingredients or side effects. The other HIV/AIDS drugs announcements are discussed in
this report and in Sihanya, 'Patent Wars Raging over Aids Cure'.

[51] *Kenya AIDS Society* v. *Professor Arthur Obel,* HCCC No 1079.

[52] Civil Appeal No. 188 of 1997.

allegedly contributed biological materials (herbs) and their traditional knowledge.[53]

What of the efficient use of external and internal resources? Donor funds are being sought and received to battle against the scourge. According to a communication from Dr Patrick Orege, the Director of the National AIDS Control Council (NACC), in the media on 1 July 2004,[54]

> Kenya's war on HIV/Aids has received a major boost after the World Bank on 30 June released KSh 300 million to fight the disease. The Director said his organization would pay out the bulk of the money – KSh 248 million – to community-based groups while AIDS control units in various ministries would get the rest. The KSh 300 million is part of the KSh 1.7 billion which the Bank had earlier withheld until it got an audit report for the past financial year.

The World Bank is the leading donor to the AIDS Council, and is providing about KSh 4 billion ($50 million) over a five-year period. The loan programme, under the Kenya National HIV/AIDS Strategic Plan, was signed in 2001 and expires in 2005. The fact is that even if patents are an obstacle to getting drugs, at least there are funds to pay royalties and accountability should be encouraged.[55] Kenya should learn from past failures.

Other non-IP strategies that can facilitate access to AIDS drugs in Kenya

1. *Therapeutic value pricing.* This has been adopted mostly in Australia. The buyer or the state Pharmaceutical Benefit Scheme determines the drug price based on therapeutic value. When a new drug becomes available, they examine it and if it is an improvement on the original, they may allow it to be sold at, say, 10% more.

2. *Pooled procurement.* For small economies, whereby several countries combine to purchase drugs together, this procedure may be of immense

[53] See Sihanya, 'Patent Wars Raging over Aids Cure'.

[54] Mike Mwaniki, 'HIV Aids War Gets Shs 300m Boost', *Daily Nation*, 1 July 2004.

[55] Kenya in 2002 had failed to qualify for AIDS aid funding under the World AIDS Fund to tackle AIDS, tuberculosis and malaria. The reasons cited included lack of accountability in Kenya's proposal. Other countries that received a boost included South Africa, Zambia and Zimbabwe. Sources within Kenya's NGO sector said that among the things that were working against the country getting any support for HIV-related programmes from such organizations as the Global Fund is the fact that the country's AIDS programme falls under the Office of the President, and not the Ministry of Health. See Dagi Kimani, 'Aids Funds: Ministry of Health Fails Test', *East African*, 29 April 2002.

value. In the Caribbean it has halved the prices of drugs. Kenya can try using this through the regional trade arrangements established under the East African Community (EAC) and the Common Market for Eastern and Southern Africa (COMESA).

3. *Negotiated procurement.* This is where large organizations such as WHO buy drugs in large quantities. In doing so they get huge discounts from the pharmaceutical companies. WHO and WTO member states can derive enormous advantages from this. Concerted international procurement efforts on vaccines and contraceptives have reduced the prices of some drugs. For example, the price of the oral polio vaccine which is sold to developing countries at 33.3 times lower than to the US government. Likewise, the oral contraceptive prices are 130–240 times lower in poor countries than in the United States. The same could be negotiated for antiretrovirals.

4. *Planned donations.* WHO and other organizations have done well in establishing guidelines for drug donations. For example, Kenya in 2002 received 1 million doses of Nevirapine, an ARV that helps prevent mother-to-child transmission of the HIV/AIDS virus.[56] This will go a long way in saving the lives of millions of Kenyans.

5. *Government commitment.* The commitment shown by the Brazilian and Indian governments in the campaign for access to drugs is overwhelming. If the Kenya government were to exhibit such commitment the question of access to drugs would be significantly improved.

The former South African President, Nelson Mandela, has persuasively argued that an effective strategy for combating the AIDS problem requires the engaged commitment of national leaders to provide not only for prevention but also for anyone who needs drugs 'wherever they may be in the world and regardless of whether they can afford to pay or not'.[57]

---

[56] In Kenya mother-to-child transmission is a major cause of AIDS. Researcher Anna Coutsoudis startled her colleagues at the thirteenth International AIDS Conference in Durban, South Africa, with the following information: in a study of 551 mother-and-child pairs, first published in the prestigious peer-reviewed journal *The Lancet* (7 Aug. 1999), her group found that mothers who breastfed their babies for at least three months had no more chance of transmitting HIV to their children than mothers who never breastfed at all. Even more surprising, children who received a mixed diet of formula and breast milk had the highest HIV rates over a period of six months. Coutsoudis followed these children for more than fifteen months, and the results remained the same. See Anna Coutsoudis et al., 'Method of Feeding and Transmission of HIV-1 from Mothers to Children by Fifteen Months of Age: Prospective Cohort Study from Durban, South Africa', *AIDS* 15 (2001): 379–7. See www.virusmyth.net, accessed on 24 Aug. 2004.

[57] Nelson Mandela, 'Care, Support and Destigmatisation', preliminary address to the XIV International AIDS Conference, Barcelona, Spain, 7–12 July 2002.

Kenya has shown some commitment by setting up an anti-Aids campaign dubbed TOTAL WAR ON HIV/AIDS; President Kibaki chairs the committee.[58] In January 2004, Charity Ngilu, the Minister of Health, met with various NGOs and interest groups to get their support, which she did, on the fight at grass-roots level.

The government has also committed itself to fighting AIDS through the AIDS Bill,[59] s. 19 of which commits the government to ensuring that everyone who needs to gets access to AIDS drugs.[60] Remarkably, in 2004 the price of ARVs in public hospitals became as low as KSh 500 a month, down from KSh 6000 a month only a year previously and available in private hospitals only. The government's policy on prevention through condoms and family life education has been weak. It imported condoms in an effort to reduce the rate of infections, against a backdrop of protests by a section of the Catholic Church who for a long time argued that condoms and family life education would encourage promiscuity.

According to one Catholic activist,

> Condoms are also promoted in Kenya as barriers against STDs [sexually transmitted diseases]. This is despite the countless STDs condoms cannot prevent. These include HPV, which causes genital warts and cancer of the cervix. This is a deadly cancer, very common in Kenya, especially among poor, malnourished, and disadvantaged women. Screening for this cancer is not practical because the health sector has been moribund for a long time. Other STDs condoms cannot prevent include clamydia, which causes sterility, Hepatitis B and C which cause pain and liver cancer, Herpes genitalis, chancroid, and syphilis. Most of these diseases are incurable: the consequences on those treatable are permanent. Condom users are not aware of these facts; those who distribute them dishonestly withhold this information. Since condoms prevent neither HIV nor STDs, those who promote them do so to make blood money as they sacrifice helpless uninformed Kenyans. How do you make informed decisions and informed choice without information? When leaders pass the message that it is all right to be immoral as long as you use a condom, promiscuity increases and

---

[58] The president appears in TV and newspaper advertisements, and posters, holding hands with ordinary citizens and saying, 'Let's Strangle [or eliminate] AIDS' in Kiswahili, the Kenyan lingua franca, 'Pamoja Tuangamize Ukimwi'. AIDS was (belatedly) declared a national disaster by President Moi on 25 Nov. 1999.

[59] *Kenya Gazette Supplement*, 76, 23 Sept. 2003.

[60] This is still a pipedream. See Orege, 'The Need for Anti-retrovirals', and Wandera, 'New Health Plan' (in which the government promises that under its proposed controversial National Social Health Insurance Scheme (NSHIF), 181,000 people living with AIDS (out of about 1.5 million) will be put on ARVs).

AIDS spreads. Asking Kenyans to use condoms is tantamount to sentencing them to death. But even if condoms were 100% protective, their use would still be illicit and below the dignity of the human person created in the image of God.[61]

6. *Differential or dynamic pricing*. Pharmaceutical companies could charge less for developing countries than in developed countries. This is consistent with the TRIPS Agreement and is backed by, among others, WHO, the EU, MSF and some corporations. The main problems now include preventing the drugs from 'leaking' back to the developed countries, and convincing the citizens of developed countries to be taxed more for the benefit of the poor.[62]

4 Lessons for others: the players' views

As already mentioned, some of the players have indicated that the problem of access to AIDS drugs is more complex, and does not only implicate patents or the WTO. Other problems include inefficient resource allocations, poverty and distribution problems, as well as government policy on public health and patents.

Significantly, the WTO agreed that the TRIPS rules be implemented by 2006. India and other countries which have been providing Kenya with drugs may stop doing so.

In August 2004 WHO delisted some of the generic drugs used for AIDS treatment, arguing that the test to determine their efficacy was conducted in dubious laboratories.[63] This is seen as a backward step, since some Kenyans depend on a particular drug, Rabanoxyl, an Indian product, which is a combination drug consisting of several individual drugs. The individual drugs, which are patented, cost a lot more when used individually. There are new drugs which experts insist are more effective, but the newer the drug the more expensive and the harder for poor Kenyans to obtain.

Activists opposed to the patenting of AIDS drugs have been criticized a lot. At the thirteenth ICASA conference, they characteristically joined

---

[61] See Stephen Karanja, 'Kenya: A Land of Graves', *Catholic Medical Quarterly*, November 2002, at www.catholicdoctors.org.
[62] See Mike Moore, 'Give the Poor Drugs and Charge the Rich', *East African*, Business Opinion, 12 March 2001.
[63] Dagi Kimani, 'Key AIDS Drugs Dropped from WHO List', *East African*, 9–13 Aug. 2004.

in the protest.[64] The Kenyan government, which the activists have cursed, in 2003 published an AIDS Bill with non-discrimination clauses.[65] In addition, in the 2003 budget the government set aside KSh 3 million to fight the AIDS problem. There is sustained pressure by some activists who are unappreciative of the effort being made and are offensive. Can their strategies be effective? Is the 'one shoe fits all' confrontational approach taken by many activists, most of whom belong to local donor-funded NGOs or are in their 30s and living in the rich Nordic countries, really working to improve access? The same question can be posited to the outdated blanket condemnation of pharmaceutical companies and TNCs generally.[66]

Kenya should learn to invest in research and development, and national health law and policy as well as patent law, all of which have affected AIDS research and development.

The effort to combat HIV/AIDS must not be handled in the traditional manner of tying foreign aid to politics. Kenya must act with a sense of urgency and purpose and approach the battle against HIV/AIDS with the same resolve and commitment that the world is using to fight terrorism. Towards this goal Kenya requires leadership and local and international co-operation. Shifting goalposts and blaming non-critical factors such as patents, the Industrial Property Act, 2001, TRIPS and the WTO is not terribly helpful. Efficient policy, legal, institutional and administrative reforms of public health, research and development and patent law are all important.

---

[64] 'The cause of the disagreement was that just 4,000 of the estimated 250,000 people who are in need of ARVs have access to them on a regular basis, while in the whole of Africa just 1% of the 4 million who need the drugs receive them, despite the fact they are only generic versions.' See Dagi Kimani, 'Activists of the World, Chill Out, We Have Heard You', East African, 6 Oct. 2003.

[65] For examples, see the Bill cited above.

[66] Kimani, 'Activists of the World'.

20

Kenya's participation in the WTO: lessons learned

WALTER ODHIAMBO, PAUL KAMAU AND DOROTHY MCCORMICK*

1 The problem in context

Kenya was among the founding members of the World Trade Organization (WTO) when the Marrakesh Agreement was signed in Morocco on 15 April 1994. The notification process was completed by 31 December 1994, when accession to the WTO was completed. As a member, Kenya is signatory to all WTO agreements including the General Agreement on Tariffs and Trade (GATT), the Agreement on Agriculture (AOA), the General Agreement on Trade in Services (GATS), the Agreement on Textiles and Clothing (ATC) and the Agreement on Trade-Related Intellectual Property Rights (TRIPS).

As in many other countries, trade issues in Kenya involve a large number of stakeholders with diverse interests. For effective policy formulation, it is important that all the stakeholders are effectively involved in the decision-making process. This is because not only are trade matters, particularly WTO-related ones, complex, but they also overlap and have far-reaching consequences. While there have been bold attempts in Kenya to engage all the stakeholders in the decision-making process, the pursuit of high-level strategic objectives in trade is undermined by the lack of any effective mechanism for co-ordination and consultation. This may have undermined the country's policy stance. It may also have resulted in poor participation by some stakeholders. Like other developing countries, Kenya also lacks capacity in the formulation of trade policy.

* Walter Odhiambo and Paul Kamau are Research Fellows at the Institute for Development Studies, University of Nairobi. Dorothy McCormick is Associate Research Professor and Director of the Institute for Development Studies, University of Nairobi.

2 The local and external players and their roles

WTO trade-related matters in Kenya involve a number of stakeholders. These include the government, the private sector and civil society organizations. These stakeholders not only have varied interests, but also have varying capacities to engage in WTO matters. What follows is a brief overview of the different stakeholders and their roles.

The government

The government is obviously one of the main stakeholders in trade matters. Overall responsibility for trade matters lies with the Ministry of Trade and Industry (MTI), although other ministries handle some trade-related matters. The MTI is responsible for the WTO and Common Market for East and Southern Africa (COMESA) issues, while the Ministry of Planning is responsible for ACP–EU Cotonou matters and the Ministry of Foreign Affairs for East African Community (EAC) matters. This fragmentation of trade responsibility has undermined the development of synergies of the WTO and other trade arrangements in Kenya.

Within the MTI, the WTO Division in the Department of External Trade is responsible for co-ordinating action within government on the Doha Round of trade negotiations as well as all other WTO matters. The WTO Division has a number of professional staff both within Kenya and at the Kenyan mission in Geneva, which deals exclusively with WTO matters. Although a crucial division on trade matters, it lacks the requisite capacity to undertake analysis of trade policy issues and the implications of tariff reduction. This, in turn, has limited the country's capacity to negotiate at the WTO.

The private sector

The private sector in Kenya is becoming an increasingly important actor on trade matters, including WTO issues. It has shown a keen interest in engaging the government on trade policy issues. For long time the private sector in Kenya was not organized and was rarely represented in important policy formulation processes. However, a number of private-sector organizations have recently emerged to present and articulate the views of the private sector, and have been active on WTO trade-related matters. These include labour unions, trade associations, the Kenya National Chamber of Commerce and Industry (KNCCI), and a number of producer associations. However, the capacity of the private sector to participate varies. Most private-sector organizations lack the analytical capacity to comprehend the implications of trade measures. They also lack information on trade issues, which prevents a full understanding of trade agreements and measures. The other problem with the private sector organizations is that they tend to have different interests and do not in most cases have a common position on economic and trade issues. The private sector in Kenya generally tends to have enclave interests.

Civil society, research and academic institutions

A remarkable development of the trade policy formulation process in Kenya has been the emergence and participation of civil society organizations (CSOs), some of which include a mix of various livelihood groups, including the poor. In most cases they have sought to represent the poor in WTO issues, and a number have been active in such issues, including the Kenya National Federation of Agricultural Producers (KENFAP), Action-Aid (Kenya), Oxfam, EcoNews, Consumer Information Network, RODI, SEATINI, the Institute for Economic Affairs, the Heinrich Böll Foundation and the Kenya Human Rights Commission. The participation of the CSOs has again been constrained by a limited capacity to undertake analytical studies on the impact of trade issues. A lack of financial resources has also limited the participation of some CSOs, especially community-based organizations (CBOs). As discussed in the next section, CSOs are better organized than the private sector in finding common ground on which to engage government.

Academic and research institutions

Academic and research institutions have been the main organizations carrying out research on trade issues in Kenya. As such they have provided an important resource to government, the private sector and civil society. They also, however, face a number of challenges including lack of resources for research.

Co-ordination of WTO matters in Kenya

On acceding to the Marrakech Agreement, Kenya established the Permanent Inter-Ministerial Committee (PIMC) in May 1995 to advise the government on all matters pertaining to the WTO. However, being an inter-ministerial committee, it excluded some key stakeholders, particularly those from the private sector and civil society. In recognition of the important role these actors could play in trade, in 1997 the government restructured the PIMC by including the private sector and civil society. Subsequently the PIMC was re-branded as the National Committee on WTO (NCWTO). Thus the NCWTO is the body through which the government consults with the private sector and civil society on WTO matters, and it is also the main trade co-ordinating body.

The NCWTO was established with a mandate to:

- study and analyze the provisions of the WTO agreements and their likely effects on the Kenyan economy;
- monitor the implementation of WTO agreements by other members and recommend appropriate action for Kenya;
- provide modalities for implementation of the WTO agreements by Kenya so as to ensure maximum gains from multilateral trade;
- provide government and the private sector with the necessary analysis of new market access conditions to enable identification of immediate and potential trading opportunities created within the multilateral trade system;
- provide government with adequate information on the sectoral impact of the various agreements in order to enable it to review current and future trade policies;
- increase the government's awareness level regarding the institutional and legislative means by which it could safeguard its trade rights and obligations in multilateral trading systems;
- enhance awareness among various stakeholders through fora and training; and
- promote a dialogue between the public and private sector and build a consensus on WTO issues in Kenya.

The NCWTO is the forum in which the government, private sector and civil society engage in WTO matters. Within the government arena, the Attorney General, the Office of the President and the ministries of Trade and Industry, Finance, Planning and National Development, Health, Agriculture, Foreign Affairs, Labour and Human Resources, Environment and Natural Resources, Information and Communications, and Transport all participate actively in the NCWTO. The ministries act as the focal points for sub-committees handling relevant WTO issues, the

Ministry of Health thus being the focal point for all health issues and the Ministry of Agriculture the focal point for all agricultural-related issues, and so on. A number of state corporations and parastatals such as the Kenya Revenue Authority (KRA), the Kenya Bureau of Standards (KEBS), the Kenya Plant Health Inspectorate Service (KEPHIS) and the Kenya Sugar Board (KSB) are members of the NCWTO. Others include the Central Bank of Kenya (CBK), the Export Promotion Council (EPC), the National Environment Management Authority (NEMA), the Kenya Industrial Property Institute (KIPI) and the Capital Market Authority (CMA).

Membership of the NCWTO is by invitation only. As national co-ordinator the MTI identifies the relevant stakeholders who are then invited to become members of the NCWTO. In a few instances, members of the sub-committee can identify other relevant stakeholders that could be co-opted. A few organizations or individuals have expressed interest in joining; there are no other formalities for becoming a member, as new members are simply entered into a list and invited to attend subsequent meetings. There is no limit to the number of stakeholders that can be members of the NCWTO, although preference has been given to orga-nizations rather than individuals. There are currently around forty-five members of the NCWTO representing different umbrella organizations and institutions. Around twenty-five CSOs are members of the NCWTO, although only seven are active.

Outside the NCWTO, CSOs have organized themselves into a loose net-work co-ordinated by EcoNews (a Kenyan NGO). This network of NGOs provides a forum for civil society to consolidate their deliberations, which are then passed on to the government. In the recently concluded Cancún talks, Kenyan civil society played a pivotal role not only in developing the country's position but also in facilitating attendance for some dele-gates. According to one interviewee, 'the civil society organizations have been commissioning research projects on various trade issues whose find-ings feed into strengthening deliberations for the Kenyan trade position. Civil society also sponsors some of the activities of the NCWTO and recently sponsored the participation of a substantial number of delegates to Cancún including parliamentarians.'

As indicated earlier, the NCWTO is an advisory body for the govern-ment on WTO issues. The advice given to the government is generated through deliberations and consultation within the national committee. Because of the number and technical nature of the issues coming from Geneva, the NCWTO formed sub-committees with specific expertise to handle different issues. There are currently around ten sub-committees dealing with diverse issues. They include:

- the Agriculture Sub-committee, chaired by the Ministry of Agriculture;
- the Services Sub-committee, chaired by the Ministry of Transport and Communications;
- the Market Access Sub-committee, chaired by the Department of Industry, ULI;
- the Trade and Environment Sub-committee, chaired by the National Environmental Management Authority (NEMA);
- the Trade Facilitation Sub-committee, chaired by the Department of Internal Trade, ULI;
- the Trade and Competition Sub-committee, chaired by the Monopoly and Price Commission;
- the Trade and Investment Sub-committee, chaired jointly by the Investment Promotion Council (IPC) and the Ministry of Finance;
- the Transparency and Government Procurement Sub-committee, chaired by the Ministry of Finance;
- the E-Commerce sub-Committee, chaired jointly by the Ministry of Transport and Communication and the ULI; and
- the Trade-related Intellectual Property Rights Sub-committee, chaired jointly by KIPI and the MTI.

Membership of sub-committees is much more open than is the case with the NCWTO, as it depends on the subject being handled and the stakeholders' interests. Whenever an issue arises, relevant sub-committees will call a meeting to deliberate on the issue and forward its deliberations to the NCWTO. Each sub-committee would get most of their inputs from the focal points (see Appendix, p. 298), which have the capacity to handle technical issues. Once the sub-committees submit their guidelines to the NCWTO, a meeting of the NCWTO is called for further deliberations on these guidelines. The NCWTO then mandates the Secretariat (Department of External Trade – MTI) to submit the deliberations to the Kenyan mission in Geneva. There are, however, cases when immediate responses are of the essence and sub-committees communicate directly with the Geneva team. This is allowed within the NCWTO. Our survey revealed that NCWTO meetings are seldom convened, except to prepare for major conferences such as the Cancún Ministerial Meeting in 2003. Afterwards, very few meetings are called. Most of our respondents felt that the NCWTO should hold regular meetings for discussions, even in the absence of any WTO issues, in order to keep members abreast of the issues and enable the committee to be proactive.

Decision-making in the NCWTO is by consensus. However, when decisions cannot be reached by consensus, voting may be used. At the sub-committee level, the decision-making process begins with the focal point which will make proposals on WTO issues coming from Geneva. However, before these proposals are presented to the sub-committee, they must be ratified by either the ministries or the organizations where the focal point is based. When the sub-committee meeting is held, members consider the position taken by the focal point for further deliberations. The decision taken by the sub-committee is then forwarded to the NCWTO, where all members deliberate on the position and adopt or amend it. At this level, decisions are made by consensus. There are cases where the national committee has vetoed a position taken at the sub-committee level and adopted a completely different position. Once the national committee has ratified a position, it is passed over to the MTI, which then passes it on to the negotiating team in Geneva through the Permanent Secretary (PS).

To ensure full implementation of all WTO agreements, particularly the Sanitary and Phytosanitary Standards (SPS) and Technical Barriers to Trade (TBT) Agreements, Kenya identified a number of focal points, which are organizations with expertise and competence in particular WTO issues. These focal points serve as the nerve centre for the relevant sub-committees by providing technical input on the specific issues handled by the sub-committee. Similarly, there are national enquiry points (NEPs) established to help disseminate crucial information related to trade issues. For instance, the Kenya Bureau of Standards (KEBS) is a focal point and also the NEP on matters relating to standards of or technical barriers to trade. Likewise, the Kenya Plant Health Inspectorate Service (KEPHIS) and the Kenya Intellectual Property Institute (KIPI) are the enquiry points on issues on the SPS and Intellectual Property Rights, respectively. There are also a number of reference points that store and disseminate WTO-related reference materials. They include the Department of External Trade within the MTI, which is the reference point for the public sector; the Centre for Business Information in Kenya (CIBK) within the Export Promotion Council, for the business community; and the Kenya Institute for Business Training for academia. Recently, the National Assembly has been identified as a reference point for parliamentarians.

Negotiations in agriculture: some insights into Kenya's WTO participation

To demonstrate how Kenya participates in the WTO, Kenya's experiences in agricultural trade negotiations are presented below. Kenya's participation in the WTO largely revolves around agriculture; it forms the backbone of the economy and produces the country's major exports. This is not to say, however, that other issues are less important. Kenya has also been very active in issues related to trade in services and intellectual property rights.

Agriculture-related issues are negotiated on two main fronts. First, there are the regular responses on issues from Geneva on which members are expected to take positions. The positions members take are presented as proposals which are then defended in Geneva. The second front is during inter-ministerial meetings like the recently concluded talks in Cancún. This is where countries make major decisions on trade matters within the WTO framework. Members have tended to form groups around particular interests and to take common positions during ministerial meetings; in Cancún, there were three main groups, G20, G90 and the European Union (EU)/US axis. Kenya was in the G90 group. The positions a country takes will, therefore, to a large extent be influenced by the position of other countries. This section seeks to provide some insights into the former case where positions are largely taken internally. The focus is on the processes involved, the actors and outcomes.

As indicated earlier, Kenya maintains a negotiating team in Geneva to present Kenya's positions on various issues, as well as to monitor and relay information on a daily basis on WTO events. These include notifications by other countries. Where situations arise and Kenya needs to respond, the Geneva team relays the information to the Ministry of Trade and Industry, which also act as the secretariat to the NCWTO. Once the information is received at the ministry, the ministry contacts the relevant sub-committee, in this case the sub-committee on agriculture, which is headed by the Ministry of Agriculture. At the same time, the information is passed on to the other stakeholders awaiting deliberations in the sub-committee.

At the Ministry of Agriculture the contact is usually the WTO desk officer. There is currently one officer in the ministry handling WTO issues. The current desk officer has been in the position for the last six months after his predecessor left to work for an NGO. This epitomizes the inconsistency and lack of continuity in the ministries. The desk officer's role is essentially that of providing technical inputs into the issues from Geneva and formulating a position. Once this is done, the officer presents the position to the head of division, who may or may not moderate the position taken. The next step is then to present the position to the Director of Agriculture who is in charge of all technical matters in the Ministry. Again, the Director of Agriculture may moderate or alter the position, although no examples of this could be found. The Director of Agriculture is then expected to brief the Permanent Secretary on the position. Once the Permanent Secretary accepts the position it becomes the position of the Ministry of Agriculture. Only in a few cases is the minister involved. This happens whenever the issues are weighty and are considered to be crucial.

As the focal point, the Ministry of Agriculture then convenes the Sub-committee on Agriculture to solicit the views of the other stakeholders. At the sub-committee, it is the responsibility of the focal point, in this case, the Ministry of Agriculture, to explain the issues and lead by presenting the position of the ministry. The members are then free to deliberate on the position taken and finally reach a consensus. So far there has been no voting on any of the agricultural issues. Although members may initially differ on issues a consensus has always been reached. The position taken is often a 'negotiated' position. One of the reasons why it has been easy to reach a consensus within the sub-committee is because the issues under discussion at the sub-committee are often too technical for most members to understand. In other instances, the position of the Ministry of Agriculture prevails.

The other reason is that members are ill-prepared for the deliberations because they receive documents from Geneva either during the meeting or a few days before. In most cases, these documents are voluminous and technical. According to one of our respondents 'only a few people can understand the issues and the sessions quickly become a boring lecture'.

Once the sub-committee takes a position on an issue, it is then required to present this to the national committee. At the NCWTO the issue is opened for further discussion by all the WTO stakeholders and a position is taken through consensus. The position taken is then passed on to the Ministry of Trade and Industry who then sends it to the negotiating team in Geneva, either as it is or with amendments depending on the government's position.

3 Challenges faced and the outcome

As a founder member of the WTO, Kenya has made commendable progress in WTO matters, and has been able to build the structures necessary for the implementation of the WTO agreements. Kenya's success is reflected in the country's participation in all major WTO trade talks and the maintenance of a strong negotiating team in Geneva. Kenya has also been able to prepare position papers on a number of issues, even taking the lead at regional level in a number of cases. However, Kenya still faces a number of challenges related to its WTO participation. We discuss here some of the challenges and outcomes.

Effectiveness of the NCWTO

As earlier indicated, the NCWTO is the body through which the government consults both the private sector and civil society. However, the committee's effectiveness has been compromised by a number of factors. As constituted the NCWTO is not a legal entity, and this has compromised both its operational and financial autonomy. For example, it does not have a chief executive officer or a board of management. The Department of External Trade in the MTI provides the secretariat for the NCWTO, while the Permanent Secretary in the same ministry assumes chairmanship. Although there have been some efforts to give the NCWTO legal status, this has not been successful. It therefore remains an informal advisory body until it is legally constituted.

The fact that the NCWTO has no legal mandate has meant that the government is under no obligation to adopt its advice and recommendations. According to a programme officer for an agriculture-based organization that is a member of the NCWTO, 'the MTI downplays the submissions presented to it by the NCWTO on agriculture because it is has no obligations whatsoever to accept them'. During negotiations the Minister of Trade and Industry can overturn positions developed through the NCWTO. A case in point according to this respondent took place during the Ministerial Meeting in Cancún:

> Prior to our departure to Cancún, we held a delegates' meeting at the Safari Park Hotel. We agreed that Kenya would not negotiate on any of the four Singapore Issues until the Agreement on Agriculture was resolved. The Minister for Trade and Industry was to uphold this decision. However, in Cancún the minister allegedly changed position and was willing to negotiate on trade facilitation contrary to the earlier position we had taken in Kenya. This did not please most of us delegates and other developing countries who viewed Kenya as a torchbearer.

Functionally, the NCWTO is incapacitated because of its weak legal status. The organization has no chief executive and lacks the requisite capacity to handle some of its activities. For one, the NCWTO lacks the financial capacity to operate effectively. The Treasury has no obligation to allocate funds to the NCWTO because it is not by law a government agency, and the NCWTO does not have its own budget from the government. Other than the funding provided by the Joint Integrated Technical Assistance Programme (JITAP), which played a key role in its establishment, the NCWTO has relied on donors and well-wishers. According to a respondent, 'since JITAP I [1998–2002] ended, activities of the NCWTO have came to a standstill. It is only through the financial support of civil society organizations that a few activities have been going on.' This has led to irregular meetings, poor information flow and poor co-ordination among members. Lack of human resources makes the NCWTO rely on members of staff from the MTI, who are also required to perform other ministerial duties.

Participation in NCWTO meetings by stakeholders

Attendance at NCWTO meetings has generally been considered to be poor; attendance is relatively higher among government officials than among the private sector or civil society. It is important to note at this point that members have no obligation to attend the NCWTO meetings. The relatively high participation by public officials is because, in most cases, they play a facilitating role. The participation of public officials is, however, affected by the fact that they are transferred from one ministry to another. Participation by the private and civil society organizations is driven more by self-interest, for example profit maximization in the case of private-sector organizations. The survey revealed that private-sector organizations are more interested in the East African Community (EAC) and the Market for Eastern and Southern Africa (COMESA), since they are their major markets. Private-sector organizations are not very interested in WTO issues: a respondent in one of these organizations concurred with this position, saying that 'WTO is far off and our members concentrate on COMESA issues'; the NCWTO calls 'too many meetings, which sometimes coincide with EAC or COMESA trade meetings in which we have direct interest. We also do not have many officers who like government.' Another respondent had this to say: 'The notices for WTO meetings are never sent on time and this demotivates us.' The transfer of officials from one ministry to another impedes the smooth running of activities in the NCWTO. There is generally more consistency within the civil society than government.

The NCWTO is supposed to organize meetings for members on a regular basis. However, the survey revealed that there are spells when the NCWTO does not convene meetings; for instance it has called only one meeting since the Cancún Ministerial Meeting in 2003. This could be associated with the costs involved, so that active stakeholders felt that there is a need to look for alternative venues so that meetings can be held more regularly, otherwise interest may wane. Even though the NCWTO has been involved in training, some respondents complained that only government officials received any training; capacity development should extend to other members. Participants should be allowed to sponsor themselves if they are able. Similarly, the calendar of NCWTO events should be less closely linked to ongoing business in Geneva. Currently, the Department of External Trade in the MTI has been the main facilitator of NCWTO activities. This has been done with the support of the JITAP. Through the JITAP, a consultant was hired to work hand in hand with the MTI in co-ordinating NCWTO matters (many respondents referred us to this consultant). Although we were not able to get this person's terms of reference or obtain an interview, we were informally told that the consultant is charged with the responsibility of organizing NCWTO activities and ensuring that the members receive communications on time. While some respondents felt that this was a good effort and should be strengthened, others said that the consultant was making the NCWTO work unnecessarily complicated.

Inclusiveness and awareness

A primary reason for the establishment of the NCWTO was to ensure that all stakeholders are brought on board. Although this has to a large extent been achieved, a number of actors are still out of the loop. For example, the Kenya Fish Processors and Exporters Association (AFIPEK) is not a member of the NCWTO, and yet fish is an important export subject in WTO regulations. Asked whether they were members of the NCWTO, the respondent in AFIPEK said, 'We have never attended a single meeting organized by the NCWTO. We have never been invited. The NCWTO is purely a group of government officials. The private sector, including ourselves, have never been invited.' This comment illustrates a feeling of exclusion and a low level of awareness on WTO matters. We did not interview the Kenya Textile Manufacturers and Exporters Association, but indications were that they are not members of the NCWTO, despite the importance of textiles in external trade.

As the supreme body for the formulation of laws in the country, parliament has an important role to play in the formulation of trade policies. As an institution, parliament is not represented in the NCWTO, neither does it have direct links. Parliament's involvement in WTO issues has generally been weak, due to lack of awareness and interest. According to an interviewee, 'in 1998, the NCWTO invited all the members of parliament to an awareness breakfast session to inform them of the importance of WTO issues. To the surprise of the NCWTO only ten out of 210 MPs that were invited turned up. It is no a secret that most MPs are not conversant with WTO issues. Involving MPs in the NCWTO meetings has not been easy ... even when MPs attend WTO meetings, they hardly sit after tea break'. To increase awareness of the WTO among parliamentarians, the National Assembly has been turned into a reference point. Another interview with a member of civil society revealed that 'the inclusion of five MPs in the Kenyan delegation to Cancún (2003) was also a significant step towards creating awareness among the parliamentarians'. Some civil society organizations, particularly EcoNews, ActionAid and SEATINI, are working directly with the Parliamentary Trade and Finance Select Committee.

General public awareness of WTO issues also remains low in Kenya. Although general awareness has been increasing in the last few years, a huge segment of the population, especially those in the rural areas, remains ignorant. The NCWTO has not been very successful in its public awareness programme. A statement by a farmer in one of the awareness workshop highlights this fact: 'The WTO seems to be a very good organization. When is it coming here to build us a market?' (a respondent involved in an NCWTO sensitization seminar narrated this to us).

Notifications

Kenya has been unable to respond through the NCWTO to a single notification since 1997.[1] Even after NEPs and focal points were set up to issue notifications, performance has been poor. We found that NEPs are not interlinked and worked more or less independently of each other. A recent case in point is when the government through the Ministry of Transport

---

[1] In an effort to increase the transparency of members' trade policies, WTO regulations require that all trade laws, regulations, judicial decisions and administrative rulings be made public by informing all WTO members whose trade may be affected by the decision. This is what we call notification according to Art. X of GATT, Art. III of GATS and Art. 63 of TRIPS.

and Communication introduced measures for speed governors and safety belts to be fitted in all public transport vehicles. Ideally, Kenya should have issued a notification through the NCWTO to all WTO members who may have an interest in undertaking such activity in Kenya, but this was not done. According to one of the respondents, 'there are so many things that we need to issue notifications on but we have failed to do so. We have the format to do it but the channel of notification is clogged by the ineffectiveness of the NCWTO.' There are no formal structures to handle notifications in Kenya.

The effectiveness of the NCWTO has also been impaired by the fact that trade issues are addressed by different ministries. For instance, EAC affairs are handled in the Ministry of Foreign Affairs, COMESA by the Ministry of Trade and Industry, and ACP–EU by the Ministry of Planning and National Development. The problem is that there is no linkage between different offices. Kenya ends up making different commitments in different trade initiatives; an example of this is the tariff commitment under the EAC, which is different from the WTO commitment on the tariffs. Implementation of such agreements becomes not only difficult but also expensive for the country.

4 Lessons for other players

Kenya's participation in the WTO provides a number of lessons for other players. These are

1. *The need for an effective co-ordination and consultation mechanism.* Benefits accruing to countries from the multilateral trading systems depend on, among other things, the extent to which trade policy issues are co-ordinated at the national level and the subsequent capacity to negotiate in Geneva. Kenya's experience shows that co-ordination of WTO matters has been weak and that this could have undermined the country's position. Co-ordination at international level requires adequate legal and resource backing, something which has been missing in the Kenyan case. Lack of financial and human capacity seriously impedes Kenya's capacity to participate effectively in trade negotiations. The survey revealed that a lack of skills at NCWTO and sub-committee levels seriously affects deliberations on WTO issues.

2. *The need for analytical capacity.* The Kenyan experience indicates a lack of analytical capacity in government, the private sector and civil society. Although some of the key institutions are staffed with personnel to carry out impact assessments, their capacity is largely inadequate. In

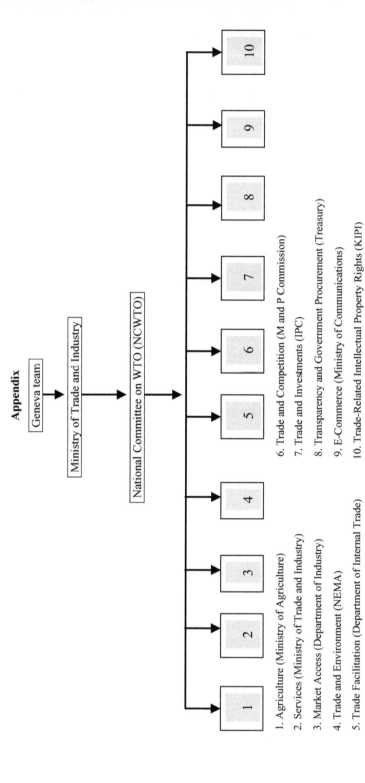

Appendix

Geneva team

Ministry of Trade and Industry

National Committee on WTO (NCWTO)

1. Agriculture (Ministry of Agriculture)
2. Services (Ministry of Trade and Industry)
3. Market Access (Department of Industry)
4. Trade and Environment (NEMA)
5. Trade Facilitation (Department of Internal Trade)

6. Trade and Competition (M and P Commission)
7. Trade and Investments (IPC)
8. Transparency and Government Procurement (Treasury)
9. E-Commerce (Ministry of Communications)
10. Trade-Related Intellectual Property Rights (KIPI)

Source: Field Survey 2004.

Figure 20.1. Structure of Kenya's participation in the WTO.

the case of Kenya, there is a need to strengthen the analytical skills of civil society organizations that are involved in trade matters and government ministries. Training in policy analysis is a necessary condition for effective policy-making by enabling policy-makers to understand the full implications of various trade proposals and agreements.

3. Fragmentation of responsibilities on trade matters. Apart from being a member of the WTO, Kenya, like many other countries, is a member of other trading arrangements, in this case the EAC and COMESA. In Kenya, the responsibility for co-ordinating these activities is with different ministries and departments and this has undermined unity in decision-making. Kenya has also not been able to exploit synergies that would be experienced through the joint and simultaneous implementation of WTO and regional trade arrangements.

References

ActionAid Kenya (2003). 'Action Forum: Trade WTO Cancún Meeting – Same Game Plan – Will Rules Change?' Issue 8, Nairobi: ActionAid.

Ikiara, G. K., Muriira, M.I. and Nyangena, W. N. (2002), 'Kenya's Trade in Services: Should the Country Fully Liberalise?', Nairobi: KIPPRA.

Ikiara, G. K., Olewe-Nyunya J. and Odhiambo, W. (2004), 'Kenya: Formulation and Implementation of Strategic Trade and Industrial Policies', in C. C. Soludo, O. Ogbu, H. Chang, eds., *The Politics of Trade and Industrial Policy in Africa: Forced Consensus?* Asmara: Africa World Press.

Kenya, Republic of (1999), 'Sessional paper No. 1 of 1986 on Economic Management for Renewed Growth', Nairobi: Government Printer.

Kenya, Republic of (2003), 'Statistical Abstract', Central Bureau of Statistics, Ministry of Finance and Planning, Nairobi Government Printer.

Kenya, Republic of (2004), 'Economic Survey', Central Bureau of Statistics, Ministry of Finance and Planning, Nairobi: Government Printer.

Odhiambo, W., and Kamau, P. (2003). 'Public Procurement: Lessons from Kenya, Uganda and Tanzania', OECD Technical Paper 208, OECD, Paris.

Stamp, Maxwell (2003), 'Republic of Kenya Trade and Poverty Programme (KTPP): Institutional Review', prepared for Ministry of Trade, Nairobi, funded by DFID, UK, June.

World Trade Organization (2000), *Trade Policy Review: Kenya*, Geneva: WTO.

21

Learning by doing: the impact of a trade remedy case in Korea

JUNSOK YANG[*]

1 The problem in context

This study deals with a particular case submitted to the WTO Dispute Settlement Mechanism (DSM) dealing with restrictions on the export of Korean[1] colour televisions sets to the United States. It is a story of how Korea used the WTO DSM as part of an overall strategy to eliminate a trade barrier that had been in place for fifteen years. It is also a story of how Korea's attitude towards the WTO changed. Thus, before we start dealing with this particular case, we need to look at some background, at what Koreans think about trade and their initial perception of the WTO.

Korean development and its attitude to trade

Like many other countries, Koreans tend to have a mercantilist view of trade, where exports are good and imports are bad. Such views are quite surprising, since the value of exports and imports in Korea usually exceed 70% of GDP, and Koreans themselves will readily admit that the country has no choice but to import raw materials, intermediate goods, capital goods and technology from abroad in order to compete in the global marketplace, as well as to fulfil domestic consumer demand. However, the average Korean often believes that Koreans must do everything they can to increase exports, while limiting imports only to 'necessary' goods. This mercantilist mindset was born in the 1960s, when Korea's average annual GDP per capita was around $150.

During the first sixty years of the twentieth century, Korea suffered thirty-six years of Japanese colonial rule. Then, at the end of the Second

[*] Professor of Economics, Catholic University of Korea, Seoul.
[1] In this paper 'Korea' refers to the Republic of Korea (South Korea).

World War, the country was split into North and South Korea, shortly followed by the three years of the Korean War. By the end of this war, much of Korea's industrial capacity was in ruins, and the country faced political chaos.

Then, in the late 1960s, Korea began an outward-oriented growth path, using exports as an engine for development. Korea joined GATT in 1967, around the time when it had embarked on the outward-oriented development strategy. While practically every Korean realizes how important exports have been, and still are, to the Korean economy, the fact that imports also played a crucial part is sometimes neglected. Korea extensively liberalized the import of raw materials and intermediate goods so that Korean manufactured goods could compete effectively in the global market.

However, Korea maintained strict controls on imports of consumer goods, in part due to the limited amount of hard currency at the time. Priority for the use of the hard currency was given to exporting firms for the import of raw materials, intermediate goods and capital goods. The government also encouraged private savings in order to provide investment funds to the up-and-coming Korean industrial sector. The attitudes built up during these years, namely a negative view toward conspicuous consumption and imports, has cast a long shadow, apparent even now, when Korea has eliminated almost all of those import barriers and achieved a GDP per capita of $10,000.

Given the mercantilist mindset and the fact that Korea is so dependent on trade for its economic well-being, Koreans often think of their country as a helpless player in the harsh global marketplace, where other countries limit imports of Korean goods for nationalist reasons and have forced Korea to open its markets before the economy is ready, resulting in massive domestic shocks. Considering that it was the gains from trade that allowed Korea to develop, this mindset may be paradoxical, but Korea is hardly alone in having such views about trade; it was, after all, only forty years ago that Korea's GDP per capita was less than $200.

Korean perception of trade disputes

In the early 1980s Korea's GDP per capita was around US$1,600–$2,000, and Korea was on its way to becoming an economic dynamo, but it was still on a weak footing. At that time, Korean companies were beginning to break into the global consumer electronics market. Electronics manufacturers, such as Samsung and Goldstar (now LG), successfully penetrated the US and European markets. However, during the same period the United States, which was Korea's largest export market, was experiencing record trade deficits, and the US press, when reporting them, often emphasized the growing economic strength of Japan and its neighbour Korea. Thus there had been strong popular feeling in the United States that the US government should limit the market access of goods from Japan and Korea, and that Japanese and Korean markets should be opened to US goods.

Such sentiments tended to strengthen the various US market restriction measures vis-à-vis Korea's exports. Especially bothersome to many Koreans were the anti-dumping measures which the United States used to limit some of Korea's most popular export items, such as consumer electronics and steel. The US anti-dumping measure on colour televisions, which is the subject of this article, was also imposed around this time.

Koreans felt that their success in the international marketplace was due to low costs and price competitiveness rather than to 'unfair' trading practices as the United States claimed. Some Koreans felt that the international trading environment was unfair, since Korea was rapidly opening up its markets, due in some cases to US pressure, while the United States was seemingly closing its own.

Partly due to the weakness of GATT and the dispute settlement mechanism at the time, these trade disputes resulted in confrontations with heavy political pressure, resulting in ill-will on all sides. People in Korea and the United States often thought of trade as an economic war, rather than a 'win–win' situation for all.

The Korean perception of the WTO

In some ways the Uruguay Round (UR) and the WTO were designed to reduce such confrontations on trade disputes. When the UR negotiations were complete and the WTO was formed, there was an expectation by Koreans that trade disputes would be solved not by political confrontation, where Korea was bound to lose to other large countries, but through a third party that would maintain neutrality and keep the global trading environment fair.

In its attempt to ensure that the WTO was such a third party, Korea paid a heavy political price domestically. Agriculture has always had a special place in Korea, and the political institutions and even consumers would support protection for agricultural goods in order to protect the

Table 21.1. *Cases brought against Korea*

Date	Case no.	Complainant	Subject
1995.4.6	DS3	United States	Measures Concerning the Testing and Inspection of Agricultural Products
1995.5.3	DS5	United States	Measures Concerning the Shelf-Life of Products
1995.11.8	DS20	Canada	Measures Concerning Bottled Water
1996.5.9	DS40	EC	Laws, Regulations and Practices in the Telecommunications Sector
1996.5.24	DS41	United States	Measures Concerning Inspection of Agricultural Products
1997.4.4	DS75 DS84	EC, United States	Taxes on Alcoholic Beverages
1997.8.12	DS98	EC	Definitive Safeguard Measures on Imports of Certain Dairy Products
1999.2.1	DS161 DS169	Australia, United States	Measures Affecting Imports of Fresh, Chilled or Frozen Beef
1999.2.16	DS163	United States	Measures Affecting Government Procurement
2002.10.21	D273	EC	Measures Affecting Trade in Commercial Vessels

Source: WTO, 'Update of WTO Dispute Settlement Cases', 26 March 2004.

farmers, even though they knew that it would result in higher prices for food. Many of these protective devices for agriculture were dismantled as the result of the Uruguay Round. Other sensitive sectors, such as services, were liberalized as well. Political repercussions from the liberalization are still being felt today.

However, Koreans were soon disappointed in the WTO. During the first few years of its operation, the United States and the European Union brought several cases against Korea. Between 1995 and 1997, eight cases against Korea were brought to the Dispute Settlement Body (DSB), and Korea usually had to accept major changes in its import regime. While these cases were lost on their merits, and even though many Koreans acknowledged that many of Korea's trade barriers were unfair, they still felt that Korea was under siege from foreign countries, and that the WTO existed for the benefit of advanced economies seeking to open the markets of developing countries. Table 21.1 shows the cases brought against Korea in the WTO DSM.

In early 1997 the European Communities (EC) and the United States filed a case against Korea which proved to be especially sensitive. In that case, known as 'Taxes on Alcoholic Beverages', the EC and the United States argued that imported spirits, such as whisky, should be charged the same domestic alcoholic beverage tax rates as *soju*, a popular Korean traditional alcoholic beverage. Koreans see whisky as an expensive luxury item. In contrast, while the alcohol content of *soju* may be closer to spirits, Koreans see *soju* as a simple, cheap and popular beverage, closer in character culturally to beer than to whisky. While the EC and the United States may have been correct in scientific terms, *soju* was certainly not thought of as being 'similar' to whisky by most Koreans, and the case caused heated arguments among Koreans. It did much to reinforce the popular conception that the WTO was a tool of the advanced countries in opening the markets of poorer, smaller countries.

2 The local and external players and their roles

In 1997, against this background, Korea brought its first case to the WTO DSB. The case concerned anti-dumping duties on Korean-manufactured colour television receivers. Korea had previously participated in the DSM as a third party, but this case was the first where Korea was the complainant.

There were three major players in this case: Samsung Electronics, producer of various electronic goods including colour televisions and one of the firms facing the anti-dumping measure; the Korean government, which brought the case to the WTO on behalf of Samsung; and the US government, specifically the Department of Commerce, which had the responsibility of reviewing the anti-dumping measure. Other players included US labour unions, which had filed an anti-circumvention suit against Samsung, and the governments of Mexico and Thailand, which became involved in the case due to the anti-circumvention suit. The Korean public was also an important, though passive, observer in the case. The background of the specific case is as follows.

In the late 1970s, Korea became a major exporter of colour television receivers due to price competitiveness. Korean exports of colour televisions to the United States had been restrained through a voluntary export restraint (VER) agreement between February 1979 and June 1982, but following the repeal of the VER in 1982, the export volume and value rose greatly. In 1983, the export volume to the United States was 1.93 million sets, 200% greater than that of the previous year, while the value of exports to the United States rose over 170% from the previous year, to $302.6 million.

In 1983 the United States initiated an anti-dumping action against six Korean colour television producers, and on 30 April 1984 it imposed anti-dumping duties on colour televisions from four of those producers, including Samsung. Investigation covered the period from April 1982 to March 1983, and while the preliminary decision showed that the dumping margins ranged between 0 and 5.31%, the final decision showed the dumping margins to be between 0 and 15.95%.[2]

From April 1985 to March 1991, exports of Korean colour televisions to the United States fell substantially and their price in the United States rose. In subsequent reviews, the United States found that dumping margins for colour television receivers produced by Samsung were below the *de minimis* margin of 0.5%. Further, Korean electronic manufacturers, including Samsung, moved much of their production abroad to Mexico and Thailand to lower production costs. Thus, from April 1991, Samsung did not export any colour television receivers from Korea. It made periodic requests for the revocation of the anti-dumping order, but the United States still maintained its anti-dumping measures on Samsung colour television receivers, arguing that there was a potential for resumed dumping. In 1996 the United States expanded, of its own accord, the anti-dumping measure to include combination television-video cassette recorder (VCR) units and high definition (HD) televisions, which were typically considered distinct from colour television receivers in terms of goods and tariff classifications.

By 1995 Samsung had made five applications for the revocation of the anti-dumping measure. Four applications were rejected on procedural grounds concerning the timing of applications. The fifth application, filed on 20 July 1995, was not acted on for eleven months. In August 1995 the United States had received a petition from several US labour unions, including the International Brotherhood of Electrical Workers, the International Union of Electronic, Electrical, Salaried, Machine and Furniture Workers, and the Industrial Union Department, which accused Korean firms of using the production facilities in Mexico and Thailand to disguise Korean exports and circumvent the anti-dumping measure.

---

[2] The original US decision can be found in US Federal Register 49 FR 18336. The details of the original decision were taken from Taeho Bark, 'Antidumping Restrictions against Korean Exports: Major Focus on Consumer Electronics Products', KIEP Working Paper, May 1991. Downloadable from the KIEP website, http://www.kiep.go.kr.

In response, the United States had initiated an anti-circumvention investigation in January 1996. While the United States decided to initiate a review of the anti-dumping measure on 24 June 1996, a year elapsed without any definite results. The US government explained that the review for revocation had to await the outcome of an anti-circumvention proceeding which had begun in January 1996.

According to Han-Soo Kim, currently a senior official in the Korean Ministry of Foreign Affairs and Trade (MOFAT), who had been involved in the colour television case, in the mid 1980s Korea, along with Japan and Taiwan, had been the most frequent target of US anti-dumping measures. Small and medium-sized firms often could not afford to fight the anti-dumping decisions because of the costs involved, and were forced to stop exporting. Thus the Korean government considered the anti-dumping measures to be serious trade barriers. When the 1984 anti-dumping measure was announced it generated much shock in Korea since colour televisions were one of its strongest export items.

While Samsung managed an exclusion from paying anti-dumping duties, the anti-dumping order remained, and Samsung had to undergo a review process every year. While Samsung, and subsequently the Korean government, believed that Samsung was eligible for revocation of the anti-dumping order, the US Department of Commerce maintained it. Frustrated with a lack of result, a consensus emerged that this case was suitable for Korea's first WTO DSM case.

According to Kim, the modifications in the dispute settlement procedures made during the UR negotiations played an important part in Korea's bringing the colour television case to the WTO DSB. Under the pre-WTO GATT, winning a case in the DSB required positive consensus where all members had explicitly to accept the panel decision, and it would have been difficult at that time for Korea to get a decision accepted by all GATT members. However, the DSM under the WTO operated under a negative consensus, which requires that all GATT members explicitly refuse the panel decision in order not to accept it. Thus the Korean government felt that the United States could not block a favourable panel decision, and felt confident enough to proceed with the DSM.

On Samsung's side, while it had moved much of its production to Mexico, it felt that the continuing use of the US anti-dumping measure was unfair, and it was also concerned with potential future exports of HD televisions. It therefore encouraged the government to bring the case, and worked closely with the government to prepare it.

3 Challenges faced and the outcome

Koreans faced several challenges in using the WTO DSM: Kim pointed to the lack of experience, language problems and budgetary concerns due to the fact that Korea had to use many foreign consultants. Because the Samsung case was the first brought to the WTO DSB by Korea, there was no real knowledge as to how to proceed. Further, there was a general dearth of Koreans with good English skills, the requisite legal skills and a good working knowledge of the dispute. The Korean officials could only learn by experience and trial and error. Recognizing these problems, Koreans hired foreign lawyers as consultants, but the high cost was an issue for the ministry.

On the bright side, Samsung and the Korean government were able to work fairly smoothly together, and co-operated to build a strong case for the WTO DSM. Samsung formed a trade dispute team to gather the necessary information and to work with the Korean government. This team is still in place today. The government and Samsung made meticulous preparations; according to one newspaper account, the amount of paperwork prepared for the case could have filled five 8-ton trucks.

The Korean case: the anti-dumping measure

Thus on 16 July 1997, the Korean government filed a request for consultations with the WTO DSB, arguing that the US actions violated Articles VI.1 and VI.6(a) of GATT 1994, and Articles 1 and 11.1 of the Anti-Dumping Agreement, which stipulate that anti-dumping measures shall be applied only if there is dumping and if it causes or threatens material injuries; and that anti-dumping duties shall remain in force only as long as and to the extent necessary. Since Samsung had not exported to the United States from Korea since 1991, and since it had been assessed only on the *de minimis* margins for the previous six years, Korea argued that the United States was in violation of these Articles.

Further, Korea argued that the United States violated Articles 2, 3.1, 3.2, 3.6, 4.1, 5.4, 5.8, 5.10 and 11.2 of the Anti-Dumping Agreement. Article 3.1 states that a determination of injury shall involve an objective examination of the volume of the dumped imports and the effect of the dumped imports on prices, and the consequent impact on domestic producers of the like product. Article 3.2 states that with regard to the volume of the dumped imports, the investigating authorities shall consider whether there has been a significant increase in dumped imports.

Korea argued that the absence of dumping for six years and the cessation of exports for the subsequent six years fully demonstrate that, under the standards set out in Articles 3.1 and 3.2, there can be no injury.

Article 5.8 of the Anti-Dumping Agreement requires immediate termination of an investigation in the case of *de minimis* dumping margins, and Article 11.2 provides for revocation of an anti-dumping order if it is no longer necessary to counteract dumping. Korea argued that having found *de minimis* margins for Samsung for six consecutive years through its annual reviews, the United States should immediately have initiated a revocation review on its own initiative and terminated the anti-dumping order. Further, Korea argued that the provision of the US Tariff Act, which defines a *de minimis* margin of less than 0.5% as eligible for revocation, is in contravention of Article 5.8 of the Anti-Dumping Agreement which stipulates a *de minimis* margin of less than 2%.

Article 11.2 of the Anti-Dumping Agreement specifies that the authorities shall review the need for the continued imposition of anti-dumping duties on their own initiative, or upon request by any interested party. Korea argued that by failing to self-initiate a revocation review and by restricting Samsung's right to request a review, the United States had evaded its Article 11.2 obligations.

Korea also argued that the failure to reach a determination in the Commerce Department's revocation review also violates Article 11.4, which provides for the expeditious conclusion of such reviews, normally within twelve months of their initiation.

The Korean case: the anti-circumvention investigation

Korea also took issue with the anti-circumvention investigation, stating that the anti-circumvention investigation initiated on 19 January 1996 was in contravention of Article VI of GATT 1994 and Article 1 of the Anti-Dumping Agreement.

Korea pointed out that Article VI.1 of GATT 1994 defines dumping as the introduction of products of one country into the commerce of another country at less than normal value, and Article 2.1 of the Anti-Dumping Agreement defines it as a situation in which the export price of the product exported from one country to another is less than the comparable price for the like product in the exporting country. Thus if another country becomes the exporting country, dumping should be separately determined. Korea argued that by effectively considering exports from Korea and exports from Mexico and Thailand as identical through its circumvention concept, the United States misinterpreted the basic concept of dumping established throughout the GATT and the Anti-Dumping Agreement. Further, Korea stated that it was a violation of Article VI of GATT 1994 and Article 1 of the Anti-Dumping Agreement to initiate an anti-circumvention investigation as an extension of existing anti-dumping measures without initiating a new dumping (and injury) investigation.

Korea also pointed out that the petitioners for the anti-circumvention investigation, namely US labour unions such as the International Brotherhood of Electrical Workers and others, were composed of employees working in various companies dealing in a diverse variety of electric or electronic products. Therefore they could not be said to represent employees of the domestic industry of the like product, namely, colour televisions. Further, Korea argued that the US authorities had neglected to examine whether the petitioners indeed represented the domestic industry, and refused Korean companies' request for such an examination, thus violating Articles 3.1, 3.6, 4.1 and 5.4 of the Anti-Dumping Agreement. Korea also stated that the failure to make a determination in the ongoing investigation after eighteen months also violated Article 5.10 of the Anti-Dumping Agreement.

Finally, Korea took issue with the fact that the United States linked the revocation review with the anti-circumvention investigation. Korea stated that it was arbitrary and illogical for the United States to respond quickly to the request for an anti-circumvention investigation while delaying for a year its response to Samsung's request for a revocation review. Korea further stated that it was unreasonable for the United States to investigate the alleged circumvention without first verifying the justification of the anti-dumping order. Further, Korea argued that the attempt to link the results of the anti-circumvention investigation with the revocation determination constituted a further breach of the proper procedural sequence. That is, a decision by the US authorities to revoke the anti-dumping order against Korean colour televisions would remove the legal basis for the anti-circumvention investigation. Thus extending the review period by making the above-mentioned linkage constituted a violation of Article 11.1 of the Anti-Dumping Agreement which requires the immediate termination of the anti-dumping order in the absence of dumping which is causing injury.

The Korean case: panel request

In July 1997 Mexico, Thailand, Hong Kong China, and the EC asked to join consultations. During the consultation phase of the DSM, Korea and the

United States held a series of bilateral meetings which were not fruitful. On 6 November 1997 Korea requested the establishment of a panel. In its request, in addition to the points made above, Korea also argued that the United States was in violation of Article X.3 of GATT, and other assorted Articles of the Anti-Dumping Agreement.

Korea argued that the initiation of the anti-circumvention proceeding violated Article VI of GATT 1994 and Articles 1, 2.1 and 3.1 of the Agreement, because it might lead to the imposition of anti-dumping duties on imports of colour televisions from Mexico and Thailand without findings of dumping and resulting injury ever having been made.

Korea also argued that the refusal by the United States to conduct a standing inquiry before initiating its anti-circumvention investigation violated Articles 3.1, 3.6, 4.1 and 5.4 of the Anti-Dumping Agreement, and the failure to make a determination in the anti-circumvention investigation for more than twenty-two months violated Article 5.10 of the Anti-Dumping Agreement.

Finally, Korea argued that the United States violated Article X.3 of GATT and Article 17.6(i) of the Anti-Dumping Agreement, because the United States had not established the facts properly and had not evaluated the facts in an unbiased and objective manner. Korea stated that Samsung had sufficient special reasons to justify its delays in requesting revocation review, including, but not limited to, the United States' consistent and excessive delays in issuing results of the administrative reviews. The United States, however, unilaterally determined that its untimeliness for the reviews was excusable, while Samsung's untimeliness was not. Korea also complained that while the initial investigation and review were proceedings for the assessment of basically the same circumstances, the United States applied different standards for determining *de minimis* dumping margins and negligible imports in the two proceedings.[3]

4 The outcome

Meanwhile, on the US side, on 31 December 1997, at the request of the petitioners, the US anti-circumvention inquiry was terminated. Before termination, the US Department of Commerce found that Samsung had

---

[3] The details of the case are taken from WTO documents WT/DS89/1 and WT/DS89/7, which were presented to the WTO by the government of Korea; see also Nae-hi Han et al. (1999), *Case Studies of Korean Trade Conflicts by Industry* (in Korean), Seoul: POSCO Research Institute.

substantial production facilities in Mexico, and several feeder plants established and operated by Korean suppliers unrelated to Samsung. From these facilities, Samsung produced colour televisions sold throughout North, Central and South America, and these televisions entered the United States duty-free under NAFTA tariff preference provisions, implying that they met NAFTA's rules-of-origin requirements.

On the same date the Department of Commerce published the preliminary results of the changed circumstances review of the anti-dumping duty order on colour televisions from Korea, in which the Department on a preliminary basis determined partially to revoke the anti-dumping duty order with respect to Samsung.[4] On 5 January 1998, as a result of this preliminary order, Korea informed the DSB that it was withdrawing its request for a panel but reserving its right to reintroduce the request. On 2 September 1998, a final determination was made by the US Department of Commerce that changed circumstances warranted revocation of the anti-dumping duty order on colour televisions from Korea as it applied to Samsung.[5] According to one Korean newspaper report, when the fourteen members of Samsung's trade dispute team heard the news that the United States had finally revoked the anti-dumping measure, they shouted for joy that their struggle, which had lasted for more than fourteen years, was finally over. At the DSB meeting on 22 September 1998 Korea announced that it was definitively withdrawing the request for a panel because the anti-dumping duties had now been revoked.

5 Lessons for others: the players' views and implications for developing countries

The Korean players' views

After the withdrawal of the request for a panel, each side touted the 'successful outcome' of the case. The United States emphasized the facts that Samsung no longer exported colour televisions from Korea and that imports of colour televisions from Korea were unlikely to increase greatly. Korea emphasized the fact that an anti-dumping measure, widely thought to be unfair and unjustifiably maintained for fifteen years, had finally been removed. While the United States claimed that the filing of the request for a panel did not unduly affect the outcome of the case, most of the Korean general public believed that the WTO petition had played a crucial role in

---

[4] These findings are taken from US Federal Register 63 FR 46759.   [5] Ibid.

the US decision to withdraw the anti-dumping measure. In this case, the anti-dumping measure had been in place for fifteen years, despite continual efforts by Samsung and the Korean government to have it revoked, but soon after the case had been filed with the WTO the measure was withdrawn. Some Korean newspapers reported that it was only after Korea had filed the WTO case that the US Department of Commerce became more responsive to the request by Samsung and Korea for the revocation of the anti-dumping order. In November 1998, Samsung started to export higher-priced televisions to the United States.

The success of the Samsung case, as well as the success of a subsequent WTO Case Concerning Anti-Dumping Duty on Dynamic Random Access Memory Semiconductors (DRAMs) of One Megabyte or Above, which had been filed against the United States at almost the same time, did much to alleviate the general concern of the Korean public about and its resistance to accepting that the WTO dispute system was fair and objective.

As a consequence, the Korean public also began to realize that the WTO was not just a tool for other countries, but was one that Korea could use as well. These two cases also did much to alleviate public concerns brought about by the non-favourable ruling on the Taxes on Alcoholic Beverages case later in 1998.[6] Most Koreans, while perhaps still not enthusiastic about the WTO, began to acknowledge that it was useful for Korea, and that it could be used to eliminate unfair trade barriers in other countries, including the advanced and powerful ones. The Korean public now acknowledges that the WTO is necessary for maintaining international trade, and while the WTO may act 'against' Korea at times, it will also act 'for' Korea as circumstances warrant. As a trading nation, Korea needs the WTO.

Han-Soo Kim of MOFAT states that the results of this case encouraged Korea to use the DSM more extensively. Other sources also state that the confidence and experience gained from these two cases encouraged Korea to take the direction of 'aggressive legalism' in handling trade disputes,[7] and it has now become one of the more active users of the DSM. While cases are still brought against Korea, Korea is now as likely to be the complainant in the WTO, as can be seen in Table 21.2.

---

[6] Dukgeun Ahn (2002), 'Korean Experience of the Dispute Settlement in the World Trading System', KDI School Working Paper 02-03, p. 17, though Ahn emphasizes the DRAM case more than the colour television case.

[7] Wook Chae and Chang-Bae Seo (2001), *Assessment of WTO and Korea-Related Trade Disputes and Policy Implications* (in Korean), Seoul: Korea Institute for International Economic Policy, p. 24, and Ahn, 'Korean Experience', p. 18.

Table 21.2. *Cases brought by Korea, and cases where Korea reserved third party rights*

Date	Case No.	Defendant	Subject
1996.6.19	DS46	Brazil	Export Financing Programme for Aircraft (by Canada) (third party rights)
1996.10.3	DS54	Indonesia	Certain Measures Affecting the
1996.10.4	DS55		Automobile Industry (by EC, Japan and
1996.11.29	DS59		United States) (third party rights)
1996.10.8	DS64		
1997.7.10	DS89	United States	Anti-dumping Duty on Imports of Colour Television Receivers
1997.8.14	DS99	United States	Anti-dumping Duty on Dynamic Random Access Memory Semiconductors (DRAMs) of One Megabyte or Above
1998.10.6	DS139 DS142	EC, Japan	Certain Measures Affecting the Automotive Industry (of Canada) (third party rights)
1998.8.3	DS141	EC	Anti-dumping Duties on Imports of Cotton-Type Bed Linen from India (third party rights)
1998.10.6	DS146	EC	Measures Affecting the Automotive Sector
1999.5.1	DS175	United States	(of India) (third party rights)
1999.7.30	DS179	United States	Anti-dumping Measures on Stainless Steel Plate in Coils and Stainless Steel Sheet and Strip
1999.11.18	DS184	United States	Anti-dumping Measures on Certain Hot-Rolled Steel Products from Japan (third party rights)
2000.6.13	DS202	United States	Definitive Safeguard Measures on Imports of Circular Welded Carbon Quality Line Pipe
2000.11.30	DS214	United States	Definitive Safeguard Measures on Imports of Steel Wire Rod and Circular Welded Carbon Quality Line Pipe (third party rights)
2000.12.15	DS215	Philippines	Anti-dumping Measures Against Polypropylene Resin
2000.12.21	DS217	United States	Continued Dumping and Subsidy Offset
2001.5.21	DS234		Act of 2000 (joint complainant)

(*cont.*)

Table 21.2. (*cont.*)

Date	Case No.	Defendant	Subject
2002.1.30	DS244	United States	Sunset Review of Anti-Dumping Duties on Corrosion-Resistant Carbon Steel Flat Products from Japan (third party rights)
2002.3.20	DS251	United States	Definitive Safeguard Measures on Imports of Certain Steel Products (Joint Complainant – along with DS248, DS249, DS252, DS253, DS254, DS258, DS259).
2002.10.7	DS268	United States	Sunset Reviews of Anti-Dumping Measures on Oil Country Tubular Goods from Argentina (third party rights)
2002.12.20	DS277	United States	Investigation of the International Trade Commission in Softwood Lumber from Canada (third party rights)
2003.6.30	DS296	United States	Countervailing Duty Investigation on Dynamic Random Access Memory Semiconductors (DRAM)
2003.7.25	DS299	EC	Countervailing Duty Investigation on Dynamic Random Access Memory Semiconductors (DRAM)
2003.9.3	DS301	EC	Measures Affecting Commercial Vessels
2004.2.13	DS307	EC	Aid for Commercial Vessels

Source: WTO, 'Update of WTO Dispute Settlement Cases', 26 March 2004.

6 Lessons for developing countries

There are aspects of Korea's experience which are useful for developing countries. One should remember that when the United States applied its anti-dumping measure in 1983, Korea was still very definitely a developing country, with GDP per capita of $2,000. The DSM under WTO is much easier to use than the dispute settlement system of the pre-WTO GATT, and developing countries should use the mechanism more actively. However, there are problems which they must consider when using the DSM for the first time.

First, close co-operation must exist between the private sector and the government. While it is the private sector which is the victim of trade barriers, it is the government which must prepare and present the case.

Thus, the private sector and the government must be able to work closely together, to gather facts relevant to the case and form a viable legal and diplomatic strategy.

Second, the WTO is useful only if it is used. Some members may be reluctant to bring a case to the WTO because of lack of experience, the costs involved and fears of reprisal. However, the Korean experience shows that gains can outweigh the possible costs. Careful preparation can reduce much of the direct and indirect costs of the case. Further, as the government deals with more cases, it will build experience, which will reduce costs in future cases. The first DSM case should be seen as an investment in the future.

Third, the successful use of the WTO can improve the image of globalization, the government and the WTO itself. Globalization is often seen as harmful because it supposedly imposes the will of stronger countries on weaker ones. Korea's experience with the WTO DSB shows that this perception is not accurate. Measures which are inconsistent with WTO Agreements can be addressed successfully by smaller countries – if they are willing to try. Thus these countries need not be passive, helpless 'victims' of globalization. Such empowerment should reduce resistance against globalization. Further, when a government uses the DSM successfully, people will gain confidence in the diplomatic, legal and economic capability of the government. Finally, the successful use of the DSM can also show that the WTO is not a one-sided tool of pro-globalization advanced countries, but rather a neutral tool for solving disputes, which can build support for trade and globalization.

However, it is vitally important that a country chooses the 'right' case, especially for its first case. Because the costs involved will be higher than for subsequent cases, and because the public perception of the WTO will depend greatly on whether the first case is won or lost, the government must choose the first case carefully, to make sure that it has willing partners in the private sector and that it has a strong legal case. The government should also use any resource that is open to it, including foreign legal help, even though it may incur high costs. The indirect benefits of winning the case, through a more favourable view of the government, and of trade and globalization, are likely to outweigh the costs of bringing the case.

22

Laos: the textile and garment industry in the post-ATC era

BANESATY THEPHAVONG, KHOUANCHAY IEMSOUTHI
AND BUAVANH VILAVONG*

1 Overview

The WTO Agreement on Textiles and Clothing (ATC) set up a transitional mechanism in 1995, with a view to phasing out quotas for trade in textiles and clothing by the end of 2004. Even though the total global imports of textiles and clothing will expand, competition is also likely to increase among many garment exporting countries around the world. It is expected that textile and garment companies in medium- to high-cost countries will reduce their manufacturing production. In contrast, those in low-cost countries with a strong competitive advantage will expand their production and export capacities to become preferred suppliers and to take advantage of liberalization. Lao textile and garment companies will be affected at different levels depending on their competitive capacities. In order to maintain its market shares or reduce losses, the garment industry needs to implement a product diversification strategy with the introduction of products in the medium to higher market segments and develop sufficient production inputs. Laos needs to develop modernized production facilities, better upstream industries (spinning and weaving) and well-trained workers to be prepared for trade liberalization. Support from the government is crucial, in particular on market access negotiations and trade facilitation. Nevertheless, a lack of capacity in terms of budget and expertise is the main constraint in the process.

2 The problem in context

The textile and garment industry is of great importance to the Lao economy. Currently, the industry comprises ninety-six factories and

* Banesaty Thephavong is Deputy Director General and Khouanchay Iemsouthi and Buavanh Vilavong are Economists, Foreign Trade Department, Ministry of Commerce.

employs more than 25,000 workers. In 2003, garment exports, valued at US$115 million, accounted for approximately a third of total exports, second to electricity. Laos exports ready-made garments to forty-two countries. As one of the forty-nine least developed countries, Laos is granted duty-free and quota-free market access to certain developed countries under the generalized system of preferences (GSP). However, the garment industry benefits very little from the GSP due to strict rules of origin, particularly related to local content requirements. Garment companies in Laos mostly depend on imported fibre, yarn and fabric for assembling as finished garments that are then re-exported.

The phasing out of quotas at the end of 2004 will lead to a dramatic increase in exports from large developing countries such as China and India. This increase could have significant implications for smaller least developed countries including Laos. One of the expected results is price competition. It is expected that the price of textiles and clothing will come down by around 20–25% when the quota abolition takes its full effect. According to Mr Bounma, the president of the Lao Fashion Garment Co., the effects of price reduction due to increased competition can be felt even now: 'Last year the price of a polo-shirt that we produced for a client in Hong Kong was US$5.50 per piece, but last week we received the order with a price offer of US$3.50.'

This is a big challenge for garment factories in Laos, where advantages in low wage costs may no longer exist. Even though the wages are relatively low workers' productivity is also low, due to the lack of proper skills training and development. Garment manufacturers in Laos have become progressively highly concentrated on low-value-added products. The exporters have market shares in selected products that are by no means in the lowest price quartile in the European market. Lower prices and better quality garments from various supply sources are expected to increase when the ATC comes to an end. Some locally owned garment factories in Laos are manufacturing-oriented and work on a CMT (cut, make and trim) basis or use sub-contractors, mainly via traders in Thailand, Singapore and Hong Kong. The working procedure is such that brand-name sportswear is designed by the brand owners, for example in Europe. The orders are placed with a Hong Kong-based representative office which will then make contact with garment suppliers in the region including China, Cambodia, Laos, Thailand and Vietnam. If the order is for 5 million pieces, for instance, it will be divided up according to each country's supply capacities. Suppliers in Laos are more likely to receive the smallest allocation in the light of their limited production capacities in comparison with those in China and Vietnam.

The other possible problem is preference erosion. In the past, apart from quota limitation, exporters from countries which are not GSP beneficiaries have to pay 12–14% import duties. This means that Lao exporters used to have the advantage of cost saving of more than 10% over exporters from other countries for categories of garments exported under the GSP. After 2005, this advantage for Lao garment exporters will be minimized. In addition, being a land-locked country, Laos faces the transportation issue; most goods are transited via ports in Bangkok or Danang. Lao garment suppliers are thus at a clear disadvantage, the transport costs for Laos being relatively high compared with its neighbours. Mr Bounma explained that 'It costs us around US$1,200 for a shipment of standard containers, while the exporters in Vietnam pay only US$250. It is estimated that taking both the preference erosion and transport costs into account, the cost-saving gap will reduce from 12–14% to only 3–5%.'

The preferred suppliers are those who will be able to take advantage of lower wages, higher labour productivity and quicker response to demand. In Laos, the labour productivity is generally low – even lower than in neighbouring Vietnam. Consequently, low productivity affects the added value of production and the capacity to diversify outputs. Given comparable clothing quality and marginal price difference, importers tend to prefer the supply sources that offer more convenience. This may be due to a cheap and large pool of labour. Easy access to sea transportation is also another crucial factor because it will affect the lead time of supply; Laos takes longer to transport goods via neighbouring countries to sea ports. From the point of view of the garment industry, the government should streamline import and export procedures to allow for fast importation of raw materials as well as quick clearance of finished garment exports. This will help to offset the disadvantage of location.

The Lao textile and clothing industry will face fierce competition in its export markets, particularly the European Union (EU), its main market for garments. Laos is not yet a member of the WTO and thus its textile and clothing trade is dependent on bilateral trade arrangements with its trading partners; membership of the WTO would give Laos its necessary predictable market access to major markets. In addition, Laos is a relative newcomer, having for example concluded a bilateral trade agreement with the United States only at the end of 2003, while its neighbours Vietnam and Cambodia have had access to the US market since 1994 and 1997 respectively.

3 The players and their roles

The key player in this case study is the Lao Fashion Garment Co., a locally owned company established in the capital, Vientiane. It employs some 230 workers, most of whom are women in their twenties, in the factory, which, equipped with 141 machines, is relatively small. Lao Fashion Garment mainly produces and exports polo-shirts, T-shirts, sweaters, jackets, brassieres and knitted items to the European market. Its performance has been reasonably successful so far. The management is aware of possible competition in the liberalized trade in textiles and garments after 1 January 2005; Mr Bounma commented that, 'We are a relatively small company which has a production capacity of 720,000 pieces per year. Lao Fashion Garment imports most of its raw materials from other countries, mainly from China and Chinese Taipei. Like most garment companies in Laos, we receive production orders from overseas partner companies in Hong Kong and Thailand.'

The textile and garment sector in Laos is composed of ninety-six factories of which fifty-seven are producers and/or exporters. Textile and garment companies can be divided into four categories, foreign direct investment subsidiaries, joint-venture companies, (locally owned) medium-sized companies and small-sized factories working as sub-contractors. There are different levels of awareness among these companies in relation to quota abolition after 2005. The foreign direct investment firms and joint-venture companies form the groups who are more likely to feel least impact. They are relatively aware of what will happen after the quota regime expires, and many of them are preparing themselves for the upcoming increased competition. They have undertaken in-house training programmes to improve labour productivity and to increase their product diversification capacity. Some companies are also looking for cheaper sources of imported raw materials. In addition, the foreign subsidiaries and joint-venture companies also have good marketing channels as a result of their connection with parent companies or foreign-based partner companies abroad.

Lao Fashion Garment falls under the third category of company, that is a locally owned factory. Producers in this category are in the group that is more likely to face the biggest challenges after 1 January 2005. As a local factory receiving orders from middle-man firms overseas, Lao Fashion Garment cannot make direct contact with importers and therefore it only works on a CMT basis. Overseas companies are responsible for marketing its exports in Europe.

In general, the most adversely affected category of garment companies is formed by the locally owned factories which are the sub-contractors for the first three categories. Given the fact that the companies in these categories are trying to cut down their production costs, one of the consequences will be to give up outside production lines and carry out all production activities onsite. As a result, sub-contractors may no longer be needed.

The Lao Textile and Garment Industry Group (LTGIG) has played a very important role in raising awareness in the garment and textile industry concerning quota abolition. The group held many workshops and invited key speakers from international organizations to talk to local businesses about the future of the world trade in textiles and garments after 2005 and its implications for the industry. 'Much more needs to be done to create a clear understanding of the possible negative impacts of the quota abolition and what should be an appropriate response from the individual company itself and the industry as a whole', commented Mr Bounma, who is president of the LTGIG.

The Lao National Chamber of Commerce and Industry (LNCCI) has worked hard to lobby the Ministry of Commerce, which is dealing with trade policy, trade negotiations and export promotion. Mr Bounma added that 'Equally important, the chamber of commerce is a business association which addresses the government with their concerns and seeks support to help the garment factories to overcome the problems.' The ministry has a direct responsibility for the promotion of exports, but it does not have sufficient funds to allow it to do so. This is unfortunate, as promotional support by government is one of the areas of support to the industry permitted under WTO regulations. This support is nearly always found in competing countries as the catalyst for helping small- to medium-sized garment companies, to move into direct exports in particular. A senior official in the Ministry of Commerce explained that 'In most of the newly developing countries, the government provides export promotion support to their garment producers. It is doubtful whether the industry in Mauritius would have reached almost US$1 billion exports if there were no promotional support from the government. Similarly, this can explain why garment suppliers in Pakistan, India, Madagascar and Malaysia are much outperformed'.

4 Challenges faced and the outcome

In general, the Lao textile and garment industry is not in the right position to face the coming competition. It is expected that global exports of textiles and garments will expand when the quotas are abolished. Lao garment companies are likely to face a considerable level of competition from larger economies such as China, Vietnam, India and Pakistan, which have the comparative advantage of a large pool of cheap labour and the production of high-quality garments. Mr Bounma said that 'In recent years, Lao Fashion Garment has received fewer and fewer orders compared with the late 1990s', expressing his concern about his own factory. This has become a sign of the keen competition in the world textile and garment market. The full effects would be realized by the end of 2004, when the quota system under the ATC was terminated and the textile and garment trade would be fully integrated into the WTO framework. Mr Bounma comments, 'Consequently, the CMT work is reducing and will not be available in the future. This would have a great impact not only on my own factory but it would also affect the whole economy of Laos, in particular the textile industry that employs more than 25,000 workforces, accounting for 20% of the total population.' This critical likely situation has obliged him to think over and over again what he should do in order to keep his factory competitive. The two burdens that he bears have inspired him to come up with some measures that will be applied in his own factory and offer this advice to the industry as a whole: 'The government should provide training courses to match the needs of the industry and improve the bureaucratic procedures to facilitate the industry to manufacture and export efficiently.'

As the owner of the Lao Fashion Garment as well as being the president of the LTGIG, Mr Bounma has some advantages over other domestic factories, as he is aware of what the Lao garment industry faces after the quota abolition. Nevertheless, he is still not very sure about the actual negative impacts. When the group organizes brainstorming workshops for responsive solutions, local factory participation is very low compared with foreign-owned or joint venture companies. The business owners hardly realize the importance of consultations and teamwork in order to discuss their concerns and find mutual solutions. Some factories usually send an office clerk or an accountant to attend these workshops. Mr Bounma emphasized, 'You need to know and understand the problems yourself in order to come up with a clear plan of action to deal with what is expected to be faced in the future.' It is more likely that the quota abolition will put many small garment factories that are sub-contractors out of business if nothing substantive has been undertaken to prevent it. Given the fact that most garment factories in Laos rely heavily on orders from third parties, importers will tend to choose those suppliers who offer them the best terms and conditions. The quality that Lao garment factories can supply may be comparable and the price may be a little cheaper, but the importers will order from the suppliers who are most convenient to deal with. Hence small suppliers in Laos can do little more than face reality and, in the worst case, may have to close down their factories.

On the other hand, the government authorities are not very aware of the impact of global competition, which requires short lead times, low prices, good-quality products and good-quality services. The garment factories expect to receive support from government authorities, particularly to provide timely import–export clearance. One area of support for productivity enhancement in the Lao garment industry is improvement in import procedures of raw materials and prompt service for the export of ready-made garments. The geographical constraint alone offers a sufficient disadvantage for Lao exporters; they should not be brought down by additional man-made difficulties. 'We would like to see the government sector working harder to improve market access for Laos as in other countries. For example, in Thailand the Ministry of Commerce and trade representatives abroad are working with key agencies to negotiate market access and make contacts for business partnerships', Mr Bounma commented. One of the biggest disadvantages for Laos, in comparison with Cambodia and Nepal, of not being a member of the WTO is that Laos is very reliant on bilateral market access. 'We are not concerned about the import tariffs because they may not come down very much after the end of the Doha Round, but the real threat for us is import quotas', added Mr Bounma. After the textile and garment trade is brought within the multilateral trade framework, any quantitative restrictions are forbidden among members. Without WTO membership, Laos has to live with bilateral trade arrangements which may be abused by importing countries even though they are WTO members.

The Lao garment industry's productivity is relatively low in comparison with its competitors due to the lack of training, skills, labour and management. The difficulties in training workers are diverse. Most factory workers are women who may finish high school and then come to the city to find jobs. The garment factories have to train them completely on site. It is indisputable that the wages in Laos are low, but the workers also have low productivity. Lao companies are only producing low-grade products.

The other challenge for Lao Fashion Garment is the lack of marketing strategies. The company is manufacturing-oriented with a passive selling approach, waiting for production orders from representative companies overseas, for example in Hong Kong or Thailand. This may be acceptable for foreign direct investment companies as they can have transfer pricing with parent companies. In contrast, it is an increasing problem for some joint ventures and certainly for 100% Lao companies such as Lao Fashion Garment.

Even though Laos is qualified under the GSP to export to many developed markets such as the EU, Japan and Canada, most garment factories are not able to take full advantage of this preferential market access. Most of Lao Fashion Garment's items are not exported under the GSP to the EU market. Mr Bounma commented that 'Due to the lack of domestic upstream industries, we import most of our raw materials such as fibre, yarn and fabric from China and Chinese Taipei.' Imported materials account for approximately 70% of total production costs and in turn these constitute quite a high proportion of the overall production costs. Due to increased competition as a result of the quota abolition, imported material cost components may not be reduced to the same extent as the garments' price reduction. Labour costs will be cut instead and in some cases the profit margin will decrease, both of which are part of the local 'value added'. The reduction in domestic value addition is a threat, especially for those who export under ASEAN cumulation rules of origin. In order to fulfil the GSP requirements of the EU, garment factories in Laos need to have local contents worth more than 50% of the total production costs.

In addition to being a non-WTO member, Laos has not yet enforced normal trade relations (NTRs) with the United States. Even though NTRs were recently rectified, many internal procedures for their effective implementation are needed. For Lao Fashion Garment and the garment sector generally, it could take six months or more to actually be able to export to the US market. In the next steps, the Lao Textile and Garment Industry Group in collaboration with the government will need to work hard to negotiate for market access for each category of garments. After Cambodia reached its bilateral trade agreement with the United States in 1997, garment exports doubled within a few years. Currently, Cambodia exports over 70% of garments to the United States and the rest go to the European market. When the ATC is ended and textile and garment trade is fully integrated into the WTO framework, the benefits of having a preferential bilateral market access may not be that great. Hence, after being granted the NTRs, the immediate positive effects on the Lao garment industry cannot be readily forecast. If Laos had had the NTRs in the last seven to eight years it would have been very useful.

For the Lao garment industry there is another disadvantage for not being able to access the US market. US buyers tend to make larger orders compared with those from the EU market. Receiving bulk orders do have economies of scale and enhance the expertise of the workers. Small quotas disrupt improvements in workers' skills. They start to become familiar with certain production settings and their productivity rises. Then, suddenly, they have to learn new skills and adapt to new settings. Progress in labour skills may take some time.

5 Lessons for others

The success of the industry during the 1990s demonstrated that it can be a significant contributor to the government's prime objective of poverty alleviation through job creation and earning of foreign exchange. For garment factories, CMT work is not sustainable and will not be available in the future. To solve these problems, strong marketing activities, as a means of having direct contact with retail buyers, are needed. Improvement in labour skills and productivity in the industry is also a key to helping Lao garment exporters stay competitive in importing markets.

Being the president of the LTGIG, Mr Bounma has actively participated in in-country and regional workshops on the issues and challenges related to trade in textiles and garments after 2005. 'Creating public awareness among locally owned garment factories, including the sub-contractors, would be an activity that needs to be undertaken immediately', commented Mr Bounma, adding that 'The Ministry of Commerce should actively work in collaboration with the Chamber of Commerce and Industry.' In order to minimize the possible negative impacts on the Lao garment industry, it is necessary for the government to make a comprehensive assessment of the potential adverse effects of quota abolition and to have a clear policy response.

Apart from raising awareness, support from the government authorities is a crucial factor. From interviews conducted with some garment factories, the general consensus is that the current legal framework should be more supportive of business operations. One example is that the government could review and improve the existing labour law. Flexible labour law is needed to allow for garment factories to compete with those in other neighbouring countries. Overtime work for workers is limited to only 30 hours per month. In addition, female workers constitute far the largest share of the workforce in the textile and garment industry but they are not allowed to work after 10 p.m. This is not enough for the factory to produce on time when bulk orders are received.

Talking about the difficulties that the textile and clothing sector in Laos has encountered, Mr Bounma had expressed some concerns resulting from his own experience and through discussions with managing directors of various other garment factories, whether wholly foreign owned, joint-venture or Lao-owned companies: almost all the companies have difficulties in developing mechanical skills, and all kinds of management skills. The result is that unit costs of production are higher than necessary, quality is inconsistent, orders are delayed and material utilization is excessive. Therefore he suggested that the government works together with the industry to create the appropriate types of vocational training institutes in Laos.

Besides, the government and the industry must work closely together to reach mutual understanding of others' difficulties. Mr Bounma emphasized that the government should negotiate bilateral agreements in order to obtain an extension to the present terms of preferential access to the world's important clothing importing markets, especially the EU, Norway and the United States. He commented further that the government should also speed up its WTO accession procedure, which will help to extend the market access for Laos on a multilateral basis. The WTO is a rule-based organization and membership will mean that Lao exporters will not run up against the risk of being discriminated against by any particular importing countries.

A regional forum to address the issue collectively is considered to be one of various means available to draw the attention of the garment importing countries. That was the view of Mr Bounma after coming back from the sixth ASEAN Federation of Textile Industries (AFTEX) meeting in mid-November 2004 in Hanoi, Vietnam, when he explained, 'I fully agreed with all the positive measures that came out from the meeting and will be submitted to the ASEAN economic ministers for adoption.' He also emphasized that there are some measures that the Lao government should undertake immediately, namely eliminating non-tariff barriers to facilitate intra-ASEAN inputs and securing the recognition of ASEAN cumulative rules of origin in all free trade area negotiations. 'The establishment of skill training, design and merchandizing centres to build capacity for the Lao garment factories will also help the Lao textile and garment industry overcome the mounting challenges', added Mr Bounma.

23

Malawi in the multilateral trading system

TONIA KANDIERO*

1 The problem in context

Malawi is a land-locked country occupying the southern part of the Rift Valley in east Africa. It is bordered by Zambia to the west, Mozambique to the south and east and Tanzania to the north. In 2001, the estimated population in Malawi was 11 million (World Bank 2003). This relatively small sub-Saharan African country is one of the poorest in the world, with GDP per capita of US$163 in 2001 and over half of the poor population living in the rural area.

Malawi is an open economy, but trade openness has not fostered economic growth, as is indicated by the declining figures for economic growth (from 6% in 1990 to −1% in 2001). Merchandise trade has declined significantly over time, with exports decreasing from US$442 million in 1999 to US$310 million in 2001, and imports from US$698 million to US$550 million in the same period (World Bank 2003). Tobacco, tea, sugar and coffee account for 90% of merchandise exports, with tobacco as the main export. There have been some efforts to diversify to non-traditional products such as fruit and vegetables and spices. On the import side, the main imports are vehicles and parts, petroleum fuels, machinery, boilers and parts, electrical machinery, fertilizer, wheat flour, pharmaceuticals, iron and steel.

Agriculture contributes a little more than a third (34%) to Malawi's GDP, while the manufacturing and service sectors account for 18% and 48% respectively (World Bank 2003). Most of the activities in the service sector are non-tradable. The importance of agriculture cannot be stressed enough: in addition to being the leading export earner, approximately half of Malawi's citizens who are in paid employment work in the agricultural sector and 85% of the population are supported by it (SADC 2001).

* University of Pretoria.

Table 23.1. *Tariffs at the end of 2000/2001 (per cent)*

Indicator	All commodities	Agriculture	Non-agriculture
Bound tariff lines	17.0	100.0	0.3
Duty-free tariff lines	4.0	11.0	2.8
Simple average applied MFN rates	13.6	15.2	13.3
Range of applied rates	0–25.0	0–25.0	0–25.0

Source: WTO, based on data provided by Malawian authorities.

From the mid-1980s Malawi made tremendous progress in trade liberalization under the structural adjustment programme and continued to do so through the 1990s. Tariffs still remain as the main trade policy instrument affecting trade. All tariffs are *ad valorem*. The maximum applied tariff rate under the two-digit Harmonized System (HS) is 25% and the average applied most-favoured-nation (MFN) tariff rate is 13.6% (see Table 23.1). The average rate in the agricultural sector is approximately 15% and in the manufacturing sector 13%. Malawi has a six-band tariff structure (0, 5, 10, 15, 20, 25), with 60% of the lines at 10% or less (WTO 2002). Tariffs between zero and 5% apply to 'necessities'. High tariffs are imposed on commodities such as coffee extracts, butter, sugar, apples, tea and consumer goods. Malawi also shows some levels of tariff escalation. Tariffs on unprocessed products are 30% lower than those on fully processed products (MG and IAWG 2003). Malawi has bound all its agricultural products at 125%, except for a few products with bound rates of 50, 55 and 65%. Only 0.3% of non-agricultural products are bound.

Malawi has removed most of its non-tariff barriers. However, a few import licences and bans for environmental, health, safety and security reasons still exist. The Ministry of Agriculture provides phytosanitary regulations, and the Ministry of Commerce and Industry issues licences for wild animals and other import licences in general. Approximately 29% of all product lines continue to face non-tariff measures (UNCTAD 2001). In the case of live fish, for example, trout face a tariff equivalent of 100%. Imports of this product line require a licence from the Ministry of Commerce and Industry. Import of live animals faces non-tariff measures of 50%. In 2001, Malawi introduced import licences on sugar and import bans on dairy produce and vegetable cooking oil. Even though sanitary and phytosanitary requirements are applied, they are not used to curtail imports. Malawi, like other developing countries, is in the process of preparing new anti-dumping measures and introducing countervailing measures (MG and IAWG 2003). Looking at exports, Malawi is a relatively open country. Since the late-1990s, all trade taxes and quotas on exports have been eliminated (WTO 2002). Export surrender remains only on tobacco, tea and sugar. Export licences are required for a few commodities such as fuel and maize for environmental protection and food security reasons. Tea and raw tobacco are also subject to export licences.

In general, Malawi faces severe trade and economic problems, including declining commodity prices, weak infrastructure, lack of technology, high cost of inputs, lack of access to financing, weak institutional and human capacity, high external debt – all of these have a major impact on trade performance.

Given this picture, what do multilateral trade negotiations mean for Malawi? Trade negotiations in the WTO offer a multilateral forum for countries to take advantage of a rules-based system for trade and development. However, Malawi is facing major constraints even as the country is engaged in multilateral negotiations. The objective of this short paper is to reveal these challenges from the perspective of the stakeholders. The study does not focus on any particular sector because most of the issues facing Malawi are across the board. And once these challenges have been addressed, Malawi will be able to grapple with more sector specific issues. To meet the objective of this endeavour, representatives from different government ministries, the private sector, non-government organizations (NGOs) and donors were interviewed. These stakeholders are presented in section two. Section three discusses the challenges faced by stakeholders. Based on their experience, the last section offers lessons for others.

2 The local and external players and their roles

Prior to 1994, Malawi was a one-party state and the government handled trade issues. In recent years, with the introduction of the multi-party system, the new governing structure has made tremendous efforts to include the private sector and non-government organizations in having a say in trade issues. Who are the main local stakeholders? The main department responsible for trade and industry policy is the Ministry of Commerce and Industry. Even though trade issues have taken centre stage in the domestic area, it is disconcerting that the Poverty Reduction Strategy (PRS) does not have a sector-specific plan for trade, meaning that when resources are allocated trade does not feature as a major priority in the development agenda. The good news is that sector-specific trade issues have been addressed in the Malawi economic growth strategy, and part of the strategy will be incorporated in the revised PRS. Other government ministries involved in trade issues include the Ministry of Agriculture, Irrigation and Food Security, which has the main task of formulating agricultural policies and the Ministry of Finance and Economic Planning, the overseer of the overall government budget as well as expenditure and revenue measures; the Malawi Revenue Authority is responsible for tax and tariff administration. The Ministry of Foreign Affairs, the Copyright Society (under the Ministry of Sports and Culture) and the Patents Office (under the Ministry of Justice) also play an important role in trade matters.

Other important public-sector players include the Malawi Bureau of Standards (MBS), the Malawi Export Promotion Council (MEPC) and the Reserve Bank of Malawi. The MBS is the designated enquiry point for the Agreement on Technical Barriers to Trade (TBT) and for the food safety aspects of the Sanitary and Phytosanitary (SPS) Agreement. In addition, the MBS is one of the regulatory authorities to formulate and implement national standards for products and services; it needs better infrastructure and more trained staff to handle these heavy responsibilities. The MEPC's major responsibility is to promote export diversification, as Malawi is overly reliant on a few commodities. In addition to the need for more skilled import and export officers, the MEPC is constrained by lack of information on foreign markets. The Reserve Bank of Malawi is responsible for monetary and exchange rate policies, as well as supervision of the financial services sector. The key private-sector stakeholders include the Chamber of Commerce and Industry, the Exporters' Association of Malawi and Textiles and the Garment Manufacturers of Malawi. These public and private players form the National Working Group on Trade Policy, a sub-group of the National Action Group. The National Working Group on Trade Policy is chaired by a private-sector stakeholder. In addition to the participation of the private and public sectors, NGOs such as the Malawi Economic Justice Network and Action Aid Malawi also participate in WTO discussions.

Multilateral and bilateral donors such as the International Monetary Fund (IMF), the International Trade Centre (ITC), the United Nations Development Programme (UNDP), the World Bank, the WTO, the Norwegian embassy/NORAD, the Department of International Development (DFID) and the US Agency for International Development (USAID), among others, have been instrumental in assisting Malawi to address some of the capacity constraints. This is being done through programmes such as the Integrated Framework (IF), Joint Integrated Technical Assistance Programmes (JITAP) and country and regional programmes. These initiatives have led to a call from donors, for example the UNDP, for technical assistance to be provided to enable Malawi to integrate into the global system. Even though trade-related technical assistance is vital to Malawi, the UNDP has stressed that issues of sustainability and making sure that the country takes ownership of the programmes still need to be addressed. As part of the consultation process, external donors also attend the National Action Group meetings.

All the stakeholders welcome the multilateral trade negotiations under the WTO. They feel that there is room for Malawi to gain significantly from participating fully in the WTO negotiations. However, in spite of the existence of the National Group on Trade Policy, there has not been a strong interaction among stakeholders. In fact, as observed by a government official, no formal discussions on the way forward or any other WTO-related issues were discussed after the Cancún Ministerial Conference. Most important discussions, it appears, tend to be tabled as high-level WTO meetings approach.

Apart from the lack of a more cohesive interaction among stakeholders, Malawi's participation is largely affected by concerns about the large financial costs that may be incurred as Malawi creates the institutions and implements the standards demanded by the trading system, as well as by capacity constraints arising from trade negotiations. These and other issues will be discussed in the next section.

3 Challenges faced and the outcome

This section presents the views and challenges faced by some key stakeholders. To start with, the Ministry of Agriculture, Irrigation and Food Security, one of the key stakeholders, considering that the country is an agriculture-based economy, recognizes the importance of Malawi's participation in the WTO. However for Malawi to benefit from the WTO process, Mr Lungu, a senior ministry official, argued that the country has to overcome some of the major domestic bottlenecks because 'if developed countries were to grant Malawi free access to their market, supply-side constraints would hinder the country from enjoying significant gains from the full access'. He went on to say that the first thing Malawi needed to do was to address the overarching issues of 'low productivity and profitability of smallholder farmers' in the agricultural sector. Productivity has been greatly affected by low-level development, poor varietal selection, declining soil fertility and poor agricultural practices. The main cause of low profitability is weak links to input and output markets. Farmers are handicapped by lack of information and weak infrastructure, resulting in high input costs and low output prices. Mr Lungu suggested that the way to deal with these challenges was to 'pursue targeted investments to improve on production frequency, yields and strengthening market linkages'.

With regard to developed countries, Mr Kabambe, a senior ministry official at the time he was interviewed (but now a permanent secretary in charge of poverty alleviation), considered that there was a need to 'level the playing field' in multilateral trade negotiations in order for developing countries to trust the system. The use of trade distorting subsidies and high tariffs on products of interest to Malawi are examples of developed countries 'not playing fair'. While there is this increased pressure for developed countries to reduce high tariffs, Dr Daudi, a senior ministry official specializing in standards at the time he was interviewed (but now a permanent secretary in the Ministry of Agriculture), cautioned that non-tariff barriers such as standards are on the rise. The challenge for Malawi, as an exporter of mainly agricultural products and venturing into exporting more processed products, is that it lacks trained manpower and equipment to address these non-tariff barriers and to comply with WTO commitments. This point was also reiterated by Dr Daudi's son at the Malawi Bureau of Standards (MBS), the designated enquiry point for the Agreement on TBT and for food safety aspects of the SPS Measures.

In addition to the constraints described above, Mr Daudi said that even though the MBS was considered an enquiry point, for effective operation they 'needed assistance in setting up and operating an enquiry point'. This could be done by learning from other established enquiry points in the region or abroad. The MBS also requires more information in order to understand TBT and SPS agreements and their obligations. Such information is also not available to other regulatory bodies which play a role in the implementation of the WTO Agreements. Another factor affecting MBS operations as a fully functioning enquiry point is its weak infrastructure. MBS is in desperate need of an effective modern information technology system for effective communication, storage and retrieval of information and reproduction of documents. Also in the area of infrastructure, the MBS lacks sufficient laboratory equipment to implement regulations effectively within the framework of the WTO Agreements.

Turning to the Ministry of Trade and Industry as the main co-ordinating body for WTO issues, the first thing that came out in interviews was that the ministry was understaffed and could not handle the massive coverage of WTO issues. Ms Musonzo, an economist in charge of WTO issues, stated that 'one staff member may be assigned to work on two or three WTO agreements on top of other assigned duties in the Ministry'. This lack of specialization, she continued, 'makes it impossible for us to fully grasp and interpret complex WTO agreements as well as submit notifications'. Mr Hara, a senior economist and a newcomer to WTO issues, commented that 'we are not sufficiently equipped in terms of manpower to carry out rigorous analytical work to analyze WTO proposals'. These in-house capacity constraints are also affected by the lack of representation in Geneva, a concern raised by all the stakeholders interviewed. As a result of the lack of representation, the ministry is not able to obtain all the information on issues discussed in meetings in Geneva. On the implications of the WTO in relation to Malawi, Mr Hara pointed out that Malawi has lower average tariff (about 15%) compared with many WTO members. However, with the lack of a proper safeguard mechanism and countervailing measures further tariff reduction can lead to dumping. Therefore, there is the need to have effective mechanisms to detect injury in case of surges of imports. Another concern, as reflected in the ministry's position papers, is the erosion of preferences due to lower MFN tariffs. According to the figures given by the ministry, Malawi is expected to lose 11% of its export earnings due to preference erosion. The ministry has begun to think about what Malawi should do when the erosion of preferences occurs. So far there is talk about preserving preferences, even if it is inevitable that preferences will be eroded due to liberalization. If the preferences cannot to be preserved, Malawi will request compensation for loss of preferences. This is also the position of the Africa group.

A senior official at the Ministry of Economic Planning and Development, Mr Mtonya, raised an important point on the cost of compliance with WTO commitments when he stressed that 'by accepting the WTO commitments Malawi takes up obligations that may impose a huge burden on the development budget. For Malawi to comply with WTO agreements it would mean the government setting aside over 50% of its budget, something not feasible considering that the country already faces budget constraints in order to meet its expenditure in many other areas. Therefore, there is need for financial and technical assistance from donors to meet the cost of compliance of WTO commitments.' To add to this concern, Mr Zimpita, also at the Ministry of Finance, expressed his concern about the revenue implications of tariff reduction as 'tariff revenue constitutes a major portion of government revenue and the reduction in collection could have serious consequences on the budget'. He felt, therefore, that rigorous analysis of WTO proposals was needed in order to assess the cost and the benefits. These sentiments were shared by the Malawi Revenue Authority.

The Malawi Confederation of Chambers of Commerce and Industry (MCCI), representing the private sector, is pushing for more public–private sector consultation. Mr Mtonakutha of the MCCI indicated that the establishment of the Trade Policy National Working Group, a body which brings together the public sector and the private sector, was a major step forward; however, he said that more still needed to be done considering that stakeholder co-ordination was a recent development. Outside Malawi, the Chamber of Commerce also widely consults with the Southern African Development Community (SADC) and the Associations of Chambers of Commerce of the Common Market of Southern and Eastern Africa (COMESA).

On the NGO side, Action Aid Malawi shared some of their documents on Trade-Related Aspects of Intellectual Property Rights (TRIPS). Action Aid formed part of the delegation of NGOs that went to the Ministerial Conference in Cancún. Action Aid's position papers on agriculture made a significant contribution to Malawi's position. Their position paper on TRIPS focused on the Agreement and its potential threat to food security and farmers' rights. The group feels that 'patents on genetic resources for food and agriculture pose a potential threat to the food security and the livelihoods of small-scale farmers. Patents will reduce access to seeds and genetic resources for farmers and breeders . . . They could also make seeds expensive due to royalty payments, restrictive contracts and increased commercialization.' This position paper by Action Aid Malawi supports the position of the Africa Aid group on 'no patents on life'. Also under TRIPS, given the public health crisis, especially in the face of HIV/AIDS, malaria and tuberculosis, Malawi is pushing for access to essential drugs on affordable terms.

Most of the stakeholders, both local and external, emphasized the importance of trade-related technical assistance. However for technical assistance to be more effective, external donors felt that several things have to be addressed. First, there was a need for close collaboration among donors in order to avoid any conflicts in policy recommendations. Second, workshops/seminars should be attended by participants working in the departments directly linked to trade negotiations. In other words, there is need for a filtering process for technical assistance to be more effective. Third, there should be a monitoring or a follow-up mechanism to track the progress of participants. Last, experts should spend enough time in the country to understand fully the problems that need to be addressed, as well as build reasonable institutional capacity so that the government can continue the process beyond the technical assistance life span.

4 Lessons for others (the players' views)

This paper has presented some of the views held by stakeholders and the challenges faced by Malawi as it participates in the multilateral trading system. Do small countries such as Malawi need the WTO? Yes, given the size of the country and resource constraints, the stakeholders are aware that the multilateral trading system offers many opportunities in terms of gains from trade and provides a strong rules-based structure to protect them against more powerful countries. And the importance of the multilateral trading system will become even greater as Malawi continues to integrate into the global economy.

So what are the lessons for others, and the areas to which Malawi should give priority in order to participate effectively? From Malawi's experience, lessons can be drawn on how to bring trade into development; how countries may effectively utilize technical assistance; the use of the safeguard mechanism and countervailing measures as liberalization prevails; how to address some of the constraints beyond tariffs and other border measures; and how to handle the issue of preference erosion.

The cost of compliance with WTO commitments is certainly a major issue for Malawi and many less developed countries (LDCs). Therefore it calls for more financial resources to assist in the compliance process. Countries must be aware that the WTO is not an international financial institution. Therefore there is need to bring trade into the development agenda. This could be done by linking sector-specific trade policies with development strategies and objectives, as well as linking assistance from international financial institutions such as the World Bank to the trade agenda. Mr Mtonya at the Ministry of Economic Planning and Development pointed out that Malawi's new Economic Growth Strategy includes a sector-specific agenda for trade which will be linked to development assistance.

Malawi has a valid concern that developed countries should reduce high tariffs and trade distorting subsidies. However, the stakeholders are aware that gains from trade will not only depend on the goodwill of the other members, but will also greatly depend on what Malawi does. As pointed out by the staff at the Ministry of Agriculture, 'aggressively improving the transport system, marketing systems, storage and distribution facilities, technology, addressing factors affecting the cost of inputs, access to trade and investment financing and exchange rate management' will assure even more gains.

Technical assistance to strengthen the institutional capacity of Malawi, including the development of human resource; strengthening the training of government officials; the training of trainers; and the retention of government staff who work on WTO issues are critical for Malawi to participate effectively. As iterated by staff, Malawi needs well-trained and specialist staff to cover each agreement. Technical assistance, however, should not be viewed as 'a form of financing', but there should be a mechanism to make sure that sustainability can be achieved and that trained employees are retained. Otherwise, countries will continue to receive technical assistance for the next ten to twenty years and nothing much will come out of the programmes. One important suggestion from local stakeholders is for donor agencies to assign personnel to spend a significant amount of time in relevant government departments to build sufficient institutional and human capacity. The sentiment of the local stakeholders is that the 'fly-in-fly-out' works up to a point but does not often leave much on the ground. And the funds used to pay consultants and personnel flying in and out of the country can be channelled to other activities on the ground. Also, given the understaffing situation in most of the government, more technical assistance in-house would lessen the staff shortages faced by government departments when staff members attend much needed trade policy courses and workshops.

Another point is that while the stakeholders welcome the fact that liberalization is here to stay, Malawi should also take serious precautions to make sure that their domestic markets are not wiped out. Mr Lungu at the Ministry of Agriculture gave an interesting example of what happened to the textiles and clothing industry. With the liberalization of the second-hand clothing market, the already deteriorating textiles and clothing industry was severely affected. The garments produced in Malawi have been found to be more expensive than second-hand clothing, and as a result, some of the major factories could not compete with the cheaper prices offered by the second-hand clothing industry and they were forced to close. Initially, the influx of second-hand clothing was seen as 'the best thing that ever happened to Malawi', but the consequences to the clothing industry were devastating. Although to some the closure of the major textiles and clothing factories can be viewed as 'injury', Malawi at the moment does apply anti-dumping measures to protect domestic industries and sensitive products. The good news is that Malawi is now in a process of preparing a new anti-dumping law and safeguard and countervailing measures.

In the case of trade preference, Malawi should focus its energy on how the country will adjust to the erosion brought about by the liberalization process. As mentioned earlier, there is a suggestion by some of the stake-holders that they should preserve preferences and if that fails, they should ask for some form of compensation for any loss of preference. Although these points are noble, countries should recognize that this could also be an opportunity to sell their commodities to other countries. Mr Banda at the Ministry of Trade and Industry pointed out that Malawi was already exporting more tobacco to Egypt and sugar to Kenya, a sign of market diversification.

Other lessons that Malawi could provide to other LDCs are to extend tariff bindings beyond agriculture to the manufacturing sector; increase programmes to enhance the participation of the private sector and other stakeholders so that supply-side constraints are addressed; and most importantly, to make sure that countries have missions at the WTO in Geneva.

References

Malawi Government (2003), Draft Issues Paper for the Fifth WTO Ministerial Conference, Lilongwe: Ministry of Commerce and Industry.

Malawi Government and the Integrated Framework Inter-Agency Working Group (MG and IAWG) (2003), Malawi-Integrated Framework: Diagnostic Trade Integration Study (draft).

SADC (2001). *Official SADC Trade, Industry and Investment Review*, Gaborone: SADC.

UNCTAD (2001), *TRAINS Database*, Geneva: WTO.

World Bank (2003), *World Development Indicators 2003* (CD), Washington, DC: World Bank.

WTO (2002), *Malawi: Trade Policy Review*, Geneva: WTO.

24

Malaysia: labelling regulations on natural rubber condoms and the WTO TBT Agreement

NORMA MANSOR, NOOR HASNIAH KASIM AND YONG SOOK LU*

1 The problem in context

When the Malaysian Standards Industrial Research Institute Malaysia (SIRIM), an organization designated as a national enquiry point for technical barriers to trade (TBT) in the World Trade Organisation (WTO), informed local manufacturers that the Ministry of Social Welfare of Colombia had proposed a new requirement for the labelling of natural latex condoms, a local company voiced its objection against such a requirement. The Draft Decree from the Committee on Technical Barriers to Trade (CTBT), received by the WTO on 15 May 2003, stated that 'each condom in the individual container shall bear at least the following information: manufacturer, trade name, sanitary register number, expiry date, batch number, the number of condoms contained, instructions for use of the condom, the statement that the condom is made of natural rubber latex that can cause irritation, instructions for the storage: "Store the condom in a cool dry place away from direct sunlight"'. The proposed regulation was to take effect from 15 August 2003.

Alarmed, Tharampal Singh, senior director (operations) of Medical-Latex (DUA) SDN BHD (ML), a Malaysian condom manufacturer, called Salmah Mohd Nordin, a SIRIM officer, to express his dissatisfaction with the new requirements. ML has been producing condoms for export since 1987, exporting 80 million condoms a year to Colombia, Venezuela and Ecuador; ML is in fact the biggest supplier in Latin America. Losing ground in these markets would adversely affect ML's profitability.

As far as Tharampal is concerned, the new requirements did not make sense. Since he joined the company in 1990, ML, which goes for niche markets, producing high-quality condoms, has penetrated some of the

* Faculty of Economics and Administration, University of Malaya, Kuala Lumpur.

European markets such as Greece, Spain, Portugal and France, with plans to expand to other European countries. Tharampal contends that 'ML aims for the most stringent standards and maintains a controlled environment for the manufacturing process and hence we could enter any market. We aim to fulfil the toughest standards.' He claimed that 'Any little news about allergies would hit the latex condom industry. Thus, we always have to be alert.' He insisted that 'Medical-Latex meets all major international standards such as ISO [International Organization for Standardization] 9001; EN 46001 (medical device directive); British Standards Institute (BSI); Laboratoire National D'ESSAIS (LNE). ML condoms carry quality seals from these highly reputable British and French standards organizations.'

Tharampal was then asked by SIRIM to put up a case for it to be discussed at the National Sub-committee (NSC) on the TBT Agreement. The NSC consists of the representatives of the ministries for Trade, Industry, Consumer Affairs, Health, Agriculture and Science, other regulatory agencies, national trade and industry associations and SIRIM as a secretariat. Among other things the NSC examines and formulates responses to WTO notifications.

After deliberating on ML's case a response was formulated and was as follows. 'There is too much information to be included on each individual condom pouch; the foil surface is not big enough. According to ISO 4074:2002(E) the labelling is separated into two parts:

The individual container shall bear at least the following information: identity of manufacturer, the lot number, the expiry date (year, month).
The consumer package (e.g. a folding pack) shall bear at least the general information in the official language of the country of destination (description of the condom, number of condoms contained, nominal width of the condom, trade name and address of the manufacturer, distributor, expiry date, instruction to store the condom in a cool dry place away from direct sunlight, whether the condom is lubricated or lubricant is perfumed or flavoured, lot number, the statement "the condom is made of natural rubber latex", instructions for use of the condom, instructions of how to dispose of the used condom, a statement that a condom is for single use.'

The comment continued, 'Our viewpoint is that the ISO allows the general information to be included on the consumer package (folding pack, envelope etc.) where the printing surface isn't a problem for complying with the requirement.'

The Malaysian economic story

The Malaysian economy has gone through rapid structural changes since Malaysia gained independence in 1957. It is one of the most advanced countries in the Third World and in recent years had experienced one of the highest growth rates, of about 8% per annum, from the mid-1980s until 1997, when the country was not spared the Asian economic crisis. However, it rebounded commendably, registering annual growth ranging from 4 to 5% since 1999. In the nineties, Malaysia with the other 'new tigers' was proud of its economic achievements and social development. Malaysia is a founder member of the WTO by virtue of its membership of GATT since 1957.

A broad historical account is necessary to describe the emergence of the little-known former British colony as a new industrialized country (NIC) almost half a century after independence. Agriculture was the main source of growth in the early phase of development. In the 1950s and the 1960s, the traditional export economy was renewed through a very successful programme of replanting rubber estates and rejuvenating smallholdings with more productive varieties of rubber trees. In spite of declining world prices, the natural rubber industry has been able to remain competitive with synthetic rubber.

In the 1960s and 1970s, import-substitution and export-oriented industrialization propelled economic growth. The most important source of Malaysian economic growth has been the development of a substantial oil and natural gas industry.

In the mid-1980s, however, the government through its fiscal policies adopted an all-out strategy of pursuing export markets to attract foreign direct investment (FDI) while at the same time enhancing domestic investment. Tax allowances and pioneer status were given to promote the secondary sector. Manufacturing and the growing service sectors were the engine of growth. In the 1990s the economy was sustained through improved productivity and industrial upgrading to higher value-added industries.

Malaysia has today become an export-driven economy spurred on by high technology, knowledge-based and capital-intensive industries, the result of opening itself to foreign direct investment. Malaysia aggressively and successfully promoted FDI, primarily through a government agency, the Malaysian Industrial Development Authority (MIDA). Today, its market-oriented economy, combined with an educated multilingual workforce and a well-developed infrastructure, has made Malaysia one of the largest recipients of FDI among developing countries. Malaysia has been transformed from a primary commodities producing and exporting country into a thriving modern economy, where manufactured products now account for more than 80 per cent of total exports, largely due to the role of multinational corporations (MNCs).

The rubber industry and condom manufacturing

The Malaysian rubber industry has maintained its forward march into the twenty-first century. However, because both latex and field coagulum harvested from rubber plantations are highly susceptible to degradation by contamination, rubber has to be processed into marketable forms that will allow for safe storage and marketing. Nonetheless, it has achieved overall expansion through increasing the range of products manufactured and the number of units, as well as through technological sophistication. Total rubber production in 2004 is expected to increase by 17.6%, to 1.16 million tones (in 2003 it had increased by 10.6% to 986,000 tonnes).

The importance of rubber ever since it first appeared, and the decisive role that it has played in the development of modern civilization prompted much interest in discovering its chemical composition in order to synthesize it. Through these research projects, the tyre industry saw the possibility of breaking away from the grip of the world's natural rubber supply.

Synthetic rubber may be obtained in many different ways, and there have been dramatic changes in the global rubber consumption. Table 24.1 shows Malaysia's rubber consumption by type.

Malaysia is today a leading exporter of rubber products. Its rubber product manufacturing industry began in 1921 with a modest range of products that included tyres, tubes, footwear, rubber bands and moulded rubber goods for the domestic market. At present Malaysia is the world's major exporter of rubber gloves, condoms and catheters, and its rubber products are exported to more than 140 countries.

As well as supplying the greater part of the world's latex concentrate, Malaysia has a thriving modern latex products manufacturing industry such as medical examination gloves, both household and surgical gloves, and a wide range of medical products such as catheters. Much of the world's rubber thread production is centred in Malaysia itself: thread is used in furniture webbing, elasticised panels for shoes, men's sock tops and ladies' underwear, and many of these items are made in Malaysia.

Table 24.1. *Malaysia's rubber consumption by type*

Year	Natural rubber (NR)		Synthetic rubber (SR)		Total rubber		
	Tonnes	% of world production	Tonnes	% of world production	Tonnes	NR:SR Ratio	% of world production
1990	172,997	3.33	14,595	0.15	187,592	92.2:7.8	1.3
1995	307,750	5.13	44,145	0.48	351,895	87.5:12.5	2.3
1996	360,784	5.90	46,668	0.49	407,452	88.6:11.4	2.6
1997	360,188	5.58	48,865	0.49	409,053	88.1:11.9	2.5
1998	334,059	5.08	42,560	0.43	376,619	88.7:11.3	2.3
1999	344,447	5.19	57,587	0.56	402,034	85.7:14.3	2.4
2000	363,715	4.99	55,608	0.51	419,323	86.7:13.3	2.3
2001	400,888	5.66	57,396	0.56	458,284	87.5:12.5	2.6
2002	407,884	5.51	63,150	0.59	471,034	86.6:13.4	2.6
2003	421,781	5.47	66,452	0.58	488,233	86.4:13.6	2.5

Source: MRB's quarterly rubber consumption survey, International Rubber Study Group (IRSG)

Since 1996, latex products have formed 76–80% of Malaysian exports of rubber products. Recently the condom-making industry has become important and is growing rapidly.

In fact more than a decade ago in 1991, United Press International (UPI) forecast that Malaysia was poised to become the world's leading condom producer, mainly because Malaysia has an advantage over Japan, South Korea and other countries in its ready supply of raw latex. If the goal is reached, Malaysia could dominate a significant piece of the world market, according to Lim Beng Huat, general manager of Medilatex, a manufacturer producing 170 million condoms a year. Currently, there are fourteen condom manufacturers in Malaysia.

2 The local and external players and their roles

The concept Malaysia Incorporated, which was launched in the mid-1980s, was aimed at mobilizing the public and private sectors to work together as one big unit to achieve rapid development as Malaysia aspires to be an industrialized nation. Through its fiscal policies various incentives and heavy infrastructure investments were offered by the government to support the economy and attract businesses. Playing the role of facilitating an environment for a private-sector-led growth, the government also provides a link with export markets through various agencies such as the earlier mentioned MIDA and the Malaysian External Trade Development Corporation (MATRADE). Multi-prong strategies include attracting FDI and promoting Malaysian exports internationally.

Meanwhile, to help Malaysian manufacturing companies with technology development and quality assurance, Standard Industrial Malaysia (SIM), formed in 1969, was upgraded into a vehicle for standards and industrial promotion. The agency, now called SIRIM, is entrusted with the tasks as the prime mover in industrial research and development. It also acts as a catalyst in bringing about national economic dynamism through excellence in technology and the international acceptance of Malaysian products and services. The mission of this organization is to enhance business competitiveness through technology and quality, and to fulfil the needs of the industry. Other roles include acting as the national technology development corporation and as a vehicle for technology transfer. SIRIM Berhad was established to assist the Malaysian government in institutional and technical infrastructure, its main functions being to promote and undertake scientific industrial research, to boost industrial efficiency and development, to provide technology transfer and consultancy services, to develop Malaysian standards and to promote standardization and quality assurance for greater competitiveness, and to enhance public and industrial welfare, health and safety.

SIRIM's role was further expanded when the Malaysian government in 1993 appointed it to manage the General Agreement on Tariffs and Trade (GATT, the WTO's predecessor) enquiry and notification functions. This was most appropriate because apart from being the focal point for TBT enquiries both from Malaysia and from other WTO members, SIRIM also works closely with other government agencies and the private sector in highlighting new or amended regulations/standards issued by WTO members that would have implications for Malaysia's domestic industry. Considering the private sector's reliance on WTO rights, SIRIM plays a pivotal role in ensuring that Malaysian companies are informed of any compliance requirement.

In this regard SIRIM, as mentioned by Salmah, a SIRIM officer, would ensure that 'Any notifications that we received would be disseminated to government agencies, institutions, organizations, associations and other interested parties in Malaysia through the WTO/TBT Newsletter which is published fortnightly and circulated to a mailing list of about 400 entries. The newsletter is also posted on SIRIM's website.'

To be an effective member of the WTO, Malaysia has set up the National Sub-committee (NSC) on the TBT Agreement that will examine the effective implementation of Malaysia's rights and obligations under the TBT agreement and will co-ordinate implementation issues related to the TBT with other agencies responsible for the agreement. The NSC will also monitor the operation and administration of the TBT agreement with regard to the duties of the enquiry point and act on issues or standards of export and domestic markets that are barriers to trade. The main objective of the establishment of the enquiry point is to ensure that technical requirements are transparent and to ensure that information is readily available to those who needed it, especially the traders. Other functions of the NSC regarding the TBT Agreement are co-ordinating with other agencies or ministries on responses to WTO notifications, managing Malaysia's notification to the WTO/TBT Committee and also formulating recommendations on TBT matters.

There are several other services provided by the Malaysian WTO/TBT Enquiry and Notification Point. It will assist in answering foreign enquiries on any existing or proposed Malaysian standards, regulation and conformity assessment systems. It will also help in answering domestic enquiries and any existing or proposed standards, regulations and conformity assessment systems affecting the trade of other WTO member countries and also assist in the preparation and submission of notification on Malaysia's proposed technical regulations to WTO in accordance with TBT agreement obligations.

Programmes are also arranged for regulatory agencies to enhance their awareness on notification obligations. These may include sending reminders and organizing meetings or discussions and other awareness programmes.

However, as shown in Table 24.2 on activities at the WTO/TBT Enquiry and Notification Point, the number of notifications submitted by Malaysia to the WTO Secretariat is very small; in 2003 none was submitted, in contrast to the number of notifications received from the WTO.

3 Challenges faced and the outcome

The TBT Agreement seeks to ensure that technical regulations and standards, as well as testing and certification procedures, do not create unnecessary obstacles to trade. However, it recognizes that countries have the right to establish protection, at levels they consider appropriate with a legitimate objective, for example for human, animal or plant life or health

Table 24.2. *Malaysian WTO/TBT Enquiry and Notification Point activities, 2000–3*

Activity	2000	2001	2002	2003
Notifications submitted to WTO Secretariat	3	2	1	0
Requests for notification texts:				
Malaysian notification	64	10	5	0
Foreign texts	10	150	111	73
Co-ordination of comments/views on:				
Malaysian notifications	3	1	2	0
Foreign notifications	2	0	0	2
TBT notification received from WTO for circulation	559	402	553	783
Enquiries:				
Malaysian standard/regulations	N/A	N/A	40	28
Foreign regulations	N/A	N/A	1	2

Source: Standard Management Department, SIRIM Berhad.

or the environment, and should not be prevented from taking measures necessary to ensure those levels of protection are met. However, legitimate objectives are subject to the requirement that they are not applied in a manner that constitutes a disguised restriction on international trade, mentioned in the preamble of the WTO/TBT agreement. The agreement therefore encourages countries to use international standards where these are appropriate, but it does not require them to change their levels of protection as a result of standardization. Product standards should be based on scientific information and evidence. Mandatory product standards should be based on internationally agreed standards.

Tharampal was therefore baffled when he was informed of the Colombian draft proposal. ML, an affiliated company of a German multinational corporation, the Beiersdorf group, has been producing high-premium quality condoms for export since 1987.

The production of condoms from latex is relatively simple and since 1920 has virtually remained unchanged. Each pack carries the ISO 4074, the global standardization for condoms made from natural rubber. ISO/DIS 4074 states all the requirements and specifies the test methods to be used for male condoms made from compounded natural rubber latex. The rules were set strictly because condoms are medical devices and should be produced under a good-quality management system.

The development of condoms made from other material (non-latex condoms) has been prompted by the epidemics of HIV/AIDS and other sexually transmitted diseases (STDs), the perceived shortcoming of latex condoms, the increasing incidence of allergies to latex condoms and the advent of new technologies and materials. Japan is one of the developed countries that commercially produces synthetic condoms by using synthetic rubber, which take only 7% to 8% of the world's condom market.

The ISO certification differentiates between the natural rubber condom and the synthetic one, since non-latex condoms have physical properties different from those of latex condoms. Manufacturers have had to submit detailed information, including the full range of pre-clinical data on the materials, its manufacturing process and the safety processes adopted before conducting actual clinical studies.

Hence Tharampal saw the Colombian draft regulation as being without a legitimate objective and in direct contravention of Article 2.2 of the TBT Agreement, since there is no scientific proof that natural rubber can cause allergies. In addition, Article 2.4 of the Agreement stipulates that where technical regulations are required and relevant international standards exist members should use them. As far as ML is concerned there exists a harmonized standard that it is currently adopting. This would be in line with the principles of the WTO/TBT Agreement of transparency, non-discrimination, mutual recognition, equivalence and harmonization.

Tharampal is also concerned that in the event of the enforcement of the Colombian decree ML's expenses would be adversely affected, since the redesign of the individual container of the condom would be necessary because the existing packet is too small to accommodate the proposed labelling. Furthermore, sales could be badly affected as the warning against allergies would be given undue prominence and at the same time create panic among the consumers.

SIRIM is equally baffled by the draft technical regulation as it exceeds ISO 4074:2000(E) as mentioned earlier. In addition, the imposition of technical regulations on labelling is unnecessary, since labelling can be interpreted as standard as stated in Annex 1 of the TBT Agreement, and therefore compliance is not mandatory.

The outcome

Malaysia's notification of objection against Colombia's draft decree was deliberated and recorded by the Committee on Technical Barriers to Trade

(CTBT) at the WTO in Geneva. According to procedure the country issuing the decree should respond to Malaysia's comments and there should be some form of bilateral engagements before matters are brought to the WTO's attention. The WTO Dispute Settlement Mechanism (DSM) would only intervene should there be further disputes. In this case, Ms Salmah of SIRIM sent two reminders but received no response from the Colombian government. It was therefore assumed that as a result of the action taken by Malaysia to assert its rights under the TBT agreement, Colombia had withdrawn its decree. Both ML and SIRIM believe that the matter has been resolved, since ML continues manufacturing using its original package and continues to control the market share in Colombia.

The notification from the CTBT, dated 15 May 2003, gave the final date for comments as 6 August 2003 – giving ML under three months to respond – otherwise the decree would be adopted on 15 August 2003; there were concerted efforts by ML and SIRIM to register their objections expeditiously. Other than the routine expenses incurred in communicating with SIRIM and other government agencies ML did not have to spend on marketing campaigns or road shows to rebut the possible negative repercussions of the Colombian decree.

4 Lessons for developing countries

Recent decades have seen rapid growth in the world economy. This growth has been driven in part by the even faster rise in international trade. Malaysia is the fourteenth largest trading nation, and in its effort to achieve its development goals it has placed great emphasis on public- and private-sector collaboration. Tharampal of ML expressed this when he said, 'The irony about the WTO is that on one hand free trade is encouraged, yet it is possible for each country to come up with new conditions that were never there. So, to really benefit from the WTO it is very important for businesses to work closely with government, because businesses do not have the expertise and ready resources to negotiate internationally. Hence we have to depend on assistance from the government, given that the WTO is a body of governments.' Hence it is critical to promote collaboration in developing standards for the manufacturing fraternity exemplified by ML. Also, it is appropriate to appreciate the regular meetings held between SIRIM and various business associations such as the Federation of Malaysian Manufacturers (FMM), the

Malaysian International Chamber of Commerce and Industry (MICCI) and the Malaysian Employers Federation (MEF).

'ML is very big in research and development both in our processing and the product. As far as processing is concerned pro-active measures are taken to steer quality in every stage of the manufacturing process. At ML every member of the staff is trained and committed to achieve consistent quality in our product manufacture. Continuous training in quality management and skills for all levels of staff ensures increased productivity and value adds to our product', said Tharampal.

He added that being a member of business associations is equally important: 'We are fully committed to the development of the medical device industry in Malaysia, ML is active in the Association of Malaysian Medical Industries (AMMI). We participate actively in FMM, MATRADE, MICCI, Malaysian–German Chamber of Commerce and Industry, Malaysian Rubber Products Association (MRPMA) and MEF. By becoming a member of these associations we are exposed to changes in other industries that might directly or indirectly affect us.'

One point that came across very strongly in ML's case is the importance of obtaining certification from international bodies on standards and quality assurance. This is crucial, especially for products meant for export markets. A producer has to ensure the correct certification for manufactured products to avoid compromising on quality and non-compliance with international standards. Once this is attained any new regulations or requirements imposed by member countries are easily surmountable.

In ML's case it went beyond certification as it also participated in promoting quality standards internationally. Together with SIRIM and the Malaysian government ML is involved in developing quality standards for condoms in the international work group for ISO TC 157.

Governments should develop expertise on the various trade requirements of the WTO and enhance their capacity to meet these requirements. If they are met there is little need for DSM/WTO involvement. The national government has also to develop the capacity to negotiate internationally. The yawning gap in terms of expertise between developed and developing nations contributed to poor trading terms, thereby creating tensions in WTO negotiations.

In Malaysia there is still room for improvement. For instance, Malaysia's notifications submitted to the WTO are very small in number. Malaysian companies, in general, view the WTO as promoting the developed countries' agenda. Therefore agencies such as SIRIM, MIDA and MATRADE should increase their efforts in raising awareness of the rights of WTO members, including obligations and notification rights that could be resolved through the WTO.

Tharampal, however, had one suggestion on the role of SIRIM as the TBT national focal point: 'It would be more effective if SIRIM had a column on WTO updates in a local newspaper – this channel would reach wider members of the public and industry.'

25

Malaysia: strategies for the liberalization of the services sector

LIM CHZE CHEEN*

As Malaysia begins to position itself strategically in the knowledge-based economy, the services sector has been earmarked as its next engine of growth. This idea, in its rudimentary form at least, has been bounced around the discussion circles of policy-makers, policy scholars and various other intellectuals involved in influencing national policy for more than a decade now. Indeed, the importance of the services sector to further Malaysia's economic growth has been increasingly highlighted in the country's various development plans.

1 The services sector in Malaysia: a brief update

The tradability of services is set to be enhanced further by the development of new transmission technologies facilitating the supply of services (e.g. electronic banking, tele-education, tele-medicine), the deregulation of monopolies (e.g. voice telephony), and the gradual liberalization of hitherto regulated sectors such as financial services and transport combined with changes in consumer preferences. The share of services in the Malaysian gross domestic product (GDP) has expanded from 48.8% in 1987 to 60.8% in 2003, if construction services are included. This simple picture of services growth, painted by existing statistics, can only become more vivid in the near future.

In terms of WTO commitments, Malaysia has signed the agreement under the single undertaking rule and General Agreement on Trade in Services (GATS) as part of the whole package. Under GATS, which follows a positive list approach, Malaysia is expected to identify services sectors or sub-sectors and the modes of supply in which it is willing to make

* Malaysian Institute of Economic Research.

commitments through the process of 'scheduling', as well as to indicate any limitations on market access and national treatment.

As of mid-2005, Malaysia had received requests from twenty-one countries. Generally, the requests received covered a wide range of professional services, advertising, news agency services, telecommunications and computer-related services, and focused on areas such as the liberalization of additional sectors not committed under GATS, for example further liberalization or the elimination of restrictions placed under the current commitments (for example, limits on foreign equity and intra-corporate transferees) and transparency of policies and domestic regulatory procedures (e.g. visa approval, incentives, licensing). On the other hand, Malaysia has also forwarded its own list of requests for market access to forty-five countries covering architecture, engineering, accountancy, construction and telecommunication services. These are areas where Malaysian services providers have demonstrated the capacity to export.

In terms of sectoral commitments, foreign companies in the field of accounting, auditing, bookkeeping and taxation, as well as engineering services (joint ventures only) could enter through local partnerships or joint ventures, and their equity in the company should not exceed 30%. The same goes for distributive services such as the wholesale and retail trades, which Malaysia has yet to list in its national schedule of offers under GATS. Regarding legal services, foreign lawyers are not allowed to provide services in Malaysia. However, foreign legal firms can do so through companies incorporated in Labuan. Foreigners in the medical field can practise in private hospitals controlled by Malaysian companies. In the realm of information, communications and technologies (ICT), a Multimedia Super Corridor (MSC)-registered company can be fully owned by a foreign company.

2 Challenges for the Malaysian services sector in the wake of GATS

The adoption of WTO trade rules in services presents us with opportunities as well as threats. One thing which is certain is that the globalization process together with participation in the WTO will reduce the areas of domestic policies which can be manoeuvred, in Malaysia and other countries. In order to enjoy greater business opportunities arising from the global liberalization of services, Malaysian services industries will have to adapt to a more open market environment. In this context, the sector needs to build up efficiency, productivity, and thus competitiveness, through essentially market means as it becomes increasingly open to foreign participation and global best practice standards, including transparency of rules and regulations.

Although the pressure on Malaysia to liberalize further will always be present, the GATS provides the flexibility to open up fewer sectors and to impose specified conditionalities in the concessions on market access. Despite such flexibility, the main concern for the policy makers is that there is only a limited number of services suppliers which are competitive by international standards. The Malaysian Ministry of International Trade and Industry (MITI) agrees that the services suppliers need to be ready and approach the ongoing negotiations from the perspectives of both the external and domestic markets.

The gradual liberalization measures will inject some elements of competition and prepare suppliers to the domestic market. The commitments undertaken by Malaysia under the GATS would eventually lead to a greater presence of foreign services providers in the country. This is envisaged as creating stiffer competition to local providers, but the extent of such competition would depend, in part, on the type, quality and price competitiveness of services offered by the foreign providers. Although Malaysia has yet to make any offer in certain areas, there is already a foreign presence in Malaysia. For example, Malaysian legal practitioners are already making good indirect use of alliances with foreign legal firms.

While the multinational corporations (MNCs) and large enterprises are generally ready to deal with changes in the global landscape, most of the small and medium-sized enterprises (SMEs) still require capacity building to prepare themselves.[1] Because of the incipient stage of development of these SMEs, they will find it tough to compete in the domestic market, let alone taking advantage of the vast opportunities associated with services market openings. These SMEs, like their larger counterparts, are also adjusting and learning to cope with WTO commitments in the area of GATS, TRIPS (the Agreement on Trade-Related Aspects of Intellectual Property Rights) and other regulatory changes that are needed for compliance. An indiscriminate liberalization of the services sector can thus create a lot of problems for the SMEs, resulting in their closures, net job loss and so on.

On the other side of the coin, the ongoing negotiations will provide suppliers to the international market with the opportunity to seek further

---

[1] Although it is often suggested that only large enterprises have the capacity and capability to export their services, there might very well be some scope for SMEs in this area.

market access in both the developed and developing countries. However, these suppliers encounter various problems as well. There are two aspects of cross-border supply problems. internal and external challenges faced by services suppliers. The internal aspect deals with the capacity and capability of the services suppliers, in terms of financial, technical and human resources. These providers need to explore ways to position themselves better globally. Externally, the services exporters would benefit significantly from understanding the market destination, with respect to trade and non-trade barriers, as well as business and social culture. For example, in the area of professional services, a plethora of regulations in the guise of economic needs tests (and local market tests and management needs tests), processing of visa applications, residency requirements, recognition of educational qualifications, social security contributions, minimum capital and investment required for commercial presence, local partners, profit repatriation and other hindrances stand in the way of obtaining market access.

Thus the challenge is to reconcile the need to protect the national interest in these sectors with the need to benefit from services liberalization. The developments mentioned thus far bring to the fore new challenges for the Malaysian economy, strengthening the need for comprehensive strategies to be formulated to address them.

3 Policies and strategic initiatives to prepare the services sector

In preparing the services industry to meet the challenges posed by the globalization and liberalization process under the WTO, the Malaysian government has developed and explored various strategies to enhance the competitiveness of the Malaysian services sector. Some sectors, such as tourism, private education, promoted manufacturing services, health and construction services, have been able to capitalize on greater market liberalization, while others may face problems adjusting to the evolving landscape. These strategic initiatives are aimed at preparing services suppliers domestically and assisting thriving services exporters.

While Vision 2020 provides the general direction of Malaysia's development aspirations, the specific strategies involved are contained in the two Industrial Master Plans,[2] the three Outlook Perspective Plans, and

---

[2] The Second Industrial Master Plan (IMP2) promulgates a two-pronged development strategy – the Manufacturing Plus Plus strategy and the cluster-based development strategy. In broad terms, the cluster-based approach aims to promote specific industries in an integrated

the various five-year Malaysia Plans. Policies to promote specific services industries, such as shipping, education, tourism and, more recently, ICT, already exist. All that is needed, albeit crucially, is to tie these various industry-specific policies together in a coherent and synergistic manner so as to guarantee their efficacy, thereby providing a powerful boost to the country's economic growth and development. In the meantime, the Malaysian Industrial Development Authority (MIDA) would be responsible for the development and promotion of the services sector in the country, except for financial services (Central Bank of Malaysia, BNM) and utilities (Malaysian Communication and Multimedia Commission, MCMC).

In architectural terms, the successful construction of a building depends in large part on the quality of the blueprint and its execution. Likewise, in creating a new service-oriented economy, there is a crucial need to develop a 'services master plan' to guide its development. Up until now, the various planning documents have presented the various services as separate sub-sectors whose roles were regarded as social or facilitative in nature. As a result, the development of services in the past lacked coherence and, more often than not, proceeded in an ad hoc and fragmented manner. Although a framework for the coherent development of the services sector that takes these into consideration is still in the making, the government is profiling the services sector in an attempt to understand the sector better, while the Department of Statistics is looking into ways of measuring the sector more effectively.

To prepare services providers, one of the first steps undertaken is the creation of awareness and dissemination of information on GATS. This includes the provision of briefings and updates on the latest developments with regard to the process of globalization and liberalization, as well as making available to members critical information related to liberalization and the export of services on a timely basis. For example, the WTO Technical Trade Barrier Notifications issued by the Standards and Industrial Research Institute of Malaysia (SIRIM), which provides updates on a regular basis, would be useful. Furthermore, it would be useful to obtain feedback through periodic surveys on the needs of the services providers with regard to liberalization and WTO issues (informational

and synergized manner to spur the development of higher-value-added activities, while the Manufacturing Plus Plus strategy calls for the participation of domestic producers and service suppliers in the whole value chain of a product, from the initial stage of product design and prototyping to the production stage of processing and assembly and, finally, to distribution and marketing.

WTO digest) and export-readiness, and then fine-tune or formulate the necessary strategic response based on the findings.

Conversations with chambers of commerce and trade associations reveal that most Malaysian services providers are aware of the WTO and GATS but lack understanding of the implication of the world trading body for their businesses. Respective ministries related to the services sector are involved in the capacity-building efforts one way or another. It is thus essential for the ministries concerned to be in constant discussion with the various professional bodies, chambers of commerce, business associations, and key industry players on the services Malaysia can open up to foreigners and the services in which Malaysian providers can venture overseas. According to Stewart Forbes, executive director of Malaysia International Chamber of Commerce and Industries (MICCI), 'MICCI engages government at every opportunity to accelerate the liberalization process in the belief that this will attract new technology and processes, which can be passed on to Malaysians and act as catalysts for subsequent development'.

Moreover, MICCI's president, Jon Chadwick, feels that 'greater contact between private sectors internationally can only assist in developing a better awareness of business opportunities, a better understanding of doing business in different countries and an ability to find business matches more easily'. In this respect MICCI signed a Memorandum of Understanding (MoU) with the Chamber of Commerce of the Northern Territory (CCNT), Australia, which provides an international business linkage that it hoped would ensure that businesses in Malaysia would be aware and kept informed of trade and investment opportunities. More of such international alliance would serve as a good training ground for Malaysian companies towards full services liberalization.

As mentioned earlier, SMEs are likely to be on the receiving end. In the light of this and the fact that SMEs are most likely to play a bigger role in the services-oriented economy, efforts to encourage SMEs to concentrate on developing specific skills and competencies for the export market are most important. SMIDEC has an array of policies to promote SMEs such as the Global Supplier Programme, the factory audit scheme and Enterprise 50.

MICCI has also launched an SME development programme in the second half of 2004 to include elements such as (i) increased awareness of branding importance and assistance through a branding award for SMEs; (ii) a series of dedicated chamber-to-chamber linkages through IT with a number of other countries so as to offer new and more specific partnership opportunities to smaller companies seeking to develop overseas linkages; (iii) low-cost IT-based trade services aimed at increasing SME exposure and international credibility. The Associated Chinese Chambers of Commerce and Industry of Malaysia (ACCCIM) has set up the Science, Technology and Innovation Committee to assist SMEs by participating actively at meetings or dialogues organized by relevant government ministries and to contribute to government's formulation of policies and implementation of programmes and activities to enhance the competitiveness of SMEs.

In the context of market access, various government agencies have identified services sectors where there is current potential for exports. According to the Malaysia External Trade Development Corporation (MATRADE), these include healthcare services, education, construction and related professional services such as engineering and architectural services, printing and publishing services, as well as IT services. In line with Malaysia's needs and priorities, the government has autonomously liberalized some of these services sector.

Effectiveness in promoting services also depends significantly on the state of export readiness of the Malaysian services sector. Before the government can design programmes to enhance export capability and capacity, they need to identify the 'what, who, where' candidates, that is, what services to export, who is ready or at least keen to export and where to export to. After the identification process and the setting up of an extensive database for ease of use by budding exporters in the future, the government (through MATRADE) can educate services exporters to be aware of and compliant with the standards and guidelines in the destination market, in accordance with the WTO rules.

With the objective of supporting and promoting the export of services, the Malaysian government has set up two bodies, the NAPSEC (National Professional Services Export Council), which is responsible for the promotion of export of professional services, and the PSDC (Professional Services Development Corporation), which is tasked with the responsibility of providing capacity building to the professional services sector. The representation of various professional bodies in these two entities is a reflection of the close collaboration between the public and private sectors to promote the export of services.

The key agenda of the PSDC is to enhance the skills and knowledge of all Malaysian professionals and to promote their marketability in an increasingly borderless world. The PSDC believes that Malaysian professionals will need to stand out in the global trading sector of professional services. For them to be recognised and respected as competent, experienced, skilful and dynamic professionals, it is imperative that the PSDC develop their capability and capacity (see Box 25.1 for the role of the PSDC). According to the PSDC, the local professional services providers lack financial strength, track record, exposure, marketing skills and branding. Besides training, the PSDC is putting these professional services providers together in a consortium in bidding for projects abroad. This would serve to strengthen the providers by leveraging on each other's complementary skills.

On the other hand, the NAPSEC, which will complement the PSDC, deliberates on issues, mainly incentives for the services export sector and the identification of priority markets for the export services (see Box 25.2 for NAPSEC's functions). MATRADE, in co-operation with the relevant professional bodies and government agencies, such as the Ministry of Health, the Ministry of Education, the Construction Industry Development Board and the Ministry of Entrepreneurial Development, has organized promotional activities overseas for the promotion of the services sector.

Even Malaysia's usually conservative professional bodies, the legal, medical and engineering fraternities, are beginning to allow their members to utilize IT and the Internet to promote their services, in preparation for the eventual liberalization of services under the ASEAN Free Trade Area (AFTA) and WTO agreements. Moreover, for local services providers to venture abroad, mutual recognition arrangements (MRAs) would need to be negotiated between Malaysia and the foreign countries, ensuring harmonized benchmarks for the services rendered.

In addition, MITI has decided to repeal the Promotion of Investments Act, 1986 (PIA) and replace it with a new act including wider scope for the development of the services sector, as well as fine-tune the Industrial Co-ordination Act, 1975 (ICA) to ensure that procedures and processes add to competitiveness. The government has also identified other constraints to be reviewed such as variations in the granting of incentives, anomalies in conditions for applications of incentives and the lack of clarity on effective dates for tax relief under Pioneer Status.

Changing the attitude of 'waiting for governments' should be the next step towards dealing with the WTO. The services providers should come forward and take a pro-active role and lead government policies in countering challenges to the domestic economy. The global trends in business have exposed a nation's industry to the test of the international standards of productivity. According to Mustapa Mohamed, the Minister in the Prime Minister's Department, as quoted in the *New Straits Times* of

25.1 A background to the PSDC

The setting up of the Professional Services Development Corporation (PSDC) was initially proposed by the National Economic Action Council (NEAC), with the aim of assisting professionals in the construction industry to meet the challenges of globalization. The proposal was subsequently approved by the cabinet and the PSDC was established on 30 April 2002, with initial capital obtained from the Ministry of Finance Incorporated.

Currently, the PSDC looks into the interests of the professional bodies in Malaysia – such as engineering, architectural, legal, accounting, planning, surveying, medical and pharmaceutical – which collectively have more than 80,000 registered members.

The PSDC is tasked to assist firms to shift from providing low-value-to high-value-added services, where this 'value migration' could be done systematically and through a concerted effort. The aim is gradually to create a unique Malaysian brand of multi-disciplinary professionals to perform in the international arena. Among the strategies undertaken are branding, marketing and promoting the Malaysian brand of professionals to other countries; establishing Malaysia as a centre for the capacity- and capability-building of professionals who are competent global players; and establishing Malaysia as an information hub for the enhancement of the intellectual capital of professionals.

To operationalize the strategies, the PSDC would encourage the use of research and development output; promoting the use of best practices; strengthen financial, marketing, management and communications skills through systematic training and continuous re-learning; establish strategic alliances and international networking; promote international accreditation for professional services providers; and maintain an effective representation in the WTO and other similar international bodies. In addition, the PSDC board members provide a wide wealth of knowledge and experience, as well as an excellent track record on the local and international scenes.

In short, the PSDC aspires to be the service provider in capacity building to both foreign and local professionals, the point of reference for professional services development and enhancement (a voice for the professionals and an information hub for all local professionals), and an international hub for professional services' networking and partnering.

Source: Information obtained from the PSDC.

25.2 A background to NAPSEC

To assist MATRADE in drawing up programmes and approaches in promoting the services sector, NAPSEC (the National Professional Services Export Council) was launched by the Minister of International Trade and Industry on 20 August 2001. NAPSEC serves as an advisory council to the MATRADE (the Secretariat for NAPSEC) board of directors on matters relating to the export of professional services. It comprises representatives from the relevant professional bodies as well as the public sector. The professional bodies involved are architects, constructors, surveyors, engineers, accountants, lawyers and healthcare. With the participation of these bodies, NAPSEC provides a forum for obtaining private-sector views and inputs in the formulation of strategies and programmes for the export of professional services.

The terms of reference of NAPSEC are

to formulate and review national strategies and promotion programmes relating to the export of professional services, including construction services;

to recommend and facilitate funding for the export of professional services;

to formulate strategies to increase participation by Malaysian professionals or companies in overseas projects funded by international lending agencies;

to gather and disseminate information related to market opportunities;

to review and recommend incentives for the export of professional services;

to compile databases or directories on export-ready professional services providers with support and feedback from the industry;

to develop databases on market access issues and regulations affecting export of professional services, including facilitating mutual recognition agreements;

to identify approaches to publicize the skills and capabilities of the professional services, including construction services, in international markets;

to monitor global developments and their implications for Malaysian professional services exports; and

to monitor developments and provide inputs towards the formulation of Malaysia's position and commitment in WTO negotiations in the professional services sector.

Source: Information obtained from NAPSEC.

10 May 2004, 'there are quite a few Malaysian companies that have made good abroad, but they are small in number. To build strong companies and strong brands, companies cannot merely rely on government handouts and protection.'

With respect to human resources development, there are currently gaps in terms of what is needed to develop the services sector in Malaysia, particularly those related to highly skilled human resources in the various services industries. Mustapa suggested that 'radical changes to the country's education system are both necessary and inevitable, but this will inevitably take some time'. While currently high investments in the education sector should ameliorate the human resource problem in the medium and long term, the increasing mobility of people and the tradability of services leave Malaysia with little time to train effective human resource in the services sector. Hence a succinct and effective action plan is needed, to prepare and equip local undergraduates with competencies and skills to be globally competitive.

Coupled with the government's efforts to nurture the business community through a variety of entrepreneurial support services, MICCI has also started a series of 'industry–university' dialogues to address directly the issue of workplace readiness among graduates, and a soft skills development programme is being explored with an international leadership institute.

The government needs to ensure that domestic regulations are WTO-compliant as well as WTO-consistent. Working closely with the relevant bodies is crucial. A periodic review of the regulations, particularly on professional standards and elements of transparency, would give services providers a big helping hand in preparing for liberalization. For instance, in the area of accounting, Malaysia continues to maintain its philosophy of convergence with international accounting standards, harmonizing its standards by minimizing differences to the greatest extent possible and modelling its standards very closely on international standards.

On the multilateral front, Malaysia has always pushed for the Emergency Safeguard Measures (ESM) provision in GATS, which calls on WTO members to negotiate on measures that can be used temporarily to address the adverse impact of the increased inflow of services imports into the domestic market. Current negotiations are focused on developing modalities for ESM. Malaysia, together with some ASEAN members, submitted a proposal on possible mechanisms. The ESM is important in offering confidence to countries, particularly developing nations, in progressively liberalizing their services sector and imposing temporary safeguard measures, if needed, to prevent irreparable damage to domestic industries.

4 Conclusion

Malaysia is currently experiencing a 'shifting of gears' within the economic engine. While it is acknowledged that making the various structural adjustments necessary to realize its goal of creating a service-oriented economy will undoubtedly be a painful process, it is, ultimately, necessary.

To reiterate, a policy framework and strategies for the development of the services sector are vital for Malaysia's economy to continue to grow and develop. Crucial for the success of these policies and strategies is a supportive physical and human infrastructure. More than the agriculture or manufacturing sectors, the services sector is highly dependent on the abilities and know-how of people. Therefore human resources development must be an integral part of any services sector development plan.

The services industry needs to have a level playing field when competing with foreign services suppliers. While pressing for such privileges at the multilateral front, it is necessary for them to consider domestic reforms in various services sectors where increased competition is likely to surface in the years ahead. The WTO, in this context, provides the ambience for the creation of a credible and reliable system of international trade (in services) rules. It is important to note that services-sector liberalization is not independent of other facets of the economy, for example investment liberalization. And there are many benefits to be gained from recognizing the complementarity between efforts in these areas and undertaking effective actions. The services industry players need to undertake a proactive role rather than a reactive one and take advantage of the system.

Bibliography

Bank Negara Malaysia (1995), *Annual Report*, Kuala Lumpur: Government Printers.
Mahathir Bin Mohamad (1991), 'Malaysia: The Way Forward', working paper presented at the Inaugural Meeting of the Malaysian Business Council, Kuala Lumpur, 28 Feb. Available at http://www.epu.jpm.my/epu-mservis-v2020.html.
Ministry of Finance (1999), *Economic Report*, Kuala Lumpur: Government Printers.
Ministry of International Trade and Industry (MITI) (1996), *Second Industrial Master Plan 1996–2005*, Kuala Lumpur: Zainon Kassim.

Ministry of International Trade and Industry, Malaysia (MITI), *Annual Report*, various years.

National Economic Action Council (NEAC) (1998), *National Economic Recovery Plan: Agenda for Action*, Kuala Lumpur: Economic Planning Unit, Prime Minister's Department.

Raja Zaharaton bte. Raja Zainal Abidin (1996), 'Services Industries as Source of Economic Growth', paper presented at the National Outlook Conference organized by the Malaysian Institute of Economic Research (MIER), Kuala Lumpur, 3–4 Dec.

Romer, Paul (2000), 'Perpetual Growth', speech given at the World Knowledge Forum 2000, Seoul, 17 Oct.

Saifuddin, Sadna (2004), 'Mustapa Outlines Eight Key Areas for Malaysia to Focus On', *New Straits Times*, 10 May 2004.

Sieh, Lee Mei Ling (1991), 'Services in Malaysia: On the Threshold of a New Era', paper presented at the National Outlook Conference organized by the Malaysian Institute of Economic Research (MIER), Kuala Lumpur, 3–4 Dec.

Sieh, Lee Mei Ling (1994), 'The Role of Services in Development: The Case of Malaysia', in *Malaysia's Development Experience – Changes and Challenges*, Kuala Lumpur: INTAN, pp. 726–49.

Sieh, Lee Mei Ling (2002), 'The Services Sector as an Engine for Growth: Niches for Malaysia', paper presented at the National Outlook Conference organized by the Malaysian Institute of Economic Research (MIER), Kuala Lumpur, 17–18 Dec.

26

Mauritius: co-operation in an economy evolving for the future

ANDREW L. STOLER*

1 The problem in context

In 2004 Mauritius, a small island state located thousands of kilometres from its major markets, was facing two major challenges: the probable erosion of preferential treatment for its main export product (sugar) and a serious disruption to its textile and apparel industry, as a result of the impending expiration of the global restraint system that encouraged producers to seek out locations that could benefit from marginal quota allocations. In addition to the likelihood of less favourable access for sugar in the European Communities (EC), the Mauritian sugar industry faced the prospect of stiff competition in the future from Brazil and new-to-market entrants benefiting from the EC's 'Everything but Arms' (EBA) initiatives.

Many of the island nation's problems could have been anticipated at the time it underwent a WTO trade policy review in 2001. Paragraph 20 of the WTO Secretariat's Executive Summary put the situation well at that time:

> Mauritius' participation in the multilateral trading system and in various regional agreements reflects its interests as a small, export-oriented economy with advantages in a few products, sugar, textiles and clothing in particular. As part of its economic success is due to preferential market access granted by major trading partners, Mauritius is taking steps to adjust to changes in this international environment.[1]

Notwithstanding its considerable geographic disadvantage and the shocks sustained by the traditional pillars of its economy, Mauritius is

---

* Executive Director, Institute for International Business, Economics and Law, University of Adelaide.
[1] WTO Secretariat, *Trade Policy Review – Mauritius*, Document WT/TPR/S/90, 5 Oct. 2001, Geneva: World Trade Organization.

a success story. The degree of success achieved is particularly evident when this country is compared to other island states with similar resource limitations.

No less a judge than the Director-General of the WTO, Supachai Panitchpakdi, commented when he visited Mauritius in March 2004, 'One can quite reasonably ask – why did a small island developing country, heavily dependent on a single commodity, vulnerable to terms of trade shocks, situated at a considerable distance from world markets and faced with a rapidly growing population, succeed – where other better endowed countries have failed?'

This case study of Mauritius, based on background research and interviews conducted in Port Louis in May 2004, attempts to examine the basis for this success and to explore the future direction of the economy.

2 The local and external players and their roles

Mauritius is a multi-racial environment where the official language of business, English, is mixed freely by locals with a French-based patois that most appear to use in their day-to-day dealings with friends and colleagues. The differing ethnic backgrounds of the population, which in other parts of the world so often give rise to political strife and economic discrimination, are embraced positively in Mauritius and seem to have been melded into a distinct local culture.

One cannot help but be impressed by the degree to which the business community and government in Mauritius collaborate on projects designed to improve the country's economic and trade prospects. There is a long-standing tradition in Mauritius of addressing problems and opportunities through institutional arrangements that bring together main players from the private sector and relevant government agencies. The Chamber of Commerce was already established in the mid-nineteenth century and the Mauritius Chamber of Agriculture opened its doors in 1853.

The single most important co-ordinating body for the private sector in Mauritius is the Joint Economic Council (JEC), established in the early 1970s shortly after the country gained independence. Although dialogue between the JEC and the government was hampered initially by mutual suspicion, the body has evolved over time into an ideal forum for sharing new ideas as well as developing shared views of problems and how best to pursue the country's economic development. According to Jean Noël Humbert, the general secretary of the Mauritius Chamber of Agriculture, it was in the JEC that discussion was first initiated on turning Port Louis into a regional seafood hub (discussed below) and where the government agreed on the need to fast-track both seafood related investment approvals and fisheries permits in order to remove any practical difficulties to making the vision a reality.

Close government–private-sector co-operation is also reflected in the country's approach to policy development in areas such as trade negotiations under WTO auspices. In this regard, a standing co-ordinating committee oversees the work of nine different sub-committees where government and the private sector share responsibility for policy development. Humbert, for example, chairs the sub-committee that oversees policy development relating to trade and environment.

Crisis management is another important role of the institutional structures evolved in Mauritius. The Sugar Sector Strategic Plan (2001–5) was developed and discussed through these government–industry groupings. The non-sugar strategic plan was also formulated within these structures, as have been the various initiatives to deal with necessary adjustment in the textiles and clothing sector.

Mahmood Cheeroo, the secretary general of the Mauritius Chamber of Commerce and Industry, says that the Mauritian economy has necessarily been open and export-oriented from the start. After serious difficulties in the late 1970s, when Mauritius was the first to adjust under an IMF standby agreement, a strong government with a political mandate undertook a tough restructuring campaign and, with a structured and co-operative buy-in from the business community, charted a course for strong export-led growth in the 1980s.

Cheeroo was quick to point out that while government–industry collaboration has produced a number of sectoral success stories over the years, there also have been policy failures. An effort to cultivate rice on the island was unsuccessful, as was an attempt to develop the country as a centre for light engineering in the region. Most importantly, however, in Cheeroo's view is that the people of Mauritius are not afraid to keep experimenting and taking chances on new ideas. Where there have been real problems or failures, the people involved in the project were generally not prepared to make a total commitment to its success.

3 Challenges faced and outcomes

Mauritius is situated at a considerable distance from international markets with significant purchasing power. Transportation costs are onerous and market development can be expensive. The country has benefited importantly over the past thirty years from preferential arrangements for sugar purchases by the EC as well as from the fact that the quota restraint system for international trade in textiles and apparel helped to create a significant garment production industry on the island. But the basis for these long-standing arrangements is subject to challenge, and both the Mauritian government and the business community have accepted the fact that eventual change is inevitable and that new routes to economic prosperity need to be explored and developed.

Overcoming the disadvantages of distance: the tourism sector

Supachai pinpointed a major element when he alluded to the problems faced by small developing countries thousands of kilometres away from major markets. It is obvious to anyone who has had the pleasure of visiting Mauritius that it has major potential as a tourist destination. The question is how to develop this potential in a way that yields the maximum benefit for the local economy. Through an interview with Patrick Y.-S. Yip Wang Wing, Director of Fiscal Policies in the Mauritian Ministry of Finance and Economic Development, it was possible for the author to gain an understanding of what has been a successful strategy to develop a high-margin tourism business.

Some considerations pertinent to this strategy are obvious. Mauritius is a relatively small island with a fragile ecology and environment, especially in areas likely to attract tourist investment. Additionally, apart from the South African market, Mauritius is a long way from sources of tourists who are likely to spend significant amounts of money on beach holidays. Yip Wang Wing explained that an analysis of this situation had led to the adoption of what seems to be a very sensible national policy in respect of tourism. The official policy calls for 'low-impact', 'high-end' tourism, meaning that the ecological/environmental impact of tourist sites will be low and the tourists visiting Mauritius are likely to spend generously while in the country.

Given the cost of travelling the long distance to Mauritius combined with the many other competing destinations between Mauritius and its main cash market (Europe) that are easier and cheaper to reach, Mauritian planners recognized from the outset that the attraction of the facilities provided would need to outweigh the cost of the air tickets. In order to realize its goal, the country needs to be able to attract the investment in the tourism sector that will produce high-quality resorts.

Yip Wang Wing explained the investment strategy along the following lines.

Where the government approves a significant investment in the tourism sector, accelerated investment and amortization allowances form an important part of the package from the start. Approved investors in the sector can amortize the cost of their investment in hotel facilities over just four years and in the case of new investments, 25% of the investment is allowed as a special credit.

In addition to making certain that the right investors put the desired levels of investment into tourism in Mauritius, governmental authorities also concern themselves with the standard of service in approved high-end hotels. Measures are in place to ensure that qualified hotel schools and hotel management certification requirements are met in the sector.

These efforts appear to be paying handsome dividends. Tourism is the third-largest source of foreign exchange earnings for the country and accounts for around 8% of total employment.[2] Mauritius' international airport has registered a growth in passenger traffic of around 8% a year in recent years.[3]

Regional relations: positioning Mauritius as a strategic hub

At the time of the author's visit to Mauritius in May 2004, the country's Prime Minister, Paul Bérenger, was on an official visit to Mozambique. A major impetus for the visit was the Mauritian plan to create a regional 'seafood hub' in Port Louis. Both Mauritius and Mozambique possess vast exclusive maritime zones. In the Mauritius controlled zone, tuna fishing has produced good results but many other species are close to exhaustion. Meanwhile, other countries in the region that have greater stocks of other species often lack the technology or infrastructure to process the catch. The notion of co-operating in the development of a rationalized regional 'hub' project was laid out by the Prime Minister in his comments to the press in Maputo. 'Mauritius has the advantage of having a highly developed free port that will facilitate the transformation and processing of fisheries products, with substantial local value added before the products are exported to European and American markets.'[4]

The fisheries sector is not the only area where Mauritian industries are seeking co-operation with Mozambique and other regional neighbours in the development of value-added processing 'hubs'. Mozambique has

<hr>

[2] Ibid., p. 71.   [3] Ibid., p. 78.   [4] *L'Express*, 28 May 2004, p. 3 (author's translation).

abundant and productive land that Mauritius lacks and Mauritian enterprises are busy building productive relationships. One Mauritian company, Happy World, inaugurated a new poultry production facility and abattoir in the course of the Prime Minister's trade mission. Another firm, the Food and Allied Industries Group, directs an agro-industrial complex in Mozambique focused on the manufacture of wheat flour products and noodles. New opportunities are being sought out constantly. Humbert, who accompanied the Prime Minister on the trade mission, was quoted on his departure for Mozambique as stating that 'We are leaving with nothing specific in mind. We are going to study the possibilities and see what they have to offer to us. We will see what opportunities present themselves when we get there.'[5]

Working with the neighbours is not free of problems. Among the challenges in Mozambique cited by more than one of those interviewed for this case study are rampant corruption, a serious lack of adequate infrastructure and the need to work in the Portuguese language.

Dealing with distance: the transport sector

The efforts being made by Mauritius to position itself as an economic hub are complicated by serious logistics competition from Johannesburg and Durban, in South Africa. In order to keep the harbour of Port Louis in the market as an effective player, the government and private sector have worked hard to keep down costs. The Mauritius Marine Authority (MMA) has expanded and modernized the port facilities in recent years and periodically studies new ways of cutting costs. A recent study, referred to as the 'dwell time for cargo' study, focused on how to remove identified bottlenecks and move vessels in and out of the harbour in as short a period as possible. The MMA periodically revises port tariffs to reflect market conditions. A programme designed to increase the handling level to twenty-five 'twenty-foot equivalent units' (TEUs) per hour by 2005 is contributing to an improvement in labour productivity in the port.

The sugar sector: making the most of a changing environment

Historically, sugar has been very important for Mauritius, and there can be no doubt that the country could not have reached its current level of economic development were it not for the many years of preferential

---

[5] *L'Express*, 26 May 2004, p. 15 (author's translation).

sales of sugar to the European Community under special arrangements. Although Mauritius has a more diversified domestic economy than many other developing countries that are also reliant on sugar exports, sugar remains especially important for Mauritius both because it is the largest single beneficiary of EC preferential purchases and because the island is ill-suited to the cultivation of alternative agricultural crops.

The interviews for this case study were conducted prior to the outcome of the recent EC sugar subsidies dispute, but those interviewed were nevertheless already expecting major change to the long-standing regime and considering how to make the best of the situation through the transition. Humbert gave an overview of how the sugar industry was adapting. The overall area of land under sugar cane cultivation was diminishing, in part motivated by a restructuring plan that would allow for more profitable land use, in some circumstances potentially contributing to the industry's modernization and also cutting one-third of the workforce in the industry. At the same time, an important part of the strategy called for modernizing and preparing the industry for the future. Part of the modernization plan involves the development and marketing of speciality sugars – seventeen different types of these are now produced in Mauritius.

On a one-to-one basis, it is difficult for any sugar-producing country to compete with Brazil, where a combination of ethanol-related investment, cheap labour and suspected cross-subsidies from the government have made the country the most cost-competitive sugar producer. In recognition of this challenge, for Mauritius cutting the cost of production is a major focus of the Sugar Sector Strategic Plan for 2001–5. Among the targets for the plan are:

- a reduction in the cost of production from 18 cents/lb to 14 cents/lb. In the period from 2006 to 2008, the cost of production is to be further reduced to 10–12 cents/lb;
- a reduction in the number of sugar factories, from fourteen to seven or eight, to be realized in conjunction with a reduction in sugar losses at harvest time and in factory processing;
- the generation of as much electricity as possible from renewable resources, in particular bagasse;[6]
- taking steps to ensure that a substantial proportion of sugar-producing land that can be mechanized is prepared, and that an

---

[6] Bagasse is the leftover organic material after the cane has been processed for its sugar content.

equivalent proportion of acreage that requires irrigation is provided with irrigation water;
- the development of research and development so as to be able fully to tap the benefits of the expected quantum leaps in respect of biotechnology, biotics and cane biomass.[7]

Dr Rajpati, the executive director of the Mauritius Sugar Authority, outlined a multi-pronged strategy designed to make the best use of the country's sugar-related resources in the face of changing international competitive positions. In terms of external influences on the sector, Rajpati cited both the expected changes in the EC's preferential regime and the marketplace power of Brazil. As core elements of its strategy for addressing these challenges, Mauritius had developed speciality sugars for niche marketing, closed inefficient operations and implemented a major programme using bagasse. In Mauritius, power plants are able to burn bagasse in the process of generating electricity, and it has become a major renewable power source. In 1988, some 70 million kw of electricity were generated by burning bagasse; in 2004, bagasse was expected to enable production of some 350 million kw. Until recently ethanol had not been produced in Mauritius, but in 2004 a plant producing 18,000 litres of ethanol from 70,000 tonnes of molasses began operations.

The director of the Mauritius Sugar Syndicate, Mrinal Roy, indicated that in 2004 Mauritius would produce about 70,000 tonnes of speciality sugars which it is able to market very successfully, due to a combination of very specific attention to quality control and customer requirements and the strong image the country has acquired over the years as a supplier of quality product.

Specialization in the production of brown sugars for direct consumption has made the industry in Mauritius famous around the world. Renowned unrefined sugar varieties include 'dry demerara', 'standard demerara', 'fine demerara', 'brown muscovado', 'light muscovado', 'golden castor' and 'fine golden demerara' among others. In advertising campaigns for these sugars considerable weight is placed on the intrinsic value of a 'natural' versus 'synthetic' sweetener in a health-conscious diet. Roy points out that the country's sugar industry is not neglecting more traditional sugar exports. The syndicate he oversees charters some twenty specialized vessels to carry sugar to market and it has invested heavily in

[7] Ministry of Agriculture, Food Technology and Natural Resources, *Sugar Sector Strategic Plan 2001–2005*, Port Louis, June 2001, pp. 1–2.

port area machinery designed to load the sugar rapidly on to vessels and to minimize the costs associated with vessels' time in harbour.

As the traditional sugar industry begins to be phased out on the island, Mauritian sugar experts have turned their attention to moving production offshore, where possibilities exist for more competitiveness. An outstanding example is the Marromeu project that began with an earlier Mauritian government–industry visit to Mozambique in 1996. Three Mauritian companies, Mon Loisir, Espitalier-Noël and FUEL, made the most significant overseas investment ever by the Mauritian private sector in a sugar plantation and refinery that had been made all but defunct by the years of civil war in Mozambique. After benefiting from Mauritian investments totalling Rs 3.6 billion (US$130 million), Marromeu is producing 100,000 tonnes of sugar a year – equivalent to one-sixth of annual Mauritian production in a good year. A considerable amount of the Marromeu output benefits from access to the EC market under the 'Everything but Arms' initiative in favour of LDCs.[8]

Sugar will remain a major component in the Mauritian economy. There will be a strong and continuing effort made to develop new speciality sugars that can be marketed as differentiated products, and the industry will continue to cut costs on traditional sugar exports. But Roy emphasizes that even if no sugar could be sold commercially on world markets, it would probably continue to be cultivated in the country if for no other reason than that it has become an important resource in energy production.

Textiles and clothing production

A combination of developments in the late 1970s and early 1980s gave rise to the establishment of a significant textile and clothing industry in Mauritius. Incentives under an export processing zone scheme combined with visa-related enticements to Hong Kong-based entrepreneurs fearful at the time of reintegration with China and the existence of quota allocation possibilities led to rapid development of the export-oriented sector.

As competitive pressures have grown and rising wages in Mauritius have made the sector less viable, a number of initiatives have been undertaken in a government–industry effort to turn the sector around. One programme, TEST (Textile Emergency Support Team), initiated an approach of voluntary benchmarking of the relative productivity of textiles firms

---

[8] *L'Express*, 26 May 2004, p. 15.

with their local counterparts. The export processing zone system was revisited to assess whether it could not be made more attractive to textile firms. Labour-related legislation was changed to make it more flexible in respect of employees working in export processing zones. One observer commented that the government did its part and more, but industry has not focused sufficiently on the need to change.

Four main products account for the bulk of the sectors' output: knitwear, shirts, trousers and jeans. Local experts say that the knitted sector remains competitive today but that the other, more labour-intensive, sectors are experiencing severe difficulties. Despite the closing at regular intervals of garment factories in anticipation of the end of the global market allocation system that was largely responsible for the creation of this industry in Mauritius, at least one observer commented that this kind of factory job is not what most Mauritians want by way of employment. As relative income and education levels have risen, interest in production-line work has waned. Overall employment in the country's EPZs has fallen from 91,000 to 77,000 in recent years. Most people anticipate a continuing decline in the prospects for this sector.

Financial services

Recognizing that rising income levels and a more well-educated populace would create a demand for more employment in white-collar services industries, the government and the private sector have collaborated very effectively to create an environment in Mauritius which has allowed the financial services sector to prosper and become a major and growing part of the island's economy. The concept and supporting legislation for offshore banking were introduced in 1991, supplemented by lower tax rates for particular types of bank. In mid-2004 there were twenty-two authorized banks operating in the country, ten under a category-1 licence and twelve under a category-2 licence. From the start, the local regulatory authorities decided that maintaining a high level of credibility in the sector was important, and only foreign banks with a recognized international reputation have been approved to do business in the country. Among those banks currently holding a category-1 licence are Barclays Bank and HSBC.

Alternative agricultural activities

With sugar in a situation of long-term decline, business and government in Mauritius are discussing and experimenting with alternative agricultural

activities. Although agriculture is unlikely to form a major part of the
Mauritian economy of the future, a number of initiatives are currently
being explored in sectors that seem to offer some promise.

The production of venison is particularly interesting for a number of
reasons. Experiments have shown that deer react well to feedlot environ-
ments, and the local Hindu population has no difficulties with the farming
of deer for food purposes. One problem the Mauritians have encountered
in their efforts to commercialize the sector fully is the apparent lack of
a relevant EC food safety standard applicable to venison exports from
Mauritius.

In addition, and apart from the seafood hub activities recently
promoted by the Prime Minister, Mauritian investors are working
hard to identify land in neighbouring Madagascar, Mozambique and
Tanzania that could be purchased or leased for long-term agro-processing
operations where products such as potatoes, tomatoes and maize
could be grown in these neighbouring countries and then brought to
Mauritius for value-added processing and export to developed country
markets.

4 Lessons for others

Many of those interviewed by the author commented that there is in
Mauritius today a large level of tolerance prevailing among the populace,
notwithstanding the many different religious and ethnic groups present
on the island. The first comment from Rajpati, the executive director
of the Mauritius Sugar Authority, was that in Mauritius there is a well-
established and functioning collaboration between the public and private
sectors and that the Mauritian people are accustomed to 'pulling together'
for the common good.

The stable political environment and absence of ethnic tensions in
Mauritius were credited by many of those interviewed with having contributed importantly to the country's relative success. This, combined with
a long-standing tradition of business and government working together
to solve problems and take advantage of opportunities, has been a cor-
nerstone of the country's development.

On the international trade front that is so vital to the country's well-
being, Mauritians are well aware that they have benefited from special
preferences and circumstances over the past thirty years, but they are
also very conscious that the landscape is changing and that these special

features of their international trade cannot be counted on for the future. Their reaction has been to preserve what they can (by, for example, acting to cut costs in sugar production while developing new niche markets for speciality sugars) and, more importantly, experiment with new ideas for the country's future economic development.

27

How regional economic communities can facilitate participation in the WTO: the experience of Mauritius and Zambia

SANOUSSI BILAL AND STEFAN SZEPESI*

1 Introduction

Since the conclusion of the Uruguay Round and the establishment of the WTO, the active participation of developing countries in the multilateral trading system has increasingly been recognized as a crucial element for their development as well as an imperative to ensure the legitimacy and sustainability of the world trade regime. Yet many poor countries do not have the capacity to influence significantly the WTO negotiations or to implement the commitments agreed multilaterally. They still face major challenges to determining and defending their positions in technical negotiations, even on issues which are of key strategic interest to them. Indeed, the unprecedented depth and breadth of issues discussed in the current Doha Development Round have put the capacity of the developing countries (DCs), both at home and in their Geneva missions (for those that can afford to have one), under extraordinary pressure in effectively managing the process of their participation in these WTO negotiations.

Recognizing the key potential role of international trade for their sustainable development, many DCs entered into various bilateral and regional trade agreements and followed a dual path of multilateralism and regionalism.

The specific question addressed in this case study is the extent to which the participation of DCs in regional economic communities (RECs) has facilitated, or on the contrary hampered, their participation in the WTO. Regional co-operation and co-ordination among DCs can be construed as a way of pooling scarce resources and create synergies. Regional

* European Centre for Development Policy Management (ECDPM), Maastricht, The Netherlands. The authors are grateful to Kathleen Van Hove for her most helpful editorial support.

institutions may provide the necessary support and appropriate forum for countries to exchange views, share information, generate technical analysis and policy input, define and when relevant co-ordinate positions and identify best practices. Working at the regional level may also offer the opportunity to connect WTO positions to regional strategies and stimulate positive spillovers between these two levels of negotiations. On the other hand, regional organizations and agendas can also divert national resources away from the WTO process towards the regional integration process or bi-regional trade negotiations. In this respect, regional co-operation can proceed at the expense of participation in the WTO.

To address these issues, the study focuses on two countries, Mauritius and Zambia, and the two regional communities to which they both belong, the Common Market for Eastern and Southern Africa (COMESA) and the Southern Africa Development Community (SADC). Mauritius has a track record of being one of the most effective trade negotiators in Africa, being a key player at regional level, as well as in the African, Caribbean and Pacific (ACP) Group and in the current negotiations of an Economic Partnership Agreement (EPA). Zambia, as a least developed country (LDC), has encountered greater difficulties in its participation in international trade negotiations. Yet, in spite of serious capacity constraints, Zambia has so far managed to remain a committed player. COMESA is intending to move towards a customs union soon. SADC, whose political dimension is predominant for the time being, gives priority to the implementation of its Trade Protocol.

This two-country two-region case study offers a comparative illustration of how regional integration processes and regional negotiations affect the preparation for and participation of members in the WTO. On the basis of interviews with a range of key actors involved in the trade policy-making process at the national, regional and Geneva level, the study attempts to address some of the following questions: Does the regional dimension help countries to co-ordinate their positions at the WTO, or are national interests and non-regional alliances predominant? Do regional secretariats provide solid technical support and analysis to help member countries take positions on certain (overlapping) issues in the WTO? And is the preparation on WTO-related issues at the regional level a complement to or a substitute for national preparation? Has the increased attention and external (trade capacity building) support for regional integration and bi-regional negotiations also contributed to facilitate the analysis and formulation of positions at the WTO? Or, on the contrary, are the two levels of negotiation (WTO, regional) competing for limited domestic capacities and resources?

2 The national and regional players and their roles

Actors in the WTO trade policy process

Negotiations at the WTO take place in the Trade Negotiations Committee (TNC) and its various sub-committees or regular WTO councils present in Geneva. The actual generation of proposals and positions in the WTO is a bottom-up process whereby input is generated at national and regional levels with numerous stages of consultation and co-ordination before it is finally delivered to Geneva. Overall, this policy process involves a broad range of state and non-state actors that should have the opportunity to provide input. A simplified scheme of this policy process from the national to the Geneva level is depicted in Figure 27.1.

Many DCs, however, face considerable obstacles in this policy process. The human and financial resource constraints with respect to the dense agenda of negotiations in Geneva, their representation and the generation of substantial input at the national level constitute major hurdles. Some do not maintain a permanent mission in Geneva, and even for those that do it is still impossible to participate in the multitude of meetings and to follow the complete agenda.[1]

Co-operation, co-ordination and the pooling of resources with countries that have similar interests is therefore of vital importance for the effective participation of many DCs in the WTO. Whereas the formation of coalitions by DCs is not a new feature in multilateral trade negotiations, the most recent Ministerial Conferences in Seattle, Doha and Cancún have shown these coalitions to be better organized and more pro-active than before. They manage to share information better, preserve internal cohesion and engage in co-ordination with other groupings.[2] A brief overview of the WTO coalitions is provided in Annex I, while Table 27.1 shows the extent to which Mauritius and Zambia are involved in WTO coalition groupings, as well as the degree to which their affiliation matches those of their fellow COMESA and SADC members.

Clearly, whereas both Mauritius and Zambia affiliate to various coalition groupings, these groupings do not always match well with the strategic interests of other REC members. The fault lines of some strategic interests as represented by the coalitions cut right through the RECs.

---

[1] See also Blackhurst et al. (1999).   [2] See Narlikar and Tussie (2004).

Figure 27.1. *Input into the WTO from the capital to Geneva*

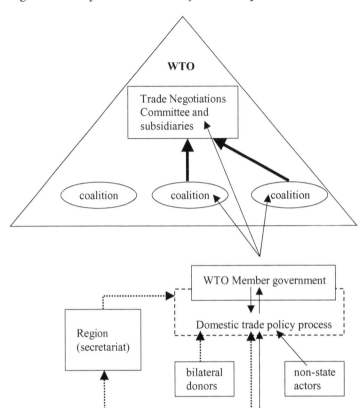

Actors at the national levels: Mauritius and Zambia

Mauritius

Mauritius has considerable human and financial resources as well as significant experience as a result of its active involvement in international trade fora over the last decades. The process of its trade and overall economic policy-making has been well documented.[3] The country has

---

[3] See, e.g., Bonaglia and Fukasaku (2002).

Table 27.1. *Participation in WTO coalitions*

WTO coalition groupings[1]	Mauritius	Zambia	COMESA (20) (number of members in coalition)	SADC (13)[2] (number of members in coalition)
	(x = member)			
G90	x	x	19	13
ACP Group	x	x	18	13
Africa Group	x	x	19	13
LDCs		x	6	6
Friends of Multi-functionality	x		1	1
G10	x		1	1
G33	x	x	5	6
Like Minded Group (LMG)	(observer)		4	1
NFIDC/LDC	x	x		
SIDS	x		1	1
SVE	x		3	1
WTO member	x	x	15 +3 observers	13

[1] All coalition groupings are issue-specific groupings, with the notable exception of the G90, ACP Group, Africa Group and LDCs which cover horizontal (cross-cutting) issues. Annex I provides a short description and membership of all the main WTO coalition groupings.

[2] After completing its accession, Madagascar will become the fourteenth member of SADC (while remaining a COMESA member).

considerable experience in participatory (trade) policy-making processes. Both private-sector and trade union representatives take part in a number of trade-related committees (e.g. the Committee of Agriculture and International Trade) and are regularly included in delegations to WTO Ministerial Conferences and regional meetings. The views of these committees flow into a core group which is chaired by the permanent secretary to the Trade Minister. At the highest level, it is the WTO's Standing Coordination Committee – chaired by the Trade Minister – that involves actors from various ministries and a number of private-sector actors. Ultimately, it is the minister who either decides on a particular position or refers the issue to the cabinet for approval or adaptation.

A position on a WTO issue can either be submitted directly to relevant WTO committees, or it can be co-ordinated and possibly adapted in a coalition grouping, after which it is submitted on behalf of the coalition. On general issues, Mauritius works mostly within the Africa Group whereas on specific issues the G10, the G33 and the Multifunctionality Group are referred to.

Zambia

As an LDC Zambia has faced more constraints on its participation, but supported by donors and international agencies it has moved to reform its policy-making process and institutions.

The Zambian Ministry of Commerce, Trade and Industry is responsible for conducting trade policy. It faces serious (human) resource constraints, in particular at the technical level.

Consultation with public- and private-sector stakeholders used to be organized in an ad hoc fashion, but since June 2004 a National Working Group on Trade (NWGT) has been established. In the NWGT, six government and six private-sector institutions have a seat. As for WTO coalitions, Zambia works predominantly with the G33 and the G90. Within the latter group it is a member of all three sub-groupings (the ACP group, the Africa group and the LDC group).

The regional level: COMESA and SADC

Mauritius and Zambia are members of both the Common Market for Eastern and Southern Africa (COMESA) and the Southern African Development Community (SADC).[4] As can be seen in Figure 27.2, membership of multiple regional organizations is common among nearly all countries in eastern and southern Africa.

COMESA

Established in 1994, COMESA currently comprises twenty member states: Angola, Burundi, Comoros, Democratic Republic of Congo (DRC), Djibouti, Egypt, Eritrea, Ethiopia, Kenya, Madagascar, Malawi, Mauritius, Namibia, Rwanda, Seychelles, Sudan, Swaziland, Uganda, Zambia and Zimbabwe. Many member states also belong to other regional organizations such as the SADC, the Eastern African Community (EAC), the

---

[4] In addition, Mauritius is a member of the Indian Ocean Commission (IOC).

Figure 27.2. *Regional groupings in east and southern Africa*

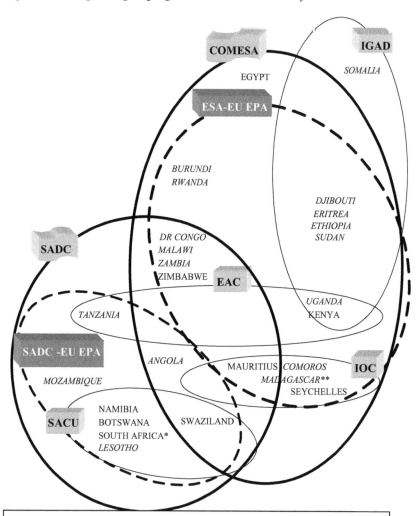

Regional and Sub-Regional Economic Integration Groupings in Eastern and Southern Africa

COMESA:	Common Market for Eastern and Southern Africa
EAC:	East African Community
IOC:	Indian Ocean Commission
IGAD:	Inter-Governmental Authority on Development
SACU:	Southern African Customs Union
SADC:	Southern African Development Community

Other acronyms:

EPA:	Economic Partnership Agreement
ESA:	East and Southern Africa
EU:	European Union

* South Africa is an observer in the SADC-EU EPA Negotiating Process
** Madagascar has initiated its accession process to SADC, while staying in COMESA.
LDC countries are in italics

Indian Ocean Commission (IOC) and the Inter-Governmental Authority on Development (IGAD).

Heads of state form the principal authority for COMESA's policy direction. The Council of Ministers, which receives recommendations from the Intergovernmental Committee, decides on operational issues and is responsible for the COMESA Secretariat. The task of the Secretariat is to provide advisory services and technical support to member states in the implementation of the COMESA Treaty.

COMESA's main focus is on strengthening regional integration through promotion of cross-border trade and investment. It has programmes on trade and transport facilitation, trade in services, free movement of persons and investment. Other features include gender policy, conflict prevention and a COMESA Court of Justice. In October 2000, nine COMESA member states moved towards a free trade area.[5] The objective is to move towards a customs union from 2004 onwards. Two other countries (Rwanda and Burundi) joined the COMESA FTA in January 2004, taking membership to eleven. All other COMESA members (except Swaziland, as a member of SACU) offer preferential access to their markets to all COMESA member states.

For WTO questions, COMESA has established a Working Group on WTO issues, which operates as a sub-committee of the COMESA Trade and Customs Committee. The core functions of this Working Group are to provide technical back-up and analysis of WTO issues and to suggest appropriate recommendations.

COMESA also facilitates EPA negotiations with the EU for sixteen ESA countries (i.e. all COMESA members except Egypt, Angola and Swaziland).

SADC

Established in 1992, the SADC currently counts thirteen member states: Angola, Botswana, DRC, Lesotho, Malawi, Mauritius, Mozambique, Namibia, South Africa, Swaziland, Tanzania, Zambia and Zimbabwe, after the Seychelles left in 2004.

SADC is a development community with a broad range of objectives varying from self-sustained development, economic growth and poverty alleviation to common political values, systems and institutions. As in COMESA, SADC heads of state and the Council of Ministers are overall

---

[5] These are Djibouti, Egypt, Kenya, Madagascar, Malawi, Mauritius, Sudan, Zambia and Zimbabwe.

responsible for the general policy direction of the organization as well as for policy implementation. The SADC Secretariat is the principal executive institution, responsible for strategic planning, co-ordination and management of SADC programmes. In 2001, SADC underwent serious restructuring, giving the Secretariat a more expanded mandate and increasing the number of staff. The previous Sector Co-ordinating Units (dispersed over the member states) are now centralized in the SADC Secretariat in Gaborone, Botswana, and merged into only four directorates.

The trade, industry, finance and investment (TIFI) cluster works on trade and economic integration and focuses on stimulating the implementation by the member states of the 1996 SADC Trade Protocol. The implementation of the Protocol should lead to the liberalization of 85% of all regional goods trade by 2008, the liberalization of regional services trade in six priority sectors, the elimination of non-tariff trade barriers, and the harmonization of standards, customs rules and procedures. The objective is to have moved by 2012 towards a customs union with a common external tariff and trade policy. The Secretariat also seeks to facilitate member states' compliance with WTO policies and agreements as well as help prepare the negotiations for a SADC–EU economic partnership agreement (EPA).

3 Regional support and co-ordination

For the participation of a country in the WTO negotiations to have any significant value, a two-stage policy process must be in place. First, countries need to be able to identify their strategic interests and be informed about the consequences of the various policy options open to them. This first stage requires proper capacity to analyze and formulate trade policy and negotiation positions. The second stage of the trade policy process consists of the identification of a negotiation strategy. This includes the formation of alliances and coalitions with partners that share common views and trade interests. Strategies must be flexible and reaction time limited, so as to adapt to the rapidly evolving negotiation environment. These two stages should not be seen as independent but rather as complementary.

In this process, the regional dimension can usefully come into play. First, regional organizations can support the preparatory work of their member states. The co-ordination of trade capacity building programmes, the organization of regional workshops, the elaboration of technical papers and the dissemination of information on WTO issues are examples of such supportive activities. Regional platforms may also contribute to facilitating the exchange of information and sharing of experiences among neighbouring countries.

Second, regional groupings may have a role to play in helping their member countries to co-ordinate their position at WTO level, in a way consistent with their regional integration and trade policy objectives. Regional organizations might co-ordinate the burden sharing among countries in following and actively engaging in a heavy WTO agenda which few, if any, DCs can adequately tackle on their own.

In the case of Mauritius and Zambia, let us consider in turn the roles that the two main regional economic communities, COMESA and SADC, have played in their participation to the WTO.

Trade capacity building support from the regions

Direct support on WTO issues

While both regional organizations have contributed to the strengthening of capacity and the preparation of national actors for WTO negotiations, there is a general recognition, in COMESA and SADC secretariats, and among key actors in Mauritius and Zambia, that more could be done.

In **COMESA**, Ministerial conferences, and high-level meetings that bring together trade experts, senior officials and Geneva ambassadors have been organized on trade and WTO issues. The purposes of such meetings have been to provide a broad overview of the state of the WTO negotiations, to discuss more technical or systemic issues of relevance to the members and, when appropriate, to formulate recommendations for the national ministers on their strategy and position for the negotiations. As such, there is no COMESA common position at the WTO (see below). These meetings are therefore primarily designed to support member countries in their preparation for the WTO negotiations. They also provide a useful platform for officials to exchange views and information.

The COMESA Secretariat has developed handbooks, conference proceedings and reports on WTO issues and distributed these to its members in preparation for WTO Ministerial Conferences. The Secretariat has conducted specific studies for trade ministries of COMESA members and has provided direct input on specific WTO issues (e.g. on WTO rules and on Ethiopia's accession to the WTO) to some of their Geneva-based missions, as well as to the Africa Group and the African Union (AU). However, this technical support has been given on an ad hoc basis as a result of specific requests.

Given that members have not often called on the COMESA Secretariat, its role has been limited in the preparation for WTO negotiations. Moreover, donors' activities on trade capacity building for WTO issues have mainly been channelled through national programmes (e.g. JITAP), somewhat neglecting the regional dimension. Nonetheless, COMESA has developed programmes and projects on trade capacity building for its members on WTO-related issues such as trade negotiations, customs valuation and facilitation, notifications and so on. Finally, it is worth noting that although the COMESA Secretariat is quite knowledgeable on WTO issues, some COMESA countries are actually better equipped and have more expertise and experience at the national level to deal with WTO matters.

In **SADC**, trade issues have traditionally received less attention than in COMESA, as SADC has a broader mandate, encompassing development and political dimensions. In addition, SADC restructuring process which is centralizing the programmes that were previously managed by the member states has not yet been fully completed. The Secretariat remains understaffed and with insufficient financial and technical means and absorption capacity to cope with an increasing regional agenda. In these conditions, it is difficult for the SADC Secretariat to contribute significantly to strengthening the trade capacity of its member states on WTO issues.

Despite the absence of an SADC programme dedicated to addressing WTO issues systematically for the region, the SADC Secretariat has organized a number of activities that have directly concerned the WTO. In response to requests from member states, and with technical assistance from UNCTAD, specific support has been provided on the issue of trade in services. The work concerned the identification of key service sectors and the drafting of a legal framework to facilitate the intra-regional liberalization of services. A study on domestic agricultural support measures was also carried out, with the aim of facilitating a regional position on this issue and was later used as background material for the WTO negotiations.

As with COMESA, the activities on WTO matters directly attributed to the Secretariat have mainly consisted of formal meetings in preparation for WTO Ministerial Conferences. In addition, the SADC Secretariat has also been collaborating with the Southern Africa Trade Research Network (SATRN). This network organizes an annual symposium on WTO issues and brings together researchers as well as policy-makers and negotiators from the SADC region to share views on WTO issues and developments.

In both **Mauritius** and **Zambia** support from COMESA and SADC has been useful, though limited. One of the main benefits of COMESA and SADC WTO-related activities has been the engagement process they have generated. Regional and national officials alike recognize that bringing national officers, diplomats and ministers together to provide general input on WTO matters has contributed to raise the political profile of WTO, and more generally trade matters. It has increased awareness on some general technical matters. At the level of Geneva missions to the WTO, the direct input from COMESA has gained visibility. Other technical support targeted trade officials in capitals, but might not always have trickled down to Geneva. Some national officials acknowledged that COMESA tended to be more responsive and proactive than SADC, the COMESA Secretariat being perhaps better equipped to tackle technical issues. In both regions, however, the support was generally provided on an ad hoc basis. It seems to have been better suited to increasing the understanding of the WTO process rather than to providing in-depth analysis which could directly input into the national technical preparation. Interestingly, the regional secretariats, COMESA in particular, noted the lack of explicit demands from member states for dedicated input on WTO issues. The secretariats therefore are left with little guidance for determining their technical work plan. This tends to suggest that the potential value added of regions in the WTO preparation of member states is not yet fully identified. It was also suggested that the regional support on WTO matters might have a greater impact on countries with weaker capacities.

More generally, awareness-raising activities and regional training of officials on trade-related matters seem to have been useful trade capacity building measures, with little distinction between WTO and non-WTO issues, generating valuable synergies in the preparation of national officials. To have a real impact on WTO negotiations, however, the support by regional organizations would have to be more specific and technical in nature, and delivered in a timely manner.

Spillovers and trade-offs between regional and WTO trade agendas

Besides the direct support on WTO issues, both COMESA and SADC have engaged in numerous trade and regional integration activities that have indirectly benefited WTO preparation and compliance.

Hence some of the COMESA activities have aimed at ensuring coherence between the regional integration process and the WTO obligations of its member states (e.g. TBT and SPS). To foster policy research COMESA has been implementing a Regional Integration Research Network Project (RIRN) which has commissioned various studies on topics such as Article XXIV, dispute settlement, on tariff schedules (GATT/WTO bindings) or the implementation of the Decision on TRIPS Agreement and Public Health.

SADC has experienced similar synergies between its preparation for regional integration and WTO issues. An example is the report and round table meeting on amendments to the Dispute Settlement Mechanism of the SADC Trade Protocol, followed up by a workshop on the WTO Dispute Settlement Mechanism.

SADC has also undertaken work to assess the compliance of its member states with WTO rules, such as the notification requirements under the WTO SPS and TBT agreements. Out of this work, draft annexes on SPS and TBT to the Trade Protocol have been developed, aimed at harmonizing regional SPS and TBT measures and regulations.

In addition, the intensive preparation for EPA negotiations, by COMESA in the context of the ESA configuration and by SADC, has also contributed to generating positive synergies with the WTO agenda.

Clearly, numerous synergies exist in the trade liberalization agenda and institutional development at the regional, EPA and WTO levels. Yet the heavy agenda in each negotiation forum, combined with the limited capacity at both the regional and national levels, have negatively affected the preparation for these negotiations. The overall issues are the same in the various trade negotiations fora, for example effective market access, trade preferences, and linkages between trade and development. However, in terms of negotiation positions, each requires specific preparation. These have increased the burden on the limited number of officials in trade and other relevant ministries. Similarly, Geneva missions to the WTO (and to some extent the Brussels missions to the EU) are often under-staffed and ill-equipped to follow the wide array of trade negotiation sessions. The degree of political commitment and the level of development of the countries do matter a great deal, as suggested by the Mauritius and Zambia experiences, the latter suffering more acutely from the lack of capacity. The same constraints are reflected at the regional level.[6]

Not surprisingly, countries with less capacity, as in the case of Zambia, have fewer opportunities to benefit from the synergies created by the multiple trade agenda, as their attention is often drawn to the most

---

[6] For a review of the SADC experience, see for instance BIDPA (2004).

urgent matter of the time. The competing trade agenda is therefore often determined by major negotiating events. In addition, donor support can also divert attention, as different steering groups are created to lead trade support programmes whose foci vary (e.g. JITAP and IF in Zambia).

For Mauritius, this is less the case, as their negotiating structure and capacities, although still insufficient and seriously strained, are more appropriate to cope with the trade agenda. The well-established tradition of significantly involving the private sector in the trade and economic policy formulation has been an important factor in Mauritius' achievement.

Initial steps towards regional co-ordination of positions

The predominance of national interests

Although both COMESA and the SADC aim to become customs unions, they have not yet established a common external tariff or developed a common external trade policy. The member countries have not had to delegate (part of) their trade authority to regional secretariats and are under no pressure to harmonize their positions at the regional level (unlike the European Union for instance).

In addition, both COMESA and that SADC have a diversified (and overlapping) membership. As indicated above, COMESA is composed of three different sub-regional groupings with some small islands, coastal countries and landlocked countries, LDCs and more advanced countries with a more diversified economy. Similarly, the SADC is also a highly heterogeneous region. Besides the overlapping membership with COMESA (seven countries being simultaneously members of the two regional organizations), it includes a more deeply integrated sub-region, the Southern Africa Customs Union (SACU), with its dominating member, South Africa, together with some of the poorest and smallest countries, such as Lesotho.

With such diverse economic, social, political and geographical characteristics, and in the absence of a strong impetus towards co-ordination, it is not surprising that national interests largely dominate the position of COMESA as well as SADC countries in the WTO arena.

The (informal) co-ordination role of the regions

In the absence of a formal mandate to harmonize the positions of WTO members, regional groupings are left with the limited option of facilitating and promoting the co-ordination of the positions of their members.[7] In these conditions, the scope for co-ordinated action at the regional level on WTO issues depends on the goodwill of the member countries, and the capacity for initiative of the regional secretariat. The main role adopted by both COMESA and the SADC has so far been to facilitate informal co-operation and stimulate co-ordination among members. Regional meetings of country trade officials and Geneva ambassadors, as well as Ministerial Conferences, have generally constituted the most appropriate (if not the only) platform for member states to exchange views and possibly co-ordinate positions at the regional level.

As discussed above, these meetings have helped COMESA members in their technical preparation, but have helped more in facilitating formal and informal consultations among member states, as well as between Geneva (and Brussels) ambassadors and senior officials in capitals. While common declarations have tended to be more general in nature,[8] stressing the development dimension of the WTO negotiations, they have contributed somewhat to the elaboration of an African position, which has then also influenced larger WTO groupings, such as the ACP Group, the Group of LDCs and the G90.

It is interesting to note that some meetings are jointly organized by COMESA and SADC, or that representatives of the other region are invited to attend. In addition, AU Commission and ACP Secretariat representatives are also often invited to participate in COMESA and SADC regional meetings. This strategy may have helped to establish better linkages between the African Group and ACP positions and the positions of COMESA and SADC members. Besides, COMESA and SADC common declarations on WTO issues have normally been presented to the AU and informed the African, ACP and LDCs Groups' positions.

From a national perspective, the common view is that regional support is more appropriate on technical issues and capacity-building initiatives than for the co-ordination of positions, which are better dealt with directly in WTO coalition groupings. Several diplomats and senior trade officials did stress that co-ordination at the regional level is better suited for delivering political messages on WTO matters. However, technical issues, where interests among member countries are more likely to differ,

---

[7] See Art. 17.8(i) of the COMESA Treaty and Art. 29 of the SADC Protocol on Trade.
[8] See, e.g., the Nairobi Declaration on Preparations for EPA negotiations and the Fifth WTO Ministerial Conference, 28 May 2003, COMESA.

are better addressed directly at WTO coalition level (e.g. G10 and G33 for agriculture and special products).

4 Main lessons

This study has sought to identify the influence of the RECs in the preparation and participation of their member (developing) countries in the WTO. In particular, looking at the experience of an LDC, Zambia, and a small island economy, Mauritius, this study attempted to identify the role of the two RECs, COMESA and SADC, in supporting and facilitating their participation in the WTO.

The main lesson is that the regional dimension in east and southern Africa (COMESA/SADC) has had little *direct* impact so far on the preparation and conduct of the WTO negotiations. Both regions have been conducting numerous useful activities to support and co-ordinate the participation of their member states: studies, reports, meetings, training and so forth. However, at least in the case of Mauritius and Zambia, the type of support provided often remains too general, with not enough specific technical relevance for member countries' specific interests significantly to inform their domestic positions on WTO matters. Besides, both COMESA and the SADC have too diverse a membership to allow for a meaningful co-ordination of their member states' positions on specific WTO issues. Common strategic interests take form within WTO coalition groupings rather than heterogeneous regional groupings. Moreover, these RECs have too small a membership (in number and economic size) to form a strong alliance within the WTO coalitions' framework, where groupings are already numerous. Since for the WTO *size does matter*, Mauritius and Zambia give priority to larger coalitions for common WTO matters (e.g. the Africa Group, ACP and LDCs Groups, and the G90). For specific-interest WTO matters, they focus on issue-dedicated groupings (e.g. the Friends of Multifunctionality, G10, G33, SIDS/SVE in the case of Mauritius). In addition, countries often rely on the Geneva channels for co-ordination and for transferring their input to WTO positions. Since neither COMESA nor the SADC have representatives in Geneva, these regional groupings are somewhat further marginalized. Nonetheless, the situation might evolve over time, as both COMESA and SADC further their integration to become effective customs unions. As COMESA and SADC remain free trade areas in the making, member states are not yet under pressure to co-ordinate their position.

Another important lesson is that regional groupings can play a much needed role in the WTO preparations through indirect means. The SADC and in particular COMESA have been instrumental in putting trade high on the regional agenda and promoting the visibility of trade matters. While the regional integration process has been the driving force, the opening of EPA negotiations with the EU and the WTO Doha Round have provided a major push. By raising awareness, by training, by providing a platform for the exchange of views and information, and by stimulating trade capacity building initiatives, COMESA and the SADC have contributed to a better preparation of their member countries on trade issues, which have had positive spillovers on their participation to the WTO. The size of these regional groupings provides good opportunities for developing useful common training and other capacity building activities to the benefit of the members.

Finally, this case study has shown that institutions with sufficient capacity have been able to benefit more from the synergy opportunities created by the multi-level trade policy interactions. Hence, COMESA, with its narrower focus on trade and economic issues, appears better equipped to support the preparation for various trade negotiations than SADC. Similarly, Mauritius officials seem more positive about the complementarity of preparations for the regional, EPA and WTO negotiations than their Zambian colleagues, who have more stretched capacities and less time to cope with this multiple agenda. Institutional capacities are therefore a key determinant in the level of synergies and trade-offs that are created by a multi-level negotiation process, in particular between the regional and multilateral level.

Annex I
ABC of WTO global coalition groupings[9]

In practice, the membership of coalition groupings evolves over time and groups can have more or fewer members than their name suggests. The current number of members is given in parentheses.

Cairns group (17): Argentina, Australia, Bolivia, Brazil, Canada, Chile, Colombia, Costa Rica, Guatemala, Indonesia, Malaysia, New Zealand, Paraguay, Philippines, South Africa, Thailand and Uruguay.

Founded in Cairns, Australia, in 1986, the Cairns Group consists of the world's largest agricultural exporters. At the 2003 Cancún Ministerial many of its key players preferred to partner along other lines, and the G20 took its place as the most influential grouping of countries in the agriculture talks.

Friends of Multifunctionality (6): EU, Switzerland, Norway, Japan, Korea and Mauritius.

This group seeks to pursue agricultural policies that encourage environmental protection, rural development and food security.

G10 (10): Bulgaria, South Korea, Iceland, Israel, Japan, Liechtenstein, Mauritius, Switzerland, Taiwan and Japan.

These are agricultural importers that maintain heavy protectionist rules for their own products and are keen to protect their domestic agricultural sector.

G20 (19): Argentina, Bolivia, Brazil, Chile, China, Cuba, Egypt, India, Indonesia, Mexico, Nigeria, Pakistan, Paraguay, Philippines, South Africa, Thailand, Tanzania, Venezuela and Zimbabwe.

A group striving for agricultural reform created at the initiative of Brazil shortly before the 2003 Cancún Ministerial and consisting solely of DCs. The varying references to the group as G20, G20+ or even G22 has been due to the fact that a few countries have joined and others – such as Peru and Colombia – have left since September 2003.

G33 (30): Barbados, Botswana, Congo, Côte d'Ivoire, Cuba, Dominican Republic, Haiti, Honduras, Indonesia, Jamaica, Kenya, South Korea, Mauritius, Mongolia, Mozambique, Nicaragua, Nigeria, Pakistan, Panama, Peru, Philippines, Senegal, Sri Lanka, Tanzania, Trinidad and Tobago, Turkey, Uganda, Venezuela, Zambia and Zimbabwe. This

---

[9] *Source:* 3D (2004), and Narlikar and Tussie (2004).

group is also referred to as the **Alliance for Special Products and a Special Safeguard Mechanism.**

The G33 consists of developing country importers of agricultural products, many of them also single-crop producers and exporters. The group advocates that DCs be granted flexibility to self-designate a number of 'special products' (SPs) on which they would not have to make any tariff reduction or tariff rate quota (TRQ) commitments. They also seek a new safeguard mechanism for DCs to enable them to counter market volatility and sudden import surges.

G90: The G90 is an umbrella group for three partly overlapping groupings:

The ACP Group, consisting of DCs from Africa, the Caribbean and the Pacific Ocean that have signed the Cotonou Partnership Agreement with the EU;

The Africa Group, consisting of the members of the African Union, which contains all African countries except Morocco; and

The Group of Least-Developed Countries (LDCs), which contains all the LDCs that are WTO members.

Like the G20, this group was also born in Cancún, among others, to oppose attempts by the US and EU to include the so-called Singapore issues – investment, competition policy, transparency in government procurement and trade facilitation – in the negotiations.

Group on Cotton (4): Benin, Burkina Faso, Chad and Mali.

Seeking a complete phase-out of developed countries' cotton subsidies.

Group of Small Island Developing States (SIDS) (9): Barbados, Cuba, Dominica, Jamaica, Mauritius, St Kitts and Nevis, St Lucia, St Vincent and the Grenadines, and Trinidad and Tobago.

Group of Small and Vulnerable Economies (SVE) (25): SIDS group plus Antigua and Barbuda, Bahamas, Belize, Comoros, Fiji, Grenada, Guyana, Haiti, Maldives, Mauritius, Papua New Guinea, Samoa, Seychelles, Solomon Islands, Surinam and Vanuatu.

Both these groups aim to put particular concerns and constraints faced by small island and vulnerable economies on the agenda.

Like-Minded Group (LMG) (13): Cuba, Dominican Republic, Egypt, Honduras, India, Indonesia, Kenya, Malaysia, Pakistan, Sri Lanka,

Tanzania, Uganda and Zimbabwe (Jamaica and Mauritius are observers).

The LMG pushes for the so-called implementation issues to be on the agenda, as well as special and differential treatment, and opposes the Singapore issues.

P5, or Five Interested Parties: United States, European Union, Brazil and India (on behalf of the G20) and Australia (on behalf of the Cairns Group).

These are the main parties involved in WTO agricultural negotiations.

References

3D → Trade – Human Rights – Equitable Economy (2004), 'Jargon Explained: Glossary of Terms Commonly Used in the WTO', July 2004, available at http://www.3dthree.org/pdf_word/m311-3D%20Glossary%20July%202004%20rev.pdf.

BIDPA (2004), 'Identification of Support for the Integration of SADC Countries into the World Trade System', fact-finding mission report, Gaborone: Botswana Institute for Development Policy Analysis (BIDPA).

Blackhurst, Richard, Bill Lyakurwa and Ademola Oyejide (1999), 'Improving African Participation in the WTO', paper commissioned by the World Bank for a Conference at the WTO on 20–21 Sept. 1999, revised November, available at http://www1.worldbank.org/wbiep/trade/papers_2000/dev_contries_wto.pdf

Bonaglia, Federico and Kiichiro Fukasaku (2002), 'Trading Competitively: A Study of Trade Capacity Building in Sub-Saharan Africa', OECD Development Centre, June 2002, available at http://www.oecd.org/dataoecd/30/55/1939825.pdf.

Narlikar, Amrita and Diana Tussie (2004), 'The G20 at the Cancún Ministerial: Developing Countries and their Evolving Coalitions in the WTO', *World Economy*, 27 (7), pp. 947–66.

28

Mexico's agricultural trade policies: international commitments and domestic pressure

ISIDRO MORALES-MORENO*

In April 2003 the Mexican government reached an agreement with more than twenty-five organizations of small-scale farmers through which a restructuring of agricultural policies was envisioned. The so-called agro-pact came after many months of peasant mobilizations in which market liberalization – scheduled to coincide with the tenth anniversary of the North American Free Trade Agreement (NAFTA) – and electoral campaign became intertwined. The flagship of peasant mobilizations was the renegotiation of NAFTA's agricultural chapter. The Mexican government did not accept this demand, but agreed to undertake a comprehensive reform of domestic agricultural policies and activated trade remedies as part of an armour plating in defence of agricultural interests. In parallel to this, Mexico joined the G20 group within the WTO and began actively to call for the suppression of export subsidies and the reduction of domestic supports within agricultural markets. This study shows how agricultural trade policies in Mexico have been modified in response to peasant mobilizations and international commitments. It also shows how Mexico's position within the WTO has maintained an equilibrium between domestic constraints and international imperatives.

1 The peasant mobilizations and their claims

After the coming into effect of NAFTA the Mexican rural sector and land tenure system were supposed to enter into a transition period of around ten to fifteen years, during which tariffs and quotas would be completely phased out. However, sensitive basic staples were protected

* Universidad de las Américas, Puebla, Mexico

under tariff-rate quotas (TRQs), to be progressively eliminated over ten years. In January 2003 most agricultural trade within NAFTA had already been liberalized and Mexico maintained TRQs for only three products: maize, beans and powdered milk – to be ended completely in January 2008.

During the 1990s a restructuring of the rural sector was anticipated through a progressive privatization of the *ejido* plots.[1] A shift from non-competitive maize or bean production to more competitive harvests, such as vegetables and fruit, was expected, as well as an increase in land productivity. Policy reforms were also implemented in the 1990s in order to dismantle price supports and protectionism in this sector. New programmes were implemented in order to cushion the impact of policy reform and trade liberalization – targeted supports for the commercialization of domestic crops through a government trading board, income supports for encouraging crop substitution for competitive farmers, income transfers for farmers producing importables in sensitive staples, and credit subsidies and official credit coverage through a development bank (Yúnez 2002: 1–8).

After ten years of trade liberalization and policy reform, two-way trade between Mexico and the United States increased at higher rates compared with the pre-NAFTA period. As expected, Mexico's comparative advantage encompasses vegetables (fresh and frozen) and fruit, where gains in land productivity are manifest. Grains and other basic crops, although their production has not collapsed, have not increased their productivity, except in plots that are irrigated.

Government supports, although they have cushioned the impact of trade liberalization for importable staples, failed to change the crop mix. Furthermore, Mexico's financial crisis of 1994–5 cancelled the availability of credits to Mexican farmers, while growing imports compensated for the shortfalls in specific products (Yúnez 2002).

Hence ten years after Mexico liberalized its agriculture no serious restructuring in this sector had been achieved. The historical divide between irrigated land and rain-fed production persists, as well as between commercial production, mostly located in the north of the country, and local crops, most of the time for subsistence purposes, located in the south. A main problem is that most of the rural population (around 18% of total) still depends on rain-fed small plots and grain-based (mainly maize and beans) traditional production.

---

[1] State-owned lands that were privatized in 1992 in a major constitutional amendment.

It is in this context that major peasant mobilizations took place in the country, from mid-2002 until the first quarter of 2003. Two major reasons propelled grassroots peasant activism. The first was the enactment of the so-called 'Farm Bill' in the United States, in the first quarter of 2002, through which more than US$70 billion would be disbursed in support for US growers during a ten-year period. The Mexican government immediately responded by launching a so-called 'agricultural armour' package which increased domestic supports already implemented by government agencies and activated the imposition of safeguards, anti-dumping (AD) or countervailing duties (CVD). In autumn that year around twelve independent grass-roots organizations formed a bloc, El Campo no Aguanta Más[2] (CNAM), whose main target was to stop the liberalization of basic staples, scheduled for 2003 under NAFTA.[3]

They also demanded the renegotiation of the agricultural chapter of this agreement in order to reverse the liberalization. It made other important requests including an increase in the agricultural budget for the years to come, a restructuring and widening of agricultural funding, the prohibition of importing genetically modified staples and the levelling of the playing field with developed partners in terms of standards and sanitary and phytosanitary (SPS) measures (El Campo no Aguanta Más 2002).

Since the rise of this movement, the position of the Mexican government was to refuse any renegotiation of NAFTA. However, Mexican officials recognized that Mexican farmers needed further supports within the 'agricultural armour plating'. After the radicalization of peasants during the first two months of 2003, President Vicente Fox signed, in April that year, the so-called 'National Agreement for the Countryside'(ANC – Acuerdo Nacional para el Campo), through which the government was committed along with major peasant organizations to a comprehensive review of agricultural policies. The ANC includes a subsection dealing with international trade negotiations, through which the Mexican government agreed to the following commitments (see Secretaría de Economía 2003):

(i) to make an assessment of the impact of both NAFTA and the US Farm Bill on Mexico's rural sector;
(ii) to consult with the United States and Canada on the possibility of creating a permanent mechanism for administering trade exchanges on white maize and beans;

---

[2] 'The countryside cannot take any more'.
[3] The staples included barley, malt, wheat, rice, copra, soybean and sunflower. Poultry and pork also became fully liberalized in January 2003.

(iii) to implement and enforce all trade defensive mechanisms contained in Mexican legislation, NAFTA and the WTO.

(iv) to plan, implement and supervise the allocation of TRQs, in consultation with peasant organizations;

(v) to reinforce, with the support of peasant organizations, SPS measures aimed at guaranteeing risk-free and healthy food;

(vi) within WTO agricultural negotiations: to defend Mexico's position as a developing country preparing for the abatement of export subsidies and domestic supports; to claim the right to impose quantitative or tariff restrictions on the basis of 'food security' or 'food sovereignty'[4] concerns, as well as the protection of rural employment and natural resources when alleging domestic injury; and

(vii) to recognize the multi-functional aspects of Mexican agriculture, featuring a cultural, ethnic, social and economic mosaic.

The ACN ended the radicalization of peasant mobilizations and opened a new stage of political and institutional negotiations in order to craft a new policy approach to Mexican agriculture, including trade positions vis-à-vis its NAFTA partners and WTO negotiations.

2 Interest groups, policy and political actors involved

The different actors and their respective positions vis-à-vis the pact negotiations and its aftermath were as follows.

Peasant organizations

Four groups could be discerned among peasant organizations: two radical groups and two rather moderate groups. The CNAM bloc, formed by twelve grass-roots organizations and representing mainly the interests of around 500,000 small farmers producing basic crops in non-competitive conditions (small plots, no irrigation, no credit, poor marketing conditions), was the most important of the radical groups. Their movement reached its climax when 100,000 farmers took part in a rally in downtown Mexico City at the end of January 2003. When interviewed, key leaders of

---

[4] According to Art. 178 of the Mexican Law of Rural Sustainable Development (December 2001), food security is understood as the permanent supply of 'basic and strategic staples' for the population (mainly poor), and 'food sovereignty' is understood when priority is accorded to national production for supplying those staples. Maize, sugar cane, beans, wheat, rice, sorghum, coffee, eggs, milk, poultry and meat, and fish are considered by this same law as 'basic and strategic staples' (Cámara de Diputados 2003: 96).

this group acknowledged that the agro-pact incorporated most of their positions. In fact, concepts such as 'food sovereignty', the multifunctional nature of agriculture, a managed-trade agreement on maize and beans and the necessity of harmonizing SPS measures were part of the banners of this group. However, its most radical claim, the renegotiation of the agricultural chapter of NAFTA, was not incorporated in the agro-pact. The other radical group was El Barzón. This association, grouping different types of members and activists (peasants and urban professional groups), supported the first group politically and ideologically by using provocative means of attracting the attention of the press and federal deputies.

The moderate peasant organization, the Permanent Agrarian Council (CAP), was founded in the 1980s and regrouped twelve organizations, including the National Peasant Confederation (CNC), which had been influential when the Partido Revolucionario Institucional (PRI) was in power.[5] Neither the CAP nor the CNC supported the tactics and some of the demands of the two radical groups. The first organization represents private growers and traders who supported pro-NAFTA reforms during the Salinas years (1988–2004), while the second represented most of the peasants who benefited from agrarian reforms under various PRI administrations.

Government agencies

The Ministry of the Economy, in charge of foreign trade negotiations and agreements, became very active following the launching of the 'agricultural armour plating'. From mid-2002 up to the present they have activated and supervised trade remedies as part of the agricultural package. The ministries of the Economy and Agriculture became the two agencies that started direct talks and negotiations once peasant mobilizations became apparent. Once the movement became politicized, it was the Ministry of the Interior, or Secretaría de Gobernación, that mediated between the executive and the peasant organizations.

During February and March 2003, Gobernación organized a series of round tables with the different blocs and groups in order to reach a consensus for an agreement. Although key actors representing grass-roots

---

[5] The Partido Revolucionario Institucional (PRI) was founded in 1929 and ruled the country with no serious electoral challenge (except in 1988) until 2000. CNC became its principal organization for controlling peasant demands.

organizations recognized tensions and impasses during the negotiation process, the four blocs were able to reach common positions in order to craft the essence and major parts of the agro-pact.[6] As some leaders phrase it, the ANC became a document in which a comprehensive restructuring of agricultural policies was drafted.[7]

Once the ANC was signed, a cabinet-level commission was created in order to supervise and follow up what was agreed.[8] However, this high-ranking commission disappeared in September 2003, and the supervisory functions were moved to the National Council for Sustainable Rural Development (NCSRD), an agency regulated by the Ministry of Agriculture.

Congressional bodies

Congress members became major actors once the institutional phase of the negotiation process started. During 2003 they put pressure on the government to collect tariffs for above-quota staples entering the country.[9] At the end of 2003, congress members agreed that those tariffs were to be compulsorily collected. They also agreed to create a special commission for supervising the enforcement of the mandates covered by the ANC. The special commission was eventually established in March 2004, and embodied seven legislative committees geared to assess and enforce the different goals of the agro-pact. This special commission opened a dialogue with grass-roots organizations in addition to those already established between them and the executive branch.

Congress members began preparing new agricultural planning legislation and creating a research centre on rural studies geared to prepare background material for further legislation.[10] As for the demand for renegotiating the agricultural chapter of NAFTA, there was no consensus on

---

[6] Interview with Max Correa, representative of Central Campesina Cardenista (CCC), Mexico City, 19 May 2004.

[7] Interview with Isabel Cruz, general director, Asociación Mexicana de Uniones de Crédito del Sector Social (AMUCSS), Mexico City, 30 June 2004.

[8] Besides the Interior, Agriculture and the Economy, the ministries of Environment, Agrarian Reform, Treasury and Social Development were also involved.

[9] Since the coming into force of NAFTA the Mexican government did not collect those tariffs recognized by the agreement during the transition period (Yúnez 2002: 9), alleging the protection of consumer interests.

[10] Interviews with Cruz López, PRI deputy president, Comisión de Agricultura y Ganadería, Mexico City, 7 June 2004, and Victor Suárez, PRD deputy secretary, Comisión Especial para el Campo, Mexico City, 17 June 2004.

this among the different legislative factions. Only the PRD supports this demand, but their members recognize the lack of political capital in boosting this claim within the national legislature.

PRD congress members consider that NAFTA has mainly benefited the agri-business vegetable-exporting sector, which represents only a minority of Mexican growers. Other farmers, including grain, fruit, beef, pork and dairy producers, were 'sacrificed' during NAFTA negotiations. That is why PRD congress members oppose a further liberalization of agricultural products within the WTO. Rather they advocate a state-led policy, whose goal would be to enhance food security, 'first of all to avoid Mexico's dependence on US food markets; this dependence could threaten Mexico's national security in the case of an embargo or a conditional restrictive access to the international food market.'[11]

Other actors

Private growers and traders were also involved in the negotiations.

They either participated through the CAP or through the Business Board on Foreign Trade (COECE). COECE was actually founded during the NAFTA negotiations and brought together the most important business associations of the country in order to interact with government negotiators. Government officials either gathered proposals from this organization or asked for its opinion. Its members participated in all the negotiation rounds and fora of the agro-pact, but they were not signatories of its final version, since the government preferred to include only the so-called 'social sector' of agriculture, that is small farmers and *ejido* tenants.[12] Nonetheless, the relationship between the COECE and the government has remained active, mainly within the Doha Round negotiations.

Finally, US agricultural growers also expressed their concerns from the start of the mobilization of Mexican farmers. In August 2002 the American Farm Bureau Federation sent a letter to the US Trade Representative (USTR) asking for a tough line to be taken vis-à-vis the 'armour plating' put into place by the Mexican government, judging it as protectionist. Once the agro-pact was signed, associations such as the US

---

[11] Interview with Suárez.

[12] Interview with Luis Ceja, board member of COECE and vice-president of CNA, Mexico City, 3 July 2004. El Barzón vetoed the participation of those organizations as not being members of CNAM, CAP and CNC. The government probably excluded COECE from the final signature of the agro-pact in order to underline the popular profile of the agreement.

National Corn Growers and the Grains Council openly opposed any re-negotiation of the agricultural chapter of NAFTA (IUST 2003e; see also IUST 2002a and 2003c).

3 Challenges to the Mexican government and the outcome

The first important challenge faced by the Mexican government was to cope with the principal demand of radical peasants to renegotiate the agricultural chapter of NAFTA. Since the beginning of the peasant mobilizations the Mexican government refused to accept this radical demand, arguing that it carried high costs (both economic and political) for the country and for US–Mexican relations. It was not easy for Mexican officials to maintain this position, due to the context in which peasant mobilizations took place. In the midst of the enactment of the US Farm Bill, and of the phasing-out of tariffs and TRQs for most agricultural products coming from the United States and Canada, poor uncompetitive farmers, comprising most of Mexico's rural population, had a powerful flagship for gaining the support of other non-agricultural political organizations. CNAM for instance was skilful enough to gain the support of unions, the media, church members and university students. Furthermore, January–July 2003 was the run-up to elections to the Chamber of Deputies. Since the radicalization of the movement took place in the two first months of 2003, political parties, mainly opposition parties, and other political organizations had the opportunity of emphasizing the peasants' demands as part of their electoral campaigns.

In order to tackle the growing politicization of agrarian claims, the Mexican government activated a two-tier strategy: it reinforced remedies in support of key products and it started negotiations with the four blocs involved in the peasant mobilizations. During 2002, AD and CVD measures were imposed on live swine, beef, apples and rice. The government also imposed SPS on pork, poultry and apples. At the end of that year, Mexican trade law was modified in order to reduce timeframes for investigations, accelerating the imposition of duties and lowering the threshold for an injury finding.

The new law also reduced the time needed for safeguard investigations.[13] In January 2003 Mexico imposed a safeguard on poultry, a few days before the ANC was announced, which ended up as a private undertaking to impose a five-year tariff-rate quota. At that point SPS restrictions were

---

[13] IUST 2002 and 4 April 2003.

also imposed on beans.[14] All these trade remedies were enforced in parallel to government negotiations with the different mobilized groups and were part of the armour plating announced in mid-2002. The government's position was consistent with its refusal to renegotiate NAFTA's agricultural chapter without at the same time renouncing the enforcement of AD, CVD measures and other remedies in order to support Mexican farmers. This position has been maintained up to the present, while domestic supports for farmers have been widened according to the commitments of the ANC.

Once the ANC was signed, the second challenge was to give a satisfactory answer to the demands for a review of the impact of NAFTA and the US Farm Bill on Mexican agriculture. It took almost a year to do so, and on 5 April 2004 the government announced the final assessments carried out by independent institutions. Experts of the International Institute for Agricultural Co-operation (IICA), an organization linked to the Organization of American States (OAS) system, undertook a thorough study of the Farm Bill. It concluded that the competitiveness of US agriculture was rather grounded in the institutional setting in which agricultural policies are crafted, and that domestic transfers in Mexico were higher (except in cotton) than the US equivalents (IICA 2004).

As for the NAFTA assessment, a well-documented study by academic experts from leading Mexican universities arrived at the conclusion that the Mexican rural sector needs a long-term state policy. the main goal of which is not protection but to increase the share of agricultural output in the country's GDP. The Mexican experts recommended an increase in direct investments in this sector, combined with the provision of 'public goods' targeting market development. Supports and subsidies ought to be better targeted, because they benefit commercial farmers more than small, subsistence-oriented farmers or rural workers. The study proposed better co-ordination of rural policies aimed at increasing productivity, income distribution and transfer efficiency for this sector. The demand for a long-term, state-based policy is grounded on the premise that trade liberalization is not enough to make Mexican agriculture competitive. The study recognizes that 'efficiency gains' have been concentrated within fruit and vegetable growing, but that an important segment of grain and oilseed farmers has not yet reaped any benefits. The productivity gap

---

[14] Poultry was supposed to be fully liberalized in January 2003. However, Mexican and US producers agreed an 80,000-ton duty-free quota with a 98% above-quota tariff. Above-quota rates will be phased out at a rate of 20% a year (IUST 2003a, 2003b).

between Mexico and its NAFTA partners has also widened, in spite of some productivity gains witnessed in Mexico. Hence the study also concludes that policy mechanisms must be put in place in order to reduce the costs for adjusting to trade liberalization, and that all relief mechanisms envisaged by NAFTA must be activated (Romero and Puyana 2004).

The two major independent studies ended by discussing renegotiating the agricultural chapter within NAFTA,[15] but framed the ongoing debate within the need to maintain a long-term state-led agricultural development policy.

The third challenge for the Mexican government was to articulate a position on subsidies and domestic supports within the WTO consistent with the ongoing domestic debate on rural development. Mexican officials recognize that export subsidies as well as domestic supports targeting the prices of staples are the most distorting in agricultural trade and affect the income of Mexican growers. They recognize, however, that the reduction of these subsidies and supports is one of the most difficult negotiations within multilateral and regional forums.[16]

Domestic supports, for instance, were accepted within the agricultural agreement of the Uruguay Round, even those that are actionable but remain below an agreed-upon threshold. This is so in the case, for instance, of the supports allowed by the US Farm Bill. One of the major mandates of the Doha Round is precisely to negotiate a further reduction of export subsidies and domestic supports.

The Mexican position was clearly stated in 2003. In agricultural negotiations Mexico will go for the whole package, wherein market access agreements shall be subordinated to the commitment of developed countries to phase out export subsidies, to 'substantially' reduce domestic supports, and to accept a special and differentiated treatment to the country due to its level of development. Although Mexico has negotiated market access in agriculture within its manifold bilateral trade agreements, disciplines on subsidies will only be negotiated within the WTO.[17] In order to strengthen its bargaining capabilities, Mexico also joined the G20 club of developing

---

[15] The possibility of eventually imposing a bilateral safeguard on beans and maize has not, however, been discarded; Mexican officials have explored the possibility (see IUST, 9 May 2003). According to Art. 801.3 of NAFTA, a bilateral safeguard can be imposed if the party affected has agreed on this and there is a satisfactory trade compensation.

[16] Interviews with Ana Aguilar, general co-ordinator, Unidad de estudios agroalimentarios y apoyo a las negociaciones comerciales internacionales, SAGARPA, Mexico City, 4 June 2004, and Héctor Hernández, director, Negociaciones Agropecuarias, Secretaría de Economía, Mexico City, 27 May 2004.

[17] Interview with Hernández.

countries, as it has been able to place the issue of the abatement of subsidies and domestic supports at the forefront of the Doha negotiations.

Mexico's position on agricultural negotiations under the Doha Round has thus become distinctive for two reasons: it has made the opening of its market conditional on the abatement of export subsidies and the reduction of domestic supports and it joined a bloc of developing countries in order to increase its leverage and negotiate a differentiated treatment as a developing country. The first issue is distinctive because Mexico had not made that type of linkage in previous trade negotiations, either bilateral or multilateral. The second is worth noting because by joining the G20 Mexico is returning to a North–South agenda that inspired its own positions when it first joined GATT, in 1986. As an official of the Ministry of the Economy put it, 'Within the WTO, Mexico participates, has participated and will keep participating as a developing country; we are not renouncing that right'.[18] To claim developing country treatment means that market opening and the enforcement of disciplines will not be symmetrical, and that the country will benefit from larger timeframes for reducing tariffs, or differentiated thresholds (in the case of the reduction of domestic supports) for reducing non-tariff barriers. This type of treatment was absent from NAFTA negotiations.

Even though Mexican officials recognize that Mexico's position under the Doha negotiations was crafted prior to the domestic peasant mobilizations and the signing of the agro-pact,[19] they acknowledge that joining G20 was a 'tactical' success: it increased Mexico's leverage in multilateral negotiations and it gained the support of disaffected peasants and PRD congress members.[20] In other words, Mexico's position in the Doha agricultural negotiations has been beneficial so far in political terms, both internationally and domestically. It is not clear, however, to what extent Mexico will be successful in negotiating its agricultural package within the WTO, but this will depend on the evolution of current alliances and the position of the United States, Europe, Japan and key developing countries currently grouped under G20. Up to now, public officials consider

---

[18] Ibid.

[19] Mexico's position on agricultural negotiations for the Doha Round was crafted by COECE in consultation with the Mexican government (interview with Ceja). According to Hernández, from the Ministry of the Economy, 'In fact, before the signature of the Acuerdo Nacional para el Campo, Mexico had decided to join the G20, because in principle and in general terms, the general goals pursued by the G20 are the same ones pursued by Mexico'.

[20] Interviews with Aguilar and Suárez.

Mexico's participation in G20 to be beneficial; however, this partnership will last only as long as Mexico's interests coincides with those of the club: 'Mexico joins a group (within the WTO) when its points of view coincide with those of the group and it ends this association when Mexico's interests do not coincide with the group any longer. This explains Mexico's position within the G20. The group has worked exclusively on matters related to market access for agricultural products and it has proved very beneficial to Mexico's concerns vis-à-vis those countries whose huge subsidies highly distort markets'.[21]

4 Lessons for other countries

Mexican public officials are convinced that NAFTA has been beneficial for Mexican agriculture, since market shares in competitive products increased once the agreement came into force. Domestic production of sensitive products (mainly grains) has not fallen and imports have balanced the growth of national consumption. Hence, they consider that there was no need for any renegotiation on the terms on which agriculture was opened vis-à-vis the United States. However, they recognize that trade liberalization is not tantamount to structural reforms. Trade openness is not enough to boost Mexico's competitiveness in lagging sectors, such as that of grains. Long-term domestic reforms must go hand in hand with the liberalization of agriculture, but must not become a substitute for the former.[22] Mexico also needs to develop its own quality standards, similar to those prevailing in developed countries, to ensure that only healthy and top-quality food and agricultural products enter the country. Standardization measures should be levelled off to US practices. 'We need to develop the institutional and legal frame for enacting so-to-say "mirror policies" related to standards, infrastructure and financing. This is not banned either by NAFTA or WTO. [Their absence] only shows that during the transition period opened by NAFTA; most of the efforts of the country went into dealing with adjacent agricultural or financial problems (e.g. the peso crisis of 1995) instead of devising and implementing long-term policies for boosting the income and competitiveness levels of Mexican growers'.[23]

Opening agriculture to the rest of the world is, however, a different matter. Mexico has hitherto preferred to negotiate à la carte market

---

[21] Interview with Gerardo Traslosheros, general director, Secretaría de Economía, Mexico City, 30 June 2004.
[22] Ibid.   [23] Interview with Aguilar.

access under bilateral terms, seeking to enhance the market shares of agricultural products. When the opening-up of trade seems not to be so favourable, as for example with most of the Latin America countries, sensitive agricultural products remain outside the negotiations. In this respect, Mexico prefers to liberalize these products within WTO negotiations, because the phasing out of barriers is longer and more gradual. Mexico also prefers the WTO forum for negotiating 'horizontal' disciplines such as subsidies and domestic supports. To negotiate them on a bilateral basis, apart from the inherent difficulties, would help outsiders to become free riders.[24] Thus, a major lesson Mexicans can offer other countries is to make the right mix between bilateral deals and multilateral positions.

Market access can be negotiated faster and more efficiently with key economies under bilateral agreements; in contrast, sensitive sectors and horizontal rules and disciplines can be better negotiated within the WTO. Finally, public officials have recognized the importance of grass-roots peasant mobilizations, since they have enlarged the domestic coalition promoting and defending policy reform in Mexico's agriculture.

Leaders of organizations of small farmers concur that their mobilizations and demands relating to the signature of the ANC were a victory for the peasants. They learned that they could put agricultural interests at the forefront of the national debate, in which public officials, academics and congress members have a say. They still perceive the ANC as the general framework for a long-term restructuring of agricultural policies. Even though they consider that trade openness has not been the cause of the lag in productivity and competitiveness in agriculture, they believe that trade liberalization has worsened the situation regarding sensitive products. Hence they call for the liberalization of sensitive products, in Mexico and elsewhere, not to be included in any bilateral or multilateral deal. They also agree that agricultural liberalization should be carried out under the basis of defending 'food sovereignty', in the sense that countries should not compete but rather complement each other and give priority to national growers.

Some leaders have recommended emulating the European example by restructuring the agricultural sector and promoting integration, giving priority to national growers, providing structural funds for reducing asymmetries among economies, sticking to imperatives such as food

[24] Interview with Hernández.

security (avoid dependence on imports) and 'land multi-functionality'.[25] As one of the leaders stated, 'we have to recognize that agriculture embodies a value-added benefit for any society; it is not only the market value of its products, but it is embedded within the cultural values, the environmental quality, social stability and cultural differences that make a society recognize itself as a nation. This becomes the backbone of a country, and thus has more than a market value.'[26]

Other leaders suggest that Mexico should take a more aggressive position within WTO negotiations. Mexico's trade negotiations agenda should put at the forefront the establishment of a 'global agrarian pact, anchored on the principle of defending the food sovereignty of nations. Each nation should be able to produce domestically its strategic staples in order to become self-suppliers. Free trade should apply to the rest of "luxury" staples. This must be the strategy to follow in order to abate famine in the world'.[27]

References

Cámara de Diputados (2003), *Compilación de leyes para el campo*, México, DF.

El campo no aguanta más (2002), 'Seis propuestas para la salvación y revalorización del campo mexicano', mimeo (12 organizations signing), November.

Inside US Trade (IUST) (2002a), 'Farm Bureau Urges USTR To Pressure Mexico on NAFTA Commitments', 23 Aug.

Inside US Trade (2002b), 'Mexico To Strictly Monitor Farm Imports after NAFTA Milestone', 20 Dec.

Inside US Trade (2003a), 'USTR Report Notes New Mexican Barriers, Quiet on EU GMO Case in WTO', 4 April.

Inside US Trade (2003b) 'US Mexico Discuss Wide Range of Farm Disputes, but not Sweeteners', 25 April.

Inside US Trade (2003c), 'Mexican Farm Plan Directs Fox Administration To Seek NAFTA Side Accords', 2 May.

Inside US Trade (2003d), 'Derbez Raises Possibilities of Mexican Safeguards on Beans, White Corn', 9 May.

Inside US Trade (2003e), 'Grassley Letter in NAFTA', 9 May

Instituto Interamericano de Cooperación para la Agricultura (IICA) (2004), *Ley de seguridad agropecuaria e inversión rural 2002 de EE.UU. y sus implicaciones*

---

[25] Interview with Federico Ovalle, general secretary, Central Independiente de Obreros Agrícolas y Campesinos AC (CIOAC), Mexico City, 19 May 2004.

[26] Interview with Cruz.   [27] Interview with Correa.

en México y en los mercados agropecuarios internacionales, downloaded at the IICA website, http://www.iica.org.mx/, 30 June 2004.

Romero, José and Alicia Puyana (2004), 'Evaluación integral de los impactos e instrumentación del capítulo agropecuario del TLCAN', accessed on 30 May 2004 from the Secretaría de Economía website: www.economia.gob. mx/pics/p/p1676/TLCAN-DOCUMENTO-MAESTRO.pdf.

Secretaría de Economía (2003), *Acuerdo nacional para el campo,* 28 April, accessed on 30 May 2004 from the Secretaría de Economía website: www.economia.gob.mx/.

Yúnez, Antonio (2002), 'Lessons from NAFTA: The Case of Mexico's Agricultural Sector', background paper prepared for the World Bank, December 2002.

29

Mongolia's WTO accession: expectations and realities of WTO membership

DAMEDIN TSOGTBAATAR*

1 The problem in context

An ill-prepared accession

Initiating the accession to the WTO was apparently among the first genuinely independent foreign political moves by Mongolia in the multilateral arena. But, after decades of COMECON (Council for Mutual Economic Assistance) membership, the pragmatic, realistic and money-driven mentality of the GATT was not quite familiar to the Mongolians, including their negotiators, at the launch of Mongolia's accession process. This lack of knowledge and understanding, coupled with a newly emerged private sector, led to a lack of political will to mobilize resources and stir a broad-based debate at national level so that the country as a whole could understand what the GATT/WTO accession could bring to the nation. As a result there was no serious economic analysis as to the consequences (be they positive or negative) of accession, except for the political objective of joining the club (i) before its two big neighbours (Russia and China); and (ii) with a view to showing the rest of the world that it was serious in its intention of embracing the market economy unreservedly.

However, the GATT/WTO was not exactly the right institution to join with a political objective of national image-building.

By taking such an 'easy' approach during the accession negotiations Mongolia did not reserve for itself sufficient transition period rights and exceptions, such as most developing member countries aim to secure. This approach also did not equip Mongolia to withstand the pressure mounted on it as to the acceptance of far-reaching concessions. Moreover, in return for its concessions, Mongolia received benefits which it could not make best use of in the near future. The chief reason for this

---

* Executive Director, Mongolian Development Strategy Institute, Unaanbaatar.

was the fact that Mongolia carried out negotiations with such countries as the United States, Canada or Mexico, with which at the moment of launching the negotiations Mongolia had virtually no trade relations. Hence, for Mongolia, undergoing arduous economic reforms, there was only a remote possibility of taking the best advantage of the concessions made by those countries, whereas the six-year accession process, along with the self-induced liberalization, made Mongolia's economy in general freer and more open, of which any country, whether it was a member of the WTO or not, could take full advantage, including Mongolia's two biggest trading partners – Russia (which remains outside the WTO) and China (at that time not a member of the WTO).

Implementation: a one-sided approach

Although the accession was not perfect, since it was a fait accompli the country ought to have focused on building the strategy through which it could still benefit from WTO membership. However, the same old lack of understanding and knowledge of the WTO observed during the accession period persevered unchanged in the post-accession period, thus causing the lack of political will (this time) to make the best use of the WTO. Besides, the domestic industry sector remained too weak and immature to be able to change the flawed attitude of the government. As a result of these factors the Mongolian government took up the unbalanced policy of focusing predominantly on bringing national trade regulations into compliance with the WTO regime; from the perspective of the WTO this is praiseworthy, but not quite so from the perspective of the industries of a developing country. In other words Mongolia, instead of keeping the balance between its own WTO-compliance efforts and the search for the ways to increase market access for its products in other countries (WTO members or non-members in the WTO queue), chose, ironically, a rather Buddhist path of self-perfection and good WTO-consistent behaviour, without regard to whether other countries were doing the same. In the real world of hard cash and profit such 'excellence' and 'idealism' gave immediate and unconditional advantage to imported goods, that is foreign producers, while there was no 'compensation' gained as a result in the form of increased market access for Mongolian exports.

It should be noted that the above argument is not put forward as a criticism of the Buddhist behaviour of Mongolia per se. It is only the one-sided, unbalanced nature of the approach and the under-exploitation of the full potential of WTO membership that is being questioned here.

Otherwise the pro-WTO measures helped the Mongolian economy to become more modern and competitive. Since a brief review of the pro-WTO measures may shed light on their actual impact on the Mongolian economy as well as the pattern of the participation of the Mongolian economy in the WTO, a selective tour of the most visible measures is offered here.

Government Resolution No. 14[1] and Prime Minister's Decree No. 6[2] were among the first decisions taken by the Mongolian government in response to the beginning of the WTO era in Mongolia. Resolution No. 14 allocated the WTO agreements to the appropriate ministries and agencies, while Decree No. 6 listed the laws and regulations that had to be modified and amended in order to bring them into conformity with the WTO.

Decree No. 6 was an ambitious attempt by the government to introduce comprehensive changes at one sweep into the trading regime of Mongolia, including, inter alia, the development of a double-column (MFN and non-MFN) customs tariff system, review of the customs valuation rules, reform of the internal taxation system, simplification of export and import procedures, elimination of bans on certain products and modification of the intellectual property protection regime. However, as the government set about implementing the decree it became evident that building a WTO-consistent trade regime was a laborious, continuous process with a beginning, but no end. Nevertheless, despite hardships and obscurities, many of the objectives sought through Decree No. 6 were achieved. Such achievements were secured at times rather spontaneously, for the country was undergoing the transition to a market economy, and successive governments were persistently pursuing the policy of liberalizing the economy. Therefore most of the measures undertaken in pursuit of such policies ended with good results matching or going beyond the objectives of Decree No. 6 and the WTO commitments of Mongolia.

In sum, it could be argued that the problems described above associated with Mongolia's WTO participation make it in the eyes of the Mongolians just another international organization, which collects membership fees and with which a small country like Mongolia had better comply. The WTO appears to be seen largely as the institution with complex, superior, but alien, rules, which provide fashionable talking fora for the government bureaucrats with little relevance to the earthly needs of the Mongolian

---

[1] Government of Mongolia, Resolution No. 14, 1 *Zasgiin Gazryn Medeelel* (Government Bulletin), 74, 1997.
[2] Prime Minister of Mongolia, Decree No. 6 (1997), Ministry of Foreign Affairs Archives.

industries. Therefore domestic businesses see little use in Mongolia's WTO membership.

2 The local and external players and their roles

For a nation to benefit fully from the WTO system, there has to be a cohesive and co-ordinated interplay between the national actors. In this interplay, ideally, the first objective move to enter or to act within the WTO parameters should be coming from the grass-roots players, that is the domestic industries. In Mongolia there was a reverse pattern of interaction from the beginning. It was the government (which at the onset of the GATT/WTO negotiations was not as yet completely freed from the mentality dictated by the just-abandoned centrally planned economy) that set forth the objectives of membership of the GATT/WTO. Not surprisingly, there was little consultation with the emerging business community of Mongolia – in 1991 there virtually were no private businesses – and limited debate, if any, with civil society at the beginning of the negotiations. This trend, unfortunately, was preserved throughout the accession negotiations, although the government could have taken note of the fact that during the six years of negotiations the private sector of Mongolia had grown to represent almost 60% of Mongolia's GDP. Surprisingly, the government monopoly over WTO business still survives in Mongolia. Moreover, the government in the heat of the pro-compliance drive has time and again exploited the WTO as a scarecrow to 'chill' the calls for support coming from the local business community. The term 'WTO-inconsistent' has almost become the surest expression to discourage any troublesome request from the business community. This in turn suggests that for the government the notion of national industries being the ultimate beneficiaries of the WTO, although it is, indeed, only national governments that are vested with a legal personality under WTO law, remains vague and obsolete. Therefore, the government apparently uses the WTO to discipline national industries rather than to encourage the national producers.

The businesses, on the other hand, irrespective of their growth to represent currently almost 80% of the nation's GDP, remain distanced from WTO affairs. This does not mean that the WTO is irrelevant to them. Neither does it mean that the industries still have preserved their infantile nature, although it is still early to say that they have reached full maturity. It means, rather, that the industries still do not fully comprehend from which angle of their business the WTO rules and opportunities apply

positively to them. It also means that the industries have not got organized to set up strong and powerful sectoral associations. The current
associations are under-funded and overloaded with national-level problems. Therefore they could not extend their activities to international-level
expertise. For example, the meat industry of Mongolia (where the number of livestock exceeds the number of the population by some twelve
to fifteen times) is suffocating because of its reliance on a single buyer,
Russia. Russia is not yet a member of the WTO and hence its trade barriers, especially those applicable to agricultural products (e.g. sanitary
and phytosanitary requirements), tend to be more complex and diverse
than those of the WTO member countries. Nevertheless, Mongolian meat
has been exported to Russia with occasional difficulties for many years.
If Mongolian meat products are capable of filtering through the Russian
market strictures unbound by the WTO there is no reason why they could
not enjoy access into the supposedly more liberal markets of the WTO
members located in north-east Asia. However, this is not the case and the
meat industry association has not as yet appealed to the government with
strong demands to raise or examine the issue within the context of the
WTO.

Another reason for the Mongolian business community to remain relatively distanced from the WTO is that the lion's share of Mongolia's
exports still fall into the category of mineral commodities. The primary
products of the mining sector have enjoyed more liberal access throughout the world, irrespective of the fact of whether or not the exporting or
importing country belonged to the WTO. Therefore the mining sector,
which could not be qualified as immature, since it is one of the more
globalized sectors of Mongolian business, remains less interested in the
WTO.

In discussing the role of private business in Mongolia's WTO-related
policy-making the role of the international investors should also be
touched upon. Foreign investors bring along with their investment knowledge and awareness of the WTO system. Hence they tend to raise the issue
of the WTO with the government more frequently than any other national
player. That explains why most of the WTO-related practical debates with
the government were raised by the representatives of the cashmere industry, where the position of the investors has always been very strong.

As could be seen from what has been put forward in this section, current
WTO-related interaction between the government of Mongolia and the
business community is not exemplary in terms of its cohesion. In fact it
would perhaps not be an exaggeration to say that on the point of the WTO

the government and the business sector may be described as wandering in two separate realms. At this stage the government has a dominating role in the WTO affairs and the business community lags behind with a passive interest in and lack of belief in the use of the global body.

3 Challenges faced and the outcome

As globalization intensifies, developing countries are expected to have a stronger interest in the more consistent operation of the WTO system, to facilitate a rule-based and predictable level playing field for the benefit of every economy of the world. Therefore, it would be equally important for Mongolia to strengthen its capacity to participate efficiently in the WTO. However, such efficient participation will be possible only on overcoming the ignorance on the part of both the government and national industries. An indifferent continuation of ignorance will lead to lost opportunities, which could otherwise assist the economic growth and progress of the country. The lack of WTO expertise and of the political will to master WTO discipline have already caused problems with Mongolia's WTO accession and post-accession policy orientation. The accession and post-accession problems have also affected the mode of practical application of WTO rules.

One of the major challenges that Mongolia is facing currently with the WTO rules is the voluntarism in the interpretation of the rules. The dispute between the cashmere producers and the national customs authority as to the application of the WTO customs valuation rules may serve as a clear example of such voluntary misinterpretation of the WTO rules and the way in which it hinders trade.

In the dispute the cashmere producers complained to the General Customs Department of Mongolia that the customs inspectors responsible for applying the export tax on cashmere had been systematically rejecting the prices declared by the exporters and instead had been applying prices close to the highest registered with the customs authority in the particular year, although it was always clear that cashmere prices were subject to substantial fluctuations in the world market. The department claimed that this approach was consistent with the WTO Customs Valuation Agreement.

The cashmere industry protested against the practice on the grounds that (i) the customs authority could not invoke the Customs Valuation Agreement in its defence, for the agreement did not apply to the calculation of export taxes; and (ii) even if one assumes that the customs authority could apply the import valuation methods to export valuations with appropriate changes, it could not just use the 'higher of two alternative values'.[3]

The cashmere producers engaged in fairly intensive consultations with the customs authority; however, the latter never fully accepted the exporter's arguments. Although as a result of the consultations the customs 'concession' was to use its up-to-date database for determining the export value, it still did not disavow the opportunity to opt for a higher alternative price.

Another challenge that could be observed currently in Mongolia is its increased interest in bilateralism. Apparently the self-perfectionist approach of the government in participating in the WTO, which has no appeal to Mongolia's private sector, as well as the lack of determined leadership at the WTO in defending the interests of a small country like Mongolia, have made bilateral arrangements, such as free trade agreements, more attractive to the Mongolians. The stronger stance, support and leadership of the WTO was missed, for example, by Mongolia when it ran into a puzzle stemming from the collision of the IMF–World Bank economic policy guidelines on Mongolia with the legal rights provided to Mongolia under the WTO. Not surprisingly, cashmere, being Mongolia's most globalized industry, was again the cause of the puzzle.

Before its accession to the WTO Mongolia had in place a ban on cashmere exports, which in the course of the accession negotiations was replaced by a 30% export duty, to be gradually eliminated over ten years.[4] The cashmere producers, especially the foreign investors, knew that tariffying the ban would have a sensible effect on their industry. However, agreeing to introduce a 30% rate, without consulting the industry, was an outcome falling far short of any expected by the cashmere producers.

Furthermore, in introducing the export duty instead of the agreed *ad valorem* rate the Mongolian authorities somehow decided to impose a specific rate of 4,000 tugruks, which was roughly equal to 30% of the export value of raw cashmere at the time of introduction.[5] However,

---

[3] See Agreement on the Implementation of Article VII of the General Agreement on Tariffs and Trade 1994, Art. 7.2(b).

[4] Protocol for the Accession of Mongolia to the Marrakesh Agreement Establishing the World Trade Organization (93 Accession Protocol 94), WT/ACC/MNG/11 (1996), Art. 3, at 118; and WTO, Report of the Working Party on the Accession of Mongolia (93 Working Party Report 94), WT/ACC/MNG/9 (1996), p. 24.

[5] N. Bataa, 'The Present Situation of the Cashmere Processing Sector', in *The Cashmere Summit* (Gobi Regional Economic Growth Initiative, Ministry of Agriculture and Industry, 2000), p. 8.

with a serious rise in the world price for cashmere the 4,000 tugruk rate often slumped down to a level which ranged below 10% of the value of cashmere. The cashmere producers, both the Mongolian companies and foreign investors, in reaction to that started pressing the government to transform at least the specific rate into the proper 30% *ad valorem* rate to discourage the virtually unrestricted export of raw cashmere, which left the local industry with a serious shortage of raw material. The introduction of the *ad valorem* rate would have been consistent with Mongolia's WTO commitment. However, at this point another global institution, the IMF, which has a leading role in Mongolia in (i) facilitating donor community support, and (ii) promoting liberal economic policies, intervened by opposing any change.

The Mongolian government turned to the WTO Secretariat for support,[6] referring to the co-operation agreement between the WTO and the Bretton Woods institutions on achieving greater coherence in global economic policy-making,[7] under which the WTO could seek respect of its legal rules by the IMF and World Bank. Mongolia argued that in its view, for the sake of true inter-institutional coherence the legal rights protected under the WTO should not be jeopardized, if not respected. Moreover, for Mongolia the 30% *ad valorem* rate was the result of six years of negotiations and, if it were to accept easily the power of another international organization in questioning its WTO rights, then for Mongolia the value, integrity and reliability of the entire WTO multilateral legal system would have been put in doubt.

In responding to the Mongolian request the WTO Secretariat confirmed in a very round-about manner that Mongolia would indeed be free to apply an export tariff at a rate not exceeding the 30% limit.[8] At the same time it went on to state that the issue should be resolved in the context of Mongolia's consultations with the IMF and the World Bank, thus distancing itself from the debate and leaving Mongolia face to face with the IMF. The outcome of such a stand-off was predictable – the specific rate remained intact.

---

[6] See Letter from the Prime Minister of Mongolia, Mr N. Enkhbayar, to the Director-General of the WTO, Mr Mike Moore, dated 20 March 2001, Ministry of Foreign Affairs Archives.

[7] See, e.g., Declaration on the Contribution of the World Trade Organization to Achieving Greater Coherence in Global Economic Policymaking, in *Legal Texts: Results of the Uruguay Round of Multilateral Trade Negotiations* (1999), 386–7. See also Singapore Ministerial Declaration, WT/MIN(96)/DEC (18 Dec. 1996), p. 5.

[8] See Letter from the WTO Director-General to the Prime Minister of Mongolia, 18 May 2001, Archives of the Ministry of Industry and Trade.

This sort of indecisiveness on the part of the WTO Secretariat under-standably did not contribute to the consolidation of Mongolian confi-dence in the WTO. Also the lack of progress on substantiating the GATT provision on freedom of transit transportation, always a serious need for Mongolia, a land-locked country, is not making Mongolia more enthusi-astic about the WTO.

Besides these challenges another seems to be looming to press the gov-ernment in the future. With the growth of the economy and the strength-ening of national industries the pressure to increase tariffs is likely to mount. Initially the government will have little difficulty with such pres-sure, for there is sufficient gap between its ceiling binding rate of 20%[9] and the applied rate of 5%.[10] However, once the gap is closed a continuous tug of war between the government and national industries may begin. However, based on the government's present reasoning and behaviour pattern, it may be hoped that the government, in the interest of ensuring long-term economic growth, would not go beyond the limit of its WTO commitments.

4 Lessons for others (the players' views)

As one can see from the review of the selected issues relating to Mongolian membership of the WTO, Mongolia's 'marriage' with the global trade organization was not perfect and free of flaws. However, these flaws and problems do not constitute sufficient grounds to provoke Mongolia into wishing to leave the club. Nowadays it is clear that no country in this ever globalizing world could afford to stay in seclusion outside the universal trading system. This is especially true of a small economy like Mongolia, since without the WTO rule-based system such a player would be doomed to stay confined to its limited markets, while the WTO system opens the doors of opportunity created by economies of scale to the entities in that small economy.

Moreover, the WTO itself is not the cause of the problems faced by Mongolia in its membership. It is rather the flawed approach of Mongolia to the WTO which is triggering the problems; once Mongolia fixes the problems its participation should become more efficient. The possibility of confusing the issue should always be borne in mind, for failure to do

---

[9] Schedule CXXXIV-Mongolia, Part I 96 Schedule of Concessions and Commitments on Goods, WT/ACC/MNG/9/Add.2 (1996).

[10] Parliament Resolution No. 27 (3 June 1999).

so leads to needless frustration and an unjustified lack of interest in the WTO.

Mongolia should therefore undoubtedly continue to retain its commitment to the WTO, while rectifying its strategies in respect of its participation. First of all the government should put an end to the lack of knowledge and understanding of the WTO and seriously start focusing on the build-up of its capacity to master the WTO's disciplines. Otherwise, Mongolia will never be able to avoid the risk of (i) choosing inappropriate policy lines; or (ii) trotting down the path of voluntarism in the interpretation of WTO rules.

Bearing in mind (i) above, the government should also rapidly change its one-sided pro-compliance policy into a balanced approach, which envisages more aggressive efforts to improve market access for national products and services. Given the fact that Mongolia's businesses, which could in fact benefit from the WTO, have not as yet organized the effective defence of their interests (despite their relative growth and gaining in strength), the government should without delay take up the leadership in setting up the habit of regular consultations with business through which it could formulate optimum policy positions on WTO matters. At this stage merely waiting for the emergence of a system whereby the policy positions on various matters are urged by the grass-roots will lead to further loss of opportunities and time.

In the meantime, Mongolian industries should work harder on getting better organized and strengthening their associations so that they could better and more accurately articulate their interests. It is also important for the industries and their associations alike to learn to get their message across to the government. In parallel with those efforts the industries should try to make the best use of foreign investors, which could assist significantly in identifying the opportunities that the WTO may offer.

These changes would bring the government and businesses, currently living in two separate realms, closer. Such an alignment would stimulate Mongolia's improved participation in the WTO.

In addition to the measures elaborated above, the government needs to carry out thorough research as to the gains realized by Mongolia as a result of its participation in the WTO. If the government at the end of the accession negotiations was able to get away without having to sell to the public the outcomes of the negotiations, now that the enthusiasm for the WTO is moderating in both camps, that is the government and business, it should now display hard evidence as to the gains that Mongolia has achieved. Without such research it will be hard to respond to the surge of bilateralism or the potential increase in the demand by domestic industries for protectionist barriers to be raised. It would be better if the research is carried out in co-operation with the WTO Secretariat, for Mongolia may indeed lack expertise in carrying out such a job. It may, for example, be included in the agenda of the trade policy review scheduled to be undertaken by the Trade Policy Review Body of the WTO in 2005.

Finally, all the lessons learnt from Mongolian participation may turn out to be useful for other countries operating under similar conditions and in similar situations.

30

Nepal: the role of an NGO in support of accession

P. R. RAJKARNIKAR*

1 The problem in context

Nepal is a small landlocked country situated between China and India. Access to sea is only through India, and India is also Nepal's major trading partner. Trade with India constitutes 55.9% of total trade, according to 2003 data. A bilateral trade treaty between Nepal and India governs the trade between these two countries, and similarly the transit treaty between two countries provides Nepal with access to the sea.

The treaties could not be renewed in 1989, when they lapsed, due to certain disputes, and the impasse resulted in a serious shortage of goods in Nepal, including critical inputs to the manufacturing sector and goods meeting basic needs. The difficulties that Nepal had to face because of bilateralism compelled it to seek entry into the multilateral trading system. Thus shortly after the trade and transit treaties with India lapsed, Nepal applied for accession to the General Agreement on Tariffs and Trade (GATT – the WTO's predecessor).

The impasse with India lasted for fifteen months. In 1990, there were political changes in Nepal; a multiparty system was restored and a new government came to power, which successfully renegotiated the Nepal–India trade and transit treaties. After this, the urgency for Nepal to accede to GATT, to be protected under Article V on transit rights, lessened and its interest in accession waned.

Until the mid-1980s, Nepal had adopted heavily inward-looking development strategies. In 1985 it introduced an economic reform programme in a modest way, and from the early 1990s geared up the process of economic reform and renewed its commitment to WTO membership,

---

* Executive Director, Institute for Policy, Research and Development, Kathmandu. This study was prepared on the basis of secondary information and in consultation with Ratnakar Adhikari, executive director, SAWTEE. As the title suggests this case study is focused on SAWTEE, but in no way does this mean that the role of other NGOs is less important.

realizing that the membership of the WTO would help its better integration into the global economy, thereby making available wider markets for Nepalese exports and more sources of foreign investment.

Nepal gained GATT observer status in 1993 and participated in the final meeting of the Uruguay Round. In 1995 Nepal again presented a formal application to accede to the newly created WTO, this time with a desire to globalize the economy, not just to be protected with transit rights.

In 1998 Nepal, in accordance with WTO procedure for accession, submitted a memorandum of its foreign trade regime. This was followed by the formation of the working party for Nepal's accession to the WTO, and the government was engaged in follow-up activities to expedite the process. However, as in other developing countries, there was fear in certain sections of Nepalese society that it would be difficult for the country to face the challenges that might emerge in the aftermath of WTO accession. Furthermore, a sizable section of society took the view that accession to the WTO would result in adverse effects on the Nepalese economy, resulting in closure of domestic industries due to weaker competitive strength and in an increase in unemployment. There was also the problem that the WTO was not completely understood: the pains were well understood but the gains were not. Thus public opinion was not strongly supportive of the membership bid. Against this backdrop, a smooth accession could not be expected, and it was feared that there might even be domestic opposition.

Some civil society organizations, including South Asia Watch on Trade, Economics and Environment (SAWTEE), were strongly in favour of Nepal's obtaining WTO membership. They had faith in the multilateral trading system and took the view that Nepal would gain from it. Meanwhile, they were also critical of the 'WTO-plus' conditions often imposed by existing members on an acceding country. They were aware of the fact that countries wishing to accede to the WTO have to follow not only multilateral but also bilateral negotiations, during which applicant countries are asked to undertake 'WTO-plus' commitments. In their opinion the WTO is inherently power-based, which is the very antithesis of the WTO's credo that countries do not receive what they desire but what they negotiate. Therefore they were concerned to build the strength and skill in negotiation of the Nepali negotiating team. They were also concerned about domestic preparations.

There was a legal provision under Nepal's parliamentary system, according to which agreements made by the government with international organizations become effective only after ratification by the House of Representatives. In March 2002 Prime Minister Sher Bahadur Deuba had dissolved it, creating additional problems or uncertainty in obtaining WTO membership.

The fifth Ministerial Conference of the WTO held in Cancún in September 2003 approved Nepal's accession to the WTO and offered membership, subject to ratification by the government. Nepal was required to ratify the protocol of accession by 31 March 2004, as per the terms of its accession. But since there was at the time no House of Representatives and the government was non-representative, ratification became uncertain. On one hand, the political parties could oppose ratification by a non-representative government on political and legal grounds, but on the other hand it would be disastrous for Nepal to defer ratification for the reason that Nepal would not be able to maintain the policy flexibilities it had been able to acquire during the tough negotiation process in any future attempts to gain membership. Deferring the accession process would mean additional commitments in such areas as investment, the environment, trade facilitation, transparency in government procurement, competition and most of the other areas which had been negotiated in a single package during the Cancún Ministerial Conference.

2 The local players and their roles

SAWTEE was one of the non-governmental organizations (NGOs) which played an active and positive role in Nepal's accession to WTO. It is a non-profit-making organization which was established in December 1994. It operates as a regional network through its secretariat in Kathmandu and eleven network institutions in five south Asian countries, namely Bangladesh, India, Nepal, Pakistan and Sri Lanka. Its mission is to enable south Asian communities to benefit from and minimize the adverse effects of changing regional and global economic paradigms. Its broad objective is to build the capacity of concerned stakeholders in south Asia by equipping them with knowledge, information and skills to voice their concerns in the context of globalization and liberalization. One of its specific objectives is to enhance the participation of developing countries, in particular least developed countries (LDCs) and landlocked countries, in the global trading system.

Of the member countries of SAWTEE, until its accession in April 2004 Nepal alone was not a member of the WTO. As it is within the scope of their work, SAWTEE, along with other NGOs, made a remarkable contribution to Nepal's accession to the WTO.

Though critical of it, SAWTEE understood the WTO not only as a threat or challenge but also as an opportunity for Nepal. Its executive director, Ratnakar Adhikari, took the view that the survival of the multilateral trading system is more important for the developing countries than the developed countries, so that it is necessary for the former to support the system. He believed that SAWTEE should play a positive and active role in facilitating Nepal's accession to the WTO, mainly for the following reasons.

- The WTO trading system provides a degree of certainty of market access. Trade becomes more predictable, which in turn encourages trade and investment in the country. In this context, he recalled the bad experience of the sharp decline in Nepalese exports of woollen carpets to Germany when it unilaterally banned import of carpets from Nepal on the pretexts of the use of child labour or of azo dyes. WTO membership provides access to its dispute settlement procedure and legal recourse to contest capricious trade policies imposed by trading partners.
- The WTO rules grant transit rights to the member countries. This is a most important benefit of WTO membership for a landlocked country such as Nepal. It has a crucial impact not only on Nepal's foreign trade but also on the whole process of its development. An unhindered and cost-effective transit facility enhances the competitive strength of the economy.
- There are several other international conventions on transit rights. But they are less effective in implementation, and also lack an effective regulatory authority, whereas the WTO provides a strong regulatory mechanism to enforce its rules.
- WTO membership enforces a rules-based trade regime, increasing transparency and reducing corruption and uncertainties in trading activities.

SAWTEE played its role of facilitating Nepal's accession to the WTO mainly in two areas, namely (i) creating a critical constituency, and (ii) strengthening the government's hand. It launched a massive advocacy effort through its regular publications and monthly forum on globalization and the WTO, organized jointly with Action Aid Nepal (AAN),[1] to create a critical constituency.

---

[1] Action Aid has been in Nepal since 1982. From the very beginning, AAN has been working with the poorest and most downtrodden. It encourages communities to take an active role in their own development process and aims to develop links by working with the government and with NGOs. It is also geared towards advocating the rights of the poor and influencing policy in their favour.

SAWTEE publishes occasional briefing papers on various topics related to its mission. It published several papers on different aspects of the WTO and brought out a study report on the gender implications of Nepal's accession to the WTO. In 2002, on the eve of Nepal's accession, it published a briefing paper entitled 'The Challenges of the WTO: Rethinking Strategies'. This paper offered the message to its readers that globalization was not an option for the developing countries, and that they should have strategies to adjust themselves to and manage the challenges of globalization. It had also published a book in July 2003, *The Road to Cancún*, which analyzed WTO agreements in the context of Nepal's accession.

SAWTEE also brings out quarterly printed newsletters and monthly electronic newsletters. These, with a large readership including policymakers, academics, media professionals and civil society activists, covered a wide range of issues related to Nepal's accession.

From February 2003 SAWTEE and AAN started jointly organizing a monthly forum on globalization and the WTO in Kathmandu. These included as participants a wide range of stakeholders including policymakers, the private business sector, academia, the media and civil society and activists. The one-year programme focused on various issues and agreements affecting Nepal's accession and the way forward, and the regional agreements signed by Nepal and their pros and cons. The reports of monthly fora were posted on the official website and included in the e-newsletters.

On the part of strengthening the government's hand in the process of accession, SAWTEE provided the government with suggestions on different issues, including the protection of farmers' interests, anti-competitive and monopoly practices. Adhikari was included in the official delegation to the Cancún Ministerial Conference. He took it as a recognition of SAWTEE's contribution on WTO issues and the co-operation it extended to the Nepalese government during the accession process.

3 Challenges faced and the outcome

The advocacy of SAWTEE and other NGOs had a positive impact in favour of WTO membership. Negative attitudes towards the WTO declined. People realized that entry into the WTO was inevitable, albeit they were concerned about the threat of 'WTO-plus' conditions and about the domestic preparations needed to ensure that accession would be favourable for Nepal.

In the course of the accession process, challenges emerged in three main areas, namely (i) tariff binding for agricultural products, (ii) resisting pressure to join UPOV, and (iii) domestic political support for ratification of the accession agreements. However, with the help of NGOs including SAWTEE, Nepal managed to meet the challenges successfully, which ultimately resulted in positive outcomes.

Tariff binding for agricultural products

Agriculture is the mainstay of the Nepalese economy; it is the source of livelihood for more than 80% of the population. But Nepal's applied tariffs on agriculture were very low, ranging from zero to 10%. NGOs in Nepal including SAWTEE had realized the need to protect Nepalese farmers through an appropriate level of tariff binding at the time of accession to the WTO. At the initiative of AAN they formed a loose network of NGOs with the Federation of Nepalese Chambers of Commerce and Industries (FNCCI) and the Ministry of Agriculture and Co-operatives (MOACS) in April 2003. The network convinced the government of the need to protect Nepalese farmers and the food security of the Nepalese people by providing adequate tariff protection to sensitive agricultural products. They worked out the appropriate tariff bindings for sixty agricultural products with proper justifications and submitted them to the government. With this background, Nepal proposed binding tariffs on agricultural products at an average of 30%. Initially, developed member countries opposed the proposal in view of the existing applied rate, but with the help of the detailed work done by the Network, the Nepalese negotiators convinced them of the need to create a policy space for protecting the agriculture sector. Finally, the average tariff binding on sensitive agricultural products was fixed at 51% for the transition period and 42% thereafter. This was a remarkable achievement in view of the prevalent low level of the applied rate, at 10%.

Resisting the imposition of UPOV

At the final stage of its accession negotiations Nepal was under pressure from one trading partner country to become a member of the International Union for the Protection of New Varieties of Plants (UPOV). UPOV is seen as providing a high level of protection to plant breeders but as severely weakening the position of farmers, restricting their rights to save, reuse, exchange and sell seeds. This proposal came to the notice of the Nepalese authorities on 9 August 2003, only a day before the Nepalese delegation had to leave for Geneva to finalize its accession to the WTO.

After receiving this proposal the government authorities asked a member of SAWTEE to prepare a briefing for them. The brief, 'Why Nepal cannot and should not join the UPOV', was handed over to the head of the WTO Division of the Ministry of Industry, Commerce and Supplies at 10.30 p.m. on 9 August 2003, giving various reasons for not joining.

Government officials made a public announcement that they would not compromise the interests of Nepalese farmers while obtaining WTO membership. Prior to their departure for Geneva, they promised that they would deal with the issue bilaterally and close the chapter once and for all.

Members of SAWTEE remained in constant touch with the government delegates by phone. NGOs were seriously concerned about the possible infringement of the rights of Nepalese farmers over seeds and local biological resources as a result of Nepal's entry into UPOV. A meeting of core members of the National Alliance for Food Security – Nepal (NAFOS)[2] was organized on 11 August to discuss possible future strategies. One of the major decisions of the meeting was to publish articles in various newsletters highlighting the need to ward off the pressure to join UPOV. Two members of SAWTEE published three articles within four days in two of the leading national dailies. Similarly, two posters, one in Nepali and the other in English, were also published and distributed to all the concerned stakeholder groups.

The NGOs also organized a press conference in Kathmandu on 13 August under the banner of NAFOS. Journalists from all the leading media organizations, farmer's groups, lawyers and other stakeholder groups participated in the conference.

The press coverage of the event was among the best during the NGOs' advocacy campaign. The next day, almost all the media provided prominent coverage, and it also came to the notice of the trading partner country's trade representative's office in Geneva.

On the final day of the accession negotiation, 15 August 2003, it was agreed to include only minimal text in the final working party report, which states:

---

[2] NAFOS is a network of NGOs and INGOs working in Nepal for the cause of protecting and promoting food security and farmers' rights. It was founded by Action Aid Nepal, together with other like-minded organizations, including SAWTEE, in 1999. SAWTEE is currently the secretariat of this network.

Nepal would also look at other WIPO and IP-related Conventions, e.g. Geneva Phonograms Convention, UPOV 91, WIPO Copyright Treaty and WIPO Performances and Phonograms Treaty, in terms of the national interest and explore the possibility of joining them in the future, as appropriate.

Ratification of the agreement on accession to the WTO

After an effort lasting more than a decade and several rounds of both multilateral and bilateral negotiations, Nepal finally received an offer of WTO membership on 11 September 2003, subject to ratification of the protocol of accession by the Nepali government by 31 March 2004. According to the legal provisions of Nepal the protocol needed to be ratified by the House of Representatives.

The offer came at a time when the country was in a state of political turmoil. The House of Representatives had been dissolved by the then Prime Minster a year previously. The incumbent government, appointed by the king, was hence non-representative, and political parties were protesting in the street against it. The task of ratification was thus politically and legally challenging.

As it was uncertain when the country would have a House of Representatives in place, the government was also not in a position to ask for extension for the ratification period, since it could not ask for an indefinite extension. It had an option to amend the legal provisions through promulgation of an ordinance, but the political parties, including the Nepali Congress and the Nepali Congress (Democratic), who were in the government as a united party at the time of applying for the membership, were likely to oppose such a move on political and legal grounds. In such a critical situation NGOs, including SAWTEE, through their various advocacy mechanisms, were able to persuade public opinion to be in favour of not deferring accession to the WTO. Through their articles and deliberations in different fora they expressed the view that if Nepal missed the opportunity of entering the WTO, it would cost the country very dear.

Towards the third week of March 2004 the government promulgated an ordinance paving the way for ratification, and were not opposed by the political parties. On 24 March 2004 Nepal notified the WTO that the process of ratification and acceptance of the protocol of accession had been completed. According to established practice, the entry into force of the protocol occurred thirty days later, on 23 April 2004. Nepal obtained membership of the WTO as the 147th member and the first least developed country (LDC) member.

4 Lessons for others

As elsewhere, people in Nepal had differing views on the WTO; the debate
on the pros and cons of the WTO system would probably never end.
However, it was widely accepted that countries need to be integrated
with the global economy through the multilateral trading system. It was
also recognized that Nepal could not remain in isolation from the fast
integrating global economic system. With membership of the WTO Nepal
would be able to participate in future important trade-related decision-
making. From Nepal's experience, it has become clear that NGOs can
play a meaningful role in influencing public opinion. It was the advocacy
of NGOs that helped people to understand the nature of the WTO and
reduce negative attitudes towards it. This created a domestic political
environment conducive to the accession of Nepal. The approach of the
NGOs created opportunities for them to work closely with the government
to some extent. This, in turn had enhanced transparency in government
activities in relation to WTO accession.

The Nepalese experience showed that even the efforts of the larger
countries to impose 'WTO-plus' conditions could be avoided with the help
of NGOs by means of networking, which had also corrected the perception
that the WTO is the tool of powerful lobbies. What is important is the
power of and skill in negotiations, through which the acceding country
can convince the working party.

Another important lesson that Nepal learned is that the approach of
networking, rather than the efforts of a single NGO, is more effective in
advocacy, and that advocacy becomes effective if it covers all stakeholders.

The commitment of the government to enact and enforce competition
law in a time-bound manner in the process of obtaining WTO membership was another important aspect of the Nepalese experience. NGOs, by
lending a helping hand to the government, can also advance the cause of
fair trade in the country.

Accession to the WTO is not only the business of government. It is
the concern of the country as a whole, including NGOs, farmers, consumers and others. Socio-economic conditions differ between developed
and developing countries. Hence the implications of WTO accession also
differ.

Based on his experience in the course of Nepal's accession process,
Ratnakar Adhikari, SAWTEE's executive director, believes that NGOs in
acceding countries should, first, conduct research on the impact of the
various WTO agreements on the poor, marginalized and vulnerable. They

should also find out which of the agreements reduce the policy space of governments seeking to protect and promote their national development priorities.

Second, NGOs should determine which 'WTO-plus' conditions the members of the accession working party are trying to impose on their countries. Third, they should work closely with the government not only to elicit the information (which is invariably otherwise kept confidential) about the terms of accession but should also provide suggestions to the government on how to fend off the pressure on them to agree to things that are 'WTO-plus' in nature. Fourth, they should gain strong public support and make use of the media to make themselves heard. Finally, if the government does not take notice of them through the regular channels, they should use other pressure tactics (campaigns, demonstrations) to make their message loud and clear.

31

Nepal: exports of ayurvedic herbal remedies and SPS issues

BIJENDRA SHAKYA*

1 The problem in context

When his company received a hefty order from a Swedish importer in August 2000, Prem Raj Tiwari rejoiced with much enthusiasm at a relatively big business deal. The single largest export order the company ever had for ayurvedic products – processed medicinal herbs – had strengthened his aim of reviving the company's languishing export trade by cashing in on the flourishing world demand for herbal products. But Tiwari's enthusiasm was soon dashed when he received an e-mail from his Narkayrd-based Swedish counterpart withdrawing the order. The mail stated that the company's product samples did not pass the 'satisfactory and sufficient' sanitary and quality standard tests for access to the Swedish market. Moreover, Tiwari was astonished to learn of the requirement for a certificate of good manufacturing practices (GMP) for each consignment.

Until this incident, Tiwari had not been aware of the requirements for such a specific test and the GMP certificate in order to be able to export the company's products. The GMP is a system of quality assurance and quality control not only for the products themselves but also for the pre- and post-manufacturing processes to ensure sanitation and the minimization of the risks inherent in food and medicinal production, processes which cannot be assessed by only testing the final products.

Tiwari's company, the Gorkha Ayurved Co. – a joint venture between Nepalese and French investors – had gained about 6% of the domestic market for herbal products. One of the major products of the company was the herbal tea sold under the established brand name Guduchi, known as a health drink. The popularity of Guduchi had, in fact, tempted other herbal firms into imitation of the brand name. Other key products manufactured

* Chief, WTO Cell, Garment Association of Nepal, New Baneswor.

by the company were about fifty herbal remedies, based on ayurvedic medicines or traditional health science. Satisfied with the sales volume in the local market, which allowed the company to break even, Tiwari, the managing director, contemplated good prospects for the export of ayurvedic medicines, as he had received business inquiries from Germany, France, Italy, Sweden, the Czech Republic and Australia over the previous couple of years.

Since Tiwari joined the company as a financial consultant in 1999, he had seen tremendous scope in this sector, for two main reasons. First, the international demand for herbal products was growing at an annual rate of 10% on average, and the global market for herbal medicines was expected to reach US$16 billion by 2005, according to a recent study. Second, Nepal had witnessed a smooth growth trend in export of herbal products, indicating one of the most potential areas of comparative advantage. That had resulted in an increased number of foreign investors – particularly the popular Indian herbal product manufacturers – being attracted to Nepal to exploit the country's favourable climate and abundance of a wide variety of aromatic plants and medicinal herbs. Nepal is endowed with more than 700 species of medicinal and aromatic plants, of which 250 species are endemic. These companies had firmly established backward and forward linkages and had exported products made from Nepalese herbs under their own brand names. However, Nepal's share in the global market for the product range remained minuscule, despite promising signs.

2 The local and external players and their roles

Although the share of herbal products in Nepal's export basket seemed to be modest, Tiwari expected three points of comparative advantage for his company to boost trade in this product line. First, the export of herbal products, including the ayurvedic remedies, did not have to face stiff price competition due to a limited number of suppliers in the world market. Second, these products had been enjoying duty advantages, as they were exempted from the customs duties under the generalized system of preferences (GSP) applying to Nepalese goods in all major international markets. Third, ayurvedic remedies had been noticeably concentrated in the European markets that accounted for almost half of the global demand for herbal remedies: Germany and France were the most prominent markets in Europe.

Despite these advantages the Swedish importer's requirement had, for the first time, put Tiwari in a very complicated situation if he was to strike a successful export business deal. If his company's products were to gain access to the Swedish market, they needed to undergo tests, in particular for organochloropesticide, fungicide and heavy metal, but also other detailed microbiological tests, which were not easily available in Nepal. In addition, the requirement of the 'stringent' GMP certification had come as a surprise to him, as he had hitherto been used only to basic laboratory tests for sanitary certificates.

In the meantime Tiwari was surprised to get an order in October 2001 from a Sydney-based importer who did not seek any such complicated tests and certification. Only a general sample test was required for the products, which were exported in the form of a single ingredient in powder form, before entering the Australian market. Since then, Gorkha Ayurved had regularly been exporting wide varieties of ayurvedic remedies without any stringent requirements.

Baffled by the two different quality and sanitary requirements for the same product range, Tiwari at first thought that the Swedish importer's conditions were 'arbitrary' and intended as barriers to trade in the importing country. Similarly, he was bewildered by the application of 'double standards' in international trade and reckoned that the buyers' requirements could possibly impede his company's export endeavours.

But soon he learned that the buyers could ask for compliance with international standard under the WTO's Sanitary and Phytosanitary Measures (SPS) Agreement. That is because the WTO recognizes internationally harmonized standards and encourages member countries to use them as a basis for their SPS measures in order to reduce distortions in market access. The SPS Agreement is consistent with the standards and guidelines of the FAO and WHO with respect to food additives, pesticide residues, contaminants, hygienic practices and methods of analysis and sampling for harmonizing international rules in this field of trade.

Thus, contrary to his initial perception, Tiwari discovered that his Swedish counterpart's requirement for GMP was in conformity to the international standards. The GMP code, developed by WHO, was in fact the internationally harmonized system for assuring quality and sanitary standards in trade related to medicinal products. In a number of advanced countries all herbal products were strictly required to be made under the GMP code. No wonder he then understood why the code of GMP had become a common requirement. Regarding the two different standards requirements, he was assured that the Australian importer was entitled to use less strict standards if they were still considered to be sufficient.

In such a situation, Tiwari understood that he had no choice other than to prepare his company to meet the international sanitary and quality standards under the guidance and support of the domestic system if he did not want to lose any lucrative business order in the future. Regarding the export of ayurvedic remedies he came to know that without the assurance of the GMP certification it wouldn't be that simple to win importers' hearts and get through the border regulations in importing countries.

Buyers in Western countries had increasingly been asking for GMP certificates for aryurvedic remedies, as these products were relatively vulnerable to contamination and unwanted substances. Meeting the quality assurances for ayurvedic remedies was comparatively complicated, because they were prepared from material of plant origin which might be exposed to a higher risk of contamination and deterioration. Unlike conventional pharmaceutical products, they may vary in composition and properties, as well as in the application of procedures and techniques. Apparently there was no exact surveillance system to be followed internationally as to standard and quality control in ayurvedic medicines. However, GMP had been considered as a basis of sanitary standards for this product category. Failure to comply with the requirements by importers in the respective countries had resulted in severe consequences: penalties, confiscation and even the rejection of consignments.

'If international buyers were entitled to ask for the quality and sanitary assurances according to the internationally recognized system, the exporters were then obliged to meet the requirement if they wanted to avoid market access complications in importing countries, and to retain exporter's positions in international markets for products like ayurvedic remedies, which indicated an increasing trend', Tiwari asserted. Keeping that in mind he contacted the Royal Drug Research Lab (RDRL), the government-owned drug quality control authority, and the Department of Food Technology and Quality Control – DFTQC (previously the Central Food Research Laboratory), the responsible government body for the inspection and accreditation of food standards, to find out if they could be of any help in preparing his company for the buyers' requirements.

3 Challenges faced and the outcome

Unfortunately, Tiwari found both institutions without any plan or policy regarding SPS standards, including the GMP certification procedures, particularly with regard to the export of products in the herbal and ayurvedic category. Although Nepal was in the process of acceding to the WTO at that time, no serious efforts were being made on policy or the institutional framework for the SPS requirements. That had resulted in a more confused situation for exporters, including Gorkha Ayurved, posing complex questions for export promotion strategy. 'How could we exploit the country's comparative advantage if the authorized bodies lacked the vigilance and departmental co-ordination to guide exporters and enforce the system recognized internationally, in the wake of Nepal's accession to the WTO?' Tiwari lamented as his problem was left unresolved.

But with endorsement of Nepal's membership to the WTO at the Cancún Ministerial in September 2003 there were reasons for Tiwari to be optimistic about his endeavour. In its accession negotiations Nepal had committed to full implementation of the SPS requirement by 1 January 2007. For that reason His Majesty's Government of Nepal (HMG) has designated the DFTQC as the national enquiry point for SPS. The DFTQC, which enforces food-related laws and code of conduct, had now been made responsible for initiating co-ordination between the government departments and the private sector regarding the implementation of the international SPS mechanism. Following that the department had expedited efforts to synergize the network and had developed a departmental structure to function effectively as the SPS national inquiry point by 2004. That required the DFTQC to implement the risk assessment mechanism and the pest detection and eradication campaigns, including the strict quarantine procedures to support Nepalese exporters in meeting the SPS standards. Among other important steps taken by the Department was promoting the awareness of FAO and WHO quality and sanitary systems among all stakeholders, to be followed by the application of the basic rules and then the fully-fledged operation of the FAO rules and WHO GMP standards in Nepal. The Department as a focal point had also actively participated in the aim of the member states of the South Asian Association for Regional Co-operation (SAARC) of implementing the FAO/WHO systems within the region by 2005.

As Tiwari went on inquiring, he found out that the Department of Drug Administration (DDA), which enforces pharmaceutical standards and quality control in Nepal, was the proper government authority to deal with the SPS system for ayurvedic remedies. However, since the DFTQC had been designated as the national SPS inquiry point, the DDA was supposed to co-ordinate with the former for policy implementation and monitoring GMP standards for products related to remedies.

Interestingly, Tiwari was surprised to know that the DDA had already made GMP mandatory for the importing of all kinds of drug-related products into Nepal since 2000. Also it had voluntarily imposed the GMP on the domestic pharmaceutical manufacturers. As soon as Nepal had acceded to the WTO, the DDA had informally instructed all pharmaceutical manufacturing companies, including the herbal medicinal producers, to abide by the WHO GMP code by the end of 2006, as a prerequisite to the SPS mechanism.

With that policy in the offing the DDA and the medicinal manufacturers both had obligations to meet. The DDA as an executing government body should have prepared itself for the accreditation of GMP certification in the country. Its organizational structure should have been strengthened to achieve the inspection and auditing capacity for effectively monitoring and evaluating the system. Additionally, it should have developed mechanisms to determine the basic requirements to be fulfilled by the firms which were obliged to operate under the GMP system. The criteria to be developed included the selection and approval of site designs, equipment selection guidelines, performance qualifications and data processing. As part of the capacity development programme, its staff have been trained by foreign experts to mobilize them as GMP auditors.

On the part of the industrial sector, businesses were required to develop the GMP-related physical facilities and implementation know-how themselves. These were supposed to be the preconditions for being officially certified for the system. Of the thirty-eight pharmaceutical manufacturers in the country, six had already made preparations for conformity with GMP before the deadline and had already requested inspection and certification from the DDA.

Although it took some time, Tiwari's untiring investigation had made him acquainted with the significance of the GMP system and its policy issues. 'Yet almost all herbal and ayurvedic manufacturers had remained unaware of its necessity because there were no genuine authorities to help them and because they lacked business advocacy skills especially within the industry concerned', Tiwari said. Nevertheless, it seemed to him that it would be worth taking his company under the GMP system to be compatible with the SPS requirements, in order to avert market access barriers in other countries and also to achieve his ambition to promote exports. His exploration of the system and policy matters gave him enough ideas for taking the necessary actions.

First of all, Tiwari raised the issue at a meeting of the company's board of directors. The meeting had been called to discuss the possibility of shifting the company's final processing units from Gorkha district, where its entire manufacturing processes had been taking place, to Kathmandu, for direct supervision. He took this opportunity to inform the other board members about the importance of SPS requirements and advised the building of the necessary infrastructures within the proposed plan for compliance with the GMP and SPS systems. The board members approved Tiwari's proposal without any hesitation.

Accordingly, Gorkha Ayurved launched the project by purchasing land in Kathmandu. It planned to utilize the company's capital reserve and external financing to meet the 'huge' project cost, estimated at Rs 25 million (approximately US$338,000). Tiwari informed us that 'We had contacted a specialist from Italy for the consultancy services on GMP technical inputs, among others. It required additional funding of Rs 900,000 (US$12,000) for a month of services that would be an extra financial burden to the company.' If the financial constraint was not an obstacle and the government was fully committed to the policy implementation, Gorkha Ayurved would be equipped with the GMP process to meet the international SPS standards within the stipulated time – Tiwari was confident about that.

4 Lessons for others (the players' view)

Tiwari explained what he had learned.

> I encountered difficulties in meeting the importers' requirements that inspired me to delve into the issue of quality and sanitary standards in international trade. It was indispensable for me to gain in-depth knowledge about the application of the provisions, domestically and internationally, in order to overcome the market access problem to meet my goal for export promotion.
>
> Without a constant follow-up and vigilance I wouldn't have successfully convinced the company board members about the benefit of assembling the GMP facility within my company's proposed plan to build a processing unit in Kathmandu. Of course, the DDA's instruction for GMP application and Nepal's systemic commitment to full implementation of the SPS measures in its accession protocol to WTO membership had actually given me ample reasons to raise the issue at the company board meeting.
>
> I think that was the key to success for getting approval from the board to make the company prepare itself for the internationally recognized standards, despite the initial requirement of huge financial and technical investments.
>
> Including the constraints of initial investments to the companies like mine, there were a number of internal challenges to effectively implement

the SPS standards. First of all, the government's commitment to meet the SPS regulation within the stipulated timeframe can only be determined by the financial resources and technical expertise at its disposal.

He pointed to one of the studies that calculated that the Nepalese government was seeking more than US$12 million to introduce an improved SPS regime. 'It's difficult for the government to easily adopt the internationally recognized policy and build capacity for the purpose unless financial and technical assistance from international donors is forthcoming.'

The government has received assurances of support from different international donors. Remarkably, the European Union (EU) had approved technical assistance for SPS national capacity building for Nepal. Tiwari's suggestion was that the technical assistance should at the same time be diverted to develop the DFTQC as the fully-fledged SPS national inquiry point and to the capacity-building of the SPS-related departments, including the DDA, which was the body responsible for enforcing the GMP.

Tiwari commented that 'The private sector should also benefit from the technical assistance, as it had an immense role to play in the awareness and business advocacy on Nepal's entry into the WTO and its commitment to the SPS mechanism. Many stakeholders, including the business community, thought they did not have roles to play in the multilateral trading system. They need to be able to understand the possibility of unfavourable consequences in international business if trade rules are not well understood.'

> There were two things to be done urgently in this regard. First of all there should have been regular government–private-sector interactions to exchange their views on the multilateral trading system. One of the objectives of the purpose should have been to listen to the voice and concerns of the Nepalese business community. However, that would not have been achieved until the private-sector associations came forward to lead in their respective fields.

Considering the rapidly changing global trading environment, Tiwari recently took the initiative in establishing the Ayurvedic Medicine Producers Association of Nepal (AMPAN). He has assumed the post of general secretary of the association with much pride.

But it is early days yet and there is still much the Association hopes to achieve in advocating the needs of its members.

32

Import prohibition as a trade policy instrument: the Nigerian experience

ADEMOLA OYEJIDE, OLAWALE OGUNKOLA AND
ABIODUN BANKOLE*

1 Trends in import prohibition

From the mid-1970s onwards, Nigeria's main trade policy instruments shifted markedly away from tariffs to quantitative import restrictions, particularly import prohibition and import licensing. As a reflection of this shift, Nigeria's customs legislation established an import prohibition list for trade items and an absolute import prohibition list for non-trade items. While the trade list covers the full range of agricultural and manufactured products, the non-trade list relates to goods and services that are considered to be harmful to human, animal and plant health, as well as public morals. Typical examples of products which feature on this second list include weapons, obscene articles, airmail, photographic printing paper, base or counterfeit coins and second-hand clothing. Furthermore, the customs legislation empowers the government to modify these lists at its discretion, by adding or subtracting items through customs and excise notices and government announcements.

Based on this legislation, the government placed seventy-six broad groups of import items on the import prohibition lists in 1978. The number of items placed under import prohibition increased further, particularly during 1982–5. Hence, at the beginning of 1986, roughly 40% of agricultural and industrial products, in terms of tariff lines, were covered by import prohibitions. This sharp increase in the coverage of import prohibitions abated somewhat during the second half of the 1980s; by 1989, import prohibition covered about 29% of agricultural products and 20% of industrial products measured, again, in terms of tariff lines (GATT 1991).

---

* University of Ibadan.

Although particular items moved in and out of the import prohibition lists over the next ten years, the general trend in reduction in the number of items whose importation was prohibited was broadly sustained. Hence, by 1998, only 127 (out of 5,147 tariff lines, or 2.5%) remained on the import prohibition list for trade. But with effect from late 2001 and continuing until early 2004, another upsurge in the number of items placed under import prohibition has occurred. In particular, the number of broad product groups under import ban rose from twenty-seven in February 2003 to thirty-five in January 2004.

In terms of sectoral coverage, import prohibition has focused on such agricultural products as fruit, vegetables, grains, meat and fish, as well as manufactured products including rubber, wood and cork, textiles and chemicals. In 1989, for example, close to 96% of the tariff lines for textiles and clothing were subjected to an import prohibition regime, with similar coverage ratio for several other sectors being as follows: furniture (93%), wood and wood products (45%), rubber (5%) and chemicals (1%) (GATT 1991). During 1982–5, the import prohibition coverage ratio for food, beverages and tobacco was over 50%.

The pervasive use of import prohibition as an instrument of trade policy in Nigeria derives from a long-standing import policy regime which was designed to promote industry, employment and balance-of-payments objectives in the context of an import substitution–industrialization strategy (Oyejide 1975). Key elements of this regime include protecting existing domestic industries and reducing the country's perceived dependence on imports, while at the same time ensuring the availability of raw materials and capital goods which cannot be obtained from domestic sources. With specific reference to the agricultural sector, trade policy has generally been aimed at discouraging importation of all food and raw materials that the county is deemed to have the resources to produce. In the case of the manufacturing sector, a major goal has been to increase the local content of Nigerian industrial output through enhanced use of local raw materials. The achievement of this goal is promoted by the government through various measures and incentives, including import prohibition.

Sectoral coverage of import prohibition has obviously varied over time. But it has been determined largely by the general policy that imports of certain products could be prohibited either if they are judged to be 'not essential' or when they compete with domestically produced goods that are available in adequate quantities.

The various motivations for using import prohibition have, however, not been fully reflected in the justifications periodically offered by the government when import prohibition notices are issued. For instance in April 1982, when a wide range of products was placed under import prohibition, the Nigerian government notified the General Agreement on Tariffs and Trade (GATT) of the measures taken with the claim that the measures had been necessitated by unfavourable external circumstances, including a deterioration in the terms of trade and sharp declines in the country's oil revenue and foreign exchange reserves. But import prohibition was periodically used for other purposes. The almost permanent ban on the importation of textile and clothing products since the late 1970s can be explained primarily in terms of protecting local industries; while import prohibition applying to such items as gypsum, kaolin, bentonites and barytes reflects attempts to promote local sourcing of raw materials for manufacturing in Nigeria. Thus when in March 1998 Nigeria notified the WTO Committee on Safeguards that the import prohibitions on wheat flour, sorghum, millet, gypsum and kaolin were imposed for safeguard reasons, there was credible reason to question the claim.

The pervasive use of import prohibition in Nigeria has another, perhaps equally important, reason: it is administratively easier. In Nigeria's responses to the questions raised on this matter during discussions at various GATT and WTO fora, it has been argued that import prohibitions are easier to monitor than price-based measures, since the presence of the banned products on local markets is, in principle, sufficient for enforcement.

2 Local and external players and their roles

It is well established that any trade policy change is likely to generate both winners and losers, even if the overall net impact is positive. Economic agents and other stakeholders involved with, or affected by, any trade policy change can be classified broadly into two groups; they are either local (domestic) or external (foreign). Each of these broad groups can be broken down into more specific interest groups, such as producers, importers, exporters, traders, workers and consumers. With specific reference to the import prohibition policy in Nigeria, local stakeholders range from the policy-making and enforcement agencies through producers of the banned imports and their workers to the importers and consumers of banned products.

On the external front, direct stakeholders include countries whose export products are denied market access in Nigeria as a result of the import prohibition policy, as well as regional and multilateral institutions (such as the Economic Community of West African States (ECOWAS), the IMF, the World Bank and the WTO) which exercise policy surveillance mandates in this area.

In capturing the perceptions and views of local and external players directly involved in and affected by Nigeria's import prohibition policy, primary reliance has had to be on published official documents and the print media. Given the period over which the policy has been tracked, interviews would have focused too narrowly on more recent events and be biased by the possibility of perception, revision and rationalization. In addition, interviews may not yield useful results, as officials of government and quasi-government agencies in Nigeria are often unwilling to go on record with views that may be critical of current public policy posture.

Local players

Among local players, the government and its agencies have played a prominent role in the initiation and sustenance of the policy of import prohibition. Much of the local opposition to import bans has generally been voiced by importers and traders. The consumers who ultimately bear the burden of the resulting higher prices and poor quality and limited variety of locally produced alternatives have remained largely silent, probably because they have not been organized. By contrast, the producers of import-competing goods and their employee unions have generally supported import bans.

On the side of government, policy statements and policy actions with respect to import prohibition have not always been synchronized and consistent. In particular, the apparent and often repeated decision to move away from the use of quantitative trade restriction measures has not been implemented in practice. In the 1970s, of course, policy statements and actions reflected the same restrictive trade policy posture. Thus, Roland Adeleye, Federal Commissioner for Industries, correctly reflected both policy and action when he stated in 1977 that 'the federal government will not import into Nigeria anything that is produced in adequate quantity by Nigerian industrialists' (*Nigerian Tribune* 1977).

Divergence between policy statement and policy action has been particularly strong since the late 1980s. For instance, in a policy statement submitted to the WTO by the Nigerian government in 1998, it was indicated that 'the list of items removed from import prohibition ... continues to lengthen' (para. 14), and that 'necessary steps are being taken by government to comprehensively eliminate all existing items on the import prohibition list as soon as possible' (para. 17). Along the same lines, President Olusegun Obasanjo's foreword to the *Trade Policy of Nigeria* (Federal Ministry of Commerce 2002) envisages a 'dynamic trade reorientation which will signify a clear departure from past regimes of controls and intervention'. Furthermore, this document affirmed that 'government shall, within the limits of its rights and international obligations and agreements, strive to eliminate quantitative trade measures' (p. 10). In practice, however, import bans actually increased in scope and coverage until 2004.

This policy had several negative effects as far as the importers of and traders in a wide range of products on the import prohibition list were concerned. Thus, the Refrigerator and Air Conditioner Dealers Association (RADA), in its statement, 'condemned the ban on importation of these products because it would lead to substantial losses of income and jobs, and further aggravate the unemployment situation' in Nigeria (*Guardian* October 2001). Similarly, the Motor Dealers Association of Nigeria (MODAN) issued a statement which argued that 'the ban on used vehicles would destroy four million jobs' (*Guardian* December 2001). In the same vein, the Embroidery Lace Dealers Association of Nigeria (ELDAN) claimed that 'an immediate enforcement of the ban on importation of textiles would inflict colossal financial loss on textile imports and eliminate three million jobs' (*Guardian* March 2004).

The domestic producers of banned imports and the workers' unions associated with them not only generally lobby government to impose and maintain its import prohibition policy but also articulate its advantages. Thus, in its reaction, the National Association of Cottage Industrialists of Nigeria (NACIN) urged the government to 'ensure strict implementation of the ban on imported products as a means of guaranteeing the survival of small and medium-scale enterprises and to create employment for the nation's teeming graduates' (*Guardian* February 2004). In the statements of the Manufacturers Association of Nigeria (MAN), this point of view was pushed further by 'proposing a minimum lifespan of five years for the current import restrictions policy as a means of ensuring that it achieves the desired results' (*Guardian* March 2004). Finally, the National Union of Textile, Garment and Tailoring Workers of Nigeria (NUTGWN) 'considered the textile ban as the best development in the textile industry in recent

times because of its beneficial impact on local output and employment'
(*Guardian* April 2004).

External players

The key external stakeholders that have played active roles in the discussions surrounding Nigeria's import prohibition policy include several
countries whose exports have been directly affected and a number of
multilateral organizations. Between 1980 and 1991, at least three countries lodged formal complaints against Nigeria with respect to import
prohibitions: Norway submitted a complaint on Nigeria's import ban on
stockfish, Côte d'Ivoire on the import ban on textiles, and the United
States on the import ban on wheat and rice. While both Norway and
the United States cited violation of GATT rules in their complaints, Côte
d'Ivoire's case rested on a violation of the ECOWAS treaty. These complaints were settled through bilateral negotiation and consultation. More
recently, both the European Union (EU) and Benin have raised issues with
Nigeria with respect to its import prohibitions. Speaking on behalf of the
EU, Claude Maerten, an official of the EU Trade Directorate-General,
argued that 'Nigeria's import ban was not compatible with, and indeed
forbidden by, WTO rules' (*Guardian* July 2003). In the case of Benin, the
country's ambassador, Benoit Adekambi, issued a statement in which he
claimed that 'Nigeria's import bans, particularly on textile products, had
dealt a severe blow to the economy of the Republic of Benin' and 'constituted a violation of the Memorandum of Understanding between the two
counties regarding continuous trade liberalization' (*Guardian* November
2003).

The three multilateral organizations which have expressed views on
Nigerian import prohibition policy can be classified in two categories. In
one of these are the World Bank and the IMF, while the other consists
of the WTO. Both the World Bank and the IMF have only an advisory
role with respect to trade and other policy matters in Nigeria. It is in this
context that both organizations encouraged the liberalization of Nigeria's
policy regimes.

The resurgence of import prohibition represents a sharp reversal of
the trade liberalization programme initiated in the mid-1980s with the
support of the IMF and the World Bank. Both organizations provided
technical and policy advice, and the World Bank also provided support
through its lending programme. In particular, the World Bank made two

quick loans to promote trade liberalization: the Trade Policy and Export Development Loan of US$450 million in 1987, and the Trade and Investment Policy Loan of US$500 million in 1989 (World Bank 1994) Both had as part of their objectives the reduction and eventual elimination of import prohibition. Although these loans were fully disbursed, subsequent evaluations concluded that the import regime reform encountered strong opposition both within and outside the government and that Nigeria had, in general, displayed a poor implementation record and commitment to import liberalization (Castillo 1993). More specifically, the World Bank, in its assessment of Nigeria's trade policy reform, sketched the following sequence of events (1994: 11–12):

> Prior to the introduction of the SAP [structural adjustment programme], imports were subject to quantitative controls implemented through a combination of outright bans on agricultural and manufacturing goods and a comprehensive licensing system
>
> ...
>
> Under the SAP, between 1986 and 1988, import and export licensing was eliminated, the list of prohibited imports was shortened, and price and distribution controls on agricultural exports were removed.
>
> ...
>
> As it transpired, the SAP's attempts to achieve transparency and stability in the incentive system were overtaken by events. The list of banned imports was once again extended so that by 1991, about 20% of industrial imports and 30% of agricultural imports were affected. About 1,000 of the harmonized system of 5,000 six-digit imports, furthermore, remained subject to conditional import prohibitions, which could be invoked on the basis of balance-of-payments considerations.

Nigeria's import prohibitions and their justifications in terms of balance-of-payments problems have triggered many discussions in GATT and then the WTO since the early 1980s. Nigeria first invoked GATT Article XVIII:B on import restrictions for balance-of-payments reasons in 1982. This led to the first consultation with the GATT Committee on Balance of Payments Restrictions in April 1984. In notifying its import restriction measures to GATT in April 1982, Nigeria emphasized their temporary nature. The Committee recognized the serious balance-of-payments problems faced by Nigeria in calling for the introduction of the restrictive measures, but encouraged it to pursue more appropriate economic stabilization policies. Follow-up simplified consultations with the Committee were held in October 1986, October 1988 and March 1991.

At these meetings it was noted that in spite of the removal of some of the restrictive measures, several import bans introduced for balance-of-payments reasons remained in force. Finally, in 1996, the WTO Committee on Balance of Payments Restrictions decided that Nigeria's import prohibitions could not be justified under the balance-of-payment rules of GATT 1994. The consultations in February 1998 discussed Nigeria's import bans on maize, vegetable oils, barytes and bentonites, as well as plastic articles. Although the consultations closed without agreed conclusions regarding Nigeria's phase-out programme for the restrictions, members of the Committee stressed, once again, that the import bans were not consistent with WTO rules. Thus Nigeria's use of import prohibitions as a trade policy instrument has been a source of friction with its trading partners; this practice has also been repeatedly condemned for its inconsistency with GATT and WTO rules.

3 Challenges faced and the outcome

In using import prohibition as a major trade policy instrument, Nigeria has hoped that its balance-of-payments problems would be alleviated, and that the protection offered would induce increased output and employment of the domestic industry. Against these postulated positive outcomes must be set several possible negative consequences of import prohibition, including raising the domestic prices of import-banned products, disrupting other sectors which use the prohibited imports as raw materials, depriving government of tariff revenue and creating vested interests among domestic producers of prohibited products and among smugglers.

Nigeria's balance-of-payments situation is determined primarily by developments in the world oil market; hence it has not been amenable to changes induced by import prohibitions. In any case, it seems clear that protection of domestic producers is the real force behind the use of this policy instrument. But there is little evidence that it has produced the desired result here either. For instance, a recent study of the textile sector – the single most important target of import prohibition policy of the past twenty years – shows that both its output and employment have stagnated or declined (Oyejide et al. 2003). In addition, a survey of manufacturing-sector performance conducted by the Manufacturers' Association of Nigeria (1989) does not support the view that the level of capacity utilization was positively related to the degree of local sourcing of raw materials – one of the major channels through which import prohibition was expected to promote increased output and employment.

There appears to be recognition both within government and among producers that the import prohibition policy is rendered virtually impotent by large-scale smuggling and that this has continued in spite of stiff penalties imposed on those involved with the importation, transportation, storage, display or sale of prohibited items. This recognition has not, however, led to the abandonment of the policy. Rather, pressure has mounted to enhance its stricter implementation. According to Moses Gbadebo, president of the National Union of Chemical, Footwear, Rubber, Leather and Non-Metallic Product Employees, 'it is not enough to say we have banned items, the government's words must be backed with action ... the law should be properly enforced' (*Guardian* January 2004). Similarly, according to Nasir Lawal, president of the National Union of Textile, Garment and Tailoring Workers, 'if you place a hundred bans and your borders still remain porous, it will only help in increasing the income of smugglers and their agents' (*Guardian* January 2004). This concern is, apparently, fully shared by Olusegun Obasanjo, the Nigerian president, who recently accused the Nigerian Customs Service of 'making nonsense of government's import prohibition policy'. In frustration, he was reported to have said 'we just have to beg them. I think other than begging, I don't know what else I can do. If it is possible to run a nation without customs, I will do it' (*Guardian* January 2004).

The apparent reluctance to abandon prohibition policy is reflected in Nigeria's responses to issues raised during various GATT and WTO discussions on this matter. For instance, during the consultations in 1984, Nigeria pledged to eliminate its import prohibitions quickly. Over time, many of these import bans were indeed lifted, but the policy itself was not abandoned. Following the 1996 decision by the WTO Committee on Balance of Payments Restrictions that Nigeria's import prohibitions could not be justified under WTO rules, Nigeria offered to eliminate all such measures by early 1997 – only to begin to notify additional ones in 1998. A further proposal was made by Nigeria to phase out all remaining import prohibitions by 2005 under an eight-year elimination programme (WTO 1998). This proposal argued that this period was necessary to allow time for the ongoing customs and port reforms to take root so as to ensure the effective administration of the resulting price-based measures and to allow the economy to consolidate the recent gains in the area of inflation, external reserves, interest and exchange rates. The upsurge in the use of import prohibitions during 2001–4 raises considerable doubt with respect to Nigeria's commitment to its own import prohibition phase-out programme.

4 Lessons

Several lessons can be drawn from Nigeria's import prohibition policy experience. Perhaps the most general of these is that the coherent and consistent pursuit of good trade policy requires not only a robust and appropriate domestic institutional framework and process for trade policy-making but also a supportive and institutionalized multilateral arrangement for trade policy surveillance. Weaknesses in both of these may be responsible, in varying degrees, for the persistence of Nigeria's import prohibition policy. Nigeria's internal trade policy surveillance mechanism consists largely of the domestic framework and trade policy-making process, both articulated at length in the *Trade Policy of Nigeria* (Federal Ministry of Commerce 2002). However, the country's actual trade policy-making deviates quite substantially from what this document stipulates. These deviations largely explain the lack of coherence between policy statements and policy actions; this probably also derives from the absence of local ownership of the trade liberalization policy which appears to have been induced by the World Bank–IMF supported structural adjustment programme.

Within the internal trade policy surveillance mechanism in Nigeria, vested interests built around the use of quantitative import restrictions have acquired tremendous powers, and no effective counterweights have evolved over time, perhaps because consumer groups and other civil society organizations are not sufficiently well organized. Furthermore, the mechanism lacks effective feedback systems in the articulation, implementation and evaluation of trade policy. In particular, trade policy initiatives are not routinely subjected to cost-benefit analysis; and no explicit system of monitoring and evaluation is used for modifying or changing trade policies which do not produce desired results efficiently.

Nigeria's membership of the WTO provides it, in principle, with a strong external trade policy surveillance mechanism. But the role of the WTO as an 'agent of restraint' in favour of good trade policy is feasible only to the extent that two important conditions are met. First, the government whose behaviour is to be 'restrained' must be committed to good trade policy and thus be willing to tie its own hand and use an external treaty obligation to strengthen its hand against local vested interests. Second, the external agent must have adequate sanctions which it is able and willing to use to punish deviations from the pursuit of good trade policy. Neither of these conditions appears to have been effective in dissuading Nigeria from the continued use of its import prohibition policy.

The basic problems inherent in the framework and process of trade policy-making in Nigeria and its surveillance are not unknown. Some of these are eloquently summarized in a recent statement by Olusola Faleye, president of the Lagos Chamber of Commerce and Industry (*Guardian* April 2004):

> We have no query with the principles of protection, but with the process. We are concerned that the recent import prohibition policy was not preceded by sufficient consultation. Import prohibition... is a major trade policy decision which requires wide-ranging consultations, capacity surveys and the advice of trade and economic development experts before being pronounced as policy. Sufficient account was not taken of the local capacity vis-à-vis local demand and issues of policy transitions and implications for existing treaties to which Nigeria is signatory.

Any sustained effort to eliminate import prohibitions in Nigeria is unlikely to be permanently successful if it does not first address these underlying problems.

References

Castillo, G. (1993), 'TEP Study on Trade Policy Reforms in Sub-Saharan Africa: The Case of Nigeria', mimeo, Washington, DC: World Bank.

Federal Ministry of Commerce (2002), *Trade Policy of Nigeria*, Abuja: Federal Government of Nigeria.

GATT (1991), *Trade Policy Review: Nigeria, 1991*, vol. 1, Geneva: GATT.

Guardian (Lagos) (2001), 'Refrigerator Importers Condemn Governments' Ban on Importation', 4 Oct., p. 19.

Guardian (2001), 'Ban on Used Vehicles Will Affect 4m Jobs, Say Dealers', 31 Dec., p. 7.

Guardian (2003), 'EU Faults Government's Ban on Imports', 21 July, pp. 1–3.

Guardian (2003), 'Ban on Textile Products Import Hurts Beninois Economy, Says Envoy', 20 Nov., p. 3.

Guardian (2004), 'Banned Items: Workers Want Government to Empower Customers' Capacity', 13 Jan., p. 67.

Guardian (2004), 'Obasanjo Accuses Customs of Foiling Import Ban Policy', 15 Jan., p. 7.

Guardian (2004), 'Industrialists Want Strict Implementation of Import Ban Policy', 25 Feb., p. 38.

Guardian (2004), 'Manufacturers Canvas Five-Year Import Restriction Regime', 2 March, p. 3.

Guardian (2004), 'Winners, Losers as Government Forecloses Textile Ban Policy Review', 28 April, p. 44.

Manufacturers' Association of Nigeria (MAN) (1989), *Sample Survey of Performance of the Nigerian Manufacturing Sector, 1987–1989*, Lagos: MAN.

Nigerian Tribune (1977), 'Nigerians Assured: We'll Protect You', 26 May, p. 2.

Oyejide, T. A. (1975), *Tariff Policy and Industrialization in Nigeria*, Ibadan: Ibadan University Press.

Oyejide, T. A., E. O. Ogunkola, A. Jerome, A. Adenikinju and A. S. Bankole (2003), *The Impact of Trade Liberalization on Nigeria's Textile Sector*, Abuja: Report for the World Bank.

World Bank (1994), *Structural Adjustment Program: Policies Implementation and Impact*, Report No. 13053 – UNI, Country Operations, Western African Department, Washington, DC: World Bank.

WTO (1998), *Trade Policy Review: Nigeria 1998*, Geneva: WTO.

33

The Pacific island nations: towards shared representation

CHAKRIYA BOWMAN*

1 The problem in context

Most small economies find it difficult to operate alone in the global economy, and less developed economies face particular hurdles in their quest for prosperity. The global trading environment is becoming increasingly integrated, and the last decade has seen a number of regional groupings form to capitalize on the benefits of more efficient use of resources and economies of scale. While this integration has been most evident in the major economies of Europe (the European Union) and North America (the North American Free Trade Agreement), similar moves towards economic integration are being explored in Asia and South and Central America, in a sign that many countries are recognizing the benefits of a shared approach to trade and development. As the world's major economies move towards greater trade and economic integration, many smaller, less developed economies are at risk of being left behind. In recognition of this, the World Trade Organization is paying particular attention to the needs of smaller economies.

The economies of the Pacific island nations are among the most disadvantaged in the world today. These nations, composed of islands that are often little more than specks of land in the vast expanse of the Pacific Ocean, are at the forefront of concerns about countries being left behind in the current tide of global economic development. Of the three WTO member nations in the South Pacific (Fiji, Papua New Guinea and the Solomon Islands), Papua New Guinea is by far the largest. Part of one of the largest islands in the world, the country itself is around the size of

---

* Research Fellow, Pacific Policy Project, Asia Pacific School of Economics and Government, Australian National University.

California, but the contrast between their economies could not be greater. Papua New Guinea is classified by the World Bank as a least developed country, and 46% of its population of 5.3 million live on less than US$1 a day.[1] It is difficult for impoverished countries like Papua New Guinea to participate fully in the global economy. In particular, with its limited human resources, the demands of providing representatives at myriad international organizations such as the WTO are a significant public burden. Despite being a founding member of the WTO, Papua New Guinea has been unable to afford permanent representation in Geneva. Neither have the two other permanent members of the WTO, Fiji and the Solomon Islands, nor the Pacific island nations with observer status – Tonga, Samoa and Vanuatu. For all the Pacific island nations, even the largest, joining the WTO involves significant costs, not only in financial terms but also in the diversion of scarce human capital and leadership skills to international affairs.

The WTO has recognized this problem and has sought to address it in a number of ways. The Advisory Centre on WTO Law was established to assist developing countries in representing their interests in the multilateral trading system, and it provides legal advisory services to countries engaged in dispute settlement proceedings. Another initiative, the Work Program on Small Economies, is aimed at framing responses to the trade-related problems of small vulnerable economies like those of the Pacific islands. The WTO also provides training courses and technical assistance on issues affecting small developing countries, including accession and trade policy reviews.

In addition to these initiatives, it was recognized that there is still a need for countries to maintain representation in Europe in order to address the bureaucratic aspects of WTO negotiations, and to ensure that they remain up to date with the issues addressed in WTO meetings. However, the costs involved in maintaining European representation, even at the most fundamental level, have proved to be prohibitive for Pacific island nations, resulting in a disengagement from the multilateral process. The WTO has recognized this issue, and has assisted in the establishment of a shared representative office for Pacific island nations. Based in Geneva, the office will represent the member nations of the Pacific Islands Forum. The office is being shared with the Organization of East Caribbean States, which is similarly a representative body for small island nations.

[1] World Bank.

2 Local and external players

The Pacific Islands Forum Secretariat is the peak representative body for the small island nations of the Pacific. Based in Fiji, it represents sixteen countries (Australia, the Cook Islands, the Federated States of Micronesia, Fiji, Kiribati, Nauru, New Zealand, Niue, Palau, Papua New Guinea, the Marshall Islands, Samoa, the Solomon Islands, Tonga, Tuvalu and Vanuatu), of which five are WTO members (Australia, New Zealand, Fiji, Papua New Guinea and the Solomon Islands). While Australia and New Zealand maintain a significant role in the Forum, its overarching aim is to promote and represent the interests of the small island nations of the Pacific. Development is a major concern in the South Pacific, and the Forum is closely focused on developing international trade to improve the quality of life for the inhabitants of member countries.

The move to create a shared representative office in Geneva for the Pacific island nations was spearheaded by the Pacific Islands Forum Secretariat at the Forum Trade Ministers Meeting (FTMM) in June 1999. The ministers recommended that a forum delegation be established in Geneva to facilitate representation of member countries, both WTO and non-WTO members, in WTO negotiations. A Forum representative would be present at all WTO meetings, and would be tasked with observing WTO operations and reporting on all issues affecting member states. The WTO welcomed this initiative, and assisted in the provision and establishment of the office.

The issue of shared representation is a significant one for the Pacific. There is recognition throughout the region that the duplication of a wide range of government-provided services is making significant drains on the scarce operating resources of island economies. The Pacific Plan, commissioned by leaders at the Pacific Islands Forum in August 2004, and now being developed by ForSec and a taskforce of senior officials from Forum governments, has identified further work to be done in pursuing the aim of regional co-operation in aviation, shipping, fisheries and counter-terrorism. Duplication of infrastructure, in particular, is an area of significant regional concern. The Australian Minister for Trade, Mark Vaile, recently highlighted the need for greater merging of regional carriers: 'running national carriers which drain national budgets is counterproductive and an inefficient use of resources'.[2] Australia has been actively pursuing a policy of encouraging Pacific co-operation in the areas of

---

[2] 'Fiji and Australia: New Economic Partners', speech to the 17th Australia–Fiji Business Forum, Gold Coast, Queensland, 18 Oct. 2004.

shipping, aviation and economic management. The establishment of the Pacific Islands Forum Representative Office, though a small step in and of itself, is nonetheless a significant sign of emerging recognition among the Pacific island nations of the need for greater regional co-operation and pooling of resources.

If shared representation is successful in multilateral trade negotiations it will set a powerful precedent regarding regional co-operation that will enable improved outcomes for the region when engaging on issues of international significance. Such an outcome can only enhance regional unity, and may serve as a model for co-operation in other areas.

3 Challenges faced and the outcome

Duplication of resources and high bureaucratic overheads make effective participation at important global fora difficult for small economies, especially those of the Pacific that are often isolated, under-populated, and have low levels of literacy and education. Regional bureaucratic integration is being pursued to manage more effectively the international rights and obligations of the Pacific island nations.

The Pacific Islands Forum Representative Office in Geneva, sponsored by groups from developed nations including the European Communities, officially began operations in July 2004. According to former European Trade Commissioner, Pascal Lamy, the establishment of the office was an important development not only for the Pacific island nations themselves, but also for the WTO, because it would enhance its deliberations. 'The WTO negotiations have to be accessible to all, including the smaller members who have special needs and constraints', said Lamy. 'The establishment of the Pacific Islands Forum Representative Office will help the Pacific region to be better represented in [the] WTO.'[3] A major strategic purpose of the Office is to follow closely developments in the WTO negotiations and to act as a channel of communication between the WTO and the Forum members. The representative office will also facilitate rotating six-month placements in Geneva for trade officials of Pacific island nations. These placements, the first of which commenced in April 2004, enable trade officials from member states to work closely with the WTO on issues important to their countries, and promote capacity-building across a range of trade issues. It is envisaged that, at the conclusion of their placement, trade officials will return to their countries and assist their governments in managing their multilateral trade agenda.

[3] Press release, Delegation of the European Commission of the Pacific, 28 June 2004.

Not only will the Pacific Islands Forum Representative Office enable member countries to improve their participation in the WTO negotiation process, it is an important first step towards greater integration of their bureaucratic systems. Greg Urwin, secretary general of the Pacific Islands Forum Secretariat, recently spoke of the need for a shared approach to institutions and bureaucracy, saying that 'It seems to me impossible to deny that enhanced regional co-operation and pooling of resources is required.'[4] In the past, small nations have had great difficulty representing their interests effectively at international trade negotiations, and a shared representative approach is being shown to provide significant benefits.

4 Case study of the shared representative approach

Kava root is a traditional medicine used throughout Pacific societies as an analgesic, tranquillizer and anti-depressant. It was also used as a beverage in traditional ceremonies, and has a long history of use throughout the Pacific. The medicinal qualities of kava root were recognized by the neutraceutical industry, with kava root being developed for use in herbal supplements and medicines world-wide. A significant Pacific kava industry evolved during the late 1990s, with kava root being processed and packaged primarily for the United States and European markets. Production peaked in 1998, and kava farms are now well established in Vanuatu, Fiji, Samoa and Tonga. The kava market is estimated to contribute around US$200 million annually to Pacific economies,[5] and around 10,000 hectares are under cultivation for kava production. Not only does the kava industry play an important role in the economies of the Pacific, it provides a sustainable income based on a traditional crop that can be developed in an ecologically sensitive manner. Kava production now plays a significant role in providing incomes and promoting development in the rural communities of the Pacific islands, many of which remain among the least developed in the world.

However, in 2002 public health authorities in Germany (BfArM) instituted a ban on kava products, based on evidence linking the consumption of kava to a range of liver problems. This prompted a number of other European Community members to review the effects of kava products

---

[4] Greg Urwin, 'Globalization and its Impact on the Pacific Islands Region', presentation at the Reserve Bank of Fiji Symposium, 15–16 July 2004.
[5] *Kava Report 2003: In-depth Investigation into EU Member States Market Restrictions on Kava Products*, Centre for the Development of Enterprise, 2003.

in more detail, and market recalls were instituted. Exports of kava products were effectively halted, significantly affecting the livelihood of many Pacific farmers and stifling the further development of the industry.

The sudden withdrawal of kava products from the world market resulted in great hardship for many rural Pacific communities. Adimaimalaga Tafuna'i, the executive director of Women in Business Development in Samoa, noted the problems faced by rural communities as a result of the ban: 'The growers are very disillusioned. The boom in exports meant that they had planted thousands of plants, involving much time and very hard work... Many of them have no other source of income, and (now) have to rely on family members for their livelihood... A new wave of poverty is definitely being experienced because of the ban.'[6] Throughout the region, subsistence farmers face a soul-destroying loss of livelihood as a result of the adverse medical findings.

Leaders in the Pacific responded quickly to this economic threat. Recognizing the difficulties each country would face if they were to fight the ban alone, the Pacific Islands Forum Secretariat moved to address this problem with the establishment of a joint representative body, the International Kava Executive Council (IKEC). This body comprises stakeholders from the four affected Pacific nations alongside European representatives from the manufacturing and marketing industries, including drug associations, extraction manufacturing associations and nutritional supplement associations. This group is innovative as a significant shared representative body, including both public and private organizations, formed to address moves by foreign countries to restrict trade in kava. After Pacific nation ambassadors consulted with the WTO it was decided to approach the issue from a health perspective, and as such the World Health Organisation (WHO) took the lead role in the ongoing dispute. The Advisory Centre on WTO Law was also a source of legal advice for the Pacific island nations as they contested the ban through dispute settlement proceedings.[7]

A comprehensive survey of the medical literature was then commissioned by IKEC; it questioned the scientific basis of the argument used to ban kava products. Medical reports were reviewed by Dr Joerg Grunwald, director of Phytopharm Consulting and a medical scientist specializing in phytopharmaceuticals and dietary supplements. The main author of the *Physician's Desk Reference for Herbal Medicines*, the international reference work for botanical medicines, Dr Grunwald is an expert on natural medicines and their safety. His report found that the dangers of kava

---

[6] Ibid.   [7] Ibid.

products had been significantly overestimated by the German health authorities, and he questioned the scientific basis of the studies used to justify the ban on kava. With this report as evidence, IKEC approached the WHO to request an independent scientific evaluation be made to determine the veracity of the German claims. As a result, in November 2003 the WHO decided to re-evaluate all existing studies of the health effects of kava to determine which studies provided accurate scientific evidence.

In early 2004, representatives of IKEC met with the German Health Ministry to discuss a way forward in the dispute resolution process. A decision was made to initiate new studies into the health effects and safety of kava products, with a view to this independent evidence being used to re-evaluate previous findings. Dr Grunwald is confident that studies will demonstrate that kava is safe and effective. 'Now we finally have the opportunity to prove the safety of kava conclusively',[8] he said.

The co-operative and shared approach developed by the Pacific island nations to the kava ban, particularly through IKEC, was a major factor in successfully convincing the German health authorities to review their ban. The director of Kava Traders in Vanuatu, Frank King, said that 'the German minister, Dr Schroeder, admits that the review of the kava position had been brought about by pressure from Pacific island states and organizations friendly to those states'.[9] Grunwald believes that the shared advisory group will play an active role in the resolution of similar disputes in future. When questioned with regard to the ongoing kava dispute, Grunwald said: 'We certainly would hope that the WTO Pacific representative office in Geneva would further support our activities and [we] are sure that . . . it will be of benefit to the Pacific Island nations.'[10]

5 Lessons for others

There is no doubt that small island economies are uniquely disadvantaged by the size of their economies and the resources available to them, both in human and in financial terms, when they come to compete in the global economy. It is essential that small economies are able to maintain a level of representation at an international level that ensures that their prospects for future development are not overshadowed or neglected by wealthier, more powerful countries. The formation of shared representative

---

[8] 'Kava Back – International Kava Executive Council (IKEC)', *Port Vila Press*, 21 April 2004.
[9] Ibid.
[10] E-mail conversation with author, 13 Oct. 2004.

groups has been shown to assist significantly the process of international representation, and the work of the International Kava Executive Council has demonstrated that a combined, co-operative approach to international issues can create an environment for the effective resolution of issues affecting Pacific livelihoods and economies. Asif Chida, private-sector advisor to the Pacific Islands Forum Secretariat, said that the shared approach taken by the Forum had proved to be very effective: 'It has brought together stakeholders in both the Pacific and Europe to discuss the problem and map out a strategy for the way forward that is aimed at eventually removing the bans and restrictions currently in place. Similar approaches ... will continue to be made, upon the request of Forum members.'[11]

The Geneva office will be able to take a lead role in future trade negotiations and provide direction and guidance to those participating in review processes. In the near future, the representative office will provide Pacific countries with better representation during the implementation of the Doha Development Agenda (DDA), which seeks to promote trade liberalization and provide commitments to strengthen assistance to developing countries. The DDA aims to allow the WTO to play a more active role in pursuing economic growth and poverty reduction in developing nations, and the Pacific island nations have been active in discussions relating to the agenda. The office will play a key role in facilitating the participation of the Pacific nations in this important initiative. As former EC Trade Commissioner Pascal Lamy observed at the opening of the office, '[The office will] facilitate the active participation of the small islands and economies in our joint efforts to move the Doha Agenda forward.'[12]

Further, the Cotonou Agreement, which covers aid, political issues and trade between the European Communities and seventy-seven developing countries, including those of the Pacific, will be renegotiated between 2002 and 2007. The Cotonou Agreement will create a free trade area between these developing countries and the European Communities from 2008, resulting in significant market liberalization by the developing nations and an end to many preferential purchasing arrangements for exports from less developed countries. Pacific leaders are very aware of the impact the removal of preferential agreements will have on their economies. Sir Michael Somare, Prime Minister of Papua New Guinea, observed that 'Unless Pacific island countries actively participate in these negotiations,

---

[11] E-mail conversation with author, 4 Nov. 2004.
[12] Delegation of the European Commission of the Pacific, press release, 28 June 2004.

we will run the risk of further marginalizing our capacity to trade with Europe as a result of dissipating trade preferences on which many of us rely.'[13] The shared representative office will address these concerns by playing a leading role in future trade negotiations. In a statement in late 2003, the Pacific Islands Forum Secretariat expressed hope that the new office will play a role in the negotiation of issues arising from the agreement, and emphasized 'It [is] important for PICs to ensure that their trade interests [are] considered in a new trade arrangement and in the WTO rules.'[14] With shared representation in Geneva, the people of the Pacific islands can be confident that they will speak with a louder voice at the negotiating table.

[13] Office of the Prime Minister, press release, 17 May 2003.
[14] Pacific Islands Forum Secretariat,*Forum Monthly Review*, March 2003.

34

Victory in principle: Pakistan's dispute settlement case on combed cotton yarn exports to the United States

TURAB HUSSAIN*

On 24 December 1998 the government of Pakistan received a Call Notice from the US government for consultation regarding the establishment of quantitative restraints on Pakistani exports of combed cotton yarn (Category 301). The basis of this was the allegation on the part of the United States that the exports of Pakistan were causing verifiable harm to the US textile sector. The legal grounds employed by the United States were the transitional safeguard measures sanctioned under Article 6 of the Agreement on Textiles and Clothing (ATC) of the WTO.[1] This was the first time in the trade history of Pakistan that a case went through all the stages of the WTO dispute settlement mechanism.[2] After the failure of bilateral consultations as the first stage of the case, Pakistan had to take the case to the Textile Monitoring Board (TMB) and finally to the Dispute Settlement Board (DSB) of the WTO.

Although the eventual outcome was in Pakistan's favour, the pursuit of a positive decision was a challenging task manifested by an array of problems relating to co-ordination and co-operation between the public and the private sectors. The objective of this case study therefore is not just to narrate the events which occurred in this case but also to highlight the various obstacles faced by the government and the business players in

---

* Lecturer, Department of Economics, Lahore University of Management Sciences.

[1] These safeguard measures allow the establishment of quota restraints by a member country if it is 'able to demonstrate that a particular product is being imported into its territory in such increased quantities as to cause serious damage or actual threat to its domestic industry producing like and/or directly competitive products.

[2] The first time the United States tried to impose transitional safeguard measures on Pakistani exports was in 1996, on the same variety of combed cotton yarn. However, Pakistan was able to defend its case at the bilateral negotiation stage and the United States chose not to impose the quota restraints.

contesting the case at each stage of the dispute settlement process. This is done so as to underline the lessons that Pakistan learned about both its trade policy administration and the role and value of the WTO in the management of an important dispute.

1 The problem in context

Since 1995 there has been a world-wide increase in textile trade, primarily due to the phasing out of the Multi-Fibre Agreement (MFA) and the introduction of the Agreement on Textiles and Clothing (ATC) under the WTO. Under the new regime the previously high quota restraints on the textile and clothing exports of developing countries were to be gradually reduced to bring this sector into compliance with the WTO rules. The textile sector of Pakistan responded positively to the general reduction in quotas by the developed world. The existing manufacturers embarked on an expansion strategy by investing in the enhancement of their production capacity. At the same time new manufacturers entered the industry increasing total production and the volume of exports.[3] Consequently in that period Pakistan became the second-largest exporter of combed cotton yarn to the United States, inadvertently giving cause to the United States to employ the transitional safeguard measures sanctioned by the ATC.

The importance of the textile sector, often referred to as the backbone of the Pakistan economy, cannot be overstated. It is the country's largest manufacturing sector with an 8.5% share in the nation's GDP. The sector's contribution to employment is 38% and it generates a phenomenal 60% of the total export earnings of Pakistan.[4]

Within the textile sector those directly affected by the quota restrictions were the exporters and manufacturers of combed cotton yarn. These restrictions not only threatened their and the country's economic well-being but also significantly increased the scepticism of local business and government towards the West's commitment to free trade. As this was the second time the United States had employed transitional safeguard measures, the general feeling among the business players in the post-MFA era was that the US government was using this as an alternative policy instrument for protecting its textile manufacturers, putting at stake the viability of the Pakistan textile industry. The prevailing views of the business players about the quota restraints can be summed up by the following

---

[3] Information provided by Anis-ul-Haq, secretary, All Pakistan Textile Mills Association (APTMA).

[4] Government of Pakistan, *Economic Survey 1998–99* (dates relevant to the period of the case).

comment by an exporter: 'On one hand the West has been strongly advocating free global market, but on the other they are imposing such restrictions which themselves negate their actions and deeds.'[5]

Moreover, the type of role played by the dispute settlement mechanism of the WTO was of paramount importance. Notwithstanding the fact that in 1996 Pakistan was able to deter the United States from employing the safeguard measures at the bilateral negotiations stage, there was still scepticism amongst local business players about the WTO. The primary reason for this was the paucity of information within the private sector about the workings and the objectives of the WTO and a generally held notion of it being more representative of Western trade interests. Thus this was an occasion which could instil the credibility of the organization locally by removing the prevalent doubts about its effectiveness in maintaining the principles of free and fair trade between unequal partners.

Beside the direct economic benefits of lifting the quota restraints, the importance of this case also hinged on the legal precedent which it could potentially establish. In the words of Akbar Sheikh, the local consultant representing the government of Pakistan at the various stages of the case,

> The legal grounds on which the quota restrictions were imposed by the United States had to be challenged as these could have led to the establishment of a precedent causing long term problems not only for Pakistan but for the rest of the developing world in future dispute settlement cases within this sector.[6]

Thus the role of the local players involved in effectively managing the case at the various stages of the dispute settlement mechanism of the WTO was crucial. The significance of a positive outcome stemmed from both the restoration of confidence of the local business in the new global trading environment and in affecting the future trade policies of larger countries such as the United States.

2 The local and external players and their roles

All Pakistan Textile Mills Association

The business/industry players, both exporters and manufacturers, were represented by the All Pakistan Textile Mills Association (APTMA). This

---

[5] *Pakistan Economist*, 15 Aug. 1999.

[6] The definition of domestic industry employed by the United States in the case was challenged by Pakistan. This according to Akbar Sheikh was the crucial legal definitional issue on which the entire case of the United States rested. For details see Report of the Appellate Body, WTO, WT/DS192/AB/R, 8 Oct. 2001.

is a broadly based body whose members come from all categories and types of textile and clothing manufacturers and traders. In 1998, when the quota restraints were imposed by the United States, the association had a standing committee on anti-dumping and WTO affairs.

The objective of this committee was initially to co-ordinate with the Ministry of Commerce in the identification and hiring of appropriate consultants and lawyers to represent Pakistan in the bilateral negotiations with the United States and then in the dispute settlement stages of the WTO.

Second, in order to facilitate the preparation and proceedings of the case, the committee and hence APTMA had to act as a liaison between the government and the business players. This was done by providing trade and industry information to the local and international consultants representing the government. Also, the committee had to keep the members of APTMA abreast of the developments in the case.

Finally, APTMA, in consultation with its members and the Commerce Ministry of Pakistan, had to formulate an acceptable mechanism for the payment of the high legal fees involved in the case.

The Ministry of Commerce

The Ministry of Commerce, as the relevant ministerial arm of the Pakistan government, was directly involved in all the stages of the case – the bilateral negotiations with the United States, the TMB review and finally at the DSB. The ministry's Export Promotion Bureau (EPB) had to co-ordinate with APTMA in the payment of the legal costs incurred during the case.

At that time there was no effective institutional framework within the Ministry of Commerce which could deal with WTO-related dispute settlement cases. Due to the lack of internal expertise, the ministry had to engage the services of a local consultant, Akbar Sheikh. He acted as a representative of the government at the WTO along with Nasim Qureshi, Joint Secretary at the Ministry of Commerce.

The basis for Akbar Sheikh's selection was his past experience at the level of bilateral negotiations and an in-depth knowledge of the textile sector of Pakistan. His role was to build the defence case for Pakistan along with the international consultants and lawyers and to present it effectively at both the TMB review and the DSB stage. For this purpose he had to work closely with both the Commerce Ministry (Nasim Qureshi) and APTMA.

The international lawyers and consultants

The lack of local expertise in international trade law and WTO-related issues had led Pakistan to hire the services of international consultants and lawyers in previous dispute settlement cases. In the 1996 combed cotton yarn case APTMA and the Pakistan government had hired the services of International Development Systems (IDS), a Washington-based consultancy firm. IDS had successfully defended Pakistan's case during the negotiations with the United States. Hence in 1998, when the United States issued the call notice for a second time, APTMA, in consultation with the government, again engaged IDS. The consultant from IDS was Brenda Jacobs, both at the bilateral negotiations with the United States and at the TMB review. Along with IDS another Washington based law firm, Travis, Sandler and Rosenberg, was engaged for the TMB review.

However, once the case went to the final DSB stage the Ministry of Commerce decided to engage the services of lawyers based in Geneva, where the dispute settlement proceedings of the WTO are held.

3 Challenges faced and the outcome

The TMB review

At the proceedings

After the failure of the bilateral negotiations between Pakistan and the United States, on 5 March 1999 the United States notified the Textile Monitoring Body (TMB) pursuant to Article 6 of the ATC that it had decided to impose the quota restraints for three years. This measure came into effect from 17 March 1999. The matter was taken up at the 54th meeting of the TMB held in April 1999. The Pakistan side was represented by Akbar Sheikh, Brenda Jacobs of IDS, and Travis, Sandler and Rosenberg.

This was apparently one of the longest cases at the TMB, lasting for around six days. As mentioned earlier, this was the first time Pakistan had gone to the TMB review, hence there was a certain degree of anxiety about the nature and result of the proceedings to follow. According to Akbar Sheikh the US team, owing to their numbers, initially looked quite formidable. There were US government functionaries, textile experts and trade lawyers and consultants present during the review. Moreover, the importance the United States was giving to this case was evident from the fact that the US chief textile negotiator, ambassador Don Johnson, who is normally not required to attend such meetings, was present even during the extended time of the sessions. The case was strongly contested by both sides, as it was clearly regarded as establishing a precedent.[7]

The questions and discussions were found to be fairly challenging by Pakistan, but according to Akbar Sheikh they were able to rebut most of the arguments put forward by the US side. Pakistan's case focused on the 'spurious' definition of domestic industry employed by the United States and therefore on the viability of the data used to draw an alleged causality between the imports from Pakistan and the decrease in US textile production. The legal precedent aspect of the case was the definition of domestic industry employed by the United States. The United States had defined its domestic industry as the producers of yarn for sale in the merchant market, excluding from the data vertically integrated producers that were producing yarn as an intermediate good. Pakistan claimed that this definition violated Article 6.2 of the ATC, as it resulted in the failure of the United States to consider its entire domestic industry.[8]

After six long days of deliberations, arguments and counter-arguments the efforts of the Pakistan team bore fruit and the TMB, accepting Pakistan's central arguments, gave a ruling in favour of Pakistan and recommending an immediate lifting of the quota restrictions.[9]

The positive decision at the first ever TMB review was a major achievement by Pakistan. The co-ordinated efforts of the government, APTMA and the business players had been successful, although as the TMB recommendations are non-binding on the countries, the United States did not rescind the quota restraints and appealed against the decision. The appeal was rejected, however, and the recommendation to lift the quota restraints was reiterated by the TMB panel.

Behind the scenes

The failure of the bilateral negotiations had made it evident to the Pakistan government and APTMA that for the US government this was a critical case, since it could lead to the establishing of a legal precedent which could be utilized against Pakistan at least for the duration of the ATC.[10]

---

[7] Correspondence between Akbar Sheikh and APTMA, 16 April 1999 (2nd Call Notice CAT-301 Combed Cotton Yarn, APTMA Files).

[8] For details of the case see the TMB report of the WTO.

[9] The TMB concluded that 'the United States had not demonstrated successfully that combed cotton yarn was being imported into its territory in such increased quantities as to cause serious damage, or actual threat thereof, to its domestic industry producing like and/or directly competitive products'. WTO WT/DS192/1, 3 April 2000.

[10] At the end of 2005 the ATC expires, bringing to an end all quota restraints sanctioned under different measures such as transitional safeguards.

Moreover, Pakistan's response to the US action had to be determined and strong so as to give a signal that in the post-ATC era (after 2005) employing contingent measures such as anti-dumping duties would not go unchallenged. These important aspects, to an extent, were conveyed successfully by APTMA to the local business players involved, exporters and manufacturers, which was reflected by their willingness to play a pro-active role during the TMB review stage.

The first example of co-operation of the business players with APTMA and the government was the provision of relevant export and production data by the combed cotton yarn manufacturers and exporters. This helped in the formulation of Pakistan's defence case at the TMB review and later at the DSB stage.

However, the lack of relevant experience on the part of APTMA and the absence of an effective institutional structure in the Commerce Ministry in terms of handling dispute settlement cases meant that there was no set rule when it came to the payment of the high legal fees charged by the international lawyers and consultants. Hence APTMA had the onerous task of coming up with an acceptable formula for sharing the costs. After some discussion and bargaining with the Commerce Ministry, it was decided in a meeting held with the Export Promotion Bureau (EPB) that 50% of the costs were to be paid by APTMA and the other 50% by the EPB. APTMA's 50% share was to be divided equally between the affected members (the exporters of combed cotton yarn) and the non-affected members of APTMA.

The willingness to share the financial burden at this stage to some extent reflected the realization amongst members of APTMA of the significance of the case and its long-term benefits. The following excerpt from a letter written by one of the large manufacturers and exporters of combed cotton yarn is indicative of the willingness to co-operate with APTMA:

> The Textile Industry is deeply indebted to your good selves, and your TEAM on the strong stand that you have taken to resist the imposition of QUOTA and the steps taken by APTMA, are highly appreciable ... We wholeheartedly support your actions, and steps taken for the waiver of quotas, and further extend our availability for any kind of help and assistance which is required by APTMA to take up this issue with the TMB.

While most of the affected exporters or manufacturers of combed cotton yarn finally did contribute their respective share, the EPB paid only 31% of their share of the costs, thus reneging from their initial commitment to paying 50%. The shortfall resulted in a five-month delay in the payment to Travis, Sandler and Rosenberg, which charged a premium of 1.5% per month for the delay.[11]

Finally, the collaboration between APTMA and the Ministry of Commerce was to a large extent facilitated by Akbar Sheikh's good personal links with both Nasim Qureshi and the Pakistan ambassador to Switzerland, Munir Akram. The co-operative role played by these two government representatives was a key reason for the success at the TMB review. Thus in the absence of any institutionalized co-ordination and collaboration between the public and the private sectors, it was individual links which mattered in achieving a positive outcome.[12]

The DSB stage

Delay in taking the case up to the DSB

As the United States refused to comply with the recommendation of the TMB review, failing to do so even after their appeal was rejected in June 1999, the only course of action left for Pakistan was to take the case to the WTO's Dispute Settlement Board (DSB). This was the final and hence most important stage of the case, as unlike the TMB review the decision by the panel at DSB is binding on the countries involved. However, it took the government almost an entire year to request the establishment of a panel at the DSB. After the success at the TMB review such a delay at this critical stage came at a large cost to the exporters and manufacturers of combed cotton yarn. In the international market the demand for combed cotton yarn was picking up, so that the quota restraints were inhibiting Pakistan's potential exports and foreign exchange earnings even more.[13]

Immediately after the TMB review there was a meeting of the APTMA standing committee on anti-dumping and WTO affairs to give a briefing on the proceeding at the TMB. The convenor was of the view that 'in the case that the US action is not rescinded within fifteen days, the Pakistan government must apply to the Dispute Settlement Body of the WTO'. In August 1999 the United States in a letter to TMB renewed its determination to retain the quota restrictions, thus rendering the TMB review unresolved.

---

[11] After the payment of US$32,175 to IDS, Washington, there were not sufficient funds left to settle the invoice of US$28,125.16 of Travis, Sandler and Rosenberg (APTMA paper on USG call notice on combed cotton yarn (CAT 301)).

[12] Information provided by Akbar Sheikh.

[13] The export of cotton yarn to the United States had increased from 599,926 kg in April 1999 to 2,380,545 kg in December 1999 (2nd Call Notice CAT-301 Combed Cotton Yarn, APTMA Files).

Following the failure of the TMB review, in a letter in September to the APTMA chairman, Nasim Qureshi reiterated that both APTMA and Pakistan government 'may start preparations immediately for initiating the dispute settlement process'. In the letter it was also stated that after consultation with the Pakistan mission in Geneva, the ministry had decided to hire the services of a Geneva-based firm. The expected total cost of preparing, filing and contesting the case was quoted as $125,000, which according to the ministry thus was far less than the $200,000 quoted by the US-based law firm. According to Akbar Sheikh the reasons for hiring Geneva-based lawyers was to avoid the large miscellaneous costs (travel, board, etc.) of hiring consultants based in Washington.[14] Thus the reason for switching lawyers at the last stage of the case seemed purely financial. Though hiring the lawyers was to take place immediately, it was not until 1 March 2000 that APTMA and the Pakistan government signed a contract with the Geneva-based legal adviser, Frieder Roessler.

Another likely reason contributing to the delay could have been the bilateral consultations between the United States and Pakistan held in November 1999 and then in January 2000. The hope of getting the quota restraints lifted after bilateral negotiations might have caused the Pakistan government to wait till the outcome of these talks. According to Akbar Sheikh there were some indications from the US side of the possibility that the quota restraints would be lifted, hence it was thought inappropriate to file a case with the DSB close to the scheduled talks.

As the bilateral consultation failed, in hindsight Akbar Sheikh felt that it could have been a delaying tactic employed by the United States. The quota restraints had been imposed for three years, and the United States was strategizing to buy time to cover as much of this period as possible.[15] Finally, in April 2000, the Pakistan government took the case to the DSB, which established a Panel at its request.

The raising of funds to contest the case at the DSB

As this was the first time Pakistan was contesting a case at the DSB level there was no institutional set-up or guidelines for the payment of the expenses involved. As with the TMB stage, APTMA and the Commerce Ministry had to come up with an agreement. APTMA's proposal of a cost-sharing formula was finally accepted in February 2000 by the Commerce

---

[14] The actual charges of the Geneva-based legal adviser, Frieder Roessler, were approximately US$60,000. The expected amount quoted by the government must have included miscellaneous expenditure, i.e. travel, board, etc. of the government consultants and representatives (2nd Call Notice CAT-301 Combed Cotton Yarn, APTMA Files).

[15] Information provided by Akbar Sheikh.

Ministry. It was decided that out of the estimated total cost of $125,000 APTMA was to contribute the first $50,000, the balance to be given by the EPB using the revenue generated from the Export Development Fund (EDF).[16]

The next stage for APTMA was to get the concerned exporters/ manufacturers to contribute their share so as to raise the agreed initial amount of $50,000. Unlike at the TMB stage, there was a problem within APTMA in getting the concerned business players to contribute a second time for the legal expenses at the DSB stage.

Some large manufacturers/exporters of combed cotton yarn saw beyond their immediate economic interest and understood the value of persisting with the case at this last and most important stage. These players were willing to contribute whatever was required of them. At the same time there were others who had contributed at the TMB stage but because of a lack of understanding of the mechanism of dispute settlement at the WTO and frustration owing to US non-compliance saw no reason to contribute in order to pursue the case further. It is safe to say that these players did not quite appreciate the significance of the case in terms of the long-term benefits of pursuing to the end a positive decision. The following excerpts are an example of the degree of divergence of views within the members of APTMA:[17]

> Pakistan must move its case to the Dispute Settlement Board. In my opinion, however expensive and cumbersome these processes may be, we must do our utmost to fight these cases to protect our existing and potential markets. In this connection I would request you to call a meeting of the concerned members to develop a strategy to contest the above case. (From a letter written to APTMA by a co-operating large manufacturer/exporter)
>
> Please note that we already are the largest quota holders in this category from Pakistan. It is not in our interest to have this quota removed as its imposition creates a barrier to entry for others. It does not make any economic sense for us to 'pay to cut our own feet'. We therefore feel that it is unjust for APTMA to ask us to pay for this contribution. (From a letter written to APTMA by a non-co-operating large exporter/manufacturer)

These financing problems were eventually resolved and APTMA was able to meet its commitment of paying the initial $50,000 of the cost incurred at the DSB. In the words of Akbar Sheikh on the issue of financing at the DSB, 'Such disagreements within the association are quite common

[16] The Export Development Fund (EDF) is collected by the government (by the EPB) by charging the exporters a certain proportion of their export earnings.

[17] 2nd Call Notice CAT-301 Combed Cotton Yarn, APTMA Files.

and thus were anticipated. The important thing was that in the end the business players, APTMA and the government got together to contest the case successfully at the DSB.'

The proceedings

The first hearing of the case was held in Geneva on 16 and 17 November and the second hearing on 13 and 14 December 2000. The hearings were before the three-member panel established by the Dispute Settlement Body of WTO.[18] A three-member team consisting of Akbar Sheikh, S. I. M. Nayyar (counsellor, Pakistan permanent mission in Geneva) and Frieder Roessler represented Pakistan. A ten-member team represented the US government. According to Akbar Sheikh the proceedings of the DSB were quite different from those at the TMB review. While at the TMB there was a lot of discussion and argument, at the DSB there was more paper work, that is questions during the hearings were focused on the written submissions by the United States and Pakistan.

Pakistan contested the case successfully, and on 31 May 2001 the Panel in its report recommended an immediate lifting of the quota restrictions by the United States.[19] The United States appealed against the decision on 9 July and the appeal hearing was held on 16 August, when the Panel upheld its earlier decision and recommended an immediate lifting of the quota restraints.

Finally, complying with the recommendations of the DSB and the Appellate Body of the WTO, the US government in November 2001 lifted the quota restriction on Pakistani imports, much to the relief of the Pakistani manufacturers and exporters. The whole process, from the day the quota restraints were imposed to the day they were lifted, lasted for almost two years and nine months, covering almost the entire period of the three-year transitional safeguard measure–quota restraint employed by the United States. The following comment by Akbar Sheikh after being congratulated by Ambassador Don Johnson for winning the case aptly summarizes the feeling at that time.

> At the end of the day both parties won, Pakistan because it got a decision in its favour and the United States because it was able to keep the quota restraints for almost the entire three-year period, thanks to the duration of the case.

---

[18] The panel consisted of the chairman and two members, one from the EU and the other from India.

[19] For details of the panel's decision see the WTO, Panel Report, 31 May 2001.

4 Lessons learnt

The government

The first major lesson which came out of the case was that the government should in future play a much more proactive role in trade-related disputes than it has done in the past. In this particular case the primary factor behind the relatively high degree of co-ordination and co-operation between the Ministry of Commerce and APTMA (business players) had been the good personal relationship which Akbar Sheikh enjoyed with the two important functionaries in the government – the Joint Secretary, Ministry of Commerce, and the Pakistan ambassador to Switzerland. There was an absence of any institutionalized co-ordination between the government and APTMA specifically relating to such trade disputes and WTO affairs.

Akbar Sheikh was of the view that in order to facilitate institutional-level co-ordination in WTO-related dispute settlement cases the government should have a properly functioning and effective cell within the Ministry of Commerce. The government seemed to have learnt that lesson right at the start of the DSB proceedings in Geneva, when in October 2000, just before the hearings, a WTO cell was established at the permanent mission office in Geneva.[20] The cell was created to 'safeguard Pakistan's export and other interest in international trade by communicating the changes in the system and rules to the relevant authorities in Pakistan'.[21] The Ministry of Commerce almost simultaneously opened a WTO wing which now has a functioning cell. This cell has six working groups on different WTO agreements.[22]

Although these steps by the Pakistan government are in the right direction, Akbar Sheikh was of the view that there is still room for improvement in developing an effective institutional framework to contest future dispute settlement cases. He pointed out that the WTO cell should provide appropriate guidelines on both trade-related and dispute settlement issues to the players involved. Research should be conducted within the cell to

---

[20] Nasim Qureshi, who was the Joint Secretary, Ministry of Commerce, during most of the duration of case, was appointed as the deputy chief of the Pakistan mission in Geneva and head of this new WTO cell. Since the cell was created right at the end of this particular case, it could not contribute substantively to the proceedings of the case.

[21] http://dawn.com/2000/10/08/ebr9.htm.

[22] According to the 2002 Trade Policy Review of Pakistan by the WTO, these steps by the government to change and modify the existing institutional framework have strengthened the Ministry of Commerce in dealing with future trade-related issues.

keep it up to date with the current dispute settlement cases around the world. At the same time the cell should maintain an archive of past cases and rulings. According to Akbar Sheikh this would be immensely helpful to the private and the public sector in developing the right strategy for contesting future cases.

One of the central problems in this cotton yarn dispute case was the hiring of expensive foreign consultants and lawyers. According to Akbar Sheikh, the type of findings which some of these firms produced could very easily have resulted from research undertaken locally, had there been some basic level of legal expertise relating to international trade and the WTO. Hence he suggested that the government should invest in the training of lawyers and consultants who in future could handle dispute cases without the government resorting to hiring expensive foreign firms.

APTMA

During the course of this case APTMA already had a committee on anti-dumping and WTO issues which was supposed to act as a liaison between the business players and the government. However, as mentioned before, it had been the personal links which Akbar Sheikh had with both the government and APTMA which largely facilitated the co-ordination and co-operation between the two. In order to rectify the lack of an effective institutional structure APTMA has recently opened a WTO cell, which according to the APTMA secretary, Anis-ul-Haq, is still in its formative stage. The cell has currently hired a law firm which advises the APTMA members regarding WTO issues. Anis-ul-Haq considers that the primary objective of the cell should be to co-ordinate with the parallel WTO cell at the Ministry of Commerce, so that future dispute cases are handled smoothly. Also, this cell should advise the concerned members of APTMA on the prevailing trade environment and international trade law so as to pre-empt any action taken internationally against the local business players.

A major problem in the cotton dispute case was the collection of funds to meet the expenses involved. Both Anis-ul-Haq and Akbar Sheikh were of the opinion that rather than the existing ad hoc case-by-case approach there should be some set criteria established by the government and APTMA. This would significantly reduce the costs in terms of saving time currently wasted in coming up with an acceptable distribution of the financial burden. Along with this, APTMA as an organization should have a pool of resources allocated specifically to meeting the expenses of future dispute settlement cases. This common resource pool could be generated if APTMA helps to develop and foster the concept of mutual insurance amongst its members, who, often because of conflicting interests, are not willing to contribute.

The business players

The positive and effective role played by the dispute settlement mechanism of the WTO in resolving this trade dispute between two unequal partners helped reinvigorate the confidence of the local business players in the global trading environment. According to Akbar Sheikh it also helped in improving the image of the WTO at the level of both the government and business and enhanced its credibility as an institution aimed at fostering free and fair trade.

However, the fact remains that the quota was rescinded just three months before the expiry of the three-year period of the safeguard measures. Thus the cost to the local business players was not just in terms of contesting the case but also in the form of the lost revenue/earnings due to the length of time the restraints were in place. The fact that at the DSB stage quite a few business players initially refused to participate in financing the case indicates a prevalent frustration with the duration of the dispute settlement process. There was also a certain amount of scepticism about the ability of the WTO to make countries like the United States comply with its recommendations and decisions. Finally, there was still a general feeling that even after the DSB decision there was no guarantee that the United States would comply, since it could not be credibly threatened into compliance by a small economy like Pakistan even if retaliatory measures were sanctioned by the WTO.

35

Pakistan: the consequences of a change in the EC rice regime

AMIR MUHAMMED AND WAJID H. PIRZADA*

1 The problem in context

Pakistan's is primarily an agro-based economy, with the agriculture sector contributing around 25% towards GDP. Rice is the third-largest crop in terms of area in Pakistan after wheat and cotton, and in 2003–4 was grown on 2.46 million hectares.[1] It is one of the key non-traditional export commodities of Pakistan. Basmati and irri are the two main types of rice cultivated, consumed in and exported from Pakistan. Basmati is a traditional, long-grain (*indica*), aromatic variety especially suited to the Kalar tract of Punjab province. Although its grain yield is lower than the coarse-grained, short-statured irri rice, the net income per unit area to the growers is about equal from both types, for the market price of basmati is two to three times higher than the irri varieties. Pakistan enjoys a natural comparative advantage in basmati rice production, which has an assured market in several foreign countries where aromatic, long-grain rice is preferred.

Pakistan's annual rice exports average 1.5–2 million tonnes. During 2003–4, they were valued at US$627 million, registering a growth of 12.8% over the preceding year. Pakistani basmati has a market niche because of its characteristic aroma and cooking qualities. Super basmati, which is an extra-long-grain aromatic rice evolved from a cross between basmati 370 and basmati 320, with almost double the yield potential of basmati 370, remains the key export commodity. The European Union (EU) is one of the leading export destinations, partly because a sizable population

---

* Amir Muhammed is Rector, National University of Computer and Emerging Sciences, Islamabad. Wajid Pirzada is Director of Research/National Co-ordinator, WTO–Food- and Agriculture-Related Matters (WTO–FARM) Cell, Pakistan Agricultural Research Council, Islamabad.
[1] *Pakistan Economic Survey 2003–4*, Government of Pakistan, Finance Division.

from the subcontinent lives in the EU and relishes basmati rice. Pakistan exports basmati rice worth US$531 million to the EU, 80% of which is super basmati. The performance of this crop, on both production and export counts, therefore has long-term implications for both a sizable number of small farmers and the national economy.

In the recent past Pakistan has faced trade restrictions on its super basmati because of recent changes in the EU rice trade regime, resulting in the withdrawal of a duty abatement of €250 a tonne, an import duty derogation earlier allowed against normal duty of €264. This study, in the context of the WTO regime on agriculture, examines the need for and aims of such a restriction, and also its possible implications for various stakeholders, including farmers, processors, traders and of course the overall national economy.

The EU agricultural imports policy

The legislative text of the agreement on reforms of the much disputed EU Common Agricultural Policy (CAP) was finally adopted by EU Agriculture Ministers on 29 September 2003. This agreement stipulates inter alia a 50% reduction in the intervention support price for paddy rice (to €150 a tonne), and an annual purchasing limit of 75,000 tonnes on the volume of rice that could be imported into the EU (100,000 tonnes in 2003–4) under this intervention. EU rice farmers are to be compensated by the provision of area-based support payments, to be paid at a rate based on national/regional reference yields multiplied by €177 a tonne. Accordingly, the subsidy payable to EU rice producers is to be increased from €52.65 a tonne to €177 a tonne, of which €102 a tonne will be included in the single payment scheme. Council Regulation No. 1785/2003 of 29 September 2003 identifies in paragraphs 3, 5, 10 and 11 the reasons for and the form of such a change:

> Having regard to the Treaty establishing the European Community . . .
>
> . . .
>
> (3) The European rice market is in serious unbalance. The volume of rice stored in public intervention is very large, equivalent to about a quarter of Community output, and is likely to increase in the long run. The imbalance has been caused by the combined effect of an increase in domestic output, which has stabilized in recent marketing years, the continuing growth of imports and by the restrictions on exports with refunds in accordance with the Agriculture Agreement. The present imbalance is to be exacerbated even further and probably to reach an

unsustainable level, in the course of the years to come as a result of increasing imports from third countries due to the implementation of EBA [Everything but Arms] Agreement.

...

(5) It appears that the most suitable solution is to decrease strongly the intervention price and to create, as compensation, an income payment per farm and a crop-specific aid reflecting the role of rice production in traditional production areas. The latter two instruments are incorporated in Council Regulation (EC) No. 1782/2003 of 29 September 2003 on establishing common rules for direct support schemes under the common agricultural policy and establishing support schemes for the farmers.

...

(10) In order to prevent or counteract adverse effects on the Community market, which could result from the imports of certain agricultural products, imports of one or more of such products should be subject to payment of an additional import duty, if certain conditions are fulfilled.

(11) It is appropriate, under certain conditions, to confer on the Commission the power to open and administer tariff quotas resulting from international agreements concluded in accordance with the Treaty or from other acts of the Council.

Under Article XXVIII of GATT 1994 it was obligatory on the part of the EU to undertake negotiations with the WTO member countries expected to be affected, before making such a change in the rice import regime. The CAP reforms therefore mandated the Commission to open negotiations about modifying import arrangements, so as to modify existing variable levy arrangements for rice and replace them with a new system of tariff rate quotas (TRQs).

The aim of these negotiations with EU trading partners, to be carried out under Article XVIII of GATT, was to modify the mechanism for setting EU rice import duties, and thereby restrict the import of rice into the EU markets. The Commission in fact wanted to end the current mechanism, based on the link between the intervention support price for rice and a maximum duty paid on import price (head Note 7 of the WTO Schedule), for setting EU rice import duties. This mechanism would, under the agreed rice regime changes (WTO Schedule for implementation from 2004–5), result in a significant reduction in the level of import duty applicable to both husked and milled rice imports. Council Regulation (EC) #3072/95 of 22 December 1995 on the Common Organization of the Market in Rice (Article 3 stating, 'the reduction in the custom duties must be accompanied by a fall in the Community prices to enable the competitiveness of the Community products') substantiates this argument.

In so notifying the WTO of its intention to modify the import duty mechanism, the Commission indicated its intention to negotiate with the main supplier countries of rice some form of 'proportionate compensation' for abandoning the 'import duty setting mechanism' inherent in Head Note 7 of the WTO Schedule. Drawing on the precedent of how the similar 'import duty mechanism' for cereals was amended in 2002, it was understood that the EC would try to limit the flow of rice imports into EU member countries by providing additional tariff-free or reduced tariff access to the EU market subject to TRQs.

In respect of EU rice imports, there are currently TRQs applicable to imports principally from Thailand and the United States (and also Australia), that compensate for the impact of Austria, Finland and Sweden the joining EU in 1995, plus a number of bilateral/multilateral quota-restricted preferential access agreements with African, Caribbean and Pacific (ACP) countries and overseas territories of EU countries, Bangladesh and Egypt. Lastly, within the existing import duty mechanism, unlimited imports of husked basmati from India and Pakistan could enter the EU, at an import duty concession of €250 a tonne, reducing the net import duty from €264 a tonne to €14 a tonne.

To offset the likely surge of imports from India and Pakistan, because of substantial reduction in tariff from €264 a tonne to €14 a tonne because of duty abatement, the EU regime on rice was modified on the approval of the Cereal Experts Committee (CEC) of the EU in a meeting held in Brussels on 20 November 2003. The proposal of the withdrawal of abatement of duty concession was presented by EU Farm Commissioner Franz Fischer and the import arrangements for basmati rice were amended; the abatement concession of €250 a tonne on the import of Pakistan's super basmati was withdrawn from 1 January 2004. In so doing the EU maintained that Pakistan's super basmati was not a pure basmati and that the action was taken to counter alleged abuse and fraud in relation to the duty abatement.

Consequently Pakistan's export of super basmati was subjected to the total import duty of €264 a tonne. The abatement concession, however, was allowed, through a subsequent derogation, on the import of kernel basmati and basmati 370 from Pakistan (and India), the two varieties that did not command a significant export share, for three months starting 1 January 2004 (to 31 March 2004), provided that sales contracts were concluded (signed) between the suppliers from those countries and the European Community traders by 31 December 2003;

certificates of authenticity, to be issued in the case of Pakistan by the Trading Corporation of Pakistan, valid for 90 days, were already issued for the relevant contracts before 31 December 2003 or were so issued no later than 31 March 2004;

the consignments should land before 30 June 2004.

In the sections that follow we discuss the factors that prompted the EU to review the duty abatement for rice and to put pressure on Pakistan to institute such measures as DNA testing and the protection of super basmati under geographical indications (GIs).

Reason for the withdrawal of the abatement and its likely impact

The duty abatement was allowed earlier inter alia to help EU millers to polish imported brown rice in their modern mills and thus compete with white basmati in the market. The intended effect of any mechanism to reduce the level of EU import duty applying to imports from a specific source of supply is to reduce the entry price and thus improve the competitive position of supplies from the beneficiary suppliers.[2] Also, with mounting pressure for steep cuts on tariffs and the removal of other (trade) distorting and restrictive measures by countries in the North, it is tempting for them to use (higher) health and hygiene and ecological and environmental standards, coupled with regulations such as those on intellectual property and investment rights, to protect their industry and especially their agriculture, which had enjoyed preferential protection and support for several decades.[3]

Super basmati constitutes 80% of Pakistani rice exports to the EU. Pakistan used to export 50–60 thousand tonnes of husked basmati rice annually under the EU abatement scheme. Consequent upon withdrawal of abatement, a bound tariff rate of €264 a tonne as against €14 a tonne under the abatement concession would be applicable to Pakistani husked super basmati, making it uncompetitive. Such a restriction could

---

[2] Graham Brookes (2003), briefing note: 'Impact of Tariff Rate Quotas (TRQs) on the EU *Indica* Rice Market', Brookes West, Jasmine House, Canterbury Road, Elham, Canterbury, Kent, UK.

[3] Wajid H. Pirzada (in press), 'Market Access and Standards', *Journal of Science Technology and Development*.

potentially lead to the ousting of Pakistan from the European rice market, inflicting heavy losses on Pakistan's economy and depriving poor farmers of their livelihood. It is worth pointing out that Pakistan had earlier accepted conditions imposed by the EU on the export of brown rice from Pakistan that included (i) fixing a quota ceiling, (ii) fixing a minimum export price, and (iii) strict quality checks. Despite these preconditions Pakistan competed effectively and (for example) utilized its full quota of 9,000 tonnes of brown rice in 1996–7,with an increase in foreign exchange earnings of US$2 million compared with the previous year.

Linking geographical indications with trade in basmati rice

It is not clear why the EU was pressing so hard for the protection of basmati under GIs except that the EU was interested in the expansion of GIs, currently limited to wines and spirits, to agricultural products to win over more supporters for the EU within the WTO system. Section 3 of the WTO Agreement on Trade-Related Intellectual Property Rights (TRIPS) is dedicated to geographical indications (GIs). It is the first multilateral agreement dealing with GIs as such.

The TRIPS Agreement contains a clear triple distinction in the level of protection for (i) GIs related to all products; (ii) wines and spirits; and (iii) wines only. Article 22 of TRIPS defines GIs as

> indications which identify a good as originating in the territory of a Member, or a region or a locality in that territory, where a given quality, reputation or other characteristic of the good is essentially attributable to its geographical origin.

India and Pakistan experienced the need for and the importance of the protection of GIs in the basmati rice case. The problem arose when the US Patent Office issued patents in 1997 for three new strains of rice. These strains could be sold under the name 'basmati', referring to a particular form of long-grained and aromatic rice associated with the plains of Punjab. In 1998 the US Rice Federation submitted that the term basmati was generic and referred to a specific type of aromatic rice. In response, Pakistan and India jointly filed a petition seeking to prevent US-grown rice from being labelled or advertised as 'basmati'. The US Department of Agriculture and Federal Trade Commission rejected the petition in May 2001, maintaining that labelling rice as 'American-grown basmati' was not misleading, and deemed 'basmati' to be a generic term. After India and Pakistan's protest against the use of the name 'basmati', the US Patent

Office barred the patent holder from using the generic name 'basmati'. This rice can now be only sold as 'Texmati' or any other name that clearly informs the consumer that the rice is not from the Punjab region.

In this regard it is worth mentioning that some multinationals have succeeded in securing patents on basmati rice, which is tantamount to a violation of GIs, as thousands of years ago Aryans developed this unique variety of rice with its special aroma, and named it 'basmati' – 'fragrance of a virgin'. The origin of basmati has been traced back to the Kalar tract of Punjab, Pakistan, where it has been grown for centuries. As such, it is a classic example of a GI, qualifying on the basis of both traditional knowledge and place, being highly localized in character. The very name 'basmati', because of its origin, identifies the product, for which provision has been made under TRIPS.[4]

DNA testing

In 1998 the UK government started a project, 'DNA Testing of Basmati Rice for Purity'. For the first time, Indian rice multinational trade companies proposed the strains basmati 370, Type 3 Dehraduni, Haryana 19 (HBC19), Tarori and Karnaal as pure line basmati rice: basmati 370 and Dehradun basmati are a common heritage of both India and Pakistan, and there has been no issue over them.[5] However, because of inadequacies in analytical and human resource capacity, coupled with financial limitations, developing countries such as Pakistan face difficulty in carrying out high-tech certification based on DNA testing.

2 Local and external players and their roles

The change in the rice import regime made unilaterally by the EU understandably generated strong protests from the affected stakeholders and governments in the developing countries. The most vigorous protests were made by the government and the rice exporting community of Pakistan, who estimated an annual loss of US$45 million to Pakistani exporters as a consequence.

---

[4] Wajid H. Pirzada (2003), 'A Log-Frame of Sui Generis System to Protect Farmers' Rights: Pakistan's Perspective', in Ratnakar Adhikari and Kamalesh Adhikari, eds., *Farmers' Rights to Livelihood in the Hindu Kush Himalayas*, Nepal: South Asia Watch on Trade, Economics & Environment (SAWTEE).

[5] Syed Faisal Hassan (2004), 'India Commercially Exploits Pakistani Basmati', *The Nation*, 23 Feb.

The Pakistan government

The Commerce Minister, Humayoon Akhtar Khan, assured Pakistan's rice exporters that Pakistan would oppose any unilateral amendment in the rice import regime that would affect Pakistan's export of super basmati to EU member countries. Pakistan's mission to the WTO took the position during negotiations with the EU of not accepting any unfavourable deal, particularly one including TRQs. It maintained that TRQs not only were trade distorting in nature but could never compensate for the loss of Pakistan's current unlimited access to the EU market.[6]

During his visit to Brussels after the withdrawal of the duty abatement, Pakistan's Commerce Minister asked the EU Trade Commissioner, Pascal Lamy, to seek Pakistan's opinion before making any changes in the rice import regime. Lamy was reported as assuring the Pakistani minister that the EU would further consult Pakistan in the matter before any final decision was taken. Consultations on this issue continued until September 2004, when a mutually acceptable deal on the issue was reportedly struck through an exchange of letters.

The private sector

The Rice Exporters Association of Pakistan (REAP) in its formal reaction said that the change in the EU regime on rice imports would affect Pakistan's exports to the EU and asked for the status quo to be maintained until Pakistani traders were to be adequately compensated. REAP deemed the proposal a violation of the code approved by the UK Grain and Food Trade Association (GAFTA) at a meeting where the Pakistani basmati variety was declared to be pure rice. They were of the view that Pakistan would not be in a position to receive substantial quota under the TRQs system worked out on the basis of previous export performance, which in Pakistan's case stood at 20–30% only.

Barrister Syed Najaf Hussain Shah, the chairman of REAP, while detailing the official stance of REAP, said that the government was fully supporting rice exporters and REAP had been assured that it would protest at the highest forum against the decision of the EU Cereal Experts Committee (CEC).[7] He said that the withdrawal of the concession would continue till September 2004, and after that all rice exports to EU member

---

[6] Ministry of Commerce (2003), 'Impact of TRQs on Basmati Rice', official document, 21 Aug.
[7] Noshad Ali (2003), *Daily Times*, 30 Dec.

countries would be free from any duty. Shah added that the withdrawal of the concession, while a shock to rice growers and exporters in the short term, would serve as a blessing in disguise in the longer run with the possibility of more value added and as the rice exporters gradually switched to the export of polished rice, which would not only add profit but also increase employment opportunities in the country. Mr Shah went on to say that Pakistan would not lose any of its market for super basmati because it would not be substituted by Indian Pusa basmati, a similar quality rice which has been given the same treatment for import purposes.

As against the above stance, the convenor of the Rice Export Committee of Lahore Chamber of Commerce and Industries, Agha Javed, said that the country could face a shortfall of 90,000 tonnes of rice export after the EC's decision. He said that the Commerce Minister had already lodged a protest with the EC and promised that the government would take precautionary measures. The co-convenor of the Committee, Zahid Khawja, said that Pakistan should not take any hasty decision in this regard and should continue to maintain that the EC decision to withdraw the concession in import duty on basmati rice was unjustified.[8]

Leading Pakistani rice exporters too, while showing their serious concern over the change in the EU rice import regime, expressed the hope that the CEC would set aside the draft proposing the new definition of basmati rice and that the old system would continue, since India too had decided to oppose the draft.

3 Challenges faced and the outcome

It had been suggested[9] that if the outcome of the EC's WTO negotiations to modify the current rice import duty mechanism focused on the additional use of TRQs to replace the current import duty setting mechanism inherent in Head Note 7 of the WTO Schedule, this would inevitably result in a reduced level of the market and of economic efficiency, to the detriment of established suppliers like Pakistan and consumers in the EU market. It was further suggested that any alternative form of agreement (including the current mechanism) that at least maintained the current level of market access outside TRQs (e.g. reduced import duty market access for basmati that was unrestricted by volume) was preferable, because it would avoid adding further losses and inefficiencies associated with TRQs. A non-tariff

---

[8] Rizwan Ali (2003), *The News*, 8 Dec. (http//www.jang.com.pk).   [9] Brookes (2003).

solution was therefore to be commended as an approach to take in the
WTO negotiations between the EU and the third-country suppliers.

On a bilateral basis, both the EU and Pakistan continued interacting
both formally and informally, and it was reported formally in August
2004 that exports of Pakistan's super basmati would resume from the
beginning of the EU fiscal year in September 2004, as the EU had decided
through an exchange of letters to re-include super basmati in its duty
rebatement list with the condition of DNA testing, and had agreed as
follows:

- the tariff rate for husked rice (CN code 1006 20) shall be €65 a tonne;
- with respect to the import regime for husked rice (CN codes 1006
  20 17 and 1006 20 98) of the varieties kernel (basmati), basmati 370,
  Pusa basmati and super basmati, the EC's specific bound rate of duty
  shall be zero.

The following measures have been agreed to implement this agreement.

- A Community control system based on DNA analysis at the border
  shall be created.
- Pakistan shall actively co-operate with the EC to set up such a control
  system and the EC shall provide the appropriate technical assistance
  in this matter.
- Pakistan will protect basmati rice as a geographical indication. The
  EC would welcome an application for protection as a GI of basmati
  rice under Council Regulation (ECC) No. 2081/92 of 14 July 1992 on
  the protection of geographical indications and designation of origin
  for agricultural products and foodstuff.[10] The EC shall process any
  such application as expeditiously as possible. The EC shall provide
  any necessary technical assistance in the matter.

As a transitional arrangement, the following has also been agreed to
by both the parties.

- As from 1 September 2004 and until the date of entry into force of
  the above-mentioned Community control system, the EC would put
  in place a transitional regime with regard to husked rice (CN codes
  1006 20 17 and 1006 20 98) of the varieties described above based on
  the following elements:
  - The EC's autonomous applied rate of duty shall be zero. However,
    if market disturbance occurs, the EC will consult with Pakistan's

---

[10] Ibid.

competent authorities to agree to an appropriate solution. If no agreement is reached, the EC reserves the right to revert to the bound rate of €65 a tonne for husked rice (CN code 1006 20).

- The EC shall establish separate tariff lines for basmati rice of the varieties indicated in the agreements with India and Pakistan.
- The competent Pakistani authorities shall continue to issue the authenticity certificates prior to the issuance of import licences, meaning that the current system of administration of the certificates of authenticity shall be maintained.

Consequently, free access for Pakistani basmati rice was allowed with effect from September 2004, partially endorsing the viewpoint of the Chairman REAP, who is on record as stating that the present restriction would cease to be effective after September 2004, when full access to Pakistani rice would be provided.[11]

The EU, however, has not yet withdrawn the condition of DNA testing nor has the issue of GIs so far been settled. Meanwhile, the EU has clarified to the Pakistani authorities that should the imports from Pakistan increase to a level of disturbance, then imports beyond certain limits would be subject to the normal tariff applicable to rice in the EU. Commission Regulation (EC) No. 1549/2004 of 30 August 2004, derogating from Regulation No. 1785/2003, indicates in paragraphs 1–5 the arrangements for importing rice and laying down separate transitional rules for import of basmati rice:

> Having regard to the Treaty establishing the European Community,
>
> ...
>
> Having regard to Council Decision 2004/618/EC of 11 August 2004 on the conclusion of an Agreement in the form of an Exchange of Letters between the European Community and Pakistan pursuant to Article XXVIII of GATT 1994 relating to the modification of concessions with respect to rice provided for in Schedule CXL annexed to the GATT 1994, and in particular Article 2 thereof,
>
> Whereas
>
> (1) Decision 2004/619/EC modifies the import regime for husked rice and milled rice in the Community. Decisions 2004/617/EC and 2004/618/EC lay down conditions for importing basmati rice. This change in regime makes it necessary to amend Regulation No. 1758/2003. In order to enable those Decisions to be applied on 1 September 2004, as provided for in the Agreements approved by those Decisions, it is necessary to

---

[11] Noshad Ali (2003).

derogate from Regulation (EC) No. 1785/2003 for a transitional period expiring on the date of entry in to force of the amendment to that Regulation, and no later than 30 June 2005.

(2) Decisions 2004/617/EC and 2004/618/EC also provide for a transitional import regime for basmati rice to be set in place until the entry into force of a definitive import regime for this type of rice. Specific transitional rules should be laid down.

(3) In order to be eligible for zero import duty, basmati rice must belong to a variety specified in the Agreements. In order to ascertain that basmati rice imported at zero rate of duty meets those characteristics, it should be covered by an authenticity certificate drawn up by the competent authorities.

(4) In order to prevent fraud, provision should be made for measures to check the variety of basmati rice declared.

(5) The transitional import regime for basmati rice provides for a procedure for consulting the exporting country in the event of disturbance on the market and possibly applying the full rate of duty if a satisfactory solution has not been found at the end of the consultations. It would be appropriate to define from what point the market may be considered to be disturbed.

4 Lessons for others

Despite the inflated claims by key players since the inception of trade liberalization under the WTO in 1995, trade distortions and restrictions continue to be rampant in the global market. A country like Pakistan, with limited exports, can hardly afford to adjust to sudden shocks because of changes like the one imposed by the EU through reforms in its rice trade policy. Trade and economic superpowers such as the EU also use their economic and trade weight to influence in their favour negotiations with developing countries such as Pakistan. In this case too, a year-long restriction on Pakistan's super basmati inflicted heavy losses on both the national economy and the farmers. Nevertheless, the proactive engagement on the part of the public and private sectors helped resolve the issue temporarily. The temporary solution, however, will result in a quota-restricted preferential treatment in terms of duty-free market access. Such solutions are not sustainable, for trade preferences are bound to erode in the long run under the WTO regime. The strategic advantage that Pakistan currently enjoys after the events of 9/11 will also not last for too long. Moreover, the TRQs system does not augur well for trade liberalization under the WTO; in fact developing countries have already been protesting about non-transparency in the administration of TRQs. As a measure for contributing to the liberalization of trade and improving market efficiency TRQs have several weaknesses. It would be in the best interest of developing countries such as Pakistan to

- strive for reduced import duty market access, rather than quota-restricted, duty free (preferential access) import for basmati rice;
- develop legal, trade and economic analyses and research capacity to face squarely issues like trade restrictions;
- develop quality infrastructure that will help realign with the standard economy;
- undertake proactive legislation on GIs that can potentially benefit Pakistan, with the ability to sell basmati rice with confidence and certainty since GIs promote consumer confidence;
- diversify, in terms of both agricultural production and processing, which will give the country economic resilience and farmers a more dependable source of income; and
- vertically integrate agricultural production in general and of high-value crops in particular, rather than depend on mono-crop culture.

Such initiatives in turn will help to counter technical barriers to trade such as DNA testing and linking trade with issues such as GIs, as such issues will continue to surface in future. Pakistan should also avail itself of the offer of the EU in developing a DNA testing service and also towards legislation on GIs in this regard.

Moreover, the present agreement between Pakistan and the EU is not definitive, and there is every likelihood that after June 2005 Pakistan may have to face a similar situation. Efforts therefore need to be directed at resolving such issues proactively on a bilateral basis. The Dispute Settlement Mechanism (DSM) under the WTO is a time-consuming and costly proposition, besides the fact that resorting to the DSM needs legal and technical capacity which most developing countries including Pakistan lack at present. It would be in the long-term interest of these countries to build such capacity, pooling their human and material resources.

36

Philippines: stakeholder participation in agricultural policy formation

DONAH SHARON BARACOL*

1 The problem in context

Agriculture is a major contributor to the Philippines economy, accounting for 21.5% of its gross domestic product (GDP),[1] generating exports valued at over US$1.5 billion,[2] and providing one third of all employment, or 11 million jobs.[3] Its contribution increases when 'all economic activities related to agro-processing and supply of non-farm agricultural inputs are included, (as) the agricultural sector broadly defined accounts for about two-thirds of the labour force and 40% of GDP'.[4] The strategic importance of this sector makes it compelling for the government to enact a stakeholder-based process that will fully and effectively render legitimacy not only to its domestic economic policies but to its international economic commitments as well, such as to the WTO.

In 1995 the Philippines acceded to the WTO in the belief that its membership of the rules-based body would bring about economic benefits, primarily to the rural sector, through increased efficiency of industries required by exposure to global competition. Jobs were promised and new industries were expected to emerge.

With the implementation of the WTO Uruguay Round commitments in 1995 came also the increasing realization, especially by the agriculture

---

* Senior Economist, Philippines Sugar Millers Association, Manila.
[1] National Statistical Co-ordination Board, *National Income Accounts 1st Quarter 2004*, available at www.nscb.gov.ph.
[2] 2001 data for agro-based products, *2002 Philippine Statistical Yearbook*, National Statistical Co-ordination Board.
[3] *National Income Accounts 1st Quarter 2004*.
[4] V. Bruce Tolentino, Cristina David, Arsenio Balisacan and Ponciano Intal Jr, 'Strategic Actions to Rapidly Ensure Food Security and Rural Growth in the Philippines', 29 March 2001, as cited by Walden Bello, 'The WTO and the Demise of Philippine Agriculture', *Focus on the Global South*, 20 June 2003.

stakeholders, that the promised gains were not forthcoming. The liberalization implied by the commitments was perceived as too fast and beyond the country's capacity to comply, and so found poor general acceptance. Serious accusations were made about the government's lack of consultation with the affected sectors, and blame directed towards government negotiators whom stakeholders felt were not only vastly uninformed about the situation in the field, but were also regarded as 'blind' advocates of rapid liberalization and therefore insensitive to their needs. Stakeholders believed that inadequate consultation had resulted in this serious disconnection between the government negotiating position and the complex realities in the field. There was an immediate call for a participatory and bottom-up approach to the domestic process in agricultural trade negotiations.

The opportunity to transform the function of formulating the negotiating position into an inclusive process was provided by the preparations needed for the upcoming WTO Seattle Ministerial in late 1999. Stakeholder participation and work could be focused around a central objective, which was to prepare for the Ministerial Conference and the global negotiations towards a new agreement on agriculture.

The Task Force on WTO Agreement on Agriculture (Re)negotiations (TF-WAR) was therefore established amidst increasing public clamour, led by farmers and people's organizations, as well as industry groups, for transparency and representation in the formulation of the Philippine negotiating position in the new round of WTO talks.

2 The local and external players and their roles

The creation of the TF-WAR

On 28 September 1998, the then Secretary of the Department of Agriculture (DA), through Special Order No. 538[5] duly constituted the Task Force on WTO Agreement on Agriculture (Re)negotiations, a multi-sectoral task force composed of twenty-eight representatives from farmer groups, industry associations, business federations, non-government organizations, people's organizations and other relevant government institutions and agencies.[6] The main responsibility of the TF-WAR was to consider,

---

[5] Issued by the Office of the Secretary, Department of Agriculture, 28 Sept. 1999.

[6] Original members included: from the government, the National Agriculture and Fishery Council (NAFC), Minimum Access Volume (MAV) Secretariat, DA Planning and Monitoring Service. From the private sector, representatives from the Philippine Chamber of

develop, evaluate and recommend Philippine negotiating positions and strategies for the new round of negotiations.

Other functions of the TF WAR included evaluating existing policies and programmes in the agriculture sector and providing policy and programme recommendations to address gaps that erode the benefits of WTO membership; reviewing General Agreement on Tariffs and Trade (GATT) adjustment and competitive enhancement measures (safety nets) drawn prior to the Philippines accession in 1995; and identifying projects and sources of funds to enhance the competitiveness of Philippines agriculture.

The TF-WAR reports to the DA Secretary, and is chaired by the DA Assistant Secretary for Policy and Planning. An elected private-sector representative serves as vice-chair. The decision on the final composition of the TF-WAR was a collective decision of the body.

During the course of the preparations for the Seattle Ministerial, the TF-WAR functioned as a formal group much like a standard inter-agency and multi-sectoral committee in the department, following the provisions of the Special Order. With the increasing demands required by the faster pace of developments on the run-up to the Seattle Ministerial, when gathering the entire membership more frequently became difficult, an ad hoc technical working group was formed to examine specific issues needing immediate feedback and comment.

In late 2001, after the new WTO Round was launched in Doha, the structure and organization of the TF-WAR underwent changes following reorganization and movement of personnel in the DA who were involved in the TF-WAR. A new Special Order was issued to reconstitute the TF-WAR.[7] While the stakeholder membership remained intact, this time it was a less formal organization and it was streamlined to involve only those government agencies which had key participation in trade policy-making. The secondary functions of the TF-WAR were removed, and its work now focused on the sole responsibility of formulating national

Food Manufacturers, National Onion Growers Co-operative, Philippine Association of Hog Raisers, Inc., Federation of Free Farmers, Coffee Foundation of the Philippines, National Federation of Hog Farmers, Inc., Philippine Association of Meat Processors, Inc. From the NGOs, the following were represented, Sanduguan, Pambansang Kilusan ng mga Samahang Magsasaka, CODE-NGO, Philippine Business for Social Progress. Membership expanded to include the grain, sugar, poultry and fishery sectors. The last eventually formed their own task force as fishery negotiations are being conducted separately in the WTO.

[7] Special Order No. 450, issued by the Office of the Secretary, September 2001.

negotiating position in agriculture. A significant new feature, however, was the formation of a core group in early 2002.

The constitution of the TF-WAR core group

The TF-WAR core group was formed to improve technical and policy work to support the TF-WAR, and to enable a quick response to developments in the negotiations, expected to become more intensive as the talks progressed. The chair recalls that 'The process ... recognized the unwieldiness of the plenary/general assembly system.' TF-WAR members who had good knowledge of a key sector and had some technical competence were invited to join the core group as a 'permanent representation, on a voluntary but committed basis'. Representatives sit in the group in an individual capacity and therefore do not represent a particular sector or interest. They may represent the country in the negotiations in Geneva, when resources permit, as official delegates and advisers. As members, they are expected to render objective analysis on the issue at hand, with the overarching consideration that any recommendation put forward is the optimal position regarded as best representing the interests of the entire Philippines agriculture. The core group members are always on call, required to convene at short notice, and consulted directly by the Geneva office in real time when necessary.

The TF-WAR core group was constituted through Special Order No. 231 dated 2 May 2002.[8] The members include the chairman of the task force, five representatives from the private sector, and staff from the DA Policy and Planning Office acting as technical secretariat. Specific tasks include detailed evaluation of proposals submitted by WTO members, in-depth analysis of both the overall and specific impacts on Philippine agriculture, and the formulation and elaboration of specific proposals based on these analyses guided by the general policy direction decided in the TF-WAR.

3 Challenges faced and the outcome

The creation of the TF-WAR redefined the consultation process in the Philippines on issues of national significance such as trade negotiations. It is unique in that it empowers the stakeholders by giving them a central role,

---

[8] Issued by the Office of the Secretary, Department of Agriculture.

Figure 36.1. *The agriculture trade negotiation process.*

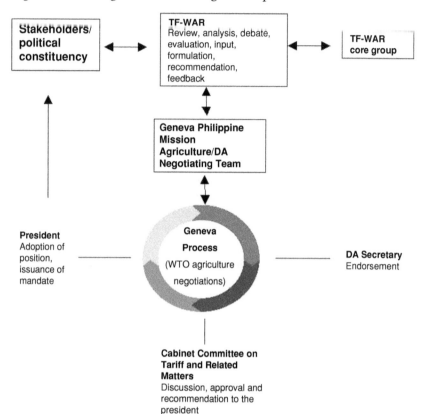

involving them from the very start of the process and throughout the entire negotiations, going much farther than the token exchange of views that had characterized previous consultation processes by the government.

A. The agriculture trade negotiation process

Figure 36.1 illustrates the process of formulating the Philippines national negotiating position on agriculture, and the institutions involved. The entire negotiation process involves a complex two-level dynamic, first among the domestic institutions involved, and second within and among members of the WTO, aimed at reaching a consensus on what is known as the Geneva process. The Geneva process of negotiations in agriculture drives the TF-WAR process.

Any new work by the TF-WAR begins with a specific development in the WTO agriculture negotiations. The Agriculture Office of the DA in Geneva regularly transmits developments in the negotiations to the TF-WAR. This, together with the reports by the DA Assistant Secretary for Policy and Planning, who is both the capital-based negotiator as well as the chair of the TF-WAR, of results of special negotiating sessions in Geneva, is the basis for the continuing work of the TF-WAR. The capital-based negotiator plays a pivotal role in the negotiations, being the link between the internal process and the external process. This entire dynamic is illustrated in the diagram, where the Geneva Philippines mission/agriculture negotiating team receives from and feeds into the TF-WAR process on one hand, and receives from and feeds into the Geneva process on the other.

After an assessment of these developments by the TF-WAR, further work is passed on to the core group, whose recommendations go back to the bigger group for evaluation and approval. These are then formally confirmed by the chair of the TF-WAR to the DA Secretary for transmittal to the Cabinet Trade and Related Matters (TRM) Committee or, in the case of specific positions within established negotiating mandates, to the Geneva-based negotiators. Discussion on recommendations or issues brought to the TRM are reported back to the TF-WAR.

The agriculture negotiating team is guided by a negotiating mandate developed with the TF-WAR and with clearance from the president. Issues within the mandate and clearance level of Geneva-based staff are merely reported back to the capital. Meanwhile, issues needing clearance at the level of the DA senior official are transmitted to the capital for a decision. The core group is convened at short notice and the issue(s) evaluated. Cleared instructions and alternatives are then issued to Geneva. For major issues that require a political decision,[9] the issue is transmitted to the capital for evaluation and recommendation by the core group and the entire TF-WAR membership, and for a final clearance and mandate by the Secretary. Ministerial Conference mandates are obtained through a further route to the cabinet TRM and the president.

The essence of stakeholder participation in the negotiations is reflected on the left-hand part of the diagram, which shows that the mandate of the TF-WAR flows from the stakeholders which they represent and whose position they endorse. When the president adopts it as the national position, it reflects the accountability of the office to an important political

---

[9] Such as joining the G20 (Group of 20) or organizing the SP and SSM (Special Products and Special Safeguard Mechanism) Alliance.

constituency, recognizing that its real mandate stems from this exercise of democratic governance.

B. The TF-WAR process

The following activities characterize the TF-WAR process.

Regular meetings. This is the heart of the domestic process. Aside from regular updating meetings, the chair meets the TF-WAR before and after each meeting of delegations in Geneva to discuss the proposals of WTO members, to report the results of WTO special sessions, and to provide the assessment of the negotiating team and its implications for the Philippines negotiating position. Issues discussed are organized along the structure of the Agreement on Agriculture. Discussion ensues mainly on the substance of the ongoing talks and possible issues to be raised, and the negotiating strategy to adopt. Members provide feedback on the possible impact of these developments or decision points on their respective sectors.

Issues are explained with emphasis on decision points. Members recommend positions and attempt to reach a consensus. If none is reached, further discussions are held if there is still available time. If not, the issue is examined more closely by the core group, who will look into the technical merits of each individual position and at other arguments to try to balance the opposing views.

The TF-WAR deals with sensitive issues of national significance, and in order not to compromise the integrity of a position, members adhere to strict guidelines for security and confidentiality of information. Information is released according to levels of confidentiality.[10]

Consultations. Consultations with their respective membership are held individually by each TF-WAR member organization. Inputs and recommendations arising from these consultations are gathered by the secretariat and discussed in the core group meetings, where views are consolidated. These are then presented in the TF-WAR and duly recommended to the Secretary. Interaction with stakeholders not represented in

---

[10] The guidelines state that 'in deciding the level of confidentiality to be accorded an information, the body shall judiciously consider the twin issues of the right to public information and national security – to strike a balance between safeguarding the basic right of people to public information on matters of public concern and access to official records, on the one hand, and the need to protect vital secrets and information affecting national security and interest, on the other... Any breach of faith regarding a commitment to confidentiality is ground for removal of membership from the Task Force ... Task Force may take legal action against the offending party', Department of Agriculture, *Guidelines for Confidentiality*, March 2000.

the TF-WAR may be through DA-initiated national and regional consultations with organization leaders, direct consultations with stakeholders or public fora.

Workshops. The core group holds one-day or two-day workshops when the issues require more study and analysis. For issues requiring technical expertise otherwise not available within the group, it invites resource persons from other government agencies or institutions and practitioners from the private sector for input.

Technical work and research. The Core Group is responsible for this, and is assisted by the secretariat, which undertakes research and the gathering and consolidation of data, processing them into the format required for analysis by the core group with the use of simple economic tools to assist in the evaluation of alternative scenarios arising from various possible negotiating positions.

Approval process and recommendation. The TF-WAR approves a final recommendation, after which the position is recommended to the DA Secretary, which then recommends it to the TRM. After deliberation, this is recommended to the president, who adopts it as the Philippines negotiating framework. This framework defines the parameters within which the DA negotiating team is mandated to work. It forms the basis for Philippines submissions to the WTO, such as proposals or statements.

The Task Force has produced at least five proposals submitted to the WTO Committee on Agriculture–Special Session since 1999, none of which has been rejected by the Secretary of Agriculture, the cabinet or the president. Assistant Secretary Segfredo R. Serrano, chair of the TF-WAR, recalls that 'Many of the developing country blocs' operational concepts of SND and even the current negotiations vocabulary owe much to TF-WAR deliberations: Strategic/Special Products (SPs),[11] Special Safeguard Mechanism (SSM),[12] automatic countervailing/counterbalancing mechanisms, the concept of interlinkage of pillar commitments, among others.'

---

[11] Special Products (SP) is a new concept introduced in the current Round and agreed by Members as a modality for further elaboration in the recently adopted framework agreement for the famous July 2004 Package. It is a special and differential treatment (SND) mechanism providing flexibility for developing countries in recognition of the inherent difficulties they face in implementing their WTO commitments, and a way of addressing the food security, livelihood security and rural development objectives aimed at by the Doha Development Agenda. Under the SP, developing countries will have less onerous commitments in reducing barriers for certain sensitive products, the number and modality of which are to be agreed.

[12] The July 2004 Package also specifies that a special safeguard mechanism (SSG) will be established for use by developing countries. The modality is yet to be developed in the next phase of negotiations.

4 Lessons for others (the players views)

The existence of such a group, representing various parochial interests, strengthens the recommending authority of the DA Secretary and lends greater legitimacy to the mandate of the president, to whom all recommendations are submitted, to proceed with the negotiating position in the WTO, the position having emanated from his or her wider constituency. This is perhaps the strongest feature of the TF-WAR process. More specific observations follow.

The institutionalized participation of stakeholders is ensured

The DA has institutionalized the participation of stakeholders in trade negotiations, not only through the formal creation of the TF-WAR by a Special Order, but by making it the central player in the negotiation process, thus ensuring the continued active involvement of these interested parties.

For TF-WAR members, 'the process is participatory and consultative, it enables members to input into the negotiation process'. 'It provides a venue to air our concerns regarding the impact of liberalization on our respective sectors.' 'The recommendation truly reflects the situation on the ground.' 'Industries feel they are heard and their interests recognized by government.' 'The mechanism thus far has been effective in addressing the systemic mistake in the past Round wherein stakeholders played a relatively passive role in the formulation of negotiating position.' 'There are less accusations from the industries that they were not heard.'

Moreover, the TF-WAR experience has proved that deeper involvement by stakeholders in the negotiating process can be obtained at very minimal financial cost to the government, an important consideration for developing countries with limited resources. Members join on a voluntary basis and through representation enable the government to reach out to more sectors without having to hold individual consultations each time.

A more informed, balanced and credible negotiating position is adopted

Stakeholders' experiences from the implementation of Uruguay Round commitments provide very useful and practical insights on the possible consequences of adopting a certain position. Members perceive that with the TF-WAR process, the sensitivity of agricultural interests is better reflected in the positions adopted. There is, moreover, a practical importance to involving the private sector, as they can better identify specific trade opportunities and barriers to Philippine exports, or threats to their markets.

The TF-WAR has members representing upstream and downstream users of agricultural commodities,[13] and can therefore be regarded as a balanced group. As each member, however, is encouraged to be parochial in advancing their interests and concerns, conflict between different sectors is unavoidable. The chair observes, 'Conflicting interests are discussed openly. Differences in views are debated, and are judged on substantive and technical merit. Any resolution must be consistent with the existing negotiating mandate. If the government decides to break the impasse, it can do so and would still need to generate consensus.' While these conflicting interests result in dynamics that are difficult to manage, the resolution of any issue gains more acceptance from all sectors when an equal opportunity to defend individual interests has been given. The TF-WAR, therefore, is a venue that 'neutralizes' the extreme positions that may be pushed for by opposing sectors.

Stakeholder experience, insights, and better knowledge of markets, balanced membership of TF-WAR, and adoption based on consensus, all ensure that the negotiating position adopted is informed, balanced and credible. It enables members, moreover, to feel ownership of the positions adopted and proposals forwarded. '[This] ownership is the bedrock of widespread political support which in turn gave those positions and proposals, and the TF-WAR, longevity and resilience in terms of official government support', a member observes.

A transparent process provides equal access and a neutral venue for stakeholders

Many stakeholder groups are not able to advance their position with policy-makers in a continuing and sustained advocacy, since very few sectors are organized enough to fund it and carry it out. The TF-WAR process provides equal access and opportunity to all stakeholders to be heard on agricultural trade issues in a sustained manner. The process is transparent and is devoid of the politicization that usually favours the more influential sector. The neutrality of venue and this openness minimize the mutual mistrust that often characterizes government and private-sector relations,

---

[13] For example, sugar and food processing, corn and livestock/poultry.

and lends greater credibility to the position that is eventually adopted by the government.

The commitment of all actors ensures credibility of position

Sectors involved in the formulation are committed to the position adopted and, as one member observes, can support the government in explaining and advocating it to the public. Maintaining consistency of and commitment to a position is built in to the process. Any change or adjustment in the TF-WAR adopted position that the government intends to advance in the WTO must be referred back to the stakeholders and subjected to the entire process of approval.

According to Assistant Secretary Serrano, 'Many developing countries have traumatically experienced frequent changes in position and thus the problem of credibility and principled consistency. The TF-WAR process solved that for the Philippines, even effectively insulating the country's negotiating positions from strong pressure from external forces including the major parties in the negotiations. Effectively, the internal pressure generated has always been stronger than those coming from other quarters.' He further explains that

> for a small country like the Philippines to advance its national interests in the negotiations successfully, it must use its meagre negotiating resources to influence other negotiating parties to its orbit. Allies, especially the developing countries, can only be generated at critical mass if there is credibility, statesmanship and consistency – roughly about 75% of small country negotiating resources. The Philippines is a strong member of the Cairns Group, the G20 and the SP and SSM Alliance [G33] and has thus attained a high level of influence in the negotiations representing developing country interests. The Philippines is now also a consistent participant in the select Green Room process, a level of influence never attained in the Uruguay Round nor in the other negotiating areas of the Doha Round.

The TF-WAR supplies stability to the negotiations effort

The Department leadership frequently changes, on average every eighteen months. Introducing the TF-WAR and obtaining a fresh mandate can take time, which affects the continuity of work. Traditional and conservative leaderships have also become a problem in this respect.

As the capital-based negotiator puts it,

On the part of the Department, anticipating the inevitable pressures on the government in any trade negotiation and the frequent changes in leadership at the ministerial and senior official level, the design of the TF-WAR provides stability to the negotiations effort. As the decisions on recommendations to the government are arrived at through consensus in the TF-WAR, mirroring the WTO process, ... repudiation of or changes in domestically negotiated positions can be very costly politically. While this mode of arriving at recommendations is most difficult and can only eventually come after an intense education of members on the language and nuances of the negotiations, and the difficult process of negotiations among themselves, joint ownership by stakeholders and government provides a most robust and sustainable anchor.

Broader dissemination of information domestically and alliance-building internationally are ensured

The multi-sectoral membership, which includes civil society, benefits the process at two levels – dissemination of information to a wider constituency through their local networks and advocacy at the international level through their international networks. This way, it is possible to bring the position of developing countries closer to each other, if not into convergence, when stakeholders in their respective countries are persuaded to advocate similar positions. At the WTO level, the advocacy of developing countries may even be strengthened, through a consistent and coherent position around issues of common interest to stakeholders across developing countries, which creates an 'informal' or silent alliance between these same countries when they articulate and advocate their views in Geneva.

In addition, the civil society groups in the TF-WAR also help in linking up Philippine negotiators with their international counterparts. This greatly helps in generating support among the WTO membership, particularly the developing countries.

Stakeholders improve their understanding of the international trading system

The TF-WAR increases awareness of developments in the international trading system, which helps industries to identify specific gains from trade negotiations. Without such advocacy, the sectors have only vague notions of benefits or, worse, may get a 'bad' deal. Sectors are able to determine how their interests can best be promoted or defended through the negotiations if they have a closer understanding of its process and substance. It also helps to avoid unreasonable demands being made on the government, and gives the private sector a chance to evaluate and, if necessary, alter its recommendation to the government, in order to get the optimum deal

The TF-WAR core group ensures responsiveness and timeliness of feedback

Technical issues become unwieldy if discussed in the bigger group. The core group enables the DA to respond quickly to developments in the negotiations as new issues are immediately brought to its attention for evaluation and study. In addition, since the convenor of the core group is also the chair of the TF-WAR as well as the negotiator, there is a seamlessness in the flow of the work being undertaken, in terms of depth of familiarity with the subject, and an established presence in Geneva and other negotiating circles, which enables core group response and feedback to be obtained as fast as is needed by Geneva.

Technical experience that complements Geneva expertise is accumulated

The Agriculture Office in Geneva has acknowledged the contribution of the core group to the quality of interventions and proposals by the Philippines. With the Geneva Office having a very limited number of people dedicated to handling all related concerns, the core group becomes all the more important as the capital-based working group which can make a more detailed and in-depth analysis of the issues at hand, at the same time providing a more comprehensive perspective based on their deeper understanding of sectoral concerns.

Moreover, prior to the creation of the core group only a few key personnel at the DA and very few from the private sector had a good grasp of the Agreement on Agriculture and the intricacies of the negotiations. Since then, the core group has become a pool of resource persons, competent in their understanding of the Agreement. The members are regularly invited as speakers and lecturers to relevant fora and meetings organized by the government or the private sector. They also complement the negotiating team in Geneva as advisers.

The quality of trade policy-making is improved

The rigid exercise of providing input, obtaining consensus, clearance, and feedback that all negotiating position is subject to at all levels in the process of negotiation ensures the quality of policy formulation from the Philippine side.

Public support for the positions taken in the negotiations, including by international civil society groups, is proof that the positions have gained wide acceptance on their own merits. According to Assistant Secretary Serrano, the Task Force also has a perfect score in terms of positions recommended and adopted by the president. A good number of these positions, expressed as formal proposals submitted to the WTO, have likewise gained widespread support among developing countries. All these attest to the effectiveness of an improved domestic process in handling agriculture negotiations.

Weaknesses

1. It is a very tedious process, since all parties have to be consulted, according to one member. The process is inherently slow and encourages contentiousness.

2. Most members believe that the participation of members can still be improved. In the assessment of the chair, 'In its early, "getting at the learning curve" stages, participation was uneven, given the openness of participation. Likewise, when developments appear to be encouraging or trust in government negotiators has been firmly established, participation tends to suffer. Being voluntary and interest-based in nature on the part of private sector stakeholders, some groups have not been represented or representation is uneven.'

A smaller group addresses these problems but sacrifices representativeness and the participation of some sectors. While manageability will be an important consideration, a complementary process or modality must be developed to attain optimal inclusivity.

3. The limited technical expertise of the core group may not be sufficient to address the more detailed level of technical work necessary to support future work in the negotiations. Not all members have formal training in trade and the WTO Agreements. Moreover, even if created through a Special Order, involvement is voluntary, so that the level of involvement is dependent mainly on individual commitment and availability. As such, there is no assurance of continuity even of this limited expertise. The quality of outputs may also be compromised owing to individual responsibilities in the members' regular jobs.

4. There are limitations in resources to undertake more detailed work, such as the lack of technical personnel in the DA Policy and Planning Office to handle WTO negotiations, the lack of a good information database, and the unreliability of funding sources. This last is important for other activities supporting the basic function of the TF-WAR, such as wider

information dissemination and education through workshops, seminars and perhaps the attendance of members and the core group at formal training sessions on WTO issues and negotiating skills, the hiring of consultants and experts when rigorous analytical work is necessary, and the conducting of studies, as well as travelling to the regions for consultations and to Geneva for the negotiating sessions.

5. There is a lack of an overall feedback mechanism. A member observes that 'feedback at the sectoral and organizational level is ensured. At the grassroots, this is largely dependent on the member organizations' fulfilling their downstream feedback and consultative responsibilities. On this score, much improvement needs to be made.'

Sectors, moreover, will benefit most from this process if within the TF-WAR member organizations themselves, there is a mechanism for internal consultation and feedback on the issues raised in the TF-WAR. Views expressed by their representatives in the TF-WAR will have the added benefit of having gone through a validation process. This demands much of the leadership, but, if observed widely, will enable sectoral interests to be more accurately represented in the formulation of the national position and will certainly improve understanding and perhaps generate more acceptance of the widely misunderstood workings of the WTO.

5 Conclusion

The words of the Task Force chair summarize well the benefits of the TF-WAR mechanism:

> This process is transparent, fully participatory beyond being merely informative or consultative. It also resulted in positions and evaluations that fully reflect the concerns and ambitions of stakeholders with full confirmation by the government. More important, positions have greatly benefited from the widest possible political support. In the Uruguay Round, the Philippines was an insignificant 'follower' and 'take-it-or-leave-it-but-has-no-choice-but-take-it' country. Its negotiators suffered the humiliation of waiting outside the small select group 'green rooms'. It never could claim any intellectual contribution to the negotiations. The concessions it obtained and the commitments it made were condemned and repudiated by the stakeholders although sustained by the country's political leaders. Now, the Task Force has turned all of that around and much more. The country is now in an infinitely better position to influence the negotiations in accordance with its national interests.

The TF-WAR mechanism has its limitations and constraints. It has proved, however, that stakeholder participation in the trade negotiations process has no substitute in terms of accurately and effectively harnessing the insights, concerns and ambitions of civil society in a developing country context. It is cost-efficient, effective and gives flesh to real democratic governance in action.

37

Philippines: adopting the transaction basis for customs valuation

RAMON L. CLARETE*

This study describes the challenges faced by customs officials in the Philippines when they adopted transaction valuation to facilitate imports, and the way in which they overcame these challenges. The Philippines government needed to adopt its international treaty obligations into domestic law, and it did that with two laws. It enacted Republic Act (RA) 8181 in 1997, which enabled transaction valuation reform. However, various obstacles hindered the implementation of this law, and so in 2001 the government adopted RA 9135 to fix the problem in RA 8181 so as to authorize post-entry audit systems.

There had been two major concerns in the Philippines regarding the country's obligations to shift its customs values from notional published values to transaction values. On the part of the customs authorities, they expected customs collection to go down as importers took advantage of their legal rights, undervalued their imports with fake invoices knowing that customs authorities would never know on time that they did so and so paid lower duties and taxes than they ought to. On their part, domestic producers were fearful that implementation of this obligation would erode their trade protection. The Philippines has nevertheless implemented its obligation and has used transaction values in customs assessments since 2000.

Three and a half year later, the then Customs Commissioner, Antonio M. Bernardo, has been pleased to see that customs collections have been going up. However, domestic producers are still concerned and keep adjusting to these changes. This study documents the policy reform process, assesses the impact of the reform and highlights the tasks yet to be done to implement transaction valuation reform effectively and properly.

* Professor of Economics, University of the Philippines.

1 Why reform customs valuation?

In 1996, when the Philippines enacted RA 8181, its customs valuation procedures deserved a major overhaul, at least from the perspective of reducing corruption and facilitating trade. Its pre-reform rules virtually allowed customs authorities to exercise wide discretion and compel importers to make deals with customs authorities to secure the most privately profitable terms for their businesses, in particular because of high tariff protection. Multiple customs valuation rules had been a tradition since RA 1937 in 1958, when customs authorities could legally calculate duties and tax assessments based on wholesale prices in exporting countries, with domestic prices adjusted appropriately to make these comparable to border prices or invoice values. That was because the law failed to specify when a particular rule should be employed. Because it also prescribed high tariff protection in order to protect domestic industries, RA 1937 sowed the seeds of corruption in customs administration in the Philippines.

The reforms following RA 1937 aimed at undoing the abuses of customs officials. Since 1972 there have been efforts made to publish home consumption values, defined to be the wholesale price of the good at about the time of exportation from the principal markets of the exporting country, and to delegate to the Philippine consular office staff the task of gathering data on home consumption values (HCV) and certifying the authenticity of these values. The list of published values failed to halt the problem because the values were not updated with the market, only 20% of the imported merchandise had published values, and only 10% had correct home consumption values.[1] Although importers could obtain consular certification of the authenticity of values to spare them the extra cost of an outdated and incomplete list of published values, this remedy nonetheless continued the regime of virtually multiple valuation rules, increased business transaction costs with the customs agency, and possibly spread the integrity problem rooted in customs administration to consular offices.

The next initiative came in March 1987, when through Executive Order (EO) 186, customs authorities used fair market values, which were defined as the wholesale price of the merchandise being exported to the Philippines in the principal market of the exporting country at the time of exportation

---

[1] Cited in E. Medalla, Loreli C. de Dios and Rafaelita M. Aldaba (1993), 'An Evaluation of the Home Consumption Value System', *Journal of Philippine Development*, 20 (2), the information was from a survey done in 1987 by the Société Générale de Surveillance (SGS).

or, in the absence of that information, that of a similar good being sold in the Philippines. The EO also ordered the use of the actual cost of freight and insurance instead of an across the board 10% surcharge to cover such costs and incorporate other expenses needed to bring the goods to the Philippines to obtain the dutiable value. The Bureau of Customs continued to maintain a list of published values of HCVs, but stopped making consular officials responsible for customs administration functions.

With hardly any resulting improvement, EO 186 had to be complemented by a pre-shipment inspection (PSI) requirement to authenticate the declared values of imported merchandise. In 1987 the government contracted the services of the Swiss-based Société Générale de Surveillance (SGS) to do pre-shipment inspections for imported merchandise with a value of at least US$500 coming from Japan, Hong Kong and Taiwan. The SGS issued a Clean Report of Findings (CRF) to the Bureau of Customs, which indicated the validated dutiable value after conducting an inspection in the exporting country. The coverage of the SGS pre-shipment inspection contract was extended to all countries and all imported merchandise in 1992.

Although PSI was generally regarded as a protection against the abuses of customs officials, the Philippines was not getting value for the 2 to 3 billion pesos a year it spent on this contract, say PSI critics, who remained unconvinced of the company's contribution to customs collection. Thus, in April 2000, when the Philippines had to implement RA 8181, the government decided not to renew the contract with SGS and stopped PSI altogether.

What was seen as the promising reform needed to weed out corruption and reduce business transaction costs with the customs agency, was to implement the WTO's transaction valuation rules. As a founding member of the WTO, the government planned to adopt the rules into its domestic law. The rules require members to use transaction value in customs assessments, which is defined as the price actually paid or payable for the goods when sold for export to the territory of the importing country. Besides the invoice value, transaction value covers as well brokerage fees, cost of containers, packing, cross-border transportation including loading, unloading and handling charges, and the cost of insurance. Expenses which may not be reflected in the invoice but are generically part of the cost of making the goods available to the consumers in the importing country include commissions, royalties and licence fees. These are counted as part of the transaction value of the merchandise. The positive point regarding these rules is their anticipation of the likely situations when computing transaction values. The rules prescribe six methods of computing transaction values and the conditions for using each method.

2 RA 8181: a good attempt given the constraints

When the Philippines government incorporated into domestic law its legal obligations under the WTO's transaction valuation agreement in 1996, the political atmosphere in the country was become increasingly hostile to WTO compliance laws. To give legal weight to these obligations only served to sustain the confrontation between those against globalization and those behind the integration of the economy into the global trading system.[2]

The chairman of the Ways and Means Committee of the Senate in 1996, Senator Juan Ponce Enrile, assumed the primary task of shepherding the bill on transaction valuation through the eleventh Congress. The House of Representatives had approved House Bill (HB) 3946 on transaction valuation reform and passed this on to the Senate for its consideration. The timing of this bill was good. The congressional leadership at that time and then President Fidel Ramos fully backed its authors. After all, compliance with the country's WTO obligations was the order of the day for all developing country members of the WTO.

Senator Enrile had previously served as Commissioner of Customs in the government of former President Ferdinand Marcos. As with all customs commissioners, he focused on increasing customs collection by reducing technical smuggling and corruption. Reportedly, Marcos had personally asked him to take the Commissioner's post when customs collection was seriously declining in the 1970s. He knew how tax evaders and corrupt officials worked and that there was still a good number of them in the country and at the Bureau of Customs. Thus he was convinced that the proposed transaction valuation reform had to have a safeguard to assure successful reform.

The action taken by the Senate was to retain the use of published values to deter undervaluation, even as transaction values were ordered to be

[2] The ratification of the Uruguay Round Final Act came first in late 1994. This was followed by legislation on the agriculture tariffication in 1996, which rekindled the 1994 political skirmishes on becoming a founding member of the WTO. When transaction valuation was considered by Congress, the legislators were considering at least four other such WTO laws, including subsidies and countervailing measures, anti-dumping measures and safeguard measures.

used for customs valuation purposes starting in 2000. The use of published values per se is in compliance with the WTO's transaction valuation rules, if the prices published are transaction values at the time the merchandise is imported. In the Philippines, however, the published values were home consumption values, not updated in line with the market,[3] neither were the data comprehensive enough to cover all possible imported merchandise. Thus it was likely that the use of published values as ordered in RA 8181 would be inconsistent with transaction valuation rules.

The Bureau of Customs officials in 1997 had pointed to the likely legal problem of including in RA 8181 the use of published values and the likely implications for customs administration in having two valuation rules. The chairman of the Ways and Means Committee in the Senate appreciated this concern and asked customs officials to suggest an alternative safeguard. Since the officials were unable to propose any at that time RA 8181 was approved including published values.

Adjusting import assessment procedures

The customs agency adjusted its import assessment system to implement RA 8181. Pre-shipment inspection had to go, customs officials having concluded that retaining the PSI for valuation purposes would only create problems; they decided not to extend their PSI contract with SGS. The Commissioner, however, extended SGS services for three months or until 31 March 2000 to give the bureau the opportunity to master the new systems and procedures under RA 8181. There would be shipments in those three months that would continue to be processed using the PSI system and others that would then be covered by the customs orders implementing RA 8181.[4]

The value range information system (VRIS) was introduced to deter attempts to undervalue imported merchandise. The system consists of

---

[3] As of Feb. 1999, the list of published values reflected 1996 values according to customs officials.

[4] The Bureau officials were not quite ready to abandon pre-shipment inspection, and the week following the approval of HB 8011 they met to adopt a contingency plan to reduce the risk of undervaluation. Customs management planned to outsource the pre-shipment inspection services for three years in order to calculate transaction values to be used to check on the authenticity of the declared values. The competitive bidding for this PSI would take place on 1 April 2000, or after the end of SGS contract. The bidding, they conjectured, might take half a year, during which the bureau would be without any third-party pre-shipment inspection. If it could implement the transaction valuation in that period, the officials would not go ahead with a three-year PSI contract.

a database giving high and low transaction values of the merchandise imported in commercial quantities to the Philippines. If the declared value of a given shipment falls outside the range, the importer would have to show the relevant documents to the Valuation and Classification Review Committee (VCRC) to support his declared value. According to Philippines customs authorities, Article 17 of the WTO Customs Valuation Agreement allows the use of the VRIS for validation purposes. If the documents presented failed to remove reasonable doubt, the importer would need to post a bond to support the conditional release of the shipment.

As SGS's PSI contract ended in March 2001, the Super Green Lane (SGL) facility became operational. The SGL is a facility meant for regular importers, most of whom were concerned about harassment in the post-PSI import processing system. To use this facility, an importer would need to be accredited by the bureau as a low-risk importer. In theory, the SGL goods require only an hour to process, and processing simply involves the matching of payment of duties and taxes with assessment.

SGL merchandise does not go through the bureau's selection system. Examination of goods may be conducted at random and at the premises of the importer. SGL importers are subject to post-release audit, the purpose of which is to verify whether their import activities are in accord with the bureau's and other government agencies' regulations and to help these importers improve compliance.

RA 8181 had two valuation rules: published official and transaction values. If they differed, customs authorities chose the higher of the two.[5]

3 RA 9135: improving the law

The Philippines customs officials realized that using published values as laid down in RA 8181 would only complicate customs administration. However, they needed a proposed alternative to published values before they went back to Congress to ask for an amendment of the law. When the chairman of the Senate Ways and Means Committee asked them for an alternative to published values to assure revenues, the customs officials were not ready with a good answer. They had heard about customs audits from training programmes sponsored by the Asia Pacific Economic Cooperation council (APEC) and executed by individual governments, but did not know how the audits were carried out in the countries that used them.

---

[5] See Customs Administrative Order No. 2-96.

The Bureau of Customs took a political gamble in asking Congress to amend the law by removing the use of published values and giving the bureau the power to undertake customs audits. There were those who advised customs officials to fix the problem of RA 8181 with appropriate regulations and not ask Congress for an amendment. However, the customs officials thought they could win the amendment they sought for, having gone through the implementation issues with respect to RA 8181 and improved their understanding on the concept and operational aspects of post-entry audits.[6]

Post-entry audit: a licence to abuse?

In late August 1999 the House of Representatives Ways and Means Committee, then chaired by Representative Danilo Suarez, held its first public hearing on HB 8011, supported by the Bureau of Customs, seeking to amend RA 8181.[7] In this bill, the customs authorities sought to replace published values with post-entry audits to assure revenues. Before RA 9135 became law in 2001, customs authorities did not release goods to their owners until they had determined that such goods complied with the customs code of the Philippines, the implementing regulations thereof and relevant regulations of other government agencies. The transaction valuation rules of the WTO, however, conferred legal rights on importers with respect to valuation. The declared transaction value, supported appropriately, is the dutiable value, unless the customs authorities have evidence to the contrary. This then implied a paradigm shift in customs supervision from front-end to back-end control, which facilitates trade. Post-entry customs audit is the primary tool of the latter approach.

The Chamber of Customs Brokers, headed by Leonides David, supported HB 8011 but opposed a provision related to post-entry audit obliging his members to keep import records for five years and assigning penalties for failure to do so. David pointed out to the committee that

---

[6] In 1998, the US Agency for International Development in the Philippines provided the bureau technical assistance to make them more familiar with the selection of importers to be audited, operational aspects of post-entry audits and other implementation issues related to transaction valuation. Experts on post-entry audit trained customs officials on how to set up an audit unit, on the selection of importers to be audited and the preparation of the audit plan, the conduct of actual audits, and on the management of the entire post-entry audit function. A few officials went on a study tour sponsored by USAID/Philippines to the United States to see how the US Customs Service conducts post-entry audits.

[7] Based on author's transcription of the House of Representatives (HOR) Ways and Means Committee first public hearing on HB 8011 on 29 Aug. 1999.

although brokers were in possession of authenticated copies of original import documents, they could not ascertain whether the document they processed contained truthful declarations by their importer-clients.

David's concern was typical of the private sector's general discomfort with the Bureau of Customs' proposed audit powers. With a negative perception of tax audits as carried out by internal revenue auditors and of the integrity of customs officials, importers saw in customs audits opportunities for abuse, harassment and corruption at their expense.

Members of the committee expressed reservations about a possible abuse of the power to audit. Representative Bueser, a committee member, sought to limit the proposed audit powers of the bureau. Representative Jesli Lapuz, a co-author of HB 8011, leaned towards limiting these powers to 'questionable imports', which the then Deputy Customs Commissioner Villanueva said could amount to as much as 10% of total imports, and towards reducing the legally prescribed period during which import transactions could be audited. Lapuz declared that the bill should be worded to allay fears that the shift to transaction values meant that importers and brokers would have to be alert for five years waiting for a possible audit by the bureau. Representative Suarez preferred the use of compulsory acquisition to deter undervaluation but remained open to the idea of audits.[8] The brokers' association disagreed with compulsory acquisition, saying that this would dampen trading.

These concerns significantly shaped the plans as to how the bureau intended to implement custom audits. Those to be audited, said Villanueva, would be selected following the risk selection criteria that the Department of Finance would have to approve and the bureau would implement using information technology and in a manner that was transparent. The selection of those to be audited and the preparation of the audit agenda covering the audit issues that needed to be raised during a field audit would be undertaken by a different unit from that of field auditors. The bureau requested an additional appropriation to upgrade its computer system. The prescriptive audit period was reduced from five to three years, but the brokers failed to get an exemption. Villanueva declared that the bureau was ready to let pre-shipment inspection go and instead use post-entry audit. In the fourth and final public hearing of the

---

[8] A resource person on one of the APEC-sponsored training courses on transaction valuation agreement of the WTO brought the idea to the Philippines. According to a provision in New Zealand's customs law which has never been used, compulsory acquisition gives a legal right to a customs agency to purchase the merchandise.

committee,[9] the bill's co-author, Representative Herminio G. Teves, assured the committee that the post-entry audit was a compliance assistance and revenue assurance measure.

'Going beyond our commitment'

Amending RA 8181 was 'going beyond our commitment', said Bernardo Mitra, representing the Petro-chemical Manufacturers Association of the Philippines (PMAP) during the second public hearing by the Senate Ways and Means Committee.[10] The leaders of a few domestic producer groups, such as Joseph Francia of the Federation of Philippine Industries (FPI), went as far as to ask for a postponement of the implementation of even RA 8181, because the government, he asserted, was not ready. The FPI was concerned about giving a legal right to importers with respect to value declaration when the government was not prepared to prevent undervaluation and did not have an equivalent substitute to pre-shipment inspection. FPI members were concerned about the erosion of trade protection which transaction valuation rules, he believed, would induce.[11]

During the Senate public hearing representatives of domestic producer groups made their case that RA 8181 was better because it incorporated the government's standard on valuation with published values. If customs authorities wanted post-entry audit powers, then the bill ought to have this as its sole purpose and not amend RA 8181. They took issue with the six methods of determining customs values, which, they said, widened the discretionary powers of customs officials.

The need to improve RA 8181

The prevailing message at the Senate hearing was that while RA 8181 enabled transaction valuation, it had to be improved in order to reduce discretion, make valuation more transparent and provide the customs authorities with a post-entry audit system to improve compliance and assure revenues. Rey Nicolas, a customs collector, explained that the six

---

[9] Based on the author's transcription of the HOR Ways and Means Committee fourth public hearing on HB 8011 on 28 Sept. 1999.

[10] Based on author's transcription of the HOR Ways and Means Committee third public hearing on House approved HB 5623 amending RA 8181 on 15 Aug. 2000.

[11] Based on author's transcription of the HOR Ways and Means Committee third public hearing on HB 8011 on 7 Sept. 1999.

methods were alternate, exclusionary and hierarchical methods, and that the proposed bill in fact limited discretion by making the law more systematic and clear on when and on what to use each method. Senator Enrile, answering a representative of the PMAP, said that the Senate wanted to improve RA 8181. If declared transaction values were truthful, no problem would arise. However, if mistakes occurred, the post-entry audit process would sort these out and help importers improve their compliance in subsequent import transactions.

President Arroyo signed RA 9135 into law on 28 April 2001. Besides enabling transaction valuation in the Philippines, this Act is more transparent and more compliant with the WTO customs valuation agreement, removes unnecessary discretion and assures revenues more positively than does RA 8181.

4 Transaction valuation reform: an assessment[12]

The effect on customs collection

With these reforms in place, customs revenues appeared to increase and not fall, as had been expected. *Ex ante* studies on the relationship of transaction values and revenues observed that customs revenues would decline from 3.95% to 6.5%.[13] With customs collection accounting for 20% of the government's income from taxes, the customs authorities had been concerned about undervaluation and what this would do to their collection.

Using the data on collection relating to the three major ports of the country (Port of Manila, Manila International Container Port and Ninoy Aquino International Port) for the period before and after the implementation of the reform (1998–2001), the *ex post facto* effect of transaction valuation on revenues indicates revenue gains of about 3.7 billion pesos or 2.6% of the 2000–01 collection of the three ports. The analysis suggests that the transaction valuation reform brought down the unit values of imports, which then expanded the base of import tariffs and border taxes. The results suggest that the use of home consumption values ostensibly to preserve, if not increase, tax incomes, ironically appeared to moderate

---

[12] See R. Clarete (2004), 'Customs Valuation Reform in the Philippines', paper prepared for the World Bank, mimeo, April.

[13] Medalla, de Dios and Aldaba (1993).

any increase in tax collection at the border, if not reduce it, by impeding the flow of trade.

The effect on customs administration costs

Transaction valuation reform is among the prominent measures that effectively facilitate commerce. Under the auspices of the WTO, the reform is an important step on the road to higher predictability and accountability of procedures world-wide for determining the dutiable value. Because almost all trading countries of the world implement the WTO customs valuation rules, importers and exporters are in a better position to know in advance the amount in duties payable, probably reducing the number of disputes and resulting delays.

It was estimated that before the transaction valuation reform and when the bureau required pre-shipment inspection the total clearance time for imported cargoes ranged from 6.43 to 11.43 days. This period dropped to an average of 5.43 days when the customs valuation reform was implemented, indicating a saving of from one to five days.[14] These improvements enabled the Bureau of Customs to save an average of about 3.7 billion pesos a year, or US$67 per trade declaration. The savings come mainly from terminating pre-shipment inspection: under this reform the work can be done without paying for the valuation-related services of a pre-shipment inspection firm.

5 Concluding remarks: lessons learned

The Philippines customs authorities and private businessmen had serious concerns about this reform. The customs agency feared that its revenue collection would be reduced, since it expected the majority of importers to take advantage of its poor capacity for enforcing compliance. Importers would undervalue their merchandise and pay lower duties and taxes. If government officials were worried that undervaluation would reduce collection, Filipino domestic producers were concerned about the erosion of trade protection. Those in the private sector who stood to benefit from the reform were in no position as yet to fathom out the positive

---

[14] The numbers reported here have been obtained from UPECON Foundation (2003), 'A Study on the Measurement of the Time Required for the Release of Goods in the Republic of the Philippines', report submitted to the Bureau of Customs and Japan International Co-operation Agency.

consequences. Thus the prospects of poor collection and import competition dominated the policy discussions at the time the government was adopting this reform.

Three and a half years later revenues have gone up, but domestic producers are concerned. Officials tend to underestimate the business response to price changes and accordingly create implementation problems for themselves. There appears to be a correlation rather than a trade-off between trade facilitation and revenue collection. In pursuit of trade facilitation, customs administration has become cost-effective.

Domestic producers are concerned, particularly those facing potential adjustment costs because of increased imports. However, there are those whose businesses are doing well because of sensible adjustments made by their owners in the face of increased imports due to the reform. Unfortunately, those producers with serious asset specificity problems continue to hope that these reforms can be undone and import competition reduced.

This case study gives the reader an insight into the policy process. Economists tend to focus their analytical energies on defining the equilibrium which promises to bring real income improvements to an economy. It is, however, also important to understand the process of how to get from where we are to the recommended improved state of things. In the Philippines case, transaction valuation reform was carried out twice, the second reform amending the first. It may be useful to draw a few conclusions from this experience.

The policy process is a political transaction involving two groups of stakeholders, each of which takes up and advocates its position in a given spectrum of views about the reform. Other stakeholders at the start of the process are uncommitted; each group of advocates works to form a dominant coalition with the latter in support of its position. At an appointed time, policy-makers and in this case the Philippines Congress decide on a politically acceptable course of action, that is, that which is supported by the dominant coalition.

The process itself involves the raising of relevant issues by a group of advocates to which the other group would have to respond well in order to win over the larger group of uncommitted stakeholders. In the case of RA 8181, those who preferred the status quo formed the dominant coalition. But, interestingly, they did not get all they wanted, which was to block the reform itself and continue with published home consumption values and pre-shipment inspection. They had to compromise and accept some aspects of the law that enabled transaction valuation. The reformers did not succeed because they did not provide good answers in respect of the risk of undervaluation. The resulting law enabled transaction valuation, so decided because policy-makers reached a decision. The synthesis of the policy process was RA 8181.

The exchange of the raising of issues and the responses to them tended to improve the quality of the law. Ideas on how to implement post-entry audits properly were the outcome of brokers and importers asking for safeguards. The number of years during which an importer was legally auditable was reduced from five to three. The law required that the selection of importers to be audited ought to be transparent and replicable and not arbitrary. How to organize the audit group in a way in which discretion was reduced, transparency improved and accountability defined – all these suggestions surfaced because of the policy debates in Congress and clearly improved the initial ideas of the customs authorities about post-entry audits.

The process is a continuous one, and every policy reform has its proper time. The Philippines experience demonstrates that RA 8181 was a poor political transaction measure and as such becomes a stimulus to a continuation of the reform process. True enough, the reformers came back in 1999, this time presenting post-entry audit as a better substitute to published values. They succeeded and RA 9135 amended and improved the 1996 transaction valuation law.

Locking the reform in

The reform does not end with a piece of legislation. There are its implementation and enforcement, which brings this study to a parting remark. It is important for the present Customs Commissioner George Jereos to ensure that there is an impartial assessment of the implementation of customs audits and of the way in which the young post-entry audit group (PEAG) at the Bureau of Customs has dispensed its duty under RA 9135 and EO 160, which created it. The risk to watch out for is that the audit group goes down the path of arbitrary selection of those to be audited and in the search for importers' violations of the Tariff and Customs Code. The cost of failure of post-entry audits is reduced collections, the lack of or incomplete implementation of regulations, and corruption.

There are other improvements in implementation that the Commissioner may want to consider. One is to improve its product description convention so that it becomes more precise and the list is regularly adjusted in line with the market. This reduces unnecessary friction between customs authorities and importers regarding the use of the value range information system. Finally, the super green lane facility that started out as a means of appeasing anxious regular and honest importers when pre-shipment inspection ended turns out to have been a useful innovation in customs administration. The facility has to be brought up to its full trade facilitation potential and institutionalized, and the appropriate bureau resources appropriately dedicated to the maintenance and upgrading of the facility.

38

The reform of South Africa's anti-dumping regime

NIEL JOUBERT*

This case study examines the development and reform of South Africa's anti-dumping regime as an example of a country's participation in the WTO. The long history of the use of trade remedies by South Africa illustrates the fact that developing countries can successfully participate in the global trading system. By using the WTO's Anti-dumping Agreement (ADA) as a model for its own anti-dumping system, South Africa also serves as an example of how a country can make use of WTO instruments to ensure that its domestic legislation is complying with its international obligations.

The first section takes a brief look at the history of the use of trade remedies in South Africa, international developments on anti-dumping rules and the various legislative changes South Africa has undertaken in the past century that have helped shape its current anti-dumping system. It examines the factors that necessitated the reform of the South African anti-dumping regime, and briefly discusses the impact of the change in regional dynamics on the anti-dumping process in South Africa.

Section 2 gives an overview of the government, business and civil society players involved in the process of reforming the South African anti-dumping system. It also briefly touches on the roles of the various parties responsible for the administration of the system in the pre-apartheid and post-apartheid periods.

Section 3 identifies the challenges faced by these different players in the process of reforming the existing anti-dumping regime. Special attention is given to the impact of regional developments on the progress of South Africa's reform. It evaluates the suitability of the new regime that is currently being put into place and the rationale behind the design of

* Researcher, Trade and Law Centre of Southern Africa (Tralac).

the new system to administer anti-dumping duties. Finally, it takes a look at whether the interests and concerns of various stakeholders were adequately addressed in the new system.

Section 4 concludes the study by reflecting on the process South Africa has been through and identifying the experience that can be transferred to other countries. This section argues that proper consultations between government and the various national stakeholders are important for effective policy-making.

1 The problem in context

The history of the use of trade remedies in South Africa

South Africa is one of the earliest users of trade remedies in the world. The first references to such remedies as anti-dumping actions, subsidies and countervailing actions can be found in section 8 of the Customs Tariff Act of 1914.[1] These remedies were administered by the then Customs Department, which later became the South African Revenue Service (SARS).[2]

The responsibility for dealing with anti-dumping remedies was taken over by the Board on Trade and Industries (BTI) in September 1923. South Africa was a very early and prolific user of anti-dumping measures; in the period between 1921 and 1947 more than 90 anti-dumping and countervailing investigations were undertaken, while another 818 investigations were undertaken between 1948 and October 2001.[3] The exact number of anti-dumping investigations cannot be ascertained, as prior to 1992 no distinction was made between anti-dumping and countervailing investigations. The first anti-dumping investigation considered the imposition of anti-dumping duties on cement.

At the time of the negotiation of the International Trade Organization (ITO) and the General Agreement on Tariffs and Trade (GATT) in the 1940s, anti-dumping as a trade remedy was a well-known and accepted practice, and was included in the GATT of 1947 as Article VI:

---

[1] Act 26 of 1914. The Act also referred to 'subsidies' and 'countervailing action' as 'bounties' and 'bounty anti-dumping duties'.

[2] International Trade Centre (ITC) (2003), 'Business Guide to Trade Remedies in South Africa and the Southern African Customs Union'.

[3] Gustav F. Brink (2002), *Anti-dumping and Countervailing Investigations in South Africa: A Practitioner's Guide to the Practice and Procedures of the Board on Tariffs and Trade.*

> The Contracting Parties recognize that dumping, by which the products of one country are introduced into the commerce of another country at less than the normal value of the products, is to be condemned if it causes or threatens to cause material injury to an established industry in the territory of a contracting party or materially retards the establishment of a domestic industry.

As Article VI only included some basic rules for the determination and imposition of anti-dumping duties, contracting parties to the GATT agreed to its review. This led to agreement on the Anti-dumping Code (to which South Africa was not a signatory) in the Kennedy Round of multilateral trade negotiations that ran from 1963 to 1967, which in turn was replaced by the Agreement on the Implementation of Article VI of the General Agreement on Tariffs and Trade (Anti-dumping Agreement) in the Tokyo Round ending in 1979.

In 1977 the BTI recommended in its annual report that all anti-dumping duties in place in South Africa should be withdrawn as of 1 January 1978. They argued that these measures had been in place for such a long time that their removal would not pose any threat to South African industries, and that any disruptive competition could be addressed through the use of formula duties.[4] In the five years leading up to the recommendation the board had only twice approved the imposition of anti-dumping duties. The decrease in the use of anti-dumping measures during the 1970s and 1980s is explained by the fact that South African producers were protected by very high tariff barriers.[5] Trade sanctions imposed on South Africa because of its apartheid policies also encouraged the government to provide protection to industries it considered to be of 'strategic' importance.[6] Import surcharges, among other things, were used for this purpose and diminished the need for anti-dumping measures.

This situation led to the decision by South Africa's then Minister of Trade and Industry to remove all existing anti-dumping duties as of 1 January 1978, as he considered that the high tariffs in place at the time provided sufficient protection for domestic companies.[7] All incidents of disruptive competition after 1978 were therefore treated as tariff cases. Whenever the prices of certain imports would drop below a specific

---

[4] ITC (2003), p. 2.   [5] Brink (2002), p. 3.
[6] Barral et al. (2004), 'Anti-dumping in Brazil, China, India and South Africa – Rules, Trends and Causes', p. 49. National Board of Trade, Sweden.
[7] Brink (2002), p. 4.

point, a formula duty would apply which effectively would increase to a pre-determined level the price of the imported goods.[8]

The Board on Tariffs and Trade Act replaced the BTI with the Board on Tariffs and Trade (BTT) in September 1986.[9] In 1992 a Directorate of Dumping Investigations was established within the Department of Trade and Industry (DTI) to assist the BTT by conducting anti-dumping and countervailing investigations on its behalf.[10] The BTT published a 'Guide to the Policy and Procedure with regard to Action against Unfair International Trade Practices: Dumping, Subsidies and other forms of Disruptive Competition' in 1992. This was followed by a second guide in 1995 entitled 'Guide to the Policy and Procedure with Regard to Action against Unfair International Trade Practices: Dumping and Subsidized Export'. The latter guide was, however, withdrawn from the South African Customs Union (SACU) in 1996.[11]

South Africa's increasing use of anti-dumping measures

South Africa returned to the global community in the early 1990s after facing decades of trade sanctions. Its transformation to a democracy led to the removal of these sanctions. It started opening its economy to become more competitive and to integrate into the world economy. South Africa actively participated in the Uruguay Round of trade negotiations and was a founding member of the WTO.

South Africa embarked on a process of rapid liberalization by introducing tariff offers aligned with those of developed countries. This left domestic firms facing increased competition from both fair and unfair international trade. South Africa's average most favoured nation (MFN) tariff rates for all goods fell from over 14% in 1996 to 8% in 2001; the MFN rates for industrial goods also fell by 50% and 55% for textiles and clothing respectively over the same period. The weighted average MFN tariff rate came down from a level of 8.6% in 1996 to 5% in 2001.[12]

With tariff protection falling away, trade remedies such as anti-dumping and countervailing measures became increasingly important for domestic producers, to protect them from the rise in imports. This led to a sharp increase in South Africa's application of trade remedies, in

---

[8] Interview with Gustav Brink, director, trade remedies policy, ITAC, 31 Aug. 2004.
[9] Act 107 of 1986.
[10] Board on Tariffs and Trade Amendment Act 1992 (Act 60 1992) and the Customs and Excise Amendment Act 1992 (Act 61 1992).
[11] ITC (2003), p. 2.   [12] Barral et al. (2004), p. 51.

particular anti-dumping measures. South Africa reported initiating 157 anti-dumping investigations and applying 106 anti-dumping measures between 1 January 1995 and 30 June 2002.[13] This makes it the fifth-largest user of anti-dumping actions (after the United States, the European Union (EU), India and Argentina).[14]

South Africa's obligations under the WTO

By joining the WTO South Africa became a party to all WTO agreements, including the Agreement on Implementation of Article VI of GATT 1994 (the Anti-dumping Agreement). Article VI of GATT 1994 provides for the right of contracting parties to apply anti-dumping measures, that is measures against imports of a product at an export price below its 'normal value' (usually the price of the product in the domestic market of the exporting country) if such dumped imports cause injury to a domestic industry in the territory of the importing country. Even though all the WTO agreements were ratified by the South African Parliament, they do not form part of South African public law, as they were never promulgated. The South African Constitution, however, explicitly states that international agreements should be used as reference and guidelines in the interpretation of domestic laws.[15]

Article 1 of the ADA requires that members will only apply anti-dumping measures under the circumstances provided for in Article VI of GATT 1994 and only after investigations which have been initiated and conducted in accordance with the provisions of the Agreement. The ADA provides detailed rules in relation to the method of determining whether a product is dumped; the criteria to be taken into account in a determination that dumped imports cause injury to a domestic industry; the procedures to be followed in initiating and conducting anti-dumping investigations; and the implementation and duration of anti-dumping measures. Where a member country institutes measures that are not in accordance with the WTO rules, these measures are subject to dispute resolution in the WTO.

Article 16 of the ADA establishes the Committee on Anti-dumping Practices (CADP). It requires members to notify the Committee immediately of all preliminary and final actions taken in anti-dumping investigations and to submit semi-annual reports of any anti-dumping actions

---

[13] See Annex I.
[14] WTO (2002). SACU Trade Policy Review, WT/TPR/S/114, p. 34.   [15] ITC (2003), p. 3.

taken in the previous six months.[16] Article 18(4) furthermore requires WTO members to bring their laws, regulations and administrative procedures into conformity with the ADA by the date of entry into force of the Agreement.[17] Under Article 18.5, members are also required to notify the CADP of any changes in their anti-dumping laws and regulations and in the administration of these laws and regulations.

Already in 1994 South Africa's National Economic Forum (NEF) – a tripartite body consisting of representatives from business, government and labour – stressed the need for national legislation on anti-dumping and countervailing measures and the need to establish an anti-dumping authority.[18]

The Board Amendment Act of 1995 made small amendments to South African legislation in an effort to bring the country's anti-dumping regime more in line with the ADA.[19] The definition of dumping was changed to correspond with the definition of dumping in the ADA, and certain new concepts such as 'normal value' were introduced. It still, however, did not provide for any procedural framework or regulations for the conducting of anti-dumping investigations. As mentioned earlier, the BTT did publish a guide on anti-dumping procedures in 1995, but it was withdrawn in 1996.[20]

With the growing use of anti-dumping measures, South Africa started experiencing increased pressure from other WTO members to bring its legislation and the administration of these measures in line with the ADA. In April 1996 South Africa announced in the WTO Committee on Anti-dumping Practices that it intended to amend its legislation on anti-dumping to ensure its compliance with the relevant WTO agreements.[21]

The South African Ministry of Trade and Industry subsequently instructed the BTT to investigate the restructuring of the South African anti-dumping regime. Small amendments were made to existing

---

[16] Art. 16(4) of Anti-dumping Agreement.

[17] The Anti-dumping Agreement, as with all the other WTO agreements concluded during the Uruguay Round, came into force on 1 Jan. 2005.

[18] The NEF was replaced by Nedlac on 18 Feb. 1995. See further below for a discussion of Nedlac. Interview with Brink.

[19] Brink (2002), p. 5.

[20] 'Guide to the Policy and Procedure with Regard to Action against Unfair International Trade Practices: Dumping and Subsidized Export'.

[21] WTO SACU Trade Policy Review p. 33, WT/TPR/S/114. Under the 1969 SACU Agreement, South Africa's customs tariffs and legislation on trade remedies were directly applicable to all SACU countries.

legislation in 1997 to give the minister the power to make regulations on trade remedies and to provide for the application of provisional safeguard measures.[22]

Professor Colin McCarthy, acting head of the International Trade Administration Commission (ITAC), highlighted the fact that South Africa had always done its best to act in strict conformity with the WTO rules in conducting anti-dumping investigations; the requirements of Article VI of GATT and the ADA, especially the notice requirements, have always been strictly adhered to.[23] Although this might have been the case in practice, South Africa's existing legislation did not fully reflect South Africa's obligations under GATT 1994 and the WTO. The Department of Trade and Industry's invitation for comments on South Africa's draft anti-dumping regulations stressed the fact that proper legislation and regulations were required to inform all stakeholders of the substance and the procedures involved in anti-dumping investigations.[24]

The restructuring of the anti-dumping regime finally became a reality with publication of the International Trade Administration (ITA) Act on 22 January 2003, creating a new body, the International Trade Administration Committee (ITAC), for the administration of trade remedies within South Africa. This was followed by the promulgation of detailed anti-dumping regulations in November 2003 to guide ITAC in conducting its anti-dumping investigations.

Changes in regional dynamics

South Africa concluded in 1999 a free trade agreement – the Trade, Development and Co-operation Agreement (TDCA) – with the EU that provisionally entered into force on 1 January 2000. It also entered into a free trade agreement with eleven members of the Southern African Development Community (SADC) on 1 September 2000 by becoming a member of the SADC Trade Protocol. These free trade agreements provide preferential access to the South African market for all EU and SADC member states, and bring with them increased competition for domestic producers. Both these agreements contain provisions on anti-dumping, countervailing and safeguard measures.

---

[22] ITC (2003), p. 4.
[23] Interview with Professor Colin McCarthy, acting head of ITAC, 31 Aug. 2004.
[24] Comments on anti-dumping law invited, 4 April 2003, Trade Law Centre for Southern Africa, www.tralac.org.

South Africa is a member of SACU together with Botswana, Lesotho, Namibia and Swaziland (BLNS countries). These countries signed a new SACU Agreement in 2002 that entered into force on 15 July 2004. Negotiations for this agreement were officially launched soon after South Africa elected its first democratic government in 1994. The aim was to democratize SACU and to create institutions that would enable the BLNS countries to participate more fully in the decision-making processes in the customs union.

The new SACU Agreement has important implications for the anti-dumping regime within the customs union. It changed the way in which tariff decisions, including anti-dumping tariffs, are made, and it also requires member states to develop legislation on contingency trade remedies such as anti-dumping for the region, and to establish national bodies to administer these remedies within the different countries.

As mentioned above, South Africa enacted the ITA Act in January 2003.[25] Its aim is to provide an institutional basis for the conduct of trade policy and the application of customs tariffs in line with South Africa's obligations under international agreements, that is agreements under the WTO, the Southern African Development Community (SADC) and SACU. We take a more detailed look below at the implications of this change in the administration of international trade affairs in South Africa.

2 The local and external players and their roles

Anti-dumping in South Africa under the 1996 SACU Agreement

Under the 1996 SACU Agreement, South Africa was solely responsible for the setting of customs duties, as well as any anti-dumping, countervailing and safeguard measures for the customs union. As members of the customs union BLNS countries were obliged to apply these measures, although they were not always beneficial to the BLNS countries since the relevant items were mostly not produced by their domestic industries.

As the body in South Africa responsible for the determination of customs duties and the administration of anti-dumping measures,[26] the BTT initiated anti-dumping investigations at the request of a domestic industry within SACU. Importers, exporters and foreign producers would then be provided with an opportunity to submit information for consideration in any such investigation. After conducting the investigation the

---

[25] Act 71 of 2002.   [26] Board on Tariffs and Trade Act, Act 107 of 1986.

BTT would make a recommendation to the South African Minister of Trade and Industry, and that ministry would then request the Ministry of Finance to Impose anti-dumping duties. In 1992 a Directorate for Dumping Investigations was established within the Department of Trade and Industry to assist the BTT by conducting anti-dumping and countervailing investigations on its behalf. As the board never had a set of published regulations to work from, it made use of its enabling legislation – Article VI of GATT and the ADA – to conduct its investigations.

Anti-dumping under the 2002 SACU Agreement

ITAC was established on 1 June 2003 by the ITA Act. ITAC replaced the BTT and will act as South Africa's national body in terms of Article 14 of the 2002 SACU Agreement. It currently acts as the tariff body for the whole of SACU and is responsible for previous BTT functions such as the investigation and evaluation of applications for the amendment of customs duties, duty and tax concessions, and import and export controls, and for administering anti-dumping, safeguard and countervailing measures.

The 2002 SACU Agreement provides for a number of new institutions for the customs union. SACU will now have a Council of Ministers, a Secretariat (based in Windhoek, Namibia), a Tariff Board, a Tribunal, a Customs Union Commission and a number of technical committees. When South Africa wants to impose an anti-dumping measure, ITAC is responsible for conducting the investigation, and under the new SACU Agreement, ITAC is now obliged to make any recommendations directly to the SACU Tariff Board.

The Tariff Board will be a supra-national SACU institution, consisting of experts drawn from member states. It will make its own recommendation to the council based on that of the national body. The final decision will then lie with the Council of Ministers, comprising at least one minister from each member state. Council decisions are then referred back to the member states for implementation. As the new SACU Agreement is still far from being fully implemented, member states have agreed upon an interim solution. The current situation is discussed in more detail in section 3 below.

The domestic adoption of the International Trade Administration (ITA) Act and the SACU Agreement

The ITA Act had to be adopted by Parliament for it to become law in South Africa. A series of briefings and public hearings were held jointly by the Parliamentary Portfolio Committee on Trade and Industry and the Economic Affairs Select Committee to explain the rationale behind the Act to stakeholders and to address their concerns. Submissions were received from the South African Chamber of Business (SACOB) on behalf of the private sector and from the Congress of South African Trade Unions (COSATU) on behalf of organized labour. After extensive consultations and debates both inside and outside Parliament, the bill was passed in November 2003.

The 2002 SACU Agreement had to be ratified by Parliament before it could enter into force in South Africa, as required by section 231 of the South African Constitution.[27] The Parliamentary Portfolio Committee on Trade and Industry again held a number of briefings and public hearings to give all stakeholders the opportunity to comment on the proposed ratification. Written submissions were received from SACOB, the Trade Law Centre for Southern Africa (Tralac), academics, the National Economic Development and Labour Council (Nedlac), COSATU and from Agri-SA on behalf of agricultural producers.

Nedlac submitted its report after holding discussions in its Trade and Industry Chamber on both the new SACU Agreement and the ITA Act. Nedlac is South Africa's primary institution for social dialogue and organizes exchanges between the business community, government, trade unions and civil society on issues of social and economic policy.[28] Nedlac has to consider all proposed labour legislation before it is introduced into Parliament, as well as any legislation that may have a significant impact on social and economic policy.[29] It is also the primary forum for discussion on all trade agreements. Nedlac provides a platform on a national level for these different stakeholders to reach consensus on these issues. The aim is to make economic decision-making more inclusive and to promote the goals of economic growth and social equity. Other chambers in which Nedlac's work is conducted are the Labour Market Chamber, the Development Chamber and the Public Finance and Monetary Policy Chamber.

Nedlac's predecessor, the NEF, has also played a very important role in the formulation of South Africa's policies. It provided valuable inputs in the determination of South Africa's tariff offers to other WTO members when South Africa joined the WTO in 1995. Since then the effectiveness of Nedlac in the formulation of policies has been in steady decline. Nedlac needs to be refocused and reorganized and also to be better resourced.

---

[27] Act 108 of 1996.   [28] Nedlac's website: www.nedlac.org.za.
[29] Ss. 4(1)(c) and (d) Nedlac Constitution.

3 Challenges faced and the outcome

Defending South Africa's anti-dumping legislation in the WTO

The promulgation of the ITA Act and the anti-dumping regulations for ITAC was an attempt to bring South Africa's anti-dumping legislation in line with the requirements of the WTO.[30] ITAC published the draft anti-dumping regulations for public comment in March 2003. It used the ADA as a model and it looked at the anti-dumping regimes of the EU, the United States, New Zealand and Australia as examples in drafting the regulations.[31] ITAC's investigations are therefore based on the ADA, while the regulations serve as a procedural guide. Inputs on the draft regulations were received from several lawyers from Canada, the United States and New Zealand, as well as local lawyers and academics. According to Professor McCarthy the draft regulations were discussed and commented on in detail within ITAC as well.[32] The regulations in their final form were approved by the Minister of Trade and Industry on 12 November 2003.

As required by Article 18(5) of the ADA the anti-dumping regulations, together with the new International Trade Administration Act were notified to the WTO's Committee on Anti-dumping Practices (CADP) on 20 January 2004.[33] These notifications included the full texts of the relevant laws and regulations, and are, like other official WTO documents, made available by the WTO to members in all three WTO languages for purposes of the review.[34]

The new legislation and regulations were subject to review in the CADP. This review takes the form of written questions from other members; questions can also be put to the notifying country during the meeting of the CADP. ITAC had to provide satisfactory written answers to all these questions and ITAC officials had to appear before the CADP to address additional questions put forward by members.[35] Written questions were submitted by the EU, the United States and Venezuela, with additional questions tabled in the CADP by Turkey. South Africa successfully defended its new legislation and regulations in the CADP by

---

[30] Comments invited on law on 4 April 2003, Trade Law Centre for Southern Africa, www.tralac.org .

[31] Interview with McCarthy.   [32] Interview with McCarthy.

[33] WTO G/ADP/N/1/ZAF/2, 20 Jan. 2004. The official WTO languages are English, French and Spanish.

[34] Interview with Brink.

[35] For the detailed questions and answers, see WTO documents G/ADP/Q1/ZAF/2, G/ADP/Q1/ZAF/4, G/ADP/Q1/ZAF/3, G/ADP/Q1/ZAF/5 and G/ADP/Q1/ZAF/1.

providing members with satisfactory answers and explanations addressing all their noted concerns.

Implementing the new anti-dumping system in SACU

The new SACU institutions have not all been established. The Secretariat is
currently in the process of being set up in Windhoek, Namibia. The Council of Ministers exists ipso facto, but the Tariff Board, the Tribunal and the
Customs Union Commission still need to be established. South Africa is
also the only member state of SACU that has established a national body
to date. According to Professor McCarthy it is important for the BLNS
countries to establish these bodies, as only they can make recommendations through to the SACU Tariff Board. The Tariff Board will not be able
to function unless such national bodies are in place. In the light of these
difficulties, the SACU Council of Ministers requested ITAC on 1 July 2004
to continue with the administration of anti-dumping investigations for
an interim period of twelve months. The only proviso was that all anti-
dumping investigations should be undertaken in consultation with the
BLNS countries.[36]

One of the main objectives of the new SACU Agreement is to democratize the decision-making process within the customs union. The final
decision on matters such as anti-dumping duties lies with SACU's supreme
decision-making mechanism, the Council of Ministers. This means
that decisions by all SACU institutions 'shall be made by consensus'.[37]
This amounts to a right of veto for member states; as there are only five
this should facilitate consensus, but they have divergent interests.[38]

This change in the process of imposing anti-dumping duties has been a
cause of serious concern to various stakeholders in South Africa. Business
and labour associations have raised several issues during the public hearings on the ITAC Bill regarding the new SACU institutions, particularly as
these would affect the functioning of ITAC.[39] The South African Chamber of Business (SACOB) pointed out in its submission to Parliament
that it remains concerned about potential delays in decision-making in
other SACU member states with regard to anti-dumping and other trade
remedies, due to the cumbersome and time-consuming decision-making

---

[36] Interview with McCarthy.   [37] Art. 17, SACU Agreement 2002.
[38] Gerhard Erasmus (2004), 'New SACU Institutions: Prospects for Regional Integration',
available at www.tralac.org, p. 5.
[39] Briefing on the Southern African Customs Union Agreement, Trade And Industry Portfolio
Committee, 16 April 2003.

structure. The competitiveness of South African industry and that of the region is highly dependent on the speed of decision-making, especially in these times of increased trade liberalization and globalization.[40]

This issue was also taken into account in the drafting of the anti-dumping regulations for ITAC, as the ADA prescribes strict time periods for the conducting of anti-dumping investigations. The regulations therefore include stricter timelines for the allowed duration of investigations.

ITAC aims to complete its investigations within twelve months, although the anti-dumping regulations allow investigations to take up to eighteen months.[41] In practice these deadlines are often missed. Colin McCarthy has pointed out that there are valid reasons for this: the Commission plays an active role in these investigations; it often has to refer submissions back to the parties involved when it is not entirely happy with the contents, and this creates delays. Interested parties also take maximum advantage of the opportunity to ask for a postponement.[42] SACU's new decision-making process is not yet in place; no one has, therefore, had the opportunity to evaluate its effectiveness. We shall have to wait and see whether or not the concerns about the process are justified.

4 Lessons for others

Countries should always keep in mind that it is the private sector that trades, not governments. A common problem faced by all countries is a lack of proper consultation between government and stakeholders to ensure that their concerns are addressed when government determines trade policies. It is important that a government establish opportunities for public–private dialogue in order to involve all spheres of society in its decision-making processes, as policy-making cannot take place in a vacuum.

South Africa has a number of existing national frameworks in place, such as Nedlac and the parliamentary hearings described above, to ensure the effective participation of different stakeholders in the legislative process. The question is, however, whether this amounts to effective consultations and to what extent government takes note of stakeholders'

[40] Comments by SACOB on the Proposed Ratification of the Final SACU Agreement by South Africa, November 2003, para. 2.2.
[41] Reg. 20, ITAC anti-dumping regulations.   [42] Interview with McCarthy.

concerns. In SACOB's submission to the Parliamentary Portfolio Committee on the new SACU Agreement, it expressed concern that the parliamentary hearings only served to rubber stamp something which had already been decided upon. It based this concern on the fact that very few of business's concerns on the draft SACU Agreement had been taken into account in the final Agreement signed by the government.

While these are legitimate concerns, it must be remembered that the SACU Agreement is a product of lengthy negotiations with other member states and that this limits the government on what it can seek to have included in the Agreement. A need exists for better consultations between government and stakeholders. According to Marion Hummel, SACOB's international trade and investment executive, SACOB is often not given sufficient time by government to consider and comment on important issues affecting business.[43] SACOB, along with other organizations, has capacity constraints and cannot give quality inputs without adequate time for research and discussions.

The whole policy-making process needs to take more of a bottom-up approach. There should be a free flow of information between government and stakeholders, as they cannot anticipate all upcoming issues. The government should also move away from its individual approach to business issues. Business cannot be neatly divided into sectors, as this often leads to cross-cutting issues being disregarded.

Discussions with stakeholders should not only focus on micro issues, but also strive to include issues that will affect the whole economy. Currently there is a lack of strategic multi-sectoral planning by business and government in South Africa. This should include debate on South Africa's national trade policy. The various business sectors have to become more involved. The recent restructuring of business associations in South Africa has had a negative impact on this process of co-operation, but this should now improve.

The use of the ADA as a model for South Africa's legislation is an example of how a country can make use of WTO instruments to ensure that it complies with its WTO obligations. Countries can adjust these instruments to suit their various needs without having to reinvent the wheel. The history of the use of anti-dumping measures by South Africa and the whole process it has undergone, both domestically and in the WTO, shows that developing countries can successfully participate in the world trading system.

---

[43] Interview with Marion Hummel, international trade and investment executive, SACOB.

Annex I

Anti-dumping measures, January 1995 to June 2002

(a) Number of cases initiated and measures in force

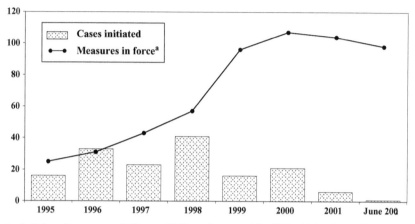

a   Anti-dumping measures in force on 31 December, except for 2002, which refers to 30 June.

(b) Initiations by product
Per cent

(c) Initiations by origin
Per cent

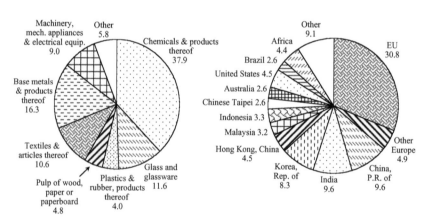

Source: **Notifications to the WTO; and information provided by South Africa.**

Bibliography

Barral et al. (2004), Anti-dumping in Brazil, China, India and South Africa – Rules, Trends and Causes, Sweden: National Board of Trade.

Brink, Gustav (2002), *Anti-dumping and Countervailing Investigations in South Africa: A Practitioner's Guide to the Practice and Procedures of the Board on Tariffs and Trade.*

COSATU (2003), 'Submission on the Southern African Customs Union (SACU) Agreement', 20 Nov.

Erasmus, Gerhard (2004), 'New SACU Institutions: Prospects for Regional Integration', available at www.tralac.org.

Erasmus, Gerhard (2004), 'The New SACU Structures Get Under Way', available at www.tralac.org.

International Trade Centre (2003), 'Business Guide to Trade Remedies in South Africa and the Southern African Customs Union'.

SACU Trade Policy Review, WTO 2002 WT/TPR/S/114.

South African Chamber of Business (SACOB) (2003), 'Comments on the Proposed Ratification of the Final SACU Agreement by South Africa', November.

'Southern African Customs Union Agreement: Briefing. Trade and Industry Portfolio Committee, 16 April 2003', available at http://www.pmg.org.za.

39

The impact of GATS on telecommunications competition in Sri Lanka

MALATHY KNIGHT-JOHN AND CHETHANA ELLEPOLA*

The telecommunications industry's potential for prompting socio-economic growth has spurred massive changes in telecommunications sectors the world over; Sri Lanka has followed this path, and ever since the mid-1990s the industry has inched towards liberalization. As in several other developing countries, Sri Lanka liberalized the domestic segment of its telecommunications market before introducing competition in international telephony. In addition, liberalization and the setting up of a regulatory body preceded the partial privatization of the incumbent operator.

Telecommunications sector reforms have undoubtedly had a positive impact on the industry and on the Sri Lankan economy. Tele-density has increased over the years with the number of fixed lines per 100 people rising from 0.73 in 1991 to 4.9 in 2003, while mobile penetration has increased from 0.01 to 7.3 over this same period. As indicated in Table 39.1, in the years 2002 and 2003 alone, mobile density shot up from 4.9 to 7.3.[1] Investment in the telecommunications sector over the past two decades meanwhile has amounted to over US$1.3 billion (Zita and Kapur 2004). According to the Central Bank of Sri Lanka (2003) the telecommunications sector remains one of the highest growth sectors in the economy, expanding from 19.3% in 2002 to 24.5% in 2003.

In line with its commitment to liberalization, Sri Lanka is a signatory to the WTO Agreement on Basic Telecommunications Services and has fully adopted the Telecommunications Reference Paper[2] that sets out the

---

* Institute of Policy Studies, Colombo, Sri Lanka. The views expressed in this paper are those of the authors and do not necessarily represent those of the Institute of Policy Studies.
[1] Telecommunications Regulatory Commission of Sri Lanka, available at http://www.trc.gov.lk.
[2] Available on the WTO website at http://www.wto.org/english/tratop_e/serv_e/telecom_e/tel23_e.htm. The Schedule of Sri Lanka's Specific Commitments is available at http://tsdb.wto.org/wto/.

Table 39.1.

Category of service	Operator	Subscriber base							
		1996	1997	1998	1999	2000	2001	2002	2003
Tele-density percentage	Fixed	1.4	1.8	2.8	3.5	4	4.4	4.7	4.9
	Cellular	0.4	0.6	0.9	1.3	2.2	3.6	4.9	7.3
	Total	1.8	2.4	3.7	4.8	6.2	8	9.6	12.2
Data communication	Internet and e-mail	2,504	10,195	18,984	25,535	40,497	62,159	75,000[1]	85,500[1]
Public pay phone booths		3,002	3,682	4,761	5,799	8,222	6,801	6,681	6,440
Radio paging		10,721	10,829	10,511	10,300	7,009	6,178	3,541	2,851
Trunk mobile radio		–	–	–	–	–	504	579	137

[1] Provisional.
Source: TRCSL at http://www.trc.gov.lk/stat_subscribe.html.

regulatory principles for the effective implementation of this Agreement as well as the Annex on Telecommunications Services.[3] The Reference Paper deals with issues such as the provision of essential facilities, competition safeguards, interconnection procedures, universal service obligations, publicly available licensing criteria, independent regulators and the allocation and use of scarce resources. Sri Lanka's Telecommunications Act, No. 25 of 1991, and its successive amendments are all in line with the commitments in the Telecommunications Reference Paper.

Despite these moves towards an open market, however, Sri Lanka's liberalization efforts have centred mainly on the core Modes of Supply under the General Agreement on Trade in Services (GATS). Sri Lanka's adherence to the regulatory principles set out in the Reference Paper has tended to be weak in practice, rendering a gap between global and domestic regulatory governance and leading to the perception amongst stakeholders in the policy and regulatory space that these WTO commitments are of little substantive significance.

This study addresses Sri Lanka's management of its telecommunications commitments with respect to interconnection under the Reference Paper. It seeks to determine the current status of the interconnection regime in Sri Lanka and the degree to which Sri Lanka keeps to its GATS commitments; to analyze the roles played by various interest groups in perpetuating, influencing and finding solutions to the interconnection problem; and to gauge the impact this issue has had on industry, consumers and the economy. Section 1 of the study lays down the background and evolution of the telecommunications sector in Sri Lanka, particularly in relation to interconnection. Section 2 sets out the information on interconnection received from key market players by way of interviews,[4] and is followed by a section dealing with the political and economic reasons behind the current status of Sri Lanka's interconnection regime.

---

[3] The Telecommunications Annex elaborates a framework of principles and rules affecting the regulatory environment established by governments vis-à-vis telecommunications network operators and other basic service providers. The Annex provides notes and supplementary provisions to the General Agreement on Trade in Services (GATS) (Asia Pacific Telecommunity 2003).

[4] The eight people interviewed included representatives from the Department of Commerce, the Telecommunications Regulatory Commission, fixed operators including the incumbent, mobile operators, data operators, the Attorney General's Department and consumer organizations.

1 The background to and the evolution of Sri Lanka's telecommunications industry

Reforms in the telecommunications industry in Sri Lanka began in the early 1980s, with the shift away from the post, telegraph and telephone (PTT) model where the state owned and operated posts and telecommunications services (Jayasuriya and Knight-John 2002). Although the de-linking of posts and telecommunications services initiated telecommunications sector reforms, it was the Sri Lanka Telecommunications Act, No. 25 of 1991, that enabled sector reforms to pick up speed. This piece of legislation transformed the then incumbent operator, the Department of Telecommunications, into a government corporation, Sri Lanka Telecom (SLT) and, in an effort to foster growth in the industry, created the Office of the Director-General of Telecommunications (ODGT) as a regulatory authority (Samarajiva and Dokeniya 2004).

In 1996, the Telecommunications Act of 1991 was amended as the Sri Lanka Telecommunications Act, No. 27 of 1996. The amended legislation strengthened the autonomy of the regulatory agency and created the Telecommunications Regulatory Commission of Sri Lanka (TRCSL). That year also saw further steps in the liberalization process of the telecommunications sector, as two wireless local loop (WLL) operators, Suntel and Lanka Bell, were licensed to operate in the area of fixed telephony. By 1997, Sri Lanka Telecommunications changed its name to Sri Lanka Telecommunications Limited (SLTL) and in a step towards partial privatization, sold 35% of its shares to Nippon Telegraph and Telephone (NTT) of Japan, while also handing over full control of management to them. Consequently, after an initial public offering (IPO) in late 2002, NTT received 35.2% of shares, the public 11.8% and employees 3.5%, while the government retained 49.5% of SLTL's equity.

The telecommunications industry in Sri Lanka today has a widely varied structure, as evidenced in Table 39.2. While the incumbent SLTL dominates the fixed wireline sector, there is a distinct duopoly[5] in the fixed wireless sector. Market shares in the fixed wireline sector are divided among these three operators, with SLTL controlling 85% of the market, Suntel accounting for 9% and Lankabell claiming the remaining 6% (Zita and Kapur 2004). The mobile sector, meanwhile, remains competitive

---

[5] According to the provisions of the amended Act of 1996, however, the incumbent SLTL was permitted to provide wireless local loop (WLL) services within the specific frequency band of 800MHz.

Table 39.2. *Licensed telecommunications system operators (as at 20 May 2003)*

Service	Operator
Fixed telephony	Sri Lanka Telecom Ltd.
	Suntel (Pvt.) Ltd.
	Lanka Bell (Pvt.) Ltd.
Mobile telephony	Lanka Cellular Services (Pvt.) Ltd.
	Mobitel (Pvt.) Ltd.
	MTN Networks (Pvt.) Ltd. (Dialog GSM)
	Celltel Lanka Ltd.
	Lanka Communications Services (Pvt.) Ltd.
	Electroteks (Pvt.) Ltd.
Facilities-based data communications services	
	SITA- Societe Internationale De Telecommunications Aeronautiques
	Lanka Internet Services Ltd.
	Ceycom Global Communications Ltd.
	ITMIN Ltd.
Switched and non-switched data communication service providers/internet based data services (internet service providers) (non-facilities based)	
	Eureka Online (Pvt.) Ltd.
	Pan Lanka Networking (Pvt.) Ltd.
	Millennium Communications (Pvt.) Ltd.
	Project Consultants International
	MTT Networks
	DPMC Electronics (Pvt.) Ltd
	Celltel Lanka Ltd.
	Dynaweb Services (Pvt.) Ltd.
	Victra-soft (Pvt.) Ltd.
	East West Information Systems Ltd.
	Lanka Global Online (Pvt.) Ltd.
	Visual Internet (Pvt.) Ltd.

Table 39.2. (*cont.*)

Service	Operator
	Dynanet Ltd.
	MTN Networks (Pvt.) Ltd.
	Internet Service Point Lanka (Pvt.) Ltd. (ISP Lanka)
	I-Net Corporation (Pvt.) Ltd.
	Sierra Information Technologies Ltd.
	Inonosphere Lanka (Pvt.) Ltd.
	Sri Lanka Telecom Services (Pvt.) Ltd.
	Tritel Services (Pvt.) Ltd.
	Mobitel (Pvt.) Ltd.
	Sunray Electronics (Pvt.) Ltd.
	Metropolitan Telecom Services (Pvt.) Ltd.
Public payphone services	
	The Pay Phone Company (Pvt.) Ltd.
	TSG Lanka Ltd.
Paging services	
	Infocom LankaLtd.
	Fentons Ltd.
	Intercity Paging Services (Pvt.) Ltd.
	Equipment Traders (Pvt.) Ltd.
Trunked radio	
	Dynacom Engineering (Pvt.) Ltd.
Leased line services	
	MTT Network (Pvt.) Limited
	Skytel Global Services (Pvt) Limited
	MTN Networks (Pvt) Limited
	Navamaga Enterprises (Pvt) Limited
	Electroteks Limited
	Electroteks Global Networks (Pvt) Limited
	Suntel Limited
	Lanka Bell (Pvt) Limited
	Sierra Information Technologies Limited
	Celltel Lanka (Pvt) limited
	Sass (Pvt) Limited
	Lanka Cellular Services (Pvt) Limited

(*cont.*)

Table 39.2. (*cont.*)

Service	Operator
	SonicNet Technologies (Pvt.) Limited
	Network Communications (Pvt.) Limited
EGO/international operators licences	
	Ionosphere Lanka (Pvt.) Limited
	Scion (Pvt.) Limited
	United Networks International (Pvt.) Limited
	Lanka Internet Services (Pvt.) LTd.
	Access Netcard Systems Private Limited
	DPMC Electronics Private Limited
	MTT Networks Private Limited
	Data Access Private Limited
	GCJ Air Services Private Limited
	Mobitel Private Limited
	Tritel Services Lanka Limited
	Star world Telecom Private Limited
	Dynaweb Services Private Limited
	East West Telecom Private Limited
	Vectone Lanka Private Limited
	VSNL Lanka Ltd,
	Finco Limited
	Golden Key Communication (Pvt.) Ltd
	Electroteks Network Services (Pvt.) Ltd.

Source: TRCSL at http://www.trc.gov.lk.

with four operators, Lanka Cellular Services, Mobitel, Dialog GSM and Celltel, possessing mobile sector market shares of approximately 3%, 15%, 60% and 22% respectively.

Following in the steps of most other developing countries, Sri Lanka made efforts to liberalize its domestic market before introducing competition to its international telecommunications market. Under a licence granted by TRCSL the incumbent SLTL reigned as the sole provider of international telephone services until August 2002. The issuing of thirty-two external gateway operator (EGO) licences however, marked the end of this monopoly era for SLTL and opened up the international segment.

Table 39.3. *Sri Lanka: distribution of population and fixed lines*

Province	Population	Fixed lines
	%	
Western (Colombo)	29	64
Central	13	9
Southern	12	7
North Western	12	6
Sabaragamuwa	10	4
Eastern	8	3
Uva	6	3
North Central	6	2
Northern	6	1

Source: Kapur and Zita (2004).

Nevertheless, in spite of this move, regulatory weakness and the lack of a working interconnection agreement has resulted in little or no progress being made in this segment. Of the licensed EGO operators for example, only ten have working interconnection agreements. Seven of these ten operators are already fully established telecoms operators in the industry, and only three are new entrants.

Despite the telecommunications industry's positive impact on the economy and its progressive steps towards further liberalization, Sri Lanka still faces a multitude of hurdles. Regional imbalances in telecommunications penetrability and accessibility, for example, are very disconcerting. As Table 39.3 indicates, fixed line users are concentrated mainly in the Colombo metropolitan area, with the rural areas in the country having only marginal levels of access to telecommunications facilities. Meanwhile, the extremely low rate of internet penetrability is also worrying; only 4.4 per 1000 people had access to the Internet as at 2003 (Central Bank of Sri Lanka 2003).

The most fundamental and sizable hurdle in the telecommunications industry, though, is the incumbent's control over bottleneck facilities and the dominance this affords to this player. SLTL's dominance over other telecommunications operators has bestowed on the incumbent the opportunity to use interconnection as the tool with which to take discriminatory and anti-competitive action; thus, rules have been flouted and anti-competitive behaviour, such as unfair interconnection regimes, have thrived. Cellular companies, for example, were initially confronted with burdensome termination charges while the WLL operators have had a number of interconnection disputes with the incumbent. Meanwhile, despite Sri Lanka's WTO commitment to provide interconnection on a non-discriminatory and reasonably priced basis, non-facilities-based operators (particularly Internet service providers (ISPs)) have had great difficulty accessing SLTL's backbone. The regulatory weakness that has coexisted with this issue has inhibited the progress of liberalization further by aggravating the intractable nature of the problem.

Although Sri Lanka's WTO commitments dictate that interconnection be provided on non-discriminatory terms, in a timely fashion and at cost-oriented rates that are transparent and sufficiently unbundled,[6] implementing a fair interconnection regime has remained challenging. The failure to implement it has been primarily due to the fact that a lacuna between the Telecommunications Reference Paper and the amended Telecommunications Act of 1991 has existed thus far. Interconnection among connectable operators, for example, was not mandatory under the prevailing legislation. Meanwhile the level of transparency in interconnection agreements among operators was also debatable. While these exclusions clearly highlight the gap between Sri Lanka's WTO commitments and Sri Lanka's prevailing telecommunications legislation, it has also resulted in enhancing the incumbent's market power and therefore worsening the issue of unfair interconnection.

Given that interconnection remains the most critical instrument in facilitating a competitive telecommunications market, the lack of a working interconnection agreement in Sri Lanka has caused a number of interconnection disputes. In November 1996, following the failure of SLTL and the WLL operators to reach an agreement on interconnection, the TRCSL issued a determination that included the terms as indicated in Table 39.4. This determination clearly disadvantaged the WLL operators, however, for not only is inbound traffic in Sri Lanka much greater than outbound traffic but also the TRCSL had provided exclusive gateway rights in the international segment to SLTL. The TRCSL was thus called on again, to make a new determination that included terms that were more advantageous to WLL operators. This determination came into effect in 1998. None of the three fixed line operators, however, was satisfied with this new determination. While the WLL operators complied with this directive, SLTL continued with the pre-1998 arrangement and eventually took the

---

[6] See WTO Telecommunications Reference Paper.

issue to court. Although SLTL eventually agreed to comply with the determination, the WLL operators later alleged that the SLTL was blocking calls originating from WLL networks and succeeded in obtaining restraining orders on SLTL (Jayasuriya and Knight-John 2002).

As Table 39.4 indicates, before a 1999 determination by the TRCSL, mobile operators had a particularly oppressive interconnection regime. The new determination, however, made an effort to recognize the thus far absent peer-status of mobile operators and addressed some of these anti-competitive elements. Despite this, the proposed implementation of a calling-party-pays (CPP) system still remains undecided. Under the current system of mobile-party-pays (MPP), mobile operators pay SLTL for calls terminated on its networks while SLTL does not pay the mobile operator for calls terminated on mobile networks; mobile users therefore have to bear the cost of this termination charge in the form of incoming call charges. In the case of outgoing calls, unless the call is intra-network, mobile operators charge a fixed rate for the call. Mobile operators have called for the implementation of the CPP system on the basis that CPP schemes are the emerging international standard and that MPP schemes result in low call completion rates due to users keeping their phones switched off to avoid incoming call charges. Fixed telephony operators, on the other hand, oppose implementation, arguing that a CPP system will pose a greater burden to fixed-access users (Jayasuriya and Knight-John 2002). Although the TRCSL announced that a CPP regime would be implemented in March 2004, considerable opposition on the part of fixed telecommunications operators regarding the manner in which the regime would be implemented has resulted in its delay.

In 2003 the TRCSL framed and implemented a set of Interconnection Rules under s. 68 of the amended Telecommunications Act, No. 25 of 1991. While these new rules were created to stamp out some of the shortcomings in the Act with regard to interconnection, it was also formulated because the interconnection rules prior to this were inadequate to fulfil Sri Lanka's commitments under the Agreement on Basic Telecommunications Services (Venugopal 2003). As mentioned before, under the preceding rules interconnection among connectable operators and the disclosure of operators' interconnection regime to the TRCSL were not mandatory. The new rules, on the other hand, made both these compulsory while also enabling the regulator to fix charges on a cost-oriented basis in the instance where operators fail to negotiate an interconnection agreement amongst themselves. The new rules also include a provision to resolve interconnection disputes; under this provision all disputes are

Table 39.4.

Year		Fixed to WLL	Fixed to mobile	WLL to mobile	WLL to WLL	Mobile to mobile
1996	Local	Sender-keeps-all (SKA) principle.	Treated as large customers and charged above cost national retail rates for interconnection; no discounts for international calls; limited points of interconnection; mobile party pays scheme.	SKA principle	SKA principle with operators splitting costs on a 50:50 basis	SKA principle
	National	SKA principle.				
	International	WLL operators granted 35% rebate on the collection rate for outgoing calls originating from their networks. No payment for incoming international calls; cost of physical links fully borne by the WLLs.				
1998	Local	SKA principle replaced by the Mutual Compensation Arrangement set out in Table * below.	Same terms as above		SKA principle with operators splitting costs on a 50:50 basis	SKA principle
	National	SKA principle replaced by Mutual Compensation Arrangement set out in Table * below.				
	International	WLLs to remit 80% of SLTL's collection rate to SLTL for all international calls originating from the WLL's network; SLTL to pay 'National Extension Fee' of Rs 9.50 a minute incoming international calls terminated in the WLL networks; WLL to				

1999					SKA principle	SKA principle	SKA principle

		provide physical interconnection links and bear full costs of installing and maintaining the apparatus up to the interface units; SLTL to provide interface units.					SKA principle
1999	Local	Same terms as those in 1998 determination	Interconnection charges same as those between Fixed				
	National	Same terms as those in 1998 determination	Same as those between Fixed and WLL operators, See Table *				
	International	Same terms as those in 1998 determination	Discount of 20% on SLTL's collection rate for international calls; mobile operator to bear full cost of installing and maintaining apparatus up to interface unit; SLTL to provide interface unit.				

*

SLTL tariff band	Local call termination charge	National transit and termination charge
	(Rs per minute)	
Peak	0.6	1.50
Standard	0.4	0.75
Economy	0.2	0.38

referred to the TRCSL, which must make a determination within thirty days of receipt of the complaint.[7]

2 The perceptions of market players of Sri Lanka's interconnection scenario

Interviews conducted with key market players indicate that whether the newly promulgated interconnection rules are being followed by market players remains an issue open to debate. According to the TRCSL, the interconnection rules were implemented on 7 March 2003, and the seven public switched telecommunications network (PSTN) operators signed an agreement to implement these rules. Nonetheless, according to one of the leading mobile operators, these rules, particularly the call termination charges, have been shelved and instead the seven telecommunications operators have formed a memorandum of understanding (MOU) regarding interconnection among themselves. This MOU stems from the fact that when mobile operators tried to implement the termination charges specified in the interconnection rules, the three fixed operators declined to pay out the mobile termination charges unless that cost was passed on to the consumer. Although the regulator did not consent to this, the mobile operators 'empathized' with the fixed operators' concerns and thus agreed to negotiate an agreement where a 'sender-keeps-all (SKA)' arrangement is pursued. Thus, the current interconnection regime between mobile and fixed operators is a 'temporary SKA' arrangement until the 'end-user tariffs can be adjusted to include the interconnection costs recommended in the rules'. Termination charges between mobile operators are, as before, on a sender-keeps-all basis. In the case of termination charges among the fixed operators, meanwhile, one of the key WLL operators maintains that while there is no formal written interconnection agreement among them, the three operators have agreed to continue with the conditions of the 1998 TRCSL determination, despite its having expired. The WLL operator also confirmed the mobile operators' claim that termination charges between the WLL and mobile operators is on a sender-keeps-all basis. This interviewee pointed out, however, that the termination charges between the mobile operators and the dominant operator are an 'asymmetrical revenue sharing arrangement' that is more favourable to the incumbent and clearly indicative of the power the incumbent wields over other operators in the industry.

[7] See Annex I for salient features of the Interconnection Rules of 2003.

The Interconnection Rules of 2003 enhanced the regulatory role played by the TRCSL not just by providing a dispute resolution mechanism but also by affording it the power to decide termination charges on a cost-oriented basis. All market players acknowledge the TRCSL's role in resolving disputes and its right to determine interconnection charges when operators fail to agree. Under the new rules, the TRCSL is able to scrutinize more closely the interconnection agreements between operators. The dominant operator, for example, has to submit a Reference Interconnection Agreement (RIO) before an interconnection regime can be approved and implemented. There is general concurrence among the key market players, however, that the regulator is still a weak entity in need of improvement and much more regulatory clout. The regulator's power, for example, is greatly undermined by the fact that in most cases operators do not abide by the rules. They oppose the regulator not so much by legally appealing against the directives but rather by opting to ignore and not follow the directives issued by the regulator. Although the TRCSL can enforce the implementation of a determination by prosecuting anyone who does not comply, the actual process of doing so is an unlikely option as it is both time-consuming and expensive, due to the state and structure of the legal system in Sri Lanka. The regulator's strength is considerably weakened by this state of affairs. Market players point out that the efficacy of the TRCSL is undermined by the fact that there is a 'dearth or non-existence of individuals in authoritative positions capable of using commitments and regulations to steer the industry forward. The lack of specific knowledge, strategy and commitment has also contributed to this downfall in regulatory governance'.

As mentioned before, the Interconnection Rules of 2003 enable the regulator to solve interconnection disputes. Market players in the industry observe that the only interconnection disputes that currently exist are ones between the PSTN operators and the newly licensed EGO operators. Access seekers, for example, have raised the issue of the value of bank guarantees; the new rules state that an access seeker needs to provide a bank guarantee as a form of security for the payment of interconnection charges. The exact value of these bank guarantees, however, are determined commercially and not by the regulator. According to the dominant operator, however, TRCSL's 'silence' on the value of the bank guarantee has led to a number of disputes and thus a delay in the implementation of EGOs. The TRCSL concurs with the dominant operators' claim, saying that the issue of EGO implementation is pending due to issues with bank guarantees. Since most of the thirty-two EGO licensed operators are small and as the value of commercially determined bank guarantees is high, the whole process of implementation has been sluggish. Nonetheless, according to a key mobile operator, these disputes are minor and are reflective merely of 'teething troubles' in the liberalization process of the newly opened-up international market. WLL operators support this hypothesis, stating that the number of interconnection disputes have progressively reduced, primarily due to the fact that the dominant operator has gained maturity over time.

While there are conflicting opinions about the extent to which Sri Lanka has met its GATS commitments, most market players agree that on paper at least, Sri Lanka's GATS commitments regarding interconnection have been met. The Interconnection Rules of 2003, in particular, attempt to incorporate some of the commitments that Sri Lanka had thus far failed to include in the amended Telecommunications Act, No. 25 of 1991. Market players are quick to point out, however, that these commitments are 'to a greater extent limited only to words'. As the regulator points out, these new rules were imperative because the interconnection rules preceding them did not provide adequate power to the regulator. For example, even after Sri Lanka initially made the commitment to ensure the transparency of its interconnection arrangements, there were instances where operators had interconnection agreements which were 'kept completely outside the control and purview' of the TRCSL. One example of this lack of transparency can be seen in the fact that although the dominant operator admits, in its Initial Public Offer (IPO) document of 2002, to signing an agreement with the WLL operators in order to avoid illegal traffic termination, when the regulator requested that the operator submit this agreement for approval, SLTL failed to do so. Regulators emphasize that this type of non-compliance and cloudy interconnection agreements would not be possible under the new rules, for the level of transparency has increased as operators have to submit all interconnection agreements to the TRCSL for approval. Although rules to ensure transparency are in place, the success and effectiveness of these rules have yet to be determined; SLTL has complied with the new interconnection rules and submitted a Reference Interconnection Offer to the TRCSL, but the decision as to whether the offer conforms to the rules is still pending.

While there is general consensus that in terms of regulation the Interconnection Rules of 2003 meet Sri Lanka's GATS commitments, market players are divided over the extent to which Sri Lanka has met its commitments. SLTL, for example, states that although most of the new rules are still being implemented, access is available on a reasonable and non-discriminatory basis as is stipulated by the amended Telecommunications Act of 1991. The regulatory body is also confident that the rules are in the process of being implemented, but emphasizes that in order to implement these faster and thus adhere to the commitments, telecommunications operators must 'co-operate'. One of the leading WLL operators and a consumers' association in the industry, on the other hand, believe that the authorities have not made serious efforts to meet these commitments, and point out that regulatory weakness is the reason behind this.

Since opinion on the extent to which these commitments have been met is mixed, it is unnecessary to say that market players have differing opinions on the effects these rules have had on the industry, on consumers and on the economy in general. The incumbent SLTL, for example, believes that Sri Lanka's GATS commitments have been met for the 'most part and as a result, the industry has improved as a whole; liberalization has resulted in consumers' access to lower prices, better quality of services and innovative product offerings'. However, this operator emphasizes that there 'currently exists a trend towards consolidation and the need for smaller players to exit the market; as such, regulators should accept these trends and thereby create avenues to make it possible for these market occurrences to happen'. The regulator maintains that since the incumbent 'upgraded its services and increased its capacity, congestion has decreased'. Mobile operators state, meanwhile, that while there has been growth in the industry, 'improved regulatory governance will stimulate further growth'. Leading WLL operators hold, however, 'that foreign investment, which depends on consistent policies, on regulatory issues and on the seriousness with which these policies are implemented, has fallen drastically due to the lack of both these factors in Sri Lanka's telecommunications industry. Network rollout and expansion, both of which require huge investments, have slowed as a result of this fall in investment and consumers are the ones who suffer as a result of this, for it is ultimately they who receive poor quality services.' Further, WLL operators maintain that 'the overall economy suffers as a result of ineffective regulatory governance and the sector in particular has seen a reduction in activity' due to these factors.

Sri Lanka's move towards opening up the international market was a massive step forward in the liberalization process. However, although thirty-two EGO operators have been legally licensed to operate, only a handful of these operators have in reality been given interconnection. Small-time EGO operators failed to realize that being granted a licence to operate does not necessarily entail interconnection. Thus far, of the thirty-two licensed EGO operators, only the seven PSTN operators and three non-PSTN operators have been granted interconnection. According to one leading data operator, the only players who benefited from the opening up of the international telephony market were the PSTN operators. According to this interviewee, they formed a cartel amongst themselves to provide interconnection in the international telephony segment. The three non-PSTN operators, meanwhile, have been given interconnection primarily due to 'political connections' that guarantee both influence and political clout in the industry. This data operator also states that SLTL refused to sell any interconnection facility to them, despite Sri Lanka's GATS commitment to provide interconnection to all licensed operators; a complaint to the regulator regarding this issue went unheeded. The TRCSL, meanwhile, maintains that SLTL has agreed to grant interconnection to three other EGO operators, VSNL, Inosphere and Vectone. Despite this, implementation is still 'pending'.

3 The political economy of Sri Lanka's telecommunications industry

The most evident trait in Sri Lanka's telecommunications industry appears to be the implicit collusion among the three fixed-line and four mobile operators. Whether this agreement is couched under the term 'MOU' or directly hailed as a 'cartel', all market players acknowledge its presence. Some market players cite the lull in interconnection disputes among the seven operators as evidence of this tacit collusion. Others claim, meanwhile, that since the TRCSL is a weak entity most operators try to resolve issues among themselves and thus come to arrangements among themselves. Regardless, there is little doubt that the new interconnection rules attempt to commit more stringently to Sri Lanka's GATS commitment; the rules' provisions to increase the level of transparency are particularly progressive steps towards making the market more open and accessible. The implementation of these rules, however, poses a problem, for it is apparent that not only is there a collusive agreement among the seven PSTN operators but that this collusion is buttressed by regulatory weakness.

There is little doubt that weak regulatory governance accounts for the existence of this arrangement among the operators. Despite the 2003 Interconnection Rules' best attempts at increasing the regulator's strength, regulatory governance is Sri Lanka is still very feeble. Market players observe that despite Sri Lanka's commitment to have an independent regulatory body, the TRCSL remains a highly politicized entity given to being influenced to a great extent by 'politics and politicians'. The structure of the regulatory body itself encourages this politicization, for according to the amended Telecommunications Act, No. 25 of 1991, the Regulatory Commission is appointed by the ministry; the ministry not only nominates three independent commissioners, but also appoints the same individual to serve simultaneously as the secretary to the Ministry and the chairman of the TRCSL. The fact that the ministry has the authority to approve or reject TRCSL licensing decisions also compromises the regulatory body's level of independence.

The incumbent operator's ownership of critical infrastructure and bottleneck facilities also subverts the power of regulatory governance to a great extent. EGO licences, for instance, can be issued by the regulator, but this does not necessarily mean that the incumbent will grant EGO operators interconnection. The fact that of the thirty-two licensed operators, only three non-PSTN operators have interconnection agreements thus far seems to reflect the dominant operator's intransigence with respect to interconnection, and highlights the power that the incumbent wields within the industry and over all market players. While the incumbent points out that the delay in the process is due to issues with bank guarantees, this delay is also indicative of the upper hand that the incumbent has over other operators when it comes to the ownership of bottleneck facilities. The dominant fixed wireline operator's acquisition of the mobile operator Mobitel has also led to considerable concern among other operators in the industry. Market players claim that the ownership of this can result in a number of anti-competitive moves such as cross-subsidization and unfair access to resources. The acquisition of Mobitel[8] has also raised concerns that the main players' dominance in the market will expand even further. SLTL currently owns 85% of the fixed line market and claims 66% of total phone market revenue (Zita and Kapur 2004) and, needless to say, the fixed operator's transgression into the mobile sector will increase its market power even further.

The anti-competitive actions of the incumbent, the incumbent's domination of the market and the politicization of the regulatory body all lead to the question as to whether rent extraction exists in the market. It is significant to note that the government owns the majority of the incumbent

---

[8] Prior to this acquisition, SLTL owned 40% of the firm. Mobitel was launched as a joint venture between Australia Telstra and SLT. In 2002 SLTL bought out Telstra's 60% and converted Mobitel to a fully owned subsidiary of SLTL.

firm's equity, while the composition and mandate of the regulatory body are highly politicized. While there is little evidence to show that the regulatory body and the incumbent are anything but independent entities, there is a very real possibility that those who control the company can also influence the regulatory decisions.

Despite these seemingly anti-competitive elements in the industry, statistics show that the telecommunications industry has seen much growth within the last two years. The subscriber network for both fixed access and mobile cellular phones grew by 29% in 2003, as opposed to 21% in the previous year. The mobile sector in particular showed sharp expansion, as mobile penetration shot up by 50% as it grew from 4.9 to 7.3 per 100 people; improvements in cellular telephone technology, affordable initial costs, aggressive competition and the quick supply and expansion of coverage have accounted for this growth (Central Bank of Sri Lanka 2003). Consumers in rural areas in particular have benefited greatly as a result of mobile sector expansion. Farmers and fishermen, for instance, have been able to evade the wiles of middlemen using mobile phones to bargain directly with buyers to get a fair price for their produce. Mobile phones eliminate the necessity for one to be on the waiting list for a wireline telephone connection and this has been one of the primary reasons for the increased demand for mobile phones. On the supply side, meanwhile, mobile operators have been able to cater to the increasing demand, due to the fact that most of these companies are subsidiaries of foreign companies and thus have deep pockets. Other sectors of the telecommunications industry have also grown, although not at the same impressive rate at which the mobile sector has grown. Internet and e-mail services, for example, increased from 14% in 2002 to 22% in 2003 (Central Bank of Sri Lanka 2003).

Investment in the industry, on the other hand, has seen a declining trend. While the initial peak in investment, particularly in fixed sector investment during the 1996–9 period, was primarily due to the fact that the telecommunications industry had just opened its gates to liberalization and investment was needed to establish networks and meet competition (Samarajiva and Dokeniya 2004), a decline[9] in the years following 1999 (see Figure 39.1) reflects the global telecommunications bust, the uncertainty of the political situation in Sri Lanka and regulatory uncertainty (Zita and Kapur 2004).

---

[9] Investment has declined from US$303 million in 1999 to US$103 million in 2001 to US$87 million in 2002 (Zita and Kapur 2004).

Figure 39.1. *Telecommunications investment in Sri Lanka.*

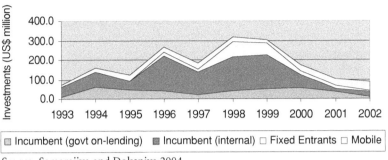

Source: Samarajiva and Dokeniya 2004.

A closer look at investment on the basis of sector, however, reveals mixed results, for investment by the dominant operator has declined over the past three years as investment by the other operators (particularly mobile operators) has increased. In 2002, for the first time, investment by other operators exceeded the level of investment by the dominant operator. While this increase in investment can be ascribed to the fact that a number of revolutionary technological changes are taking place within the sector, it is also indicative of the deep pockets for investing that mobile operators have. The decline in investment by the incumbent operators can be explained for the most part by the fact that the government owns the majority stake in SLTL, and despite privatization remnants of the practice of the government on lending have remained: investment decisions are thus determined to an extent by government decisions (Samarajiva and Dokeniya 2004).

4 Conclusion

Despite the Interconnection Rules of 2003 and the telecommunications industry's attempts to commit more stringently to Sri Lanka's WTO commitments, its existing status has hampered any real effect the rules may have had in liberalising the telecommunications market further. The incumbent's dominant position in the market and implicit collusion among the seven PSTN operators make it harder for any real liberalization efforts to take place. Regulatory weakness has meanwhile increased the incumbent operator's power in the market.

There is little doubt that Sri Lanka's 'liberalized' telecommunications market is still in need of massive reforms. There is ample room for the industry to grow and it is vital that the industry does indeed expand because of the various positive knock-on effects the telecommunications sector has on other segments of the economy. If the industry is to grow, however, it is imperative that all players in the policy and regulatory space commit more seriously towards liberalising the market. The regulator should, for example, resolve its internal issues and function more effectively and efficiently; currently, the TRCSL has a number of vacancies that remain unfilled because of the time that the ministry takes to appoint new people. In some cases, more deserving and capable people may be overlooked for those with political connections. Timbales in implementing policies should also be eliminated if one is to gauge accurately the effects of the new rules and ensure further liberalization in the market. Fixed and mobile operators meanwhile have to abide more strictly by the regulations set by the regulatory body. It is of vital importance that the telecommunications industry undergoes these changes if it is to progress and be sustained as an engine of growth for the rest of the economy.

Annex I
Salient features of the Interconnection Rules of 2003:

1. The Rules apply to every connectable licensed operator who is authorized to connect at any interconnected telecommunications system (Rule 2).

2. Interconnection service is mandatory among connectable operators and is required to be provided on an efficient, non-discriminatory and cost-oriented basis (Rule 4).

3. Every Access seeker must enter into an Interconnection Agreement with the Access Provider on such terms as are set out in the Rules (Rule 5(2)(a)). The terms and conditions on which interconnection are provided, both price and non-price terms, must represent world's best practice (Rule 5(4)(e)).

Where the Access Provider fails to provide information, which is necessary to negotiate an agreement, to the Access Seeker within five working days, the Access Seeker may inform the TRCSL. The TRCSL would then make its determination (Rule 5(7)).

All parties to a negotiation must sign a non-disclosure agreement prior to commencement of the negotiations.

No interconnection Agreement comes into effect until the TRCSL issues a certificate that it conforms to the Rules (Rule 5 (11)). Rule 15 sets out the role of the TRCSL with respect to agreements entered into with the dominant operator.

Activities, including concealment or misinterpretation as to the origin or nature of traffic, are prohibited under Rule 9.

TRCSL would determine interconnection charges where parties fail to reach an agreement (Rule 10).

All disputes are referred to the TRCSL, which must make a determination within 30 days of the receipt of the complaint (Rules 5(16), 7(2) and 8(2)).

Source: Venugopal, 2003.

References

Asia Pacific Telecommunity (October 2003), 'Guide to Telecommunications Trade Principles, WTO Commitments and Doha Development Round Negotiations'.

Asia Pacific Telecommunity (February 2004), 'Survey of Telecommunications Development Strategies, Policies and WTO Commitments of Asia-Pacific Economies'.

Central Bank of Sri Lanka (2003), *Annual Report 2003*, Colombo: Central Bank of Sri Lanka.

Dharmawardena, Sumathi (February 2004), 'Sri Lanka's Experience in Interconnection and Liberalization of International Telecommunications Segment', *SAFIR Newsletter*, 15, 2–7.

Jayasuriya, Sisira and Malathy Knight-John (January 2002), 'Sri Lanka's Telecommunications Industry: From Privatization to Anti-Competition?', Working Paper 14, Manchester: Centre on Regulation and Competition, University of Manchester.

Samarajiva, Rohan and Anupama Dokeniya (February 2004), 'Regulation and Investment: Sri Lanka Case Study', discussion paper, WDR 0303, World Dialogue on Regulation for Network Economies, available at http://regulateonline.org/2003/dp/draftpapers/html.

Sri Lanka Telecommunications Act, No. 25 of 1991, as amended by Sri Lanka Telecommunications (Amendment) Act, No. 27 of 1996, available at http///:www.trc.gov.lk.

Venugopal, Krishnan (October 2003), 'Telecommunications Sector Negotiations at the WTO: Case Study of India, Sri Lanka and Malaysia', paper presented at the ITU/ESCAP/WTO Regional Seminar on Telecommunications and Trade Issues, October 2003, Bangkok, Thailand, available at www.unescap.org/tid/mtg/ituwtoesc_s51b.pdf.

World Trade Organization (1997), 'Schedule of Specific Commitments of Sri Lanka', WTO Reference Paper, available at http://tsdb.wto.org/wto/.

World Trade Organization (1997), 'Telecommunications Reference Paper', available at http://www.wto.org/english/tratop_e/serv_e/telecom_e/tel23_e.htm.

Zita, Ken and Akash Kapur (April 2004), 'Sri Lanka Telecommunications Brief', USTDA South Asia Communications Infrastructure Conference, New Delhi, April 2004, available at http://topics.developmentgateway.org.

40

Thailand: conciliating a dispute on tuna exports to the EC

NILARATNA XUTO*

Tuna is arguably one of the most well-known and abundant of fish, found in large quantities at supermarkets and convenience stores around the world. It is such a popular sight in its canned form that one may have even dissociated it from its origins as a fish, until reminded of the amusing slogan-cum-brand, 'chicken of the sea'. As such, it is safe to say that tuna enjoys as much popularity among consumers as the humble and ubiquitous chicken.

On the production side, easy accessibility and popularity translates into big business, thriving markets and fierce competition. For producers of canned tuna, the fish is their livelihood, an important source of income and an industry of serious economic significance, contributing as it does to the national balance of payments, the employment rate and, subsequently, a productive and healthy social climate.

This is especially true in the case of Thailand, the world's third-largest producer of canned tuna and the largest exporter, accounting for 31% of the global volume of exports. As of 2000, the United States has remained Thailand's biggest export destination, followed by the European Community (EC) and then Canada.[1] Since Thailand's tuna industry is export-oriented, with almost all its production intended for overseas markets, foreign import restrictions and regulations wield considerable impact on its growth and overall dynamism. This is where Thailand encountered difficulties with one of its major trading partners – the EC.

Despite its impressive world ranking, producers of canned tuna in Thailand were convinced that their industry was capable of considerably better performance given more equitable access to the EC market. This

---

* International Institute for Trade and Development, Bangkok.
[1] Rabobank International, 'The Dynamics of the Thai Tuna Industry', Industrial Note IN 044-222, February 2002, pp. 1–3.

inequity existed primarily in the form of a preferential tariff granted by the EC to canned tuna producers from the African, Caribbean and Pacific states (ACP countries), a status consolidated in the Cotonou Agreement (ACP Agreement) of 3 February 2000 between the EC and the ACP countries. While ACP countries were enjoying zero tariffs on tuna imports, other countries such as Thailand were continuing to face an inhibiting tariff of 24%, which was proving detrimental to the legitimate economic interests of Thailand as a major producer of canned tuna. Furthermore, zero import tariffs for ACP countries encouraged investors increasingly to view the ACP countries as a favourable investment destination, in contrast to Thailand, undermining the cost and other comparative advantages that Thailand has to offer.

This case study illustrates the manner in which Thailand raised the issue and challenged the EC tariff within the framework of the Dispute Settlement Understanding (DSU) provided for in the WTO Agreement. There are three major stages to the DSU: consultation between the concerned parties, adjudication by Panels and, if necessary, the Appellate Body, and implementation of the ruling. However, it is not always necessary for every case to follow this trajectory and to be taken to Panels. In fact, the preferred path is for members to settle the dispute between themselves, through consultations.[2]

To this end, the DSU provides good offices, conciliation and mediation which may be requested by members if consultations fail to produce an acceptable solution. These options serve as an intervening step in which an independent third party is engaged to help members resolve the dispute at hand, thereby avoiding Panel proceedings which can be the most costly and time-consuming stage of the DSU procedures.

The events concerning this case study span approximately three and a half years, dating back to the conclusion of the ACP Agreement in 2000, followed by the WTO consultation and mediation process and concluding with the EC's new Council Regulation of 5 June 2003. As the first case in WTO history to be settled through mediation, it sets a valuable example for fellow member countries, demonstrating that disputes may be resolved within the WTO without resorting to formal litigation.

Although this is a recent case, it is worth noting that the EC–ACP relationship dates back almost forty years to 1963. During this time a number of agreements were produced through which the EC granted ACP countries trade benefits on a number of products, including canned tuna.

---

[2] Dispute Settlement Training Module, ch. 6, WTO website, http://www.wto.org.

Thus, for this particular product, ACP countries had been enjoying free access to the EC market for almost thirty years prior to the ACP Agreement of 2000. By the mid-1990s, Thailand's tuna industry was increasingly feeling the negative impact of this preferential trading arrangement, as reflected in revenue, investment and opportunity losses.

With the formal establishment of the WTO in 1995 and the entry into force of the GATT 1994 rules came a more favourable climate in which to address such preferential or discriminatory trading relationships in the international arena. One of the basic principles of the WTO legal framework is the MFN (most-favoured nation) principle, which states that 'all WTO Members are bound to grant to each other treatment as favourable as they give to any other Member in the application and administration of import and export duties and charges. A tariff concession made to one Member must therefore be extended immediately and unconditionally to all other Members.'[3] Thus, with regard to the EC's preferential tariff rates, the legal impetus and the framework within which Thailand could challenge the discriminatory tariff were in place. It would be up to the concerned parties of Thailand to take up the cause, and to gather the information, personnel and determination necessary to see it through to a satisfactory conclusion.

1 The players

The countries concerned here are Thailand and the Philippines on the one hand and the European Community on the other. The Philippines, as a fellow ASEAN and WTO member facing similar difficulties, joined with Thailand in this landmark attempt to prove that preferential tariffs had long been impairing their economic interests, and to seek appropriate redress or compensation from the EC. For the purposes of this case study, however, the focus will remain on Thailand and its actions, although the term 'complainants' will be used to refer collectively to Thailand and the Philippines when necessary.

Throughout this process, close collaboration and co-ordination was a vital element between private-sector players – that is representatives of the complainants' tuna industries – and their respective governments. In Thailand's case, it was the Ministry of Commerce specifically that provided a strong link between the tuna industry and the Thai permanent mission

---

[3] Dickson Yeboah, 'Course Material for Intensive Course on Trade Negotiations Skills', *WTO Principles and World Trade Negotiations*, January 2004.

to the WTO in Geneva, where the mediation took place. At the WTO proceedings, the role of negotiator was assumed by the Thai ambassador to the WTO, who thereby served as the official voice of Thailand.

The Thai tuna industry was represented by Chanintr Chalisarapong, in his capacity as chairman of the Thai Tuna Packers' Group/Thai Food Processors' Association. Chanintr acted as a focal point in consolidating industry data and information, as well co-ordinating efforts and co-operation from the private sector side. Since the matter involved issues of international law and practice, lawyers were also hired. Although this was a WTO case, the complainants were challenging the EC, whose headquarters is located in Brussels. Therefore the Thai side chose to engage a law firm based in Brussels, which is where the first round of consultations was also held. Finally, although this case was treated as strictly confidential, no such dispute can exist entirely in a vacuum; therefore, external forces in the form of political pressures from some EC governments had their impact as well.

From the start, the role of each of the major players was well delineated, with each playing to their natural strengths. The major task for the private sector was to provide industry data, information and support in every form possible to the Ministry of Commerce. The Ministry of Commerce, on the other hand, examined the legal and related aspects associated with the negotiation process, as well as providing an official link to Geneva and the WTO proceedings. The Brussels law firm provided in-depth legal counsel and professional backing in writing official submissions, although it did not participate in the actual mediation.

Constructive co-operation between the public and private sectors was a key element for a number of reasons. First, a strong, mutually supportive partnership created a sense of solidarity in a shared pursuit. Second, the government alone would not have been able to allocate the funding necessary for an endeavour of this nature. Therefore, where financial resources were needed, the private sector pooled its funds. Third, the sharing of industry data and information – from sources such as the Customs Bureau, and FAO and EC statistics – enabled the team to build a much stronger case than would otherwise have been possible, which allowed them to maintain consistency and confidence in their positions and arguments throughout the lengthy process. In sum, a vital component of success was the readiness of the affected industry to contribute to its own defence, in terms of funding and manpower.

Of their working relationship with the Thai government Chanintr remarked, 'We launched into the process of seeking redress, confident in our just cause, equipped with the factual tools and reassured by the full support of the government and its willingness to take the lead in negotiations and in lobbying efforts at all levels.' This willingness on the part of the government was matched by the private sector's own efforts: 'When we saw that there was not enough legal expertise in the ministry, we, the private sector, gathered the funding needed to hire a law firm in Brussels. While representatives of the government engaged actively in the negotiations, we continuously provided factual evidence and helped to formulate appropriate ways to respond to the rebuttals and counter-arguments throughout the consultation and mediation processes. This kind of Cupertino isn't always in place with other industries.'

2 Challenges and the outcome

The initial challenge faced by Thailand was, indeed, how to persuade the EC to enter into discussions on the matter. On 2 March 2000 the EC requested a waiver of its MFN obligations with regard to the ACP Agreement. In the eighteen months following the request until the adoption of this waiver, Thailand had on numerous occasions expressed its concerns relating to the implementation of the ACP Agreement and the negative effects that it would have on their canned tuna exports. They received no response.

At the Doha Ministerial Conference, however, a give-and-take situation presented itself. The EC–ACP Agreement could not be extended without the consensus of all WTO members in approving the adoption of the requested waiver. Realizing that Thailand would not concede, the EC agreed to hold consultations with Thailand and the Philippines (the complainants) to examine their differences. In the end, Thailand agreed to concede on the waiver, on condition that their case be taken up in an appropriate forum, with the aim of resolving the conflict of interest.

Thus on 14 November 2001, the day the waiver was adopted, EU Trade Commissioner Pascal Lamy addressed a letter to Manuel A. Roxas, the Philippines Secretary of Trade and Industry, and Adisai Bodharamik, the Thai Minister of Commerce, to express the EC's willingness to enter into full consultations with the Philippines and Thailand. The letter stated that the aim of the consultations would be to 'examine the extent to which the legitimate interests of the Philippines and Thailand are being unduly impaired as a result of the implementation of the preferential tariff treatment for canned tuna originating in ACP countries'.[4] The complainants were not satisfied with the promise of consultations; they had wanted full arbitration. At Thailand's insistence, therefore, the letter also included the option of taking the matter beyond consultations. Since the EC insisted on avoiding arbitration, the parties compromised and decided that, should consultations fail to deliver an acceptable resolution, 'the Community would be open to recourse to the mediation procedure as provided under Art. 5 of the WTO's DSU'.[5] In this manner, the dispute process was initiated.

Shortly afterwards three rounds of consultations were held, the first in Brussels (6–7 December 2001), the second in Manila (29–30 January 2002) and the third in Bangkok (4–5 April 2002). The Ministry of Commerce did not enlist the direct participation of the private sector until the second and third rounds, when the latter contributed to the discussions and negotiations. Although government officials are usually entrusted to do the talking during consultations, in this case Chanintr and other private-sector representatives were given the opportunity to provide factual support and to tell their story. Throughout these consultations, complainants demonstrated preparedness and commitment in responding to the numerous rebuttals and arguments springing back and forth between the parties. Nevertheless, as anticipated, a satisfactory solution was not to be had at this stage.

On 4 September 2002 the parties jointly submitted a formal letter to the Director-General of the WTO, requesting mediation. Agreed-upon working procedures were attached to the letter, committing both parties to issue a written submission to the WTO Mediator on 21 October 2002. The written submission would provide a comprehensive picture of the dispute, as well as explain in detail the arguments and positions maintained.

A period of intensive collaboration followed, during which the written submission was drafted. Thailand, the Philippines, their respective governments and the Brussels lawyers held in-depth brainstorming sessions and communicated constantly by e-mail. By the end of that same month, their joint submission was virtually completed. At a meeting with the mediator on 5 November 2002, the WTO ambassadors of each party delivered oral statements in which they presented their main arguments and requests. The mediator alternately called on each party, giving both

---

[4] Letter from EU Trade Commissioner Pascal Lamy to the Ministers of Commerce of Thailand and the Philippines, 14 Nov. 2001.
[5] Ibid.

sides ample opportunities to rebut arguments and to direct questions at one another.

Having alleged economic injury, the major challenge for the complainants was to confirm the merits of their claims, and to convince the mediator that the preferential tariff had substantially negative effects on their tuna industries. The complainants consolidated and analyzed data and worked out a sound methodology by which to make an accurate, quantitative estimate of these adverse economic effects. In doing so, they noted that the EC market – already the largest single market in the world for canned tuna – was continuing to grow and that, while the ACP countries' market share experienced substantial growth in keeping with the expansion of the EC market, the volume imported from Thailand decreased by 46% between 1994 and 2000, according to Chanintr.

The complainants were able to show that this decrease was not due to lack of competitiveness on their part, as exports to other markets in North America, Australia and the Middle East either remained stable or experienced positive growth; if they had lacked competitiveness, they would have experienced similar losses in other markets to which they were exporting. Furthermore, imports from 'non-preferred' countries other than the complainants showed similar downward trends. Even with the advent of the Asian financial crisis in 1997, which drove the Thai currency down to such levels that canned tuna imports from Thailand were even less expensive than usual compared with those of its competitors, Thai export performance vis-à-vis the EC did not improve.

The complainants concluded that the 24% import tariff so distorted the conditions of competition between the complainants and their ACP counterparts that the complainants' products were essentially displaced from the EC market. In such circumstances it would be almost impossible for the complainants to reach their full export potential, and the growth of their canned tuna industries was evidently threatened. According to them, the fact that they managed to maintain a notable EC market presence despite the 24% handicap, while ACP countries were enjoying free access, was in itself a direct testament to the competitiveness and productivity of their industries.

Another challenge related to WTO members' rights and obligations and the difficulty in striking a balance between what one might characterize as a 'legal' versus a 'political' spin on the situation. Legally speaking, Thailand had a solid right to pursue dispute resolution. Politically speaking, however, one must recall that in the WTO there are certain forms of 'positive' discrimination which are acceptable; that is, discrimination in favour of the poorest countries. In the light of this, Thailand argued that, while the preferential tariff was perhaps justifiable in the 1970s as a means of support for least developed countries (LDCs), greatly improved investment and economic situations in the ACP countries by the 1990s no longer warranted it. Thailand did not refute the rationale behind 'positive' discrimination, but maintained that favourable treatment should not be extended to any developing member to the detriment of another developing member.

Once all the arguments and rebuttals had been presented, it was time for the mediator to formulate an advisory opinion as to how the matter should be resolved. This required the mediator to make a thorough examination of the logic and reasoning behind claims made by both parties, for which they consulted with economists. On 20 December 2002, the mediator came out with an advisory opinion that the EC open up a new quota of 25,000 tonnes at a tariff rate of 12%, to be allocated to four beneficiaries: Thailand (for 52% or 13,000 tonnes), Philippines (36% or 9,000 tonnes), Indonesia (11% or 2,750 tonnes) and other third countries (1% or 250 tonnes).

The mediator's opinion indicated that the merits of the complainants' case had been acknowledged and accepted. The complainants were satisfied by this outcome, but the work was not yet over. The WTO mediation advisory opinion, after all, is not a legal, binding decision. Therefore the EC had every right to reject the advisory opinion and to maintain what had become the status quo as far as imports from the complainants were concerned. Of course, the EC had to take into account that doing so might prompt the complainants to take the case to Panel, which would have turned the matter into a fully-fledged legal battle.

Nonetheless, the complainants' actions in this next phase following the advisory opinion would prove every bit as decisive as the mediation itself. Chanintr characterized this phase as a period of 'quiet lobbying' – no small task, as the EC consisted of fifteen separate governments, each of which had to be convinced to support the mediator's opinion.

Discreet lobbying required tact and diplomacy. Here again, the close link between the private sector and the government proved indispensable. said Chanintr offered the following comment.

> Through close collaboration our cause was raised everywhere, be it Doha, Brussels or Geneva. Thai ambassadors and officials maintained a constant dialogue, formally or informally, with their EC counterparts everywhere. Of the fifteen EC members at the time, northern Europe supported our cause,

as they had no tuna industry of their own to protect. Spain and Portugal, on the other hand, were extremely opposed to the mediator's opinion. In between were France and Italy. We realized that France's opinion carried so much weight among EC constituents that it could have turned the majority vote within the EC either way. Fortunately, our Prime Minister paid an official visit to France at the time and he raised the issue with President Jacques Chirac. He also held discussions with the French Prime Minister and some of his Cabinet members. France ended up supporting our case – this was the real turning point. We knew then that our case had achieved success in concrete terms.

These concrete terms were set out in the EU Council Regulation No. 975/2003 of 5 June 2003, in which the tariff-rate quota suggested by the mediator was officially adopted. The Regulation specifies that the 'tariff quota shall be opened annually for an initial period of five years. Its volume for the first two years shall be fixed as follows: 25,000 tonnes from 1 July 2003 to 30 June 2004, and 25,750 tonnes from 1 July 2004, to 30 June 2005.'[6] The regulation also allowed for a revision in the second year after the tariff quota is opened, so that the volume of the quota could be adapted to the market needs of the EC, if necessary. The regulation entered into force following its publication in the *Official Journal of the European Union*, and is 'binding in its entirety and directly applicable in all [EU] Member States'.[7]

3 Lessons

This case is a good example of how developing country members were able to use their WTO rights to secure more equitable treatment from a developed country trading partner. Once the positive resolution had been reached, EU Trade Commissioner Pascal Lamy travelled to Bangkok to inform Thailand's Minister of Commerce, Adisai Bhodharamik, an indication of continued good relations between the two trading partners. Indeed, Chanintr emphasized that, although the tariff situation was

---

[6] Council Regulation (EC) No. 975/2003 of 5 June 2003, opening and providing for the administration of a tariff quota for imports of canned tuna covered by CN codes 1604 14 11, 1604 14 18 and 1604 20 70. Published in the *Official Journal of the European Union*, 7 June 2003.

[7] With the addition of ten new member countries to the EU on 1 May 2004, the complainants are set to revisit tariff negotiations with the EU, which provides an opportunity to lower further the 12% rate and to discuss forms of compensation, since new member countries are required to employ the EU tariff, which in some cases is a marked increase from their usual rate.

of great importance to its canned tuna industry and national interests, Thailand made a conscious effort to maintain good relations with the EC throughout the proceedings. He said that 'in resorting to the dispute settlement process, we did not seek to confront, but opted for friendly persuasion and understanding. After all, the EC is one of our major trading partners, and a very important consumer not only of Thai tuna but in other sectors as well. We intended to avoid at all costs doing anything that would jeopardize our long-standing and good relationship with the EU.'

On a broader level, it is well accepted that taking action can itself be a sticking point for developing countries wary of investing the time, energy and financial resources in a consultation and mediation process which may not even produce any binding outcomes, let alone taking the matter to Panel proceedings. This is often the case for other sectors within Thailand as well. Chanintr nonetheless encourages countries to pursue action if it feels that it has a strong case. An adverse outcome to a dispute is not always a complete loss. The country will at least have made itself heard, which can have positive effects on negotiations in other fora. On the other hand, if the country wins, then the economic returns on the invested time, money and energy will surely come back to it many times over. In Chanintr's opinion, Thailand's main objective was to show the international community that an unfair practice was being directed at the complainants and that they were serious about challenging it.

Regarding obstacles, Chanintr sees them as inevitable and should therefore inspire action rather than inertia. Instead of simply dwelling on them, efforts should be made to overcome obstacles because they are and always will be an inherent part of disputes and negotiations. Above all, this means that economic players must collect data and maintain consistent industry information. Without solid factual evidence, any attempts to make a legal impression would be seriously undermined from the start, as every claim and argument put forth could be challenged or rejected by the opposing side. Certainly, the EC initially rejected just about every argument made by the complainants, but Chanintr reassured Thailand's ambassador to the WTO that the private sector would not back down, and that they would continue to support the government. Another major obstacle is the issue of unity within a given industry or sector, which is often lacking, resulting in poor co-ordination and teamwork. Therefore, efforts must be made to achieve the level of commitment and the momentum necessary to support the industry throughout the dispute settlement process.

This case sets a precedent for other member countries, demonstrating that even without full court proceedings, a binding result could ultimately be achieved. Though some observers may comment that a 12% tariff is still too high, for Chanintr and his team, 'Compromise was the best outcome, and we are satisfied with the result. We wanted a win–win situation where trade would be managed as fairly as possible. We didn't want to take advantage of our opponent, or to simply turn the tables on them.'

The overriding lesson to take away from this case is that co-operation between a well-represented tuna industry and the Thai government made it possible for the team to overcome obstacles that so often prove to be insurmountable stumbling blocks for other industries or sectors. The public–private sector collaboration utilized in this case sets a positive example for negotiations in other fora. Chanintr emphasized that

> Government and the private sector working hand in hand can be the best weapon to defend our national interests. The government cannot negotiate effectively without good information and support from the private sector. The two sectors must work together and determine very clearly how much time and resources they have to spend and, if they win, how much the industry will benefit as a whole. Combining strengths made our case more solid, which led to much greater bargaining power. We could not have done it alone.

41

Uganda's participation in WTO negotiations: institutional challenges

NICHODEMUS RUDAHERANWA AND
VERNETTA BARUNGI ATINGI-EGO*

Uganda is heavily reliant on agricultural activities – in large part dominated by smallholder farmers – and is a key player in regional integration, bilateral and international negotiations as developments in the multilateral trading system continue to evolve rapidly. Uganda is a founding member of the WTO, and a party to the African, Caribbean and Pacific countries (ACP)–European Union (EU) Cotonou Agreement, the Common Market for Eastern and Southern Africa (COMESA), the East African Community (EAC) Customs Union and, most recently, the African Growth and Opportunities Act (AGOA) and 'Everything but Arms' (EBA) initiatives. Uganda actively participates in these multilateral and bilateral trade initiatives, which carry with them new opportunities and challenges. The effective use of these trade initiatives depends very much on how Uganda prepares for (and effectively participates in) the negotiation process in order to articulate and defend its interests. This is possible if preparations for (and the conduct of) the trade negotiations are well structured, co-ordinated and include all stakeholders, namely the government, the private sector, civil society and academia.

Trade negotiations vary in scope and content but generally depend on the structure of the economy of a particular country. Uganda, like many other developing countries, is trying to diversify away from traditional exports; the trade negotiations in which it is involved are therefore aimed at securing markets for new products (namely tea, tobacco and cotton), in addition to markets for the traditional exports. Trade negotiations

* Research Officers, Economic Policy Research Centre (EPRC), Kampala. Any matters regarding this paper should be addressed to Nichodemus Rudaheranwa. We are very grateful to all those representing institutions in the IITC and others who took the time to respond to our interview questions. Views expressed in this paper, however, are entirely our responsibility.

are also aimed at obtaining the co-operation of trading partners on the technical and financial assistance required to meet market preferences and to comply with health and technical standards as well as other customs or entry requirements. In the broader context of development support, negotiations can also be targeted at obtaining assistance to developing countries such as Uganda to address production and supply constraints, so as to develop fully and increase their production potential for both domestic and export markets.

An effective trade policy framework requires the formulation of trade policy and strategy, the preparation and execution of negotiating strategies, the implementation of agreements, and the monitoring and evaluation of policies and agreements. This short study attempts to identify Uganda's current capacity to prepare for, and participate in, WTO trade negotiations. It considers the processes taking place on national, regional and international levels and how they affect the formulation and co-ordination of Uganda's participation in trade negotiations. This study is expected to contribute to a better understanding of the country's trade capacity and its ability to co-ordinate and participate in trade development negotiations. Policy actions to improve and strengthen capacity among various stakeholders and the development of a sound trade policy in Uganda are suggested.

1 Consultation processes in Uganda for trade negotiations

Consultations are important for formulating and executing an effective trade policy, negotiating effectively, implementing trade agreements, meeting ongoing trade obligations and defending the country's trade-related rights (OECD 2003: 32). The consultation process helps to ensure that Uganda's negotiating position is realistic and pragmatic. Uganda's share in global trade is small and cannot, therefore, influence the final outcome of trade negotiations; however, the quality of the information obtained in the consultation process could be of significant value in informing the country's negotiating position. The consultation process ensures that a country's position covers all areas and allows for an open and transparent exchange of ideas among stakeholders.

The consultation process often has a number of objectives, including but not limited to (i) seeking the views of stakeholders on how the negotiations could help their various constituencies in achieving their goals; (ii) building consensus among stakeholders on key current and emerging issues affecting the country's negotiating position; and (iii) keeping stakeholders informed of the country's negotiating positions as they are being developed. Interest-based discussions provide stakeholders with an opportunity to discuss their needs, desires, concerns and fears, and provide the potential for greater creativity and consensus on common goals.

Uganda's preparation and participation in WTO trade negotiations take place at WTO meetings abroad (most often in Geneva) or in the capital, Kampala, where the lead ministries on WTO issues are to be found, as well as the various domestic stakeholder institutions in the private sector, academia and among civil society groups. A link has been established between representatives taking part in the negotiations abroad and ministry officials and support institutions in the capital. The latter are expected to provide timely information in support of the negotiating positions adopted, to enable Uganda's representatives in Geneva, or elsewhere abroad, to argue the country's positions. The support groups are briefed on the twists and turns of the negotiations and are expected to provide feedback and input to the negotiators regarding the way forward.

The process of preparing for trade negotiations in Uganda is largely a consultative process co-ordinated by the Inter-institutional Trade Committee (IITC), which includes government institutions, the private sector, academia and civil society organizations.[1] The IITC is a broad-based national body that formulates trade policy and negotiating positions for Uganda; its members are expected to present the views of the constituencies they represent. The Ministry of Tourism, Trade and Industry (MTTI), which chairs the IITC and acts as its secretariat, is the chief government negotiator. It co-ordinates the negotiation process by consulting stakeholders during the formulation of the country's negotiating positions, linking stakeholders with the government (before, during and after the negotiations), and articulating and defending Uganda's interests during the negotiation process. The MTTI is also responsible for the implementation of the WTO Agreements.

The way in which consultations are structured and co-ordinated, however, is as important as the seriousness with which the stakeholders regard the process; participants should represent the views of their constituencies faithfully and ensure that the consultations serve to inform the trade policy process. The key objective of the stakeholder consultations in Uganda is to reach a consensus on national development goals and the means

---

[1] Six government ministries participate in the IITC. Other participants include representatives from the private sector, academic institutions, NGOs and eight trade associations (see Annex I for the current composition of the IITC).

available to achieve them, as well as to refine the negotiations strategy in response to progress and changing circumstances in the negotiations. To get a sense of the actual preparation and development of the negotiation process in Uganda, views on this were sought from stakeholders using structured interviews and focused group discussion. The following section presents the challenges for trade negotiations by Uganda as identified through these interviews.

2 The challenges of participation in WTO trade negotiations

As noted above, the MTTI is mandated to co-ordinate trade matters including the preparation and co-ordination of negotiations, representing Uganda in the negotiation process, and the implementation of agreements. Its mandate was defined in the 1995 Constitution of the Republic of Uganda. Other government ministries, specifically those of Finance, Planning and Economic Development (MFPED), Foreign Affairs (MOFA), Agriculture, Animal Industry and Fisheries (MAAIF), and Justice and Constitutional Affairs are also key players in the negotiation process.

The country's preparation and participation in regional and multilateral trade negotiations faces a number of challenges. The first of these is that the IITC is not yet formally established, which makes it difficult to obtain government funding for its activities. Consequently, most of its activities are donor-funded, while others are covered by the MTTI's budget (Mugyenyi and Nuwamanya 2003; Mangeni 2004).

However, efforts are under way to get the IITC formally established, and it is envisaged that it will be Uganda's representative body in all trade negotiations. The IITC has a core team of specialists whose daily activity brings them in contact with trade issues. This core team is mandated to speak on behalf of the government and attends negotiations, while the larger grouping provides the backup. This arrangement is expected to introduce a degree of homogeneity in the positions of government ministries and departments and among trade organizations. However, inadequate negotiating skills, low technical expertise and limited funding for trips to participate in the trade negotiation are obstacles to the implementation of this strategy.

Trade negotiations at the WTO take place between governments, so that non-government IITC members are not involved in the actual processes. Nevertheless, the views of non-government members as expressed in the IITC are expected to form an integral part of national positions. A number of IITC stakeholders we interviewed felt that their contribution had a substantial influence on Uganda's position in trade negotiations.[2]

Essentially, the process for collecting these inputs into the negotiations is as follows. The MTTI liaises with stakeholders to collect their views, which are then used by technical staff in the ministry to compile cabinet papers; these are then presented to the cabinet by the MTTI. It is on the basis of this process that cabinet comes up with national positions for trade negotiations. After this, the MTTI goes on to present, articulate and defend Uganda's negotiating positions in the various negotiating fora.

For any country to participate effectively in trade negotiations, it needs to have sufficient numbers of technically trained members of staff and negotiators. In the case of Uganda, they are members of the Ugandan missions to the WTO in Geneva and to the EU and ACP in Brussels. Uganda's missions are insufficiently staffed so that capital-based negotiators regularly participate in negotiations in Geneva, especially when a topic of interest to Uganda is on the agenda.[3] Capital-based negotiators are kept abreast of developments at the WTO through the local mission and through direct contacts with the WTO Secretariat. In addition, the Secretariat circulates to WTO members documents concerning the trade regimes of the various Members, documents on notifications, etc., which helps the capital-based negotiators formulate negotiating positions. Bilateral negotiations (within the framework of the WTO) are conducted through a series of requests and offers. These requests and offers are sent to the Ministry of Tourism, Trade and Industry, which then co-ordinates with stakeholders. Field interviews show that technical expertise in formulating these requests and offers is lacking in the relevant ministries, as well as in private-sector and civil society participants in the process.

The MOFA has tended to concentrate on political affairs, while MTTI has focused on trade affairs; the MOFA does not have a library with reference material for ongoing trade negotiations. The reference centre for the WTO, located in the MTTI, contains publications and online

---

[2] According to a number of those we interviewed, the major problem (beyond limited capacity and awareness) has been political influence on making the final decision during the negotiation process.

[3] Even this arrangement is not adequate. The MTTI has only five officers based in Kampala covering the entire WTO as well as other organizations. There are a few other officials who have also been trained in WTO issues, however; although they do not handle WTO issues on a daily basis they are called upon in case of need. MOFA maintains two officers in Geneva to cover the WTO and all other Geneva-based international organizations, but there are no specific trade officers. Trade officers are maintained in MTTI, since it is mandated to handle trade issues. The MTTI and MOFA work closely together.

documentation. It is, however, unsustainable because it was established and run by the Uganda Programme for Trade Opportunities and Policy (UPTOP) and the Joint Integrated Technical Assistance Programme (JITAP) for African LDCs, among others, and does not have a specific budgetary allocation within the ministry's budget. It ceases operations in 2005.

Trade negotiations are a give-and-take exercise and even the best negotiator can hardly achieve 100 per cent of his or her negotiating targets. Numerous positions have to be formulated as one prepares for negotiations, and regular consultations have to be undertaken even during the negotiation process. The IITC is regularly updated on the progress of trade negotiations and invited to provide feedback. Any new ideas which may emerge need to go through the same procedure (i.e. endorsement by cabinet) before they are validated as national negotiating positions. Information obtained from interviews, however, indicates that the mechanism of providing feedback is inadequate, since representatives do not consult members of their institutions before providing feedback to ITTC, because they have insufficient time for consultations, too little background information, often provided too late, and not enough in the way of analysis, synthesis and briefing papers. Hence some important views are left out.

An additional challenge is that, despite the fact that the IITC plays a crucial role in trade negotiations, the knowledge base of most IITC members on the multilateral trading system and trade negotiations is very weak.[4] This means that they cannot adequately help in formulating national negotiating positions. Consequently, technical staff in MTTI are obliged to examine carefully any suggestions put forward by the IITC and put them in context before they go ahead to draft national positions for cabinet approval. It is in the light of this that plans are under way to conduct briefings regularly to inform members of the IITC. Technical assistance in the form of training for IITC members has also been sought from the WTO (e.g. the recently concluded video conferences on negotiations on non-agricultural market access, trade in services and agriculture, and the workshop on trade in services).

Trade negotiations involve a number of disciplines including economics and law. It is in this context that other factors, such as social issues, are taken into account in the negotiations. Uganda has no specialists in international trade law,[5] so that the country's negotiating team is largely

---

[4] One government ministry official was of the view that some suggestions from some sections of IITC sound too radical, with little of the flexibility essential in the negotiation process.
[5] There is only one known specialist in this area (a trade lawyer) in Uganda.

composed of trade economists; this means that the legal implications of
certain agreements may not be duly taken into consideration during the
negotiations. This probably explains why it has taken such a long time
for WTO agreements to be introduced into national laws; for example,
the WTO Implementation Bill has remained a bill since 2000 (see WTO
2001).

Given the country's weak negotiating capacity, Uganda has recently
tended to team up with several other countries to try to make its voice
heard through the decision-making process in the WTO, where it is possible for Uganda to block any measure that it considers to be against
its interests (decision-making at the WTO is by consensus).[6] Uganda's
negotiators are, in most cases, not adequately funded and facilitated
by the government. Often donors, including some involved in negotiations, assist the country's negotiators, and the potential dangers associated with this arrangement are obvious. For example, the donors may
(intentionally or otherwise) book a flight ticket in such a way that at
the time of making important decisions, an opposing negotiator is on
his/her way out of the capital hosting trade talks. A combination of its
limited share in global trade and inadequate support for its trade negotiators undermines Uganda's capacity to pursue national interests in trade
negotiations.

A number of meetings are held on a regular basis under the auspices of
the WTO. While Uganda's permanent representative at the WTO attends
some of these meetings, since several may take place simultaneously it is
impossible for the small Ugandan mission to attend them all. This is a
problem for most African countries, and is worse for those who do not
have a mission in Geneva but must have meetings covered by representatives stationed in Brussels or elsewhere in Europe. To address this problem,
African representatives in Geneva share responsibilities and attend different meetings and then meet and brief each other and formulate the way
forward in consultation with their capitals (note the advantage of negotiating as a bloc). In the case of Uganda, the MTTI is in constant contact
with the Geneva mission, and the Geneva- and capital-based negotiators
regularly meet either in Geneva, Brussels or Kampala or at any other trade
negotiations venue.

---

[6] See Art. IX of the WTO Agreement. A footnote to the article says, 'the body concerned
shall be deemed to have decided by consensus on a matter submitted for its consideration,
if no Member, present at the meeting when the decision is taken, formally objects to the
proposed decision'.

3 The way forward

Trade negotiations are an integral part of international and national development strategies. The capacity to prepare adequately for such negotiations and the level and manner of participation have an important bearing on the outcome of trade negotiations for any economy. It is not the trade negotiation per se that can drive an economy to development, but rather the post-negotiation handling or adjustments that are made to take advantage of the opportunities created by negotiations. For example, all the WTO agreements have longer transition periods for, and give special and differential treatment to, LDCs. However, most LDCs, including Uganda, seem not to have taken full advantage of, or benefited from, these opportunities. This is largely attributable to the failure of these countries to reorient national policies in a direction that can help them tap the opportunities arising from trade negotiations, such as tariff cuts under the Uruguay Round, the use of subsidies in one of the boxes (specifically, the green box) under the Agreement on Agriculture, and so forth.

Uganda's current Poverty Eradication Action Plan (PEAP), for example, does not have trade issues as a priority so as to tap trade opportunities created by the Uruguay Round. Tapping these opportunities had not been a national priority since the first PEAP was developed in 1997. Only in the recently concluded PEAP revision exercise of 2003/2004 were trade issues included in national development plans. The way forward is for Uganda to prepare its development policies in such a way as to enable the country to benefit from the trade opportunities arising from numerous trade negotiations. Mainstreaming trade development strategies in the overall national development policy framework, a process that has just begun, should be strengthened.

The government's handling of trade negotiations is still wanting. This could partly be due to the fact that trade issues have not yet been placed at the centre of national development objectives. It is important that the government views trade negotiations as an important development tool in which it needs to invest. There is a need to provide technical expertise in missions to trade bodies so the members of such missions can handle a number of issues at the same time, while also co-ordinating in time with the ministry (MTTI).

The government needs to fund its own negotiators so that their capacity and the attention paid to negotiations are not compromised. Foreign-funded and facilitated negotiators affect the preparation process: if the funding body delays confirmation of funding, the negotiator has the uncertainty of not knowing whether he or she will be able to attend the negotiations.

The diverse composition of the IITC is good for the consultation process, but the knowledge base of the members is still wanting. It is imperative that they are trained in trade issues, specifically on the multilateral trading system, so that they can adequately push for the interests of their constituents and properly advise government during the consultation phase in preparation for trade negotiations.

The need also exists for increasing awareness of the importance of WTO negotiations among stakeholders, particularly the private sector and civil society. Manufacturing and farmers' associations (e.g. the Uganda Manufacturers' Association) could be targeted in the process of raising awareness. Stakeholders should be well informed as to WTO requirements and their implications, so as to obtain a good understanding of the negotiation process.

Annex I

Table 41.1. *Uganda's current Inter-Institutional Trade Committee membership*

Institution	Number of representatives
Government ministries (6)	
Tourism, Trade and Industry	6
Finance, Planning and Economic Development	2
Foreign Affairs	1
Health	1
Agriculture, Animal Industry and Fisheries	2
Justice and Constitutional Affairs	1
Government departments (10)	
Exports Promotion Board	2
National Bureau of Standards	2
Revenue Authority	2
Law Reform Commission	1
Bank of Uganda	1
Investment Authority	1
National Agricultural Research Organisation	1
National Environmental Management Authority	1
Civil Aviation Authority	1
President's Office	1

Table 41.1. (*cont*)

Institution	Number of representatives
Academic institutions (4)	
Law Development Centre	1
Makerere University Business School	1
Economic Policy Research Centre	1
Makerere University Faculty of Law	1
NGOs (6)	
Actionaid Uganda	1
ACODE	1
DENIVA	1
SEATINI	1
Food Rights Alliance	1
Uganda Consumer Protection Association	1
Trade associations (8)	
Uganda National Farmers Federation	1
Private Sector Foundation Uganda	2
Uganda Manufacturers Association	1
Uganda National Chamber of Commerce and Industry	1
Uganda Fish Processors and Exporters Association	2
Uganda Services Exporters Association	1
Uganda Clearers and Forwarders Association	1
Uganda Law Society	1
Total public-sector institutions: 16	Total 44
Total private-sector institutions: 17	
Overall total: 33	

Source: Adapted from Mangeni (2004).

Bibliography

Kasekende, L. A., C. Abuka and P. K Asea (1998), 'Trade Policy, Manufacturing Efficiency and Exports in Uganda', unpublished report for African Centre for Economic Growth, Nairobi.

Mangeni, F. (2004), 'The Challenges of Multilateral and Regional Trade Negotiations for African Countries', mimeo, Kampala.

Maxwell Stamp (2003), 'Review of Trade Policy Institutions and Capacity', draft report for consultation prepared for Ministry of Tourism, Trade and Industry, Kampala.

Morrissey, O. and N. Rudaheranwa (1998), 'Ugandan Trade Policy and Export Performance in the 1990s', CREDIT Research Paper 98/12, University of Nottingham.

Mugenyi, O. and Nuwamanya D. (2003), 'Challenges for Enhancing the Role of Non-State Actors', ACODE Policy Research Series No. 7.

OECD (2003), 'The DAC guidelines: Strengthening Trade Capacity for Development, International Development', available at www.SourceOECD.org.

Republic of Uganda, *Background to the Budget* (various issues), Kampala: Ministry of Finance, Planning and Economic Development.

Republic of Uganda, *Statistical Abstract* (various issues), Entebbe: Uganda Bureau of Statistics.

UNCTAD (2003), *FDI in Landlocked Developing Countries at a Glance*, New York: United Nations.

WTO (1995, 2001), *Trade Policy Review: Uganda*, Geneva: WTO.

42

Uruguay in the services negotiations: strategy and challenges

SOLEDAD SALVADOR AND PAOLA AZAR (WITH THE COLLABORATION OF CLAUDIA RUCCI)*

1 The problem in context

Uruguay is a small South American country lying between Brazil and Argentina. In relation to the rest of the continent, it is a small country with a land surface of approximately 176,000 sq km; it is also small in demographic terms – its population is only 3 million – and in economic terms – gross domestic product (GDP) in 1998 was around US$23 billion. However, Uruguayan society enjoys high social integration and low levels of inequality.

As in other countries, the services sector represents two-thirds of employment and about 60% of GDP. During the 1990s the sector was an engine for national exports and its share in the total volume of exports increased threefold. Uruguay is a net exporter of commercial services (travel, transport and 'other commercial services'),[1] which account for 34% of global exports (the average for Latin American countries is 20%). Those classified under 'other services', including communications, construction, financial intermediation, business services, information-technology-related services, as well as royalties and property rights, have been the most dynamic.

The international expansion of the services sector seems to be a promising alternative to the exploitation of the country's natural resources. Yet the small size of its domestic market poses a challenge to efforts to

---

* Interdisciplinary Center for Development Studies, Uruguay – CIEDUR, Montevideo. We should like to acknowledge the contribution of Claudia Rucci, who was contracted by CIEDUR for this work
[1] The available figures of trade in services from the balance of payments underestimate the true extent of the fields covered by the General Agreement on Trade in Services (GATS).

liberalize the sector. Deregulation should be followed by re-regulation in order to ensure the effective operation of competition in the domestic market. The decision-making process needs to be founded on a sound basis (with good regulatory frameworks and appropriate institutions), with appropriate evaluations of risks and opportunities.

From this perspective it is important to ensure that policies and strategies are being co-ordinated and supported by the major players; this would help trade negotiations to become effective in empowering the country's international presence. Ideally, the actors involved should include policy-makers from the trade and services sector; firms from the services sector, professional associations, trade unions and civil society organizations.

During the first round of the GATS negotiations – the Uruguay Round (1986–94) – Uruguay, along with other developing countries, did not have a clearly defined strategy. This partly explains why their interests were barely reflected in the results emerging from that process. During negotiations Uruguayan negotiators claimed to have taken a defensive attitude; in the Doha Round (opened in 2001), local negotiators claim to have adopted a more assertive and liberalizing negotiating position.

This gives rise to the need to address the following questions:

How have the actual strategy-building and decision-making processes been designed in the light of the new round of services negotiations?
What lessons can be learnt from the first round of negotiations on the General Agreement on Trade in Services (GATS)?

At first glance, the level of interest shown in the GATS appears to have grown, as compared with the situation during the first round. Hence government actors have shown themselves to be eager to interest the general public and the private sector. They point to the fact that their central challenge lies in making the range of players aware of the 'commercial nature' of services.

Services firms are not completely aware of the GATS, its relevance and potential. Those firms that have been engaged in selling their goods abroad have done so by pursuing informal channels (such as personal contacts) rather than using institutional backups.

Actors from civil society more acquainted with the trade agreements alert the public about the scant information on the negotiations, on the confidentiality of the decision-making process at the government level and the need to open up the debate.

2 The strategy-building and decision-making process

The players and their roles

The government institutions directly involved in the trade policy design process as well as in the negotiations themselves are the Ministry of Foreign Affairs (MFA), the Planning and Budgeting Bureau (OPP – Spanish abbreviation)[2] and the Ministry of Economics and Finance (MEF). Depending on the nature of the issues under negotiation, these bodies ask for the participation of sectoral bodies related to the activities under discussion. The MFA is responsible for the negotiations and the decision-making process at the WTO, and it therefore provides the Uruguayan delegation in Geneva with directives and co-ordinates the participation of the different national actors.

Uruguay's positions vis-à-vis WTO negotiations are discussed in a body known as the 'National Section on the WTO'; this body groups representatives from the ministries, the OPP, regulatory agencies and the Central Bank of Uruguay. As multilateral negotiating strategies are discussed there, the position on GATS is also part of the agenda.

Within this general structure the OPP played a particular role in the GATS negotiations, as it was in charge of preparing the requests and offers to be presented to the other members of the WTO.

Multilateral negotiations have, to date, focused on financial and telecommunications services; this has meant that the Central Bank of Uruguay (CBU) and the Communication Services Regulatory Agency (URSEC)[3] have been frequently consulted on a variety of issues. The Ministries of Tourism, Transport and Education have also been asked to assist in elaborating issues to be discussed. The latter, in turn, consulted public and private tertiary education institutions to know their positions.

There is no single institutional channel to communicate with the private sector, such as entrepreneurs, trade unions and civil society. This is equally true for general WTO negotiations as for specific ones such as GATS.

As described above, those responsible for elaborating requests and offers have principally consulted government bodies. M. A. Peña, head of the integration and trade policies department at the OPP, has pointed out that if there is a 'macro policy' designed by the government in certain areas, it is taken as the 'rule' and there is no need to make further contacts. In other cases, the government tries to consult with the private sector.

---

[2] The OPP is an advisory organ operating under the auspices of the President's Board.
[3] The URSEC regulates and controls the telecommunication and postal services.

Hence in May 2002 the MFA and the OPP co-ordinated various rounds of contacts between public- and private-sector representatives involved in a range of service activities. The objective was to disseminate information about the ongoing negotiations and gather any demands that might be made and data needed to support the preparation of requests and offers. The meetings were attended by representatives of the Uruguayan Chamber of Information Technologies (CUTI, a strong exporter of software and related services), members of maritime transport associations, the Chamber of Construction, the Association of Private Promoters of Construction, professional associations and delegates from the country's universities.

In the view of the MFA's representatives, private-sector firms needed to be exporting already in order to show interest. They affirmed that 'if firms are not exporting, they don't feel any need to participate'. But probably the lack of awareness about GATS and its possible implications has been the main cause.

The firms interviewed for this case study represent the main players in the newly emerging services export sector; examples of these companies include an advertising agency, an audiovisual producer and a consulting engineering company, all of which said that they had never been contacted by the MFA. On the other hand, CUTI, a pillar of Uruguay's services export sector, acknowledges that it has developed better communications with the MFA, although 'we are not informed about the negotiating process and the decisions adopted'.

Professional consultants (in architecture, engineering, medicine and construction management) involved with Mercosur's negotiations through the CIAM,[4] have taken different approaches to the GATS negotiations. Health professionals did not participate in a systematic manner in the consultations, even though they eventually exchanged information with government representatives. The construction management firm was invited to participate in some of the consultations, but did not consider that the matter was important to them. The architects' association was questioned by the MFA but did not provide any answers because their members felt very detached from the negotiations and claimed not to have been informed about its progress. Finally, representatives of the engineers' association attended all the meetings they were invited to but pointed out

---

[4] Commission for the Integration of Surveying, Agronomy, Architecture, Geology and Engineering of Mercosur (Comisión para la Integración de la Agrimensura, Agronomía, Arquitectura, Geología e Ingeniería del Mercosur).

that they had not received any further information on the progress of the negotiations, and asked for an ongoing exchange of information.

Trade unionists[5] were only invited to participate in a seminar which took place before the WTO Ministerial Conference in Cancún. The government presented the current state of play in the negotiations and the general contours of the national strategy. The union's reaction with regard to the talks is summed up by one its representatives, J. Silva: 'That mechanism would only serve government to legitimize its actions with the civil society.'

Non-governmental organizations (NGO) neither participated nor were consulted on the negotiations. They demanded more 'space' since 'the MFA has never paid attention to our claims and proposals'.[6] Conversely, the contact between NGOs and the Congress is more fluid, thanks to personal connections and informal exchanges of information. NGOs and workers' representatives maintained that new trade-related issues (such as services) are not usually discussed at the legislature, 'not even in the congressional international affairs commission', revealing the existence of information gaps. In fact, the Congress has not participated in any of the decision-making processes related to WTO negotiations. This would take place only if some foreign entity presented a demand or claim that justified the call for the Minister of Foreign Affairs to give an explanation to Congress members.

Government actors working at the elaboration of the national strategy and the decision-making process on services are the same for all the different levels of integration. This has contributed to the co-ordination of negotiations, but also to the accumulation of experience. The Mercosur negotiations have provided a good background for the negotiations on GATS. Its institutional mechanisms have been successfully used to integrate the different actors (trade unions, firms and civil society) in negotiations, promote awareness and engage various concerned parties with the matters discussed.

Relevant features of the strategy-building process

The MFA's authorities have said that up to now trade in services was not a tough issue to negotiate: 'most of the countries are hardly consolidating their status quo', 'the present negotiations are at the stage of bilateral

---

[5] There is a single umbrella organization (PIT-CNT), formed by the different sectoral unions (from both the public and the private sector).

[6] Eduardo Gudynas, director, Latin American Centre of Social Ecology (CLAES).

exchanges, and ... their progress is very slow, because it is mainly determined by progress in the agriculture negotiations'. However, Julio Lacarte Muró, a former Uruguayan economic and commercial advisor in Geneva, said, 'we are being encouraged to use the services liberalization to obtain the agriculture liberalization'.

The need for a strategy for participating in the negotiating process has now been accepted by the actors involved. Ernesto Medina (from the MEF) said, 'at first, there was a defensive attitude, as it was assumed that the WTO was a "rich countries' club" created to further their interests. Afterwards, in government circles this image was altered, and a change was made towards taking a more pro-active and positive attitude that extended into other trade negotiations. Currently, a more active stance is being pursued.'

Carlos Pérez del Castillo, special advisor on international trade negotiations to the president of Uruguay, stressed the shift towards a more aggressive and liberalizing position as reflected in the attitude of the Uruguayan delegation in the Doha negotiations compared with the Uruguay Round: 'Our country was the first developing economy to submit the initial offers. It means that we have important advantages compared with the rest of Latin American countries.' Hugo Cayrús, a negotiator in Geneva and the person behind this change, has remarked that this was the best way to gain a better negotiating position.

All government actors have highlighted that this attitude was not reflected in any similar changes in domestic institutions or regulations. In fact, according to comments from MFA officials, 'all that we have submitted is already subject to liberalization and it is only an initial offer that does not imply many changes in relation to the Uruguay Round commitments'. They also added that 'for the time being, nobody is thinking of consolidating the liberalization beyond the status quo'. However, this sort of statement co-exists with clear difficulties for the government in assessing the current regulatory framework for the services sectors and modes of supply covered by GATS.

Up to now Uruguayan offers have included some competitive services which are already exporting and are liberalized domestically (e.g. software and tourism-related activities such as hotels, restaurants), and those where protection against foreign competition is not regarded as relevant (e.g. real estate services, designers). M. A. Peña argues that the rationale is that 'if it is the case of a competitive sector or a sector in which Uruguay has not a specific qualification, there is no need to be protectionist'.

The government's survey of the demands formulated by the private sector showed that professional associations were concerned about the harmonization of basic curricula at the regional level and, mostly, about the need to create an agency or institution responsible for the recognition of local qualifications abroad. This would be considered under Mode IV, traditionally regarded as the most interesting one for developing countries. They were also interested in knowing which discriminatory rules were already included in existing regulatory frameworks.

In relation to companies, the government was aware that their reaction, where information was not easily available and the situation therefore uncertain, was generally cautious. Entrepreneurs have suggested to negotiators that 'in case of doubt, it is preferable not to offer any commitment'. Finally, the MFA's officials pointed out that firms exhibit 'great difficulty in considering strategies of access to extra-regional markets'. Meanwhile, as M. A. Peña has pointed out, 'Uruguayan requests were generally focused on developed countries'.

Some of the interviewed entrepreneurs who had developed an export-oriented strategy were in favour of liberalization and aware of the possibility of developing services exports because of their good quality and low costs. They were interested in greater openness because they felt confident about their chances to compete, and are likely to make a contribution to the offers put forward by Uruguay in the course of negotiations. They also stated that up to the present, asking for government support or establishing direct contact with official authorities was not part of their business strategy. For instance, the director of the advertising agency said that their export strategy was built on personal and informal contacts and considered that these sorts of network really worked. The same applied to executives or consultants working in the audiovisual, engineering and construction sectors.

In the case of software exporters, the government stated that these firms act autonomously: 'they know what they want and they move in the fields they know in order to get it'. However, CUTI's representatives expressed it differently: 'we have a rather discontinuous relationship with ministries. We have received some calls from time to time, but after we answered their questions we were not told about the steps that have been taken'. They mentioned that the government had contacted them to find out about the opportunities and barriers that they had faced in the bilateral exchanges.

3 Challenges faced and the outcome

The non-tradable nature of services, the lack of experience in assessing the effects of trade policy and the non-existence of an institutional machinery to construct links between the different actors are but some of the challenges faced by Uruguay. M. A. Peña said that 'it is hard to deal with this subject, because the tradable nature of services has not been assumed yet. It has not been integrated into the popular wisdom... Developed countries have a wider experience in this approach as regards to regulations and opportunities. But developing countries tend to look at the matter with certain apathy.'

Despite the political shift brought about by the government's decision to comply with the GATS schedule, more was needed to keep the process on track. To devise a trade policy agenda aimed at finding out the advantages and costs of the process means that as many players as possible need to be considered. Uruguayan policy-makers have attempted to address this matter through the implementation of some rounds of consultations. However, their outcome was rather limited (in both the government's and the firm's view). Whether the mechanisms chosen for consulting the private sector were not the best ones or the policy-maker's conviction about the benefits of a wider participation was not strong enough, the result is that the construction of an inclusive commercial strategy is still far from being achieved.

Private-sector agents and civil society representatives have expressed their willingness to improve communication channels with government negotiators. They pointed to the convenience of setting up an information flow with government agencies to exchange ideas and suggestions. They claimed that effective participation in the decision-making process not only requires asking about the expected effects or benefits of certain measures, or the detection of particular problems; it really needs to involve social and business entities in the daily strategic decision-making process. A more fluid contact between all the actors would ease the dialogue by translating trade policy rules and technical foundations of WTO agreements into a more comprehensible and attainable language.

From this perspective private-sector and government representatives held contrasting views of the mechanisms to institutionalize consultation and participation. The former stated that government demands for information are too specific and are not followed by any lesson-learning or inclusive-exchange process. The latter admitted the need to facilitate closer collaboration and partnership with other actors. However, apart from recognition that the situation existed, the interviewed policy-makers did not refer to any concrete measure that might be taken to enhance and promote joint activities with other important players.

Roberto Bissio[7] considered that the most critical challenge is to acknowledge the core significance of the subject, something which the government has not completely embraced. He held that 'Trade in services possesses characteristics that make it different from goods and requires careful deliberation and attention in the liberalization process because it entails irrevocable changes in national legislation...Consequently, the debate about these questions must not remain secret.' He stated that 'keeping the trade issues in the shadow is part of a deliberate strategy'. The 'secret' avoids debate on the strategies, which could complicate the course of the negotiation: 'Less awareness imposes less pressure.'

Lacarte Muró emphasized another aspect of the same point. For him, the most serious difficulty the country had to overcome was 'the disregarding attitude of the government', related to the prevailing ignorance on the real relevance of these negotiations for Uruguay. He said that it was necessary to identify the sectors involved in this trade and hear their messages. Besides, he considered that 'communication channels at the government level frequently do not work properly and the decision-making processes are less structured than was envisaged'. So the negotiating team in Geneva was deemed to be rather 'isolated' from local bodies.

The absence of a clearly designed strategy-building and decision-making structure usually left the communication channels subject to the personal qualities of the actors. In the view of both the private sector and the government, the changes in personnel in leading positions affected progress.

Different civil society, private-sector and government actors agreed that the country's trade strategy has no clear direction. Asked about this, government officials said that 'Discussions about trade in services are framed in the absence of sectoral policies. The country does not have any long-term agreed development policies.'

All those interviewed highlighted the excellent qualifications of the Uruguayan delegation, as well as its long and rich experience in multilateral negotiating fora such as the WTO. But this expertise needed to be complemented with a well-prepared strategy. The substantive content and the outcome of the country's trade strategy are affected by the lack of a distinct 'macro-economic policy orientation'. This might affect the final negotiating positions in reflecting personal ideas and convictions independently of the interests of the majority of actors involved. Hence while the MFA's representatives adopted a cautious position, other government

---

[7] Director, Third World Institute (ITEM), Uruguay.

actors considered that liberalization 'is always good and favourable'. On the other hand, Lacarte Muró observed, 'unbridled trade liberalization is not wise. Countries must develop and retain the ability to make strategic choices.'

Furthermore, he pointed out that none of the local actors really knew about Uruguay's domestic regulations: 'The United States and the European Union [EU] have a deep knowledge about their regulatory frameworks and seek to adapt WTO's norms to those already applied in their countries in order to avoid introducing changes to their local rules. While the United States and EU negotiate in full awareness about their legislation, in our case international commitments are automatically integrated as national law.'

The lack of human and material resources undermines the evaluation of the potential risks and gains of liberalization and the compliance of domestic regulations. In Lacarte Muró's words, 'that is why Uruguay finds it so difficult to identify where the real advantages lie', and 'our ignorance about the local and international regulations leaves us very little leeway to negotiate'. Indeed, some government officials have observed that 'the lack of clear regulations on competence and consumer protection makes the situation worse and should inhibit the benefits of liberalization as new practices could affect rights which were not considered up to that moment. It damages our negotiating position before countries with clear and consolidated regulations.'

The multiple negotiating fronts at bilateral, regional and multilateral levels and the diversity of issues under discussion bring new complexities. In particular, in the case of services, building a strategy implies a full understanding of the rules, disciplines and commitments included in the different modes of supply by each sector, and a good command of the sectoral classification list used in the negotiations.

The targeted markets have not been the same for policy-makers and for the private sector. Until now, professional consultants and firms have oriented their business strategy towards regional or developing countries. While government actors have been concerned in putting forward offers to developed countries, the private sector sees that as complex and restrictive. Ultimately, during the 2004 International Trade Centre Conference,[8] Cayrús pointed out that 'current negotiations should not be seen as a North–South, or developing versus developed countries issue. They must

---

[8] International Trade Centre (ITC) UNCTAD/WTO, Latin America and the Caribbean Regional Conference, 'Business for Development', Rio de Janeiro, Brazil, 8–9 June 2004.

be seen as an excellent opportunity for developing countries to negotiate commitments in sectors and modes of supply, of their interests in order to contribute with their national realities.'

Uruguay's services negotiating position is subject to what is gained in agriculture. Nevertheless, the real impacts and effects of this posture have never been truly analyzed. Here inertia is again present: the country seems to 'go with the flow'. No resources are systematically devoted to the collection and examination of data to assess the comparative effects in terms of employment and added value of trade in services against trade in agriculture. Therefore there is no evidence to support the present strategy, or discussion about the effective competitive advantages for the country.

Government actors have said that WTO negotiations progress at the speed imposed by developed countries. 'Developed countries push the process. If they don't make requests, the rest of the countries don't move forward... So our countries act as a reflex of that push.' In this sense, officials declared that it was hard to follow a fixed line of action, as 'we have to act in response to pressures, because we are a little and poor country'.[9]

According to some of those interviewed, if Uruguay has not been a target of international pressures it is because its position has been generally in line with what was 'expected'.

4 Lessons for others

The supposed change in the country's negotiating posture appears as a response to its inaction during the Uruguay Round. It is intertwined with knowledge gained about managing the services negotiations, what the rights and obligations of the countries are, and the government's capacity to implement the provisions of the Agreement. Government delegates suggested that the advantages of such a shift have not been appreciated by most developing countries.

The 'offers' and 'requests' were carefully elaborated. In contrast to the Uruguay Round, this time the interests of the services sector were considered. It was further noted that the expertise derived from the practice at Mercosur's negotiations on the subject contributed to an improvement in the government's relationship with firms. This suggested that Uruguay was abandoning its earlier dismissive attitude, evident in the inclusion

---

[9] These ideas were expressed by various trade officials.

of 'the fewest sectors possible' during the Uruguay Round, for a more considered one, more concerned to accommodate the country's interests.

However, the 'new strategy' alleged by the government did not seem to be noticed by the rest of the consulted actors. The still limited contact between policy-makers and other players involved in the process (mainly service sector firms and civil society) might result in the government's engagement in defending interests far from what the private sector has identified as relevant. If this is not realized before liberalization intensifies, the performance and development of the liberalized services sectors will be prejudiced.

Despite the fact that government and private-sector actors recognize the need to bridge the information gaps and to use surveys and assessments to determine the exact nature of the ongoing regulation as well as the potential effects of modifications of trade measures, no actions or resources have been devoted to meet these needs effectively. This is especially evident in the absence of any review of the regulatory framework in Uruguay, in contrast to what has taken place in Argentina and Brazil, for example.

In this sense, the services negotiation by negative list agreed with Mexico implies the identification of those sectors to be excluded. This seems to be inconsistent with the unclear regulatory norms and national interests.

Given the absence of open debate on trade in services and the lack of information on the progress of negotiations, it is difficult to expect entrepreneurs 'spontaneously' to gather together and claim a space for participation. Those who are already participating are those who have clearly identified advantages in international trade and are interested in being considered in the negotiations. Thus the ongoing mechanism of consultation with private actors seems to have reached only those firms that government has recognized as potential exporters, while it has left the rest 'invisible'.

The option to establish an institutional mechanism in local trade policy formulation and implementation which would involve entrepreneurs and civil society could be successful, as in the case of Mercosur. For instance, the professionals taking part in CIAM have had the opportunity to exchange ideas and analyze the potential advantages and disadvantages of regional integration, which has successfully involved them in the negotiating process.

One critical aspect is related to the role of stakeholders in determining negotiation mandates and monitoring the process. General opinion has been that the local delegation is well prepared. However, the research has shown that local agents need to be trained not only to improve the scope of their political interventions but also to widen and deepen inter-agency collaboration and civil society involvement. Several players referred to the experience of joint participation of government actors, entrepreneurs and civil society in the case of Brazil and Chile as a pattern to be followed.

In the words of Pérez del Castillo, 'trade in services is the negotiation of the future'. However, there is no sign that any future opportunities to promote research, to look for access to new markets or even to build a solid and distinguishable strategy will be taken. No long-term strategies are being constructed, despite the shared conviction that there is need of them.

Bibliography

Cayrús, H. (2004), 'Trade in Services Negotiations at the WTO', speech at 'Business for Development', International Trade Centre (ITC) UNCTAD/WTO, Latin America and the Caribbean Regional Conference, Rio de Janeiro, 8–9 June.

De Brun, J. (1994), 'Assessment of the Effects of Liberalization on Regional Trade in Services at the Mercosur: The Uruguayan Case', report for the Inter-American Development Bank, November.

Direction of International Economic Organisms, Ministry of Foreign Affairs (2004), Report on Services Negotiations at the WTO.

Vaillant, M. (1998), 'Trade Policy on a Country Basis and the Uruguay Round: The Case of Uruguay', mimeo.

World Trade Organization, Trade Topics, Services, Sector by Sector, documents available at www.wto.org/english/tratop_e/serv_e/serv_sectors_e.htm.

Hoekman, B., A. Mattoo, and P. English, eds. (2002), *Development, Trade and the WTO: A Handbook*, Washington, DC: World Bank.

43

Vanuatu's suspended accession bid: second thoughts?

DANIEL GAY*

1 The problem in context

The background to accession

Vanuatu began its WTO accession process in July 1995, and the main momentum towards membership came in 1997 with the advent of a structural adjustment package known as the Comprehensive Reform Programme (CRP).[1] This set of reforms aimed to improve governance, enhance the role of the private sector, increase economic growth and further liberalize the economy. As part of this last process the programme was directed at reducing trade barriers within the context of WTO membership.[2] The import-substitution policy, followed since independence in 1980, was failing. The economy was generally closed, while Vanuatu had always run a visible trade deficit; some policy-makers and politicians felt that the economy should integrate more into the global economy.

A further impetus towards accession was that all Vanuatu's neighbours and principal trading partners were WTO members – Fiji, the Solomon islands, Papua New Guinea, Australia and New Zealand. There was a feeling that trade relations would be enhanced under the WTO framework.

Economic conditions

The CRP did not meet many of its objectives. Growth in gross domestic product (GDP) declined in the following five years:[3] per capita GDP was no higher in absolute terms in 2003 than in 1998, and is now about

---

* Overseas Development Institute, London.
[1] See *Comprehensive Reform Programme* (1997), Port Vila: Comprehensive Reform Programme Co-ordination Office.
[2] Ibid.   [3] Department of Finance and Economic Management.

US$1,150.[4] Exports fell 40% during the same period,[5] incoming investment fell faster than world-wide foreign direct investment trends[6] and government expenditure increased as a proportion of GDP.[7] This failure of economic performance provoked strong opinions from some government officials: 'The CRP was a complete waste of time. It paid for the salaries of a few consultants and did nothing for the country.'[8]

As Table 43.1 shows, Vanuatu had consistently run a visible trade deficit since independence in 1980. Whilst cutting the deficit was a motivation for WTO membership, the failure of the CRP to deal with this problem or to improve the economy helped undermine public support for WTO accession.

In the eyes of local business people, many civil servants and some of the public, the WTO was tarred with the same brush as the CRP, and the decline in economic performance reinforced protectionist attitudes.

Reasons for the suspension of the accession

In 2001, just before the Doha Ministerial Conference, when Vanuatu was due to accede, the Minister of Trade withdrew a finalized working party report, citing 'technical reasons'.[9] During the subsequent two years little progress was made towards accession, although in 2004 Vanuatu began another attempt.

Local players cite several reasons for the suspension of accession apart from the general economic downturn and the failure of the CRP. The most immediate reason was that a general election was due in May the following year, and the Minister of Trade was concerned about protectionist pressures from a small number of business interests, particularly in the area of wholesale and retail trade.[10]

The leader of the negotiating team, Roy Mickey Joy, admits that negotiators did not communicate enough with ministers, partly as a result of frequent political change. Others confirm this view: 'Political instability was ... a problem. Different ministers also had different views on the

---

[4] Department of Statistics; population is around 200,000 and GDP approximately US$230 million.
[5] Department of Trade, Industry and Investment.
[6] Vanuatu Investment Promotion Authority.
[7] Department of Finance and Economic Management.
[8] Interview with Roy Mickey Joy, Director of Trade, Industry and Investment.
[9] WT/ACC/VUT/14.
[10] Interview with unnamed senior government official, 2004.

Table 43.1. *Vanuatu trade trends, 1983–2002*

Year	Exports[1]	Imports[2]	Trade deficit as % of GDP
	million vatu		
1983	2,583	4,338	16
1984	3,939	4,826	7
1985	2,753	5,257	19
1986	1,806	4,849	24
1987	1,937	6,157	29
1988	1,559	5,883	28
1989	1,609	6,727	31
1990	1,783	8,854	38
1991	1,600	7,128	26
1992	2,027	7,131	23
1993	2,140	7,406	23
1994	2,402	8,203	23
1995	2,552	8,507	23
1996	2,708	8,647	22
1997	3,565	8,613	17
1998	3,907	8,931	15
1999	2,907	9,989	22
2000	3,214	9,821	20
2001	2,302	10,357	24

[1] Merchandise.
[2] Cleared for home consumption.
Source: Department of Statistics; author's calculations.

WTO. There were insufficient consultations between the political level and the civil servants ... We were going into negotiations without consulting other line departments. There were insufficient consultations between the Ministry and the Department.'[11]

The political system is unstable, with constantly shifting coalitions in office for a few months at a time. Institutional memory is short, which made it difficult for negotiators to keep ministers informed. In Vanuatu ministries are separate from departments, which meant that the Department of Trade, which deals with technical matters and line duties, had

[11] Interview with Timothy Sisi, former Assistant Collector, Department of Customs and Inland Revenue, now Principal Trade Officer, Department of Trade, Industry and Investment.

minimal contact with the ministry. It has been suggested that when the Minister of Trade suspended the accession process in 2001 it was the first time that he was fully aware of the contents of the accession package.

A number of players believe that the accession process was too burdensome for a small, least-developed country (LDC). Only around five members of staff, based in the departments of Trade and Customs, were available to deal with accession. They had no prior experience of General Agreement on Tariffs and Trade (GATT) or the WTO.

Funding was scarce, particularly at a time of economic downturn and fiscal austerity. No resources were available for a social or economic impact study. Vanuatu had no mission in Geneva. The numerous trips to Geneva necessary for membership were difficult to fund, and cost an estimated total of VT 20 million (US$150,000). Vanuatu has never paid its annual fees as a WTO observer, which in 2003 were 23,070 Swiss francs,[12] representing around 14% of the total annual Department of Trade budget.[13]

There was particular pressure on Vanuatu because it would have been the first LDC to join the WTO. Members of the working party, in particular the United States, extracted the maximum concessions possible – what some have termed 'WTO-plus'.[14] Those involved with accession believe that the negotiation process was stacked in favour of incumbents, a particular problem for small, capacity-constrained Vanuatu: 'At present, accession is a power-based process within which the applicant – even the largest and seemingly most powerful, such as China – has no real power to inflict any marginal cost on a demandeur.'[15] There was also a fear among local people that, following independence in 1980, Vanuatu was re-selling its country to foreign interests. At least two prominent civil society and NGO members have expressed fears of 're-colonization'.[16]

In sum, Vanuatu did not have sufficient ownership over the outcome of negotiations. In the absence of consultation and information, the logical option for doubters was to oppose the entire WTO process.

This lack of ownership was due to the asymmetry between members and acceding countries. Also to blame were the problems typical of small, developing countries – a lack of experience, insufficient communication

---

[12] Source for all figures here: Department of Trade, Industry and Investment.

[13] Author's calculations.

[14] R. Grynberg and R. M. Joy (2000), 'The Accession of Vanuatu to the WTO', *Journal of World Trade* 34 (6), pp. 159–73.

[15] Ibid., p. 172.

[16] See also J. D. Salong (1998), 'Reform or Recolonization: Vanuatu's Comprehensive Reform Programme under the Microscope', *Tok Blong Pasifik*, March/June 1998.

between negotiators and politicians, and limited resources. The ability of politicians to distance themselves from the final result meant that accession was always vulnerable to protectionist pressures from prominent business and civil society interests.

It might be asked why Vanuatu wanted to join the WTO if the costs were so high. However, it is only through the protection of a rules-based system and access to the dispute-settlement mechanism that many Vanuatu officials felt the country could function successfully in the world economy. As globalization proceeded – meaning, for example, the erosion of Vanuatu's trade preferences as an LDC – many believed that it was important to be a part of the multilateral trading regime.

2 Some local and external players and their roles

Government and public sector

The Council of Ministers

Vanuatu had nine different governments between 1995 and 2004;[17] political instability made it very difficult for the negotiating team to keep the Council of Ministers informed of developments. Although its members knew that Vanuatu was joining the WTO, most were unaware of any details of the accession package and did not understand the role of the WTO. A lack of confidence in representatives has made many civil society actors cautious about WTO participation: 'One of my concerns is our ability to participate effectively in WTO meetings. For instance our parliament has fifty-two members, but you only ever hear three talking throughout the year. How confidently can we participate? If we can't participate effectively we might as well not be included.'[18] Some members of the Council of Ministers acted on behalf of a handful of outspoken business people. Non-governmental organizations (NGOs) had little impact on the Council of Ministers.

Ministers of Trade

Six different Ministers of Trade took office between 1995 and 2001. Two of the most pro-active were Willy Jimmy Tapanga Rarua, then a member of the francophone Union of Moderate Parties (UMP) but now deputy leader of the centrist National United Party, and Rialuth Serge Vohor, former UMP Prime Minister and Trade Minister in 2001.

---

[17] Parliament library.   [18] Interview with Dickinson Tevi, Vanuatu Association of NGOs.

Vohor can be said to be neither particularly pro- nor anti-WTO. His concern in 2001 was primarily re-election the following year. It is also alleged – although difficult to prove – that he was influenced by the powerful Dinh business family.

Tapanga Rarua, again the Minister of Trade for the first half of 2003, is more well-disposed towards WTO membership. He was also from the same Wantok (extended family) as many in the negotiating team, a relationship which improved communications between the team and the ministry. The greatest progress towards membership was made during his time in office.

The Director General and political advisors

The Director General of Trade and Foreign Affairs, in office since 1997, provided important stability. This position was created with the aim of mediating between the department and ministry and providing guidance alongside advisors appointed by the minister.

Political advisors were motivated primarily by a concern to remain in employment, as their jobs finished when the minister left office. They were therefore conservative and did not push for WTO membership.

The Director General of Trade was answerable to three ministers – for Industry as well as Foreign Affairs, and Trade and Commerce – who were often from different political parties. He had wide-ranging responsibilities and attempted to achieve a compromise between the differing policy stances.

Director of Trade

Roy Mickey Joy, Director of Trade, Industry and Investment since 1998, has provided the strongest impetus towards accession of any official or politician. He led the negotiating team, alongside the Director of Customs, and communicated with foreign capitals during bilateral discussions. The Department of Trade is the WTO focal point.

Joy is one of only a handful of civil servants or politicians who are trained and experienced in WTO matters and can operate successfully on the international stage. With a team of only five officials, however, split between two departments, he was over-stretched during accession: 'We were basically dealing with goods, without realizing that other important aspects were not addressed, such as agriculture or services. The suspension of accession was timely. It gave us an opportunity to do more work, and to realize the costs and benefits.'

As for any acceding country, terms of membership were decided during accession. The rules were particularly unclear for Vanuatu as potentially the first LDC to accede. This absence of clear guidelines or rules meant that despite his best efforts the Director of Trade found it difficult to comprehend the implications of many points of negotiation.

Technical advisors

Pacific Islands Forum Secretariat representative at the WTO

The part-time Forum Secretariat representative helped to formulate the negotiating position and was involved with some bilateral discussions. His prior WTO knowledge made up for the lack in domestic experience. Correspondence makes it clear that this source of technical help was important,[19] and shows the benefits of pooling resources within the Pacific region. The consultant, who understood Melanesian cultural and economic priorities, was able to prioritize local demands.

WTO Secretariat, Accessions Division

The accessions office provided technical input during accession. A major motivation was to bring the negotiations to a swift conclusion. Some commentators have called into question the independence of the secretariat, suggesting that in order to enhance the development credentials of the WTO following Seattle, WTO officials as well as prominent members wanted countries from the three official levels of development to join at Doha: Taiwan, a newly industrialized country, China, a developing country, and least-developed Vanuatu.

> The WTO official was, in my view, representing one big player when he came here. There was no face-to-face bilateral; we were only exchanging correspondence ... The WTO Secretariat appeared not to be acting independently – it was pushing on behalf of a particular country.[20]

While these are serious allegations, it seems particularly important for national officials to see the WTO Secretariat as strictly impartial. Face-to-face negotiations, rather than the secretariat only delivering responses, may help. Rushing responses forced Vanuatu into making ill-considered decisions.

---

[19] Department of Trade files.   [20] Interview with Sisi.

The private sector

Chamber of Commerce

The Vanuatu Chamber of Commerce is unusual in that it is funded by government. Because they pay no fee, corporate members take a varying interest in its operations. Although in favour of WTO entry, the Chamber was relatively uninvolved in the accession process. Officials believe that they should have been consulted more closely: 'People weren't sure what the WTO was. They didn't know what the benefits were for Vanuatu... The private sector and NGOs were not consulted on the process. That's why there wasn't any support from the stakeholders.'[21]

The Chamber of Commerce argues that Vanuatu has insufficient domestic production to be able to take advantage of increased market access. The argument is not that WTO entry would be damaging, but that it is not currently relevant.

Companies

Around six vocal manufacturing companies form a powerful lobbying interest. Most of these firms have sheltered behind high trade barriers since independence, despite manufacturing comprising only 3% of GDP.[22] Under the Melanesian Spearhead Group Free Trade Area, a regional trade agreement, each company has managed to negotiate protective import tariff rates of 35% for their main product, including ice-cream, wooden furniture, toilet paper, fruit juice, corned beef and sawn timber.[23]

Manufacturing companies were broadly hostile to WTO membership. However, most did not grasp that the average negotiated bound tariff rate was 40%, with applied rates for their products below bound rates.[24] This lack of awareness was partly due to the dearth of information provided by government, but the facts were never denied to companies had they wished to find out.

NGOs

Initially NGOs groups were uninformed about the implications of WTO membership for Vanuatu. Aspects of their analysis, based on information from European NGOs, were opposed to the interests of Vanuatu. For

---

[21] Interview with Sowany Joseph, Principal Trade and Investment officer, Port Vila Chamber of Commerce.
[22] Department of Finance and Economic Management.
[23] 'MSG Trade Negotiators Agree to Re-impose Protective Customs Tariff', *Vanuatu Trading Post*, October 2002.
[24] See WT/ACC/VUT/13/Add.1.

instance, some European NGOs were lobbying against a reduction in domestic agricultural support because it would increase unemployment. This is true for Europe, but local NGOs failed to realize that it would make Vanuatu farm products more competitive in the European market. One local NGO published an inflammatory article in the newspaper, taken from a European anti-WTO website, just before Vanuatu was due to sign the working party report.[25]

> Prior to recent awareness sessions I didn't read much about WTO matters. Before I had an opinion without reasoning. I heard everyone else talking about the WTO ... But now I also have other views about the WTO. I know that a country like Vanuatu can have a say on any issue.[26]

With an increase in awareness about the WTO after 2001, NGOs have been able to tailor their analysis to the domestic context. A VANGO representative has attended several domestic and overseas WTO workshops and distributed local literature on the WTO to members. Most NGOs, however, remain sceptical about WTO entry.

The media

At the time two newspapers, the *Trading Post* and the *Port Vila Presse*, were published three times a week. Both played a key role in forming attitudes towards the WTO. The expatriate editor of the *Trading Post* (now the *Daily Post*) has opposed WTO membership in the belief that it would increase unemployment. The newspapers were purportedly motivated by sales and had a minimal political agenda – both were owned by foreign investors.

A number of articles reprinted from foreign publications served to spread misperceptions about the WTO, although a publicity campaign by the Department of Trade is now increasing awareness.[27]

The New Zealand and Australian High Commissions

Australian and New Zealand diplomats based in Port Vila intervened during accession as part of their close donor relationship. Both countries, however, have major economic and political interests in the Pacific. Vanuatu officials found it difficult to separate technical assistance from self-interest. This was reflected in the marked difference between the

---

[25] *Port Vila Presse*, 2001.   [26] Interview with Tevi.
[27] See, e.g., 'Speak Your Mind on the World Trade Organization', *Daily Post*, 24 Aug. 2003; 'Vanuatu Restarts WTO Negotiations', *Daily Post*, 6 May 2004.

roles of the respective development agencies – AusAID and the then New Zealand Overseas Development Agency – and their departments of trade.

> I remember walking into negotiations in Canberra thinking we were talking to friends, when suddenly we were hit by a barrage of aggressive negotiating demands. We had no negotiating position worked out beforehand.[28]

Correspondence indicates that Australia and New Zealand had specific demands during Vanuatu's accession, including, as expected from members of the Cairns group, opposition to agricultural export subsidies.[29] The dual role of these countries as both donors and demandeurs undermined the final outcome.

3 Challenges faced and the outcome

Vanuatu had to make major commitments on goods and services in compensation for its inability fully to meet demands on issues such as land ownership. Although no single concession alone was responsible for the decision to suspend accession, services commitments, and in particular the liberalization of wholesale and retail trade, were among the most important.

Export subsidies

Vanuatu periodically used aid payments to subsidise copra exports when international prices were low. Farmers in remote outer islands have no other source of income. Article 15 of the Agreement on Agriculture excludes LDCs from reduction commitments under the agreement, and yet some WTO members argued that they would not permit new countries to join with export subsidies.[30] Vanuatu was forced to agree to discontinue its periodic export subsidies if it wanted to join the WTO. Although it never used domestic funds as subsidies, the result was an unpopular restriction on policy.

Goods

As a tax haven, Vanuatu derived the biggest single share of government revenue from import duties, leaving a lot at stake in goods negotiations.

---

[28] Interview with Joy.   [29] Department of Trade files.
[30] Grynberg and Joy (2000), pp. 166–7.

Again, the issue of preparedness arises. No country can consider the accession process entirely holistically because accession takes years, during which period the economic structure evolves and administrations change. Yet Vanuatu did not take an overall view, instead treating each element of negotiations discretely.

> We were responding to requests and they were responding with high demands. We could not defend our positions, so we just had to give in. For example hydrocarbon oil duty rates, when converted to *ad valorem* from specific rates, were about 200–300%. At the moment they are well below, at 75%. We were pushed hard to convert them from specific to *ad valorem* and they were too high. Revenues on fuel are well below what we were collecting before.[31]

Although Vanuatu negotiated a higher average bound rate than some other acceding LDCs, this absence of an overall negotiating strategy meant that the outcome did not meet expectations. Vanuatu eventually agreed to bind 100% of tariffs, more than many developed and developing country members.[32] The agreed tariff peak of 75% was also much lower than many WTO members, as was the average tariff rate of 40%.[33]

Among other difficult areas in goods negotiations were duty rates for alcohol and tobacco, both of which generated significant revenue for the government. Owing to its small size and lack of capacity the Department of Customs and Inland Revenue has found it difficult to collect excise and value added tax.

Services

The leader of the negotiating team, Roy Mickey Joy, now admits that services received insufficient attention. This was for the simple reason that local officials were unfamiliar with the GATS system; it was left mostly to the temporary outside consultants.[34]

In the final schedule of commitments on services, Vanuatu agreed to include ten general areas out of a possible eleven, with fifty specific commitments.[35] These commitments are higher than those of most

---

[31] Interview with Sisi.
[32] For instance Australia has bound only 95% of tariffs and Cameroon 13.3% of tariffs.
[33] Egypt, e.g., has a peak tariff of 3,000% on agricultural goods and the United States 350%. The Maldives has an average bound rate of 300%.
[34] Confirmed in interviews with the Director of Trade and Principal Trade Officer.
[35] WT/ACC/VUT/13/add.2.

neighbouring economies and above the average for WTO members. The Solomon Islands included nine general areas and Fiji only two.[36]

One of the most controversial areas was wholesale and retail trade. Tonga, which was in the early stages of acceding, requested that Vanuatu make minimal commitments in these areas for fear of setting a precedent for its own accession.[37] Vanuatu officials also wanted to promote local ownership of the numerous small shops operating in the remote outer islands. In the end, however, distribution services were largely opened up.[38]

Land ownership

For customary and traditional reasons the Vanuatu constitution prohibits the freehold ownership of land. Leasehold lasting seventy-five years is allowed in some, mostly urban, areas. Yet the United States requested the revision of land laws. To allow freehold would have been politically suicidal and culturally unacceptable, so negotiators could not compromise on this issue. Provisions prohibiting foreign freehold ownership of land were made under the horizontal section of the services schedule of the final report.[39] As a result, significant concessions had to be made in other areas.

Special and differential treatment

WTO members argued that since Vanuatu was not yet a member of the WTO it could not use special and differential treatment (S&D) provisions. This has already been seen in the case of export subsidies, yet it also meant that Vanuatu could not take full advantage of transition periods for Trade-related Aspects of Intellectual Property Rights (TRIPS) or customs valuation.[40] Negotiators found it difficult to understand why they could not make full use of these sources of flexibility.

The decision on the accession of LDCs adopted by the WTO General Council on 10 December 2002 was partly a response to Vanuatu's

---

[36] Grynberg and Joy (2000), p. 170.   [37] Discussion with temporary consultant.
[38] WT/ACC/VUT/13/add.2.   [39] Ibid.
[40] Vanuatu was allowed two years to adopt these agreements, while Cambodia and Nepal were allowed three years or more.

predicament, both as a capacity-constrained country experiencing difficulties in negotiations and in its inability to take advantage of S&D.[41]

Document WT/L/508 recommends that 'WTO members shall exercise restraint in seeking concessions and commitments on trade in goods and services from acceding LDCs, taking into account the levels of concessions and commitments undertaken by existing WTO LDCs' members.' It allows acceding LDCs to take advantage of special and differential treatment, streamlines the accession process and improves access to technical assistance and capacity-building.

4 Lessons for others

Coping with limited capacity

The WTO accession process was too onerous and power-based for a small, capacity-constrained country. Vanuatu officials were forced to make concessions that politicians were not prepared to sustain in the long run and which were greater than many developed and developing WTO members. This is in the interests neither of WTO members in general nor of Vanuatu.

Whatever degree of training and capacity-building assistance is provided, and however high the quality, small countries and many LDCs will always struggle to negotiate effectively with big players. Not only do small countries and some LDCs simply lack manpower, but even when fully trained officials often move jobs. Out of Vanuatu's original five-member WTO team, three have now taken up new positions. This means that negotiating capacity is little better than at the start of accession in 1995.

The accession of Nepal and the finalization of Cambodia's working party report in 2003 show that LDCs have negotiated with varying degrees of success, and yet the outcomes showed limited true flexibility, for example on telecommunications, audiovisual and wholesale and retail.[42]

Despite the 2002 General Council decision on LDCs, 'There is a continued need for clear, objective rules and disciplines for accession negotiations.'[43]

A set of basic rules and disciplines would help overcome capacity limitations. These rules could – at least – lay down fixed transition periods for

---

[41] WT/L/508; This has been confirmed in informal conversations with officials from the WTO Secretariat.

[42] See, e.g., the working party report of Nepal, WT/ACC/NPL/16.

[43] UNCTAD (2004), *The Least-Developed Country Report 2004*, Geneva and New York: United Nations, p. 63.

adoption of the TRIPS, Customs Valuation and sanitary and phytosanitary measures (SPS) agreements; suggest guidelines on import tariff reduction commitments; and put in place maximum required service-sector commitments.

Of course some room for manoeuvre is required, and there can be no blueprint for accession. However, in reality the existing procedure allows limited flexibility because of the standard demands of big players. Most local players involved with Vanuatu's accession believe that excluding certain issues from negotiations would improve the overall outcome.

Using international resources

Most local players agree that technical assistance was vital. The Pacific Islands Forum Secretariat consultants had both prior experience of the WTO and local knowledge, a combination which was particularly important in the case of land laws. A key lesson here is that technical assistants are more help if they have country or regional experience.

Since 2001 Vanuatu has been able to take better advantage of technical assistance. The increase in awareness has allowed key officials to take a step back from the nitty-gritty, looking instead at the overall costs and benefits.

Government officers have attended many overseas training courses organised by the WTO, UN agencies and others. However, it is important to ensure that training is targeted at the appropriate personnel. In a low-wage country, *per diems* comprise a significant incentive, even if the training is not directly relevant.[44] Overseas trips are often distributed as bonuses to favoured staff.

The only obvious way around this problem is for international agencies to establish contact with ministries other than the WTO contact point and to target training at officials with relevant responsibilities. This may cost more, but it would be better to conduct a handful fewer training sessions and spend the resources on targeting the sessions than to train the wrong people. 'We need to send key stakeholders on WTO workshops so that they can help the Department of Trade.'[45]

The Chamber of Commerce has suggested that members of the private sector and NGOs should have attended awareness seminars at an early

---

[44] A middle-ranking Vanuatu government officer earns VT 1.1 million a year, about US$10,000. An average WTO *per diem* for a one-week course is therefore about 65% of the monthly salary.

[45] Interview with Joseph.

stage. This would have prevented misunderstandings about the WTO and enabled tailoring of analysis and strategy to the local context.

A lack of understanding among politicians also hindered Vanuatu's accession. A suggestion is that parliamentarians involved with the productive sectors – trade, finance, industry and tourism – should attend more training seminars on the WTO.

Training sessions must also be customized to local circumstances. General awareness of WTO rules is only half of the story; it is also crucial for people to understand the implications for their own country. It would make sense for any training seminar to involve in-depth prior country research, good-quality regional consultants and knowledgeable country officials.

Often Vanuatu trainees did not find it relevant to analyze in detail the legal meaning of individual WTO agreements or articles – the sort of scrutiny that happens in Geneva; more important was a basic understanding of how the WTO agreements would affect the country and region.

Consultation and transparency

A problem mentioned by almost every player involved in Vanuatu's accession was the lack of consultation: 'there was minimal consultation with or information provided to civil society, government and NGOs'.[46] The reasons were twofold: first, officials were simply stretched too thin. They did not have the time or resources for adequate consultation. Second, there was simply not enough understanding that accession must be based on the true interests of the country rather than the desires of government officials.

Politicians must also be briefed regularly, even if the news is bad. The Minister of Trade found it easy to withdraw from accession because there was so little domestic ownership or understanding of the issues.

Consultation must take two forms: first, individual talks aimed at determining private views, and second, frequent national seminars aimed at stimulating debate and arriving at an overall viewpoint. The former type of consultation focuses more on deciding the content of negotiating proposals; the latter aims mostly to create a sense of public ownership. If local players feel that they have been consulted, they are more likely to commit to any final outcome even if they disagree with it.

---

[46] Interview with Roy.

Since 2001 Vanuatu has created an inter-departmental WTO committee chaired by the Environment Unit. This involves key government and NGO players and ensures that the process does not revolve entirely around the Department of Trade.

Consultations, however, do not mean that all views can be accommodated. It is likely, for example, that some NGOs will disagree with companies. As seen in Vanuatu's goods negotiations, there was no aggregated strategy. This was the result partly of a lack of strong leadership – someone needs to say 'no' to particular demands, which is often culturally difficult in Pacific countries. There must come a time when a small group of officials, or a politician, finalizes strategy. A lack of domestic direction in Vanuatu's accession allowed other players to dictate proceedings.

Trade negotiations strategy

Negotiations strategy is a large area with a significant literature, and it is difficult to say much in a few words. However it deserves mention because it is one of the areas in which Vanuatu's accession displayed the most weakness.

The main problem was that there was no overall plan. Negotiators had not worked out a position in advance. For example, there was no development of an ideal-case, expected and worst-case scenario, either for the overall outcome of accession or for individual discussions. Negotiators had not prioritized issues. There was little attempt to quantify the impact of changes other than to recognize the importance of tariff cuts for government revenue. 'There was very, very little preparation done. In terms of opening up the economy, which affected revenue, we were under-prepared.'[47]

As has been discussed in section 3, an overall strategy is difficult when policy is unstable, the economy is changing and negotiations have few obvious parameters. However, even if strategy alters with every new administration or change in economic structure, it is better than no strategy at all.

Because most officials had only previously negotiated with co-operative neighbouring Melanesian countries, they did not appreciate the self-interested nature of international negotiations. It is a very basic point, but working out the agenda of the other party in advance is of paramount importance. Research on the local and foreign economies is vital,

47 Ibid.

including the development of accurate data. Training on negotiations would be useful: 'There are skills involved – the theoretical aspects of negotiations can be studied in behavioural sciences, or in negotiating skills training in management courses.'[48]

A particular lesson which Vanuatu learnt from accession was that there is no rush. To this extent officials disagree with the current proposal by the LDC group to put in place a three-year timetable for accession. The only way in which this would work would be if objective rules were put in place as suggested under 'Coping with limited capacity' above, and the accession procedure was mostly formal in nature rather than open to negotiation.

Acceding in three years under current circumstances would force negotiators into making hasty decisions. The range of issues that must currently be covered is too large to be covered by a small administration. Three years is not enough time for a small country to build ownership or to conduct sufficient research.

[48] Former Director of Customs.

44

Public and private participation in agricultural negotiations: the experience of Venezuela

RITA GIACALONE AND EDUARDO PORCARELLI*

1 The problem in context

The significant changes experienced by Venezuela in recent years have had an important impact on the structure and the position it has adopted in trade negotiations, especially in agricultural negotiations. These changes can be classified in three major areas: political, constitutional and institutional.

In 1999, Lieutenant-Colonel (retd) Hugo Chávez came to office after winning the December 1998 presidential election. Chávez defined his government as military, leftist and populist, and supported by the majority of the deputies of the National Assembly (Congress). An agenda for the agricultural sector was formulated within the broader context of the National Plan for Economic and Social Development (NPESD) (2001–7). It was based on a new economic model of agriculture-related matters, and sought to guarantee an adequate food supply to the majority of the population.[1]

The NPESD established the following guidelines:

(a) promotion of the rational use of land for agricultural purposes, and respect for private property, but eradicating large landed estates and penalizing holders of unused land;
(b) reorganization and regulation of the agricultural marketing and commercial system;

---

* Rita Giacalone works for the Grupo de Integración Regional (GRUDIR) – Universidad de Los Andes (ULA), Mérida. Eduardo Porcarelli is Legal Adviser to CONAPRI (National Congress of Private Investment) and Professor of the Graduate School of Law, Universidad Central de Venezuela.
[1] Ministerio de Planificación y Desarrollo (2001), *Plan Nacional de Desarrollo Económico y Social (2001–2007).*

(c) prioritization of infrastructure construction; and
(d) adjustment of commercial policies to the National Agriculture and Food Plan, among other actions.[2]

In addition to this, the reinforcement of national sovereignty and the promotion of a multi-polar world are given as important objectives in the chapter dedicated to the international aspects of the NPESD. The government's objective regarding national sovereignty has had a particularly important influence on its position on commercial agriculture. This is because the government considers that the commercial agricultural negotiations that took place in the period before 1999 were one of the main factors to have negatively influenced the agricultural sector as well as national sovereignty.

Changes in Venezuela's position on commercial agriculture have forced negotiators to adopt a hardline position in World Trade Organization (WTO) negotiations. This lack of flexibility was already in evidence in the months leading up to the Doha Ministerial Conference in 2001. In the months following Doha the Venezuelan position in commercial agriculture negotiations became remarkably rigid, because agricultural policies were focused on short-term issues. For example, the government focused its efforts on enlarging the national market for domestic producers, rather than on medium- to long-term issues such as the development of export options for agriculture.

The Venezuelan Constitution of 1961 had contained general positions on agricultural matters related to the need to improve the living conditions of the rural population; mention was also made of the fact that large estates were not in the public interest, and of the government's responsibility to help agricultural workers to obtain the necessary resources to work.

The Constitution of 1999 contains more specific dispositions regarding agriculture, including the following:

- the promotion of favourable conditions for integrated rural development;
- the optimized use of land by means of infrastructure, credit facilities, training and technical assistance;
- the opposition of large landed estates to social interest and provision of land of their own to workers;
- the promotion of sustainable agricultural growth as the first step to rural development;

---

[2] Ministerio de Planificación y Desarrollo (2001), *Plan Nacional de Desarrollo Económico y Social (2001–2007)*.

- the development of national farming production as part of a stable and permanent movement to guarantee an adequate food supply to the population; and
- the consideration of activities related to food production as part of Venezuelan national interest, with the purpose of achieving national self-sufficiency.

The dispositions cited are connected with Article 301 of the Venezuelan Constitution, which provides that 'The State reserves the use of commercial policies to defend public and private national companies'. This article has been used by senior officials at the Ministry of Agriculture and Land to justify maintaining a defensive position in WTO negotiations and other regional integration schemes of which Venezuela is a member. The Agriculture Marketing Law, which was approved in 2001, contains dispositions on commercial agriculture negotiations, based on the articles of the new Constitution. Five years later, these constitutional changes have not been put into practice (Dalke 2004).

Constitutional changes are important, because, according to a public official, in many cases when no specific guidelines for negotiation are provided, high-level officials resort to seeking such guidelines in the Constitution. Carlos Abello, former Director-General of the Venezuelan government's agricultural marketing branch, and therefore negotiator over agricultural issues in different for a, including the WTO, for over ten years, considers that the legal and constitutional changes in this matter have been positive. However, Abello points out that they have been politically focused and have become a negative element, acting against Venezuela's negotiation processes by failing to assemble good negotiating teams and implement a negotiation strategy which is in line with the country's economic and productive reality.

Another former public official, who was involved in the negotiation process but wants to remain unnamed, also states that 'Venezuela's position in commercial negotiations that have taken place in the last five years obeys political and ideological changes more than constitutional and legal ones'.

2 Local and external players and their roles

Along with the political and constitutional changes, institutional ones also took place. Between the mid-1970s and the negotiations on commercial agriculture in 1996, matters were handled by the Institute of External Commerce (ICE) in co-ordination with the Ministry of

Agriculture (MAC). In 1997 the Ministry of Industry and Commerce (MIC) was created as a result of the merger of the ICE with the Ministry of Development. Co ordination between MIC and MAC persisted until 2000, when they were merged into the newly created Ministry of Production and Commerce (MPC). In 2002, the portfolio for agriculture was separated from the MPC to create the Ministry of Agriculture and Land (MAT). These developments have meant that co-ordination in agricultural commercial negotiations between the MPC and MAT were significantly affected.

Former Director-General Abello considers that, before the first merger in 2000, important efforts were made to unify positions between MAC and the ICE and between MIC and MAC. Relations between the employees of each institution became difficult, due to several structural changes that took place after 2000. In Abello's opinion, institutional decay began after the merger, and made the positions held in the agricultural commerce negotiations all the more difficult to defend. Decay was fostered by structural changes that did not improve the efficiency of the institution, and by the rotation of competent officials and negotiators to other functions due to the need to accommodate new political appointees. In the opinion of another officer, the negotiations became political after these structural changes took place. The country's position in commercial negotiations was affected because the government had lost sight of the whole Venezuelan economy when it adopted an uncompromising position regarding agriculture.

Luis Ferraz, a former Deputy Minister of Agriculture (2001) thinks that the merger of the ministries of Agriculture and Commerce into a single institution was a positive development, as it favoured the co-ordination of negotiation positions, but that it was not properly managed. Antonio Frances (1999) agrees, and gives as a reason the fact that MIC had a streamlined and highly trained staff with a competitive orientation, whereas MAC was overstaffed and had developed a very defensive position in agricultural commercial negotiations. As a consequence it became difficult to develop coherent positions and to find a minister with a sound knowledge of both industrial and agricultural matters.

According to Abello, the frequent changes in the negotiating team have resulted in improvization and inconsistencies. This, together with the lack of specific guidelines for mid-level officials, and especially the teams' inadequate structure, has put in risk the negotiation process. Defective communication between the responsible government departments has prevented the building of a clear-cut agricultural position. He also points out that, even though the highest level decision-makers were properly informed, in most cases they did not fully understand the positive and negative implications of the negotiations for the country, due to lack of experience in this area.

The official involved in negotiations mentioned above points out that the frequent changes in the team members of the MAT and the MPC have not only affected the emphasis placed on each issue, but also the way in which they are addressed. Due to the difficulties encountered when new officials seek clear and specific institutional guidelines on negotiation issues, they tend to adopt a very rigid position; in this way they avoid assuming too much responsibility and are able to protect their jobs.

An anonymous former official considers that not only was the co-ordination level between institutions better before 2000, but also that the commercial negotiations that took place before this year were seen as a chance to create opportunities for the Venezuelan private sector, while the contrary is now the case. Now there is little or no institutional co-ordination, and the private sector's interests are not taken into account by the government. Richard Dalke (2004) agrees that, before 2000, negotiations were conducted in a more efficient way than in the period that followed. Also, while in theory the government currently gives more attention to agricultural negotiations in the WTO, in practice this has never been the case.

All the former officials who were interviewed consider that despite the fact that negotiations were not conducted in a perfect manner before 2000, co-ordination made it easier for the institutions involved to agree on a common position. Additionally, mid- and high-level officers had a more technical than political background, and a better understanding of Venezuela's internal and external agricultural agendas. They feel that at present public officers devote more attention to the internal agricultural agenda.

An additional problem originates in the structure of the Venezuelan mission at the WTO in Geneva, which reports to the Ministry of Foreign Affairs. The officials who work there work for the Ministry of Foreign Affairs, but receive instructions not only from that ministry but also from any other ministry which has an area of competence covered by the negotiations at a given time. In addition to the Ministry of Foreign Affairs, the other two ministries that are involved in the process are the MPC and MAT. The continuing changes, not only in the structure but also in the personnel of these three ministries, and the resulting lack of clearness in guidelines and instructions, make the mission's work extremely difficult.

The participation of the Venezuelan private sector in commercial negotiations has been affected by its high degree of dependence on the state.
In an oil-based economy, in which petroleum exports make up more
than 80% of total exports and its proceeds go to the state – which uses
them to pay for public contracts, salaries and other mechanisms – the
private sector has to choose carefully in which areas to make demands,
as it is unable to refuse the government's leadership in agricultural matters. Commercial agricultural negotiations in the WTO in the last few
years offer a good vantage point from which to analyze this behaviour,
as well as the deterioration of government–private-sector relations in
Venezuela.

For representatives of ASOVEMA (Venezuelan Association of Rice
Mills), the last meeting with private-sector participation was organized
when the then Minister of Commerce and Production, Jesus Montilla,
made a very short presentation on the Venezuelan position which was to
be taken to Seattle. When Luisa Romero was minister, ASOVEMA was
not invited to participate in discussions to formulate or make comments
on the Venezuelan position for the Doha meeting. Since then, they have
learned of government positions through the press, and have had access
to official documents published on the ministry's website. They have had
more access in negotiations between the Andean Community of Nations
(ACN – Bolivia, Colombia, Ecuador, Peru and Venezuela) and Mercosur
(Argentina, Brazil, Paraguay and Uruguay), and attribute this to the fact
that the ACN encourages the participation of business together with government representatives by creating ad hoc groups and asking for advice
from the Andean private sector (Salas 2004).

Another representative of a business association has reported that,
although she has been working in ASOGRASAS for the past sixteen years,
the association was never invited to participate in activities related to the
WTO agricultural negotiations, neither have they followed what is discussed there. However, they participated until April 2002[3] in activities
related to the negotiation of a free trade agreement between the ACN and
Mercosur. Since that date the government has stopped inviting them to
any activities, although informal contacts were made once again at the
end of 2003 by the MPC. Meanwhile the association has been able to

---

[3] In that month the President was removed from power for 48 hours by a civil-military
movement and the President of FEDECAMARAS, the umbrella organization of the private
sector, took up the position of President during that time, before armed forces loyal to
Chavez reinstated him.

follow the ACN–Mercosur negotiations, as well as those of the Free Trade Agreement of the Americas (FTAA), by participating in meetings of the ACN Secretariat and in the Business Forum of the Americas, and by means of their close relations with Colombian businesses (González de Useche 2004).

Two problems seem to affect business participation in the negotiating process. First, agro-food industry and primary producers do not share the same view of the negotiations, and not all associations are concerned about what is going on at multilateral or WTO levels and, second, they tend to concentrate their efforts on concrete aspects of bilateral or group negotiations, such as those between the ACN and Mercosur or in the FTAA. While the agro-food industry is more competitive and may accept tariff reductions if the government gives guarantees of its willingness to provide an adequate framework for their activities, primary rural producers are not in the same situation. Thus the latter had a more defensive (protectionist) position vis-à-vis the WTO and the former a more proactive one. The second problem may be the result of a combination of lack of human resources to follow different negotiating processes simultaneously and the perception that Venezuela had had little leverage in the multilateral agricultural negotiations, and that in smaller regional groupings there were more opportunities of having demands taken into account, especially when Venezuelan associations co-operate with those of similar countries.

Difficulties experienced inside the government sector have not made communications with the private sector any easier. This is not only due to the constant changes in contact personnel in each public entity – the opposite occurs in the private sector, where there is more stability and contact personnel tend to remain in the same job for long periods of time – but it is also due to a lack of intra-government communication. This lack of communication between the responsible government institutions does not provide the private sector with a coherent and consistent message. In addition, communication between public and private sector was practically cut by the political events of December 2002, when a private-sector general strike seriously affected economic activity, and even paralysed the state-owned oil company .

In addition some government officials and former officials think that the private sector is trying to exert its influence on agricultural and commercial issues to the benefit of their respective sectors without understanding that this might be counterproductive for intrinsic or extrinsic reasons. Abello and another official involved in the negotiations indicate that the internal struggle caused by the antagonistic positions held by the primary producers and the agro-food industrialists has resulted in a general weakening of the private-sector position. And other former public officials comment that some representatives of the private sector do not know the contents of multilateral rules and procedures, especially the effects that negotiations might have on their sectors. This is due not only to problems in the information flow between the sectors (which have become very serious after the general strike of December 2002 mentioned above) but also to the lack of interest and the poor organization of the agricultural private sector.

3 Challenges faced and the outcome

Venezuela's position since becoming part of the WTO (1995) until the beginning of a new round of agricultural negotiations in the first quarter of 2000 could be classified as evolving from 'moderate offensive' to 'moderate defensive'. In general terms, before 2000 Venezuela requested the opening of developed countries' markets, in exchange for a moderate opening of Venezuela's domestic market. Most of the former officials who were consulted agreed that Venezuela negotiated its agricultural questions effectively when it joined the WTO, counting on the active participation of the private sector, the agro-food industry more than primary producers, who were not well organized at that time.

After the beginning of the new round of negotiations, Venezuela's position became considerably more, even totally, defensive, with little interest in taking the offensive. Some of the elements of Venezuela's current position are:

- favouring the interests of primary agricultural producers over those of the agro-food industry;
- making no compromises further than a limited tariff reduction for some specific products;
- making more effective use of the mechanisms of special and differential treatment;
- adopting horizontal and unlimited dispositions in non-commercial issues;
- having longer transition periods;
- maintaining agricultural safeguards;
- emphasizing resolving the problems of rural poverty, unemployment, food supply and the environment;

- applying a tariff reduction formula with low impact on the primary agricultural producers;
- eliminating export subsidies and reducing trade distorting measures of domestic support in developed countries.

These result from the emphasis on the political and the ideological in negotiations, especially the first and last points.

Another observer[4] has stated that, since the Chávez administration came to power in 1999, and especially since the signing of the new Constitution, the Venezuelan government's position on agriculture had been more supportive of the interests of primary rural producers, to the detriment of the interests of agro-food producers. This is reflected in the fact that since 1999 ministers of agriculture have been consistently more radicalized than ministers of production and commerce. This may also explain the hardening of the Venezuelan position between Doha and Cancún, based more on political than economic reasons. However, the fact that Venezuela is a net importer of food products limits its capacity to sustain a coherent position within the ongoing WTO negotiations.

On many occasions the interests of primary producers and the agro-food industry differ because if the former were to ask for protection and receive it, the agro-food industry would then be harmed by being limited in its access only to inputs from domestic producers (Salas 2004). This is of particular importance since the agro-food industry imports most of its inputs, except in the case of rice – although rice mills can buy rice abroad, they cannot depend on the exports of China, India and Thailand, because bad weather in those countries can sharply curtail their supply. In addition, the Venezuelan rice sector is highly industrialized and has made important investments at the levels both of primary producers and of the agro-food industry. Some of the differences between primary producers and the agro-food industry may well arise from the fact that, except for the establishment of protective tariffs, agriculture has never been encouraged by government, while the agro-food industry was explicitly promoted by some administrations (Salas 2004).

María Eugenia Salas (2004) has been in charge of following commercial and integration negotiations for ASOVEMA since 1997. According to her, between 1997 and 1999 the government facilitated agro-food industry participation in those negotiations by organizing seminars and other meetings in which private-sector representatives had access to

---

[4] Formerly employed in the public administration.

information. Since late 1999, however, this co-operation has been lost and the private sector learns about discussions taking place by means of the press and/or official papers with no input from the agro-food industry.[5]

An example from the earlier stage of relations is the agricultural workshop organized by the MPC in November 1999, in order to present the preliminary position that the Venezuelan government would take to the WTO Millennium Round (Programa de Formación 1999). At that time the main challenges to Venezuela were defined as the liberalization of agricultural markets, the laggard technological performance of agriculture, and the need to create a sustainable base for its development and alter the low nutritional level of the population. The document put forward by the government also recognized that it was imperative to reconcile the interests of Venezuelan agricultural producers, the agro-food industry, and traders and consumers (Programa de Formación 1999: 26). Accordingly, the proposal called for the strengthening of the position of agriculture vis-à-vis trade liberalization, promoting new markets for Venezuelan agricultural exports, and also supporting policies for rural development, environmental protection and food security. Special emphasis was put on co-ordinating with the rest of the Andean countries (Programa de Formación 1999: 32–3).

If in the Doha and Cancún meetings the Venezuelan government asked for the removal of domestic agricultural subsidies by the developed countries, the position changed from mentioning the general removal of subsidies in Doha to supporting the continuation of subsidies for developing nations in the Cancún meeting. Thus the government moved from asking that developing nations be granted the possibility of a gradual elimination or phasing out of subsidies (Programa de Formación 1999) to claiming that developing nations could not be asked to put an end to their own subsidies (Rosales 2003). Accordingly, Venezuela sided with the G20 on this question. When after the Cancún Ministerial Conference Colombia,[6] Ecuador and Peru left the group, Venezuela and Bolivia remained,

---

[5] A former official who does not want to be named disagrees with this statement. For him after 1999 the participation of the private sector began to lessen, but it did not deteriorate until 2002. In the case of WTO negotiations, business participation has usually been low because those negotiations are conducted by country missions in Geneva. Moreover, neither Venezuelan primary agricultural producers nor agro-food industry representatives have ever presented to the government a coherent national position distinct from that of their individual sector or company.

[6] Colombia is a member of the Cairns group that has consistently called for the opening of all markets to agricultural goods (Hugueney 2004).

ending the co-ordination of their negotiating positions in agriculture at the WTO.

According to Salas, public-sector participation in the WTO negotiating process is weak, due to the fact that the government has general positions but no specificity because it does not know what to promote, what to protect and what to reconvert, and no negotiator can hope to succeed without a clear state policy behind him. The only point at which Venezuela had a clear policy line was when it joined GATT, but that line has, in the intervening period, been blurred and lost due to lack of definition and continuity. This is why negotiators have fought for protection, but not for the promotion of Venezuelan agriculture, and Venezuelan producers have made efforts to protect themselves but not to prepare themselves for access to a global economy.

The absence of communications between business associations and the government since 2000, and the latter's defence of an autarkic position regarding food security – hard to sustain because the government is importing large amounts of food free from tariffs – means that the evolution of the Venezuelan position between 2000 and 2003 was predicated more on ideological than on economic terms. Although the government's position in the WTO is faultless from the private sector's point of view because it demands an end to agricultural subsidies in developed countries, it is also uncompromising and thus denies all possibility of negotiation in favour of those Venezuelan agro-food products that may have a chance in the international market (Salas 2004).

At the same time, several contradictions exist in Venezuela's position at the WTO: it defends special and differential treatment, such as the maintenance of agricultural subsidies for developing nations, but has never gone beyong making declarations and designating rice as a so-called 'flag sector' at the beginning of the present administration. Primary producers whose production techniques have become more industrialized have achieved this by means of their own investments, or by integrating themselves with the agro-food industry. The only subsidies rice producers get are indirect (cheap water in certain areas and cheap energy everywhere). Also, by supporting in the WTO the maintenance of developing countries' agricultural subsidies, Venezuela is supporting nations that are big agricultural producers, and can support those subsidies, to the detriment of its own rice producers which could face competition from subsidized rice from Thailand and India (ibid.).

Without a clear and defined agricultural programme there is no possibility of sustaining a concerted and coherent position, not only in the

WTO, but also in regional negotiations. Salas (ibid.) does not see any coherence and/or continuity in agricultural policies, when abrupt changes of technical staff in the ministries risk putting an end to the 'historical memory' of negotiation processes. Another important limitation is that the government and the private sector have not sat down to define a development programme for agriculture and the agro-food industry (ibid.). And the situation has been exacerbated since the strike of 2002, after which the government started importing food products with zero tariff – to the detriment even of primary agricultural producers – so that currently Venezuelan food security is being predicated on cheap imports paid for by high oil revenues.

In summary, political, legal and institutional changes after 2000 have had an important effect on Venezuela's position in commercial negotiations in general, and more specifically in agriculture. In addition to constitutional and legal provisions that do not allow flexible positions, political context and institutional changes have made the negotiation process more difficult, due to the lack of public–public- and public–private-sector co-ordination. The ministries related to commerce and agricultural negotiations (MPC and MAT) have experienced structural and functional changes. Departments and working teams have been reorganized and officials have been rotated or substituted. In a four-year period (2000–04) there have been five ministers of agriculture, five ministers of commerce, five deputy ministers of agriculture, six deputy ministers of commerce, three directors general of agricultural marketing and three directors general of foreign trade. New officials, in general, require training, time to learn about their new posts and experience (especially if they have none previously, as is the case with the majority of the new political appointees), and team co-ordination. In most cases, when taking up their post each high-level official reorganizes tasks and teams, and even sometimes substitutes experienced officials with new ones with no relevant experience but safer in political terms.

Additionally, private-sector participation in the WTO agricultural negotiations seems to have been consistently slight, and has been practically reduced to zero in the last couple of years due to domestic political problems. In the years when private-sector representatives have had access to government negotiators, contacts between them seemed to have been informal (joint participation in workshops and seminars and the circulation of documents and information), and neither public officials nor the sector's associations have made efforts to institutionalize their co-operation in foreign commercial negotiations. This has not prevented private-sector representatives from blaming the government for any perceived flaw in the outcomes of the WTO process, especially when political polarization has freed them from their usual restraint in relations with the state apparatus.

4 Lessons for others: the players' views

From the different interviews conducted it is clear that there are many lessons that could be learned in order to improve Venezuela's WTO negotiations. We will sketch first the general ones, and afterwards the lessons for the public- and private-sector actors.

Several key points were signalled by most of the interviewed regardless of their public/private-sector origin.

Public officials need to consult frequently with the private sector with regard to aspects of negotiating that affect their performance, and also to have a better understanding of the different strategies and alternatives that can be carried out.

The construction of communication channels between them is a common responsibility of both public and private sector. There will not be balanced negotiations in the national interest if the representatives of the public and private sectors cannot agree on a minimum consensus base.

The organization of teams with relevant experience in the different areas of trade negotiations is a priority, as frequent changes of institutions and removal of public officers place the country at a disadvantage.

A consensus in agriculture-related issues should be reached between the public and private sectors; this is needed in order to introduce practicable domestic policies that strengthen negotiations and their results.

The following are key points for public-sector actors.

High-level officials involved in negotiations need to review carefully the positive and negative implications for the economy as a whole, as well as reviewing in detail WTO agreements in order to have a better understanding of the legal scheme of negotiations.

The politization of technical negotiating teams should be avoided.

Co-ordination between ministries should be improved, and officers need to know clearly who is in charge of the final decision-making process.

The following are key points for the private-sector actors.

Improvements in communication should be made inside and between private-sector associations, in order to balance the interests of the primary producers and the agro-food sector.

Some associations need more trained staff in order to follow properly the negotiating process.

Associations need to improve their links with their members in order to represent their interests in a more effective manner, keep members informed of what is being negotiated and obtain their support when dealing with the government.

In conclusion, the lessons are clear. There should be concentration on communication flows, the development of human resources for negotiations and follow-up, the need to establish positions supported by domestic consensus and on the avoidance of politization by both the public and the private sector. Thus a state position should be developed separately from a government one, and private-sector associations should carefully navigate the waters of domestic politics in order to have the right to participate in shaping Venezuela's position in agricultural commercial negotiations at the WTO.

References

Abello, Carlos (former Agriculture Marketing Director and negotiator for ICE/ MIC/ MPC/MAT) (2004), interview in Caracas, 18 June.

Arellano, Fèlix Gerardo (CAVIDEA) (2004), interview in Caracas, 9 June.

Briceño, Germàn (FEDEAGRO) (2004), interview in Caracas, 8 June.

Dalke, Richard (former Agriculture Marketing Director, MAT (1993–8); FEPORCINA) (2004), interviews in Caracas, 8 June and 6 July.

Ferraz, Luis (former Deputy Minister of Agriculture, in office in 2001) (2004), interview in Caracas, 12 July.

Frances, Antonio (1999), 'La fusión MAC–MIC', *El Universal*, 5 Sept.

Gonzàlez de Useche, Morelia (ASOGRASAS) (2004), interview in Caracas, 9 June.

Hugueney, Clodoaldo (2004), 'The G-20: Passing Phenomenon or Here to Stay?', *Dialogue on Globalization*, FES Briefing Paper, March.

Programa de Formación de Negociadores Económicos Internacionales (1999), *Propuesta preliminar de posición de Venezuela para las negociaciones comerciales de la Ronda del Milenio de la OMC*, Caracas: CIET-PDVSA.

Rosales, Manuel (2003), 'Posición de Venezuela ante la OMC', 11 Sept., available at www.aporrea.org.

Salas, María Eugenia (ASOVEMA) (2004), interview in Caracas, 30 June.

45

Preparation by Vietnam's banking sector for WTO accession

PHAN VAN SAM AND VO THANH THU[*]

1 The problem in context

This paper focuses on showing how Vietnam will meet its trading partners' expectations that it will liberalize its economy through commercial legislation and regulatory changes and, more specifically, will liberalize its financial institutions and markets by the time of the country's planned accession to the WTO in 2005.

Since 1975 until recently, Vietnam has maintained an almost isolationist economic policy. It has not, as a result, had much success in improving the efficiency of its commercial sector in a way that contributes to significant or consistent economic growth. Vietnam is now a country clearly wanting closer connections with the rest of the world, but policies to promote and finance international trade or to attract adequate foreign investment have lacked direction. As the country progresses towards joining the WTO, economists are debating how to improve the country's investment efficiency, especially through financial market reform.

In this context, the BTA (US–Vietnam Bilateral Trade Agreement) exposed the lack of competitiveness of the Vietnamese banking sector. Vietnamese enterprises that have tried to improve their competitiveness in world markets (such as the fishing industry) have found that the lack of banking competitiveness and competence has held them back. They fear that this will continue to happen when the Vietnamese market is opened up as a result of WTO membership.

The Vietnamese banks themselves realize (partly as a result of the BTA) that they have to reform or lose even more business to foreign banks and financial institutions. They understand that the WTO or the General

* Phan Van Sam is Dean, Mekong University, Vietnam. Vo Thanh Thu is at the University of Economics, Ho Chi Minh City.

Agreement on Trade in Services (GATS) does not require Vietnam to open up its banking market (unlike the BTA, for example, which does have such provisions), but they can see that this is likely to happen in future because their own customers – who will face competition in their markets after WTO accession – will be demanding to use foreign banks. Vietnam is considering liberalization of its banking system for its own purposes, so that its companies and its banks can survive WTO-enforced trade liberalization.

Some analysts have also expressed concern about the falling proportion of foreign capital in the country's private investment structure and the increasing levels of state investment, sometimes considered to be associated with inefficiency or misallocation. This topic is still being debated, but some economists consider that increasing investment by state-directed or state-owned companies might be associated with Vietnam's import substitution and protectionist policies which in turn negatively affect resource allocation.

The world economy generally has seen changes in trading practices aimed at reducing protectionist policies. Lower protection translates into better use of internal resources. But in Vietnam, in contrast with more developed economies, the policies needed to ensure higher levels of economic growth include not only the more efficient use of internal resources but also financial and banking laws that will attract more external resources.

For example, there appears to be a need to raise or even remove the 30% ceiling on foreign investors' stakes in listed business organizations. When the government first opened its doors to foreign investment some twenty years ago there were many restrictions concerning where foreign investors could invest their money. Back then, Vietnam wanted to attract foreign capital to areas and activities where capital was needed most without threatening Vietnam's national interests. This policy, to some foreign investors, protected the capital of state-owned enterprises (SOEs) and locally owned private enterprises rather than effectively encouraging the development of overseas and international business. Over time, banking restrictions have also prevented the owners of local enterprises from realizing the true value of their investments because they were unable to access global capital markets.

The opportunity for foreign-invested companies to undertake bigger commercial activities in Vietnam is now more widely recognized.

The local press claims that this is something which is compulsory under the BTA and other international commitments Vietnam has made; they also suggest that a government decision to lift the cap on foreign participation in local business was to be made in 2004. However, as of the time of writing nothing has happened. Is this the old Vietnamese comment, 'maybe tomorrow'? However, liberalization of the restriction on investment will encourage and facilitate a more specialized domestic production schedule which would flow on to changed international trading patterns, replacing Vietnam's previous focus on import substitution.

Warwick Cleine, a senior partner of the international consultancy firm KPMG, is among those foreign analysts who felt greatly encouraged when they heard that the Ministry of Finance (MoF) was considering proposing that the government raise or even remove the investment 30% cap. 'It doesn't make sense to restrict foreign capital in the domestic sector. If they do not remove the cap, private local companies will suffer over time', he says.[1]

Since the State Securities Commission (SSC) was transferred to the MoF's management earlier this year, the MoF has understood that its task of developing the fledgling stock market – which has only twenty-four listed firms with a total capitalization of less than 10 billion dong ($US 634 million) – has become more urgent than ever.

Adjustments of the investment cap would, however, require many changes to both the Foreign Investment Law (FIL) and the Enterprise Law. There is clearly a role for Vietcombank (the Bank for Foreign Trade of Vietnam) in this area.

According to Tony Foster of the Freshfields law firm, the government has distinguished between the FIL and the Enterprise Law in order to make sure that foreigners invest under the control of the FIL: 'If foreigners could invest more than 30%, the FIL would lose importance – which may happen when the FIL and Enterprise Law are merged next year anyway. That is why I assume the government is considering lifting the ceiling now.'[2]

In general, foreign analysts believe that the government has slowly been moving towards a unified legal system for foreign-invested and domestic enterprises. This is a natural part of Vietnam's intended integration into the world economy: the source of the capital is not important, but rather the use to which it is put. 'This means government policy will become more focused on how enterprises invest their money rather than how the enterprise raises its capital', says Cleine of KPMG.

The most important action for the MoF is to work with industries to adjust its Decree 58. Once this decree is adjusted, the regulations will

---

[1] Interview with Warwick Cleine, 5 June 2004.   [2] Interview with Tony Foster, 6 June 2004.

define in which business sectors the state can hold a 100% stake and which can be invested in by foreign companies, translating into a liberalization of the investment banking system.

These developments indicate slowly changing thinking within the government about their regulations and their operation of the previously state-controlled financial and banking system. It also reflects an increasing acknowledgement of a need for Vietnam to join the 'world economy'.

Financial institutions are now realizing that GATS did not force administrators, particularly in developing countries, to liberalize their financial system to encourage further investment. However, if these state institutions cannot update it is unlikely that they will be able to compete with other private financial companies within Vietnam.

For example, Dong a Bank, a private commercial bank, was established fifteen years ago. Its capital has increased ten times and, in foreign exchange transactions, accounts for 70% of total foreign currencies in Vietnam; Vietcombank – the largest state-owned bank – has not achieved this. The BTA agreement with the United States has induced the government to undertake that, by 2010, US banks will operate without any constraints in Vietnam. Under competitive pressure for survival, institutions must restructure, adjust and change operational procedures, and even change their form of ownership to assist in the country's economic development. The financial system clearly needs overhauling to achieve these objectives.

According to the BTA, Vietnam has to liberalize its financial and banking services for US banks in compliance with the 'road map' agreed by the two parties. Vietnam must comply with the ASEAN Free Trade Area (AFTA) 'road map' for tariff removal, implement the BTA guidelines for banking services, train banking staff, and apply information technology (IT) and other technologies in banking services so that Vietnamese banks can compete in the future.

Vietnam has to implement its road map in the following terms and in the 2001–10 time framework, including allowing insurance services to become more effective: US investors can set up joint services ventures and there will not be any constraints in penetrating the market by US insurance companies. Other major developments so far have been that

- all US financial providers (except banks and leasing companies) have been entitled to set up joint ventures with Vietnamese partners in providing their financial services in Vietnam;
- from December 2004 US-owned banks will be entitled to expand their commercial services;

- from 2009, US financial institutions will also be entitled to issue credit card facilities and enjoy the national treatment policy. They can receive deposits in Vietnamese dong; and
- from 2010, US banks will be entitled to set up 100% US-owned banks in Vietnam, and to set up joint venture banks in Vietnam, but the US capital contribution shall not be lower than 30% and not exceed 49% of joint venture registered capital.

Clearly, all these development changes and procedures are progressive and longer term, but there is a distinct role for and need for the reform of Vietnamese banks in this process.

2 Challenges faced by the Vietnamese banking sector

During this integration process, the Vietnam banking system will be heavily influenced by the international financial market in terms of exchange rates, interest rates and foreign currency reserves, while they must simultaneously carry out international obligations and commitments. Competition will probably become much stronger when foreign banks expand their scale and scope of operations in the Vietnamese market. Vietnamese commercial banks will need to cope with many difficulties in expanding their banking activities in the world and competing with foreign banks.

As noted earlier, the BTA exposed the lack of competitiveness of the Vietnamese banking system. The Vietnamese banks came to realize that they had to reform or lose more business to foreign banks and financial institutions. Liberalization became of interest to both Vietnam's commercial and banking sectors to assist in surviving WTO-enforced trade liberalization (although not specifically liberalization of the banking sector).

Historically (some fifteen years ago), the Vietnamese government still operated a centrally planned economy; Vietcombank was one of the three banks entitled to undertake international payments. With its monopoly in this external financial relationship, Vietcombank played an important role and obtained a large market share of international payments, albeit in a relatively small market. In general, its business operation was advantageous at that time, but not now.

There was also a low development level in technology, organization, management and professional skills in the Vietnamese banking industry. Hence the speed of opening up the economy remained low, as was the ability to mobilize internal capital with the country's underdeveloped strategies for expanding into the international market. Some of this bureaucratic 'overseeing' remains.

Related to this, Vietnam's legal system still operates restrictions in quantification, and there is confusion in relation to finance and credit which is contrary to some requirements of GATS and the BTA. The State Bank still has not met the operational requirement of a unified banking system; banking policies remain uniformed and do not create a competitive business environment.

One of the major challenges now facing Vietnamese banks is the role of foreign banks. The foreign banks' strength of capital, technology, services and global operational scale provide them with potential advantages. For example, in Ho Chi Minh City, the biggest finance centre in Vietnam, the foreign-invested banks have a high growth rate, leading to a high percentage of the market share in the finance business, while the state commercial banks' percentage share has now fallen (see Tables 45.1 and 45.2).

Table 45.2 also indicates the fall in the bank loan market share of state commercial banks while the foreign banks' share of loans has increased.

A further problem exists with the Vietnamese (in)ability to provide adequate capital for economic development, and this is also in comparison to other countries in the region. The registered capital of leading state commercial banks only accounts for 3–4% of the total capital of all commercial banks; their financial capacity is too low to meet the country's economic development requirements. Capital provision is also over too short a period for the longer-term nature of many commercial projects. This point is summarized in Table 45.3.

There is also an increasing amount of overdue commercial debt, as summarized in Table 45.4. There are debt problems between commercial business and state-owned banks, often resulting from inexperience in dealing with secured commercial lending. The Vietnamese banking system must improve commercial practices, including the renunciation of delinquent claims. The EPCo and Tanimex Companies are two typical cases where the owners are insolvent and unable to repay loans to Vietnamese banks.

There are some signs of gradual banking reform. In 1998, the Committee for Banking Reform was established (Decision No. 337/QD-NHNN) and implemented in 2001. A major objective is to ensure that the commercial banking system is both effective and sustainable; for example, the commercial banks must deal effectively with secured commercial lending from a sound financial management team.

Table 45.1. *Share of borrowed capital from banks in Ho Chi Minh City in 2003*

Banking system	Market share of borrowed capital				Increase or decline compared with 2002	
	2002		2003			
	Amount (billion dong)	Percentage	Amount (billion dong)	Percentage	Amount (billion dong)	Percentage
State commercial banks	43.163	50.2	57.506	49.4	+14.343	33.2
Joint stock commercial banks	24.712	28.7	32.707	28.1	+7.995	32.4
Joint venture banks	3.272	3.8	4.724	4.1	+1.452	44.4
Branches of foreign banks	14.849	17.3	21.533	18.5	+6.684	45.0
Total	85.996	100.0	116.470	100.0	+30.474	35.4

Source: State Bank of Vietnam, 2003.

Table 45.2. *Market share of bank loans in Ho Chi Minh City in 2003*

| Banking system | Market share of bank loans | | | | Outstanding increase or fall compared with 2002 | |
| | 2002 | | 2003 | | | |
	Amount (billion dong)	Percentage	Amount (billion dong)	Percentage	Amount (billion dong)	Percentage
State commercial banks	38.001	51.2	48.426	48.0	+10.245	27.4
Joint stock commercial banks	19.814	26.7	29.160	28.9	+9.346	47.2
Joint venture banks	2.783	3.7	3.946	3.9	+1.163	41.8
Branches of foreign banks	13.645	18.4	19.354	19.2	+5.709	41.8
Total	74.243	100.0	100.886	100.0	+26.643	35.9

Source: State Bank of Vietnam, 2003.

Table 45.3. *Duration of capital mobilization of banks in Ho Chi Minh City, 2002–3*

Duration of capital mobilization	2002		2003	
	Amount (billion dong)	Percentage	Amount (billion dong)	Percentage
Over 12 months	17.098	19.88	22.582	19.39
Under 12 months	68.898	80.12	93.888	80.61
Total	85.996	100.00	116.470	100.00

Source: State Bank, Ho Chi Minh City.

Table 45.4. *Overdue debt of the Vietnamese banking sector, 1995–2000*

	1995	1996	1997	1998	1999	2000
	(billion dong)					
Vietnam banking sector	7.9	9.3	12.4	12.0	13.2	13.1
State commercial bank	9.1	11.0	12.0	11.0	11.1	11.0
Private commercial bank	3.3	4.2	13.5	16.4	23.0	24.0

Source: IMF, *Vietnam: Statistical Appendix and Background Notes*, IMF Staff Country Report No 00/116, August 2000, Table 21.

One main objective of any central bank is to maintain the soundness and security of its country's financial system as an aid to economic development. This work requires specialized knowledge of controlling a sound monetary economy devoid of obvious politics. The Central Bank of Vietnam has to establish requirements and procedures for the establishment of improved financial institutions. Their activities should be limited to fields in which they have certified competence and the central bank must supervise and monitor financial institutions on an acknowledged financial/accounting basis.

In short, the Central Bank of Vietnam must set standards for the establishment of financial institutions to ensure that applicants have enough resources and adequate systems in place.

The impact on import-competing industries

In the country's own interest, Vietnam needs to reform its banking and financial sector so that its import-competing food and manufacturing sectors will have the support they need to become globally competitive in the markets being opened to the world by the WTO. Some examples in support of this point follow.

Nguyen An, director of Seafood Processing Enterprises in Ho Chi Minh City, the largest economic centre in Vietnam, mentions his difficulties in borrowing a large amount of capital from Vietcombank for investment in his company. He says, 'Access to Vietcombank for a bank loan was a difficult task. Vietcombank's monopoly made it difficult for me to access sources of foreign currencies.'[3]

To Kien Hanh, the owner of a business manufacturing electric fans, cookers and so on, said, 'Although my company has the need to borrow money from banks, I have not borrowed such money since my company's establishment seven years ago. When I need capital for production and investment I just mobilize capital from my relatives and my friends.'[4]

Nguyen Van Tuyen, director of a company providing labour protection devices, said that he had already approached the bank but had been refused due to his lack of mortgage property.

Tran Trong Tuong, director of an export company of wooden furniture, is in a more favourable situation as he has a big house for collateral and could get a bank loan. However, he complains that the bank's collateral valuation is only equal to half the market price of the house and the bank loan is only for 70% of their collateral valuation. This cannot meet his company's financial needs.

There are many other reasons why small enterprises cannot persuade banks to lend to them, and for security banks often impose tighter measures to prevent commercial enterprises from accessing banks.

Duong Phuc Hau, a director of Fosta Enterprises, specializing in anti-absorbent materials, expresses his objective opinions on (these) bank restrictions and, also, that business enterprises should provide more binding obligations.

3 Facing the challenge of liberalization

The Vietnamese banking system has so far been partly reformed but is still weak. The state-owned banks still dominate the banking system; the

---

[3] Interview with Nguyen An, 2 April 2004.   [4] Interview with To Kien Hanh, 15 April 2004.

overdue loan rate is increasing; Vietnamese commercial banks have limited lending capacity, and so the story continues.

Coupled with this, and sometimes due to inadequate banking and foreign investment laws, most Vietnamese-owned enterprises are under-capitalized. Once Vietnam liberalizes its trading economy many industries will have to compete with foreign entrants to the Vietnam market, maybe for the first time. In such a situation, their competitive strength in their own market will depend a lot on better access to more economically competitive banking services.

In April 2004 there were nearly 40,000 small and medium-sized enterprises in Vietnam. According to a recent survey conducted by the Vietnam Chamber of Commerce and Industry (2004) these enterprises cannot clearly realize the constraints of the integration process and the banking industry, although they understand well the problems their private enterprises can have with current banking services in Vietnam. Resolving the difficult situation of small and medium-sized enterprises by effectively accessing their sources of capital and therefore gaining more commercial benefits is a current problem.

With over 90% of Vietnamese enterprises falling into the small or medium-sized categories and people generally having low incomes, the current capacity for capital mobilization by banks is limited. If the banking system is permitted to be equitized and to sell stocks widely to foreign markets, additional foreign capital is likely to increase and help boost the country's economy and economic development.

To reform the banking sector and facilitate the liberalization of the commercial process, the government of Vietnam has announced the Internationally Integrated Programme of the Banking Industry, and is committed to implement it when Vietnam joins the WTO. Vu Viet Ngoan, managing director of Vietcombank, has observed that 'The Programme of Integration into the international economy initiated by the Vietnamese government has created opportunities and challenges for Vietcombank.'[5]

This is reflected in other comments. Banking operations will be expanded, especially with a view to attracting investment capital. Ngoan also said 'the securitization project of Vietcombank shall be deployed "favourably" because Ms Le Thi Bang Tam, Vice Minister of Finance, has submitted to the Vietnam government "the plan" allowing Vietcombank to sell its stocks widely to investors in foreign countries. If and when this happens, then the mobilization of long-term capital for Vietcombank

---

[5] Interview with Vu Viet Ngoan.   [6] Ibid.

will be easier, and the funding capacity for big commercial projects can be increased.'[6]

He added that 'Joining WTO can help Vietcombank, a large foreign trade bank, to have more opportunities to co-operate in banking fields such as monetary planning and risk management, and, through this, Vietcombank's prestige will likely be improved in the fields of international financial transactions.'[7]

In sum, several things are needed to achieve this.

The Vietnamese banking industry must mobilize capital, access new technology and retrain its management and staff to match the development requirements of other financial markets.

With tougher competition, Vietcombank must further specialize in professional banking skills to enhance the efficiency of enterprise capital usage.

New banking services need to be developed and made more rapidly accessible. In this way Vietcombank can exploit and more effectively apply its (developing) banking services to contribute to economic growth and an increased share in both the international and domestic financial markets.

Vietcombank can take advantage of its wide network of branches to match the managerial and business styles of foreign banks.

Internationally integrated banking operations can help support these reforms and also increase the transparency of the Vietnamese banking system to meet the needs of integration and implement the commitment to (other) financial institutions and the WTO.

When Vietnam joins the WTO, foreign-invested and private banks will have better operational conditions there. Vu Viet Ngoan further stated that 'besides submitting the plan of the bank's securitization to mobilize more capital, Vietcombank must improve its competitiveness by all the measures' (speech given at the Vietnam Banking Conference, April 2004).

Banking services techniques and technology must be improved and service charges reduced to attract more customers.

Staff professional skills must be improved so that Vietcombank (and other banks) will be both a currency trader and an investor, thus helping commercial enterprises to develop. The growth of these enterprises should become a foundation for banking development.

---

[7] Ibid.

4 Lesson from Vietnam's experience

To achieve its successful planned economic/financial integration, Vietnam needs also to fill the development gap with other countries in the region. Vietnam is carefully opening its market step by step to maintain some sustainable development.

Because of the requirements of the BTA, Vietnam is opening its financial and banking market and therefore making WTO access and further developments more feasible.

Being a WTO member will bring some well-defined obligations requiring more open markets. But the WTO does not tell individual economies what they need to do to succeed. They have to adopt some practices and procedures that go beyond WTO requirements. In Vietnam, the liberalization of banking and financial services is going beyond GATS requirements, but this seems to be necessary to make an economic success of WTO membership.

Development and practical changes as a result of macro thinking are sometimes slow in Vietnam. However, it is possible that some developing countries can benefit from the Vietnam experience. Now that guidelines have been set out for joining the WTO, it will be interesting to watch developments in 2005 and beyond.

INDEX